A Companion to Ramon Llull and Lullism

Brill's Companions to the Christian Tradition

A SERIES OF HANDBOOKS AND REFERENCE WORKS ON THE
INTELLECTUAL AND RELIGIOUS LIFE OF EUROPE, 500–1800

Edited by

Christopher M. Bellitto (*Kean University*)

VOLUME 82

The titles published in this series are listed at *brill.com/bcct*

A Companion to
Ramon Llull and Lullism

Edited by

Amy M. Austin
Mark D. Johnston

Translated by

Amy M. Austin
Alexander Ibarz
Mark D. Johnston

BRILL

LEIDEN | BOSTON

Names: Austin, Amy M., editor, translator. | Johnston, Mark D. (Mark David),
    1952- editor, translator. | Ibarz, Alexander, 1974- translator.
Title: A companion to Ramon Llull and Lullism / edited by Amy M. Austin, Mark
    D. Johnston ; translated by Amy M. Austin, Alexander Ibarz, Mark D.
    Johnston.
Description: Leiden ; Boston : Brill, [2018] | Series: Brill's companions to
    the Christian tradition ; volume 82
Identifiers: LCCN 2018034269 (print) | LCCN 2018040100 (ebook) | ISBN
    9789004379671 (ebook) | ISBN 9789004226227(hardback :alk. paper)
Subjects: LCSH: Llull, Ramon, 1232?-1316. | Llull, Ramon,
    1232?-1316--Influence.
Classification: LCC B765.L84 (ebook) | LCC B765.L84 C66 2018 (print) | DDC
    189/.4--dc23
LC record available at https://lccn.loc.gov/2018034269

Typeface for the Latin, Greek, and Cyrillic scripts: "Brill". See and download: brill.com/brill-typeface.

ISSN 1871-6377
ISBN 978-90-04-22622-7 (hardback)
ISBN 978-90-04-37967-1 (e-book)

Printed by Printforce, the Netherlands

Contents

Preface to *A Companion to Ramon Llull and Lullism*

Any student or scholar who encounters, for the first time, the voluminous work of the medieval Majorcan lay theologian and philosopher Ramon Llull (ca. 1232–1316), or any of its multifarious adaptations in later centuries, may rightly find them overwhelming, if not incomprehensible. Llull's idiosyncratic theologico-philosophical system, his self-styled "Great Universal Art of Finding Truth," and its diverse use at the hands of many subsequent generations of Lullists, are undeniably difficult to understand, even for experts well-versed in the philosophical, religious, literary, or scientific traditions of medieval, Renaissance, and early modern Europe. The chapters of this volume seek to present Ramon Llull's work and examples of the major manifestations of his legacy in terms comprehensible to academic readers who are familiar with those traditions. Toward this end, the design of this handbook strives to obviate several basic obstacles commonly faced by readers not familiar with Llull or Lullism, in their first encounter with these subjects.

First among those obstacles is the sheer size of Llull's own encyclopedic oeuvre, which includes almost 300 writings on nearly every branch of medieval knowledge, and the equally vast corpus of material produced by Renaissance and early modern devotees of Llull's system and ideals. Despite over a century of labor by modern scholars, perhaps fifteen percent of Llull's own writings still remains available only in manuscript or in early modern editions. Even cursory mention of every text by Llull would therefore be impossible and undesirable in a survey of this kind; published inventories of his oeuvre can provide interested readers with some idea of its depth and scope.[1] In order to satisfy best the needs of those readers not specialized in study of Llull and Lullism, the chapters in this volume on Llull's own work are limited to synthesizing its major features or to analyzing his best-known writings, explaining these with reference to commonly-known philosophical, theological, and literary norms from his era. Similarly, the chapters on later Lullism describe synthetically or analyze in detail major examples of its cultivation within the philosophical, religious, and literary cultures of the Renaissance, early modern, and modern eras, so that students of those periods can appreciate the diverse manifestations of Llull's work and thought from the late Middle Ages through the Enlightenment.

---

1   Bonner, *SW* 1257–1313; Fernando Domínguez Reboiras, "Works," in *Raimundus Lullus: An Introduction to his Life, Works and Thought*, (eds.) Alexander Fidora and Josep E. Rubio (Turnhout: 2008), 125–242.

Second, if the quantity of writings produced by Ramon Llull and later Lullists appears daunting to readers not familiar with Llull and Lullism, the vast body of scholarship on these fields will surely seem overwhelming. The available print and online bibliographies of that scholarship already catalog many thousands of items, and their number grows monthly.[2] The unconventional character of Llull's work prompted controversy even during his own lifetime – several of his own writings suggest that contemporaries derided him as a "fool" – and later Lullists sometimes faced caustic criticism, if not actual Inquisitorial persecution, for advocating his methods and doctrines. Echoes of those past conflicts perhaps persist today among modern experts in their divergent interpretations regarding certain aspects of Llull's work or the later Lullist endeavors that it inspired. The chapters in this volume strive to offer a balanced synthesis of current scholarly interpretation concerning Llull and Lullism, with a correspondingly balanced bibliography of secondary literature, in order to provide the general orientation most useful to readers not specialized in the study of Llull and Lullism.

A third, very practical, obstacle for many readers may simply be language. Llull's native vernacular tongue was Catalan, and several of his writings exist only in that idiom, many only in Latin, and some in both languages. (He also prepared Arabic versions of some of his writings, but none of these are known to survive.) Although Llull for modern Catalans is a figure comparable in importance to Chaucer in English or to Dante in Italian, his native language and its long literary history are not well-known today outside Catalonia. Moreover, much of the modern scholarship on Llull and Lullism is written in Catalan or Spanish. Among Anglophone academic audiences, even knowledge of the latter is not always common outside Hispanic studies. Following the norms of Brill's series "Companions to the Christian Tradition," all chapters in this volume are written in English, with quotations from primary or secondary sources translated as needed. Wherever possible, contributors identify and cite published English translations of Llull's works, but much of the most relevant scholarship cited in this volume exists only in other languages. For Anglophone readers, this volume happily includes contributions from several major European scholars whose work has not previously appeared in English. The

---

2   Rudolf Brummer, *Bibliographia Lulliana: Ramon-Llull-Schrifttum 1870–1973* (Hildesheim: 1976) and Marcel Salleras i Carolà, "Bibliografia lul.liana (1974–1984)," *Randa* 19 (1986): 153–98, provide exhaustive inventories for the years indicated. The online "Base de Dades Ramon Llull (Llull DB)" from the University of Barcelona (http://orbita.bib.ub.edu/llull/) is a comprehensive searchable database, regularly updated. As a guide to major studies, see "Selected Bibliography on Ramon Llull," *Raimundus Lullus: An Introduction*, 517–537.

editors and translators of these chapters are deeply grateful to their authors for their patience and advice in preparing the English versions of their work.

Finally, the fourth – and perhaps most formidable – obstacle for non-specialist readers seeking to understand Llull or Lullism is the deliberately idiosyncratic, alternative nature of Llull's Great Art. Conceived as a comprehensive method for both fostering devotion to God and for demonstrating the truth of Christian doctrine to unbelievers, the Great Art: (1) relies on a limited, fixed number of basic concepts that Llull believed acceptable to Christians, Jews, Muslims, and pagans alike; (2) rejects the Aristotelian logic of Llull's Scholastic contemporaries in favor of manipulating his Great Art's basic concepts through sometimes complex analogical arguments and an *ars combinatoria*, as the preferred means of analyzing any subject; (3) rarely cites any authorities other than Llull's own writings; and (4) uses a peculiar terminology of Llull's own invention. Many of his literary works, although not based explicitly on his Great Art, incorporate some or all of these features, which several chapters in this volume strive to explain. As a result, even readers proficient in Catalan or Latin, if unfamiliar with the system of Llull's Great Art and its singular methods or terminology, may still find his writings unintelligible.

A Reader's Guide to This Volume

Practically speaking, few readers from the fields of philosophy, theology, or literature are likely to know, or will care to know, the entire scope and scheme of Llull's work, unless they intend to specialize in the study of Llull or Lullism. Thanks to Llull's application of his Great Art to all branches of knowledge, readers who consult this volume are more likely to be interested in some specific contribution by Llull or his later enthusiasts within a particular sphere of intellectual or spiritual activity. The organization of this volume attempts to anticipate those spheres of interest where readers might want to understand better such contributions. Its design also assumes that most of these readers probably seek only an introduction to the endeavors of Llull or later Lullists in one sphere of interest, rather than a comprehensive understanding of Llull and Lullism across the centuries. Reading this entire volume cover-to-cover will certainly provide that comprehensive knowledge, but the editors and contributors have attempted, in so far as possible, to craft each section of this volume, and their component chapters, as more or less self-contained and self-explanatory expositions of how Llull or later generations of Lullists participated within a specific sphere of philosophical, theological, or literary activity. Each section includes at least one chapter that offers an overview of that section's general subject, accompanied by chapters on topics of interest to specialists in particular aspects of each subject. This tactic has necessarily created considerable redundancy among the chapters, but enhances, we hope, this volume's utility as a reference work to consult piecemeal, if desired, without the need to read sequentially all of its chapters.

The initial section on "Llull as Philosopher and Theologian" reviews his life and work. To readers seeking simply an introduction to Llull and his achievements, we recommend Johnston's brief account of Llull's life, followed by Berlin's review of the contemporary thinkers most often compared or contrasted to Ramon Llull. Batalla analyzes more specifically his unusual role as a lay philosopher and theologian, with a concise explanation of his Great Art. Finally, readers who want or need a full understanding of Llull's system will find all of its principles and methods clearly explained in the chapter by Rubio. We especially recommend the latter to any student or scholar of early modern thought who needs to understand the particular elements of Llull's Great Art that later Lullists adapted and promoted.

The section on "Llull as Evangelist" reviews the aspect of Ramon Llull's work most often mentioned in modern histories of the European Middle Ages, namely his life-long campaign to convert unbelievers, especially Muslims and Jews, to the Christian Faith. His efforts in this pious endeavor have inspired many (sometimes very speculative) claims about his ideals and tactics, not to mention some colorful apocryphal legends. In the first chapter of this section, Stone reviews the evidence of Llull's familiarity with Islam, summarizing the features of Llull's Great Art that, arguably, best reflect his efforts to craft arguments acceptable to Muslim audiences. Next, Mayer judiciously analyzes Llull's announced tactics for debating and disputing with non-Christians, also reviewing how these tactics informed the design of his Great Art. Last, Beattie carefully reviews exactly what Llull says (and does not say) about crusading as a strategy for promoting the Faith, another aspect of his evangelizing ideology that continues to stimulate scholarly debate.

The section on "Llull as Vernacular Writer" reviews another of Ramon Llull's major contributions to medieval European culture, namely his prolific composition of works in his native vernacular, often known to non-specialists from their translations into other languages in later centuries. Readers interested in medieval poetics, literary theory, and the development of national literatures will find in the chapter by Aragüés Aldaz the most comprehensive analysis available to date in English of Llull's sometimes peculiar discursive methods, especially his efforts to meld genres of exemplification with the exemplarist metaphysics of his Great Art. For comparatist students and scholars of

medieval narrative, Ibarz provides a very accessible review of Llull's two famous "spiritual romances," *Blaquerna* and *Felix* (*Libre de meravelles*). Finally,
Franklin-Brown also offers for comparatists an overview of Llull's many encyclopedic writings, some of them especially important to the development
of later Lullism, and critical to understanding Llull's participation in the lay
learned culture of his era.

As the sections on evangelism and literature show, the apparent idiosyn-
crasy of Llull's work typically results from his application of the peculiar methods of his Great Art. The debt of those methods to specific Christian, Jewish,
and Islamic sources is a question that will continue to occupy modern scholars
of his Great Art, but is not essential for non-specialists to engage, except as
evidence of the cultural and intellectual interaction possible among the major
religious communities of the Western Mediterranean during Llull's lifetime.
Meanwhile, as every chapter in this volume stresses, Llull's broader social and
religious ideals – such as reforming Christian society and the Catholic Church
or promoting the evangelization of unbelievers – are hardly unique in his era,
and so familiar to any student of Western European society and culture around
1300.

The section on "Renaissance and Modern Lullism" surveys the widespread
diffusion of Ramon Llull's methods and ideals among European devotees from
the late 15th through the late 18th centuries. For reasons of economy, these
chapters on Lullism cannot treat in detail such interesting, but isolated, late
medieval or early Renaissance examples of Lullist activity as the persecution
of 14th-century Aragonese Lullists by the Dominican Inquisitor Nicholas Eymerich; the operations of a Lullist school in 15th-century Barcelona; or the adaptation of Llull's work by Nicholas of Cusa and Raymond of Sabunde. Readers
interested in these specific examples should consult the relevant scholarship
cited in the chapters from this section. Likewise, this section excludes analysis
of the many alchemical, magical, cabbalist, or hermeticist works that circulated under Llull's name in the Renaissance and early modern era.[3] The teachings of these pseudo-Lullian texts generally owe little to Llull's own methods
or ideals; their existence serves mostly as testimony to the magnitude of his
reputation in that era. To serve best the needs of readers seeking to understand

---

3   Michela Pereira, "'Vegetare seu transmutare:' The Vegetable Soul and Pseudo-Lullian Alche-
    my," in *Arbor scientiae: Der Baum des Wissens von Ramon Lull*, (eds.) Fernando Domínguez
    Reboiras, Pere Villalba, and Peter Walter (Turnhout: 2002), 93–119, and many other studies
    by Pereira (few in English) offer detailed analysis of the major pseudo-Lullist traditions. Still
    useful as introductions in English to these traditions are Bonner, *SW* 72–89; Peter J. French,
    John Dee: The World of an Elizabethan Magus (New York: 1972); and Frances Yates, *Giordano
    Bruno and the Hermetic Tradition* (Chicago: 1964) and *The Art of Memory* (Chicago: 1966).

the development of Renaissance and early modern Lullism, this section begins with Báez Rubí's account of the critical decades in the early 16th century when collaboration between certain French and Spanish thinkers revived interest in both Llull's Great Art and his evangelizing ideals; her chapter especially serves the needs of students and scholars of Golden Age Spain, by updating much obsolete information and claims about Spanish Lullism in this era. For readers seeking to understand the diffusion of Lullism throughout Europe during the early modern era and Enlightenment, Ramis-Barceló offers the most comprehensive account available in English. Finally, for the Anglophone readers whom this volume primarily serves, Albrecht analyzes notable examples of Lullist influence in 17th-century England.

The last section on "Lullist Missions to the New World" may yield surprises even to specialists unaware of, for example, the Lullist inspiration of the first missionaries that accompanied Columbus or the Lullian training of the recently canonized Saint Junípero Serra. This section presents in chronological order the most notable known examples of Lullist evangelism in the Americas. For students and scholars of the Columbian voyages, Dagenais first recounts the case of little-known friar Bernat Boïl, who accompanied Columbus in 1493, evidently inspired by contacts with the French and Spanish Lullists described by Báez Rubí in chapter eleven. Next, for readers especially interested in the diffusion of Lullism to New Spain, Báez Rubí continues her account of its development with examples such as Juan de Zumárraga, first archbishop of Mexico, and Diego de Valadés. This section, and our volume, fittingly ends with Dagenais's account of Junípero Serra, whose career perfectly illustrates how the Lullist schools surveyed by Ramis Barceló still motivated missionary zeal into modern times.

Any companion volume on Llull and Lullism, no matter how carefully designed, cannot adequately represent the richness of Llull's work or the myriad intellectual and spiritual endeavors that it inspired in later centuries. The editors and contributors hope that its chapters nonetheless satisfy some needs of those readers seeking, for the first time, information about Ramon Llull or Lullism, and perhaps inspire them to further study of Llull's fascinating work and long legacy. Many, many details of that work and legacy still demand further investigation; some aspects of Llull's unique enterprise, and its interpretation by later Lullists, will always remain issues of scholarly debate and controversy. In so far as possible, the contributors to this volume have sought to acknowledge those issues, while providing guidance in evaluating them for non-specialist readers. Any errors of fact or omission that remain are entirely the responsibility of the editors.

Works Cited

Primary Works: Llull

Selected Works of Ramon Llull, (ed.) Anthony Bonner (Princeton: 1985).

Secondary Works

"Base de Dades Ramon Llull (Llull DB)," University of Barcelona (http://orbita.bib. ub.edu/llull/).

Brummer, Rudolf, *Bibliographia Lulliana: Ramon-Llull-Schrifttum 1870–1973* (Hildesheim: 1976).

Domínguez Reboiras, Fernando, "Works," in *Raimundus Lullus: An Introduction to his Life, Works and Thought*, (eds.) Alexander Fidora and Josep E. Rubio (Turnhout: 2008), 125–242.

French, Peter J., *John Dee: The World of an Elizabethan Magus* (New York: 1972).

Pereira, Michela, "'Vegetare seu transmutare:' The Vegetable Soul and Pseudo-Lullian Alchemy," in *Arbor scientiae: Der Baum des Wissens von Ramon Lull*, (eds.) Fernando Domínguez Reboiras, Pere Villalba, and Peter Walter (Turnhout: 2002), 93–119.

Salleras i Carolà, Marcel, "Bibliografia lul.liana (1974–1984)," *Randa* 19 (1986): 153–198.

Yates, Frances, *The Art of Memory* (Chicago: 1966).

Yates, Frances, *Giordano Bruno and the Hermetic Tradition* (Chicago: 1964).

Acknowledgements

A work of the size and scope of this volume is necessarily a collective endeavor, relying on contributions by many colleagues. First among these is Julian Deahl, retired senior acquisitions editor at Brill, who first suggested this volume during conversations in 2004 at the annual International Congress on Medieval Studies. Without his persistent support and encouragement, this volume would certainly not now exist. Our subsequent efforts to prepare and produce this work would likewise have been fruitless without the constant assistance and guidance provided by Christopher Bellitto, Ivo Romein, and all the editorial and production staff at Brill. The editors are especially indebted to the expert work of James Joshua Pennington, who copyedited the entire volume. To Alexander Ibarz and Rosa Gallagher we owe particular thanks for their assistance as translators.

Each of the thirteen colleagues who contributed portions of this volume also provided, in addition to their individual chapters, much useful advice concerning its overall design: their suggestions certainly improved its plan and scope. Above all, we are grateful for their patience during the long process of gathering, translating, and editing the huge body of materials required to fulfill the plan of this volume.

Preparation of this volume was possible in part thanks to the generous support of: DePaul University, the Spanish Ministry of Education, the University of Texas at Arlington, and the Spanish Ministry of Economy, Industry, and Competitiveness research project MICINN FFI2017-83960-P (AEI/FEDER, UE). The Biblioteca de Catalunya and the New York Public Library graciously supplied illustrations from works in their collections. The Archivo Histórico Nacional (Osuna, Spain) and Santa Barbara (Calif.) Mission Archive and Library also provided access to their collections for research critical to several chapters in this volume.

After so much effort by so many collaborators, any deficiencies or infelicities that remain are entirely the responsibility of the editors.

Amy M. Austin
Mark D. Johnston
June, 2018

Illustrations

Abbreviations of Frequently Cited Works

Bonner, *AL*   Anthony Bonner, *The Art and Logic of Ramon Llull: A User's Guide* (Leiden: 2007).

Bonner, *SW*   *Selected Works of Ramon Llull*, ed. Anthony Bonner (Princeton: 1985).

EL   *Estudios Lulianos* [subsequently *SL*] (Palma: 1957–1990).

Hillgarth, *RLL*   Jocelyn N. Hillgarth, *Ramon Lull and Lullism in Fourteenth-Century France* (Oxford: 1971).

Johnston, *SL*   Mark D. Johnston, *The Spiritual Logic of Ramon Llull* (Oxford: 1987)

Johnston, *ER*   Mark D. Johnston, *The Evangelical Rhetoric of Ramon Llull* (New York: 1996).

MOG   *Raymundi Lulli Opera omnia*, ed. Ivo Salzinger, 8 vols. (Mainz: 1721–1742; repr. Frankfurt: 1965).

NEORL   Nova edició de les obres de Ramon Llull, 14 vols. to date (Palma: 1991-present)

OE   Ramon Llull, *Obres essencials*, ed. Miquel Batllori et al., 2 vols. (Barcelona: 1957–1960).

ORL   Obres de Ramon Lull, edició original, 21 vols. (Palma: 1906–1950).

PL   Patrologia Latina, ed. J.-P. Migne, 221 vols. (Paris: 1841–1865).

ROL   Raimundi Lulli Opera Latina, Corpus Christianorum – Continuatio Mediaevalis (Palma and Turnhout: 1959-present).

SL   *Studia Lulliana* [previously *EL*] (Palma: 1991-present).

Figures from Llull's Great Art

Figures From the Quaternary Phase of Llull's Art

From: Josep E. Rubio, "Thought: The Art," in *Raimundus Lullus: An Introduction to his Life, Works and Thought*, ed. Alexander Fidora and Josep E. Rubio (Turnhout: 2008), 301–08.

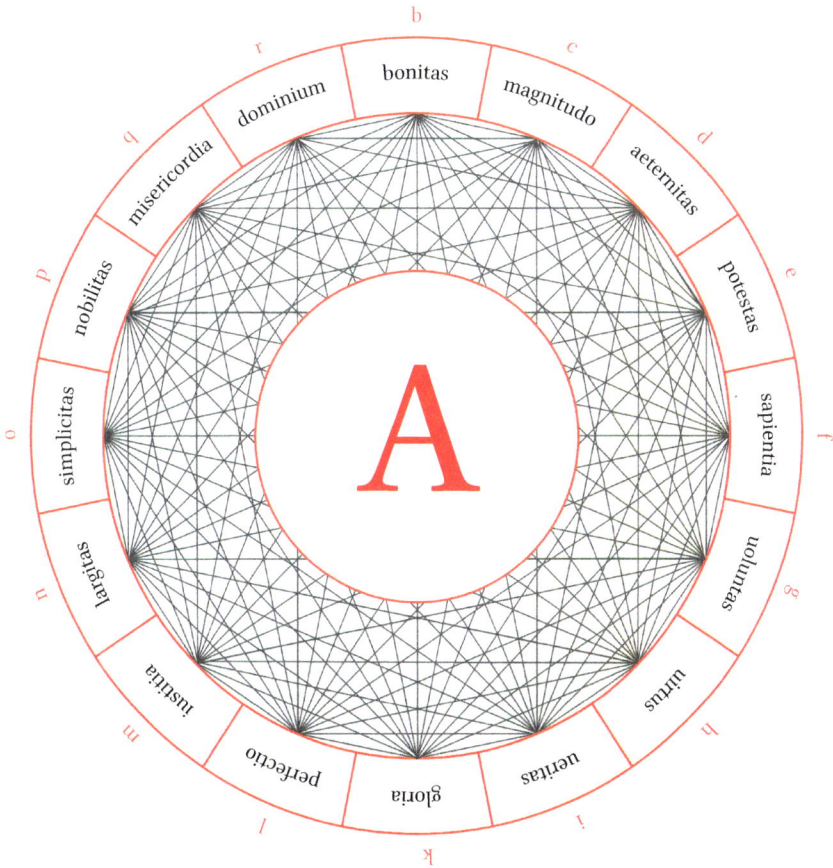

Figure A

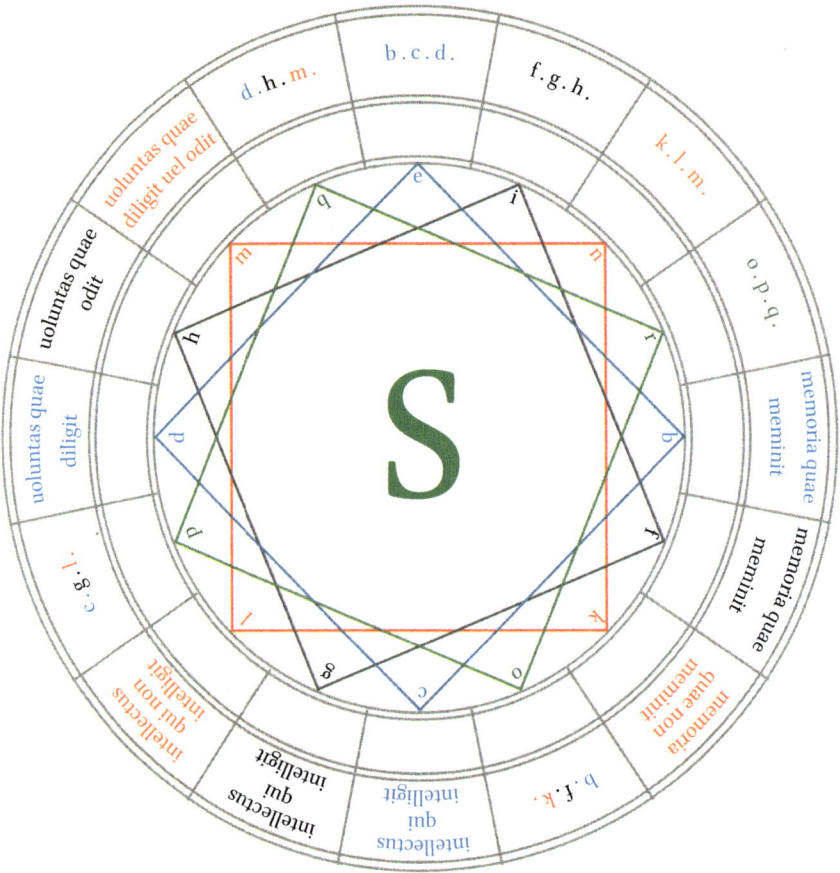

Figure S

Figure T

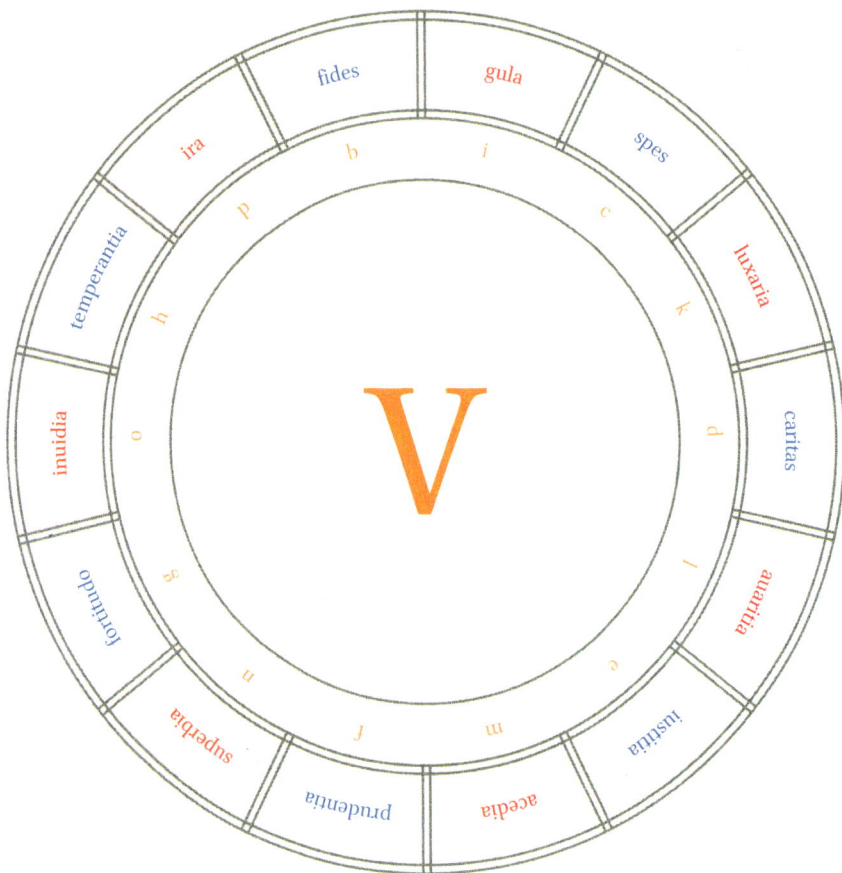

Figure V

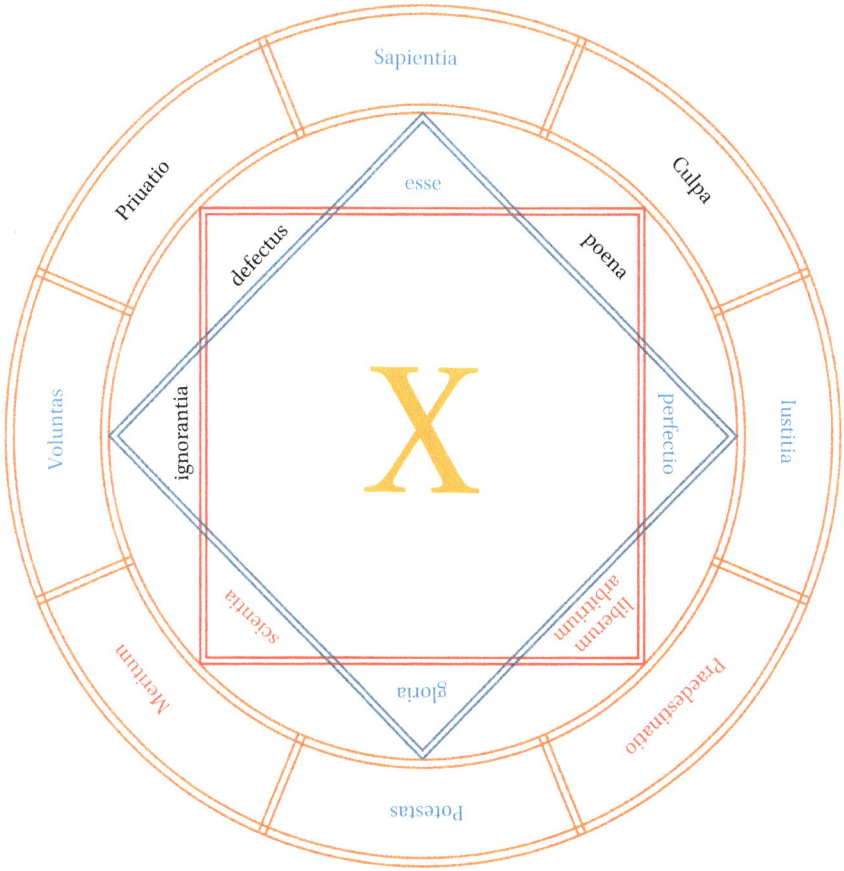

Figure X

De figura aeris

Terra	Aqua	Ignis	Aer
Aqua	Terra	Aer	Ignis
Ignis	Aer	Terra	Aqua
Aer	Ignis	Aqua	Terra

De figura terrae

Ignis	Aer	Aqua	Terra
Aer	Ignis	Terra	Aqua
Aqua	Terra	Ignis	Aer
Terra	Aqua	Aer	Ignis

De figura ignis

Terra	Aqua	Aer	Ignis
Aqua	Terra	Ignis	Aer
Aer	Ignis	Terra	Aqua
Ignis	Aer	Aqua	Terra

De figura aquae

Ignis	Aer	Terra	Aqua
Aer	Ignis	Aqua	Terra
Terra	Aqua	Ignis	Aer
Aqua	Terra	Aer	Ignis

The Elemental Figure

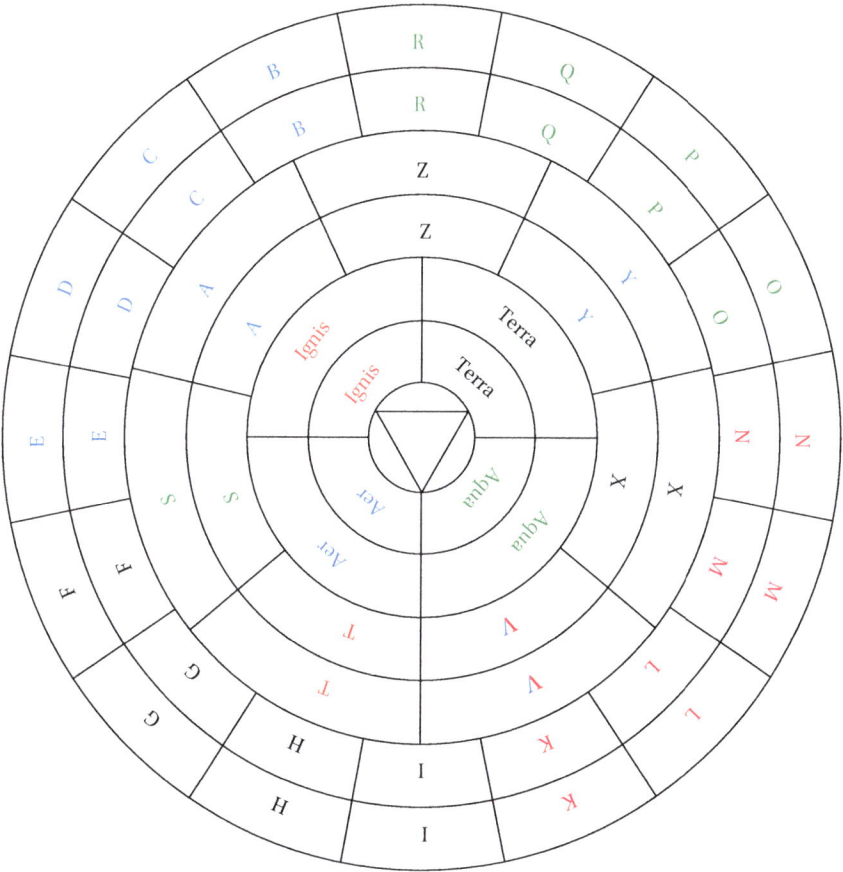

The Demonstrative Figure

Figures from the Ternary Phase of Llull's Art

From: MOG 5 (1729; repr. Frankfurt: 1965), s. p. [prelim. p. x]

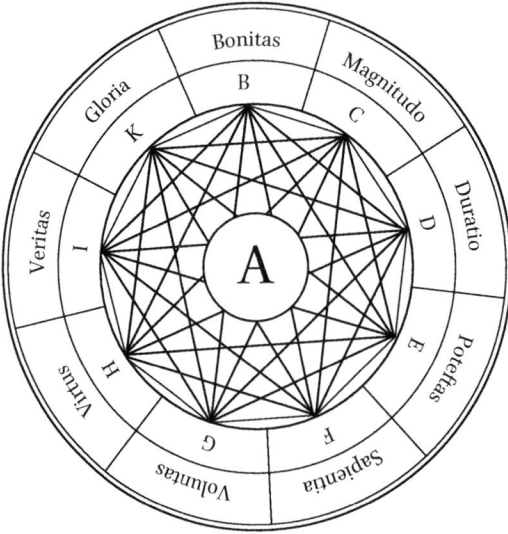

Figure A

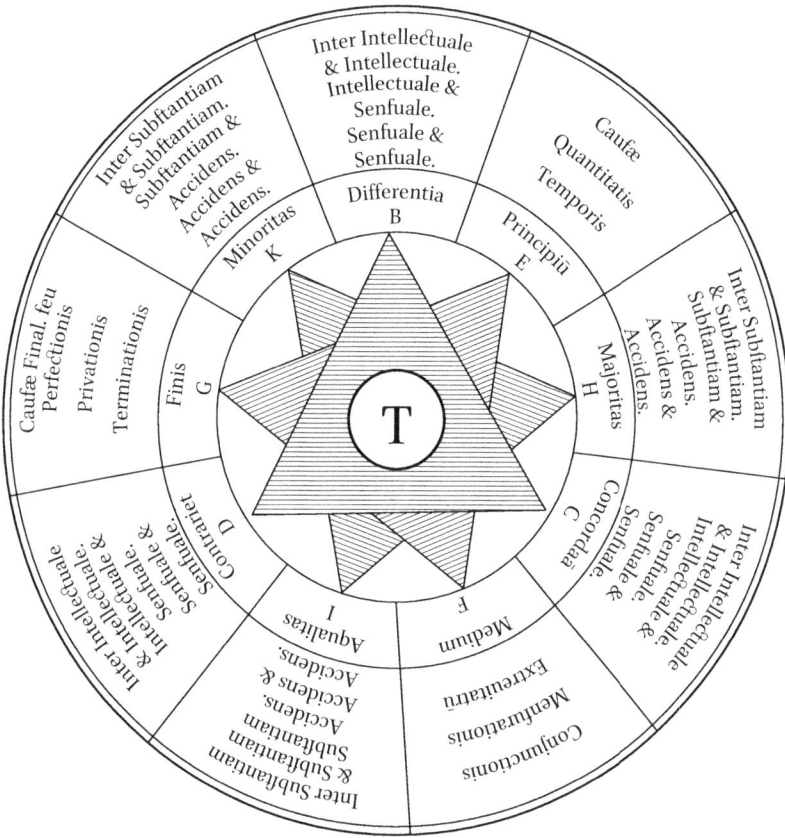

Figure T

Third Figure

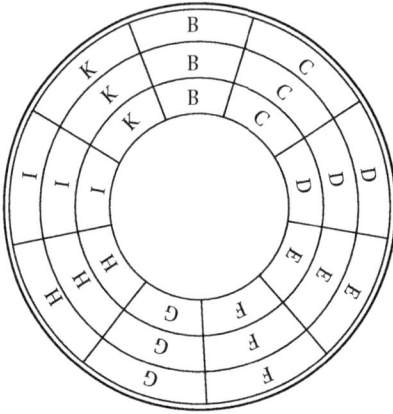

Fourth Figure

The Lullian Alphabet from the Ternary Phase

From: Johnston, *SL* 25.

	PRINCIPIA ABSOLUTA	PRINCIPIA RELATIVA	QUAESTIONES	SUBIECTA	VIRTUTES	VITIA
B	Bonitas	Differentia	Utrum ?	Deus	Iustitia	Avaritia
C	Magnitudo	Concordantia	Quid ?	Angelus	Prudentia	Gula
D	Aeternitas	Contrarietas	De quo ?	Coelum	Fortitudo	Luxuria
E	Potestas	Principium	Quare ?	Homo	Temperantia	Superbia
F	Sapientia	Medium	Quantum ?	Imaginatio	Fides	Acidia
G	Voluntas	Finis	Quale ?	Sensitiva	Spes	Invidia
H	Virtus	Maioritas	Quando ?	Vegetativa	Charitas	Ira
I	Veritas	Aequalitas	Ubi ?	Elementativa	Patientia	Mendacium
K	Gloria	Minoritas	Quomodo ? Cum quo ?	Instrumen-tativa	Pietas	Inconstantia

PART 1

Llull as Philosopher and Theologian

∴

Ramon Llull, ca. 1232–1316

Mark D. Johnston

1.1 Introduction

For any modern scholar of Ramon Llull's life and work, one of the most vexing impediments to studying his career is the very incomplete biographical information available about him, a disparity especially exasperating in the case of an author so prolific and so long-lived. For example, we know such details as the name of a street (Rue de la Bûcherie) where he lived during his last visit to Paris in 1311; the exact date (Pentecost, 1293) of one of his several "spiritual crises;" and the exact terms of his will. Yet we do not know the date of his birth, scarcely anything about the first thirty years of his life; where or how he attained his knowledge of philosophy and theology; or the precise date and circumstances of his death.

These disparities in our knowledge of Llull's life reflect, in part, the disparate nature of our three chief sources of information about his career:

(1) The most important by far is a quasi-hagiographical *Vita*, evidently composed in 1311, from Llull's own recollections, by friends at the Carthusian house of Vauvert near Paris.[1] It begins by proclaiming its intention to recount Llull's "conversion to penitence and some of his other achievements" (*conversione sua ad poenitentiam, et de aliquibus gestis eius*).[2] Written in a learned Latin style that Llull himself never mastered, the *Vita* highlights the events from his life that best illustrate his piety and evangelical zeal, almost surely in order to promote his personal authority as he prepared various proposals for the Council of Vienne later that year.[3]

(2) Next are the various autobiographical references found in Llull's own writings. Some are perhaps *topoi* of medieval Christian confessional literature and narratives of personal salvation, but others are very specific recollections – in works such as his *Desconhort* [Discouragement] and

---

1   *Vita coaetanea*, ROL 8:269–309.

2   *Vita* 1.1, ROL 8:272.

3   Mario Ruffini, "Il ritmo prosaico nella *Vita beati Raymundi Lulli*," *EL* 5 (1961): 5–60, analyzes exhaustively how the *Vita* adapts features of the medieval *cursus*.

© KONINKLIJKE BRILL NV, LEIDEN, 2019 | DOI:10.1163/9789004379671_002

Cant de Ramon [Song of Ramon] – of the frustrations or challenges that
he faced during his career. Especially helpful are the brief colophons that
he began adding, after 1294, to virtually all his writings, indicating their
place and date of composition or revision.

(3)   Finally, there survives a corpus of several dozen records concerning the
legal and financial concerns of Llull's family, as well as a precious handful
of documents regarding his own affairs. The latter include his will and
letters of recommendation from princely and ecclesiastical authorities.[4]

In addition, there also exist a few, but certainly not enough, texts by Llull's contemporaries that mention him or allude to his activities. The dearth of material
testifying to the contemporary reception of Llull's Great Art is especially exasperating but, as scholars in all fields become more familiar with his doctrines
and methods, we can hope that more will recognize, in the materials that they
study, allusions or reactions to his work and endeavors.

The following synopsis of Ramon Llull's career synthesizes, from existing
scholarship, the known, or reasonably plausible, information about his life.
Readers interested in the exact sources of that information, or in the range
of expert conjectures about the more obscure periods in his life, can consult
several helpful major studies.[5]

1.2   Early Life and "Conversion to Penitence"

Ramon Llull was born in the city of Majorca, probably in 1232. His father was
a wealthy merchant from Barcelona, one of many who settled on that island
after assisting its capture in 1229 from the Muslims by King James I "the
Conqueror" of Aragon. We know virtually nothing about Llull's upbringing or instruction, although some modern scholars have speculated that the
first chapters of his novel *Blaquerna* describe, in idealized terms, the kind

---

4   Jocelyn N. Hillgarth, *Diplomatari lul·lià* (Barcelona: 2001), gathers all the documents known
to date.

5   Hillgarth, *RLL* 1–134 remains the best critical account of Llull's career. Fernando Domínguez Reboiras and Jordi Gayà Estelrich, "Life," in *Raimundus Lullus: An Introduction to his
Life, Works and Thought* (Turnhout: 2008), 3–124, offer the most ambitious, and speculative,
attempt to contextualize all known details about Llull's life within the cultural, economic,
political, and social events of his era. Bonner, *SW* 3–52, provides a less detailed, but also less
speculative, account. Brief readable summaries in English include Bonner, *AL* 1–10, and Johnston, *SL* 10–15. For editions and translations of the works cited below, readers should consult
the online "Base de Dades Ramon Llull (Llull DB)" from the University of Barcelona (http://
orbita.bib.ub.edu/llull/).

of education that Llull considered most appropriate for a youth of his socio-economic status. He was probably an only child, and so supposed to perpetuate his family's wealth and position. In 1257 he married Blanca Picany, daughter of another wealthy merchant family, and they subsequently had two children, Dominic and Madeleine.

The *Vita* of 1311 begins its narrative by recounting how Llull was serving as a courtier (*senescallus mensae*) for the future King James II of Majorca (1243–1311). It would have been uncommon for a young man of Llull's social class to attain such a position at court, but the term "seneschal" used in the *Vita* may in fact be a slur, intended to emphasize Llull's sinful lifestyle, since seneschals were common targets of satire and criticism in contemporary literature. In any case, the *Vita* recounts how Llull saw, while occupied over several days writing a love song for a lady, repeated visions of Christ crucified. These convinced him to abandon worldly affairs and to serve God. The best way to do so, he decided, would be to seek the conversion of all Muslims and other unbelievers to Christianity, especially by: (1) risking even death to evangelize the infidels; (2) writing a book, "the best in the world" (*meliorem de mundo*) against their errors; (3) and asking the pope and Christian rulers to found monasteries for training preachers in the languages of the infidels. For three months Llull did nothing to pursue these goals. A sermon, delivered by a bishop in the Franciscan church on the feast-day of Saint Francis, finally convinced him to act. He sold his possessions, though reserving some resources to support his family, then confirmed his resolution with pilgrimages to Rocamadour, Compostela, and "various other holy places" (*diversa alia loca sancta*).[6] Thus the *Vita*, from its first chapter, organizes the trajectory of Llull's "conversion to penitence" and subsequent exploits according to those practices, such as pilgrimage, and those models, such as Saint Francis, most likely to impress the ecclesiastical and academic leaders who would assemble at Vienne in 1311. A clear, conventional definition of his piety was especially necessary in order to counter any reservations that authorities may have harbored about the orthodoxy or pretensions to spiritual and intellectual authority of a layman such as Ramon Llull.

1.3   Study and Training

The problematic basis of that authority may explain the somewhat disjointed character of the next paragraphs in the *Vita*, which cover one of the most important, yet still obscure, periods in Ramon Llull's life.

---

6   *Vita* 1, ROL 8:272–278.

The *Vita* reports that, once returned from his pilgrimages, Llull wanted to study in the schools of Paris. However, family members and friends, especially former Dominican Master-General Raymond of Penafort (1175?–1275), famed as compiler of the *Decretals* of Pope Gregory IX, dissuaded Llull from this proposal, urging him instead to return home to Majorca. This "name-dropping" mention of the renowned Master-General, along with his achievements in canon law, perhaps helped to validate Llull's training through private study, rather than through formal education at Paris, and so to legitimate his authority as a learned layman. Returned to Majorca, Llull cast off his "usual clothes" (*vestibus sollemnioribus*) in favor of a robe fashioned from coarse fabric, then devoted himself to learning "a little Latin" (*parum de grammatica*) and to studying Arabic with a Muslim slave purchased as his tutor.[7]

The encounter with Raymond of Penafort perhaps occurred at Barcelona in 1265. The *Vita* next describes how, nine years later, the slave attacked Llull after his master rebuked him for blaspheming the name of Christ. Llull imprisoned the slave, unable to bear seeing him executed. The slave subsequently hanged himself, while Llull was in seclusion at a nearby abbey, usually identified with the Cistercian house of La Real.[8] Apart from dealing with a violent slave, what else was Llull doing during these nine years? This remains one of the most critical unresolved questions regarding his intellectual and spiritual formation. Hillgarth conjectured that Llull studied at La Real, based on analysis of its surviving library catalogs, which record respectable, though not extensive, holdings in theology and philosophy.[9] However, only a few works from the abbey's collections really relate directly to the interests, arguments, or methods found in the several texts that Llull evidently composed during this period. The latter include a compendium of the *Logic* of Algazel and the *Libre de contemplació en Déu* [Book of Contemplation of God], the seminal text of his entire oeuvre.

The *Vita* instead suggests a source of knowledge that Llull – like so many medieval mystics, devout laypeople, or heterodox religious – often invoked: divine inspiration. After the death of his slave, Llull ascended a nearby mountain, always identified with Mount Randa. For eight days he contemplated the heavens, until God "suddenly illuminated his mind, giving to him the form and method of making the aforementioned book against the errors of the infidels."[10]

---

7   Ibid. 2.10–11, ROL 8:278.
8   Ibid. 2.11–13, ROL 8:279–280.
9   Jocelyn N. Hillgarth, "La biblioteca de La Real: fuentes posibles de Llull," *EL* 7 (1963): 5–17.
10   *Vita* 3.14, ROL 8:280: "subito Dominus illustravit mentem suam, dans eidem formam et modum faciendi librum, de quo supra dicitur, contra errores infidelium."

Offering thanks to God, Llull returned to La Real, where he began composing the first redaction of his Great Art, the *Ars compendiosa inveniendi veritatem*, with the familiar circular diagrams and combinatory mechanics that were the foundation of its unique methods. Its reliance on components organized like the four elements of medieval natural science defines the first, so-called "Quaternary" phase in the development of Llull's Great Art. With a draft of his work completed, Llull returned to the place of his original illumination on Mount Randa and built a hermitage for himself. One day, a young, joyful, and handsome shepherd, unknown to anyone in that area, visited Llull and provided in one hour as much wonderful knowledge about God, the heavens, and the angels as a normal man could relate in two days. Before departing, this obviously celestial messenger fulsomely blessed Llull and his books.[11] Immediately after this manifestation of divine approval for his work, the *Vita* turns to describing its endorsement by human authorities.

In his will of 1272, James I "the Conqueror" of Aragon confirmed the eventual division of his realm into two kingdoms. Upon his death in 1276, his son Peter III inherited Aragon, Catalonia, and Valencia, while his other son became King James II of Majorca, with additional territories in southern France, such as Montpellier. In 1274 or 1275, Prince James, having heard about Llull's "good writings" (*libros bonos*), summoned his former "seneschal" to Montpellier for examination by a Franciscan friar. Llull's visit to Montpellier initiated four decades of nearly constant peripatetic existence – a life-long *peregrinatio* – with only occasional return visits to his native island. His last years on Majorca and first years in Montpellier were also a period of prolific literary production that included such popular vernacular texts as his *Libre de l'orde de cavalleria* [Book of the Order of Chivalry], *Doctrina pueril* [Instruction for Children], and *Libre del gentil e dels tres savis* [Book of the Gentile and Three Wise Men].

1.4   Llull's Western Travels and First North African Mission, 1275–1293

The Franciscan friar who examined Llull at Montpellier, evidently impressed in particular by his *Libre de contemplació*, approved his writings, pronouncing them "replete with prophecy and Catholic devotion" (*prophetia et devotione catholica plenas*). According to the *Vita*, Llull subsequently composed a new version of his Great Art, the *Ars demonstrativa*, which he "taught publicly" at Montpellier (*legit ibidem publice*) and wrote numerous other works. At the same time, Prince James agreed to support a monastery for training thirteen

---

11   Ibid. 3.14–15, ROL 8:280–281.

Franciscan missionaries at Miramar on Majorca, thus fulfilling one of Llull's three original goals. A papal bull confirmed its foundation in 1276.[12] The eventual failure of this project at Miramar, which the *Vita* never mentions, became a bitter disappointment to Llull. By emphasizing instead the initial clerical approval of Llull's writings and royal support of his plans to train missionaries, the *Vita* demonstrates, for its Parisian readers in 1311, how his project had enjoyed official support from the earliest years of his career.

The *Vita* then says nothing about the next dozen years in Llull's life. We do know that his wife requested legal authority in 1276 to administer their family estate, claiming that her husband had become too "contemplative" (*contemplativus*) to manage their affairs,[13] but Llull nonetheless witnessed a property transfer on Majorca in 1278.[14] More importantly, we know that these years, perhaps divided between Majorca and Montpellier, were intensely productive for Llull as an author: he wrote some three dozen works on theology, missionizing, and philosophy, perhaps intended for instructing the friars at Miramar. Above all, around 1283 he completed his first major "spiritual romance," the novel *Libre d'Evast e d'Aloma e de Blaquerna* (commonly known simply as *Blaquerna*).

The *Vita* resumes its narrative in 1287, with Llull visiting Rome to seek papal support for his projects, but the death of Honorius IV (3 April 1287) frustrated his intentions. He remained in Rome at least long enough to compose his poem *Cent noms de Déu* [Hundred Names of God], offered as a Christian improvement over the 99 names of God from the Koran, and the *Liber Tartari et Christiani*, a dramatization of inter-faith dialog.

Llull turned next to Paris, hoping "there to communicate to the world the Art that God had given to him" (*communicandum ibidem mundo, quam sibi dederat Deus, Artem*).[15] By special request of University Chancellor Berthaud, Llull read his work in the Chancellor's "lecture hall" (*aula sua*). The *Vita* neglects to mention Llull's documented efforts to obtain support from King Philip IV "the Fair" of France, which included composition of his second vernacular "spiritual romance" for lay readers, the extraordinary *Libre de meravelles* (also known as *Fèlix*, from the name of its hero).[16] At the university, Llull perhaps first met those masters, such as Peter of Limoges and Thomas Le Myésier, who later studied or promoted his work. He certainly encountered there also the so-called "Latin Averroists," whose doctrines he vigorously contested in many later writings.

12   Ibid. 3.17, ROL 8:282. Hillgarth, *Diplomatari*, 39–40.

13   Hillgarth, *Diplomatari*, 36–37.

14   Ibid., 41.

15   *Vita*, 4.18, ROL 8:283.

16   *Libre de meravelles* 8.89, ed. Salvador Galmès, 4 vols. (Barcelona: 1931–34), 4:107–108, describes, in third person, Llull's efforts at Paris.

Meanwhile, James II of Majorca had lost the island to his nephew Alfonso III of Aragon. Consequently, Llull found James at Montpellier in 1289. Perhaps motivated by the difficulties that he faced when explaining his system at Paris, Llull overhauled the Great Art in a new redaction, the *Ars inventiva veritatis*. Based explicitly on three-fold schemes of components, this new version initiates the "Ternary Phase" in Llull's ongoing development of his idiosyncratic system. From this period evidently date as well Llull's association with the Spiritual Franciscans and Ramon Gaufredi, the Franciscan Minister-General deposed in 1295 for tolerating the Spirituals. Gaufredi provided Llull in 1290 with a letter of recommendation, authorizing him to teach his Great Art at Franciscan convents in Italy.[17] While visiting Genoa en route to Rome, Llull perhaps also made his first contacts with members of the Spinola family, whom he later counted among his strongest supporters. The *Vita* claims that he prepared at Genoa an Arabic translation of the *Ars inventiva*, apparently for use in planned missions among the Muslims.[18]

Events in the Eastern Mediterranean dictated Llull's next actions. Loss of the last Crusader strongholds in the Holy Land, especially the fall of Acre in 1291, alarmed the Christian West. Llull responded with renewed attention to methods of missionizing and even considered the role of armed crusades. In 1292 he offered to Pope Nicholas IV his *Tractatus de modo convertendi infideles*, but the pontiff's death and "obstacles in the Curia" (*impedimenta curiae*) again upset Llull's efforts to attract papal interest in his schemes.[19]

Llull returned to Genoa, where the *Vita* reports, in one of its longest episodes, that he suffered the most intense spiritual crisis of his career. Although the Genoese enthusiastically supported Llull's preparations for a mission to North Africa, at the last minute he shrank from setting sail, overcome by fear that Muslims there would either kill him or imprison him for life. Ashamed of causing a "scandal against the faith" (*scandalum contra fidem*) among the Genoese, Llull fell into such a profound depression of remorse that he became ill and bed-ridden with a fever. On Pentecost of 1293 he had himself carried to the Dominican church where, after hearing the friars intone the hymn "Veni, Creator," he wondered whether God would ever save him. Taken after mass to a bed in the friars' dormitory, Llull saw a bright light and heard a voice say "In this Order you can be saved" (*In ordine isto posses salvari*). Only the absence of the friars' prior prevented Llull from professing in their Order. He returned to his lodgings, where he recalled the strong support shown to him by the

---

17   Hillgarth, *Diplomatari*, 60–61.
18   *Vita* 4.19, ROL 8:284.
19   Ibid.

Franciscans. Once again he saw the light and heard the voice aver that he could find salvation only with the Dominicans. Knowing that the latter would not accept his Great Art, Llull opted instead for association with the Franciscans, even if this assured "his own eternal damnation" (*damnationem sui ipsius aeternam*), a choice deemed "super-wonderful" (*supermirabile*) by the *Vita*. The warden of the local Franciscan convent promised Llull that he could take their habit when closer to death. As an outward demonstration of good faith, Llull then made confession, prepared his will, and went to mass. At the moment when the priest offered him the Host, he felt a hand pull his head away and heard a voice say "You will be punished as you deserve, if thus you now accept me" (*Poenam condignam patieris, si tu me sic nunc susceperis*). Immediately he felt a hand pull him back to face the Host; falling to the ground, he kissed the priest's feet and accepted the Host, hoping "at least through this feigned devotion to save his Great Art" (*ad hoc quod ipse saltem sub tali devotione ficta salvaret Artem*).

The import of this episode, literally central within the plot structure of the *Vita*, scarcely requires comment. The text nonetheless explains jubilantly how, from this "wonderful temptation" (*mirabilis tentatio*), comparable to God's testing of Abraham, "it is obvious" (*evidenter colligitur*) that Llull loved God and neighbor more than himself, since he chose to save the souls of others, through his Great Art, rather than to seek his own salvation.[20]

Thus confirmed in his resolve to evangelize Muslims overseas, Llull departed for Tunis, despite his continued illness and his friends' efforts to discourage him. He arrived there, fully restored to health in body and mind, by autumn of 1293. The *Vita* describes in detail the evangelizing tactics that he adopted, and often dramatized in his other writings. After slowly recruiting some local "experts in the faith of Mohammed" (*peritioribus in lege Machometi*), Llull promised them that he would convert to their religion if they could demonstrate its superiority to Christianity. He then successfully countered all their eager arguments with those of his Great Art, which the *Vita* neatly summarizes thus: (1) the best faith is that which most fully accounts for the revelation in Creation of the innate attributes of the Godhead; (2) the Christian doctrines of the Trinity and Incarnation most fully accomplish this; (3) therefore Christianity is the superior faith.[21] In support of his arguments, Llull began writing his *Tabula generalis*, the fullest schematic expression of the methods of his Great Art. The *Vita* next claims that, just as Llull appeared to achieve some success from these tactics, a "famous" (*famosus*) Muslim denounced him to the king of Tunis and recommended his execution. One member of the royal council convinced the

---

20   Ibid. 4.19–5.24, ROL 8:284–288.
21   Ibid. 6.25–27, ROL 8:289–291.

king simply to expel Llull from Tunis. Deliberately delaying his departure to Italy, Llull suffered "much abuse" (*multa opprobria, verbera et aerumnas*). After an angry mob almost killed another Christian who resembled Llull, he relunctantly abandoned his efforts, and returned to Naples.[22]

1.5   Travels West and East, 1294–1312

At Naples in early 1294, Llull completed his *Tabula generalis* and several other new works, most notably his *Disputació dels cinc savis* [Disputation of Five Wise Men]. He also wrote there one of his strangest treatises, the *Liber de sexto sensu*, in which he argues that speech (which he terms *affatus*) deserves recognition as a "sixth sense" because it is the only corporeal faculty capable of grasping God. Llull also obtained permission from royal authorities to proselytize Muslims in the town of Lucera.

News of the election of Pope Celestine V (5 July 1294) prompted Llull to visit Rome, but he arrived only to find Celestine abdicated and replaced by Boniface VIII. Llull addressed his *Petitio Raymundi* to Boniface as he followed the itinerant pope to Anagni and elsewhere. After "many frustrations" (*multas angustias*), Llull abandoned his attempts and returned to Rome.[23] There, between late 1295 and early 1296, Llull composed his encyclopedic *Arbor scientiae*, one of his longest, most elaborate, and most popular works. Once again despairing of support for his projects, Llull poured out his frustration in the 828 vernacular verses of his poem *Desconhort*. He subsequently visited Genoa, met with King James II of Majorca (perhaps at Montpellier), and then reached Paris, for the second time, in the autumn of 1297.

Llull apparently stayed in Paris for almost two years, but the *Vita* reports merely that he taught his Great Art, wrote several books, presented his proposals to the king, and then departed, seeing that his efforts would "accomplish little or nothing" (*parum vel nihil super talibus obtinere*).[24] This terse account scarcely represents the scope of Llull's efforts in Paris, which yielded at least sixteen new writings, including such important works as his *Liber de articulis fidei, Tractatus novus de astronomia, Arbor philosophiae amoris*, and *Cant de Ramon*, another vernacular poem venting his frustrations. His disappointment perhaps resulted from lack of response by the academic community to his writings – such as the *Declaratio Raymundi* (his treatment of the

---

22   Ibid. 7.28–30, ROL 8:291–293.
23   Ibid. 8.31–32, ROL 8:293–294.
24   Ibid. 8.32, ROL 8:294.

positions condemned at Paris in 1277), *Disputatio Eremitae et Raimundi*, and *Liber super quaestiones Magistri Thomae Attrebatensis* (for his friend Thomas Le Myésier) – in which he clearly sought to rouse the masters' interest in the theological and philosophical issues that he deemed most urgent.

From Paris Llull turned homeward. In 1299 he visited Barcelona, where King James II of Aragon granted him permission to proselytize Muslims and Jews within the king's realms.[25] By 1300 Llull returned to Majorca, which his former patron James II had now recovered, and where in the following year James definitively closed Llull's old foundation at Miramar.[26] The *Vita* notes only that on Majorca Llull wrote "many books" (*libros nonnullos*) and strove, through disputation and preaching, to convert the "innumerable" (*innumeros*) Muslims living there.[27] In fact, the Muslim population of Majorca was no longer so large, and local authorities did not encourage, for social and economic reasons, converting those who remained on the island.

Once again, news from the East – the alleged capture of Syria and Palestine by the Mongols, considered potential allies against Islam by Western Europeans – inspired Ramon Llull to action. In 1301 he traveled to Cyprus, only to learn that news of the Mongol conquests were untrue. Resolving not to waste his time on the island, he sought permission from the king of Cyprus, Henry Lusignan II, to proselytize Eastern Christians there, as well as the "sultan ... and king of Egypt and Syria" (*Soldanum ... atque ad regem Aegypti et Syriae*), but Henry ignored his requests. The *Vita* also notes, almost incidentally, that Llull met at Limassol with Jacques de Molay, last Grand Master of the Knights Templar. Llull also escaped a plot, contrived by his two traveling companions, to poison and rob him.[28] Based on references to Jerusalem in Llull's writings, later biographers have conjectured, very optimistically, that he also took this opportunity to travel in the Holy Land.

The *Vita* states only that he returned to Genoa, evidently by 1303, writing there many books, and then went again to Paris, where he taught and wrote more. No other evidence exists for this visit to Paris; many of Llull's works from this period instead indicate Montpellier as their place of composition. His nearly two dozen writings from Genoa and Montpellier in these years cover a wide range of topics, including such major contributions as his *Logica nova* (a comprehensive revision of Aristotelian logic), *Disputatio fidei et intellectus*, *Liber de lumine*, *Liber de praedicatione* (a complete annual cycle of sermons), *Liber de ascensu et descensu intellectus* (the best summary of Llull's epistemology),

---

25   Hillgarth, *Diplomatari*, 71–72.
26   Ibid., 73.
27   *Vita* 8.32, ROL 8:294.
28   Ibid. 8.33–34, ROL 8:294–296.

Liber de demonstratione per aequiparantiam (a fundamental feature of his dialectic), and *Liber de fine* (a concise statement of his missionary and crusading ideals). By autumn of 1305, Llull was again in Barcelona, where he wrote a *Liber praedicationis contra Iudaeos* (a manual of sermons for Jewish audiences), one of his few works specifically concerned with evangelizing Jews. After his alleged stay in Paris, the *Vita* next places him in Lyon, where he sought to present his usual proposals, as explained in the *Liber de fine*, to Pope Clement V. This probably occurred at the pontiff's coronation in November of 1305.[29]

Llull again returned to Majorca, and from there departed in 1307 to the North African city of Bugia (modern Bejaia), seeking to evangelize its Muslim population. His attempts to preach in public provoked a violent response and his immediate incarceration. Once again, the *Vita* rehearses neatly the arguments from his Great Art that Llull delivered to the city's Muslim "bishop" (*episcopus*) and other authorities. It also emphasizes his persistence in the face of physical abuse and harsh conditions of imprisonment. While in jail, Llull received frequent visits from local Muslim "clergy and emissaries of the bishop" (*clerici vel nuntii episcopi*), who promised him material rewards and conjugal pleasures for converting to their religion. Ultimately, several consented to a literary duel in which each side would put in writing its arguments for the superiority of its faith. While Llull was busy with this endeavor, the king of Bugia ordered his expulsion.[30]

En route to Genoa, the ship carrying Llull went down in a severe storm near Pisa. He escaped to shore, but lost all his possessions, including his many books. One of the first that he wrote out again was the *Liber disputationis Raimundi christiani et Homeri saraceni*, which depicts a debate with one of his Muslim interlocutors while in jail at Bugia. Llull remained only six months in Pisa, but finished there two of the best-known and most important works in his entire oeuvre, the *Ars generalis ultima*, the last redaction of his Great Art, and its epitome, the *Ars brevis*. The *Vita* also reports that Llull received enthusiastic promises of material support for his projects from the Pisan city council, as well as from noble citizens of Genoa, where "pious matrons and widows" (*devotae matronae atque viduae*) thronged to hear him. The two cities also provided Llull with letters of support, addressed to Clement V, resident since 1309 at Avignon.[31]

The *Vita* relates that Llull abandoned this plan as unlikely to yield results, and instead continued to Paris. However, we know that he spent some, if not most, of the time between May 1308 and April 1309 in Montpellier, thanks to

---

29   Ibid. 9.35, ROL 8:296–297.
30   Ibid. 9.36–10.40, ROL 8:297–300.
31   Ibid. 10.41–42, ROL 8:300–302.

the colophons of several important works from this period: the *Ars compendiosa Dei*, *Liber de novis fallaciis*, *Liber de convenientia quam habent fides et intellectus in obiecto* (his clearest explanation of the relationship between faith and reason), and *Liber de acquisitione Terrae Sanctae* (a restatement of his proposals for missions and crusades). He found time as well to meet with Christian Spinola in Genoa, and to correspond with King James II of Aragon, to whom he sent the vernacular *Proverbis d'ensenyament* [Proverbs of Instruction] as a kind of *speculum principum* for the monarch's sons.

Llull evidently intended several of the works composed at Montpellier to serve as manifestos of the methods, proposals, and doctrines that he planned to defend at Paris, where he arrived by November of 1309. The *Vita* depicts Llull teaching there his Great Art to a "multitude of masters and students" (*tam magistrorum quam etiam scholarium multitudo*).[32] Documentation of his activity includes letters of commendation from: (1) King Philip IV, with whom he met; (2) forty masters from the Faculties of Medicine and Theology; and (3) University Chancellor Francesco Caraccioli.[33] The latter document is interesting for its use of Biblical tropes, such as the "widow's mite" (Mark 12:41–44, Luke 21:1–4), commonly cited to praise the faithful who display great devotion by offering to God's glory whatever they can, even if very humble or modest. Such a comparison probably reflects well the estimation of Llull's work by many of the university's masters and students. The *Vita* specifically mentions Llull's effort to combat, by "scientific and demonstrative means" (*via demonstrativa et scientifica*) the Averroists' alleged position that matters of faith are impossible to understand intellectually. Disputing with them, he "frequently led them into self-contradiction" (*eos ad redargutionem multipliciter reducebat*).[34] The 27 works that Llull composed at Paris naturally include new anti-Averroist treatises, such as the *Disputatio Raimundi et Averroistae* and *Sermones contra errores Averrois*, but also some of the last important works of his entire career: *Ars mystica theologiae et philosophiae* ("mystic" here means "mixtic" or "unified"), *Metaphysica nova*, *Liber correlativorum innatorum* (the essential presentation of this fundamental Lullian doctrine), *Liber de conversione subiecti et praedicati et medii* (further elucidation of his concept of "proof"), and *Liber lamentationis philosophiae* (an allegorical dialog on the abuse of philosophy, addressed to Philip IV), among others. Llull's two years at Paris constituted, arguably, his last major period of original literary production, since so many of the works from the last five years of his life are much less ambitious.

---

32   Ibid. 10.42, ROL 8:302.
33   Hillgarth, *Diplomatari*, 85–86.
34   *Vita* 10.43, ROL 8:302.

Parisian readers of the *Vita* would easily have been able to assess for themselves its claims about Llull's achievements during his final stay in their city. However, the *Vita*, like many of Llull's own writings and efforts from his last year at Paris, already anticipates another purpose and audience: presenting his proposals to the churchmen assembled at the council convoked by Clement v for October of 1311 in Vienne. The *Vita* ends by listing the three requests that Llull planned to present at the Council: (1) creating language academies for missionaries; (2) consolidating all the military orders into one; and (3) appointing a papal commission to review the doctrines of the Averroists. After noting that forty years had passed since Llull devoted himself to God's service, the *Vita* cites a string of Biblical passages to praise his constant written production, especially the Arabic versions of his works, and mentions the collections of his texts deposited with (1) the Charterhouse at Paris, (2) a certain nobleman of Genoa, and (3) a certain nobleman of Majorca. As an appendix, it then lists the titles of 124 of Llull's writings.[35]

After September of 1311, our knowledge of Llull's activities depends on the colophons to his writings and a handful of documents. Although he dated at least three of his writings from Vienne, the actual extent of his participation in the council remains unknown. His Catalan poem *Lo concili* [The Council] sets forth ten proposals: these include the three noted in the *Vita* along with others regarding such diverse issues as the restriction of usury, evangelizing Western Muslims and Jews, and ecclesiastical reforms. After the Council, his dream vision *Liber de locutione angelorum* (written at Montpellier in May of 1312) expresses his satisfaction that the Council had decreed the creation of language schools for missionaries at the papal court and at major universities (Paris, Oxford, Bologna, and Salamanca) and commanded transfer of all property of the Templars to thc Hospitallers. The *Liber de locutione angelorum* is the first of many addressed to King Frederick III of Sicily (1272–1337), whose patronage Llull now sought to enlist, probably encouraged by Frederick's sympathy for the Spiritual Franciscans, efforts to reform clergy in his kingdom, and interest in overseas missions.

By summer of 1312 Llull returned to Majorca for the last time. He continued writing copiously, mostly short treatises expounding his "proofs" of Christian dogma. He also composed several major texts extending the application of his methods: *Liber de participatione christianorum et saracenorum*, *Liber de novo modo demonstrandi* (a final explanation of his epistemology), *Liber de virtutibus et peccatis* (136 sermons on the virtues and vices), and *Ars abbreviata praedicandi* (despite its title, a miniature version of the Great Art). However,

---

35   *Vita* 11.44–16, ROL 8:302–309.

by far the most important text produced by Llull during his time on Majorca is his will, dated 26 April 1313. Then at least 80 years old, and planning yet another mission overseas, Llull finally recognized the need to settle his temporal affairs. He provided: (1) legacies to his children, Dominic and Madeleine; (2) bequests to local religious houses and churches; and above all, (3) instructions for making parchment copies of all his works, along with single-volume anthologies for the monastery of La Real, Percival Spinola in Genoa, and his son-in-law Pere de Sentmenat.[36]

With these arrangements in place, Llull departed to Sicily, arriving in Messina by August of 1313. There, he continued writing furiously, producing some three dozen small works in less than a year. Few of these short treatises, most devoted to rehearsing familiar arguments, offer new insights into Llull's doctrines and methods. None illuminates his interactions with Frederick III or their outcome.

Llull's next dated works place him in Tunis by the summer of 1315. Correspondence with King James II of Aragon shows Llull now seeking assistance from this monarch.[37] We know nothing about his activities there, a lacuna that later legends filled with stories of his martyrdom, probably adapted from accounts of his previous visits to North Africa in the *Vita*. At Tunis Llull wrote at least seven short works, all addressed to the local *qadi* and devoted chiefly to expounding Llull's arguments for the Trinity and Incarnation. The last of these little treatises is dated December 1315.

The date and circumstances of his death are unknown. His body was buried at the Franciscan church on Majorca, where he probably died by March of 1316.[38]

Works Cited

Primary Works

Hillgarth, Jocelyn N. (ed.), *Diplomatari lul·lià* (Barcelona: 2001).
Vita coaetanea, (ed.) Hermogenes Harada, ROL 8:269–309.

Primary Works: Llull

Libre de meravelles, (ed.) Salvador Galmès, 4 vols. (Barcelona: 1931–34).

---

36   Hillgarth, *Diplomatari*, 87–90.
37   Hillgarth, *Diplomatari*, 91–100.
38   Hillgarth, RLL p. 134, n. 369; Johannes Stöhr, "Introductio generalis," ROL 1:18.

Secondary Works

Domínguez Reboiras, Fernando and Jordi Gayà Estelrich, "Life," in *Raimundus Lullus: An Introduction to his Life, Works and Thought*, (eds.) Alexander Fidora and Josep E. Rubio (Turnhout: 2008), 3–124.

Hillgarth, Jocelyn N., "La biblioteca de La Real: fuentes posibles de Llull," *EL* 7 (1963): 5–17.

Ruffini, Mario, "Il ritmo prosaico nella *Vita beati Raymundi Lulli*," *EL* 5 (1961): 5–60.

Stöhr, Johannes, "Introductio generalis," ROL 1:10–68.

University of Barcelona, "Base de Dades Ramon Llull (Llull DB);" (http://orbita.bib .ub.edu/llull/).

CHAPTER 2

Ramon Llull and His Contemporaries

Henry Berlin

> And what is more wonderful, there is the inspiration given to human minds, so that simple and untutored persons, filled with the gift of the Holy Spirit, come to possess instantaneously the highest wisdom and the readiest eloquence.
>
> THOMAS AQUINAS, *Summa contra Gentiles* 1.6.1

2.1 Introduction

There is no doubt that Ramon Llull was and remains a singular figure in medieval history and literature, one whose prodigious evangelizing labors inspired both devotion and derision. In this chapter, it is my aim to situate this singular figure within a web of relations both biographical and intellectual. By "contemporaries," I understand figures whose most important work took place during Llull's lifetime and not merely figures with whom Llull interacted directly. Thus, while I discuss in some detail, for example, the Aragonese physician and apocalyptic thinker Arnold of Villanova, who served and petitioned the same kings and popes as Llull, I also include thinkers such as Roger Bacon and Thomas Aquinas who moved in substantially different institutional circles. I am guided, then, not only by biography or direct textual citation, but by conceptual threads productive for comparative intellectual history. The chief threads in question, which structure the chapter, are attitudes toward language and authority in mission; the relationship between exegesis, philosophy, and spiritual knowledge; and ideas of creation, theology, and signification. These broad areas include, in turn, more detailed consideration of subjects such as the relationship between reason and faith and specific questions of doctrine (ideas concerning the Incarnation and the Trinity; attitudes toward philosophical positions attributed to the Parisian Averroists). Although some of these threads undoubtedly arise individually in other chapters in this volume, my hope in drawing them together is to contextualize Llull's thought in a way that allows scholars to approach its undeniable idiosyncrasies with a more critical – perhaps even deflating, in some cases – eye.

It is axiomatic by now to point out that mission is the organizing principle of Llull's thought about what otherwise are topics of the greatest diversity, and it has guided me in the material synthesized here. Furthermore, although Llull spent a significant portion of his active life away from the crown of Aragon, there is no question that his missionary strategy was shaped by intellectual developments centered around the Aragonese Dominicans. Interreligious polemic and disputation were not new in the 13th century, but Raymond of Penafort (d. 1275) and his disciple, Raymond Martí (d. 1285), forged a new approach based on serious engagement with rabbinic texts in particular, as well as on the serious language study necessary to make that engagement possible. Meanwhile, it is believed that it was Martí, whose own *Pugio fidei* (1278) was a landmark text of anti-Jewish polemic, who communicated to Thomas Aquinas (d. 1274) Penafort's request that Aquinas compose his own polemical text, the *Summa contra Gentiles* (ca. 1270).[1] In the *Summa contra Gentiles*, Aquinas is less concerned with matters of language and authority; the missionary context of the text's production does, however, guide his more metaphysical approach to areas that overlap significantly with Llull's concerns. Another master at Paris and, later, Oxford, the Franciscan Roger Bacon (d. 1294), combines in his *Opus maius* reflections both exegetical and metaphysical, analyzing, like Aquinas, the role of philosophy in theological study and in mission. Finally, Arnold of Villanova (d. 1311), Llull's strictest contemporary and companion in heterodoxy, a product of Martí's language *studium*,[2] is surprisingly instructive as a counterpoint to Llull in his approach to theological reflection and to the role of language and exegesis therein. In what follows, I will not discuss these figures sequentially, but rather organize their thought along conceptual threads. The first such thread will be language, a fundamental concept that opens into questions of authority, rhetoric, disputation, and signification as such.

2.2   Language and Authority in Mission

Llull famously convinced King James II of Majorca to found, in 1276, a monastery at Miramar where Franciscans could study both Llull's own Art and the "languages of the infidels."[3] Much later in his career, for example in his *De fine* of 1305, Llull continued to advocate the founding of further monasteries for the study of the languages of the Muslims, Jews, schismatics, and Tartars and

---

1   John V. Tolan, *Saracens: Islam in the Medieval European Imagination* (New York: 2002), 242.

2   See the introduction to Villanova, *Tractatus de prudentia catholicorum scolarium,* (ed.) Jaume Mensa i Valls, *La* Prudència de l'escolar catòlic *i altres escrits,* trans. Jordi Raventós, (Barcelona: 2002), 19. Villanova himself refers to Martí's inspirational "religious zeal" in his *De significatione nominis tetragrammaton*, ibid., 51.

3   Hillgarth, RLL 48.

other pagans.[4] Earlier in the 13th century, Raymond of Penafort, who was confessor and chaplain to Pope Gregory IX from 1230 to 1238, master general of the Dominicans from 1238 to 1240, and thereafter spiritual adviser to King James I of Aragon, was at the head of a Dominican project to found language *studia* as part of the order's apostolic mission.[5] The aims of this mission, in Aragon and beyond, were varied, however, and while Penafort did lobby for the obligatory attendance of Muslims and Jews at missionary sermons, he was also instrumental in establishing an inquisition in Aragon whose focus was on the elimination of heresy, not on conversion. Indeed, although Penafort never served as an inquisitor, his own writings give the impression of a man much more preoccupied with the problem of heresy than with the unbelievers. Thus, at a 1242 council at Tarragona, Penafort was the main drafter of a minute taxonomy of heretics, such as *insabbatati*, who would not swear oaths, *suspectus*, who prayed at the same time as the *heretici*, or *celatores*, who saw and recognized *insabbatati* without reporting them to the proper authorities.[6] The punishment for most of these heretics was excommunication, although Penafort generally favored persistent attempts at reconciliation before that point was reached.[7]

Penafort's focus on the policing of heresy is, in fact, characteristic of the 13th-century Dominican approach as a whole, "the protection and nurturing of the faithful rather than conversion of unbelievers."[8] Indeed, the primarily missionary purpose of the language *studia* themselves has recently been called into question. Iberia seems to have constituted a space for pedagogical innovation for the Dominicans. In 1250, for example, small groups of friars in Compostela and Zamora were assigned to study logic, and the language *studia* themselves may have served a similarly philosophical purpose: "Arabic and Hebrew may have been useful to missionaries, but along with Greek and Latin these were also the languages *par excellence* of medieval philosophy and theology."[9] Still, Penafort himself provides guidance for mission to the unbelievers in his *Summa de paenitentia*, noting that Jews and Muslims should

---

4   *Liber de fine* 1.1, (ed.) Alois Madre, ROL 9:252–255.

5   Tolan, *Saracens*, 234.

6   For a detailed analysis of this document, see Damian Smith, *Crusade, Heresy and Inquisition in the Lands of the Crown of Aragon (c. 1167–1276)* (Leiden: 2010), 196–198. The document itself can be found in Penafort's *Diplomatari*, (ed.) Ferran Valls i Taberner (Zaragoza: 1991), 13. A similar, but less developed set of definitions can be found in Penafort's earlier (1225–27) *Summa de paenitentia* 1.5.1, (eds.) Xaverio Ochoa and Aloisio Diez (Rome: 1976), 317–318.

7   Smith, *Crusade, Heresy and Inquisition*, 190.

8   Robin Vose, *Dominicans, Muslims and Jews in the Medieval Crown of Aragon* (Cambridge: 2009), 7.

9   Vose, *Dominicans, Muslims and Jews*, 104; on the Dominican study of logic in Iberia, see also 100–102.

be converted by the use of "authorities, arguments, and blandishments," rather than coercion, to the Christian faith.[10] The prominent place of authority in his instructions anticipates the primary missionary purpose to which the Dominicans' language study would be applied: a new, "professional" engagement not only with the Old Testament in Hebrew, but with rabbinic texts as well.[11]

Later in the *Summa*, Penafort notes that Christians may eat with Muslims, but should neither eat nor socialize in any way with Jews; this is because the latter, making an incorrect use of Scripture, attack Christians more with their misguided dietary laws.[12] This small challenge to Jewish exegesis presages the much greater one carried out in the writings of Penafort's most celebrated disciple, Raymond Martí, whose *Capistrum Iudaeorum* (1267) and *Pugio fidei* (1278) demonstrated the new tactic of challenging traditional Jewish understandings of the Old Testament and rabbinic literature. In fact, exegesis constitutes the center of Martí's missionary strategy, to the exclusion of other (for example, philosophical) possibilities, as the writer seeks both to prove elements of Christian doctrine and attack elements of Jewish doctrine through the exclusive use of texts whose authority Jews grant.[13] The earlier *Capistrum Iudaeorum* focuses largely on the Old Testament, although Martí explains that he will use rabbinic literature when Jews raise an interpretative, rather than purely philological, objection.[14] The *Pugio fidei*, meanwhile, has been held up as "the high-water mark not only of the mid-13th-century missionizing effort but, in many ways, of medieval Christian proselytizing argumentation against the Jews altogether,"[15] but it is important to recognize that even this much later text follows

---

10   *Summa de paenitentia* 1.4.2, 309: "Debent ... tam iudaei quam sarraceni auctoritatibus, rationibus et blandimentis, potius quam asperitatibus, ad fidem christianam de novo suscipiendam provocari, non autem compelli, quia coacta servitia non placent Deo."

11   Robert Chazan, *Daggers of Faith: Thirteenth-Century Christian Missionizing and Jewish Response* (Berkeley: 1989), 116.

12   *Summa de paenitentia* 1.4.3, 310: "Circa eos debent se habere christiani hoc modo, secundum quosdam: non debent comedere cum iudaeis, neque habitare, neque recipere eos ad convivia sua; cum sarracenis, tamen, possumus manducare. Ratio diversitatis est, quia iudaei, per abusionem Scripturarum et contemptum ciborum nostrorum, magis fidem nostram impugnant."

13   Chazan, *Daggers of Faith*, 117, 129.

14   Raymond Martí, *Capistrum Iudaeorum*, praef., 2, 1:54, (ed.) and trans. Adolfo Robles Sierra (Würzburg: 1990): "Contra secundum vero, collegi in Talmud, et ex aliis libris authenticis apud eos, quaedam dicta magistrorum suorum antiquorum inducentium vel exponentium auctoritates huiusmodi, et alia verba prophetarum, Dei dispositione, ut arbitror, non sua intentione ad propositum nostrum."

15   Chazan, *Daggers of Faith*, 136.

almost exactly the agenda set by Pablo Christiani for his disputation with Moses Nahmanides in 1263. Like Pablo in Barcelona, Martini begins his attack upon the Jews with evidence for his claim that the messiah has come; he then proceeds to argue for the trinitarian nature of God and the need for a messiah both divine and human; and he concludes with a discussion of the incarnation and life of Christ, as the messiah who suffered and died to save mankind.[16]

The Barcelona Disputation focused exclusively on the Old Testament and rabbinic texts, resulting in the tactical advantage that "the truth of Christianity was in no sense under investigation,"[17] but also attempting, at least, to avoid the simple exchange of conflicting authorities. Thus, the *Pugio* remains simply the most exegetically sophisticated product of the Dominican realization that verbal mission of any kind requires some form of shared ground.

Penafort and his disciples argued on the common ground of Old Testament and even rabbinic authority, but they rarely sought a common ground *beyond* scriptural authority.[18] This is the error that Llull attempted to avoid in proposing, in his Art, a shared *inventive* language for disputation, and his early *Libre del gentil e los tres savis* [Book of the Gentile and the Three Wise Men] (ca. 1272) shows that he perceived the use of authority to be an error even as Martí was still writing. As the *Libre del gentil's* Jewish wise man explains,

> Christians and Saracens indeed believe that God gave the Law to Moses, and each believes that our Law is true. But because they believe other things that are contrary to our Law, therefore, and insofar as they believe these things contrary to our Law, they disbelieve our Law. Moreover, we and the Christians agree on the text of the Law, but we disagree in interpretation and commentaries, where we reach contrary conclusions. Therefore, we cannot reach agreement based on authorities and must seek necessary arguments by which we can agree.[19]

---

16   Jeremy Cohen, *The Friars and the Jews: The Evolution of Medieval Anti-Judaism* (Ithaca: 1982), 136.

17   Robert Chazan, *Barcelona and Beyond: The Disputation of 1263 and its Aftermath* (Berkeley: 1992), 52.

18   Cohen, *Friars and the Jews*, 132, notes that Martí does engage with pagan and Muslim philosophers in the first part of the *Pugio*.

19   *Libre del gentil e los tres savis* 2.3, (ed.) Sebastián Garcías Palou, *OE*, vol. 1 (Barcelona: 1957), 1080: "Certa cosa és que·ls crestians e·ls sarraïns creen que Déus haja donada la lig a Moisès, e cascú ha creença que la lig nostra sia vera. Mas car ells creen en altres coses qui són

I return to the crucial concept of "necessary arguments" later in this chapter; for now, it is important to note that Llull was not alone in expressing broad skepticism toward the utility of authority in disputation, and certainly not the first. Indeed, forgoing authoritative arguments is at the root of what would become Franciscan spiritual rationalism, as expressed in the prologue of Anselm of Canterbury's famous *Monologion* of 1076, perhaps the first articulation of the well-known ontological proof for the existence of God:

> [Some of my brethren] ... specified (on the basis more of their wishes than of the task's feasibility or my capacity) the following form for this written meditation: nothing whatsoever to be argued on the basis of the authority of Scripture, but the constraints of reason concisely to prove, and the clarity of truth clearly to show, in the plain style, with every-day arguments, and down-to-earth dialectic, the conclusions of distinct investigations.[20]

It is important, however, not to conflate what are really two reasons for eschewing arguments based on authority. The above quotation from Anselm illustrates the more radical approach, adopted by Llull, in which authority is altogether avoided. The more moderate critique, based on the absence of shared scripture, is articulated by Aquinas in the opening chapters of the *Summa contra Gentiles*:

> [Correcting those in theological error] is difficult because some of them, such as the Mohammedans and the pagans, do not agree with us in accepting the authority of any Scripture, by which they may be convinced of their error. Thus, against the Jews we are able to argue by means of the Old Testament, while against heretics we are able to argue by means

---

contràries a nostra lig, per açò, en quant creen ço qui a nostra lig és contrari, descreen nostra lig. Mas descovenim-nos en la exposició e en les gloses qui són contràries; e per açò no·ns podem concordar per auctoritats, e cercam raons necessàries on nos puscam acordar." English translation *Book of the Gentile and the Three Wise Men* 2.3, trans. Bonner, *SW* 1:170.

20 Anselm of Canterbury, *Monologion* Prolog., trans. Simon Harrison, in *The Major Works*, (eds.) Brian Davies and G.R. Evans (Oxford: 1998), 5; *Monologion*, (ed.) P. Franciscus Salesius Schmitt (Stuttgart-Bad Cannstatt: 1964), 26: "Cuius scilicet scribendae meditationis magis secundum suam voluntatem quam secundum rei facilitatem aut meam possibilitatem hanc mihi formam praestituerunt: quatenus auctoritate scripturae penitus nihil in ea persuaderetur, sed quidquid per singulas investigationes finis assereret, id ita esse plano stilo et vulgaribus argumentis simpliceque disputatione et rationis necessitas breviter cogeret et veritatis claritas patenter ostenderet."

of the New Testament. But the Mohammedans and the pagans accept neither the one nor the other. We must, therefore, have recourse to the natural reason, to which all men are forced to give their assent. However, it is true, in divine matters the natural reason has its failings.[21]

Reason's failings lead Aquinas to adopt, in the *Summa contra Gentiles*, an approach similar to that of Martí that nevertheless reserves a larger role for demonstrative arguments. Those truths that are susceptible to rational investigation must be demonstrated, but the "truth which surpasses reason" will be defended by "answering the objections of its adversaries and setting forth the truth of faith by probable arguments and by authorities."[22] Aquinas, then, will follow Martí's two-pronged strategy of attacking error and supporting dogma with authority, having already conceded that "[t]he sole way to overcome an adversary of divine truth is from the authority of Scripture."[23] In this way, he remains firmly in what we may think of as the Dominican camp, although he makes a much more ambitious use of demonstrative argument than his Aragonese brothers.

The Franciscans were also aware of the difficulties that arise in disputation among those who share no sacred text. On the occasion of the 1254 dispute at the Mongol capital of Karakorum between Catholics (represented by William of Rubroek, a Flemish Franciscan), Nestorian Christians, Muslims, and Buddhists (organized by the Khan), William of Rubroek scolded the Nestorians for relying too much on authority, noting that "if you recite one Scripture our enemies will

---

21   Thomas Aquinas, *Summa contra Gentiles* 1.2.3, trans. Anton C. Pegis (New York: 1955), 62. *Summa contra Gentiles*, Editio Leonina Manualis (Rome: 1934), 2: "[Q]uia quidam eorum, ut Mahumetistae et pagani, non conveniunt nobiscum in auctoritate alicuius Scripturae, per quam possint convinci, sicut contra Iudaeos disputare possumus per Vetus Testamentum, contra haereticos per Novum. Hi vero neutrum recipiunt. Unde necesse est ad naturalem rationem recurrere, cui omnes assentire coguntur. Quae tamen in rebus divinis deficiens est."

22   Aquinas, *Summa contra Gentiles* 1.9.3, 78. *Summa contra Gentiles*, Editio Leonina Manualis, 8: "[A]d illius veritatis manifestationem procedemus quae rationem excedit, solventes rationes adversariorum, et rationibus probabilibus et auctoritatibus, quantum Deus dederit, veritatem fidei declarantes." These two kinds of truth are sometimes referred to by Aquinas as the *mysteries of faith*, "taken to be true solely on the basis of revelation," and the *preambles of faith*, which, "while they are included in revelation, can be seen to be true apart from that setting;" see *De unitate intellectus contra Averroistas*, (ed.) and trans. Ralph McInerney, *Aquinas against the Averroists:* On There Being Only One Intellect (West Lafayette, Indiana: 1993), 160–161.

23   Aquinas, *Summa contra Gentiles* 1.9.2, 77. *Summa contra Gentiles*, Editio Leonina Manualis, 8: "Singularis vero modus convincendi adversarium contra huiusmodi veritatem est ex auctoritate Scripturae."

reply with another."[24] This example is particularly relevant here because William of Rubroek seems to have met Roger Bacon and discussed the dispute with him.[25] Their discussion, among other things, may have laid the groundwork for Bacon's own ambivalent approach to authority, to which I will now turn.

For Bacon, as for Aquinas, the question of the use of authority in mission is inseparable from the question of philosophy's role in theology. Whereas Aquinas articulates the question in terms of reason's capacity to know God (a point to which I will return), Bacon approaches the problem from a disciplinary perspective, writing much more about "philosophy" than about reason itself. Bacon and Llull have sometimes been compared because of their shared encyclopedic ambitions and for the practical reason that both advocated the teaching of foreign languages for missionary purposes,[26] a point made plainly by Bacon in Book Three of the *Opus maius*:

> [T]he knowledge of languages is necessary to the Latins for the conversion of unbelievers. For in the hands of the Latins rests the power to convert. And for this reason Jews without number perish among us because no one knows how to preach to them nor to interpret the Scriptures in their tongue, nor to confer with them nor to dispute as to the literal sense, because they have both the true letter and their own ancient expositions according to [blank space in manuscript] and of other men of wisdom as much as the literal exposition requires, and in general as much as it requires for the spiritual sense.[27]

This picture of Jews as exegetically self-sufficient but still open to persuasion if only someone could confer with them in their own language is equally valid for schismatics, Muslims, Tartars, and pagans:

---

24   Cited in R.W. Southern, *Western Views of Islam in the Middle Ages* (Cambridge, Mass.: 1962), 49.

25   Southern, *Western Views of Islam*, 51.

26   See, for example, Hillgarth, *RLL* 42–45. They have also been compared in the context of the broader Franciscan approach to mission; see, for example, E. Randoph Daniel, *The Franciscan Concept of Mission in the High Middle Ages* (Lexington, Kentucky: 1975), 55–75.

27   Roger Bacon, *Opus maius* 3.13, trans. Robert Belle Burke (New York: 1962), 110. Bacon, *Opus maius*, (ed.) John Henry Bridges, 3 vols. (Oxford: 1897–1900), 3:120–121: "[L]inguarum cognitio necessaria est Latinis propter conversionem infidelium. Nam in manibus Latinorum residet potestas convertendi. Et ideo pereunt Judaei inter nos infiniti quia nullus eis scit praedicare, nec scripturas interpretari in lingua eorum, nec conferre cum eis nec disputare juxta sensum literalem, quia et veram literam habent [et] suas expositiones antiquas secundum [sententiam ...] et aliorum sapientum quantum literalis expositio requirit, et in universali quantum ad sensum spiritualem."

Then the Greeks and the Rutheni and many other schismatics likewise grow hardened in error because the truth is not preached to them in their tongue; and the Saracens likewise and the Pagans and the Tartars, and the other unbelievers throughout the whole world.[28]

Bacon's diagnosis of the challenge of Christian missionaries – his picture of those who need conversion – is strikingly similar to that of Llull, expressed not only in programmatic texts such as the *Liber de fine* [On the Goal (of Converting non-Christians)] or *Liber de passagio* [Book on Passage (to Converting Unbelievers)], but also in disputational and devotional texts such as the *Disputació de cinc savis* [The Disputation of Five Wise Men][29] and the *Libre de sancta Maria* [Book of Saint Mary].[30] For Llull, Christian unity must be achieved as a precursor to successful universal mission: "For, if they were united, they could easily conquer and destroy all the world's Saracens, and, after that, they could subjugate the Tartars and other pagans to the holy Christian faith."[31] Bacon couches this missionary rationale in a much broader epistemological and even liturgical appeal, arguing first and foremost that knowledge of Hebrew, Chaldean, and Greek is simply necessary for Christians to understand their own Scripture and the philosophical teachings that enrich Christians' spiritual knowledge.[32] And it is important for Christians to have a thorough philosophical grasp of their theology precisely because, as Bacon explains in Book Two of the *Opus maius*, arguments from authority are of little use in mission:

---

28 Bacon, *Opus maius*, 3.13, 111. *Opus maius*, (ed.) Bridges, 3:121: "Deinde Graeci et Rutheni et multi alii schismatici similiter in errore perdurant quia non praedicatur eis veritas in eorum lingua, et Saraceni similiter et Pagani, ac Tartari, et caeteri infideles per totum mundum." Bacon makes a similar point with regard to the Greeks specifically earlier in the text at 3.2, 78: "If the books of these authors had been translated, not only would the learning of the Latins be augmented in a glorious way, but the Church would have stronger supports against the heresies and schisms of the Greeks, since they would be convinced by their own sacred writers whom they cannot contradict" (ed.) Bridges, 3:70: "Et si libri istorum translati essent, non solum augmentaretur sapientia Latinorum, sed haberet Ecclesia fortia adjutoria contra Graecorum haereses et schismata, quoniam per sanctorum eorum sententias, quibus non possunt contradicere, convincerentur").

29 *Liber de fine*, (ed.) Aloisius Madre, ROL 9:233–291; *Liber de passagio*, (eds.) Blanca Garí and Fernando Domínguez Reboiras, ROL 28:255–353; *Disputació de cinc savis*, (ed.) Josep Perarnau i Espelt, *Arxiu de Textos Catalans Antics* 5 (1986): 7–229.

30 *Liber de sancta Maria*, (eds.) Blanca Garí and Fernando Domínguez Reboiras, ROL 28:3–241.

31 *Disputació de cinc savis* Prolog., (ed.) Perarnau i Espelt, 24–25: "Car, si s'unien, leugeramén purien uensre e destruir tots los saraïns del món e, aprés, los tartres e·ls altres pagans purien subiugar a la sancta fe crestiana."

32 Bacon, *Opus maius*, 3.1, 75–78.

And since they deny Christ, it is not strange if they deny the authorities of the Christians. Now persuasion in regard to the faith is necessary, but this can be accomplished in only two ways, either by miracles which are above believers and unbelievers, concerning which no one can presuppose, or by the road common to believers and unbelievers, but this is only by philosophy. Therefore philosophy must give the methods of proof of the Christian faith. But the articles of this faith are the principles belonging to theology; therefore philosophy must enter into the proofs of the principles of theology, although less deeply than into the principles of other sciences.[33]

The skepticism expressed by Bacon toward the missionary utility of authority is mitigated, on the one hand, by Bacon's disciplinary mindset, and, on the other, by his belief in the extraordinary power of careful exegesis to produce spiritual knowledge.

Bacon studied at Oxford and taught at both Paris and Oxford during his long career.[34] Sometime before becoming a Franciscan in 1250, he was "seized by the desire ... to reorganize the whole of Christian learning, giving particular emphasis to its practical applications."[35] This desire, along with a request from Pope Clement IV, led to the massively ambitious *Opus maius*, a critical taxonomy of the human sciences that also proposed their Christian utility. When the text did not receive the desired response, however, Bacon scaled back his ambition (while also evincing considerable bitterness in his later texts):

Perhaps at this point, reflecting on the unique ways in which the various sciences had been described as useful for theology in the *Opus maius*, he recognized that there was one science which theologians could not escape, with which they were already familiar, and of which they were in desperate need, and it was the science of language. Biblical exegesis

---

33 Ibid., 2.18, 71. Ibid., (ed.) Bridges, 61–62: "Et etiam quia Christum negant, non est mirum, si auctores Christianorum negent. Persuasio autem fidei necessaria est; sed non potest hoc esse nisi duobus modis, aut per miracula quae sunt supra fideles et infideles, de quibus nullus potest praesumere; aut per viam communem fidelibus et infidelibus; sed hoc non est nisi per philosophiam. Ergo philosophia habet dare probationes fidei Christianae. Articuli vero hujus fidei sunt principia propria theologiae; ergo philosophia habet descendere ad probationes principiorum theologiae, licet minus profunde quam ad principia aliarum scientiarum."

34 For an excellent, concise biography of Bacon, see the introduction to *Compendium studii theologiae*, (ed.) and trans. Thomas. S. Maloney, *Compendium of the Study of Theology* (Leiden: 1988), 2–13.

35 Ibid., 4–5.

requires a proper understanding of the many modes in which words can signify and so does the proper conduct of a disputation on *questions*. In this area theologians were still holding linguistic theories which he considered erroneous ... If theologians were ill-prepared to see the relevance of all sciences to theology, perhaps they could be brought by one last effort to see the value of the study of language, a proposal far more modest than the grand scheme of the *Opus maius* but one standing in relation to it as the part to the whole.[36]

This shift in focus in the career of Bacon from encyclopedic ambition, including a substantial commitment to exegesis to the philosophical study of signification, provides an opportunity to shift this chapter's focus from authority and mission to exegesis and the broader epistemologies of Llull, Bacon, and Villanova. Because those views are tied inextricably to their respective cosmologies, this will also provide an opportunity to discuss the question of the divine nature and its knowability, a discussion in which Aquinas will also be of particular importance as a midpoint between Llull's optimism and Villanova's pessimism.

2.3   Exegesis, Philosophy, and Spiritual Knowledge

In the prologue of part one of the *Compendium studii theologiae*, Bacon explains in an apparently even-handed manner that because the language of theology is "still aired through authorities, arguments, and solutions of philosophy (as is known to all sufficiently literate), thus to conform myself to others I desire to use authorities and philosophical reasons abundantly."[37] In the prologue of part two, however, Bacon asserts reproachfully that "theologians are more prone to receive a treatise on *questions* than on the text [of sacred scripture]."[38] This tone of reproach is easy to understand if one takes into account the great power accorded to exegesis in the *Opus maius*, especially in the way it helps Bacon read philosophy into the history of Christianity.

---

36   Ibid., 12–13. One might note here a similarity to Llull's continued refinement and simplification of his Art after its initial rejection at Paris; see Bonner, *AL* 93–120.

37   Bacon, *Compendium studii theologiae*, lib. 1, Prologue, 2, 32–33: "[E]t reliqua pars, quae est in terminis theologiae, adhuc ventilatur per auctoritates et argumenta et solutiones philosophiae, ut notum est omnibus sufficienter literatis, ideo, ut conformem me aliis, auctoritatibus et rationibus philosophicis uti cupio abundanter."

38   Ibid., lib. 2, Prologue, 17, 48–49: "[P]roniores sunt theologi ad recipiendum tractatum de quaestionibus quam de textu."

For Bacon, "there is only one perfect wisdom, which is contained wholly in the Scriptures, and is to be unfolded by canon law and philosophy,"[39] the two disciplines that compose theology.[40] Philosophical language is not just useful in interpreting scripture, but constitutes an original element of scripture's revelation:

> I say, therefore, that the power of philosophy was given by God to the same persons as the sacred Scripture, namely, the saints at the beginning, so that there thus appears to be one wisdom in its entirety necessary for mankind. For the patriarchs and prophets alone were true philosophers, knowing all things, to wit, not only the law of God, but all the parts of philosophy.[41]

Throughout humanity's history, however, knowledge of philosophy has fluctuated according to our moral deserts, disappearing when the wise came to be worshipped as gods and reappearing in devout figures such as Solomon.[42] For Bacon, this means that some pagan philosophers (Thales, Pythagoras, Socrates, Plato, and Aristotle) were privy to at least some of this revelation.[43] Their philosophical knowledge is thus relevant to exegesis:[44]

> Those philosophizing should not be surprised, therefore, if they must need raise philosophy to the level of divine things and theological truths and the authorities of sacred writers, and employ these freely whenever the occasion arises, and prove them when necessary, and by means of these prove other matters; since without doubt philosophy and theology have much in common. The sacred writers not only speak as theologians, but as philosophers, and frequently introduce philosophical

---

39   Bacon, *Opus maius*, 2.1, 36. *Opus maius*, (ed.) Bridges, 1:33: "[U]na tamen est sapientia perfecta, quae in sacra scriptura totaliter continetur, per jus canonicum et philosophiam explicanda."

40   Ibid., 2.2, 37.

41   Ibid., 2.9, 52. Ibid., (ed.) Bridges, 1:45: "Dico igitur quod eisdem personis a Deo data est philosophia potestas quibus et sacra scriptura, videlicet, sanctis ab initio, ut sic appareat una sapientia esse completa et omnibus necessaria. Soli enim patriarchae et prophetae fuerunt veri philosophi qui omnia sciverunt, non solum legem Dei, sed omnes partes philosophiae."

42   Ibid., 2.14, 64.

43   Bacon even claims, ibid., 2.16, 68, citing Augustine's authority, that Plato had knowledge of the Old Testament.

44   Ibid., 2.14–18, 64–71.

subjects. Therefore Christians desiring to complete philosophy ought in their works not only to collect the statements of the philosophers in regard to divine truths, but should advance far beyond to a point where the power of philosophy as a whole may be complete. And for this reason he who completes philosophy by truths of this kind must not on this account be called a theologian, nor must he transcend the bounds of philosophy; since he can handle freely what is common to philosophy and theology and what must be accepted in common by believers and unbelievers.[45]

Bacon is here carving out space for philosophical exploration of traditionally theological questions, while arguing that theologians should not feel that their position in the hierarchy of knowledge is under threat. If philosophy has always been a part of revelation, then it does not "transcend its bounds" when it is brought to bear on scriptural revelation or, indeed, on the contemplation of the divine through the study of creation.

Early in part two of the *Opus maius*, on philosophy, Bacon asserts the primacy of scripture through the extended metaphor of a tree:

But the roots of all these matters and the erect stalk itself are found in the Scriptures; the branches belong to the expositors of the same, so that in the body of the canons are to be had the leaves, flowers, and fruit bringing salvation. For the pleasing embellishment of the language of the canon is compared to leaves according to the Scriptures, but the utility of the flowers and fruits is comprised in the four divisions already mentioned under their appropriate metaphors. And for this reason the canons are merely the golden heads of grain, and the branches, the ripeness of the grapes, are to be offered through the virtue in their own Scriptures. Since therefore canon law is thus subject to Scripture, it is contained in one body,

---

45   Ibid., 2.19, 73. Ibid., (ed.) Bridges, 1:63–64: "Non igitur mirentur philosophantes, si habeant elevare philosophiam ad divina et ad theologiae veritates et sanctorum auctoritates, et uti eis abundanter cum fuerit opportunum, et probare eas cum necesse est, et per illas alias probare; quoniam proculdubio philosophia et theologia communicant in multis. Et sancti non solum loquuntur theologice, sed philosophice, et philosophica multipliciter introducunt. Et ideo Christiani, philosophiam volentes complere, debent in suis tractatibus non solum dicta philosophorum de divinis veritatibus colligere, sed longe ulterius progredi, usquequo potestas philosophiae totius compleatur. Et propter hoc complens philosophiam per hujusmodi veritates non debet dici theologicus nec transcendere metas philosophiae; quoniam ista quae sunt communia philosophiae et theologiae potest secure tractare et ea quae communiter habent recipi a fidelibus et infidelibus."

just as the body of a single tree is composed of roots and stalk, branches, flowers, and fruits.[46]

This metaphor is particularly interesting to the Llull scholar, who may be struck by the resemblance to Llull's *Arbre de sciència*, although, of course, Llull replaces the language of scripture with that of his Art.[47] That is no small difference, yet it still allows for important methodological similarities to emerge. After expressing what is fundamentally a philological preoccupation with the elimination of errors in the Latin scriptures,[48] Bacon argues that knowledge of other languages will also allow ecclesiastics to see how Latin itself encodes the present and future of Church history, just as

> the individual letters of the Hebrew alphabet had significance respecting the ancient people, and how they show the numbers of centuries through which the state of that race passed as regards the different periods and ages, in accordance with the special powers and potencies of the letters; and then the progress of the Church of the Latins is shown by the virtues of the Latin letters.[49]

Bacon's clear allusion to Kabbalistic practice initially raises the perennial question of Llull's own adaptations of Jewish and Islamic mystical practices, particularly regarding Llull's divine *dignitates*.[50] Llull's interest here was,

---

46   Ibid., 2.2,, 38. Ibid., (ed.) Bridges, 1:35: "Sed horum omnium radices et ipsa stipes erecta apud sacram scripturam reperiuntur. Rami vero penes expositores ejusdem, ut in canone folia, flores, fructus salutiferi capiantur. Nam sermones canonici suavis ornatus foliis comparantur secundum scripturam. Flores autem et fructus sunt segetum aurei palmites et uvarum maturitio. Et ideo jus canonicum sine potestate scripturae in uno corpore continetur, sicut unius arboris corpus ex radicibus et stipite, ramis, floribus, et fructibus constituitur."

47   Trees are also, of course, fundamental to the disputation at the heart of the *Libre del gentil*, and Cynthia Robinson has argued that trees constitute one of the most important intellectual and artistic metaphors for medieval Iberia's interconfessional context: "Trees of Love, Trees of Knowledge: Toward the Definition of a Cross-Confessional Current in Late Medieval Iberian Spirituality," *Medieval Encounters* 12 (2006): 388–435.

48   Bacon, *Opus maius*, 3.5–6, 89–99.

49   Ibid., 3.11, 108. Ibid., (ed.) Bridges, 3:118: "[S]ingulae literae alphabeti Hebraei signabant super populum antiquum, et ostendunt numerum centenariorum annorum quibus decurrebat status illius gentis juxta singulas aetates et secula, secundum speciales vires et potestates literarum; et deinde decursum Ecclesiae Latinorum per virtutes literarum Latinarum."

50   For a general discussion of these resemblances, see Miguel Cruz Hernández, *El pensamiento de Ramon Llull* (Valencia: 1977), 72–78. On the dignities and the Kabbalah's *sefirot*,

however, primarily theological, whereas writers such as Bacon and Villanova adapted specifically exegetical practices to demonstrate the truth of Christian doctrine.

Villanova is a particularly instructive case here in that his condemnation of the abandonment of biblical exegesis is much stronger even than Bacon's, grounded as it is in an apocalyptic discourse. Villanova's career can be divided into three principal (and overlapping) phases: doctor, diplomat, and church reformer.[51] In 1281, already serving as physician to King Peter III of Aragon, Villanova studied with Raymond Martí and translated some Arabic medical texts. In the last decade of the 13th century, teaching medicine at Montpellier and serving as physician to King James II of Aragon at the same time, he composed his own series of medical texts. However, during this period he also became interested in apocalyptic thought, circulating his *Tractatus de tempore adventu Antichristi* during a 1299 embassy from James II to Paris. The text was rejected as heretical, and when Villanova sought the protection of Popes Boniface VIII and Benedict XI, his medical expertise was acknowledged but his theological doctrines rejected.[52] Nevertheless, Villanova remained in the service of James II until 1310 and of Frederick III of Sicily until his death. Several of his theses were posthumously condemned in 1316 by the Inquisitor of Tarragona and other clergy, a condemnation confirmed by the provincial council in 1318.[53]

Llull is known to have consulted with Villanova while promoting crusade against Granada in 1308;[54] J.N. Hillgarth has summarized the similarities between the two figures:

> Both Llull and Arnau claimed to have received divine revelations; both were often considered "fantastic" by their contemporaries; both, perhaps, to a certain extent enjoyed the appellation and regarded it as a compliment,

see Harvey Hames, *The Art of Conversion: Christianity and Kabbalah in the Thirteen Century* (Leiden: 2000), 118–189, particularly 118–131. On the dignities and the Islamic *ḥadras*, see Robert D.F. Pring-Mill, *El microcosmos lul·lià* (Palma: 1961), 124–125.

51   Mensa, intro. to Villanova, *La Prudència*, 14.

52   Miquel Batllori, *Arnau de Vilanova i l'Arnaldisme* (Valencia: 1994), 264.

53   For a brief overview of Villanova's life and work, see Mensa, introduction to *La Prudència*; for a longer treatment, see Batllori, *Arnau de Vilanova i l'Arnaldisme*, 3–147.

54   Hillgarth, RLL 70. For Llull's approach to crusade, see Benjamin Kedar, *Crusade and Mission: European Approaches toward the Muslims* (Princeton: 1984), 189–199; Fernando Domínguez Reboiras, "La idea de cruzada en el *Liber de passagio* de Ramón Llull," *Patristica et Mediaevalia* 25 (2004), 45–75; and Gabriel Ensenyat, "Pacifisme i croada en Ramon Llull," in *Ramon Llull i l'Islam: L'inici del diàleg* (Barcelona: 2008), 232–245.

coming from men of the world. Arnau is known to have seen Lull and himself as the "two modern messengers" of truth.[55]

It is nevertheless the case that, although Llull and Villanova may have shared a heterodox temperament, they were almost diametrically opposed in epistemological and cosmological terms. Villanova always emphasized Scripture as the source of wisdom, noting that this is where the "prudent" scholar will seek the teachings of the "eternal Master."[56] In fact, one of the chief reasons that Villanova has sometimes been called an "anti-Scholastic" is that he frequently accuses scholars and ecclesiastics not only of alleging false authorities in support of their arguments, but, echoing Bacon, of disdaining Scripture in favor of secular intellectual pursuits: "They study questions, sophisms of logic and nature, and secular sciences much more than the text of the Bible."[57]

In his *De significatione nominis tetragrammaton* (1292), Villanova holds that the letters of the Hebrew name of God disclose God's trinitarian nature:

[T]he meaning of the letters found in the name of the tetragrammaton according to Hebrew writing is as follows: in God there is the beginning that has no beginning, that gives its own origin and sound, that conceives itself first and always and breathes out an angle that knots together or unifies indissolubly two equal sides; there is also in Him the beginning that proceeds from a beginning that is eternal like Him, who always accompanies Him and who breathes out the same angle as Him.[58]

---

55 Hillgarth, *RLL* 97.

56 Villanova, *La Prudència*, 86. For the contraposition of philosophy and wisdom in Villanova, see Eusebi Colomer i Pous, *El pensament als països catalans durant l'Edat Mitgana i el Renaixement* (Barcelona: 1997), 43.

57 Villanova, *Confessió de Barcelona*, (ed.) Miquel Batllori, *Obres catalanes*, vol. 1 (Barcelona: 1947), 131–132: "[M]olt més studien en qüestions e en sophismes de lògica, e de natures, e en sciències seglars, que en lo test de la Bíblia." On Villanova's "anti-Scholasticism," see Batllori, *Arnau de Vilanova i l'Arnaldisme*, 261–272; Francesc J. Fortuny, "Arnau de Vilanova: Els límits de la raó teològica: Arnau en oposició a Averrois, Maimònides i Tomàs d'Aquino," *Estudi General* 9 (1989), 31–60; and, for a comprehensive discussion, Jaume Mensa i Valls, *Les raons d'un anunci apocalíptic: la polèmica escatològica entre Arnau de Vilanova i els filòsofs i teòlegs professionals (1297–1305): Anàlisi dels arguments i de les argumentacions* (Barcelona: 1998).

58 *De significatione nominis tetragrammaton*, (ed.) Mensa i Valls, *La* Prudència, 63–64; *Allocutio super significatione nominis Tetragrammaton*, (ed.) Josep Perarnau i Espelt, *Arnaldi de Villanova Opera Theologica Omnia* (Barcelona, 2004): 3:156: "Est, ergo, in summa significatio litterarum que sunt in nomine Thetagramaton secundum hebraycam Scripturam quando propriis uocabulis explicantur, ista: In Deo est principium sine principio principians et per se sonans et seipsum primo et semper concipiens et spirans angulum nodantem

Villanova will make a similar trinitarian claim for the Latin letters of the Tetragrammaton;[59] for him, however, this trinitarian reading of scriptural language does not translate into a trinitarian reading of creation. In the *Tractatus de prudentia catholicorum scolarium* (before 1297), he writes that teachers other than God may be able to "engrave on the mind teachings about some truth," but only God can grant the faculty of understanding.[60] The contemplation of sensible objects can be beneficial, but philosophers contemplate in those objects "the proper reasons of their essence," whereas the faithful contemplate them "as they relate to their first cause" and are thereby incited to feel affection for the divine.[61] The philosophical underpinnings of this statement are expressed in the later *Allocutio Christini de hiis quae conveniunt homini secundum propriam dignitatem creaturae rationalis* (1304–5), a work dedicated to Frederick III:

> Undoubtedly, God gave man reason and intelligence. But he was given intelligence so that, through it, he might know God in Himself. [This is] because God, being spirit and only intelligible, is only apprehensible in Himself through the intelligence. On the other hand, he was given reason so that, reasoning from the sensible to the intelligible, he might know how to perceive the excellences and perfections of God through what he knows of created things, so that, in this way, knowing God in Himself as much as possible in this life and knowing his perfections, his soul might burn with ardor to love him and, loving Him, be incited to praise Him ... For this reason, anyone who wants to be incited to love God must contemplate the divine perfections in creatures, but must become

---

siue indissolubiliter colligantem duo latera equalia et in eo, inquam, est principium ex principio coeternum ei, uel semper concomitans ipsum et spirans eundem angulum quem et ipsum." In translating Villanova's Latin treatises into English, I have, where possible, consulted Jordi Raventós's Catalan translations from *La* Prudència, 191–208.

59   Ibid., 64.

60   Ibid., 87. *Tractatus de prudentia catholicorum scolarium*, (ed.) Perarnau i Espelt, *Opera*, 3:211: "Ceteri namque possunt instruere, hoc est, menti aliqualia imprimere documenta de qualibet ueritate, sed intelligendi potentiam dare nequeunt ullo modo [...]."

61   Ibid., 96. *Tractatus de prudentia*, (ed.) Perarnau i Espelt, *Opera*, 3:227–228: "Quoniam ipsa sensibilia possunt considerari secundum id quod sunt in se, et tunc in eis considerantur rationes entitatis ipsorum: et hoc modo considerat ea philosophus [...] Alio modo possunt considerari sensibilia, secundum quod referuntur in Causam Primam: e tunc attenditur qualiter in eis reluceant potentia, sapientia et bonitas creatoris. Et per talem considerationem inflammatur in Deum affectus: qualis consideratio pertinet ad fideles."

accustomed to meditate upon them with even more attention in the Scriptures.[62]

Villanova's divine knowledge is not that of Llull, or even of Bacon or Aquinas. The emphasis on contemplation and meditation, on the one hand, and love and affection, on the other, indicate that for Villanova, very little is actually knowable about the divine in this world, barring an infusion of grace. There is something of the divine in creation, but it is matter for acquiring spiritual wisdom – not philosophical knowledge – through meditation and prayer. And even so, the study of Scripture is a superior vehicle for the faithful student. Furthermore – and here, Villanova is clearly completely at odds with Llull – although the contemplation of the divine perfections in nature may incite our devotion, human language is incapable of articulating those perfections: "the condition of his glory transcends all the things of the sensible world and, therefore, all the words and all the names of this world."[63]

Villanova's assertion of the absolute unknowability of the divine, outside of revelation, marks a definitive break from all strains of 13th-century rationalism.[64] But it is just the "divine perfections" (dignities) that Llull believed to have been revealed to him. In this sense, one can say that Llull's personal rationalism is founded on grounds that Villanova accepts: divine self-revelation. Villanova would dispute, however, that such a revelation could be shared through human language. For Llull, it was exactly a correspondence between human language and the divine nature that had been revealed, and it was for this reason that doctrines such as the Incarnation and the Trinity could be explained and proved by necessary reasons.

---

62   *Allocutio christini de hiis quae conveniunt homini secundum propriam dignitatem crea-turae rationalis*, (ed.) Josep Perarnau i Espelt, *Arxiu de Textos Catalans Antics* 11 (1992): 77–82: "Dedit igitur Deus homini rationem et intellectum. Sed intellectum dedit, ut per ipsum cognoscat Deum in Se. Quoniam Deus, cum sit spiritus et res solum intellectualis, solo intellectu apprehenditur in Se ipso. Rationem vero dedit ei, ut a sensibilibus ad intel-ligibilia ratiocinando, sciat Dei excellentias sive dignitates animadvertere per ea, que in sensibilibus experitur, ut sic, per cognitionem ipsius in Se, quantum possibile est in pre-senti vita, et per cognitionem suarum dignitatum, incalescat eius animus ad amandum eum et amando sollicitetur ad laudandum eundem ... Unde, quicumque voluerit inflam-mati ad amandum Deum, diligenter in creaturis debet contemplari dignitates divinas, sed diligentius in scripturis divinis studio meditationis se ipsum exercitare."

63   Ibid., 91: "Status autem illius glorie transcendit omnes res huius mundi sensibilis et per consequens omnes voces et omnia nomina mundi huius."

64   Fortuny, "Arnau de Vilanova," 36. As the same author notes, 31, it also marks the beginning of a "total rupture" between Judaism and Islam, on the one hand, and Christianity, on the other.

2.4   Theological Doctrine and Signification

By 1290, Llull's Art was thoroughly trinitarian in structure.[65] Not only was the divine essence, understood and communicated through its dignities, a Trinity, but creation and language were, by ontological analogy, trinitarian as well.[66] This real relationship between creation and Creator, based on "participated resemblance," renders metaphor itself unnecessary – which is why Llull often refers to it as "signification."[67] It also means that doctrine can be proved with demonstrative arguments,[68] and not just the "probable arguments and authorities" in Aquinas's arsenal.

It should be noted that this is a point of proximity between the thought of Llull and Bacon. As Maloney has noted, the latter was an "extreme realist" who held that "universals exist outside the mind and they exist in things," because "the world was created to be both universal and particular at the same time … When we think of it as a unity (at any level of genus or species) we are not simply playing a mental game or talking abstractly. We can think of the unity of the world, because there within things are their common (universal) natures. From Bacon's point of view, Porphyry's tree is a useful tool for thinking about the world precisely because it is the metaphysician's view of the stratigraphy of the world."[69] Llull made use of Porphyry's tree, describing it in his earliest work on logic, the *Lògica del Gatzell posada en rims* [Logic of Algazel Versified].[70] But Llull's illumination (as he understood it) provided him with a much more detailed picture, with specific semantic content, of the relationship between the universal (divine) and the particular.[71] Johnston describes Llull's "worldview" thus: "Lullian metaphysics is insistently 'superrealist' in both a subjective and an objective sense: it tends to conflate the content of understanding or expression with the actual concept or word itself. Since for Llull that understanding or expression includes the perception of so many spiritual truths, this superrealist metaphysics is already a virtual *allegoria in rebus*. Applied globally

---

65   Bonner, *AL* 117–120; Jordi Gayà Estelrich, *La teoría luliana de los correlativos: Historia de su formación conceptual* (Palma: 1979), 79.

66   Josep Maria Ruiz Simon, "De la naturalesa com a mescla a l'art de mesclar (sobre la fonamentació cosmològica de les arts lul·lianes," *Randa* 19 (1986), 71.

67   Ibid., 90.

68   Josep Maria Ruiz Simon, "'Quomodo est haec ars inventiva?' (L'Art de Llull i la dialèctica escolàstica," *SL* 33 (1993), 82.

69   Thomas S. Maloney, "The Extreme Realism of Roger Bacon," *The Review of Metaphysics* 38 (1985), 827–828, 837.

70   (Ed.) Jordi Rubió i Balaguer, "*La lògica del Gazzali posada en rims* per en Ramon Llull," *Anuari de l'Institut de Estudis Catalans* 5 (1913–14), lines 1543–65.

71   On participated resemblance and signification in Llull, see Johnston, *ER* 34–35, 38.

to things, concepts, and words, it is in fact a universal allegory, a kind of meta-physics of meaning."[72]

The trinitarian structure of Llull's theology is in part based on Llull's theory of three "correlative" principles that exist in all beings.[73] As Pring-Mill explains, in the divine essence, each of the dignities is divided into three "subordinate principles – active, passive, and the act itself," making the divine essence itself constantly active.[74] These principles are reflected in creation – although each can no longer be predicated of the other – such that man, for example, can be defined as a "manifying animal," composed of a "manifying" form, "manifiable" matter, and the act of "manifying."[75] As Pring-Mill has argued, divine activity is fundamental to Llull's trinitarian arguments,[76] as can be seen in the following example from Llull's *Liber praedicationis contra Iudaeos* of 1305:

> In truth, God could not be one without being three. For if He were one and not three, his unity would be empty and imperfect, because without deifying it would be idle, just as his intellect without the understanding, the understood, and [the act of] understanding, and his will without the willing, the willed, and [the act of] willing ... and so on with all of his dignities.[77]

Later in the same text, Llull argues that there must be some trinitarian resemblance in men, because God would otherwise be "alien" to humanity.[78] The linchpin of this argument is, in fact, the Incarnation. On the one hand, God's activity (as first cause of creation) is proof of the Incarnation;[79] on the other,

---

72 Ibid., 34. On resemblance and signification, see also Josep M. Vidal i Roca, "Significació i llenguatge," *Catalan Review* 4 (1990), 329.

73 On the complicated development of this trinitarian ontology throughout Llull's career, see Gayà Estelrich, *La teoría luliana de los correlativos*.

74 Pring-Mill, *El microcosmos lul·lià*, 38–39.

75 Ibid., 151. The example is from Llull's *Logica nova* of 1303.

76 Ibid., 141–142.

77 *Liber praedicationis contra Ivdaeos*, sermon 4, (ed.) Aloisius Madre, ROL 12:19: "Deus uero non posset esse unus, nisi sit trinus. Si enim esset unus et non trinus, sua unitas esset uacua et imperfecta, quae sine deificante esset otiosa, sicut suus intellectus sine intelligente, intellecto et intelligere, et sua uoluntas sine uolente, uolito et uelle ... et sic de aliis suis dignitatibus."

78 Ibid., sermon 6, 22. The *Liber praedicationis* is an example of Llull's increased use of authorities in his later career; the authority in question here is Ex. 34:14, "Non habeas Deum alienum."

79 *Liber de trinitate et incarnatione* 2.19, (ed.) Alois Madre, ROL 12:135: "Omne illud ens, per quod primitiuae causae habent maiores actus in causis primis creatis, est incarnatum. Sed Deus est huiusmodi; ergo Deus est incarnatus."

the Incarnation serves as the "mirror" of the Trinity,[80] establishing a "middle" between the divine and the human "through high and sublime participation."[81] Participated resemblance also plays a crucial role in Llull's rhetorical theory, as when he argues in the *Rhetorica nova*: "Someone who says 'The queen is beautiful,' speaks beautifully by putting a substantive before an adjective in this speech. This is because a substantive has greater essence and nobility than the adjective predicated of it, which would lack a place to exist without it."[82] The ontological level of the signified determines the aesthetic quality and proper order of the signified. This participation is, of course, crucial for salvation, and it is therefore, and relatedly, the basis for knowledge of the divine: the Incarnation made possible the system of participated resemblance through which the divine essence can be contemplated in this world.[83]

A useful comparison can be drawn here between Llull and Aquinas, who also developed a sophisticated model of participation in his understanding of creation. According to Aquinas, the revelation of the Trinity was necessary in order to have a true picture of creation and a correct understanding of mankind's salvation.[84] The Trinity in God, in which "procession means personal communication of the fullness of the divinity," has its analogy in creation: "Thomas considers creation to be the participation of creatures in the divinity's being and perfection. It is on this level of the *communication of being*, implying the doctrine of analogy, that we find trinitarian causality."[85] And this causal participation is crucial to Aquinas's concept of spiritual knowledge. For Aquinas, as apparently for Llull, causal participation creates a similitude between

---

80   *Disputació de cinc savis* 3.1, (ed.) Perarnau i Espelt, 83–84.

81   *Liber Praedicationis*, sermon 6, 22: "[E]st ergo Deus incarnatus, ut non sit nobis Deus alienus, ut sit medium inter ipsum et nos per participationem altam et sublimem." For a detailed discussion of the role of the Incarnation in Llull's theory of signification, see Robert D. Hughes, "Speculum, Similitude, and Signification: the Incarnation as Exemplary and Proportionate Sign in the Arts of Ramon Llull," *SL* 45–46 (2005–6): 3–37.

82   *Rhetorica nova* 2.3.3, (ed.) and trans. Mark D. Johnston, *Ramon Llull's New Rhetoric: Text and Translation of Llull's* Rethorica nova (Davis, Calif.: 1994), 14: "Et qui dicit 'Regina est pulcra' dicit pulcrum verbum propter hoc quod ponit in predicto verbo substantivum ante adiectivum, quoniam substantivum habeat maiorem essentiam et dignitatem quam adiectivum quod predicatur de ipso et sino ipso locum in quo esset habere non posset."

83   *Liber de trinitate et incarnatione* 2.20, 136: "Omne illud ens, per quod Deus intelligit se magis intelligibilem et amabilem erga suam creaturam, oportet esse in Deo. Sed incarnatio est illud ens, per quod Deus intelligit se magis intelligibilem et amabilem erga suam creaturam, ut probabo; ergo incarnatio est in Deo."

84   Gilles Emery, "The Doctrine of the Trinity in St. Thomas Aquinas," in *Aquinas on Doctrine: A Critical Introduction*, (eds.) Thomas Weinandy, Daniel Keating, and John Yocum (London: 2004), 45.

85   Ibid., 60.

creation and the divine essence. In Aquinas's thought, however, there is no real metaphysical continuity between creation and the divine essence itself:

> God's essence remains "unparticipated and uncommunicated" (*imparticipata et incommunicata*). Creatures do not result from a differentiation of the divine essence in many parts, but they are the many partial "similitudes" into which the similitude of God's essence is distinguished and multiplied. It is through its *similitudo* that the divine cause is "propagated and multiplied" in his creatures (*propagatur et multiplicatur*).[86]

Thus, "participation" in Aquinas names a fundamental difference between Creator and creation, and the similitude that does exist between them is "deficient:" "The intelligible connection between creature and creator is not such that the form of a creature enables us to say positively what the 'form' of God is."[87]

It is in this context that we should consider, finally, the accusation of extreme rationalism that was sometimes directed at Llull in his own lifetime. Llull certainly does believe that the contemplation of creation allows us to make true statements about the divine essence, whereas Aquinas argues in the *Summa contra Gentiles* that the divine substance is ultimately unknowable:

> For the human intellect is not able to reach a comprehension of the divine substance through its natural power. For, according to its manner of knowing in the present life, the intellect depends on the sense for the origin of knowledge; and so those things that do not fall under the senses cannot be grasped by the human intellect except in so far as the knowledge of them is gathered from sensible things. Now, sensible things cannot lead the human intellect to the point of seeing in them the nature of the divine substance; for sensible things are effects that fall short of the power of their cause.[88]

---

86   Rudi A. te Velde, *Participation and Substantiality in Thomas Aquinas* (Leiden: 1995), 93.

87   Ibid., 96. See also Johnston, *SL* 154.

88   *Summa contra Gentiles*, 1.3.3, 64. *Summa contra Gentiles*, Editio Leonina Manualis, 3: "Nam ad substantiam ipsius capiendam intellectus humanus naturali virtute pertingere non potest: cum intellectus nostri, secundum modum praesentis vitae, cognitio a sensu incipiat; et ideo ea quae in sensu non cadunt, non possunt humano intellectu capi, nisi quatenus ex sensibilibus earum cognitio colligitur. Sensibilia autem ad hoc ducere intellectum nostrum non possunt ut in eis divina substantia videatur quid sit: cum sint effectus causae virtutem non aequantes."

The likeness (*similitudo*) between creation and Creator does not allow for demonstrative arguments, but it does allow for probable ones. The value of making these arguments is not primarily intellectual, but affective:

> Yet it is useful for the human reason to exercise itself in such arguments, however weak they may be, provided only that there be present no presumption to comprehend or to demonstrate. For to be able to see something of the loftiest realities, however thin and weak the sight may be, is, as our previous remarks indicate, a cause of the greatest joy.[89]

For Llull, probable arguments were not enough; it was necessary to prove Christian doctrine demonstratively.[90] Llull often put the desire for "necessary reasons" in the mouths of Muslims and other "unbelievers;" his *Disputatio fidei et intellectus* of 1303, for example, opens with Intellect recounting the example of the Muslim king who, his own faith having been disproven by a Christian wise man, offered to convert himself and all the Muslims of his kingdom to Christianity if its truth could be demonstrated by necessary reasons, only to become enraged when the Christian told him this was impossible.[91] In fact, reason is indispensable for convincing schismatics as well, since, unlike Muslims, Jews, and pagans, they already have Christian faith.[92]

When Aquinas affirms that there can be no conflict between reason and faith, he is at least in part addressing the so-called "double truth" of the Parisian Averroists.[93] His opposition to doctrines held by the Averroists, such as the unity of intellect, is based not only on his interpretation of Aristotle, but on questions of salvation (and perdition): "Take away from men diversity of intellect, which alone among the soul's parts seems incorruptible and immortal, and it follows that nothing of the souls of men would remain after death except a

---

89   Ibid., 1.8.1., 76. Ibid., Editio Leonina Manualis, 7: "Utile tamen est ut in huiusmodi rationibus, quantumcumque debilibus, se mens humana exerceat, dummodo desit comprehendendi vel demonstrandi praesumptio: quia de rebus altissimis etiam parva et debili consideratione aliquid posse inspicere iucundissimum est, ut ex dictis apparet."

90   See, for example, Llull's *Liber de passagio* 3, ROL 28:343.

91   *Disputa entre la Fe i l'Enteniment* 1.1, (eds.) Josep Batalla and Alexander Fidora (Turnhout: 2011), 88.

92   Ibid., 1.14, 112–114.

93   *Summa contra Gentiles*, 1.7.1, 74. On the question of Aquinas' knowledge of Averroes's actual teachings, see Alain de Libera, *Raison et foi: Archéologie d'une crise d'Albert le Grand à Jean-Paul II* (Paris: 2003), 246–254. Libera argues that there is no "missionary" intent in the *Summa*, although there is a real desire to counter a "radicalized" account of the views Averroes and the Parisian Averroists such as Siger de Brabant and Boetius of Dacia actually held.

unique intellectual substance, with the result that reward and punishment and their difference disappear."[94] Llull, on the other hand, takes the threat of Averroism as another occasion to champion his view that Christian doctrine can be demonstrated, arguing, for example, that if men shared one intellect, they would also share one will and one memory, causing a "disorder" that would not correspond to the divine as "most ordered" first cause.[95] For him, there is no conflict between reason and faith because, as Intellect explains in the *Disputatio fidei et intellectus*, the two are in fact inseparable, each depending on the other to function properly and both, in turn, depending on grace.[96] In this sense, Llull is not a rationalist at all, but, as Eusebi Colomer has argued, an Augustinian who thinks as if Aquinas had never existed.[97] The very idea that faith and reason should be opposed or separately delineated threatens to undo the unity of Christian thought and provoke a return to paganism.[98] This anachronistic view, more proper to the 11th century than to the end of the thirteenth, has been said to be the most truly distinctive feature of Llull's thought.[99] It is here, then, that Llull is farthest from Villanova, whose anti-rationalism was grounded in the inaccessibility of the divine essence to reason.

Without disputing this view, I would like to conclude by suggesting that there is another area in which Llull distinguishes himself even more clearly from his contemporaries: his literary activity. Detailed analysis of his lyric and narrative works appears elsewhere in this volume, but one literary genre has already been briefly discussed: the *exemplum*. The well-known example discussed above of the Muslim who has lost faith in Islam and is frustrated in his desire to have the truth of the Christian faith demonstrated to him receives, in the vernacular *Disputació de cinc savis*, a slightly different treatment. Here, rather than becoming enraged and exiling the Christian wise man, the disappointed Muslim replies that "it is a grave thing for a man to leave one faith for another, as a matter of belief, but it is an easy thing to abandon a belief

---

94   *De unitate intellectus* 1.2, 18: "Subtracta enim ab hominibus diuersitate intellectus, qui solus inter anime partes incorruptibilis et immortalis apparet, sequitur post mortem nichil de animabus hominum remanere nisi unicam intellectus substantiam; et sic tollitur retributio premiorum et penarum et diuersitas eorundem."

95   *Liber reprobationis aliquorum errorum Averrois* 2.6, (ed.) Helmut Riedlinger, ROL 6:305–310.

96   *Disputatio fidei et intellectus*, 1.2–3, (eds.) Batalla and Fidora, 88–96. See Johnston, *SL* 297, and Carles Llinàs, "La teoria lul·liana del coneixement de Déu: una introducció," *Ars brevis* s.n. (1998), 75.

97   Colomer, *El pensament als països catalans*, 147, 151.

98   Fernand van Steenberghen, "La signification de l'oeuvre anti-averroïste de Raymond Lulle," *EL* 4 (1960), 127.

99   Colomer, *El pensament als països catalans*, 237.

because of a necessary demonstration or proof."[100] The narrative genre allows Llull to convincingly portray the interiority of the "infidel," and to explore, as in the case of these variations on the same story, the role of affect in belief. In bringing to bear his courtly upbringing on matters of mission and theology – in crafting a "divine" chivalry[101] – Llull could express matters of particular subjectivity in such a way that they completed his grand Artistic project.[102] Narrative also served as a basis for popular conversation, which Llull hoped to guide toward disputation using his Art's terms.[103] Like faith itself, literature complements the rational in Llull both strategically and cosmologically.

Works Cited

Primary Works

Anselm of Canterbury, *Monologion*, (ed.) P. Franciscus Salesius Schmidt (Stuttgart-Bad Cannstatt: 1964).

Anselm of Canterbury, *Monologion,* trans. Simon Harrison, in *The Major Works,* (eds.) Brian Davies and G.R. Evans (Oxford: 1998), 5–81.

Aquinas, Thomas, *De unitate intellectus contra Averroistas*, (ed.) and trans. Ralph Mc-Inerny, *Aquinas against the Averroists:* On There Being Only One Intellect (West La-fayette, Ind.: 1993).

Aquinas, Thomas, *Summa contra gentiles*, Editio Leonina Manualis (Rome: 1934).

Aquinas, Thomas, *Summa contra gentiles*, trans. Anton C. Pegis (vol. 1), James F. Ander-son (vol. 2), Vernon J. Bourke (vols. 3–4), and Charles J. O'Neil (vol. 5), *On the Truth of the Catholic Faith (Summa contra gentiles)*, 5 vols., (New York: 1955).

Bacon, Roger, *Compendium studii theologiae*, (ed.) and trans. Thomas S. Maloney, *Compendium of the Study of Theology* (Leiden: 1988).

Bacon, Roger, *Opus maius*, (ed.) John Henry Bridges, 3 vols. (Oxford: 1897–1900).

Bacon, Roger, *Opus maius,* trans. Robert Belle Burke, 2 vols. (New York: 1962).

Martí, Raymond, *Capistrum Iudaeorum*, (ed.) and trans. Adolfo Robles Sierra, 2 vols. (Würzburg: 1990).

Raymond of Penafort, *Diplomatari*, (ed.) Ferran i Taberner Valls (Zaragoza: 1991).

---

100   *Disputació de cinc savis* Prol., (ed.) Perarnau i Espelt, 29: "[G]reu cosa és que hom leix una fe per altra, segons manera de creensa, mas leugera cosa és que hom leix creensa per nescessària demostratió o probatió."

101   Cruz Hernández, *El pensamiento de Ramon Llull*, 52.

102   See, for example, on the role of lyric in the "double translation" of Algazel's logic: Domi-nique Courcelles, *La parole risquée de Raymond Lulle: Entre le judaïsme, le christianisme et l'islam* (Paris: 1993), 56.

103   As explained in the prologue to his *Liber de sancta Maria*, 41.

Raymond of Penafort, *Summa de paenitentia,* (eds.) Xaverio Ochoa and Aloisio Diez (Rome: 1976).

Arnold of Vilanova, *Allocutio christini de hiis quae conveniunt homini secundum propriam dignitatem creaturae rationalis,* (ed.) Josep Perarnau i Espelt, *Arxiu de Textos Catalans Antics* 11 (1992): 7–135.

Arnold of Vilanova, *Allocutio super significatione nominis Thetagramaton,* in *Arnaldi de Villanova Opera Theologica Omnia,* (ed.) Josep Perarnau i Espelt, vol. 3 (Barcelona: 2004), 139–204.

Arnold of Vilanova, *Obres catalanes,* (ed.) Miquel Batllori, 2 vols. (Barcelona: 1947).

Arnold of Vilanova, *La* Prudència de l'escolar catòlic *i altres escrits,* (ed.) Jaume Mensa, i Valls, trans. Jordi Raventós (Barcelona: 2002).

Primary Works: Llull

Disputa entre la Fe i l'Enteniment, (ed.) and trans. Josep Batalla and Alexander Fidora (Turnhout: 2011).

Disputació de cinc savis, (eds.) Josep Perarnau i Espelt, *Arxiu de Textos Catalans Antics* 5 (1986): 7–229.

Liber de fine, (ed.) Aloisius Madre, ROL 9:233–291.

Liber de passagio, (eds.) Blanca Garí and Fernando Domínguez Reboiras, ROL 28:255–353.

Liber de sancta Maria, (eds.) Blanca Garí and Fernando Domínguez Reboiras, ROL 28:3–241.

Libre de sancta Maria, (ed.) Fernando Domínguez Reboiras, trans. Elisenda Padrós Wolff, *Das Buch über die heilige Maria* (*Libre de sancta Maria*) (Stuttgart-Bad Cannstatt: 2005).

Liber praedicationis contra Iudaeos, (ed.) Alois Madre, ROL 12:1–78.

Liber reprobationis aliquorum errorum Averrois, (ed.) Helmut Riedlinger, ROL 6:287–318.

Liber de trinitate et incarnatione, (ed.) Alois Madre, ROL 12:79–137.

Libre del gentil e los tres savis, (ed.) Sebastián Garcías Palou, *OE* 1:1057–1142.

Libre del gentil e los tres savis, (ed.) and trans. Anthony Bonner, *SW* 1:91–304.

Logica nova, (ed.) Walter Euler, ROL 23:1–179.

Lògica del Gazzali, (ed.) Jordi Rubió i Balaguer, "*La lògica del Gazzali posada en rims per en Ramon Llull,*" *Anuari de l'Institut d'Estudis Catalans* 5 (1913–14): 311–54.

Rhetorica nova, (ed.) and trans. Mark D. Johnston, *Ramon Llull's New Rhetoric: Text and Translation of Llull's* Rethorica Nova (Davis, Calif.: 1994).

Secondary Works

Batllori, Miquel, *Arnau de Vilanova i l'Arnaldisme* (Valencia: 1994).

Chazan, Robert, *Barcelona and Beyond: The Disputation of 1263 and its Aftermath* (Berkeley: 1992).

Chazan, Robert, *Daggers of Faith: Thirteenth-Century Christian Missionizing and Jewish Response* (Berkeley: 1989).

Cohen, Jeremy, *The Friars and the Jews: The Evolution of Medieval Anti-Judaism* (Ithaca: 1982).

Colomer i Pous, Eusebi, *El pensament als països catalans durant l'Edat Mitjana i el Renaixement* (Barcelona: 1997).

Courcelles, Dominique, *La parole risquée de Raymond Lulle: Entre le judaïsme, le christianisme et l'islam* (Paris: 1993).

Cruz Hernández, Miguel, *El pensamiento de Ramon Llull* (Valencia: 1977).

Daniel, E. Randolph, *The Franciscan Concept of Mission in the High Middle Ages* (Lexington, Kentucky: 1975).

Domínguez Reboiras, Fernando, "La idea de cruzada en el *Liber de passagio* de Ramón Llull," *Patristica et Mediaevalia* 25 (2004): 45–75.

Emery, Gilles, "The Doctrine of the Trinity in St. Thomas Aquinas," in *Aquinas on Doctrine: A Critical Introduction*, (eds.) Thomas Weinandy, Daniel Keating, and John Yocum (London: 2004), 45–65.

Ensenyat, Gabriel, "Pacifisme i croada en Ramon Llull," in *Ramon Llull i l'Islam: L'inici del diàleg* (Barcelona: 2008), 232–245.

Fortuny, Francesc J., "Arnau de Vilanova: Els límits da la raó teològica: Arnau en oposició a Averrois, Maimònides i Tomàs d'Aquino," *Estudi General* 9 (1989): 31–60.

Gayà Estelrich, Jordi, *La teoría luliana de los correlativos: Historia de su formación conceptual* (Palma: 1979).

Hames, Harvey J., *The Art of Conversion: Christianity and Kabbalah in the Thirteenth Century* (Leiden: 2000).

Hughes, Robert D., "Speculum, Similitude, and Signification: the Incarnation as Exemplary and Proportionate Sign in the Arts of Ramon Llull," *SL* 45–46 (2005–2006): 3–37.

Kedar, Benjamin Z., *Crusade and Mission: European Approaches toward the Muslims* (Princeton: 1984).

Libera, Alain de, *Raison et foi: Archéologie d'une crise d'Albert le Grand à Jean-Paul II* (Paris: 2003).

Llinàs, Carles, "La teoria lul·liana del coneixement de Déu: una introducció," *Ars brevis* s.n. (1998): 67–100.

Maloney, Thomas S., "The Extreme Realism of Roger Bacon," *The Review of Metaphysics* 38.4 (1985): 807–837.

Mensa i Valls, Jaume, *Les raons d'un anunci apocalíptic: la polèmica escatològica entre Arnau de Vilanova i els filòsofs i teòlegs professionals (1297–1305): Anàlisi dels arguments i de les argumentacions* (Barcelona: 1998).

Pring-Mill, Robert, *El microcosmos lul·lià* (Palma: 1961).

Robinson, Cynthia, "Trees of Love, Trees of Knowledge: Toward the Definition of a Cross-Confessional Current in Late Medieval Iberian Spirituality," *Medieval Encounters* 12 (2006): 388–435.

Simon, Josep Maria Ruiz, "De la naturalesa com a mescla a l'art de mesclar (sobre la fonamentació cosmològica de les arts lul·lianes)," *Randa* 19 (1986): 69–99.

Simon, Josep Maria Ruiz, "'Quomodo est haec ars inventiva?' (L'Art de Llull i la dialèctica escolàstica)," *SL* 33 (1993): 77–98.

Smith, Damian J., *Crusade, Heresy and Inquisition in the Lands of the Crown of Aragon (c. 1167–1276)* (Leiden: 2010).

Southern, R.W., *Western Views of Islam in the Middle Ages* (Cambridge, Mass.: 1962).

van Steenberghen, Fernand, "La signification de l'oeuvre anti-averroïste de Raymond Lulle," *EL* 4 (1960): 113–128.

Tolan, John V., *Saracens: Islam in the Medieval European Imagination* (New York: 2002).

te Velde, Rudi A., *Participation and Substantiality in Thomas Aquinas* (Leiden: 1995).

Vidal, Josep M., "Significació i llenguatge," *Catalan Review* 4 (1990): 323–344.

Vose, Robin, *Dominicans, Muslims and Jews in the Medieval Crown of Aragon* (Cambridge: 2009).

CHAPTER 3

Llull as Lay Philosopher and Theologian

Josep Batalla

3.1   Christo Integre Deservire

3.1.1   *Conversion to Penitence*

When Ramon Llull was in the fullness of his thirties (*nel mezzo del cammin di nostra vita*), his conversion (*conversio sua ad paenitentiam*) changed the course of his life.[1] It is not easy to say exactly what this event entailed, because Llull only talked of it explicitly in two poems, and in the *Vita coaetanea*, an autobiographical narrative, drafted in the style of medieval hagiography and aimed at edification (*aedificatio*). In these works, he chose to emphasize virtuous ideals, rather than to describe the internal upheavals that he suffered.[2] We will never know, therefore, what events led to his psychic fatigue (*taedium vitae*), nor the disappointments, the readings, or the conversations that caused the apparitions and visions that changed the course of his life.

Llull admitted to having a sick feeling in the presence of females ("the beauty of women is a tribulation and pestilence to my eyes"),[3] but did not reveal what his wife, Blanca Picany, meant to him. However, it is quite likely that Llull's youth was more careless than debauched, as he was led by the licentious permissiveness recommended by Andreas Capellanus (1150–1220). Nonetheless, overwhelmed by a sense of guilt (*conscientia rea*) and terrified (*territus*) before the greatness of the divine, Llull decided that he had to break with his worldly past (*relicto mundo*) and dedicate himself to serving Jesus Christ entirely (*Jesu Christo integrate deservire*).[4]

Historically, the act of spiritual conversion, with both biblical and Neoplatonic roots, was a combination of changing the way of living (ἐπιστροφή) and deciding to radically change the way of thinking (μετάνοια).[5] After conversion,

---

[1]   Cf. *Vita coaetanea* 1, ROL 8:272.

[2]   Dieter von der Nahmer, *Die lateinische Heiligenvita. Eine Einführung in die lateinische Hagiographie* (Darmstadt: 1994), 46–56: "Tugend, Heros, Aedificatio."

[3]   *Libre de contemplació* 104.16, ORL 3:10: "la bellea de les fembres és estada pestilència e tribulació a mos ulls."

[4]   *Vita coaetanea* 1.4, ROL 8:274.

[5]   Arthur D. Nock, *Conversion: The Old and the New from Alexander the Great to Augustine of Hippo* (Oxford and London: 1961); Paul Aubin, *Le problème de la conversion: Étude d'un terme commun à l'hellenisme et au christianisme des trois premiers siècles* (Paris: 1963).

the convert perceived an abyss between what he needed to do and what he did before, because he had reached a new "religious vision of the world" (*religiöse Weltanschauung*),[6] a new "root metaphor," through which he valued everything differently.

However, Llull's spiritual conversion was not, as is the case with some Neoplatonic philosophers, a simple awareness of the requirements of a rational, natural theology (*theologia naturalis*). Rather, it welcomed the demands of the Christian God revealed in Jesus Christ crucified. Therefore, we must place Llull's conversion in the wake of the great Christian converts, such as Saint Paul (ca. 5–ca. 67), Saint Augustine of Hippo (354–430), Saint Pascal Baylon (1540–1592), G.K. Chesterton (1874–1936), or Charles de Foucauld (1858–1916).

Llull's spiritual conversion was not a decision or an episodic *resolutio*, but rather a firm adoption of a new way of life that flowed from the personal center of energy that all converts discover from within.[7] His conversion—similar to Saint Paul's—was a definitive *prise de position*, surging from an inexhaustible moment. In these cases, the convert—clinging to what had upset him—sought to direct everyone towards the absolute, by meditating and contemplating divine greatness.[8]

In fact, since the 12th century, the new life that Llull adopted was known as *conversio ad paenitentiam* and focused on partially-institutionalized prayer, poverty, and fraternity. For fervent laymen, to "do penance" meant not only to confess sins and to repent them, but also involved years of practicing the evangelical precept: *Paenitentiam agite; appropinquavit regnum caelorum*.[9] More than anything, it was to "take state," that is, to commit oneself to live humbly in order to be worthy of God's love.

After his *conversio ad paenitentiam*, Llull followed the ecclesiastical customs and rules of his age, and honorably resigned himself to dress thereafter as befit a man of his class, always wearing a very simple habit made of rough cloth.[10] This externalized his decision to live ascetically. As his contemporary Jacopone

---

6   Wilhelm Dilthey, *Die Typen der Weltanschauung und ihre Ausbildung in den Metaphysischen Systemen,* in *Gesammelte Schriften*, 12 vols. (Leipzig and Berlin: 1931), 8:88–91: "Die religiöse Weltanschauung."

7   William James, *The Varieties of Religious Experience* (London: 1902), 289.

8   Jean Baruzi, *Création religieuse et pensée contemplative* (Paris: 1951), 27: "Prise de possession définitive, ravissement qui arrache soudain à une forme de vie abolie un être qui se tendra désormais vers ce moment inépuisable et y amenera les autres, tous les autres, presents et futurs, en qui ce moment medité, ou contemplativement retrouvé, provoquera selon des rythmes divers une entrée dans l'absolu."

9   Based on the Latin expression of Matt 4:17, *paenitentiam agite*, which translates the Greek command μετανοεῖτε.

10   *Vita coaetanea* 2.11, ROL 8:278: "Relictis vestibus sollemnioribus, quibus usque tunc usus erat, assumpsit sibi vilem habitum de panno, quem ipse invenire poterat, grossiore."

of Todi (1230–1306) did—when he decided to change his life, but had not yet taken the Franciscan habit—Llull decided to wear the habit of *bisocone* (penance) since "in that habit lies the foundation of saintly humility."[11]

Therefore, after abruptly abandoning his family, it is very likely that Llull quickly established a relationship with the secular penitents. These men gathered freely in brotherhoods, choosing many diverse ways of life: communal or solitary living, connected to an order (*conversi*), or living independently as hermits or urban itinerants. The Franciscan Third Order often appeared as one of these brotherhoods of penitents, and Beguines were often in close proximity.[12]

3.1.2 *Ars Contemplationis*

The lay penitents' way of life involved undertaking pilgrimages, dedicating themselves to contemplation, committing themselves to evangelism, and assuming the mission of preaching.[13] Llull was determined to develop himself spiritually in order to fully comply with (*integre*) all the requirements of his rediscovered faith. He turned to contemplation and study so intensely that, after a few years, his wife had to ask a court to assign a guardian for the family assets. The judge agreed because "after completing a thorough investigation into Llull's life and customs," it was clear that "he had opted for the contemplative life and did not take care of his property."[14]

The fruits of these years of study and contemplation resulted in two works: his *Compendium logicae Algazelis*, a summary of philosophical logic, as well as an ample and very personal meditation, and his *Libre de contemplació en Déu*, written in the form of spiritual theology. These works revealed Llull's greatest intellectual concern after his conversion, which was to develop a theological vision of the world that allowed him to account for everything: the world perceived by the senses, by inner experience, and through Christian faith.

---

11   *Le vite antiche di Jacopone da Todi*, (ed.) Enrico Menestò (Florence: 1977), 36–41.

12   Cf. André Vauchez, "Les pénitents au Moyen Âge," in *Les laïcs au Moyen Âge: Pratiques et expériences religieuses* (Paris: 2007), 105–112; Ernest W. McDonnell, *The Beguines and Beghards in Medieval Culture* (New Brunswick and New Jersey: 1954), 246–277. On the Beguines of Majorca, see José Pou y Martí, *Visionarios, beguinos y fraticelos catalanes* (*siglos XIII–XV*) (Alicante: 1966), 235–284.

13   Rolf Zerfass, *Der Streit um die Laienpredigt: Eine pastoralgeschichtliche Untersuchung zum Verständnis des Predigtamtes und zu seiner Entwicklung im 12. und 13. Jahrhundert* (Freiburg im Breisgau: 1974), 204–210.

14   Jocelyn N. Hillgarth, *Diplomatari lul·lià*, doc. 12 (Barcelona: 2001), 36–37: "Facta diligenti inquisitione super vita et moribus dicti R. Lulli, cum nobis constet ipsum R. Lullum elegisse in tantum vitam contemplativam quod quasi circa administrationem bonorum suorum no intendat ... administratorem et curatorem dictorum bonorum damus et assignamus."

Llull caught a glimpse—perhaps suddenly—[15] that through the contemplative activity of metaphysical logic, he could help produce the desired theological vision of reality. The original purpose of the Art was to account for everything from a Christian view of the world. The *Vita coaetanea* links the genesis of the Art to missionary activity when it mentions "the best book in the world" (*unum librum meliorem de mundo*) that Llull decided to write "against the errors of the infidels" (*contra errores infidelium*).[16] The *Vita* reflects, I believe, how Llull interpreted his life at 79 years old when he felt disillusioned by the failure of his missionary projects. However, it did not reveal the genesis of his Art when he was 40 for two reasons: first, because originally his apologetic work was intended to demonstrate the Christian faith, rather than to refute the errors of the infidels; and second, because in the prologues to the first versions of his Art, the conversion of the infidels was only one of its many objectives, and never considered the most important one. To affirm, then, that the conversion of the infidel was the *raison d'être* of the Art misrepresents its original purpose, which was contemplation.

Certainly, the Art was slow to widen its scope, but Llull never considered it as a logical way of thinking independent of the act of contemplation. To the extent that all of the Lullian message focused on the full recovery of faith, the Art successively explained what the life of a secular and penitent intellectual encompassed, including the imperative to understand and to love God, to live honestly, to understand and justify the faith, to rationally reveal to others what one believed, to allow for the possibility to convert the infidel, and to have the capacity to assimilate and integrate all knowledge in a religious vision of the world.

> This Art has many purposes: it teaches us to understand and to love God, to adhere to the virtues, to hate the vices and through compelling reasons to refute the erroneous views of the infidels. It also teaches us to formulate and solve questions, and also allows us to acquire other sciences in a short space of time and carry them to their necessary conclusions according to the requirements of the subject.[17]

---

15 The *Vita coaetanea* 3.14, ROL 8:280, gives it a hagiographical interpretation: "God suddenly illuminated his mind" (*subito Deus illustravit mentem suam*).

16 *Vita coaetanea* 2.6, ROL 8:275.

17 *Compendium Artis demonstrativae* Prol., MOG 3:293: "Multae sunt utilitates propter quas haec Ars est inventa: instruit enim nos intelligere et diligere Deum, adhaerere virtutibus, odire vitia et confundere cogentibus rationibus infidelium erroneas opiniones. Docet etiam facere et solvere quaestiones et alias scientias sub brevi spatio temporis posse acquiri et reduci ad necessarias conclusiones secundum exigentiam materiae."

Llull's thought had a radically Christian and unmistakably contemplative orientation, which was both deeply theological[18] and resolutely philosophical.[19] Llull began with the created reality which, when subjected to a process of reasoning, made the uncreated reality of the divinity transparent. Upon discovering this, in the *Libre de contemplació*, Llull bursts into a song of joy, expressing his delight that God exists and that He reveals His existence. Through reasoning, Llull makes it diaphanously clear that existence is the supreme good because it inspires real "ontological emotion:" "Just as for us, Lord, it is much better to exist than not to exist, so it behooves us to rejoice that we exist."[20]

In the Lullian Art, longing to know the divine predominates over mystic *affectus*, and so Llull "stresses an intellectualist and universalized understanding of *contemplatio*."[21] However, this is not a cold and purely speculative intellectualism. Almost always for Llull, thinking manifests itself in the form of a warm and loving dialogue with God. We could say that contemplation arises from the tension in which the imagination balances understanding and affection.[22] Contemplation is thus a kind of "intellectual voluntarism,"[23] which involves

---

18   On the importance of *contemplatio* for theological reflexion, see Hans Urs Von Balthasar, "Spiritualität," in *Verbum Caro* (Einsiedeln: 1990), 226–244, and *Das betrachtende Gebet* (Einsiedeln: 2003).

19   On *contemplatio* and *meditatio* as methods of philosophical reflection, cf. Descartes, *Meditationes de prima philosophia* 3, in *Oeuvres de Descartes*, (eds.) Charles Adam and Paul Tannery, 12 vols. (Paris: 1897–1913), 7:52: "Placet hic aliquandiu in ipsius Dei contemplatione immorari, ejus attributa apud me expendere, et immensi hujus luminis pulchritudinem, quantum caligantis ingenii mei acies ferre poterit, intueri, admirari, adorare." Cf. Ulrich Nolte, *Philosophische Exerzitien bei Descartes: Aufklärung zwischen Privatmysterium und Gesellschaftsentwurf* (Würzburg: 1995), 94–97: "Kontemplation," and Martin Seel, *Adornos Philosophie der Kontemplation* (Frankfurt am Main: 2004).

20   *Libre de contemplació* 2.2, ORL 2:11: "Enaixí com a nos és, Sènyer, molt mellor cosa ésser en ésser que no seria si no érem en ésser, enaixí se cové que ens alegrem molt, per ço car som en ésser." Cf. Amador Vega, "Ramon Llull: l'art d'inventar la veritat," in *Ramon Llull i l'islam: L'inici del diàleg*, (ed.) Maria-Àngels Roque (Barcelona: 2008), 209.

21   Bernard McGinn, *The Presence of God: A History of Western Christian Mysticism, vol. 3: The Flowering of Mysticism: Men and Women in the New Mysticism, 1200–1350* (New York: 1998), 135. Contemplation imples in a way that prayer achieves an "understanding of God" (Gottesverständnis des Beters); cf. Richard Schaeffler, *Kleine Sprachlehre des Gebetes* (Trier: 1988), 68–71. Cf. also Vincent Brümmer, *What Are We Doing When We Pray? A Philosophical Inquiry* (London: 1984), 72: "Religious experience entails a knowledge claim, which, like all knowledge claims, is both subjective and objective."

22   Joseph de Guibert, "Méthode et contemplation au XIIIe siècle: l'*Art de contemplation de R. Lull*," in *Études de théologie mystique* (Toulouse: 1930), 308; Amador Vega, "Die religiose Imagination bei Ramon Llull: Elemente für eine theorie des Kontemplativen Gebets," in *Deutsche Mystik im abendländischen Zusammenhang*, (eds.) Walter Haug and Wolfram Schneider-Lastin, (Tübingen: 2000), 749–772.

23   Miguel Cruz Hernández, *El pensamiento de Ramon Llull* (Valencia: 1977), 260.

all the human psyche: memory, understanding, and will. We love what we remember; we love it in so far as we understand it; and if we love it, we do it
so as not to forget it: "The more you understand, the more you can love or
unlove what you understand; and when you can love or unlove, the more you
understand."[24] Contemplation is a spiritual activity that could be described
as "thorough prayer" (*gewußtes Beten*) because, the more highly reflective one
is, the closer one is to understanding faith.[25] This is why praying introduces
"new reasons" in prayer every day, which can be seen in the *Romanç d'Evast e
Blaquerna*: "Blaquerna was praying and considering the way in which to contemplate God and his virtues; and when he had finished his prayer, he wrote on
how he contemplated God. And he did this every day. And he found new reasons in his prayer."[26] Llull's contemplative Art is expounded upon in a many of
his texts; some contain poetic images, others are written in exemplary prose or
are discursive meditations with geometric figures, tables, and abbreviations. It
is preferable, I believe, to refer to them as "abbreviations" rather than of an "algebra," as many do, because what characterizes algebra is the use of variables,
structured through constants.[27] In contrast, the letters used by Llull always
represent very specific and definite entities. A good way to navigate through
these lush texts is to use a conceptual simplification to distinguish between the
"internal system" and the "external mechanism."[28] They both form part of the
system—Lullian Dignities, Relative Principles, Definitions, Conditions, and
Rules, along with the scale of being and ethical values. They also belong to the
mechanism of thought reflected in geometric shapes, abbreviations, tables,
and empirical combinatorial processes.

We must insist that Llull's thought is found within the conceptual system of
the Art, not within its apparently logical combinatorial mechanism. To assert
uncritically that we should understand the Art exclusively from the evolution

---

24 *Libre del gentil e dels tres savis* 3.9.5, NEORL 2:136: "On més entens, més pots amar o desa-
     mar ço que entens; e on més ho pots amar o desamar, més ho pots entendre."

25 Romano Guardini, "Unmittelbares und gewußtes Beten," in *Auf dem Wege* (Mainz: 1923),
     111–130.

26 *Romanç d'Evast e Blaquerna* 100, NEORL 8:428: "Blaquerna estava en oració e considerava la
     manera segons la qual contemplava Déu e ses virtuts; e quan havia finida sa oració es-
     crivia ço en què havia contemplat Déu. E açò fahia tots jorns. E mudava en sa oració
     novelles raons."

27 Cf. Alfred North Whitehead, *An Introduction to Mathematics* (London: 1911), 15: "proposi-
     tions about *any* thing or about *some* things, without specification of definite particular
     things."

28 José Casadesús, *El Arte magna de Raimundo Lulio* (Barcelona: 1917), 3–4 and 15. The same
     distinction appears in Jean-Henri Probst, *Caractère et origine des idées du bienheureux
     Raymond Lulle* (Toulouse: 1912), 57–58.

of its "external mechanism" is to distort Llull's thought. That is, we cannot limit the study of Lullian thought to the four more "mechanical" works—*Ars compendiosa inveniendi veritatem, Ars demonstrativa, Ars inventiva veritatis,* and *Ars generalis ultima*—nor can we interpret other texts and other artistic practices as simple, theoretically irrelevant, practical changes in the formal operations of the mechanism. We must always bear in mind that the "internal system" of the Art is essentially a set comprised of the *Ars contemplationis, Ars amativa boni, Ars mystica theologiae et philosophiae,* and most definitively, *Ars compendiosa Dei.*[29]

Extracted from the "internal system" of thought for which it was designed, the "external mechanism" of the Art becomes a conglomerate of mnemonic techniques, of visual representations, and of combinatorial empirical process-es that do not form any logical, internally coherent system.[30] However, this does not mean that the "external mechanism" is irrelevant. Llull's thought is what it is thanks to its combinatorial mechanism; without this mechanism, it would be something else entirely. The constant circular movement of the figures and the relentless combination of various abbreviations give dyna-mism to the Art. Llull does not describe reality statically, but instead explains which relationships actively sustain all beings. Llull investigates reality by considering all the possible relationships between the human and divine ele-ments. The figures of the Art are not static, but revolving. The dynamism of the Art, the incessant revolving of principles (*circulatio principiorum*),[31] "is prob-ably the most significant aspect of Lullism in the history of thought,"[32] which, ultimately, serves as a "mystical philosophy in action."[33] Twirling incessantly, the "external mechanism" acts as a kaleidoscopic instrument that combines all elements of the "internal system" of the Art. Through the successive combi-nations, one can see the contemplation (σκοπεῖν) and the conceptual beauty

---

29   *Art de contemplació* (ORL 19:433–490); *Ars amativa boni* (ORL 29:120–432); *Ars mystica theologiae et philosophiae* (ROL 5:286–466); and *Ars compendiosa Dei* (ROL 13:15–331).

30   Josep Batalla, "Die lullische *Ars* als philosophische Theologie," *Jahrbuch für Religion-sphilosophie* 9 (2010): 129–158, offers a critique of the interpretation of the "external mechanism" as a self-sufficient, logically and epistemologically valid, system. Cf. *The Developement of Modern Logic,* (ed.) Leila Haaparanta (Oxford and New York: 2009), 75: "Llull never achieved any logical results, and his program rests heavily in theological premises."

31   *Ars mystica theologiae et philosophiae* Prol., ROL 5:286: "Subiectum Artis istius est circu-latio principiorum primitivorum, necessariorum et verorum, cum quibus investigabimus obiecta summa per ipsa significata."

32   Frances A. Yates, *The Art of Memory* (London: 1992), 178.

33   Cf. Tomás Carreras i Artau and Joaquín Carreras i Artau, *Historia de la filosofía española: Historia de la filosofía cristiana de los siglos XIII al XV,* 2 vols. (Madrid: 1939–43), 1:637.

(κάλλος) generated by the relationships between ideas or between divine and human forms (εἴδη) remain together.

The dynamic circularity of the Art is essentially theological, as revealed in the "first intent" (*prima intentio*) of man. This phrase unequivocally shows the religious orientation of the Art. Llull uses the term *intentio* to describe the field of theological ethics, which is the decision to direct all actions toward "honoring, loving and serving God."[34] Llull does this precisely at a time when logicians use the term *intentio* to distinguish between the concepts that refer to real things (*intentio prima* or *materialis*) and the actual meaning of the concepts (*intentio secunda* or *formalis*).[35] Llull, while admitting that the logical intention (*intentio*) involves "abstracting the form of the similarities present in that which it resembles,"[36] still considers it a secondary kind of knowledge. Llull is not interested in logic and epistemology, but in theology. He insists that, unlike his Art—which is firmly focused primarily on knowing and loving God—logic is "unstable and labile."[37] For Llull, logic does not reflect the *intentio prima*, the ultimate goal of man, but only deals with the means of achieving the ultimate goal, the *intentiones secundae*.[38] In his words, "We will speak of logic briefly because we must talk about God."[39]

3.1.3   *The Missionary as Philosopher*

In the contemplative life of penance, Llull discovered that the lucid recognition of what one believes (*confessio fidei*) is an essential requirement of evangelical life.[40]

Even during the 12th century, medieval Christianity was becoming aware of the need to confess faith. The testimonies of the new Mendicant orders and

---

34   Cf. *Libre de contemplació* 45, ORL 2:227–232.

35   Ria van der Lecq, "Logic and the Theories of Meaning in the Late 13th and Early 14th Century including the Modistae. Part II: The Logic of Intentions," in *Handbook of the History of Logic*, (eds.) Dov M. Gabbay and John Woods, 9 vols. (Amsterdam and Boston: 2008), 2:370–385.

36   *Logica nova* 4.3.30, ROL 23:91: "Intentio est forma cum qua logicus seu mathematicus abstrahit similitudines a similato, eo quod extra subiectum eas considerat, ut habitum logicalem habere possit."

37   *Ars generalis et ultima* 10.87, ROL 14:367: "Logica est scientia instabilis sive labilis. Haec autem Ars generalis est permanens et inlabilis."

38   *Logica nova* Prol., ROL 23:16: "Logici consideratio circa intentiones versatur secundas."

39   *Lògica del Gatzell* 1604–1605, ORL 19:62: "De lògica parlam tot breu / car a parlar havem de Déu."

40   Cf. Aquinas, *Summa theologiae* 2a.2ae, q. 188, a. 6, in *Opera omnia*, (ed.) Roberto Busa, 7 vols. (Stuttgart: 1980), 2:763: "Maius est contemplata aliis tradere quam solum contemplari."

fervent laymen assumed that they, as well as clerics, were also responsible for promoting the *vita apostolica*.[41] The expression *vita apostòlica* was ambivalent, meaning a return to the simple life of the early Christians and fervent apostles; it also meant making themselves available to preach the gospel to unbelievers, as the apostles and missionaries who accompanied them did.

Llull was aware of these two dimensions of the *vita apostòlica*. He clearly expressed his nostalgia for a past when the spirits of believers were "inflamed," and he also could not hide his displeasure with the present:

> When the apostles were thus imbued and inflamed by the grace of the Holy Spirit, they went to preach the Gospel of God. [...] We are far, my son, from that day when the Holy Spirit descended on the disciples and for this reason, my son, almost dead are devotion and love to preach and convert the errant infidels.[42]

Meanwhile, medieval Christendom, which for centuries had ignored the non-Christian culture represented by Islam, began to appreciate it—especially Islamic philosophy—and to imagine hastily and unfoundedly that understanding was possible and that a unifying faith was feasible. Religious unity, even if it were to be achieved by force, was an achievable "dream."[43] But the facts reveal that it was indeed a naive hope that Christians stop seeing Arabic culture as a threat to the integrity of Christianity.[44]

Llull knew these views and participated in these concerns. It is likely that as a Christian eager to evangelize unbelievers, he was somewhat influenced by the apocalyptic ideal—probably of Joachimite inspiration—whereby humanity had reached the end of history and that it was time to compel non-believers to convert.[45] However, it seems undeniable that Llull was among

---

41   Cf. Marie-Dominique Chenu, *La Théologie au douzième siècle* (Paris: 1976), 225–273: Ch. 10, "Moines, clercs, laïcs: Au carrefour de la vie évangélique" and Ch. 11, "Le reveil évangélique."

42   *Doctrina pueril* 50, NEORL 7:127: "Con los apòstols foren enaixí embeguts e aflamats de la gràcia del Sant Esperit, adoncs anaren a preicar los evangelis de Déu. ...Llunyat s'és, fill, de nosaltres aquell jorn con lo Sant Esperit davallà sobre los deixebles e per açò, fill, és quaix morta devoció e caritat a preicar e a convertir los errats infeels."

43   Robert I. Burns, "Christian-Islamic Confrontation in the West: The Thirteenth-Century Dream of Conversion," *The American Historical Review* 76 (1971): 1386–1434.

44   Richard W. Southern, *Western Views of Islam in the Middle Ages* (Cambridge, Mass.: 1962), 67–68.

45   Nicholas Eymerich, *Dialogus contra lullistas*, trans. Jaume de Puig i Oliver (Barcelona: 2002), 104–113, accuses Llull and Lullists of affirming the Joachimist doctrine of the three ages of history.

those missionaries who believed that this effort should be based predominately on intellectual methods.[46]

Llull's missionary praxis was complex because it was based on two divergent theoretical postulates. On the one hand, it served as an evangelical allegory, referring fervently to the past in order to inspire the faithful to imitate the life of the early Christians. On the other hand, it became a philosophical anagoge, which referred ideally to the future with the aim of promoting the universal spread of the Christian faith.[47] Both assumptions contained a strong utopian vision to the extent that they projected missions in a situation that was difficult to achieve: to convert not only the lazy faithful, but also the indifferent unfaithful, to the one, true Christian faith.

> And just as we have one God, one Creator and Lord, so we should have one faith, one religion, one sect, and one way of loving and honoring God, and we should love and help each other, and among us there should be no difference or contrariety of faith or of customs, because of which difference and contrariety we hate one another, and war against and kill each other.[48]

Llull took over the mission to evangelize without leaving the philosophical baggage he had gathered in contemplation, for as Llull surely believed, the missionary was a philosopher precisely because he was a missionary.[49] This did not mean that the mission of the preacher and the thinker diluted each other. Rather, according to Llull, the most effective way to evangelize was to reason, especially when "the unfaithful are not interested in the accepted authorities of the faithful, but they are interested in the reasons."[50] In these cases, one needs to use philosophical preaching, *praedicatio per moralem philosophiam*.[51]

---

46   E. Randolph Daniel, *The Franciscan Concept of Mission in the High Middle Ages* (St. Bonaventure, New York: 1992), 14–22.

47   Cf. Vicent Serverat, "Utopie et histoire: Les postulats théoriques de la praxis missionaire," in *Raymond Lulle et le Pays d'Oc* (Toulouse: 1987), 191–229.

48   *Libre del gentil e dels tres savis* Epilog, NEORL 2:207: "E enaixí com havem un Déu, un creador, un senyor, haguéssem una fe, una llig, una secta e una manera en amar e honrar Déu, e fóssem amadors e ajudadors los uns dels altres, e enfre nos no fos nulla diferència ni contrarietat de fe ni de costumes; per la qual diferència e contrarietat havem los uns enuig dels altres, e guerrejam e auciem los uns los altres."

49   Cf. Jorge J.E. Gracia, "El misionero, como filósofo," *EL* 22 (1978): 129–138.

50   *Liber de demonstratione per aequiparantiam* Prol. 4, ROL 9:221: "Infideles non stant ad auctoritates fidelium, et tamen stant ad rationes."

51   *Lectura super Artem inventivam et Tabulam generalem* Dist. 3, pars 2, quaest. 851, MOG 5:713; cf. Fernando Domínguez Reboiras, "El proyecto luliano de predicación cristiana," in *Constantes y fragmentos del pensamiento cristiano* (Tübingen: 1996), 117–132.

3.2   Philosophical Theology

3.2.1   *Popular Philosophy*

As in the *philosophia christiana* of Augustine or Bonaventure (1221–1274),[52] we can never say exactly whether Llull's Art was the work of a philosopher who wanted to rationally account for reality by proposing that reason stems from a Christian view of the world; or rather, if it came from a theologian who, through reason, proposed Christian faith as a coherent view of the world. What is known is that Llull was both a philosopher and a theologian who sought to express himself reasonably as such. His thought is a "theological philosophy," based on the unquestioned acceptance of divine reality, through which the consequences of philosophical arguments that are useful for understanding the world are deduced. But it is also a "philosophical theology" insofar as it expresses the theological content accomplished through faith, using only strictly philosophical concepts, i.e. avoiding resorting to any biblical or patristic text.[53]

Llull, conscious of being a simple layman,[54] occasionally frequented the universities of Montpellier and Paris, but his intellectual activity was never that of a scholastic master because he had not received any strict university education. He did not participate in the reception of Aristotle, he did not comment on the *Liber sententiarum*, he did not draft any *summa*, he did not formally intervene in any *disputatio*, nor was he prepared to intervene in any of the *quaestiones diputatae* taking place at universities.[55] His philosophy and his theology did not make any great doctrinal contribution. He only sought to offer a new method of reasoning to laymen, one that could be visualized and was clear and easy to follow. He wanted to develop a "spiritual logic"[56] that was accessible to educated lay people eager to "know and love God" (*cognoscere et amare Deum*):

> Since there are many men eager to acquire knowledge, we have decided to present this Art briefly, so that they can more easily obtain knowledge

---

52   Michele F. Sciacca, *Saint Augustin et le néoplatonisme: La possibilité d'une philosophie chrétienne* (Louvain: 1956); Léon Veuthey, *S. Bonaventurae philosophia christiana* (Rome: 1943), 30–45.

53   Marilyn McCord Adams, "Reviving Philosophical Theology: Some Medieval Models," in *Was ist Philosophie im Mittelalter?*, (eds.) Jan A. Aersten and Andreas Speer (Berlin: 1998), 60–68.

54   Josep Batalla, "Ego, qui sum laicus," *SL* 48 (2008): 69–92.

55   *Philosophical Debates at Paris in the Early Fourteenth Century*, (eds.) Stuart F. Brown, Thomas Dewender and Thomas Kobush (Leiden and Boston: 2009).

56   As argued by Johnston, *SL*.

of what they want to know, so that they can know and love God our Lord and attain heavenly glory.[57]

Therefore, we should consider Llull a popular philosopher who sought ways to offer understandable demonstrations for everyone.[58] The adjective "popular" characterizes Llull, but does not disqualify him in any way. Cultural historians, in studying the intellectual production of an author or a time, need to distinguish between esoteric works aimed at a scientific community—those focused on very specific topics and written in a very technical language—and exoteric works aimed at the general public—in broad terms, those written in various genres, with freely-chosen vocabulary. Aristotle made more than one reference to his exoteric or popular writings,[59] and during the German Enlightenment, there was a clear distinction between *Schulphilosophie* and *Popularphilosophie*. The former designated university texts, the latter characterized popularizing endeavors.[60]

Following the reception of Aristotle, medieval thinkers began to distinguish clearly between *philosophia*, a purely rational activity in accordance to the Aristotelian model, and *theologia*, a partially rationalizing activity of faith, received as a supernatural gift. Llull was aware of this distinction and of how his contemporaries attributed a propaedeutic function to philosophy, even in preaching:

> The sermons in this book are mostly from two sciences, which are philosophy and theology. And therefore philosophy is the light by which one finds theology, because we preach to the people through philosophy, by

---

57   *Lectura compendiosa Tabulae generalis* Prol., MOG 5:359: "Cum igitur sint plures homines qui desiderant habere scientiam, ideo nos complilamus hanc Artem ut ipsi melius possint habere cognitionem huius quod desidrant scire, ut possint cognoscere et amare nostrum dominum Deum et pervenire ad caelestem gloriam."

58   Jean-Henri Probst, "Ramon Llull philosophe populaire et franciscain," *Criterion* 2 (1926): 387–406 and 3 (1927) 182–210.

59   Cicero, *De finibus bonorum et malorum* 5.5, (ed.) Harris Rackham (London and New York: 1931), 402, states that Aristotle composed two kinds of books, the "exoteric" or popular, and others for the more learned, in the form of commentaries: "Duo genera librorum sunt, unum populariter scriptum quod ἐξοτερικόν appelabant; alterum limatius, quod in commentariis relinquebant." Cf. Peter W. Forchhammer, *Aristoteles und die exoterischen Reden* (Kiel: 1864), 58–62.

60   Helmut Holzhey, "Der Philosoph für die Welt—eine Chimäre der deutschen Aufklärung?," in *Esoterik und Exoterik der Philosophie*, (eds.) Helmut Holzhey and Walther Zimmerli (Basel and Stuttgart: 1977), 117–138; Ekkehard Martens, "Philosophie in der Spannung zwischen Esoterik und Exoterik: Zum Begriff einer Philosophie für jedermann," in *Philosophie als Thema in der Universitären Erwachsenenbildung* (Hamburg: 1981), 9–27.

the light which knowledge aims for theological understanding and to know God and His works, for the knowledge that we have of God and His works, we fall in love with God and His works.[61]

Despite being expounded as a popular philosophy, his Art sought to supersede both what philosophy makes intelligible and what faith makes believable. It was situated at a higher level of truth where all the sciences converge and harmonize, because "philosophically and theologically there is only one truth."[62] Writing informative books that used clearly understandable "sensory figures," was a challenge.[63] Llull wrote in Catalan and in Latin—even in Arabic at times— "and made continuous efforts to simplify and popularize his philosophy and to make it generally accessible."[64] He could not use rigorous scholastic terminology because neither he nor his readers had mastered it, but he demanded the readers' understanding of his Latin texts if there were nothing wrong in the writing (*si forte eis minus bene dicere videamur*) or without stumbling over an Arabic idiom (*modum loquendi arabicum*).[65] Moreover, Llull was quite aware that the vernacular language he used was not sufficiently rich and flexible:

And because we have a need for words that are not in the vernacular, therefore we use some words in Latin and also some foreign words that are not in the vulgar tongue nor in Latin.[66]

---

61   *Libre de virtuts e de pecats* Epilog, NEORL 1:298: "Los sermons d'aquest llibre són majorment per dues ciències, les quals són filosofia e teologia. E car filosofia és llum per què hom puja a teologia, deu hom preïcar al poble per filosofia, per lo llum de la qual sàpia pujar a entendre teologia e conèixer Déu e les sues obres, car per la coneixença que hom ha de Déu e de les sues obres s'enamora hom de Déu e de les sues obres." Cf. *Liber de virtutibus et peccatis* "De fine huius libri," ROL 15:432: "Sermones huius libri sunt maxime per duas scientias, quae sunt philosophia et theologia. Et quia philosophia est lumen, per quod ascenditur ad theologiam, debet praedicari populo per philosophiam, lumine cuius sciat ascenderr ad intelligendum theologiam, et cognoscendum Deum et opera eius. Quoniam per cognitionem, habitam de Deo et operibus eius, efficitur homo philocaptus de Deo et operibus eius."

62   *Liber de syllogismis contradictoriis* Prol., ROL 7:170: "non est nisi una veritas philosophice et theologice."

63   *Libre de contemplació en Déu* 364.1, ORL 7:598: "Qui vol encercar l'Art e la via vera per la qual sàpia obrir veritat o falsetat, cové que en l'encercament afigur figures sensuals ab les quals sàpia afigurar les figures entel·lectuals, per les quals e ab les quals hom pot donar obriment e endreçament a son enteniment d'entrar conèixer qual cosa és vera o falsa."

64   Hillgarth, RLL 43.

65   *Compendium seu commentum Artis demonstrativae* Epilog, MOG 3:452.

66   *Art amativa* Prol. 4, ORL 17:7: "E car havem fretura de vocables qui no són en vulgar, cové nos usar d'alcuns vocables qui són en llatí e encara d'algunes paraules estranyes qui no

All this makes Llull—much like Pierre Teilhard of Chardin (1881–1955), for example—a kind of freelance thinker who is difficult to classify. His work is thus extremely tight because it is stretched by forces that seem irreducible. It presents a rough, logical radicalism not always in keeping with the contemplative adoration that permeates most of his writing. The combinatory mechanics of his Art are surrounded by an esoteric halo, which contrasts with the clarity and simplicity of his moralizing stories. He continues to praise ecstasy in the face of Divine Goodness, but never forgets that contemplation requires preaching what one has been given to contemplate. In fact, the peculiarity of Llull's popular philosophy, full of internal tensions, paradoxically made him unpopular. Why? Because Llull's way of thinking (*Denkform*) considerably restricted the audience of his Art. His way of thinking, like that of John Scotus Eriugena, it was a kind of complex theological form (*Mischtyp*).[67] The number of readers it reached was very limited: a few secular intellectuals, both big and small enthusiasts, who had general cultural knowledge. For the simple folk, the Lullian philosophical theology was probably not understandable because of its complex speculative circularity; for the Schoolmen it must have seemed simplistic and not rigorous due to its naïve and unsophisticated symbolism.[68]

3.2.2   *Exemplarist Metaphysics*

Llull's philosophy is theological in the sense that it stems from divine reality and everything is explained through the divine properties accessible to the human mind. We could say of Llull what Gottfried Wilhem Leibniz (1646–1716) said of Baruch Spinoza (1632–1677): "Popular philosophizing started with created beings, Descartes began from the mind, and Spinoza begins with God."[69] But Llull does not arrive at the divinity through a rigorous philosophy that would rationally require its existence. For Llull, God was the patrimony common to all cultures, as Islam and Judaism show.

---

són en ús en vulgar ni en llatí;" cf. *Libre de Déu* Prol., in *Obras de Ramon Llull*, (ed.) Jerónimo Rosselló, 3 vols. (Palma: 1901–1903), 2:441: "E car nos no poríem bé declarar ni alt enteniment haver sense alguns vocables novells que direm, cové a usar d'aquells e encara d'alguns vocables los quals hom no usa en romanç."

67   Cf. Hans Leisegang, *Denkformen* (Berlin: 1928), 169–174 and 404–413. It was both circular and symbolic at the same time, according to Erhard-Wolfram Platzeck, "La mentalidad del beato Raimundo Lulio y la teoría moderna de las formas del pensar," in *La evolución de la lógica griega en el aspecto especial de la analogía* (Barcelona: 1954), 113–135.

68   Johnston, *ER* 178.

69   Ludwig Stein, *Leibniz und Spinoza* (Berlin: 1890), 83: "Vulgus philosophicum incipere a creaturis, Cartesius incepisse a mente, se incipit a Deo."

Llull believed, therefore, that philosophically questioning the theist tradition did not make sense. For him, moving between "tradition and originality,"[70] and the task of the Christian philosopher was to rethink the tradition and at the same time to remember personal experience: the experience he had gained in the contemplation of God, the experience that had enlightened his mind (*mentem suam illustravit*)[71] and that had made him understand what is essential and accidental in all things (*principia essentialia et accidentalia omnium rerum*).[72]

The *principia essentialia* are called "dignities" (*dignitates*) and also "reasons" (*rationes*), because they are the foundation that explains the existence of all things. Llull identifies them with the essential qualities or divine names (*nomina divina*) that one should attribute to God as Creator of the universe, just as Islamic and Judaic philosophers did,[73] and also as the Christian tradition had done.[74] As a result, the divine dignities appear reflected in all created beings, because "in the creation of the world each of divine reasons impresses there its likeness" (*en la creació del món cascuna de les divines raons hi posà sa semblança*).[75]

> This world is the image which signifies the great nobility and goodness of God. And the memory that is created in remembrance of God, thus, by nature they should rejoice and remember the image of God, that is knowing that the goodness of the creature is signified the goodness of God and the greatness of the creature is signified the greatness of God, and in like manner the other things like these.[76]

70   Robert D.F. Pring-Mill, *El microcosmos lul·lià* (Palma: 1961), 41–49.

71   *Vita coaetanea* 3.14, ROL 8:280.

72   *Breviculum ex artibus Raimundi electum* 1, ROL Suppl. 1:15.

73   Daniel Gimaret, *Les noms divins en Islam: Exégèse lexicographique et théologique* (Paris: 1988); Gershom Scholem, "Die Name Gottes und die Sprachtheorie der Kabbala," in *Judaica 3: Studien zur jüdischen Mystik* (Frankfurt am Main: 1973), 7–70; Moshe Idel, "*Dignitates* and *Kavod*: two theological concepts in Catalan mysticism," *SL* 36 (1996): 69–78; Ernst Cassirer, "Sprache und Mythos: Ein Beitrag zum Problem der Götternamen," in *Wesen und Wirkung des Symbolbegriffs* (Darmstadt: 1977), 71–167.

74   Dionysius Areopagita, *De divinibus nominibus*, PG 3:585–984, often glossed by medieval theologians.

75   *Proverbis de Ramon* 36.17, ORL 14:43.

76   *Libre de meravelles* 53, *OE* 1:401: "Aquest món és imatge per la qual és significada la gran bonea e noblea de Déu. E car la memòria sia creada a membrar Déu, per açò, per natura se deu alegrar com remembra la imatge de Déu, ço és saber, que per la bonesa de la criatura és significada la bonesa de Déu, e per la granea de la criatura és significada la granea de Déu, e així de les altres coses semblants a aquestes."

In the created things, everything that is particular is explained by what is universal or transcendental; that is to say, by divine dignities under which all creation has been configured. The dignities become the instruments with which God has created everything from nothing, and so constitute the fundamental structure of the universe.

However, in God the dignities remain indiscernible, are one essence, and their actions are interchangeable among each other:

> The divine dignities are one another, just as goodness is one same thing with greatness and eternity and the others, in so far as they are simply one in number and without any distinction in number, essence, nature, or the deity [...] All of these reasons are good through goodness, great through greatness, eternal through eternity, and powerful through power, wise through wisdom, willing through will, virtuous through virtue, true through truth, and glorious through glory, and not distinct in number.[77]

But Llull had discovered that, besides the *principia essentialia*, there were also some *principia accidentalia* or ancillary, that is to say, a kind of universal principles acting as relational functions (*Relationsfunktionen*)[78] to establish all the connections and all the possible dependencies between finite and infinite beings. In the final version of his Art, Llull establishes three ternary groups: difference, concordance, and contrariety; beginning, middle, and end; majority, equality, and minority.[79]

In this exemplarist metaphysics, all sensible realities are nothing more than imitation of the intelligible or archetypical realities (*exemplares*), in other

---

77 *Arbre de sciencia* "De l'arbre divinal," 1.3 and 1.5, ORL 12:278–279: "Les divines dignitats són les unes les altres, enaixí que bondat és una cosa mateixa ab granea e eternitat e les altres, en tant que el nombre és un e simplement sens neguna distinció de nombre per essència e natura e deïtat. ...Totes aquestes raons són bones per bondat, e grans per granea, e eternals per eternitat, e poderoses per poder, e sàvies per saviea, e amades per voluntat, e virtuoses per virtut, e veres per veritat, e glorioses per glòria, e no distinctes en nombre per distinció." Cf. *Arbor scientiae* 14.3 and 14.5, ROL 25:647–649: "Dignitates divinae sunt invicem numero idem, ita quod bonitas est idem cum magnitudine et aeternitate, et ceteris, in tantum quod numeras est unus simpliciter sine aliqua distinctione numeri per essentiam, naturam et deitatem ... Omnes istae rationes bonae sunt per bonitatem, et magnae per magnitudinem, et aeternae per aeternitatem, et potentes per potestatem, et scientificae per sapientiam, et amatae per voluntatem, et virtuosae per virtutem, et verae per veritatem, et glorosae per gloriam et indistinctae numero per distinctionem."

78 Erhard-Wolfram Platzeck, *Raimund Lull. Sein Leben, seine Werke, die Grundlagen seines Denken*, 2 vols. (Düsseldorf: 1962), 1:204.

79 For detailed discussion, see Chapter 4 of this volume.

words, reflections of the dignities that exist in the Godhead. Llull, in maintaining this theological metaphysics, was in the wake of Bonaventure's theology, according to which the Son is the exemplary figure (*exemplar*) of all creatures.[80]

This exemplarity could explain the nature of the necessary reasons (*rationes necessariae*) which, according to Llull, helps us to understand what the Christian faith aims to believe. In effect, if what structures the material or spiritual essence of beings is their conformity with the divine essence, what philosophically explains the uniqueness of the relationships being created also explains the uniqueness of the relationships typical of the divine. Therefore, the *rationes necessariae* discovered in created beings also explains the essence of their creator, to the extent that they are nothing more than the expression of the correspondence between God and his creatures.[81]

3.2.3   *Meaning and Demonstration*

Llull's philosophy presupposes as an indisputable fact that "creatures signify and demonstrate the great goodness and nobility" (*les creatures donen significació e demostració de la gran bonea e noblea*) of their creator,[82] which means that we must consider them a likeness or a *vestigium* of the invisible deity. As a religious philosopher, Llull begins with the assumption that the world is theologically open and meaningful. He follows Bonaventure's exemplarity,[83] and believes that, through contemplation up and down the scale of beings, one can discover the links that unite the creature with its creator.

In this sense, Llull's theological philosophy is a metaphysics based on the Neoplatonic scheme of *exitus-reditus*. Although ontologically the process of ascent and descent begins with the divine dignities, its epistemological starting point is sensible experience. Thinking religiously means to start the *via ascensus*, or to begin to contemplate sensible reality, in order to discover

---

80   Bonaventura, *Commentarium in I. Librum sententiarum* Dist. 6, art. 1, q. 3, in *Opera Omnia*, 10 vols. (Quaracchi: 1882–1902), 1:130: "Procedit ergo Filius secundum rationem exemplaritatis non sicut exemplatum per exemplar sed sicut ipsum exemplar vel ratio exemplandi cetera." Cf. Romano Guardini, *Systembildende Elemente in der Theologie Bonaventuras* (Leiden: 1964), 40–50. For detailed discussion of Llull's exemplarism, see Chapter eight of this volume.

81   Manuel Bauçà, "El ejemplarismo como clave de la teología de la *Ars Dei* de Ramon Llull," in *Von der Suche nach Gott*, (eds.) Margot Schmidt and Fernando Domínguez Reboiras (Stuttgart and Bad Cannstadtt: 1998), 399–428.

82   *Libre de contemplació en Déu* 1.10, ORL 2:8; cf. Jordi Gayà Estelrich, "Significación y demostración en el *Llibre de contemplació* de Ramon Llull," in *Aristotelica et Lulliana*, (eds.) Fernando Domínguez Reboiras, Ruedi Imbach, Theodor Pindl, and Peter Walter (Steenbrughe: 1995), 477–499.

83   Jean Marie Bissen, *L'exemplarisme divin selon saint Bonaventure* (Paris: 1929), 42, n. 1.

the traces (*vestigia*) of its creator. Then understanding, once divine reality is reached, strengthens itself with the vision that confers faith and begins its descent, the *via descensus*, along which one can "attain the true meaning of things and unravel their secrets" (*intellectus transit ad attingendum res rerum et secretum earundem*).[84] Therefore, since the two-way ascent and descent of the scale of beings can understand all reality that exists, and everything that can be the object of perception, imagination, doubt, belief or understanding, Llull considers the exposition of this process an integral part of the theological philosophy inherent in his Art. "We say that the book *De ascensu et descensu intellectus* forms part of the Art, since using the procedures of the Art (*artificialiter*), it instructs the mind to ascend and descend to the sensible, imaginable, doubtful, believable or intelligible, so that the intellect can know what they are."[85]

The Art allows understanding to have access to uncreated reality and to the *secreta* of the created because Llull developed an ontology that innovatively highlighted the relational aspect common to all reality: to the creatures, of course, but also to their creator. In the Aristotelian tradition, "relationship" (*relatio*) was understood as a category that could affect a substance. In the Augustine and Scotus speculative Trinitarian theology, "relationship" was not decisive. Llull, however, considered reality as essentially—and not accidentally—relational, and thus introduced a new way of thinking about the world.

As a result, with his ontological discovery, he elaborates his ternary theory of relationship, the theory of "correlatives," for which he created the appropriate terminology. In effect, the perfect good is not static, but the union of three moments: 1) the essence, or the ability to do good (*bonificativum*); 2) the object, or, that which can be made good (*bonificabile*); and 3) the essential activity that combines these two moments in the act of doing good (*bonificare*). We cannot separate any of these three moments—the subject, the object, and the action—because all three are universally present in both the creature and the creator.[86]

---

84   *Liber de ascensu et descensu intellectus* 1, ROL 9:23. Cf. Amador Vega, *Ramon Llull and the Secret of Life* (New York: 2003), 101–104, which considers Llull's work a "Hermeneutics of the Secret."

85   *Liber de fine* 3.2.18, ROL 9:288–289: "Liber *De ascensu et descensu ipsius intellectus* Ars dicitur eo quia ad entia sensibilia, imaginabilia, dubitabilia, credibilia et intelligibilia docet ascendere et descendere artificialiter intellectum, ut de ipsis entibus faciat scientias intellectum."

86   *Ars amativa* "Tabula," MOG 6:155: "Bonificativum est bonum quod agit bonum sub ratione bonitatis, et bonificabile est id quod est dispositum ad esse bonum, et bonificare est actus

The world thus becomes a huge polymorphic sign, inciting the philosopher, as lover of God, to find "the meaning that the creatures give to their beloved" (*les significances que les creatures donen de son amat*).[87] But the reality is so complex that the philosopher is compelled to divide it into three ontological levels (sensible, intelligible, infinite), according to which he discovers four modes of meaning:

> In the first mode, through something sensible one investigates something else sensible...; in the second, through something sensible one demonstrates the intelligible...; in the third, from something intelligible is signified something else intelligible...; in the fourth, through the intelligible one demonstrates the sensible.[88]

These four modes of meaning result in three modes of necessary demonstration:

> There are three degrees of the demonstration, namely, demonstration from the sensible, intellectual demonstration of something finite, and intellectual demonstration of something infinite. The second mode is more important than the first and the third more important than the second.[89]

When demonstration goes beyond sensible knowledge and reaches rational knowledge, it leaves behind what is simply good (*bonum*) and achieves something better (*melius*). Likewise, when we exceed what is rational and enter into what is infinite because it exceeds all good (*optimum*), we attain a reality that we cannot exceed (*optimum et maximum*) and attain the divine, the greater reality which no one can fathom (*id quo maius cogitari nequit*).[90]

---

bonitatis, et bonificatum est id quod est factum bonum;" "The *bonificativum* is the good that does good through goodness; the *bonificabile* is that which is disposed to being good; and *bonificare* is the act of goodness, and the *bonificatum* is that which is made good." Cf. Jordi Gayà Estelrich, *La teoria luliana de los correlativos* (Palma: 1979), 83–89.

87   *Libre d'amic e amat* 57, (ed.) Albert Soler, "Els Nostres Clàssics. Col·lecció B" 13 (Barcelona: 1995).

88   *Compendium logicae Algazelis*, (ed.) Charles Lohr (Freiburg: 1967), 118: "Primo enim, per unum sensuale debet investigari aliud sensuale...; secundo vero, per sensuale demonstratur intellectuale...; tertio autem, per unum intellectuale aliud intellectuale significatur...; quarto vero, per intel·lectuale sensuale demonstratur." Cf. Amador Vega, *Tratado de los cuatro modos del espíritu* (Barcelona: 2005).

89   *Libre de demostracions* 13, ORL 15:92–93: "Tres són los graus de demostració, ço és a saber, demostració sensual e demostració entel·lectual de cosa finida e demostració entel·lectual de cosa infinida. Lo segon mou és de major importància que el primer e el terç que el segon."

90   Cf. Anselm, *Monologion* 2, in *Opera omnia*, (ed.) Franz S. Schmitt, 6 vols. (Edinburgh: 1946–61), 1:101.

The jump from a lower level to a higher one becomes possible because there are situations where, because of a "excess of meaning" (*ex excessu*), a cognitive faculty is transported to a higher one.[91] Llull calls those significant excesses "transcendent points." In fact, there can be a *mirabilis rerum connexio* that connects each entity with each other.[92] The most important transcendent point is that which, in projecting what is intelligible to something higher order, allows the human mind to transcend itself and attain knowledge of God.

The world becomes a major symbol, forcing one to consider the threshold of significance. "The symbolic never belongs exclusively to the beyond (*Jenseits*) nor to the here (*Diesseits*), or the field of immanence or transcendence, but rather has a value which can overcome these opposites from a metaphysical theory stuck between two worlds. The symbolic is neither one thing nor the other, but rather one set into the other."[93]

3.3   Theological Philosophy

3.3.1   *Natural Theology*

Because "general" (*generalis*), Llull's Art was intended to be a universal science, ideal for providing a theological foundation for all knowledge (*scientia generalis ad omnes scientias*).[94] The purpose of this new universal science was to develop a theory of everything[95] which, in competition with Aristotelian epistemology, offered a new theoretical framework able to account for all knowledge deductively. With his *Ars generalis*, Llull tried to establish a *theologia naturalis universalis* that—through non-Aristotelian ways, that is, through the contemplation of dignities—allowed access to everyone, from any discipline, to the true God.[96]

Llull believed that contemplation of the divine names was the best method for knowing God, and, in knowing Him, to discover the truth of the Christian faith. For that reason, in the prologue of his *Cent noms de Déu*, he assures his

---

91   *Ars inventiva veritatis* 3.8, MOG 5:47: "Causatur enim punctus transcendens ex excessu quem alia potentiarum hominis habet supra aliam aut aliquando supra se ipsam."

92   Cf. Aquinas, *Summa contra Gentiles* 2.68.6, in *Opera omnia*, (ed.) Roberto Busa, 7 vols. (Stuttgart and Bad Cannstatt, 1980), 2:45: "Hoc autem modo mirabilis rerum connexio considerari potest. Semper enim invenitur infimum supremi generis contingere supremum inferioris generis."

93   Ernst Cassirer, *Philosophie der Symbolischen Formen*, 3 vols. (Darmstadt: 1973), 3: 447.

94   *Ars generalis ultima* Prol., ROL 14:5.

95   John D. Barrow, *Theories of Everything: The Quest for Ultimate Explanation* (Oxford: 1991).

96   Charles Lohr, "Ramon Llull: 'Logica nova,'" in *Interpretatione: Hauptwerke der Philosophie: Mittelalter*, (ed.) Kurt Flasch (Stuttgart: 1998), 337.

readers: "This book is good for contemplating and for knowing God, and for proving the Christian faith according to Him, and this book is of great consolation and pleasure."[97] Like everyone else at the time, Llull admitted that theology was an activity reserved for the clergy: "The clerics are established in the world to learn theology and to show other men, so that they love God and know how to keep themselves from sin."[98]

But given this, the *intellectus fidei*, or the analysis of the intelligibility of the faith, was not optional, but rather a divine precept, because "the understanding is obliged to understand with all its strength just as the will is to love."[99] Llull was also aware that there was a theological reflection appropriate to the laity:

> Because there are some men who are naturally perceptive, and competent in some sciences, but lazy in studying the divine trinity and the incarnation, we wrote this book to reproach them, since sloth is a mortal sin. Also, we wrote this book for those lay people who have acute intelligence and a great desire to know the divine trinity and incarnation, so that from greater knowledge of God, they can greatly love and admire Him.[100]

Llull, while accepting the possibility of a *theologia negativa*, did not admit that *theologia affirmativa* was an exclusive patrimony of faith. Llull argued that understanding, according to the capacity that he gave to it, could also make valid statements about God, which collectively comprised his philosophical theology.[101] Llull stood, thus, in the wake of the logicians of the Christian tradition. Indeed, Augustine remarked that we only believe what

---

97   *Cent noms de Déu* Prol., ORL 19:80: "Aquest llibre és bo a contemplar e a conèixer Déus, e a provar la fe cristiana segons en ell apar, e és llibre de gran consolació e plaer."

98   *Doctrina pueril* 75.3, NEORL 7:195: "Los clergues són establits en lo món per ço que aprenen teologia e que la mostren als hòmens, per tal que sien amadors de Déu e que es sàpien guardar de pecat.

99   *Libre de demostracions* 1.13, ORL 15:18: "Aitant obligat és l'enteniment a entendre a tota sa força con la volentat a amar."

100   *Liber de actu maiori* Intr., ROL 1:165–166: "Cum sint aliqui homines, qui habent subtile ingenium per naturam, et habent aliquas scientias, sed sunt accidiosi et pigri ad investigandum divinam trinitatem et incarnationem, per hoc facimus istum librum ad reprehendendum ipsos, cum accidia sit mortale peccatum. Et etiam facimus istum librum propter aliquos homines laicos, habentes intellectum subtilem et magnam voluntatem ad cognoscendum divinam trinitatem et incarnationem, ut per magnam notitiam de Deo possint ipsum multum amare et contemplari."

101   Cf. *Disputatio fidei et intellectus* 1.18, ROL 23:238.

seems credible;[102] Anselm exalted the *fides quaerens intellectum* and *credo ut intelligam*;[103] Richard of Saint-Victor (d. 1173) urged understanding what we received from faith;[104] Roger Bacon (c. 1219/20–c. 1292) argued that philosophy was part of divine wisdom so that the mission of Christian philosophers (*christiani philosophantes*) was to discover it there.[105] Finally, it does not seem unreasonable to think that Llull could have shared the intellectual guidance of the Islamic current of the mu'tazilites, according to which the first duty of the believer is to know God for reflection and speculation, since we cannot know Him, either intuitively or sensorially.[106] Also, Llull was presumably not far from Maimonides' (1135/38–1204) ideal of achieving union with God through understanding;[107] nor are certain similarities with Kabbalistic theosophism inadmissible.[108]

Llull's philosophical theology of rationalism was not aberrant, but rather was within the great tradition of natural theology that interpreted nature mystically as a book that showed the same God revealed in the Bible. In this sense, the *intellectus fidei*, the rational understanding of faith, as Llull understood it, became an *ars inveniendi*, a method by which to discover—in a manner valid for all faithful Christians, as well as infidel Muslims and Jews—the essential manifestations of the divine, epitomized in a small number of concepts, which were defined by the divine dignities. The Art thus became a "conceptual theology" (*Begriffstheologie*)[109] and also a "theological logic" (*Theologik*), that

---

102 Augustine, *De praedestinatione sanctorum* 2.5, PL 44: 963: "Nullus quippe credit aliquid, nisi prius cogitaverit esse credendum."

103 Anselm *Proslogion* 1, in *Opera omnia*, (ed.) Franz S. Schmitt, 6 vols. (Edinburgh: 1946–61), 1:97–100.

104 Richard of Saint Victor, *De Trinitate* Prol., (ed.) Jean Ribailler (Paris: 1958), 81: "Satagamus, ut dictum est, quae credimus intelligere. Nitamur semper, in quantum fas est vel fieri potest, comprehendere ratione quos tenemus ex fide."

105 Roger Bacon, *Opus maius* 3.2.3, (ed.) John H. Bridges (London: 1900), 39: "Quod autem philosophiae potestas non sit aliena a Dei sapientia sed in ipsa conclusa, manifestum est."

106 Cf. 'Abd al-Jabbar, *Kitab al-usul al-khamsa* [Book of the Five Fundamentals]: "If it is asked: What is the first duty that God imposes upon you? Say to him: Speculative reasoning (*al-nazar*) which leads to knowledge of God, because he is not known intuitively (*daruratan*) not by the senses (*bi l-mushahada*). Thus, He must be known by reflection and speculation." Cited from Richard C. Martin, Mark R. Woodward, and Dwi S. Atmaja, *Defenders of Reason in Islam: Mu'tazilism from Medieval School to Modern Symbol* (Oxford: 2003), 90.

107 Maimonides, *The Guide for the Perplexed* 3.51, trans. Moritz Friedländer (New York: 1956), 384–391.

108 Harvey J. Hames, *The Art of Conversion: Christianity and Kabbalah in the Thirteenth Century* (Leiden: 2000), 118–189.

109 Wilhelm Schmidt-Biggemann, *Philosophia perennis: Historische Umrisse abenländlischer Spiritualität in Antike, Mittelalter und Früher Neunzeit* (Frankfurt am Main: 1995), 129–143.

is to say, a theology that stemmed from the divine names and sought to make the fundamental dogmas of Christianity logically comprehensible.[110]

Llull thus anticipated the *liber creaturarum* that Raymond of Sabunde (ca. 1385–1436) rightly called *theologia naturalis*,[111] and placed himself among the thinkers who, in one way or another, have investigated the degree of reasonability that Christianity could have. Llull wanted to capture what is rational in Christianity in the same way that centuries later John Locke (1632–1704) sought the reasonableness of Christianity and Gotthold Ephraim Lessing (1729–1781) was interested in *Christentum der Vernunft*.[112]

Alfred North Whitehead points out that—unlike Buddhism, which is a metaphysical religion—Christianity is a religion—that is, a way of living morally under the guidance of supra-rational beliefs—that seeks a metaphysics it did not originally have, or a dogmatic it never quite reaches. For Whitehead, a constant element in the history of Christianity is in fact stubbornly trying to rationalize its beliefs by building a dogmatic around what is never purely rational: the faith of the believer.[113] From this point of view, Llull was a genuinely Christian thinker.

All the same, Llull was a lay Christian philosopher. The invectives that he launched during the first decade of the 14th century against the clergy of the Faculty of Arts in Paris reveal that what separated him from the *magistri artium* was their divergence at that time in defining the field of philosophical theology.[114] The *magistri artium*, radical followers of Aristotle, argued that reason, autonomously and exclusively, embraced a very wide field of reality. Faith was not denied, but had another, much smaller level. Some subtle and logical distinctions, persistently revised, marked the boundary that separated and simultaneously related the realms of faith and reason. Llull, as a Christian layman with Scholastic training, saw everything much more simply. His "conceptual theology" (*Begriffstheologie*) left no room for logical subtleties and he considered the divine names unquestionably well-defined realities. Their meaning was clear and semantically true:

> The subject of theology is God and the subject of philosophy is understanding. And since the object of understanding is truth, and God is

---

110   Jan Rohls, *Philosophie und Theologie in Geschichte und Gegenwart* (Tübingen: 2002), 237.

111   Raymond of Sabunde, *Theologia naturalis seu Liber craturarum*, (ed.) Friedrich Stegmüller (Stuttgart and Bad Cannstatt: 1966).

112   Karl Vossler, "Mittelalter Aufklärung in Spanien und Europa," in *Aus der romanischen Welt* (Krarlsruhe: 1948), 540–50, has noted the aspects of Llull's thought that can tentatively be considered "enlightened."

113   Alfred North Whitehead, *Religion in the Making* (New York: 1926), 50.

114   Ruedi Imbach, *Laien in der Theologie des Mittelaters* (Amsterdam: 1989), 102–130.

truth, it follows necessarily that true philosophy and theology must agree with one another. And therefore, for whatever is truly intelligible, its opposite is not believable; otherwise this would imply a contradiction, but contradiction is impossible.[115]

3.3.2   Ars Dei

Lullian theological philosophy is circular:[116] to explain man and nature, the theologian begins with divine reality, but only knows as divine in so far as the human soul and nature display it. This circularity is explained by the "lay style" of Lullian theology,[117] —a version of Christian Neoplatonism, based on a simple combinatory art that thinks in circles.[118] This is very different from the "clerical style" of Scholastic theology—like that of Thomas Aquinas (1225–1274), for example—concerned with theology as a science, according to Aristotelian epistemology.[119] Although Llull presents some texts as if they were *disputationes* like the commentaries on Peter Lombard's (c. 1100–c. 1161) *Librum sententiarum*,[120] these do not come from scholastic activity, but are the fruit of the spiritual theology modeled through his Art. After all, Llull did not try anything more than to promote knowledge and love of God:

> We compile this Art to understand and to love God so that human understanding through the Art ascends to divine knowledge, and consequently to love, since the intellect, unable to do anything without method, can do so methodically, though with the help of grace and divine wisdom.[121]

---

115   *Liber de efficiente et effectu* Prol., ROL 7:274: "Subiectum autem theologiae est Deus, et subiectum philosophiae est intelligibile. Et quia obiectum intelligentis est veritas, et Deus est veritas, necessarie sequitur, quod vera philosophia et theologia habeant concordantiam ad invicem. Et ideo, quidquid est vere intelligibile, eius oppositum non est vere credibile; aliter implicaretur contradictio; sed contradictio est impossibilis."

116   Nicholas of Cusa, *De docta ignorantia* 1.66, in *Philosophisch-Theologische Werke*, (ed.) Paul Wilpert-Senger, 4 vols. (Hamburg: 2002), 1:86–88: "Omnis theologia circularis et in circulo posita existit." Cf. Eusebi Colomer i Pons, *Nikolaus von Kues und Raimund Lull* (Berlin: 1961), 88–91.

117   Hans Urs von Balthasar, *Herrlichkeit: Eine theologische Aesthetik*, 3 vols. (Einsiedeln: 1962), 2/1:13, 18, and 22.

118   Platzeck, *Raimund Lull*, 1:397: "Die reine Kombinatorik ist im Grunde ein Kreisdenken."

119   Marie-Dominique Chenu, *La Théologie comme science au XIIIᵉ siècle* (Paris: 1969).

120   *Disputatio Eremitae et Raimundi super aliquibus dubiis quaestionibus Sententiarum magistri Petri Lombardi*, MOG 4:225–346.

121   *Ars compendiosa Dei* Prol., ROL 13:17: "Ad intelligendum et diligendum Deum facimus Artem istam, ut intellectus humanus artificialiter ascendat in divinam cognitionem et per consequens in amorem, quoniam intellectus, quod non potest sine artificio, cum artificio ipse potest, tamen divina gratia et sapientia mediante."

This knowledge and this love provided by theology tended to expand. The dialogue that invited the infidel to convert was initially the preferred means of propagating the Faith and love between men. However, the ideal of Christianity— which Llull shared—did not always manage to avoid belligerence.

Regarding the speculative innovations of the scholastics in the 13th century, Lullian theology did not make original contributions, but rather represented an alternative doctrine. His position was a bit eccentric. On the one hand, his innovations, such as the theory of correlatives, were only of doctrinal interest if men adopted his Art as a way of thinking. On the other hand, Llull was obligated to invent a quite peculiar vocabulary, packed with ideolects, which was less precise and more imaginative than that of the scholastics because it was aimed at cultured laymen—and also directed at non-Christians—who, even if they were educated, did not know the peculiarities of scholastic Latin nor Llull himself.

Moreover, Llull did not aspire to reflect on all of the theological questions debated at the time, but only on those articles of faith that were the most essential for Christians and most problematic for non-Christians. Essentially, these were the Trinity and the Incarnation, the two theological affirmations most abhorrent to the strict monotheism of the Islamic and Judaic faiths. His aim was to demonstrate, in the framework of a philosophical theology of the Abrahamic religions, that the Christian God was the most rationally justifiable God. The Christian layman, if he felt responsible to account for his faith, could not be exempted from the obligation to reflect upon it with as much rigor as possible: "No one is excused from doing all that it possible to connect the Trinity with divine incarnation."[122]

Reflection on the Trinity was a central theme in Lullian thought. It could explain two facts: Llull's contemplative activity, constantly focused on understanding and appreciating the dynamism of the divine; and the difficulty of transmitting his trinitarian contemplation to Christians and non-Christians in a believable way. Like all medieval thinkers, Llull began with a psychological explanation of the trinity proposed by Augustine. "Since, Lord, human thought cannot act without memory and understanding, thus is signified your Holy Trinity; and since man's thought involves three things, so it signifies that he is compelled to contemplate three things in his creator."[123] But Lullian theology

---

122   *Liber de divinis dignitatibus infinitis et benedictis* Prol., ROL 1:177: "Nullus est excusatus quod non agat secundum suum posse ad cognoscendum divinam trinitatem et incarnationem."

123   *Libre de contemplació* 246.21, ORL 6:183: "En açò, Sènyer, que la pensa humana no pot ésser en actu sens memòria e enteniment, per açò és significada vostra sancta trinitat; e per açò car la pensa de l'home és en tres coses, és significat que és obligada a contemplar en son creador tres coses."

demanded a broader philosophical basis insofar as the divine trinity was the structure of all beings, not just of the human mind. The *dignitates* or *rationes* could therefore be the ontological basis for the Trinity. They only needed to be interpreted from his theory of correlatives.

Llull's reasoning stemmed from the principle that any reality, even God, cannot remain *otiosa*. "Eternity is the eternal principle (*ratio*) that produces the eternal, that is as a principle in the Father, who is eternity and produces the eternal Son who is eternal by virtue of His eternity, since it is this principle's nature and His not to be idle."[124]

Therefore, as idleness implies ontological absence, it is necessary that all beings contain the principles that allow them to remain active. The correlative theory explains these active principles that, when applied to the Trinity, make us understand that in God there has to be a generative principle, a generated term, and a generating act. Therefore, in God three persons are necessary: Father, Son, and Spirit. However, the Art—although it offered an ontological framework that made it partially understandable that in God there could be three persons—did not explain the fundamental Trinitarian difference between the *generatio* of the Son from the Father and the *spiratio* of the Spirit from the Father and the Son. Therefore, aware of the explanatory limits of a Trinitarian theology based exclusively on the Art, Llull ultimately does not hesitate to juxtapose, without distinguishing them conceptually, elements drawn from his Art (the dignities and correlatives) and elements drawn from traditional theology (*amor* and *spiratio*):

> The second branch [of the Divine Tree] is *spiratio*, which includes the infinitives of the dignities through the act of love, which is *amare*. For example, the act of goodness requires that, from the love of the Father for the Son and of the Son for the Father, this *amare* issues, so that it can be a person, as in the Father and the Son, and its *bonificare* exist through personal *amare*.[125]

---

124   *Arbor scientiae* 14.2.3, ROL 25:646: "Aeternitas est ratio aeterno, quod aeternum producat, videlicet est ratio Patri, qui est aeternitas, qui Filium aeternum ratione suae aeternitatis producit, quae est ei ratio, ut ipsa non sit otiosa nec ipse otiosus." Cf. *Arbre de sciencia*, ORL 12:276–277: "Eternitat es raó a eternal que produga eternal, ço és a Pare qui es eternitat, lo qual produu Fill eternal per raó de sa eternitat, estant ell raó que no sia ociós de ella ni de sí mateix."

125   *Arbor scientiae* 14.4.2, ROL 25:670–671: "Secundus ramus [arboris divinalis] est spirare, sub quo sunt infinitivi dignitatum sub actu amoris, quod est amare. Sicut actus bonitatis, qui requirit, quod de amore, quem Pater habet ad Filium, et quem Filius habet ad Patrem, exeat tale amare, quod possit esse ita persona, sicut est in Patre et Filio, ut suum bonificare

As for the theological explanation that makes the mystery of the Incarnation of the Son rationally admissible, Llull's arguments, much like his explanation of the Trinity, are based on the necessary activity of the divine being. Llull contemplates Jesus Christ, the Man-God, located at the confluence of *ad intra* divine activity—which explains the Trinity—and the *ad extra* divine activity, beginning with creation and culminating in incarnation:

> In Our Lady God was made a man, in whom were contained all the goodness, greatness, etc. that are or can exist in creatures. For the humanity of our Lord God Jesus Christ is the fulfillment and end of all creatures, and any goodness, greatness, etc. that exists in a creature corresponds to the goodness, greatness, etc. of the humanity of Jesus Christ. So, in this humanity is contained the humanity of all things that God created, since He created everything for the glory and honor of this precious humanity.[126]

From this theological position, the primary purpose of the Incarnation is the necessary manifestation of divine goodness, while the secondary purpose is the redemption of humanity historically conditioned by original sin:

> They do not speak correctly who assert that the main purpose of incarnation is to redeem mankind, since then it would follow that, if there had been no original sin, God would not have been incarnate, and sin be the cause of the Incarnation, which is impossible.[127]

---

possit esse in personali amare." Cf. *Arbre de sciencia*, ORL 12:301: "Lo segon ram és espirar, dejús lo qual estan los infinitius de les dignitats sots l'actu d amor qui és amar, axí com l'actu de bontat qui requer que de l'amor que el Pare ha al Fill e que el Fill ha al Pare, ixca tal amar que ella hi pusca ésser en així persona, com és en lo Pare el Fill, per ço que el seu bonificar pusca ésser en personal amar."

126   *Liber de Sancta Maria* 22, ROL 28:188: "In beatissima virgine Maria fuit factus homo Deus, in quo contentae fuerunt omnes bonitates, magnitudines etc., quae sunt aut esse possunt in creaturis. Nam humanitas domini Iesu Christi est finis, et complementum omnium creaturarum. Et omnis bonitas, magnitudo etc., quae est in creatura, tota correspondet bonitati, magnitudini etc. humanitatis domini Iesu Christi. In ista enim humanitate habet se pro contenta humanitas de omnibus, quae Deus creavit, quoniam omnia creavit ad gloriam et honorem huius pretiosae humanitatis." Cf. *Libre de Sancta Maria* 22.3, ORL 10:165.

127   *Liber de iustitia Dei* 3.10, ROL 2:52: "Non dicunt bene illi qui asserunt, quod principalis finis incarnationis est redimere humanum genus, quia sequeretur, quod, si peccatum originale non fuisset, Deus incarnatus non esset, et quod peccatum fuisset causa incarnationis: quod est impossibile."

3.3.3 *Ars Mystica Theologiae et Philosophiae*

Lullian thought is coherent and complex at the same time: coherent, because it presents a clear unity around a few, central, easily-identifiable themes; complex, because it seeks to explain in a singular conceptual system all the aspects of reality known to a literate layman in the 13th century.

We can present this complex unity, noting five key directions and ordering them successively to see how they appeared in the life of Llull, successively emerging one from another:

1. *Reflexive Contemplation*: Llull's conscience, following his conversion, was religiously overwhelmed by nature, which appeared to him as a reflection of the divine perfections, traditionally epitomized in the "divine names."

2. *Theological Philosophy*: meditation on the names of God allowed the discovery that natural reality reflected divine reality. Therefore, in combining the divine attributes, we can discover how they engage with each other in divine essence while we discover that all beings are interrelated with both each other and the divine. Thus emerges Llull's Art: a religious vision of the world that integrates all the elements that shape reality.

3. *Philosophical Theology*: the inherent combinatorial nature of the Art highlights the internal dynamism of all beings (correlative theory), which allows a rational understanding of what is believed by faith (Trinity and Incarnation).

4. *Rational Apologetics*: the worldview obtained through the Art coincides with the fundamental features of the natural theology of the three Abrahamic religions. Consequently, philosophical theology, common to Christianity, Islam and Judaism, can demonstrate that the basic tenets of Christianity are rationally comprehensible.

5. *Mystical Encyclopedism*: the religious vision of the world through the Art assimilates all sciences into an encyclopedia that assumes that everything comes from and returns to the divine; the result is a *Ars mystica theologiae et philosophiae* that unifies all reality.

We could apply the four moments with which Jean Baruzi characterizes formation of the mystical "I" of John of the Cross (1542–1591) analogously to Llull's contemplative "I": 1) the attainment of a new vision of the world; 2) the development of a new way of thinking; 3) the regeneration of consciousness, which, in purifying itself, leads to divinization; and 4) the universal gaze that sees everything from divine fullness.[128]

---

[128] Jean Baruzi, *Saint Jean de la Croix et le problème de l'expérience mystique* (Paris: 1924), 374; Helmut Hatzfeld, "The Influence of Ramon Llull and Jan van Ruysbroeck on the Language of the Spanish Mystics," *Traditio* 4 (1946): 337–397.

Therefore, like the great mystics, Lullian philosophical thought is the fruit of religious experience. In contrast to the logical treatises of his contemporaries, Llull's *Ars magna* is mystically oriented toward what is supra-rational and not logically toward what is rational.[129] Certainly, Llull's thought is rational, but it is to the extent that it rationally presents a theoretical elaboration of the meditations achieved from contemplation. For strong thinkers, mystical contemplation can possess a "noetic quality" that shapes a "state of knowledge" that allows contemplation to become a deepening of truth, unfathomable for strictly discursive rational thought.[130]

Despite his apparent rationalism, Llull recognized that, in crafting his Trinitarian theology, understanding only worked when thought was under the guidance of divine understanding and when reasoning in accordance with its reasons:

> We have sought the Blessed Trinity, through its understanding and reasoning. Thus, human understanding becomes enlightened in so far as it cannot reasonably deny the Trinity. As a result of this enlightenment, the habituated in love, is exalted in its object.[131]

Despite the impressive cognitive apparatus that his Art provides for understanding, we remain perplexed because we never know what the divine substance is in itself, nor do we quite know who we are ourselves. "It is, Lord God, a great wonder that we are such a thing that we do not know or understand what it is itself. Hence, while knowing what we are, we lack knowledge and understanding, how much more we should fail to know what your substance is in itself!"[132] However, if, as Augustine says, "God is wisdom, through whom all things were made, as divine authority and truth have shown, the true philosopher is a lover of God,"[133] we should never forget that—as Llull says—the

---

129   Wilhelm Risse, *Die Logik der Neuzeit*, 2 vols. (Stuttgart: 1964), 1:533.

130   William James, *The Varieties of Religious Experience* (London: 1902), 380.

131   *Ars mystica philosophiae et theologiae* 7.14, ROL 5:314: "Venati sumus beatissimam divinam trinitatem cum suo intellectu, discursu per suas rationes. Propter quem discursum intellectus humanus est illuminatus in tanto quod rationabiliter ipsam non potest negare. Propter quam illuminationem, voluntas, ex caritate habituata, est obiective exaltata."

132   *Libre de contemplació* 20.9, ORL 2:98: "És, sènyer Déus, gran meravella que nos siam aquella cosa que no sabem ni entenem què s'és en si mateixa. On, com a saber la cosa que som nos defall saber e enteniment, quant més nos deu defallir a saber e conèixer la vostra substància què és en si mateixa!"

133   Augustine, *De civitate Dei* 8.1, PL 41:225A: "Si sapientia Deus est, per quem facta sunt omnia, sicut divina auctoritas veritasque monstravit, verus philosophus est amator Dei."

philosopher lover "is always happy" (*Philosophus semper est laetus*),[134] despite recognizing the insurmountable limits of his understanding.

Work Cited

Primary Works

Anselm, *Opera omnia*, (ed.) Franz S. Schmitt, 6 vols. (Edinburgh: 1946–61).

Aquinas, Thomas, *Opera omnia*, (ed.) Roberto Busa, 7 vols. (Stuttgart: 1980).

Augustine, *De civitate Dei*, PL 41: 13–804.

Augustine, *De praedestinatione sanctorum*, PL 44: 959–992.

Bacon, Roger, *Opus maius*, (ed.) John H. Bridges (London: 1900).

Bonaventure, *Commentarium in Primum Librum sententiarum*, in *Doctoris Seraphici S. Bonaventurae Opera Omnia*, 10 vols. (Quaracchi: 1882–1902), vol. 1.

Cicero, *De finibus bonorum et malorum*, (ed.) Harris Rackham (London and New York: 1931).

Descartes, René, *Meditationes de prima philosophia*, in *Oeuvres de Descartes*, (eds.) Charles Adam and Paul Tannery, 12 vols. (Paris:1897–1909), vol. 7.

Dionysius Areopagita, *De divinibus nominibus*, PG 3:585–984.

Eymerich, Nicholas, *Dialogus contra lullistas,* trans. Jaume de Puig i Oliver (Barcelona: 2002).

Hillgarth, Jocelyn N. (ed.), *Diplomatari lul·lià* (Barcelona: 2001).

Maimonides, *The Guide for the Perplexed*, trans. Moritz Friedländer (New York: 1956).

Menestò, Enrico (ed.), *Le vite antiche di Jacopone da Todi* (Florence: 1977).

Nicholas of Cusa, *Philosophisch-Theologische Werke*, (ed.) Wilpert-Senger, Paul, 4 vols. (Hamburg: 2002).

Raymond of Sabunde, *Theologia naturalis seu Liber craturarum*, (ed.) Friedrich Stegmüller (Stuttgart: 1966).

Richard of Saint Victor, *De Trinitate*, (ed.) Jean Ribailler (Paris: 1958).

Vega, Amador (ed.), *Tratado de los cuatro modos del espíritu* (Barcelona: 2005).

Primary Works: Llull

Arbre de ciència, OE 1:555–1046.

Arbor scientiae, (ed.) Pere Villalba Varneda, ROL 24–26.

Arbre de sciencia, ORL 11–13.

---

134 *Liber proverbiorum* 2.77.14, MOG 6:122; cf. *Proverbis de Ramon* 277.14, ORL 14:303. Cf. Helmut Kuhn, *Liebe: Geschichte eines Begriffs* (Munich: 1975), 141–146, and Alois M. Haas, Sermo mysticus: *Studien zu Theologie und Sprache der deutschen Mystik* (Freiburg: 1979), 409–413.

Art amativa, ORL 17:1–398.

Ars amativa, MOG 6:7–154 (text 2, sep. pag.).

Ars amativa boni, (eds.) Marta M.M. Romano and Francesco Santi, ROL 29:1–432.

Ars compendiosa Dei, ROL 13:15–331.

Ars generalis et ultima, (ed.) Aloisius Madre, ROL 14.

Ars inventiva veritatis, MOG 5:1–211 (text 1, sep. pag.).

Ars mystica theologiae et philosophiae, ROL 5:286–466.

Art de contemplació, ORL 19:433–490.

Breviculum ex artibus Raimundi electum, ROL Suppl. 1.

Cent noms de Déu, ORL 19:77–170.

Compendium Artis demonstrativae, MOG 3:293–452 (text 6, sep. pag.).

Compendium logicae Algazelis, (ed.) Charles Lohr (Freiburg: 1967).

Compendium seu commentum Artis demonstratiuae, MOG 3:293–452 (text 6, sep. pag.).

Disputatio Eremitae et Raimundi super aliquibus dubiis quaestionibus Sententiarum magistri Petri Lombardi, MOG 4:225–346.

Disputatio fidei et intellectus, (ed.) Walter Euler, ROL 23:213–279.

Doctrina pueril, (ed.) Joan Santanach i Suñol, NEORL 7.

Lectura compendiosa Tabulae generalis, MOG 5:344–358 (text 4, sep. pag.).

Lectura super Artem inventivam et Tabulam generalem, MOG 5:359–716 (text 5, sep. pag.).

Liber de actu maiori, ROL 1:161–171.

Liber de ascensu et descensu intellectus, ROL 9:20–199.

Liber de demonstratione per aequiparantiam, ROL 9:216–232.

Liber de divinis dignitatibus infinitis et benedictis, ROL 1:173–184.

Liber de efficiente et effectu, ROL 7:273–291.

Liber de fine, ROL 9:250–291.

Liber de iustitia Dei, ROL 2:39–58.

Liber de Sancta Maria, ROL 28:1–241.

Liber de syllogismis contradictoriis, ROL 7:169–198.

Liber de virtutibus et peccatis, ROL 15.

Liber proverbiorum, MOG 6:283–413 (text 6, sep. pag.).

Libre d'amic e amat, (ed.) Albert Soler, "Els Nostres Clàssics. Col·lecció B" 13 (Barcelona: 1995), 61–193.

Libre de contemplació, ORL 2–6.

Libre de demostracions, ORL 15.

Libre de Déu, in *Obras de Ramon Llull*, (ed.) Jerónimo Rosselló, 3 vols. (Palma: 1901–1903), 2:269–371.

Libre de meravelles, OE 1:319–511.

Libre de virtuts e de pecats, NEORL 1.

Libre del gentil e dels tres savis, NEORL 2.

Logica del Gatzell, ORL 19:1–62.

Logica nova, (ed.) Walter Euler, ROL 23:1–179.

Proverbis de Ramon, ORL 14:1–324.

Romanç d'Evast e Blaquerna, (eds.) Albert Soler and Joan Santanach, NEORL 8.

Vita coaetanea, (ed.) Hermogenes Harada, ROL 8:259–309.

Secondary Works

Adams, Marilyn McCord, "Reviving Philosophical Theology: Some Medieval Models," in *Was ist Philosophie im Mittelalter?*, (eds.) Jan A. Aersten and Andreas Speer (Berlin: 1998), 60–68.

Aubin, Paul, *Le problème de la conversion: Étude d'un terme commun à l'hellenisme et au christianisme des trois premiers siècles* (Paris: 1963).

Barrow, John D., *Theories of Everything: The Quest for Ultimate Explanation* (Oxford: 1991).

Baruzi, Jean, *Création religieuse et pensée contemplative* (Paris: 1951).

Baruzi, Jean, *Saint Jean de la Croix et le problème de l'expérience mystique* (Paris: 1924).

Batalla, Josep, "Die lullsche *Ars* als philosophische Theologie," *Jahrbuch für Religionsphilosophie* 9 (2010): 129–158.

Batalla, Josep, "Ego, qui sum laicus," *SL* 48 (2008): 69–92.

Bauçà, Manuel, "El ejemplarismo como clave de la teología de la *Ars Dei* de Ramon Llull," in *Von der Suche nach Gott*, (eds.) Margot Schmidt and Fernando Domínguez Reboiras (Stuttgart and Bad Cannstadtt: 1998), 399–428.

Bissen, Jean Marie, *L'exemplarisme divin selon saint Bonaventure* (Paris: 1929).

Brown, Stuart F., Thomas Dewender and Thomas Kobush (ed.), *Philosophical Debates at Paris in the Early Fourteenth Century* (Leiden and Boston: 2009).

Brümmer, Vincent, *What Are We Doing When We Pray? A Philosophical Inquiry* (London: 1984).

Burns, Robert I., "Christian-Islamic Confrontation in the West: The Thirteenth-Century Dream of Conversion," *The American Historical Review* 76 (1971): 1386–1434.

Carreras i Artau, Tomás and Joaquín Carreras i Artau, *Historia de la filosofia española: Historia de la filosofía cristiana de los siglos XIII al XV*, 2 vols. (Madrid: 1939–43).

Casadesús, José, *El Arte magna de Raimundo Lulio* (Barcelona: 1917).

Cassirer, Ernst, *Philosophie der Symbolischen Formen*, 3 vols. (Darmstadt: 1973).

Cassirer, Ernst, "Sprache und Mythos: Ein Beitrag zum Problem der Götternamen," in *Wesen und Wirkung des Symbolbegriffs* (Darmstadt: 1977), 71–167.

Chenu, Marie-Dominique, *La Théologie au douzième siècle* (Paris: 1976).

Chenu, Marie-Dominique, *La Théologie comme science au XIIIᵉ siècle* (Paris: 1969).

Colomer i Pons, Eusebi, *Nikolaus von Kues und Raimund Lull* (Berlin: 1961).

Cruz Hernández, Miguel, *El pensamiento de Ramon Llull* (Valencia: 1977).

Daniel, E. Randolph, *The Franciscan Concept of Mission in the High Middle Ages* (St. Bonaventure, New York: 1992).

Dilthey, Wilhelm, *Die Typen der Weltanschauung und ihre Ausbildung in den Metaphysischen Systemen,* in *Gesammelte Schriften,* 12 vols. (Leipzig and Berlin: 1931).

Domínguez Reboiras, Fernando, "El proyecto luliano de predicación cristiana," in *Constantes y fragmentos del pensamiento cristiano* (Tübingen: 1996), 117–132.

Estelrich, Jordi Gayà, "Significación y demostración en el *Libre de contemplació* de Ramon Llull," in *Aristotelica et Lulliana,* (eds.) Fernando Domínguez Reboiras, Ruedi Imbach, Theodor Pindl, and Peter Walter (Steenbrughe: 1995), 477–499.

Estelrich, Jordi Gayà, *La teoria luliana de los correlativos* (Palma: 1979).

Forchhammer, Peter W., *Aristoteles und die exoterischen Reden* (Kiel: 1864).

Gimaret, Daniel, *Les noms divins en Islam: Exégèse lexicographique et théologique* (Paris: 1988).

Gracia, Jorge J.E., "El misionero, como filósofo," *EL* 22 (1978): 129–138.

Guardini, Romano, *Systembildende Elemente in der Theologie Bonaventuras* (Leiden: 1964).

Guardini, Romano, "Unmittelbares und gewußtes Beten," in *Auf dem Wege* (Mainz: 1923), 111–130.

de Guibert, Joseph, "Méthode et contemplation au XIIIᵉ siècle: l'*Art de contemplation de R. Lull*," in *Études de théologie mystique* (Toulouse: 1930), 299–310.

Haas, Alois M., Sermo mysticus: *Studien zu Theologie und Sprache der deutschen Mystik* (Freiburg: 1979).

Hames, Harvey J., *The Art of Conversion: Christianity and Kabbalah in Thirteen Century* (Leiden: 2000).

Hatzfeld, Helmut, "The Influence of Ramon Llull and Jan van Ruysbroeck on the Language of the Spanish Mystics," *Traditio* 4 (1946): 337–397.

Hillgarth, Jocelyn N., *Ramon Lull and Lullism in Fourteenth-Century France* (Oxford: 1971).

Holzhey, Helmut, "Der Philosoph für die Welt—eine Chimäre der deutschen Aufklärung?," in *Esoterik und Exoterik der Philosophie,* (eds.) Helmut Holzhey and Walther Zimmerli (Basel and Stuttgart: 1977), 117–138.

Idel, Moshe, "*Dignitates* and *Kavod*: two theological concepts in catalan mysticism," *SL* 36 (1996): 69–78.

Imbach, Rudi, *Laien in der Theologie des Mittelaters* (Amsterdam: 1989).

James, William, *The Varieties of Religious Experience* (London: 1902).

Kuhn, Helmut, *Liebe: Geschichte eines Begriffs* (Munich: 1975).

Leisegang, Hans, *Denkformen* (Berlin: 1928).

Lohr, Charles, "Ramon Llull: 'Logica nova'," in *Interpretatione: Hauptwerke der Philosophie: Mittelalter,* (ed.) Kurt Flasch (Stuttgart: 1998), 333–351.

Martens, Ekkehard, "Philosophie in der Spannung zwischen Esoterik und Exoterik: Zum Begriff einer Philosophie für jedermann," in *Philosophie als Thema in der Universitären Erwachsenenbildung* (Hamburg: 1981), 9–27.

Martin, Richard C., Mark R. Woodward, and Dwi S. Atmaja, *Defenders of Reason in Islam: Mu'tazilism from Medieval School to Modern Symbol* (Oxford: 2003).

McDonnell, Ernest W., *The Beguines and Beghards in Medieval Culture*, (New Brunswick, New Jersey: 1954).

McGinn, Bernard, *The Presence of God: A History of Western Christian Mysticism, vol. 3, The Flowering of Mysticism: Men and Women in the New Mysticism, 1200–1350* (New York: 1998).

Nock, Arthur Darby, *Conversion: The Old and the New from Alexander the Great to Augustine of Hippo* (Oxford and London: 1961).

Nolte, Ulrich, *Philosophische Exerzitien bei Descartes: Aufklärung zwischen Privatmysterium und Gesellschaftsentwurf* (Würzburg: 1995).

Platzeck, Erhard-Wolfram, "La mentalidad del beato Raimundo Lulio y la teoría moderna de las formas del pensar," in *La evolución de la lógica griega en el aspecto especial de la analogía* (Barcelona: 1954), 113–135.

Platzeck, Erhard-Wolfram, *Raimund Lull. Sein Leben, seine Werke, die Grundlagen seines Denken,* 2 vols. (Düsseldorf: 1962).

Pou y Martí, José, *Visionarios, beguinos y fraticelos catalanes (siglos XIII–XV)* (Alicante: 1966).

Pring-Mill, Robert D.F., *El microcosmos lul·lià* (Palma: 1961).

Probst, Jean-Henri, *Caractère et origine des idées du bienheureux Raymond Lulle* (Toulouse: 1912).

Probst, Jean-Henri, "Ramon Llull philosophe populaire et franciscain," *Criterion* 2 (1926): 387–406 and 3 (1927) 182–210.

Risse, Wilhelm, *Die Logik der Neuzeit*, 2 vols. (Stuttgart and Bad Cannstatt: 1964).

Rohls, Jan, *Philosophie und Theologie in Geschichte und Gegenwart* (Tübingen: 2002).

Schaeffler, Richard, *Kleine Sprachlehre des Gebetes* (Trier: 1988).

Schmidt-Biggemann, Wilhelm, Philosophia perennis*: Historische Umrisse abenländlischer Spiritualität in Antike, Mittelalter und Früher Neunzeit* (Frankfurt am Main: 1995).

Scholem, Gershom, "Die Name Gottes und die Sprachtheorie der Kabbala," in *Judaica 3: Studien zur jüdischen Mystik* (Frankfurt am Main: 1973), 7–70.

Sciacca, Michele F., *Saint Augustin et le néoplatonisme: La possibilité d'une philosophie chrétienne* (Louvain: 1956).

Seel, Martin, *Adornos Philosophie der Kontemplation* (Frankfurt am Main: 2004).

Serverat, Vicente, "Utopie et histoire: Les postulats théoriques de la praxis missionaire," in *Raymond Lulle et le Pays d'Oc* (Toulouse: 1987), 191–229.

Southern, Richard W., *Western Views of Islam in the Middle Ages* (Cambridge, Mass.: 1962).

Stein, Ludwig, *Leibniz und Spinoza* (Berlin: 1890).

van der Lecq, Ria, "Logic and the Theories of Meaning in the Late 13th and Early 14th Century including the Modistae. Part II: The Logic of Intentions," in *Handbook of the History of Logic*, (eds.) Dov M. Gabbay and John Woods, 9 vols. (Amsterdam and Boston: 2008), 2:370–385.

Vauchez, André, *Les laïcs au Moyen Âge: Pratiques et expériences religieuses* (Paris: 2007).

Vega, Amador, "Die religiose Imagination bei Ramon Llull: Elemente für eine theorie des Kontemplativen Gebets," in *Deutsche Mystik im abendländischen Zusammenhang*, (eds.) Wolfram Haug and Walter Schneider-Lastin (Tübingen: 2000), 749–772.

Vega, Amador, *Ramon Llull and the Secret of Life* (New York: 2003).

Vega, Amador, "Ramon Llull: l'art d'inventar la veritat," in *Ramon Llull i l'islam: L'inici del diàleg*, (ed.) Maria-Àngels Roque (Barcelona: 2008), 207–211.

Veuthey, Léon, *S. Bonaventurae philosophia christiana* (Rome: 1943).

Von Balthasar, Hans Urs, *Das betrachtende Gebet* (Einsiedeln: 2003).

Von Balthasar, Hans Urs, *Herrlichkeit: Eine theologische Aesthetik*, 3 vols. (Einsiedeln: 1962).

Von Balthasar, Hans Urs, *Verbum Caro* (Einsiedeln: 1990).

von der Nahmer, Dieter, *Die lateinische Heiligenvita. Eine Einführung in die lateinische Hagiographie* (Darmstadt: 1994).

Vossler, Karl, "Mittelalter Aufklärung in Spanien und Europa," in *Aus der romanischen Welt* (Krarlsruhe: 1948), 540–550.

Whitehead, Alfred North, *An Introduction to Mathematics* (London: 1911).

Whitehead, Alfred North, *Religion in the Making* (New York: 1926).

Yates, Frances A., *The Art of Memory* (London: 1992).

Zerfass, Rolf, *Der Streit um die Laienpredigt: Eine pastoralgeschichtliche Untersuchung zum Verständnis des Predigtamtes und zu seiner Entwicklung im 12. und 13. Jahrhundert* (Freiburg im Breisgau: 1974).

CHAPTER 4

Llull's "Great Universal Art"

Josep E. Rubio

4.1 Introduction

The "Great Universal Art" (*Ars Magna Universalis*) is the foundation of Ramon Llull's written works regardless of genre, that is, not only his philosophical and theological texts but also those dealing with scientific topics, as well as his poetic and narrative works. Llull's Art provides a single omnivalent method of generating a theoretically endless number of meaningful propositions. Therefore, as we shall see, although the Art may not be itself reduced to a single text in Llull's corpus, it nonetheless represents a single method, since it is always present either explicitly or implicitly in the whole length and breadth of Llull's extant *oeuvre*.

It is common to find, in different eras or among different scholars, a particular work identified with the Art, with some ascribing "*Ars magna*" inappropriately to texts carrying a different title in the respective critical editions. For example, there are those who take the *Ars compendiosa inveniendi veritatem* or the *Ars demonstrativa* as their starting point for explicating the *Ars Magna*, in spite of the fact that the majority view has always been to equate the *Ars Magna* with the *Ars Generalis Ultima*. Thirty-four years stand between the first and the last of the extant written versions of the Art, according to the catalog of the Raimundi Lulli Opera Latina edition of Llull's works; but, even after the redaction of what, according to Llull himself, was the final and definitive version of the Art, the latter continues to exercise a defining role in shaping all the works that he produced thereafter.

As we have seen, then, critics use the term "Art" in two distinct senses, as a method and as an instantiation of the method in a specific text. The first usage involves the series of elements which are present in all versions of the Art: the exposition of principles divided according to *figurae*, the use of combinatory mechanics, and the proposition and resolution of questions through the combinations of first principles. In the second usage, the method is restricted to a specific formulation thereof, with its own peculiarities, and these allow us to speak of different versions of the Art. Despite the deep strength and unity of its method, perfectly anticipated from the outset, the Art acquires nuances and refinements here and there and is "re-written" in different ways so as better to

© KONINKLIJKE BRILL NV, LEIDEN, 2019 | DOI:10.1163/9789004379671_005

address the changing needs both of the moment and of Llull's audiences over time.

So, what is the Art, and what meaning did it have in Llull's own lifetime? Llull himself spoke of a method revealed to him in contemplation, as a "gift of God" (*donum Dei*) in the service of a divine mission to demonstrate the truths of the Christian faith. By its very constitution this "art" can serve as the foundation of any branch of knowledge, but its main purpose, at least for Llull, was missionary. The *Cant de Ramon* [Song of Ramon], a poem in which Llull discusses his system, says:

> A new knowledge I have found;
> from which one can know truth
> and destroy falsehood.
> Moors will be baptized
> Tatars, Jews, and many in error,
> from the knowledge that God has given to me.[1]

Posterity has of course effected many differing interpretations of the Art. Above all, the presence of the *ars combinatoria* has stimulated modern readings of the method that view it as an automated mechanism, sometimes referred to as a "mechanical logic" or "thinking machine," capable of solving all problems regarding any topic. And, indeed, the so-called *Ars Lulliana* does possess a special design, remarkable for the cultural epoch in which it was designed, and which makes it in appearance allied to the formal notations of modern symbolic logic. Interesting parallels have even been made with Artificial Intelligence. In particular, the formalization of language via the use of symbolic letters to substitute for concepts and the mechanism of combining figures makes Llull, in the opinion of some experts, a predecessor of modern information technologies.[2]

Of course, Llull innovated in formal aspects of his Art to such a degree that it became a predecessor of modern logic systems that have nothing to do with its explicit purpose. Such formal innovation was placed in the service of the transmission of content. Llull deployed a unique semiotic system to transmit

---

1 *Cant de Ramon, OE* 1:1031: "Novell saber hai atrobat; / pot n'hom conèixer veritat / e destruir la falsetat. / Sarraïns seran batejat, / tartres, jueus e mant errat, / per lo saber que Déus m'ha dat."

2 Eusebi Colomer, "De Ramon Llull a la moderna informàtica," *EL* 23 (1979): 113–135, was among the first to study the relationship of the Art to Information Technology, modern symbolic and mathematical logic. See also Alexander Fidora and Carles Sierra (eds.), *Ramon Llull: From the Ars Magna to Artificial Intelligence* (Barcelona: 2011).

the experience of a religious faith otherwise impossible to channel through the usual expressive routes of theological tradition. The insights that underlie the revelation of the Art involve the discovery of an expressive form developed little by little throughout the encyclopedic *Libre de contemplació en Deu* [Book of Contemplation of God],[3] the work from which the Art really arises. In this immense mystic encyclopedia, Llull struggles to find a language suitable for enabling communication of the *significationes* that Reason grasps intellectually, a language to reflect, in one mode of meaningful expression, both the *modus essendi* ("the way of being") and *modus intelligendi* ("the way of understanding") of reality.

This language takes shape finally in the Art. From this perspective, that is from the point of view of the exposition of the method, we may attempt a first definition, and affirm that the Lullian Art is a technical language designed for the purpose of communicating rationally the contents of the Christian faith. In this way, the Art is intended to overcome the opposition of Faith to Reason, since according to Llull, Faith can become fully manifest only with the aid of Reason. The Art may thus be defined as a rational mechanism placed in the service of religious faith, both to strengthen and to help propagate it.

Together with this missionary objective, Llull's Art possesses a more general epistemological foundation. The modifier *universalis* means that it intends to be a method upon which all branches of knowledge (*scientiae*) may be predicated, in other words, it represents the realization of the dream of a "universal knowledge" (*scientia universalis*) from the general principles of which derive all the branches of knowledge.[4] Llull became increasingly concerned with presenting his system as a *scientia universalis* applicable to any branch of knowledge, not merely theological matters. This concern seems to grow as the later versions of the Art are written, to such an extent that the prolog of the *Ars generalis ultima* refers only to the Art's epistemological function. However, the theological and apologetic character remains primary throughout, and indeed may be considered to be Llull's main objective, since in the final analysis, knowledge of the truth, any truth, stands in the service of the absolute Truth of God. The moral imperative of the "first intention" (*prima intentio*), by which Llull understands knowledge and love of God, marks the point on the horizon

---

3   *Libre de contemplació en Déu*, OE 2:85–1269.

4   Josep Maria Ruiz Simon, *L'Art de Ramon Llull i la teoria escolàstica de la ciència* (Barcelona: 1999), analyzes the epistemological connotations of Llull's engagement with the Aristotelean concept of science. Josep Batalla, "L'art lul·liana com a teologia filosòfica," *Revista de lenguas y literaturas catalana, gallega y vasca* 15 (2010): 321–344, argues against this interpretation of the Art as scientific method, and for readings that pay more attention to its theological component.

to which all human action should be directed. The Art, before all else, is intended to serve this "first intention."

Llull insists upon the universal nature of science and the epistemological purpose of the Art. One may reasonably surmise that he did so in order to adapt his discourse to an academic context, a move he thought beneficial for the spread of his ideas, especially in order to anticipate criticism a priori by non-Christian philosophers and theologians, to whom Llull was wont to address his works. From the start, Llull is keen to alleviate prejudice among any audience predisposed culturally or opposed religiously to Christianity, and this is done overtly and explicitly. It is clear that Llull knew that if he strove to anticipate criticism through the pursuit of pure reason, he might hope to produce a communicative act that would penetrate otherwise insurmountable barriers of inter-religious and inter-cultural prejudice. Therefore the Art has no recourse to authorities of any kind, not even the Bible. For all the above reasons, the very notion of a *scientia generalis* fit for the rapid acquisition of knowledge of any aspect of reality can be seen as part of this wider communicative strategy. In the words of Robert Pring-Mill, "the primary apologetic function of the Art was of course masked, if only for tactical reasons, by its more general nature as a universal *ars inveniendi veritatem.*"[5]

So, when studying any version of the Art, one must recognize that Llull's express purpose of demonstrating faith through reason provides a single and unified method across all works. In this way we avoid falling into the error of thinking that the development of the Art over time radically transforms its primary purpose, or the operation of its premises. Any changes or developments in the original system were conditioned by immutable constants integrated within the Art, which as we shall see, meant that Llull considered any adjustment an improvement, not affecting adversely the structural integrity of the whole, but ameliorating it. It is for this reason that any description of the Art must begin by accounting adequately for the underlying basic Lullian thinking. Taking the longer view, the different versions are "cornerstones of a single edifice," in the words of Tenge-Wolf.[6]

---

5 Robert D.F. Pring-Mill, "The Trinitarian World Picture of Ramon Llull," *Romanistisches Jahrbuch* 7 (1955–56): 238. Viola Tenge-Wolf, in her introduction to the *Tabula Generalis*, ROL 27:28*-32* and 105*-113*, following the same tactical interpretation of the universality of the Art, compares the Lullian exposition of the intentionality of the method in each of the versions of the Art. Johnston, *ER* 17–20, sees Llull's Art as a development of Saint Bonaventure's *reductio artium ad theologiam.* Josep E. Rubio, "Contemplation et prière, deux composantes de l'Art lullien," *Iris: Annales de philosophie* 33 (2012): 59–70, analyzes its mystical contemplative component.

6 *Tabula generalis*, "Introduction Generalis," ROL 27:113*: "Bemerkenswert ist darüber hinaus, daß in sämtlichen Prologen die einzelnen *Artes* durch Rückverweise auf ihre Vorgängerwerke

First, therefore, to facilitate the exposition that follows, we offer a chronological list of some of the works in which Llull developed the method of his
Art. The list below is not exhaustive, containing only the principal works and
those secondary ones that depend upon them. Llull rarely let the method remain in its abstract or theoretical form in any of its various versions. Hence,
he also wrote texts where the Art is applied to particular sciences, in order to
develop and demonstrate the applicability of the method detailed in his core
theoretical treatises.[7]

Ars compendiosa inveniendi veritatem (1274)
Quattuor libri principiorum: Liber principiorum theologiae, Liber principio-
rum philosophiae, Liber principiorum iuris, Liber principiorum medicinae
Ars universalis
Ars demonstrativa (*ca.* 1283)
Introductoria Artis demonstrativae
Ars inveniendi particularia in universalibus
Liber propositionum secundum Artem demonstrativam
Liber de quaestionibus, per quem modus Artis demonstrativae patefit
Lectura super figuras Artis demonstrativae
Liber chaos
Liber exponens figuram elementalem Artis demonstrativae
Compendium seu commentum Artis demonstrativae
Ars inventiva veritatis (1290)
Quaestiones per Artem demonstrativam seu inventivam solubiles
Ars amativa boni
Tabula generalis
Arbor philosophiae
Arbor scientiae
Brevis practica Tabulae generalis seu Ars compendiosa
Lectura artis, quae intitulata est Brevis practica Tabulae generalis
Ars brevis
Ars generalis ultima (1305–1308)

An important point in the development of the Art occurs in the *Ars inventiva*
veritatis of 1290. According to Anthony Bonner's classification, two phases are

---

so miteinander verkettet werden, daß der Eindruck einer organischen Entwicklung der *Ars*
entsteht. Llull konzipiert die einzelnen Versionen der *Ars* nicht als voneinander unabhängige
Neuentwürfe, sondern als Bausteine eines wachsenden Gedankengebäudes."

7   Fernando Domínguez Reboiras, "Works," in Alexander Fidora and Josep E. Rubio (eds.), *Rai-*
mundus Lullus: An Introduction to his Life, Works and Thought (Turnhout: 2008), 125–242, provides a full list of works, together with descriptions.

distinguished in the Art's development. The first is known as the "Quaternary Phase," in which the basic principles of the method are organized in groups of multiples of four. The second is known as the "Ternary Phase," so-called because these principles appear in groups of multiples of three. The Ternary Phase begins with the *Ars inventiva veritatis* in 1290.[8] The differences between the two stages go beyond the numerical structure of the basic principles. On the one hand some changes in the method can already be glimpsed in texts written before the *Ars inventiva veritatis*, which opens the "Ternary Phase." On the other hand, not all the features of the later versions of the Art are present in the *Ars inventiva veritatis,* for example, the ten *Regulae* that play such a decisive role later. On balance, the progression of the Art seems rather to be one of continuous refinement, rather than abrupt changes, although it is true that the division into two stages may indicate otherwise but is completely justifiable given the changes indicated.[9]

4.2   Llull's Art: Guiding Principles

4.2.1   *The Divine Dignities*

All of this began with contemplation. Llull recounts in the *Vita coaetanea* how he came to uncover the Art as a formal method after a period of contemplative retreat on Mount Randa near the city of Majorca. Contemplation of the divine is the origin of this revealed method for spiritual advancement. Yet, if this *illuminatio* or *illustratio mentis*, known as the enlightenment on Mount Randa, yielded what we might call the "structural" aspects of his method, we must look earlier for its foundations, its raw material, the intellectual principles and premises that found their definitive form on Mount Randa. The Art was not born spontaneously from a single moment of revelation, but from reflection and contemplation, from the intellectual and emotional effort that Llull lays out in the *Libre de contemplació en Déu*, written well before the first "official" version of the Lullian Art, namely the *Ars compendiosa inveniendi veritatem* of 1274. Gayà Estelrich has observed that "The discovery of the Art, managing to find an 'art and means' for his writing and preaching, is the consequence of a rigorous and intense effort of contemplation initiated with the renunciation of

---

8 Bonner, *SW* 1: 56–57.

9 Josep E. Rubio, "Thought: The Art," in Alexander Fidora and Josep E. Rubio (eds.), *Raimundus Lullus: An Introduction to his Life, Works and Thought* (Turnhout: 2008), 243–310, provides a detailed description of each of the versions of the Art. Bonner, *AL* 93–120, amply explains the changes between the quaternary and ternary phases.

his family and property, which, in the mind of the contemplative, is not only its own reward, but always a gift of divine grace."[10]

In the *Libre de contemplació* Llull showed how the contemplative process, which exercised such a strong hold over him, is the activity in unison of the three powers that together constitute the rational soul, namely Memory (*Memoria*), Understanding (*Intellectus*) and Will (*Voluntas*). For Llull, contemplation furnishes the appropriate means for examining all human actions, in order better to direct them toward their "first intention" (*intentio prima*). In this way, the practice of contemplation unifies the active and the contemplative lives under a single objective, namely it strives, by understanding God through "necessary reasons" (*rationes necessariae*), to stimulate the growth of love in the human subject as its primary resource, thus enabling man to be guided towards his perfection as a moral agent.[11]

For this reason, anyone who seeks in the *Libre de contemplació* a poetic spirit waxing lyrical on the topic of his mystical ecstasies, will probably be disappointed by the preponderance of its intellectual element, which always accompanies the emotional effusions that Llull directs to God. To love God one must understand Him. Llull sought through contemplation to enrich his understanding of faith, in order better to strengthen it. He hoped thus to enhance its merit, though paradoxically some of his critics saw his insistence on "necessary demonstrative reasons" as having the opposite effect, diminishing, rather than increasing, his *meritum fidei*.

Llull was well aware of the limits set by God upon mortal understanding. His was an Art that perfectly respected the unknowability of the Divine Essence. But Llull argued that if direct knowledge of God's essence is beyond reach, knowledge of His essential qualities can be gleaned indirectly. Here Llull's contemplative art derives its first axioms, the divine attributes or qualities, which Llull also referred to as "powers" (*virtutes*). These "virtues," "qualities" or "attributes" are a unique essence in God, so the fundamental principle of the Art as

---

10   Jordi Gayà Estelrich, "Introducció," in Ramon Llull, *Darrer llibre sobre la conquesta de Terra Santa* (Barcelona: 2002), 42: "El descobriment de l'Art, haver aconseguit trobar 'art e manera' per a la seva escriptura i per a la seva predicació, és el compliment d'un esforç rigorós i intens de contemplació iniciat amb la renúncia a la família i als seus béns, la qual cosa, en la consciència del contemplatiu, no és tanmateix mèrit propi, sinó sempre do i gràcia de Déu."

11   Mechthild Dreyer, "Raimundus Lullus, 'Quid sit contemplatio?,'" in Fernando Domínguez Reboiras, Viola Tenge-Wolf, and Peter Walter (eds.), *Gottes Schau und Weltbetrachtung: Interpretationen zum "Liber Contemplationis" des Raimundus Lullus* (Turnhout: 2011), 417–438, sets the Lullian attitude towards contemplation in the wider theological climate of Llull's contemporaries.

stated in the *Libre de contemplació* is the mutual agreement (*convenientia*) of the divine virtues, resulting in the lack of contradiction that obtains between them. This principle leads in turn to the concept of mutual convertibility which lies at the heart of his proposal for argumentation *per aequiparantiam*, based on the identity of essence of the divine virtues. This species of argument follows the principle of a *reductio ad absurdum*, whereby any assumption may serve as a premise, and if over the course of its logical development a contradiction of any kind results between the divine virtues, such a premise shall be automatically falsified, rendering its opposite true.

But how does Llull come to define the divine virtues as the foundation of his Art? The *Libre de contemplació* portrays contemplative activity as the intellectual ascent from material to spiritual realities, and as the search for "likenesses" (*similitudines*) that meaningfully connect visible reality with the non-visible world. In Llull's obviously exemplarist worldview, the dual sensory and spiritual planes of Creation are connected by *similitudines* upon which a whole complex set of "meanings" (*significationes*) may be established. Moreover, each of these planes includes equally meaningful *similitudines*, so that one can know an object of sensory nature through another object of the same category, and the same occurs among objects of a spiritual nature. The *similitudines* manifested across the various planes of creation lead back to God, foundation of meaning itself, first cause of all creation, who has impressed into them His likenesses. Thus, the causal relationship between God and creatures allows an intellectual ascent from the latter to the former, through the knowledge of the meanings provided by the *similitudines*.[12]

Thus one reaches the divine virtues. The existence of goodness in creatures signifies a greater good in the divine cause, in such a way that created goodness cannot exist without an uncreated goodness which precedes it as a cause; the same is true of other qualities such as greatness, duration, power, etc. Throughout the *Libre de contemplació en Déu* Llull presents a diverse series of divine virtues or qualities, the archetypes of creation itself, in which are written the similitudes. Their number is variable, depending on the context in which they

---

12   Jordi Gayà Estelrich analyzes in details this method of demonstrating theological proofs
      in the *Libre de contemplació*: "Significación y demostración en el 'Libre de Contemplació'
      de Ramon Llull," in Fernando Domínguez Reboiras, Ruedi Imbach, Theodor Pindl, and
      Peter Walter (eds.), *Aristotelica et Lulliana magistro doctissimo Charles H. Lohr septuage-
      simum annum feliciter agenti dedicata* (Steenbrughe and The Hague: 1995), 477–499; "La
      construcción de la demostración teológica en el 'Libre de contemplació' de Ramon Llull,"
      in Margot Schmidt and Fernando Domínguez Reboiras (eds.), *Von der Suche nach Gott.
      Helmut Riedlinger zum 75. Geburtstag* (Stuttgart-Bad Cannstatt: 1998), 147–171.

appear named. Llull insists always upon the fact that the divine virtues, powers or attributes alluded to can be expanded upon, as the multiplicity of the essential qualities in God is without end. In Chapter 178 for example he discusses two series of nine divine virtues respectively, which he terms "virtues essential with respect to God" (*virtutes essentiales quoad Deum*) and "virtues essential with respect to us" (*virtutes essentiales quoad nos*). The first series comprises "infinity" (*infinitat*), "eternity" (*eternitat*), "wisdom" (*saviea*), "power" (*poder*), "love" (*amor*), "virtue" (*vertut*), "goodness" (*bonea*), "simplicity" (*simplicitat*), "perfection" (*acabament*), "and the others similar to these" (*e les altres semblants a aquestes*). The second consists of "creation" (*creació*), "grace" (*gràcia*), "compassion" (*misericòrdia*), "justice" (*dretura*), "lordship" (*senyoria*), "humility" (*humilitat*), "generosity" (*larguea*), "greatness" (*granea*), and "honor" (*honrament*), "and the others similar to these."[13] The final apostille shows that the list is not closed and could be expanded. Just as one can choose any of them in order to study some aspect of the Godhead, one must recognize that, although our intellectual perception and subsequent linguistic expression might refer to a plurality of divine virtues, they are all manifestations of one indivisible divine substance.

These divine virtues are the foundation of Llull's *Ars Magna*. The interpretive tradition of the *Ars luliana* terms these attributes "absolute principles" (*principia absoluta*), which they are when predicated of God, but not when predicated of created beings, where they must be considered as semblances of the corresponding absolute principles.[14] The earliest versions of the Art call these divine realities "dignities" (*dignitates*) and, as can be seen in the illustrations of figures from the Quaternary Phase, Llull chose sixteen from among those that he was using in the contemplative system of the *Libre de contemplació* and organized them in the circular "Figure A."[15] The transition from the *Libre de contemplació en Déu* to *Ars compendiosa inveniendi veritatem* involves the numerical organization of the principles into closed lists, the lists being distributed around the diagrammatic figures of the Art, relating to each other through the combination of the principles in the construction of what Bonner has described as "a generative system, that is one which, starting from a finite,

---

13   *Libre de contemplació* 178.1–2 and 178.14, *OE* 2:514–518.

14   See Bonner, *AL* 131.

15   On the meaning and origin of the term *dignitas*, see Hélène Merle, "'Dignitas': signification philosophique et théologique de ce terme chez Lulle et ses prédécesseurs médiévaux," *EL* 21 (1977): 173–193; and Anthony Bonner, "Una nota sobre el mot 'dignitas,'" in *Studia Lullistica et Philologica: Miscellanea in honorem Francisci B. Moll et Michaelis Colom* (Palma: 1990), 35–38.

limited set of concepts can generate arguments on all possible subjects. This is what made it, in medieval terms, 'inventive.'"[16]

Before considering the next series of principles underlying the Art, it is essential to note that, for Llull, the perfection of a being necessarily implies its action, for inaction (*otiositas*) is identified with non-being and, hence, imperfection. God, supreme being and absolute perfection, is always active, and this activity is manifested in His dignities. For example, Goodness (*Bonitas*), first of the dignities in the Figure A of the *Ars compendiosa inveniendi veritatem*, is defined in a way that characterizes the dynamic nature of its essence: Goodness cannot be good without doing good, and correspondingly divine Goodness cannot be good without doing good, and eternal and unending Goodness must generate goodness everlasting and without end. Below (in discussing Llull's "universal principles") we will consider what implications the development of this dynamic concept of being will exercise over Lullian metaphysics and how it becomes the pivot around which the rest of the Art revolves, as Llull claims that the Art represents the structure of being.

4.2.2   *Meanings* (Significationes)

First we must consider the other fundamental concepts that, alongside the divine dignities, engage Llull's dynamic conception of being. If the divine dignities are what we might call the "absolute principles" of existence, Llull develops as well a series of "relative principles" that account for the meaningful relationships that connect the dignities among themselves and with their likenesses in creation. Just the principle of ontological dynamism compels Llull to consider being as never existing in isolation but as a relational dynamic that connects all its manifestations among themselves. The *Libre de contemplació* makes a special effort to systematize these conduits of influence from the ideal to the material realms of reality that, from the epistemological viewpoint, are arranged as a series of *significationes*, which the mind can traverse, both in a horizontal as well as a vertical movement of ascent and descent, from knowledge of one reality to knowledge of another reality, whether equal to, greater than, or lesser than the first.

Afresh we are faced with the concept of *significatio* ("the generation of meaning") that lies at the heart of the Lullian philosophy and the Art. It is the epistemological correlate of metaphysical exemplarity. In a world where resemblances articulate the relations among beings, knowledge of these implies

---

16   Bonner, *AL* 52. Josep E. Rubio, *Les bases del pensament de Ramon Llull: Els orígens de l'Art lul·liana* (Valencia and Barcelona: 1997), studies more extensively the connection between the two works.

discovering the *significationes* carried by those resemblances. *Significatio* is conceived of in the ambit of *relatio*, one of the *accidentia* of Aristotelian logic, and which Llull considered a substantive principle manifesting the necessary plurality of entities. His *Logica nova* defines it thus: "*Relatio* is a form indicating necessary plurality. Thus the plurality that exists between father and son [indicates] antecedent and consequent."[17] What we might call the "semiotic" value of *relatio* is patent in the phrase "form indicating," which is the cause therefore of the signifying relationship between signifier and signified: "Further, *relatio* is that form which has an indication in a subject. Thus smoke signals fire; and illness a corruptive, corruptible, or corrupting [entity]."[18]

Llull arranges his *significationes* in line with the hierarchy of levels that organize the world. He seeks to classify the different types of signifying relations obtaining between these hierarchical levels, which, as we have seen, also organize the world according to the basic division between the sensory and spiritual. The former function as a mirror that reflects *similitudines* of the latter:

> Just as the mirror represents and demonstrates the shape or shapes presented to it, thus the sensory world is a ladder and demonstration through which man ascends to the knowledge of the intellectual things.[19]
> ...
> Each intellectual thing, Lord, has an appropriately corresponding sensual thing as a subject through which it can be known; thus, some intellectual things have sensual things through which they are grasped, and other intellectual things have others; and so from one level to another, Lord, each intellectual thing has a sensual thing suitable for demonstrating it to human understanding.[20]

In the generation of meaning the significance of resemblance is revealed by the identification of the properties of the objects of sensory or intellectual

---

17   *Logica nova* 3.4, ROL 23:66: "Relatio est forma indicativa, indicans pluralitatem necessariam. Sicut pluralitas, quae est inter patrem et filium, antecedens et consequens."

18   Ibid.: "Adhuc, relatio est illa forma, quae habet in subiecto indicationem. Sicut fumus habet indicationem in igne; et infirmitas in corruptivo, corruptibili et corrumpere."

19   *Libre de contemplació* 169.1 and 169.26, *OE* 2:483: "Enaixí com lo mirall representa e demostra la figura o figures estants en la sua presència, enaixí les coses sensuals són escala e demostració per les quals puja hom a haver coneixença de les coses entel·lectuals."

20   Ibid., 169.26, *OE* 2:485: "Cascuna entel·lectualitat, Sènyer, ha apropiada sensualitat que li pusca ésser subject per la qual sia coneguda; on, les unes entel·lectuïtats han alcuns sensuals per los quals són apercebudes, e altres entel·lectuals n'han altres; e així de grau en grau, Sènyer, cascuna intel·lectuïtat ha sensualitat a ella covinent a significar e a demostrar-la a l'enteniment humà."

perception that are evaluated and subjected to comparison. The object of study is placed in relation to one that is better known, be it of the same nature or of a different one, and with which it shares some likeness. The act of comparing the properties and qualities of both objects reveals which qualities occur to a greater or lesser degree in each, or which qualities signify concord or contrariety among them, and so forth. In the final analysis, *significatio* unveils hidden meanings in the *differentia* between the qualities, differences that can signify majority (*maioritas*), equality (*aequalitas*), minority (*minoritas*), concordance (*concordantia*), contrariety (*contrarietas*), beginning (*principium*), middle (*medium*), or end (*finis*). These are the categories of meaning permitting access to knowledge of reality from a comparison of the qualities pertaining to the objects of knowledge or perception. They comprise a series of "relative" principles, because they account for the relationships among hierarchy of beings: the relationship between two objects which share a likeness may be one of similarity of concordance, contrariety, majority, equality, and so forth. In his Art, Llull groups these principles in the Figure T, which always accompanies the Figure A of divine dignities or *principia absoluta*.[21]

Significatio can be seen to be "based on a hierarchically exemplarist conception of the universe."[22] Exemplarity is based on likeness, and hierarchy upon order. To these two concepts one should add a third component: *influentia*. As Johnston explains: "Ramon Llull's Great Art of Finding Truth creates a model of universal signification based on the metaphysics of likeness, order and influence."[23] By influence is here understood the transmission of a semblance from one object to another: "This process commonly consists of transmitting a likeness from one thing to another, which thus establishes an affinity between them."[24] Llull is not speaking of direct transmission via a vertical emanation, as direct transmission through the Chain of Being would result in abolishing the necessary separation between God and created reality.[25] In all versions of the *Ars* the principles of Figure T are closely allied to the dignities of Figure A. In the earliest redaction, the *Ars compendiosa inveniendi veritatem*, Figura T is

---

21   Josep E. Rubio, "'Significatio' im 'Liber contemplationis,' oder: wie kann man durch die Betrachtung die Wahrheit finden?," in Fernando Domínguez Reboiras, Viola Tenge-Wolf, and Peter Walter (eds.), *Gottes Schau und Weltbetrachtung. Interpretationen zum "Liber Contemplationis" des Raimundus Lullus* (Turnhout: 2011), 227–237.

22   Jordi Gayà Estelrich, *La teoría luliana de los correlativos: Historia de su formación conceptual* (Palma: 1979), 23: "basado sobre una concepción jerárquicamente ejemplarista del universo."

23   Johnston, *ER* 39.

24   Ibid., 37.

25   Gayà Estelrich, *La teoría luliana de los correlativos*, 194–195.

called a "figure of meanings" (*figura significationum*) and this explains also why Llull conceives of an auxiliary Figure T containing the four natural elements: fire, air, water and earth. The connection between the relative principles and the natural elements explains their usage, according to the latter's function of conveying the meanings of the Dignities through the similitudes imprinted upon them.[26]

The study of elemental composition of the natural world is of interest too, both in the earlier redactions of the Art, as well as in works entirely dedicated to the topic, such as the *Liber chaos*. The topic is not so much of interest as part of natural philosophy, but is seen rather as the significant bearer of hidden spiritual realities, to which it is connected via the doctrine of correspondences. The elemental *figura* in the *Ars compendiosa inveniendi veritatem* is auxiliary to the *figura significationum* because it serves to generate metaphors, *exempla* and likenesses with which to resolve the questions posed about other aspects of reality, represented in the principles of the other Figures of the Lullian Art. Of course, Llull proposes studying natural philosophy in his "Elemental Figure," but this purpose is secondary with respect to the figura's main function as a bearer of *significationes* related to the content of the other *figurae*:

> The Elemental Figure has been placed into this Art with the express intention of metaphorically generating *exempla* of that which is necessary to the solution of A, V, X, Y, Z, and so that answers may be provided to questions of natural philosophy naturally according to the working and disposition demonstrated by the Elemental Figure described above.[27]

These five letters A, V, X, Y, and Z refer to the Figures representing God, the Virtues and Vices, Predestination, and Truth and Falsity. Lullian metaphors acquire a probative valency within the Art, and it is necessary to understand that Llull uses *exempla* not as literary artífice, but as an element of the utmost importance in the development of the Art. The special usage of metaphor ascribed to metaphor in the *Principia medicinae*, represents the trope as a bridge between rhetorical and logical patterns of thought, which Llull grounds upon the cognitive function of Aristotelean metaphor.

---

26   Frances A. Yates, "The Art of Ramon Llull: An approach to it through Lull's theory of the elements," *Journal of the Warburg and Courtauld Institutes* 17 (1954): 115–173.

27   *Ars universalis* 1, "De secunda Figura ipsius T, id est, de Figura Elementali," MOG 1:491: "Intentio, qua ista figura elementalis interponitur in hac arte, est, ut metaphorice detur exempla hujus, quod est necessarium solutioni ipsorum A.V.X.Y.Z., ac ut naturalibus quaestionibus respondeatur naturaliter secundum operationem et dispositionem, quae in elementali figura superius designatur."

4.2.3 *The Powers* (Potentiae)

The Elemental Figure appears in the Art as the paradigm of signification, that is, of the epistemological value of resemblance. This is why the Elemental Figure is ancillary to the Figure T. The latter, together with Figura A, comprise the core of foundational principles of the Art, but only along with others equally essential. The search for truth is an epistemological process comprising the ordered action of an intellect directed toward a goal. To obtain its desired goal, the searching subject needs certain rules of action, appropriate to that goal. Llull thus includes other principles concerning the subject's agency and the rules governing the heuristic process that the subject must follow. This subject is the rational animal, created with the "first intention" of reaching God with all its powers (*potentiae*). Through the organized action of the three powers of the rational soul, memory (*Memoria*), understanding (*Intellectus*) and will (*Voluntas*) a human being can, with the Art's help, know, love and contemplate God without error, and affirm Him beyond doubt.

We should note that Llull does not use "subject" in the modern sense that we recognize, that of an individual (usually human) agent, but rather in the Aristotelean sense of any entity that supports qualities and accidents, or the predicates in logic, by virtue of which its nature tends toward passivity. The modern sense of a "subject" as active agent, identified with a Cartesian thinking *ego*, only emerges from a long process in the post-medieval era.[28] In Llull we encounter, as we might expect, the doublet *potentia-obiectum* (not *subiectum-obiectum*), to which *actus* is added as a connective term; thus the *Ars brevis* says: "Power is the form with which the Intellect apprehends the object. Object is the subject in which the Intellect comes to rest. Act is the connection between the power and the object."[29]

Between the Figure A and the Figure T Llull places his Figure S, which embraces all the possible actions of the three powers of the rational soul that can come into play in his Art as an active aspect of the search for truth. As God created man in His image and likeness, so the structure of the Figure S reproduces this resemblance of the rational creature to its Creator, so that the principles which make it up comprise the number 16, a number matching the

---

28   Alain de Libera, *Archéologie du sujet: La naissance du sujet* (Paris: 2007).

29   *Ars brevis* 10.12, ROL 12:235: "Potentia est forma, cum qua intellectus attingit obiectum. Obiectum autem est subiectum, in quo intellectus quiescit. Actus est connexio potentiae et obiecti;" trans. Bonner, *SW* 1:622. Núria Gómez Llauger, "Estudi dels termes 'Potentia' 'Obiectum' i 'Actus' a partir del *Liber de potentia, obiecto et actu* de Ramon Llull," *Revista Internacional d'Humanitats* 19 (2010): 17–28, analyzes in detail the meaning of these terms in Llull.

divine dignities of the Figure A. The Lullian Art is thus founded on the analogy between God, humans (as microcosm), and the world (as macrocosm).[30] The 16 principles contained in Figura S are further organized in a quaternary structure, that is, distributed across four squares of four principles each. Thus the Figure S bridges God and the elements of nature, or in other words describes the mechanism connecting the Divine Dignities with the four elements. The human being, as the center of Creation, is the privileged depository of *significationes* since a human unites within itself the different natures of Creation, as can be seen from the following passage, so central to any adequate explanation of the role of analogy and metaphor in the Art:

> There is an Elemental Figure set and ordered within the structure of this Art, so that through the Elemental Figure the intellect may see the works of Nature and her secrets, by understanding the beginning, middle, and end of Nature
>
> ...
>
> and since the elements are a mirror of S (for however the elements are ordered in nature, so the powers [of the rational soul] are ordered in S) and S is a mirror of A, thus similarly is placed the Elemental Figure in this Art. Just as metaphorically S reflects A, so similarly the Elemental Figure is placed in this art, so that metaphorically S sees A in itself and similarly sees itself in this Figure, according to which the elements generate suppositions and similitudes, so that through these similitudes [S] may have knowledge of itself.[31]

Semblance and signification, as the greatest expression of concordance between God and humans, play a fundamental role in Llull's Christology, since

---

30 Robert D.F. Pring-Mill, *Ramón Llull y el número primitivo de las dignidades en el 'Arte general'* (Oxford: 1963) and "The Analogical Structure of the Lullian Art," in *Islamic Philosophy & the Classical Tradition: Essays presented to Richard Walzer on the occasion of his 70th Birthday* (Oxford: 1972), 315–326.

31 *Liber propositionum secundum Artem demonstrativam* 2, "De intentione," MOG 3:511–512: "Elementalis figura in hac arte posita est et ordinata, ut per eam intellectus videat opera naturae et eiusdem secreta, intelligendo principium medium et finem naturae ... et quoniam elementa sunt speculum S. (nam quemadmodum ordinantur elementa in natura, sic ordinantur potentiae in S.) et S. est speculum A., ideo posita est similiter elementalis figura in hac arte, ut metaphorice S. videat in se A., et ut similiter semet videat in ipsa figura, secundum quod elementa producunt supposita et similitudines, ut mediantibus illis similitudinibus habeat sui ipsius cognitionem."

his doctrine of the Incarnation must be built upon the same axioms that provide the foundational principles of his Art.[32]

What we have here then is the systemization of the possible acts of the powers of the rational soul (Figure S), the active element in the search for the truth, directed toward the contemplation of God (Figure A) – that is, toward understanding God, an understanding inseparable from love and which sustains it. These powers use in their investigation of the truth about God, centered around definitions of the Divine Dignities, a series of instrumental principles (Figure T) which systemize the possible *significationes* derived from the exemplarist structure of the universe, ordered according to the ascending hierarchy of sensory (material) to intellectual (spiritual). The Elemental Figure has the same role as the Figure T, to which it is ancillary in the first version of the Art, in so far as it furnishes "semblances, *exempla* and metaphors" through which the other Figures can be accessed. In other words, through the *significationes* one can acquire knowledge of God, of man, and of moral laws, as Llull explains in the *Ars demonstrativa*:

> Accordingly, the Elemental Figure in this art is most necessary, since through this Figure the practitioner of the Art is directed to have knowledge of the other Figures. This is because the workings of Nature signify the intrinsic and extrinsic workings of the Figures A, S & V with X & Y. For this reason this Art offers various similitudes, exempla and metaphors through the Elemental Figure, following the conditions of the Second Distinction.[33]

4.2.4   *Ethics*

The remaining *figurae* mentioned in the preceding quotation are no less important, as they exhaust the collection of principles that the first versions of the Art prescribe. The Figure V refers to human moral conduct, which is the inseparable correlate of intellectual action. According to Llull, truth cannot be known without correct moral orientation. *Memoria, Intellectus,* and *Voluntas* can only become a suitable receptacle for truth if they aspire equally to apply themselves to the pursuit of virtue and, while powers of the rational soul di-

---

32   Robert D. Hughes, "Speculum, Similitude and Signification: the Incarnation as Exemplary and Proportionate Sign in the Arts of Ramon Llull," *SL* 45–46 (2005–06): 3–37.

33   *Ars demonstrativa* 1.8, ROL 32:33: "Haec siquidem figura in hac arte quam plurimum est necessaria, eo quia per ipsam dirigitur artista ad habendum cognitionem ceterarum figurarum; hoc enim est, quia in operibus naturalibus significantur opera intrinseca et extrinseca ipsorum A S V cum X Y. Idcirco in hac arte dantur diversimode similitudines, exempla et metaphorae per elementalem figuram, sequendo conditiones secundae distinctionis."

rected toward the pursuit of vice (forgetting the *prima intentio* of humankind) will descend into spiritual disorder and falsehood. The Figure V therefore comprises two series of seven virtues and seven corresponding mortal sins in order to study their relationship with the other Figures. The appearance within the Art of the Figure V is almost always tied to the concepts of Truth and Falsehood, represented in Llull's system by the symbols Y (*Veritas*) and Z (*Falsitas*), which complete the alphabet of the Figures in the first versions of the Art. For example, V accompanied by Y signifies moral virtues in relation to the discovery of Truth, whereas the same V accompanied by Z signifies vices, sins, and falsehoods as the epistemological consequences of moral disorder.

4.2.5   *Relative Opposites*
The reader will have realized that the sense of order so dominant in Llull's system leads him to structure the principles of his Art and the Figures containing them within the limits of the Latin alphabet. In the visual presentation of these Figures and Principles one can see how he achieves this objective with nearly exact precision. Only one letter, and so one figure, remains to complete his scheme: this is the Figure X. One should not think that it serves merely to complete his alphabetical scheme. Llull presents it as the *Figura Praedestinationis* or *Figura Oppositorum* because it addresses the theological issue of predestination and free will based on the consideration of pairs of opposites. These opposites may be defined as "relative opposites," as in the case of "predestination versus free will," which cannot be considered an "absolute opposite," as this would contradict the mutual convertibility of Divine Dignities such as Wisdom and Justice, two other opposing terms included in the Figure X. If Predestination is the fruit of God's perfect Wisdom, then His perfect Justice presupposes the existence of Free Will.

The treatment of this delicate theological question makes of Figure X an important tool incorporating logic, epistemology, metaphysics, and ethics as constituted in the preceding Figures. The brothers Carreras i Artau recognized this importance in their detailed description of the *Ars compendiosa inveniendi veritatem*, by insisting on the fact that "this Figure compiles the results of the four previous Figures."[34] A quick review of the concepts that it includes confirms this judgment. In the Figura X, as depicted in the *Ars compendiosa inveniendi veritatem,* we encounter, in addition to the examples already cited, pairs such as *perfectio-defectus, meritum-culpa, potestas-voluntas, gloria-poena,*

---

34   Joaquín Carreras i Artau and Tomás Carreras i Artau, *Historia de la filosofía española: Filosofía cristiana de los siglos XIII al XV,* 2 vols. (Madrid: 1939–43), 1:379: "en esta figura vienen a recopilarse los resultados de las cuatro figuras anteriores."

esse-privatio and *scientia-ignorantia*. As Gayà explains, this represents an ontological axis (*perfectio-defectus, esse-privatio*) together with a moral axis (*meritum-culpa*). Some of the concepts coincide as well with the divine dignities of the Figure A. In the *Ars demonstrativa* Llull even introduced four new pairs of relative opposites, which "underscore the logical elements present in the method of the Art."[35] Examples are *suppositio-demonstratio, immediate-mediate, realitas-ratio*, and *potentia-obiectum*.

As always, these conceptual pairs first appeared in the *Libre de contemplació* as instruments for the demonstration of the truths of the faith. The relative pair *suppositio-demonstratio* first defines overall the logical path by which *suppositio* achieves *demonstratio*, through the components in the following pairs. The *potentia* should be directed to the *obiectum* illuminated by *ratio* in order to know *realitas*. *Ratio* is intellectual comprehension through *significationes*; *realitas* is an extra-mental independent reality superior to *ratio* and the latter depends always on *potentia*, namely, on the correct conjoint action of *Memoria, Intellectus* and *Voluntas*. Llull defines the relationship between these concepts in the following terms, where the letters E, I, N, and R symbolize the acts of the powers of the rational soul, and so refer to Figura S, while in the sphere of Figura X, they refer to the *potentia* directed to an *obiectum*:

> Reality is that entity which is, while Reason (*Ratio*) is only a light, through which E, I, N & R perceive objects, sometimes according to Reality, sometimes not, namely according to the mode of sensory or intellectual concordance or contrariety, and since Reality is inalterable, but Reason is variable, Reality involves what is greater and Reason what is lesser.[36]

The problem of the nature of the relationship between Predestination and Free Will thus leads to deeper investigation of the ontological structure of reality and its logical correlate, by proposing that their apparent contradiction is resolved through the subordination of Reason to Reality: "Every entity exists more by virtue of Reality than Reason."[37] In this way, the Figure X summarizes

---

35   Gayà Estelrich, *La teoría luliana de los correlativos*, 58: "subrayan los elementos lógicos presentes en la metodología artística."

36   *Lectura super figuras Artis Demonstrativae*, "De secunda Figura X: De Camera realitatis ratio," MOG 3:226: "Realitas est illud ens, quod est, ratio vero est lumen, per quod E.I.N.R. objecta accipiunt, quandoque secundum realitatem, quandoque non, scilicet per modum concordantiae vel contrarietatis sensualis et intellectualis, et quoniam realitas est inalterabilis, ratio vero variabilis, convenit realitas maioritati, sed ratio minoritati."

37   *Liber propositionum secundum Artem Demonstrativam* 4.1, MOG 3:528: "Omne ens majus est in realitate, quam in ratione."

the assumptions that guarantee the demonstrative dynamic of the Art. In short, that dynamic ensures the exact correspondence between Reality and Reason, so that a given *potentia*, when perceiving *obiecta*, produces the *similitudines* used in constructing Lullian *demonstratio*.[38]

The same section lists *propositiones* concerning the principles of Figura X, among which we read the following: "Because Reason and Reality are different, the universal that exists in Reason is one thing, and the universal that exists in a natural thing is another."[39] We might choose to see here a reference to the states of the universal *in re* (also termed *naturalia* or *realia*) and *post rem* (known as *logicalia*). For Llull, they are different, and the first is superior to the second because it is real, existing and participating in the universal *ante rem*. Clearly, in the light of these statements, the tendency to consider Llull as a "rationalist" needs to be nuanced somewhat, as Llull's metaphysical position may be more accurately defined as "extreme Realism,"[40] and Llull himself considered a "Realist philosopher."

4.2.6   *The Governing Principles of* Scientiae

The Figures described thus far are the main figures that organize the key concepts in the earliest versions of the Art. In the *Ars demonstrativa* Llull adds three more, without a corresponding alphabetic symbol: *Figura Theologiae*, *Figura Philosophiae* and *Figura Iuris*. These do not appear as such in the earlier *Ars compendiosa inveniendi veritatem*, but Llull had however dedicated separate works to applying his Art to the corresponding sciences: known as the *Quattuor libri principiorum*, these are the *Liber principiorum theologiae*, the *Liber principiorum philosophiae*, the *Liber principiorum iuris* and the *Liber principiorum medicinae*. Llull expresses his intention to use his Art to provide guidelines for the study of the university curriculum based solely on reason; this explains the need to enlist the aid of auxiliary *figurae* to aid students in three of the four main university courses (excluding medicine). The role played by the Figure of Medicine in the *Ars demonstrativa* is fulfilled by the Elemental Figure, which appears here as an independent Figure, no longer subordinate to the Figure T. In fact, it is given greater prominence than the other three Figures of the principles of Theology, Philosophy and Law, as it continues to be the instrument

---

38   Ibid.: "Potentiae animae sunt, ut assumentes objecta producant similitudines suae essentiae et similitudines Dei."

39   Ibid.: "Quia ratio et realitas differunt, aliud est illud universale, quod est in ratione, et aliud est illud universale, quod est in re naturae."

40   Johnston, *SL* 20.

with which the mind knows via *similitudines* or metaphors and ascends from the sensory to the intellectual planes.

4.3   The Art's Interactivity

4.3.1   *Conditiones operandi*

Taken in isolation, the Figures of Llull's Art lie dormant until they are placed in a working relationship with other Figures. This is where the combinatory mechanics of Llull's method comes into play. Llull sought to reflect the elemental *mixtio* (the scheme of the four elements again becomes the model for creating *similitudines*), to show the deep imbrication of the manifestations of being through the likenesses of the Divine Dignities that they share. The Art is a logical model that summarizes reality in order to make it comprehensible to Reason; thus it reduces every being to its constituent principles, and by combining these generates a kind of "conceptual map" to reflect the *modus essendi* of things. Ruiz Simon explains the functioning of the elemental model of *mixtio* in the configuration of the Art, noting the development over time from a more naturalistic to a more metaphysical model: "In the *Ars compendiosa*, Llull reads the 'natural mix of elements' upon which natural compounds are formed through an 'art of mixing elements' (medicine) as a 'combinatory method' and devises, metaphorically, in its likeness, an 'art of mixing combinatorily the objects of Reason' (represented by symbolic letters) for the purpose of constructing logical propositions."[41]

Arising from the ordered and systematic combination of principles is the knowledge of universals to which can be reduced the particulars investigated through Llull's Art. This knowledge is the result of the "Conditions" (*Conditiones*) deriving from each successive combination. The Conditions are an extremely important element in the dynamic of the first versions of the Art and the most direct consequence of its combinatory mechanics. The first combinations generated by the system are the binary combinations of the concepts constituting the Figures. To facilitate the constitution of the combinations,

---

41   Josep Maria Ruiz Simon, "De la naturalesa com a mescla a l'art de mesclar (sobre la fonamentació cosmològica de les arts lul·lianes)," *Randa* 19 (1986):76: "Llull, a l'*Ars* compendiosa, llegeix la *mescla natural dels elements* a partir de la qual es formen els compostos de la naturalesa a través d'una *art de mesclar els elements* (*medicina*) *segons mètode* (*combinatòria*) i confegeix, metafòricament, a semblança d'aquesta, una *art de mesclar combinatòriament els objectes de la raó* (representats per lletres simbòliques) destinada a construir composts lògics."

Llull uses mobile figures, the first of which is the *Figura Demonstrativa* of the *Ars Demonstrativa*. Each binary combination forms a chamber and is clearly represented visually in the early versions by two principles framed in a quadrangle. Via triangular figures, Llull demonstrates all the binary chambers extracted from each figura.

The Conditions define the interpretation or exegesis of each chamber, the discursive explication of their *significationes*. The *Ars demonstrativa* therefore speaks of each chamber being "conditioned" with the help of the triangles from the Figure T. In the *Ars universalis* the Conditions of the binary chambers are listed. For example, the Conditions of the chamber "Eternity Generosity" (*Aeternitas Largitas*) based on triangles from the Figure T generates a series of demonstrative "necessary reasons" for proving the dogmas of faith. In Lullian terminology, the chamber and the triangles from the Figure T instantiate a "universal," and the dogmas of faith derived from its Conditions are its "particulars," which can be known through the universal. Llull uses the term "universal" in the widest sense: in his Art, a "universal" is any Principle or combination of Principles and their corresponding definitions, or the Conditions deriving from a combination. Also the Modes and Rules, to be discussed below, are universals. In turn the "particular" is what the practitioner of Llull's Art or Artist (*artista*) seeks to know, as well as the specific formulation of the question posed to the Art for resolution:

> In this Art (*scientia*) we call "universal" any Principle and its Definition, as well as any Mode and Rule of the aforementioned Questions, because all these are universal, general principles for all branches of knowledge; hence this Art can be called "general." Likewise, we also call "universal" the mixture of Principles, as it appears in the Figures, since we call "universal" any of the chambers of the Figures. And we call "particular" the question that one poses.[42]

His argument regarding the chamber "Eternity Generosity" therefore proceeds thus:

---

42   *Lectura super Artem inventivam et Tabulam generalem* 5.10, MOG 5:368: "Dicimus autem Universale in hac Scientia quodlibet Principium et ejus Definitionem, et etiam quemlibet Modum et Regulam praedictarum Quaestionum, quia omnia ista sunt universalia Principia et generalia omnibus Scientiis; ideo ista Scientia potest dici generalis. Etiam Mixtionem Principiorum ad invicem appellamus Universale, secundum quod apparet in Figuris, sic, quod quamlibet Camerarum Figurarum appellamus Universale. Dicimus vero Particulare illam Quaestionem, quam homo proponit."

The Chamber and the regulated triangles residing within it are the universal, by which through necessary reasons may be found the Trinity, Incarnation, Resurrection, Creation and other particulars, which can be known through the aforesaid universal; for when B remembers that if Figure A can give being in red, how much more can it give being without red in *Aeternitas*; for if not, it would follow, that the chamber would not agree in majority, and that it would be greater to give lesser gifts, rather than greater ones; and if this were the case, it would be greater in red, than in this, in which red does not exist, which is incongruous.[43]

The basis of the demonstration is simple: Memory remembers (B) that if God (A) can give existence (through His generosity) to a being that has Beginning, Middle, and End (the "red triangle" from the Figure T), so much more can He give existence in Eternity (where there is no Beginning, Middle or end). Were the contrary to be true, the universals in the chamber "Eternity Generosity" which is being "conditioned" would not agree in Majority, since giving something lesser (a being with beginning, middle and end) would be greater than giving something greater (a being without beginning, middle or end). Such a scenario would be absurd, since the lesser cannot be greater than the greater, and this would be the case if a lesser gift existed without an existing greater gift, since that which exists is greater and better than that which does not exist. Thus one sees how the play of *significationes* associated with the Principles from the Figura T and applied to the chamber in question generates a set of *conditiones operandi* or "operating instructions" to which the arguments utilized must conform. Thus "conditioned," the demonstration advances to prove the Trinity, for example, as this derives "artistically" (that is, applying the methods of Llull's Art) from the necessity of the existence of divine eternal activity which gives being to an eternal reality: the generation and the procession within the Godhead are eternal actions, fruit of the eternal generosity and, if they did not exist, they would violate the truth conditions (in this case the premises) of the chamber being interrogated (something impossible according to the operation of the Art). The *significationes* of the divine virtue of Generosity,

---

43   *Ars universalis* 8.60, MOG 1:542: "Camera et trianguli regulati manentes in ipsa sunt universale, quo per necessarias rationes reperiri possunt *Trinitas, Incarnatio, Resurrectio, Creatio* et reliqua particularia, quae sunt possibilia per praedictum universale cognosci; nam cum B. recolit, quod si A. dare potest esse in rubeo, quanto magis ipsum dare potest sine rubeo in aeternitate; quia si non, sequeretur, quod camera non conveniret in maioritate, et quod major esset largitas minorum donorum, quam majorum; et si sic, major esset in rubeo, quam in hoc, in quo rubeus non existit, quod est inconveniens."

joined to those of Eternity, also demonstrate the Incarnation. Christ has two natures, the divine (eternal and generated) and the human (finite and created). Divine generosity would be less if it did not seek and was not able to unite the eternal and generated nature with the created and finite nature, i.e. one which is symbolized by the red triangle of Beginning, Middle and End:

> Moreover, the chamber gives a greater gift in red, if some particular of red is conjoined with the eternal generated in generosity, than in giving a gift without the aforesaid conjunction; and since it is more noble and greater that a gift of red is able to be given in nature, in which red does not exist, on account of this it follows that Generosity provide such a gift, better fitting with Eternity, which agrees with Majority.[44]

4.3.2   Principia, Subiecti, *and* Definitiones

The role played by the Conditions of the Chambers in forging the demonstration is the same played in the ternary versions of the Art by its Definitions (*Definitiones*) and Rules (*Regulae*). In its heart, the essence of the method continues unadulterated, requiring the setting of axiomatic or universal parameters, constraints or conditions, which the specific data studied must respect. In the development of his Art, Llull thus perfects the search for universals. The most significant change was one that allowed for greater rigor in the choice of axioms defining the universals: Llull transformed the Divine Dignities of Figura A and the relative principles of Figura T into absolute universal and archetypal principles of all Creation, and their subsequent correlative definitions. These changes were the result of a gradual revision of the Art, which began after the redaction of the *Ars demonstrativa* in 1283, and the details of which can be studied across various transitional works up to the *Ars inventiva veritatis* of 1290.[45]

---

44   Ibid.: "Praeterea majus donum camera dat in rubeo, si quoddam particulare rubei cum aeterno generato infinito in largitate conjunxit, quam in munere, quod dat sine praedicta conjunctione; et quoniam nobilius et majus donum rubei largiri potest in natura, in qua rubeus non existit, propterea necessarium est, quod largitas praebeat tale donum, in quo melius conveniat cum aeternitate, quae cum maioritate concordat."

45   On these developments, see especially: Bonner, *AL* 93–120; Josep Maria Ruiz Simon, "De la naturalesa com a mescla" and "La transformació del pensament de Ramon Llull durant les obres de transició cap a l'etapa ternària," in Maria Isabel Ripoll Perelló (ed.), *Actes de les Jornades Internacionals Lul·lianes "Ramon Llull al s. XXI." Palma, 1, 2 i 3 d'abril de 2004* (Palma and Barcelona: 2005), 167–196; and Josep Enric Rubio, "L'evolució de les figures A, S i T de l'Art quaternària en el trànsit cap a l'Art ternària," *Taula* 37 (2002): 83–98.

From the *Ars inventiva veritatis* onward, Llull established 18 Universal Principles distributed across two Figures, as follows (see the illustrations of Figures from the Ternary Phase):

> Figure A: Goodness (*Bonitas*), Greatness (*Magnitudo*), Eternity or Duration (*Eternitas* or *Duratio*), Power (*Potentia*), Wisdom (*Sapientia*), Will (*Voluntas*), Virtue (*Virtus*), Truth (*Veritas*), and Glory (*Gloria*)
> Figure T: Difference (*Differentia*), Concord (*Concordantia*), Contrariety (*Contrarietas*), Beginning (*Principium*), Middle (*Medium*), End (*Finis*), Majority (*Maioritas*), Equality (*Aequalitas*), Minority (*Minoritas*).

The other two triangles of the Figure T from the earlier versions of the Art continue to play a significant role, but outside the 18 Universal Principles: God (*Deus*), creature (*creatura*), and operation (*operatio*) will be developed into nine Subjects (*Subiecti*), while affirmation (*adfirmatio*), doubt (*dubitatio*), and negation (*negatio*) become part of the nine Rules (*Regulae*). All that exists does so implicitly thanks to the 18 Universal Principles; in the case of those from the Figure A, these signify not only divine Goodness and divine Greatness, etc., but also any type of goodness or greatness whatsoever:

> In this Figure all things are implicated. As when is said: God is good, great, eternal, *et cetera*. The Angel is good, great, durable, etc. Avarice is not good, but bad; and thus of the others accordingly.[46]

Llull's strives from the first version of his Art to establish a universal method of knowledge, and so must advance toward the presentation of a series of general principles, universal and true, to which all that exists can be reduced. The Subjects investigated according to the principles of the Art are also general ones. The previous quotation includes two of the nine Subjects included in the Art of the ternary phase, God and Angel, to which he adds seven more: Heaven (*Caelum*), Man (*Homo*), Imagination (*Imaginativa*), Sense (*Sensitiva*), Vegetal power (*Vegetativa*), Elements (*Elementativa*), and Skills and Arts (*Instrumentativa*). All that exists is implicit in these nine categories, and any particular subject that the Lullian Artist investigates with the help of the Art can be reduced to one of these nine meta-categories.

---

46   *Ars generalis ultima* 2.1, ROL 14:11: "In ista figura implicantur omnia. Sicut quando dicitur: Deus est bonus, magnus, aeternus, et cetera. Angelus est bonus, magnus durabilis, et cetera. Avaritua non est bona, sed mala; et sic de aliis suo modo."

The same occurs with the principles of the Figure T: as in the case of the Figure A, these now are universal principles to which all that exists can be reduced:

> The green triangle of Difference, Concord, and Contrariety, applies in general to all things; for whatever is, exists either in difference or concord or contrariety. In this triangle, whatever is, is implied ... The red triangle, which signifies the Beginning, Middle, and End, applies in general to all things, by virtue of the fact that it contains all things within itself, since whatever may be, either has a beginning, a middle, or an end; and no being can exist outside these three terms ... By the yellow triangle is to be understood universal Majority, under which all other superiorities are subalternated ... And the same occurs in the case of Equality, and Minority in their way.[47]

These eighteen principles can also be combined among themselves, to which end Llull adds a third and fourth figure to the two main ones, permitting binary and tertiary combinations. Ternary combinations are systematized in a table, serving as the main instrument for formulating questions and answers. Each combination of principles generates a series of axiomatic statements which can also be restated in the form of questions. These statements are also called "conditions" (*conditiones*) in the *Ars brevis*:

> The multiplication of the fourth Figure consists of this, namely that the first chamber of B C D in the fourth Figure or in the Table signifies that B has one condition with C, and another with D; and C has one condition with B, and another with D; and D has one condition with B and another with C. And thus there are in the same chamber six conditions, with which the Intellect conditions itself for seeking and finding, for objecting and proving, and for solving (*determinandum*).[48]

---

47   Ibid. 2.2, 14–17: "Triangulus viridis, qui est de differentia, concordantia et contrarietate, est generalis ad omnia; nam quidquid est, vel est in differentia aut concordantia aut contrarietate. In ipso quidem triangulo, quidquid est, implicatum est ... Triangulus rubeus, qui est de principio, medio et fine, est generalis ad omnia, eo quia omnia continet in se, cum quidquid sit, vel est in principio, vel medio vel fine; et extra istos tres terminos nullum ens esse potest ... Per triangulum croceum intelligitur una maioritas universalis, sub qua omnes aliae maioritates sunt subalternatae ... Et hoc idem est de aequalitate, et etiam minoritate suo modo."

48   *Ars breuis* 7, ROL 12:220: "Multiplicatio quartae figurae consistit in hoc, videlicet quod prima camera B C D in quarta figura sive in tabula significat, quod B unam condicionem

A definite continuity of method is thus evident with the setting of conditions in the binary chambers from the quaternary phase of the Art. This continuity is however not static but based on changes evolved for perfecting Llull's method. Hence, in the later versions of the Art, these statements or conditions are relegated to a secondary level with respect to other expressions on which they directly depend: the definitions of the principles themselves. "By a condition is meant a self-evident proposition which arises by combining two principles as the subject and predicate of a proposition. The self-evidence of the condition is due to the fact that it is an immediate proposition directly deducible from the definitions of the basic principles."[49]

Of course, the method itself does not change substantially with these changes: the particular truth that the Artist seeks must conform to the definitions of the Principles, not just to the Conditions of the chambers, since these also depend on the Principles. The universal scope of these Principles now requires a definition that explains the essence of each one, which will replace the Conditions.[50] Definitions played a key role in Aristotelean science. If Llull wanted to present his Art as a *scientia generalis*, he had to address a tenet of knowledge as central as the theory of definition. Aristotelean definition consists of a genus and limiting species, resulting in definitions such as "man is a rational animal" (*homo est animal rationale*). To this Llull adds another kind of definition that he considers more precise, because it acknowledges the essential nature of the being defined. Llull's definition expresses the essence of the being defined, in its "correlative structure." Gayà Estelrich has observed that "the Principles are inseparable from their definitions, to such a degree that, without any exaggeration, one can say that Llull's system is based on his 'artistic' definition of the Principles. The common core found in all the Principles is their active nature [*agere*] ... Llull seeks a definition that says not just what a thing defined might be, but rather how the thing defined exists."[51] Gayà

habet cum C, et aliam cum D; et C unam condicionem habet cum B, et aliam cum D; et D unam condicionem habet cum B, et aliam cum C. Et sic sunt in ipsa camera sex condiciones, cum quibus intellectus se condicionat et disponit ad investigandum et inveniendum, ad obiciendum et probandum, et ad determinandum."

49   Walter W. Artus, *The "Ars Brevis" of Ramon Lull: A Study,* Ph.D. diss. St. John's University (New York: 1967), 300.

50   Jordi Gayà Estelrich, "Els principis de l'Art lul·liana i les seves definicions." *Taula* 37 (2002): 53–71.

51   *La teoría luliana de los correlativos*, 218: "Los principios son inseparables de sus definiciones. Hasta el punto de que, sin exageración alguna, puede decirse que el sistema se funda en la definición artística de los principios. El núcleo común que enhebra los principios es el *agere* (...). La definición que pretende Llull dice algo más que el definido sea, dice cómo el definido es." Erhard-Wolfram Platzeck, *Raimund Lull. Sein Leben-seine Werke. Die Grundlagen seines Denkens* (*Prinzipienlehre*), 2 vols. (Rome and Düsseldorf: 1962), 1:128ss,

Estelrich's words summarize well the sense of the new Lullian definition. The Latin verb *agere* ("to do") deserves special attention in defining the essences of the Principles: what constitutes them in essence is their active nature, the presence in each one of three "innate correlatives" that are identified with its very essence and thus define it. Using neologisms of Llull's own invention, these correlatives express the agent, patient, and act inherent in each Principle. For example, Goodness (*Bonitas*) cannot be good without its essential correlatives of "bonificative" (*bonificativum*), "bonificable" (*bonificabile*), and "to bonify" (*bonificare*).[52] Not only are the Principles of the Art defined in this fashion, but also the Subjects and all that exists: "As in the case of a man, it befits him to humanize [*hominificare*]; a lion to lionize [*leonare*], fire to heat [*calefecare*] and in a similar fashion the rest may be defined. And such ways of defining are both very easy and useful."[53] Man (*homo*), as a universal, must "humanize" (*hominificare*), that is, activate or actualize "humanness" (*humanitas*). Llull's new approach to the science of definition is also perhaps in part inspired in the "descriptive definition" (*rasm*) employed by Muslim logicians, although the description that Llull includes develops the potential of this model further by pretending to identify the essence of the thing to be defined (*definiendum*) through its coessential correlatives.[54]

4.3.3   *Rules* (Regulae)

The definitions of the Principles are closely connected to the Rules (*Regulae*) from which they in fact derive. The Rules are another of the pillars upon which the Art is constructed in the ternary versions. Adapting the Aristotelean categories for the predicates of logical statements (*praedicamenta*), Llull elaborates a list of ten rules that are more than simply logical categories, since they also serve as ten universal questions to which any inquiry can be reduced:

> These rules comprise ten general questions, according to which every question posed by the querent must be formulated ... For just as all declinable nouns are included in five declensions, and can be declined

---

remains the standard analysis of the primariness of the Lullian definitions of the principles, that is their role as "definitions of first principles."

52   Elena Pistolesi, "Note sulle definizioni lulliane," *SL* 47 (2007): 51–69, is especially useful regarding the linguistic features of Llull's terminology.

53   *Ars generalis ultima* 3, ROL 14:23: "Sicut homini, cui proprie competit hominificare; et leoni leonare, et igni calefacere; et sic de aliis. Et talis modus definiendi est valde facilis et utilis."

54   Alexander Fidora, "Les definicions de Ramon Llull: entre la lògica àrab i les teories de la definició modernes," *Revista de Lenguas y Literaturas Catalana, Gallega y Vasca* 12 (2006): 239–252.

according to these, so too all other questions beyond those of this Art are included in these ten, and can be reduced and ruled by them, by reason of their generality.[55]

The ten questions are represented by the nine letters of the alphabet in the ternary Art, with a dual value for the letter K:

Rule B: Possibility (Whether?) [*de possibilitate (Utrum?)*]
Rule C: Identity (What?) [*de quidditate (Quid?)*]
Rule D: Matter (From what?) [*de materialitate (De quo?)*]
Rule E: Form (How?) [*de formalitate (Quare)*]
Rule F: Quantity (How much?) [*de quantitate (Quantum?)*]
Rule G: Quality (What kind?) [*de qualitate (Quale?)*]
Rule H: Time (When?) [*de temporalitate (Quando?)*]
Rule I: Place (Where?) [*de localitate (Ubi?)*]
Rule K1: Mode (In what way?) [*de modalitate (Quomodo?)*]
Rule K2: Instrument (With what?) [*de instrumentalitate (Cum quo?)*]

Llull also assigns species to each Rule. For example, Rule B has three species: affirmation (*affirmatio*), negation (*negatio*), and doubt (*dubitatio*); these are the concepts forming the first triangle of the Figure T in previous versions of the Art. Rule C regarding "what" has four species: "what a thing is in itself" (*quid est res in se ipsa*), "what a thing has in itself" (*quid habet res in se ipsa*), "what a thing is in another" (*quid est una res in alia*), and "what a thing has in another" (*quid habet una res in alia*). These four species of Rule C especially serve to help elaborate correlative definitions and complement the Aristotelian definition of the four causes (material, formal, efficient, and final). As an example, Llull defines Intellect through the four species of his Rule C:

> The first species concerns the definition and the thing defined that is interchangeable (*convertitur*) with the definition. As when it is said: Intellect is the being (*esse*) of its essence. Another example: It is that being to which understanding properly pertains; and thus with others similarly. The second species asks of a thing, what it has in itself essentially and

---

55   *Ars generalis ultima* 4, ROL 14:26: "Istae regulae sunt decem quaestiones generales, per quas oportet esse omne quaesitum ... Nam sicut omnia vocabula nominalia declinabilia includuntur in quinque declinationibus, et possunt declinari per ipsas, sic suo modo omnes aliae quaestiones praeter istas huius Artis, quae fieri possunt, includuntur in ipsis decem, et etiam ad ipsas quidem reducuntur; et etiam per ipsas regulantur ratione generalitatis, quam habent."

naturally, without which the thing cannot exist. As when it is asked: What does Intellect possess of itself coessentially and naturally, without which it cannot exist? And it must be replied, that it has the innate "intellective" (*intellectivus*), "intelligible" (*intelligibile*), and understanding (*intelligere*) ... The third species asks: What is something in another thing? And it must be replied, that this is from the genus quality. Thus intellect, which is active through its "intellectivum" when it grasps an object; and it is passive, when it accepts species ... The fourth species asks: What does one thing have in another? As when it is asked: What does the intellect have in an object? And it must be replied that it has activity and passivity [in its object], as is signified in the third species ... And it possesses goodness through moral virtues and blame through sin.[56]

As this passage explains, the Rules are directly connected to the definition of the Principles and together the Principles and the Rules constitute the twin pillars of the Art. As was the case with the definitions of the Principles, the Rules occupy a place formerly held by the Conditions of the chambers in the quaternary Art, and contribute to defining the correlatives, whose dynamic structures being; and which, consequently, are integral to the definition of the Principles so that from their definitions emerges the proof of the truth sought by the Lullian Artist.[57]

4.3.4   *The Resolution of Questions*
The Conditions, Rules, and Definitions of the Principles constitute the universals of the Lullian Art, the intelligible expression of *realitas* as a mode of being.

---

56   Ibid. 4.2, ROL 14:28–30: "Prima species est de definitione et definito, qui cum ipsa definitione convertitur. Ut cum dicitur: Intellectus est esse suae essentiae. Item: Est illud esse, cui proprie competit intelligere; et sic de aliis suo modo. Secunda species est, quando quaeritur de re, quid habet in se essentialiter et naturaliter, sine quibus ipsa res non potest esse. Sicut cum quaeritur: Intellectus quid habet in se coessentialiter et naturaliter, sine quibus non potest esse? Et respondendum est, quod habet innate intelectivum, intelligibile et intelligere ... Tertia species est, quando quaeritur. Quid est res in alio? Et respondendum est, quod est secundum genus qualitatis. Sicut intellectum, qui est activus per suum intellectivum, quando attingit obiectum; et est passivus, quando recipit species ... Quarta species est, cum quaeritur: Quid habet res in alio? Sicut quando dicitur: Quid habet intellectus in obiecto? Et respondendum est, quod habet actionem et passionem, ut in tertia specie significatum est ... Et habet bonitatem per morales virtutes, et culpam per peccatum."

57   Gayà Estelrich, *La teoría luliana de los correlativos*, 91, analyzes the importance of the Rules and the functioning of the correlatives. José Higuera Rubio, *Física y Teología (Atomismo y movimiento en el Arte luliano)* (Pamplona: 2014), 99–158, examines Llull's correlative language and its conexión to contemporary philosophers, including Robert Kilwardby.

The Art's most basic premise of operation is the regulated reduction of the particular to the universal, wherein is contained all that is. From the universal are derived all possible questions and all possible answers. Through its combinatory mechanism, the Art performs this derivation. The table containing the possible combinations deriving from the fourth Figure in the ternary arts is the instrument for generating questions and solutions. In earlier versions of the Art the binary combinations of the principles of the Figures also produced questions. Various versions of the Art end with a series of questions derived from combinations of Principles, following a schema typical of Scholastic practice, which frequently expounded doctrines through the resolution of *quaestiones*. Essentially, contemplating the terms of a *quaestio* formulated in the light of the Principles and the Rules returns the Lullian Artist to the place where the question is born, to the universals, which is where the answer resides. In other words, one has the impression that, in reality, Llull has formulated the answer *before* the question, and the battery of questions that conclude some versions of the Art are nothing more than a sample of what has been proven already.

Let us consider an example: the *Ars generalis ultima* investigates nine Subjects, each "conducted" through the Principles and Rules. Analysis of the first subject, God, through the Principle of Difference concludes:

> Concerning God, I deduce arguing *per differentiam*. The human intellect remembers the scale of difference from the second Figure.[58] It denies that the difference within God does not exist between sensual and sensual, nor between sensual and intellectual. For it is not a body, but rather exists between intellectual and intellectual, in existence essentially the same. And this shows what is said about the Principles of the first Figure. For without difference or distinction the Divine Dignities or Reasons cannot have infinite actions. And this clearly appears in Goodness. For to make good from this Goodness (*bonificare ipsius bonitatis*) without distinguishing between the agent goodness and product of goodness (*bonificantis et bonificati*) cannot be; for to act indeed without distinguishing the agent and the acted upon cannot be; thus there is no act of making good (*bonificare*) without the aforesaid.[59]

---

58   In Llull's Figure T, Difference occurs in one of three ways among all beings: between sensual and sensual, between sensual and intellectual, and between intellectual and intellectual.

59   *Ars generalis ultima* 9.1.1.5, ROL 14:201: "De Deo, per differentiam deducto. Recordatus est intellectus humanus scalam differentiae, in secunda figura positam. Et negat, quod differentia, quae est in Deo, non est inter sensuale et sensuale, neque etiam inter sensuale et intellectuale. Non enim est corpus, sed est inter intellectuale et intellectuale, existentia

Here we must take into account the Definitions of the Principles involved, in order to understand the text appropriately. For this reason the *Ars generalis ultima* begins with the presentation of the Principles and their Definitions. Specifically, Difference is defined in the following terms: "Difference is that, through which Goodness, Greatness, etc. are separate principles (*rationes inconfusae*) and likewise *bonificans*, *bonificabile*, and *bonificare* are separate."[60] Without the universal principle of difference, the Divine Dignities could not differ one from another and, what is scarcely less important, they would not possess different coessential correlatives. Goodness, for example, is defined thus: "Goodness is the entity, by reason of which the good does good" (*Bonitas est ens, ratione cuius bonum agit bonum*).[61] And Divine Goodness, says Llull, could not do good (*bonificare*) if there were no difference between that which does good and that which is made good, because it is not possible to act without distinction between the agent and the object acted upon. Eliminating the Difference between the correlatives of Goodness would strike against its essential definition, which is absurd and runs contrary to the Art's basic premise, that the Definitions of the Principles remain inviolable.

In the final section of Questions from the *Ars generalis ultima,* for each paragraph on application of the nine Subjects, Principles, and Rules there is a corresponding question. For the paragraph discussed above, Llull asks "Whether the divine principles without any distinction could possess infinite actions?" (*Utrum divinae rationes sine aliqua distinctione possint habere actus infinitos?*). Naturally the solution is provided by the text already quoted, tersely cited: "Solution in the nineteenth" (*Solutio in decimo nono*) paragraph on the Subject God.[62] Llull does not provide the answer after the question in Scholastic fashion because, in contrast to contemporary Scholastic thinkers, in the Art answers always precede questions. He systematically cites, using the formula "go to" (*vade ad*), the place where the question arises, that is, to its answer, to the universal, to the text where the Subjects are "conditioned" through combinations of his Principles and Rules. At the end of the Questions about God, Llull states:

---

idem essentialiter. Et hic manifestatur, quod de principiis primae figurae dicitur. Absque enim differentia sive distinctione divinae dignitates sive rationes non possent habere actus infinitos. Et hoc manifeste apparet in bonitate. Nam bonificare ipsius bonitatis absque differentia bonificantis et bonificati nequaquam esse posset; agere quidem sine distinctione agentis et agibilis esse non potest; sic quidem nec bonificare absque praedictis."

60   Ibid. 3, ROL 14:22: "Differentia est id, per quod bonitas, magnitudo, etc., sunt rationes inconfusae, et etiam bonificans, bonificabile et bonificare, sunt inconfusi."

61   Ibid. 3, ROL 14:21.

62   Ibid. 11.5.1, "Quaestio 360," ROL 14:422.

We laid out the Questions concerning God according to Principles and Rules. Wherefore, if a different question should arise about God, refer it to the text or relevant place and it will solve itself, taking it either affirmatively or negatively so as not to invalidate the text.[63]

Llull of course thinks that his Art can answer questions besides those created through its combinatory mechanics, but any other questions posed by one using his methods must be solved by reducing them to the "places" or universals present in the text of his Art. In reality, the entire mechanism is programmed to generate questions arising from the text. To put it another way, the Art generates questions whose answers are provided automatically by the very same process of the statement's initial production. Posing a question already yields its answer, since both arise from the same source.

In his *Tabula generalis* from 1293–94, Llull systemizes, through the ternary combination of principles, possible questions which can be posed to the Art for resolution. The resultant combinations, taking into account the definitions of the Principles involved, yield the answers. In the words of this text's editor, Viola Tenge-Wolf, "Finding Truth is not for Llull, as one might expect, primarily a matter of answering questions, but it is rather the questions themselves. The *Ars* wishes to teach how to set the parameters of questions to fit reality: if the technique of the *Ars* is correctly applied, the solutions arise almost by themselves."[64] This judgment does not, we believe, contradict the priority of the answer in the *Ars generalis ultima*. Llull strives above all to generate questions correctly and appropriately through his Art, questions whose answers appear almost by themselves in the process that generates them. This is as true in the *Ars generalis ultima* as it was in earlier versions, such as the *Ars demonstrativa*, where final questions are systematically extracted from combinations of the Demonstrative Figure, a forerunner of the Fourth Figure of the ternary Art, wherein combinations are "conditioned" in advance, and in whose conditioning is found the answer to the corresponding question.

---

63   Ibid. 11.5.1, ROL 14:424: "Fecimus quaestiones de Deo per principia et regulas. Quapropter si fiat quaestio peregrina de Deo, applicetur ad textum sive locum, ei competentem, et solvatur per ipsum, tenendo affirmativam aut negativam, tali modo quod textus non destruatur."

64   *Tabula generalis*, "Introductio generalis," ROL 27:41*: "Bei der Wahrheitsfindung stehen für Llull nicht, wie man vielleicht erwarten könnte, primär die *Antworten* auf die Fragen im Vordergrund, sondern zunächst die *Fragen* selbst. Die *Ars* will dazu anleiten, die richtigen Fragen an die Wirklichkeit zu stellen – die Lösungen ergeben sich, sofern die Technik der *Ars* korrekt angewendet wird, fast von allein."

Here we reach the end: Llull has shown his readers how, by taking the essential and dynamic structure of being as a starting point, based on real universal principles to which all beings may be reduced, they can attain rational knowledge that culminates in the truths of the Christian Faith. His Art is a method that permits one to establish, clearly and simply, the correspondence between ways of being (*modus essendi*) and ways of knowing (*modus intelligendi*), a correspondence where the doctrines of Faith find their proof, since by affirming them the human mind achieves a clear comprehension of the structure of reality, a structure so perfectly designed that it would collapse were any of these doctrines negated. In short, Llull ultimately designed his Art to serve the Christian Faith and, in spite of the purely scientific and epistemological aspects of its method, this apologetic design could not have passed unperceived by the Muslim scholars with whom Llull sought to engage in dialogue. Perhaps this is why it did not find use for the missionary objectives that its author had established. But many did recognize it, for centuries, as an important point of reference in the history of European thought: the Lullian *Ars Magna* has its own history in the evolution of Lullism after Llull.

Works Cited

Primary Works: Llull

Arbor philosophiae, (eds.) Carla Compagno and Ulli Roth, ROL 34:1–149.

Arbor scientiae, (ed.) Pere Villalba Varneda, ROL 24–26.

Ars amativa boni, (eds.) Marta M.M. Romano and Francesco Santi, ROL 29:1–432.

Ars brevis, (ed.) Aloisius Madre, ROL 12:123–127.

Ars compendiosa inveniendi ueritatem, MOG 1:433–473 (text 7, sep. pag.).

Ars demonstrativa, (ed.) Josep Enric Rubio Albarracín, ROL 32.

Ars generalis ultima, (ed.) Aloisius Madre, ROL 14.

Ars inveniendi particularia in universalibus, MOG 3:453–502 (text 7, sep. pag.).

Ars inventiva veritatis, (ed.) Jorge Uscatestcu Barrón, ROL 37.

Ars universalis, MOG 1:483–606 (text 8, sep. pag.).

Brevis practica Tabulae generalis (*Ars compendiosa*), (ed.) Carmelo Ottaviano, *L'Ars compendiosa de R. Lulle*, Études de Philosophie Médiévale 12 (Paris: 1930).

Cant de Ramon, OE 1:1031–1032.

Compendium seu commentum Artis demonstrativae, MOG 3:293–452 (text 6, sep. pag.).

Darrer llibre sobre la conquesta de Terra Santa, (ed.) Jordi Gayà Estelrich (Barcelona: 2002).

Introductoria Artis demonstrativae, MOG 2:55–92 (text 2, sep. pag.).

Lectura artis, quae intitulata est Brevis practica Tabulae generalis, (ed.) Jordi Gayà Estelrich, ROL 20:106–113.

Lectura super Artem inventivam et Tabulam generalem, MOG 5:359–716 (text 5, sep. pag.).

Lectura super figuras Artis demonstrativae, MOG 3:205–247 (text 4, sep. pag.).

Liber chaos, MOG 3:249–292 (text 5, sep. pag.).

Liber de quaestionibus, per quem modus Artis demonstrativae patefit, unedited.

Liber exponens figuram elementalem Artis demonstrativae, MOG 4:1–10 (text 2, sep. pag.).

Liber principiorum iuris, (ed.) María Asunción Sánchez Manzano, ROL 31:323–412.

Liber principiorum medicinae, (ed.) María Asunción Sánchez Manzano, ROL 31:413–564.

Liber principiorum philosophiae, (ed.) María Asunción Sánchez Manzano, ROL 31:155–322.

Liber principiorum theologiae, (ed.) María Asunción Sánchez Manzano, ROL 31:1–154.

Liber propositionum secundum Artem demonstrativam, MOG 3:503–564 (text 8, sep. pag.).

Libre de contemplació en Déu, (ed.) Antoni Sancho y Miquel Arbona, OE 2:85–1269.

Logica nova, (ed.) Walter Euler, ROL 23:1–179.

Quaestiones per Artem demonstrativam seu inventivam solubiles, MOG 4:17–224 (text 3, sep. pag.).

Tabula Generalis, (ed.) Viola Tenge-Wolf, ROL 27.

Vita coaetanea, (ed.) Hermogenes Harada, ROL 8:259–309.

Secondary Works

Artus, Walter W., *The "Ars Brevis" of Ramon Lull: A Study,* Ph.D. diss. St. John's University (New York: 1967).

Batalla, Josep, "L'art lul·liana com a teologia filosòfica," *Revista de lenguas y literaturas catalana, gallega y vasca* 15 (2010): 321–344.

Bonner, Anthony, "Una nota sobre el mot 'dignitas'," in *Studia Lullistica et Philologica: Miscellanea in honorem Francisci B. Moll et Michaelis Colom* (Palma: 1990), 35–38.

Carreras i Artau, Joaquín and Tomás Carreras i Artau, *Historia de la filosofía española: Filosofía cristiana de los siglos XIII al XV*, 2 vols. (Madrid: 1939–43).

Colomer, Eusebi, "De Ramon Llull a la moderna informàtica," *EL* 23 (1979): 113–135.

Domínguez Reboiras, Fernando, "Works," in Alexander Fidora and Josep E. Rubio (ed.), *Raimundus Lullus: An Introduction to his Life, Works and Thought* (Turnhout: 2008), 125–242.

Dreyer, Mechthild, "Raimundus Lullus, 'Quid sit contemplatio?'," in Fernando Domínguez Reboiras, Viola Tenge-Wolf, and Peter Walter (ed.), *Gottes Schau und Weltbetrachtung: Interpretationen zum "Liber Contemplationis" des Raimundus Lullus* (Turnhout: 2011), 417–438.

Fidora, Alexander, "Les definicions de Ramon Llull: entre la lògica àrab i les teories de la definició modernes," *Revista de Lenguas y Literaturas Catalana, Gallega y Vasca* 12 (2006): 239–252.

Fidora, Alexander, and Josep E. Rubio (ed.), *Raimundus Lullus: An Introduction to his Life, Works and Thought* (Turnhout: 2008).

Fidora, Alexander and Carles Sierra (ed.), *Ramon Llull: From the Ars Magna to Artificial Intelligence* (Barcelona: 2011).

Gayà Estelrich, Jordi, *La teoría luliana de los correlativos: Historia de su formación conceptual* (Palma: 1979).

Gayà Estelrich, Jordi, "Significación y demostración en el 'Libre de Contemplació' de Ramon Llull," in Fernando Domínguez Reboiras, Ruedi Imbach, Theodor Pindl, and Peter Walter (ed.), *Aristotelica et Lulliana magistro doctissimo Charles H. Lohr septuagesimum annum feliciter agenti dedicata* (Steenbergen and The Hague: 1995), 477–499.

Gayà Estelrich, Jordi, "La construcción de la demostración teológica en el 'Libre de contemplació' de Ramon Llull," in Margot Schmidt and Fernando Domínguez Reboiras (ed.), *Von der Suche nach Gott. Helmut Riedlinger zum 75. Geburtstag* (Stuttgart-Bad Cannstatt: 1998), 147–171.

Gayà Estelrich, Jordi, "Els principis de l'Art lul·liana i les seves definicions," *Taula* 37 (2002): 53–71.

Gómez Llauger, Núria, "Estudi dels termes 'Potentia' 'Obiectum' i 'Actus' a partir del *Liber de potentia, obiecto et actu* de Ramon Llull," *Revista Internacional d'Humanitats* 19 (2010): 17–28.

Higuera Rubio, José, *Física y Teología (Atomismo y movimiento en el Arte luliano)* (Pamplona: 2014).

Hughes, Robert D., "Speculum, Similitude and Signification: the Incarnation as Exemplary and Proportionate Sign in the Arts of Ramon Llull," *SL* 45–46 (2005–06): 3–37.

Libera, Alain de, *Archéologie du sujet: La naissance du sujet* (Paris: 2007).

Merle, Hélène, "'Dignitas': signification philosophique et théologique de ce terme chez Lulle et ses prédécesseurs médiévaux," *EL* 21 (1977): 173–193.

Pistolesi, Elena, "Note sulle definizioni lulliane," *SL* 47 (2007): 51–69.

Platzeck, Erhard-Wolfram, *Raimund Lull. Sein Leben-seine Werke. Die Grundlagen seines Denkens (Prinzipienlehre)*, 2 vols. (Rome and Düsseldorf: 1962–1964).

Pring-Mill, Robert D.F., "The Trinitarian World Picture of Ramon Llull," *Romanistisches Jahrbuch* 7 (1955–56): 229–256.

Pring-Mill, Robert D.F., *Ramón Llull y el número primitivo de las dignidades en el "Arte general"* (Oxford: 1963).

Pring-Mill, Robert D.F., "The Analogical Structure of the Lullian Art," in *Islamic Philosophy & the Classical Tradition: Essays presented to Richard Walzer on the occasion of his 70th Birthday* (Oxford: 1972), 315–326.

Rubio, Josep E., *Les bases del pensament de Ramon Llull. Els orígens de l'Art lul·liana* (Valencia and Barcelona: 1997).

Rubio, Josep E., "L'evolució de les figures A, S i T de l'Art quaternària en el trànsit cap a l'Art ternària," *Taula* 37 (2002): 83–98.

Rubio, Josep E., "Thought: The Art," in Alexander Fidora and Josep E. Rubio (ed.), *Raimundus Lullus: An Introduction to his Life, Works and Thought* (Turnhout: 2008), 243–310.

Rubio, Josep E., "'Significatio' im 'Liber contemplationis,' oder: wie kann man durch die Betrachtung die Wahrheit finden?," in Fernando Domínguez Reboiras, Viola Tenge-Wolf, and Peter Walter (ed.), *Gottes Schau und Weltbetrachtung. Interpretationen zum "Liber Contemplationis" des Raimundus Lullus* (Turnhout: 2011), 227–237.

Rubio, Josep E., "Contemplation et prière, deux composantes de l'Art lullien," *Iris: Annales de philosophie* 33 (2012): 59–70.

Ruiz Simon, Josep Maria, "De la naturalesa com a mescla a l'art de mesclar (sobre la fonamentació cosmològica de les arts lul·lianes)," *Randa* 19 (1986): 69–99.

Ruiz Simon, Josep Maria, *L'Art de Ramon Llull i la teoria escolàstica de la ciència* (Barcelona: 1999).

Ruiz Simon, Josep Maria, "La transformació del pensament de Ramon Llull durant les obres de transició cap a l'etapa ternària," in Maria Isabel Ripoll Perelló (ed.), *Actes de les Jornades Internacionals Lul·lianes "Ramon Llull al s. XXI." Palma, 1, 2 i 3 d'abril de 2004* (Palma and Barcelona: 2005), 167–196.

Tenge-Wolf, Viola, "Introductio Generalis," in *Tabula Generalis*, ROL 27:1*–204*.

Yates, Frances, Frances, "The Art of Ramon Lull (An Approach to it through Lull's Theory of the elements)," *Journal of the Warburg and Courtal Institutes* 17 (1954): 115–173.

PART 2

Llull as Evangelist

∵

CHAPTER 5

Ramon Llull and Islam

Gregory Stone

5.1 Introduction

Ramon Llull's idiosyncratic place in the intellectual history of the late Middle Ages is unthinkable apart from Islam. Llull's writings as well as his missionary and political efforts were dominated by a single purpose: in the words of the *Vita coaetanea*, his life's task was "converting to [God's] worship and service the Saracens who in such numbers surrounded Christians on all sides."[1] The primary impulse behind Llull's drive to convert Muslims was his hope that the establishment of "one faith and one religion" (a global unity of creed) would put an end to "rancor or ill will among men, who hate each other because of diversity and contrariness of beliefs and of sects."[2] Moreover, Llull's major philosophical innovations – the claim to offer demonstrative proof of articles of the Christian faith (above all, the Trinity and the Incarnation) by "necessary reasons" and the rational method that he deployed for that purpose – arose from his conviction that prospective Muslim converts would not be content with mere assertions of Christian doctrine or with scriptural exegesis. Llull invented his famous Art (the topic of many and the blueprint for most other of his works) because he needed an apparently neutral demonstrative discursive instrument as the ground upon which to commence dialogue with Islamic intellectuals.

Neither of these two ways in which Llull's life work is motivated by his encounter with Islam – first, his mission; secondly, his philosophical method – requires that the origins, content, or essential gist of his thinking be to any degree Islamic. The Art may well be a vehicle for the delivery, by a preacher who is purely Christian although "surrounded" by Muslims, of a Truth that is sufficiently contained within and co-extensive with Christianity itself. On the other hand, it is possible that Llull's Christianity and the method by which he aimed to demonstrate its doctrines are "Islamic" in certain significant ways – i.e., that his thinking and his Art could not have taken their essential shape

---

1 *Ramon Llull: A Contemporary Life* 1.5, trans. Anthony Bonner (Barcelona: 2010), 35.
2 *Book of the Gentile and the Three Wise Men Prologue*, in *Doctor Illuminatus: A Ramon Llull Reader*, (ed.) and trans. Anthony Bonner (Princeton: 1993), 90.

were it not for a profound influence exerted upon him by certain Muslim writings and traditions. We consider this question toward the end of this chapter.

"Llull and Islam" is a large and multifaceted topic. Rather than focus on any single one of these facets, this chapter presents an overview of several, while pointing the reader toward some of the most significant scholarship in this area of Llull studies. First, we consider Llull's mission to convert Muslims and the concerns that shaped the method by which he hoped to carry out the task. Does his reputation as a tolerant champion of interreligious dialogue actually match his own conception of his mission, which included repeated calls for a new military crusade to dispossess Muslims of the Holy Lands? Secondly, we survey Llull's various attitudes toward Islam by presenting a sample of those things that he says about "Saracens," Muhammad, the Qur'an, and the Islamic religion. Thirdly, we raise the question concerning the extent to which essential aspects of Llull's thinking may be called "Islamic." In this section, we suggest affinities between Llull and the great Islamic religious thinker al-Ghazālī. Finally, we briefly consider ways in which he adopted or rejected the views of the *falasifa*, the Islamic rationalist philosophers such as al-Farabi, Avicenna, and Averroes.

5.2   Mission and Method: Tolerance or Fanaticism?

Llull's zeal for the conversion of all Muslims to Christianity, taken along with his frequent expression of admiration for Muslims and for the value of Islamic thinking, has aptly been called "a curious mix of fanaticism and tolerance."[3] Those who view Llull as tolerant normally commend his seeming insistence that the Muslim world should be Christianized through discussion rather than through physical force, his accurate and respectful representation of Muslim beliefs, his apparent interest in non-European cultures and languages (especially Arabic), his promotion of polite interreligious dialogue, his unbiased recognition that Islamic sages and scholars had advanced at least as far as their Christian counterparts, and his goodwill in portraying Muslims as sincere, pious believers whose faith shares a great deal of common ground with Christianity.

There are indeed moments when Llull's interreligious ecumenism goes very far and when he seems to deserve his modern reputation as a hero of interfaith

---

3   John V. Tolan, *Saracens: Islam in the Medieval European Imagination* (New York: 2002), 258, and esp. 256–274, which offers an excellent summary of Llull's strategies for the conversion of Muslims.

dialogue.[4] The most notable of these is the famous *Book of the Gentile and the Three Wise Men*, a work that Llull says was written for "entering into union with and getting to know strangers and friends"[5] and that has been called a "utopian project for brotherhood among the three religions of the Book."[6] Overall, the *Book of the Gentile* gives the impression of treating the three monotheisms as equals. Book One presents the many fundamental principles shared in common by Judaism, Christianity, and Islam. The fact that there is no indication concerning which of the three sages – the Jew, the Christian, or the Muslim – is explaining these basic principles serves to emphasize the concordance between the three religions.[7] Books Two through Four, in which each of the three sages takes his turn trying to convince a gentile philosopher that the sage's particular religion is the true way to salvation and better than the religions of the other two, amounts to a remarkably non-contentious "dispute." A tone of cordiality prevails throughout and remains in place at the end: "They took leave of one another most amiably and politely, and each asked forgiveness of the other for any disrespectful word he might have spoken against his religion."[8] The book's open-ended conclusion—which Bonner calls "an ending most surprising in a piece of medieval polemical literature"[9] – refrains from proclaiming one of the monotheisms superior to the other two and might almost be called an endorsement of religious freedom. At the climactic moment, when the gentile is about to disclose which religion he prefers, the three sages ask him not to reveal his choice to them: "The three wise men answered, saying that, in order for each to be free to choose his own religion, they preferred not knowing which religion he would choose." The wise men prefer to keep the question open, so that they will continue to "have such a good subject of discussion."[10]

---

4   For a portrait of Llull as a champion of tolerance and peaceful dialogue, see Cary J. Nederman, *Worlds of Difference: European Discourses of Toleration c. 1100-c. 1550* (University Park, Penns.: 2000), 30–37.

5   *Book of the Gentile* Epilogue, (ed.) Bonner, 170.

6   Amador Vega, "Ramon Llull: L'art d'inventar la veritat," in *Ramon Llull i l'islam: L'inici del diàleg*, (ed.) Maria Àngels Roque (Barcelona: 2008), 210; unless otherwise indicated, all subsequent translations into English are my own. The essays in this volume (the most important recent collection on Llull and Islam) are also available in a bilingual English/Spanish edition, *Ramon Llull and Islam: the Beginning of Dialogue/Ramon Llull y el islam, el inicio del diálogo* (Barcelona: 2008).

7   See Anthony Bonner, "La disputa interreligiosa, la solució enginyosa de Ramon Llull," in *Ramon Llull i l'islam: L'inici del diàleg*, (ed.) Maria Àngels Roque (Barcelona: 2008), 219.

8   *Book of the Gentile* Epilogue, (ed.) Bonner, 169.

9   "Introduction," *Book of the Gentile*, in *Doctor Illuminatus*, 80.

10   *Book of the Gentile* Epilogue, (ed.) Bonner, 167.

More than once in later works Llull claims that the *Book of the Gentile* (an early work, written between 1274 and 1276) is not open-ended but rather that it proves the truth of Christianity and the falseness of Islam and Judaism.[11] The validity of this claim is questionable, since the *Book of the Gentile* does not explicitly assert that the gentile would have pronounced in favor of Christianity. Some scholars have argued that while on the surface the work's conclusion is open-ended, closer reading shows that Christianity is the gentile's only possible choice.[12] Does Llull's youthful liberality give way to a mature conservatism? Although there are signs of a certain bitterness and darkening of spirit in some of Llull's later writings, his many apparent self-contradictions are best explained by bearing in mind that Llull is nothing if not a rhetorician: he shifts his tone and even his positions so as to suit his intended audience. The *Book of the Gentile* seems to have been originally intended as palatable training in Llull's Art, meant to provide Christian missionaries with material that they might use to hold non-confrontational discussions with North African Muslims.[13] Llull reckoned that prospective converts would be more likely to listen to Christians who presented themselves as friendly toward other religions. In some cases Llull deploys tolerance as an appropriate strategy, whereas at other times he is much more stridently Christian.[14] Following one of his own tenets, he always bears in mind the "first intention" (ultimate aim or purpose) of an endeavor. His occasional openness to other religions is a "second intention" (an instrument or means) that serves his "first intention" – namely, the

---

11   See, for example, *Liber de fine* 1.5 and 3.2. See also verse 279 of the *Book of the Lover and the Beloved*, in *Romanç d'Evast e Blaquerna*, (eds.) Albert Soler and Joan Santanach, NEORL 8:500: the *Book of the Gentile and the Three Wise Men* is said to provide "knowledge that the Catholic faith is true and that the beliefs of the Jews and of the Saracens are false and erroneous."

12   See Joan Santanach, "Sobre el Llibre del gentil i la coherència doctrinal de Ramon Llull," in *Ramon Llull i l'islam: L'inici del diàleg*, (ed.) Maria Àngels Roque (Barcelona: 2008), 225–231, esp. 227–228: denying that Llull's cordiality entails tolerance for non-Christian doctrines, Santanach argues that the *Book of the Gentile* is "only apparently open-ended" and that "only a superficial reading of the work" could posit that "Ramon considers all three religions equally valid." See also Tolan, *Saracens*, 266–267: "despite all the polite language of respect," the *Book of the Gentile* implies "that Islam is fundamentally irrational."

13   Bonner, "Introduction," *Book of the Gentile*, in *Doctor Illuminatus*, 80–81.

14   Dominique Urvoy, "Ramon Lull et l'Islam," *Islamochristiana* 7 (1981): 135, remarks that Llull's "intellectual schizophrenia" is a function of the differing audiences for which he writes: those texts "intended for Muslims are respectful toward the Qur'an and the Prophet, while those texts meant solely for the use of Christians often repeat the worst commonplaces concerning Muhammad's excess sensuality, his having been educated by a heretic, etc."

conversion of the entire globe to Christianity.[15] It is irrelevant to ask whether or not Llull's tolerance is heartfelt: he designs his attitudes to fit his purpose rather than vice-versa.

The most serious manifestation of Llull's split personality involves his seeming both to discourage and to encourage the conquest of Muslim territories through military crusades.[16] On the one hand, Llull follows his Catalan predecessors, the Dominicans Ramon de Penyafort and Ramon Martí, key figures in 13th century Western Christendom's general strategic shift toward winning the Holy Land through missions rather than crusades. As recounted in the *Vita coaetanea*, Llull's initial impulse following his conversion (in 1263) is very much in line with his contemporaries' preference for converting by means of words rather than warfare. Thus in his seminal early work, the *Libre de contemplació*, Llull insists that attempting to conquer the Holy Land "through force of arms" rather than "through preaching" is a futile endeavor.[17] In various other works he makes a similar point, mentioning with approbation a supposed (probably fictitious) letter sent by the Sultan of Egypt to the Pope, in which the Sultan attributes the Christians' failure to regain the Holy Land to the fact that they attempt to reconquer by armed force (in the manner of Muhammad) rather than in the original manner of Christ and his disciples – namely, through preaching and shedding one's own blood.[18] In *Blanquerna* the eponymous hero convinces a violent armed knight that "strength of mind is nobler and greater than strength of body."[19] On the other hand, the *Vita coaetanea* also recounts how the elderly Llull (in 1307 or 1308) proposed to the Pisan council

---

15   One might even consider the possibility that the conversion of the entire globe to Christianity is itself a "second intention" in relation to Llull's genuine "first intention" – namely, world peace. This pragmatic notion of Christianity's value is implied in the Prologue to the *Book of the Gentile*, (ed.) Bonner, 90, where one of the wise men expresses his fervent hope that "all peoples could unite and become one people…under one faith and one religion." Here it does not so much matter *which* faith conquers the globe so long as the globe has *but one* single faith.

16   Chapter seven of this volume analyzes in detail Llull's several treatises specifically devoted to recovery of the Holy Land.

17   *Libre de contemplació: antologia* 112, (ed.) Josep E. Rubio (Barcelona: 2009), 122; cf. also 121–122: "I see many knights going to the Holy Land across the sea, thinking that they will conquer it through force of arms. The end result is that they are all laid to waste without attaining their aim. Thus it seems to me, Lord, that that Holy Land should not be conquered except in the manner by which it was conquered by You and Your apostles, who conquered it with love and speech and with the shedding of tears and blood."

18   For one version of this letter (and references to other versions), see Jordi Gayà Estelrich's introduction to *Darrer llibre sobre la conquesta de terra santa*, trans. Pere Llabrés (Barcelona: 2002), 37.

19   *Romanç d'Evast e Blaquerna* 2.50, NEORL 8:238.

that "their city...found an order of Christian religious knights devoted to do-
ing continual battle against the treacherous Saracens for the recovery of the
Holy Land" and how a few years later (in 1311) he petitioned the Council of
Vienne to make "all the Christian military religious orders" into a single one
"that would maintain continual warfare overseas against the Saracens until the
Holy Land had been reconquered."[20] Whether or not a younger anti-crusade
Llull changed into an older pro-crusade Llull, what is certainly true is that,
beginning in 1292, he wrote a series of works focused on persuading ecclesiastical and lay powers of Europe to launch a new and final Christian military
conquest of the Muslim Near East and North Africa.[21] The most important of
these works, the *Liber de fine* (1305), is conceived as a final summation of his
life's aim – namely, to bring about the Christian reconquest of the Holy Land
and the total Christianization of the globe.[22] Not only does Llull encourage
the undertaking of new crusades, but he also fancies himself the world's master crusade strategist, offering highly detailed plans on all aspects, including
invasion scenarios, recommendations concerning armaments, plans for the organization of supporting institutions, geo-political considerations, and numerous other suggestions (such as the appointment of a Christian "warrior king,"
leader of a military order whose members would be required to read Llull's
novels and some of his more accessible scientific writings) that his contemporaries no doubt found unusual. Llull's position on crusades is exemplified
by his reinterpretation of the political meaning of the biblical metaphor of
the "two swords" (Luke 22:38). Normally understood in late medieval European
political theory as an allegory for the distinction between lay power and ecclesiastical power – between the (temporal) power of kings and the (spiritual)
power of popes – for Llull the two swords signify two modes of papal power:
the (spiritual) power to fight with the "sword" of speech (in the manner of the
Dominican missionaries) and the (temporal) power to fight with real swords.
Llull regards *both* swords as legitimate, although the Church should commence

20   *Ramon Llull: A Contemporary Life* 10.42 and 11.44, (ed.) Bonner, 79 and 83.

21   See Tolan, *Saracens*, 274, for the view that Llull, who in his earlier writings "pushes ad-
      miration and appreciation of the religious other to its limits," changes his position on
      crusades as he comes to realize that "Jewish and Muslim infidels refuse to be convinced
      by his arguments." For an insistence that Llull's support for the legitimacy of crusades
      remains constant throughout his writings, see Fernando Domínguez Reboiras's introduc-
      tion to Llull's *Liber de passagio*, ROL 18:257–267.

22   On the *Liber de fine*, see Franco Porsia, *Progetti di Crociata: Il De fine di Raimondo Lullo*
      (Taranto: 2005). On the relative priority of mission and crusade in Llull, see Fernando
      Domínguez Reboiras, *Ramon Llull: El mejor libro del mundo* (Barcelona: 2016), 187–201.

with the former before exercising, when necessary, the latter power.[23] Llull's position on crusading is summed up in a verse from the *Desconhort*, where he says that the conversion of infidels will come about "through iron and wood and through true argument."[24]

Despite apparent self-contradictions, one thing remains constant: Llull's conviction that his Art is the one and only method for converting infidels that might possibly work. Thus crusading is not in itself a method of conversion; rather, it is one way of establishing conditions favorable for a potential conversion. Following the successful conclusion of the military enterprise, Christians will have the liberty to preach in the Holy Land without fear of being killed by Muslims. Authentic conversion must be the result of a choice freely willed by the one who converts, not the result of any coercion, for God desires that converts "come to Him of their own free will and not of constraint."[25] Ever the innovator, Llull conceives of a new purpose for crusades: conquered Muslims will be forced to listen to teachings grounded in Llull's Art! If that Art works as it should, those Muslims will then freely choose to become Christians.[26]

Llull's missionary method is a new departure from that of his Dominican predecessors and contemporaries in three ways.[27] First, "authority" (the citation of an esteemed text, such as scripture or the writing of an acclaimed thinker) plays virtually no role in the formulation of his arguments.[28] While Llull is remarkably fond of mentioning his own works, he hardly ever mentions the works of others. The failure of the famous Dispute of Barcelona in 1263 had shown Llull that one cannot enlighten one's adversary by haggling over the meaning of texts.[29] For all of his utopian idealism, Llull was also a perceptive

---

23   *Liber disputationis Petri clerici et Raimundi sive Phantasticus* 5.117. For a recent Latin edition with modern Catalan translation of this text, see *Llibre de la disputa del clergue Pere i de Ramon, el fantàstic. Llibre de la ciutat del món*, (ed.) and trans. Lola Badia (Santa Coloma de Queralt: 2008).

24   *Desconhort* 31, ORL 19:234.

25   *Romanç d'Evast e Blaquerna* 2.43, (eds.) Soler and Santanach, 213.

26   E.g. *Liber de fine* 2.6. On Llull's view that crusading is not an end in itself but an instrument for ensuring the preaching of Llull's Art, see Gabriel Ensenyat, "Pacifisme i croada en Ramon Llull," in *Ramon Llull i l'islam: L'inici del diàleg*, (ed.) Maria Àngels Roque (Barcelona: 2008), 232–245.

27   See chapter two in this volume for a review of the methods and positions advocated by Llull's contemporaries.

28   On Llull's strategic avoidance of *auctoritates*, see Josep E. Rubio, "Thought: The Art," in *Raimundus Lullus: An Introduction to his Life, Works, and Thought*, (eds.) Alexander Fidora and Josep E. Rubio, ROL Suppl. 2 (Turnhout: 2008), 482–483.

29   See Bonner, "La disputa interreligiosa," 215. On the Dispute of Barcelona, a public debate over the interpretation of the Talmud between the great Jewish Rabbi Nahmanides and

realist: he knew that telling Muslims that Christian texts tell humankind that they ought to believe Christian beliefs was, to say the least, a not very effective method of conversion. In particular, exhortations to believe Christian teachings would not be taken at all seriously by Llull's target audience: Muslim intellectuals, who, in Llull's view, did not hold mere belief in very high esteem. Thus on multiple occasions Llull tells a variant of a story in which an educated Muslim ruler is angered by a Christian missionary who cannot offer in the place of Islam anything other than a Christianity conceived of as another mere belief.[30] This leads to Llull's second important innovation: he asserts (to an extent that courted charges of heresy) that the Christian faith (and, especially, its two most essential and specific articles) can be proven, demonstratively, to be rational: reality, for "necessary reasons," demands that there be the Trinity and the Incarnation.[31] Llull offers to Muslim intellectuals a method by which they can know and understand, in the manner of a demonstrative science, the truth of these most important Christian articles of faith. But why would those Muslim intellectuals ever consent to follow the path of a method proposed by a Christian thinker? This is the problem resolved by Llull's third major innovation: the Art *per se* is not Christian, even though its very *raison d'être* is to convert all non-Christians to Christianity. That is, Llull's arguments do not proceed from or commence with Christian teachings but rather from basic monotheistic principles that are readily accepted as axiomatic by all educated Jews, Christians, and Muslims.[32] Indeed as Llull develops the Art over time he

---

a Christian convert from Judaism named Paul Cristiani, see Nahmanide, *La dispute de Barcelone*, trans. Éric Smilévitch and Luc Ferrier (Paris: 1984) and Nina Caputo, *Nahmanides in Medieval Catalonia: History, Community, and Messianism* (Notre Dame, Indiana: 2007).

30   See, for example, *Disputatio fidei et intellectus* 1.1 [4], in *Disputa entre la Fe i l'Enteniment*, (eds.) and trans. Josep Batalla and Alexander Fidora (Turnhout: 2011), 88–89.

31   Alexander Fidora, "Combinatòria i reciprocitat: Una nota sobre la vigència de l'Art lul·liana," in *Ramon Llull i l'islam: L'inici del diàleg*, (ed.) Maria Àngels Roque (Barcelona: 2008), 196, remarks that the gist of Llull's project is precisely this effort to provide rational proof of the truth of Christianity – something that Martí and Aquinas (for whom the articles of faith transcend the grasp of reason) neither tried nor wished to do.

32   Ibid., 197: "Thus Llull takes the elements that all the religions share in common and combines them ... to show that, if one understands these elements properly, they themselves will lead us to the Trinity and the Incarnation." For Bonner, "La disputa interreligiosa," 215, the greatest novelty of Llull's missionary method, totally unprecedented in medieval interreligious discussion, is the fact that its arguments are not grounded in (i.e., do not use as premises) specifically Christian doctrines.

makes it more and more neutral, more apparently universal and objective, less Christian-seeming and even less manifestly theological.[33]

Although Llull presents himself as one concerned with truth (and often refers to the Art as a method of "finding truth"), this impulse toward truth is in itself rhetorically conditioned by his contemporary circumstances. Llull's devotion to truth is not absolute, and he is not averse to lying when necessary.[34] If truth is now enlisted to serve the cause of global evangelization, it is because truth is what will *work now*. This historically specific advent of a call for truth is attributable in large part to the development of Islamic thinking. Muslim intellectuals – Llull often repeats – now demand truth; and so, following suit, humankind in Llull's view has now entered an Age of Reason.[35] The Great Universal Art of Finding Truth is conceivable in other historical times and places, and it is certainly useful for other purposes. But were it not for the level of sophistication that Islamic thinking had reached by Llull's lifetime, the Art would not have stood alone in Llull's mind as the only possible instrument

---

33   Bonner, *AL* 100–101, describes Llull's method as "a classic tactic of presenting foundations to which the adversary could not object, but which would have drawn him into a labyrinth from which he could not extricate himself without finally admitting to positions undeclared at the beginning: those involving the truth of Christianity." In addition to the detailed exposition provided in *AL*, see also Bonner's brief summary "What Was Llull Up To?" in *Ramon Llull: From the Ars Magna to Artificial Intelligence*, (eds.) Alexander Fidora and Carles Sierra (Barcelona: 2011), 5–24.

34   Thus Blanquerna, after comforting a grieving shepherd by lying to him, then teaches the shepherd the "art and method" of comforting others – the primary technique of which involves telling them lies: *Romanç d'Evast e Blaquerna* 49, (eds.) Soler and Santanach, 232–236.

35   On Llull's notion that humankind, following the lead of Muslim and Christian intellectuals, has progressed into an Age of Reason (i.e., knowledge of truth), see Gayà's introduction to *Darrer llibre*, 34–35. In his *Libre de meravelles* 1.12, (ed.) Salvador Galmés, 4 vols. (Barcelona: 1931), 1:133, Llull divides the history of human assent to religious law into three successive epochs: "In the age of the prophets, it was fitting that one converted people through belief, since they believed easily; in the age of Christ and the apostles, miracles—which are demonstrations of physically visible things – were appropriate. Now the age has come when people desire necessary reasons, because people are grounded in the great philosophical and theological sciences;" cf. *Liber de acquisitione Terrae Sanctae* 2.2, in *Darrer llibre*, 35: "If the Saracens convert, all the other peoples all over the world will easily be converted, since, in comparison, all other peoples except for us, we Christians and Saracens, know nothing at all." See also *Blanquerna* 44, (eds.) Soler and Santanach, 216, where the allegorical figure of Understanding says: "The time has come when our knowledge is exalted and the infidels demand necessary reasons and demonstrations, and they shun [mere] belief. It is time that we go and use the science that we have ... Learned Saracens have great doubt in their faith ... We have a new manner of disputing with the infidels by showing them the Brief Art of Finding Truth; and when they will have learned it, we will be able to confound them with the Art and with its principles."

of conversion. Here Llull's assessment is quite sound: Muslim intellectuals (including the highly influential al-Ghazālī, who, despite his reputation as an opponent of the Islamic philosophers, was a great champion of knowledge, logic, and reason and often expressed near-contempt for unexamined traditional religion and for mere faith that makes no effort toward understanding) did tend toward enlightened rationalism. In sum, Llull's method is *shaped by* as much as it is meant to shape the state of the thinking of his Muslim contemporaries.

Llull's very clear notion of his primary target audience also indicates that he is not entirely dedicated to the noble idea that truth ought to be known by all humankind. Time and again he specifies that the mission he promotes (and that the Art serves) is meant especially to convert Muslim elites – educated rulers and intellectuals.[36] Llull adopts a top-down, trickle-down approach according to which it does not matter exactly what trickles down: he does not much care whether the Muslim masses follow their elites in the way of knowledge, so long as those elites, once converted, will convert their rank-and-file, by whatever means they might use. Here again we see the fundamentally rhetorical nature of the Art: Llull is only interested in persuading educated Muslims that Christianity is true (demonstrable by "necessary reasons") so that they will then persuade the Muslim masses to become Christians. Truth is not the Art's end but rather its means. Llull's method is in accord with the principle of least effort: if things go as planned, Christendom itself will not have to do the hard work of converting the Muslim masses, since Muslim elites will themselves take over this task. And then there will no longer be any reason for Europeans to learn Arabic![37]

5.3   Llull on Islam, Muslims, Muhammad, and the Qur'an

The Book of the Gentile and the Three Wise Men includes Llull's most extended and sympathetic presentation of the Islamic religion. In Book 4 of that work,

---

36   *Liber de fine* 1.2, in *Darrer llibre*, 81: "If the most important Saracens convert, they will lead the least important to convert as well." For references to several instances of this theme in Llull's pro-crusade writings, see Porsia, *Progetti di Crociata*, 100, 113, 126.

37   Cf. *Desconhort* 28, ORL 19:233: Llull says that learned Muslims who through "force of reasoning" do not believe in Muhammad or value the Qur'an will be easily converted to Christianity through "force of reasoning" because "once converted, [they] will convert the people,/and it will no longer be necessary [for us] to learn their language/nor to speak ill of Muhammad."

a Muslim sage explains twelve Islamic articles of faith (for example: that there is one God; that God created the universe; that Muhammad is God's Prophet; that the Qur'an is the Law given by God, etc.). This presentation has been commended as "remarkably fair and accurate" and as a "faithful reproduction of the point of view of others."[38] The work's respectful and undistorted approach was likely intended to capture the goodwill of prospective Muslim converts who might enter into discussion with those Christian missionaries whom Llull envisioned using the *Book of the Gentile* as a sort of training manual. One must also bear in mind that verisimilitude dictates that the Muslim sage would present his own religion in a positive light.

Despite its title, a brief section of the *Liber de fine* called "Against the Saracens" does not denigrate Islam but rather emphasizes the common ground that it shares with Christianity: "They agree with us about many things."[39] According to Llull, not only are Muslims monotheists, but they also believe that Jesus is the son of God, that Jesus is the best man who ever has existed, exists, or will exist, that Jesus was conceived through the Holy Spirit and born of the blessed Virgin Mary, and that the apostles are saints. However, Muslims do not believe that Jesus *is* God (that is, they reject the Incarnation), and they do not believe in the Trinity, since they misconstrue that doctrine to mean that God is divided into three separate parts. Throughout Llull's works, the essential difference between Islam and Christianity is the former's rejection of the Trinity and the Incarnation. One often gets the impression that in Llull's view all other differences between the two religions are negligible, inflected by the accidents of history and culture, even trivial.[40] We see here why Llull, regarding Islam and Christianity as so nearly identical, seems to have believed that his project might succeed: it is a matter of uniting two faiths that are already quite close together. This task of unification is twofold: first, convincing Muslims that Islamic principles concerning God necessarily entail the Trinity and the Incarnation; secondly, showing Muslims that Christianity's two essential articles of faith are rational and provable through scientific demonstration.

---

38   Anne Marie C. Mayer, "Ramon Llull i el diàleg indispensable," in *Ramon Llull i l'islam: L'inici del diàleg*, (ed.) Maria Àngels Roque (Barcelona: 2008), 58.

39   *Liber de fine* 1.2, in *Darrer llibre*, 81; cf. Porsia, *Progetti di Crociata*, 51.

40   E.g. *Liber disputationis Raimundi christiani et Homeri saraceni*, the record of a dispute between Llull and a learned Muslim named Omar that took place in Bugia in 1307; Llull agrees to convert to Islam if he cannot prove the Trinity and the Incarnation, while Llull's Muslim hosts agree to convert to Christianity if Llull can prove those two articles of faith.

Muslims will come to realize, upon reflection, that they already are essentially "Christian."[41]

Various passages in Llull's writings bring out differences between the two religions. Islam is an "easier" religion than Christianity, and thus more appealing to the masses, while the latter is intellectually difficult. The spread of Islam throughout formerly Christian parts of Africa, Europe, and Asia is directly attributable to the fact that Christianity is "very profound and difficult to believe" whereas the Islamic creed "is not profound."[42] The difficulty in question involves belief in the Trinity, which seems to be quite irrational – so much so that there are now in the world one hundred infidels for every Christian.[43]

Llull often praises Muslims for their piety and sincere devotion to God, and he indicates that Christians would do well to imitate Muslims in this regard.[44] According to Llull, no Muslim could ever be as morally virtuous as the best of Christians, but neither could any Muslim be as wicked as the worst of Christians, and the worst torments in Hell are reserved for the latter.[45] Some Muslims are intelligent, learned, rational, and good philosophers. However, Muslims in general are defective in their faculty of reason.[46] Literate Muslims

---

41   Cf. Rubio, "Thought: The Art," in *Raimundus Lullus,* ROL Suppl. 2:245: "The secret of the Art ... consists of its demonstrating that the accepted world-view [shared by late medieval Jewish, Christian, and Muslim cultures] implies the Christian view of God, so that neither the Trinity nor the Incarnation can be denied without contradicting the cosmic order."

42   *Disputatio fidei et intellectus* 1.2 [6], in *Disputa entre la Fe i l'Enteniment,* (eds.) Batalla and Fidora, 90: Intellect tells Faith the following: "It is said that before Muhammad appeared, all of Africa and moreover Asia and Europe were ruled by Christians, thanks to the preaching of the apostles. But after Muhammad appeared, the Saracens wiped out the Christians in nearly all of those lands, because you are very profound and difficult to believe. The Saracens' belief concerning God is not profound."

43   Ibid., 1.20, 120: "For to believe that God is three and one along with everything that pertains to the Divine Trinity is more difficult than to believe in one God who is not three. People avoid difficulties and are pleased by easy things. That is why for every Christian there are a hundred infidels and gentiles."

44   E.g. *Book of the Lover and the Beloved* 148, in *Romanç d'Evast e Blaquerna,* (eds.) Soler and Santanach, 465: "The lover blamed Christians for not putting the name of his beloved, Jesus Christ, first in their letters, in order to honor him as the Saracens honor Muhammad (who was a deceiver), whom they honor by naming him first in their letters."

45   *Libre de virtuts e de pecats* 3.24 [40], NEORL 1:101–102: "Those men who can have greater faith and greater charity, and are sinners, are greater sinners than those who, because of their religion, cannot have such great faith or such great charity. Those who can have greater faith and greater charity are Christians; thus, Christians can be greater sinners than Saracens or Jews or other men ... It is thus manifest and proven that Christian sinners will have greater pains in Hell than other men."

46   Llull frequently asserts that Muslims (and infidels in general) cannot fully and properly exercise their rational faculty but rather are restricted to exercising the often-erring imaginative faculty; eg. *Libre de contemplació* 77, *Libre de virtuts e de pecats* 3.20 [36].

doubt the veracity of Muhammad and of the Qur'an.[47] Muslims are constantly trying to destroy Christians.[48] Muslim leaders train assassins to help them
accomplish their secular, political aims.[49] It is not safe to preach Christianity or
to criticize Muhammad in Muslim lands.[50]

According to the Muslim sage's discourse in favor of Islam in Book Four of
The Book of the Gentile and the Three Wise Men, Muhammad was a prophet
sent by God to enlighten the people of Mecca and Yathrib, so that they might
know Him and turn away from idolatry. One proof of Muhammad's prophet-
hood is the fact that he was a layperson who could not read or write – yet he
transmitted the Qur'an, a work of unsurpassed wisdom and beauty. Another
proof is the fact that Muhammad is so widely honored and followed throughout the world. Although the gentile does formulate some minor objections to
the Muslim sage's claims, Llull does not in this work make much of an effort to
call those claims into question. Rather, he aims to present, in an undistorted
manner, the Islamic view of their Prophet. In his *Doctrina pueril*, however, in
which Llull speaks in his own voice and for a domestic audience (the work is
addressed to Llull's young son), Muhammad appears in a much more negative
light. Muhammad was a charlatan who, having been taught a false doctrine
patched together from the Old and New Testaments by a renegade Christian
monk, used various sideshow tricks to convince the ignorant and foolish
people of Yathrib that he was God's messenger. Muhammad then converted
Mecca and surrounding territories by means of physical force. Muhammad
was exceedingly lustful: although he had nine wives, he had sexual relations
with many other women. He attracted followers to his sect by promising that in
Paradise they would have sexual relations with women, eat honey, drink wine
and milk, and have beautiful gold and silver palaces, precious gems, and fine
clothing.[51] Interestingly, this portrait of Muhammad appears in the section of
Llull's *Doctrina pueril* "On the Three Laws." Any 13th-century reader would have

---

47   Cf. *Liber de fine* 1.2, in *Darrer llibre*, 81: Llull says that few Muslim "men of letters...believe
      in Muhammad because they know quite well that he was a sinner and that he introduced
      into his Law a great many deceptions;" cf. *Desconhort* 28.

48   Cf. Prologue to the *Liber de fine*, in *Darrer llibre*, 77, and *The Book of the Beasts*, in *Doctor
      Illuminatus*, trans. Bonner, 253, where Dame Reynard tells the following fable: "There was
      once a Christian who had a Saracen whom he trusted very much, and whom he did many
      favors; the Saracen however, being against him because of his religion, was unable to bear
      him any good will, but rather was continually thinking how he could kill him." This is
      a thinly disguised autobiographical reference to the famous episode, recounted in *Vita
      coaetanea*, in which Llull is nearly killed by his Muslim slave: *Ramon Llull: A Contempo-
      rary Life* 2.11–13, trans. Bonner, 39–41.

49   *Liber de fine* 1.1, in *Darrer llibre*, 80.

50   Cf. *Desconhort* 24 and 27.

51   *Doctrina pueril* 71, ORL 1:125–128.

instantly understood the "three Laws" to be Judaism, Christianity, and Islam. But Llull, playing off against this expectation, divides this section of the work into five chapters: "On the Law of Nature," "On the Old Law," "On the New Law," "On Muhammad," and "On Gentiles." The Law of Nature is the rational ethical behavior and obedience to God exhibited by the patriarchs and prophets from Adam to Moses; the Old and New Laws are, of course, Judaism and Christianity. The gentiles are people without a Law or knowledge of God.[52] Pointedly, Llull does not consider Islam to be an authentic Law, that is, a divinely ordained religion. Rather, Muhammad's followers are situated somewhere between those peoples who have authentic Laws and those who have no Law whatsoever. Indeed, throughout his writings Llull consistently maintains that Islam was the invention of Muhammad and that the Qur'an was not a divinely revealed text – in short, that Islam is a counterfeit religion.[53]

Llull was well aware of the Islamic notion that Muhammad (unlike Christ) did not himself need to perform miracles to attract followers, since the Qur'an is itself a miracle, a book that surpasses all human powers of composition:

> The Saracens believe that they have one single necessary and authentic miracle, on the basis of which they affirm that theirs is the true Law. This miracle is, they say, that the Qur'an was dictated in such an elevated style that it is impossible that a human could have dictated it ... Thus they call the Qur'an the word of God. Indeed, I acknowledge that the style of the Qur'an is very poetic.[54]

But, Llull continues, the content or subject matter of the Qur'an is fraudulent and false, a fact which refutes those who say that the book is a miracle. In the preface to his *Cent noms de Déu* (*100 Names of God*) Llull explains that his intention is to write a book whose content surpasses that of the Qur'an, thus proving that the latter was not sent by God:

> Because Saracens think that they can prove that their Law is God-given by the fact that the Qur'an is so beautifully composed that no human could have made anything of the sort, I, Ramon, unworthy, want to try (with God's help) to make this book, in which there is better subject matter [i.e., content] than there is in the Qur'an. This signifies that just as I am able to make a book that has better subject matter than does the Qur'an,

52   Ibid. 72, ORL 1:128–129.
53   On these views regarding Muslims, see Marta M.M. Romano and Óscar de la Cruz, "The Human Realm," in *Raimundus Lullus*, ROL Suppl. 2:435–436 and 2:450–459.
54   *Liber de fine* 1.2, in *Darrer llibre*, 82.

so might someone else make a book that has more beautiful speech than does the Qur'an.[55]

Llull acknowledges that the Qur'an may well be "beautiful speech." But this is faint praise, since he reckons beautiful words to be worth very little compared to beautiful things – and in fact judges the true beauty of words according to the value of their signified meanings.[56] Llull says that his book will surpass the content of the Qur'an because it will contain one hundred names of God (whereas the Qur'an traditionally was said to contain 99). And, showing more than passing familiarity with a set of Islamic *hadith*, Llull insists that the fact that he dares name the hundredth name is not to be construed as a claim that he knows everything. This knowledge of traditions concerning the names of God and the miracle of the Qur'an shows "the extraordinary ... degree to which he is conversant with Islam ... if one compares him with earlier or even contemporary authors."[57]

5.4   The Islamic Roots of Llull's Thought

Considering the degree to which Llull is familiar with Islamic thought, he makes relatively few references to specific Islamic influences, and scholars have failed positively to identify many direct borrowings from Islamic source texts. This is no doubt an effect of Llull's resistance to naming any authors other than himself. But although one cannot say for certain which particular texts by which particular Muslim authors Llull must have read, one can clearly see the pervasive influence of Islamic concepts on Llull's thought.[58] On the most

---

55   In *Obras rimadas de Ramon Lull: escritas en idioma catalan-provenzal*, (ed.) P.J. Gelabert (Palma: 1859), 201.

56   For example, "hate" is not a beautiful word, according to Llull's *Rethorica nova* 2.6.2, in Mark D. Johnston (ed. and trans.), *Ramon Llull's New Rhetoric: Text and Translation of Llull's* Rethorica Nova (Davis, Calif.: 1994), 26.

57   Romano and de la Cruz, "The Human Realm," *Raimundus Lullus*, ROL Suppl. 2:451.

58   For an excellent general survey of this topic, see Dominique Urvoy, "Fins a quin punt el pensament de Ramon Llull va estar marcat per la seva relació amb l'islam," in *Ramon Llull i l'islam: L'inici del diàleg*, 29–47; for a more detailed study, see Urvoy's *Penser l'Islam: Les présupposés islamiques de l'"Art" de Lull* (Paris: 1980). A good summary of identifiable Islamic and Arabic sources of Llull's writings is Sebastián Trías Mercant, "Arabismo e islamología en la obra de Ramón Llull," *La Ciudad de Dios* 28 (1995): 439–452. For a brief but valuable enumeration, see Anna Akasoy and Alexander Fidora, "Ibn Sab'īn and Raimundus Lullus: The Question of the Arabic Sources of Lullus's Logic Revisited," in *Islamic Thought in the Middle Ages: Studies in Text, Transmission and Translation, in Honour of Hans Daiber* (Leiden: 2008), 433–434. For a classic book-length study of this theme from multiple perspectives, see Sebastian Garcías Palou, *Ramon Llull y el Islam* (Palma: 1981).

general and perhaps obvious level, the Art is by design necessarily Islamic (as well as Jewish and Christian). The whole idea behind the strategy of the Art is that its principles are shared by all monotheists. This common stock of ideas, the "collective substrate of the commonplaces of medieval culture, shared by Jews, Christians, and Muslims alike," guarantees that the Art is, in Llull's eyes, Islamic (not exclusively so, but deeply so nonetheless).[59]

The cornerstone of Llull's Art, the set of basic concepts from which everything else proceeds and returns, is what he calls Figure A – a graphic representation of God's essential attributes. This set changes over time (decreasing from sixteen to nine elements) as Llull develops and simplifies the Art.[60] These concepts – which Llull calls the Dignities (*Dignitates*) or Principles – are the axioms that ground Llull's various methods of reasoning. In the final version there are nine Principles: Goodness, Greatness, Eternity (Duration), Power, Wisdom, Will, Virtue, Truth, Glory. Llull's Dignities substantially resemble the divine attributes or Names of God as developed in Islamic theology.[61] More specifically, positing the Dignities as axioms allowed Llull to claim that he had found an entirely new method of reasoning, superior to Aristotelian logic.[62] Whether or not "the origin of [Llull's] *dignitates* is to be found in a Muslim method of contemplation,"[63] it is hard to deny that Llull wanted his Muslim interlocutors to regard those Dignities as identical to the attributes of God as understood in Islamic *kalam* (scholastic theology) and Sufism. Debates over whether Llull's Dignities should be traced back ultimately to Christian neoplatonic, Muslim, or Jewish sources miss the point, since, if the Art is to work as Llull wished, then its Principles must be rooted in all three traditions.[64] Given the absolute

---

59   Rubio, "Thought: The Art," in *Raimundus Lullus*, ROL Suppl. 2:254; cf. Bonner, *AL* 101.

60   See chapter four in this volume for detailed analysis of these changes.

61   See Charles Lohr, "The Islamic 'Beautiful Names of God' and the Lullian Art," in *Jews, Muslims, and Christians in and around the Crown of Aragon: Essays in Honour of Professor Elena Lourie*, (ed.) Harvey J. Hames (Leiden: 2004), 197–205, esp. 198: "among the 99 traditional [Islamic] names we can find correspondences for all the nine *dignitates* in the final version of Lull's Art." Moreover, Lohr argues that several aspects of Llull's characterization of the divine attributes, having no precedents in the Christian tradition, are rooted in distinctions from the Islamic tradition. On the development of doctrines concerning the divine attributes in Islam and Christianity, see H.A. Wolfson, "The Muslim Attributes and the Christian Trinity," *The Harvard Theological Review* 49 (1956): 1–18.

62   See Josep M. Ruiz Simon, *L'Art de Ramon Llull i la teoria escolàstica de la ciència* (Barcelona: 1999), esp. 238–295.

63   Lohr, "The Islamic 'Beautiful Names of God' and the Lullian Art," 197.

64   Bonner, *AL* 284: "Whether [the Dignities] had their 'origins' in the divine names of (PseudoDionysius the Areopagite, the primordial causes of John Scotus Eriugena, the Islamic *hadrās*, or the Judaic *sefirot* ... is perhaps less fruitful than thinking of them as something that would set up resonances with the three religions." On the Dignities as rooted in all

centrality of the Dignities in Llull's system, it is not wrong to recognize that system as rooted in Islamic thought.

Closely related to the Dignities and perhaps equally important in Llull's thought is his notion of the correlatives, the key concept in his formulation of a "dynamic ontology ... in which being and activity are inseparable."[65] This concept is the ground for his most compelling demonstrations of the Trinity and the Incarnation. For Llull, a being is not simply an essence in act (i.e., something that actually *is*); rather, co-essential to any being is its activity: something is what it does. God, for example, is not simply God; rather, God "Godifies;" similarly, lions "lionify" and plants "plantify."[66] Thus the being of anything implies three things: the thing that acts, the thing acted on, and the action itself. The Trinitarian implications of this concept are quite apparent. Man, for instance, defined by Llull as "the animal that manifies," implies man's active power to manify, man's passive potential to be manified, and man's activity or operation of manifying.[67] Again, some scholars point to Christian sources as likely influences on Llull's concept of the correlatives, while others point to Islamic antecedents.[68] It is hard to deny that Llull was influenced by Augustine's teachings, including the following from *De Trinitate*: "Love is love of something, and love loves something. Therefore, there are three: the loving, what is loved, and love."[69] Nonetheless, one could scarcely point to a more exact analogue to Llull's notion of the correlatives than Avicenna's "The First [i.e., God] is Intellect, is intellected, and intellects" – a phrasing that Llull repeats nearly

---

three monotheisms, see Mayer, "Ramon Llull i el diàleg indispensable," in *Ramon Llull i l'islam: L'inici del diàleg*, 48–60.

65   Bonner, *AL* 108. See chapter four in this volume for a detailed explanation of Llull's theory of "innate correlatives" in every being.

66   See Alexander Fidora, "From 'Manifying' to 'Pegasizing:' Ramon Llull's Theory of Definitions Between Arabic and Modern Logic," *Mirabilia* 7 (2007): 79.

67   Akasoy and Fidora, "Ibn Sab'īn and Raimundus Lullus," 443: "According to this theory, every entity is constituted by a threefold structure, i.e., an agent, a patient and an act. Divine goodness *bonitas*, for instance, implies a *bonificativum*, a *bonificabile* and a *bonificare*, and so do the remaining divine attributes. The same holds for the created realm, insofar as creation is an image of the divine. Thus the 'essential properties' of man—as Lullus sometimes calls the correlatives—are *homificativum*, *homificabile* and *homificare*, and those of [man's] understanding [are]: *intellectivum*, *intelligibile*, and *intelligere*."

68   Akasoy and Fidora, "Ibn Sab'īn and Raimundus Lullus," 443–444, remarking that "the correlatives occupy a very prominent position in debates around possible Islamic influences on Lullus," point out multiple possible sources in Islamic philosophy and theology. For Augustine's influence on Llull's correlatives, see Robert Pring-Mill, "The Trinitarian World Picture of Ramon Lull," *Romanistisches Jahrbuch* 7 (1955–56): 229–256.

69   Augustine, *De Trinitate* 8.10.14, cited in Akasoy and Fidora, "Ibn Sab'īn and Raimundus Lullus," 445.

verbatim.[70] Whether or not Llull knew Avicenna directly, he certainly knew al-Ghazālī, who himself mastered Avicenna and reports that according to the philosophers "knowledge, knower, and thing known are one."[71] But again, there is little need in trying to decide whether the correlatives are Christian or Islamic, since Llull developed this notion precisely so that it would appeal to adherents of Augustine as well as those of Avicenna.[72] At any rate, efforts to deny that the correlatives are rooted in Islamic thinking are not convincing, especially given that Llull, in introducing his *Compendium seu commentum Artis demonstrativae* to scholastic philosophers at Paris in 1289, referred to this novel doctrine as "an Arabic manner of speaking."[73]

It is no exaggeration to say that the two most important foundations of the Art – the Dignities and the correlatives – are conceived by Llull to be essentially Islamic. More precisely, one might say (to borrow an adjective from Llull) that the Christian and Islamic traditions are "co-essential" in the formation of the Art. Christianity teaches two salvific truths that are denied by Islam – namely, the Trinity and the Incarnation. These truths, however, are not principles, premises, or foundations of the Art; instead they are conclusions proven by the Art. The Art itself, prior to whatever conclusions it may be used to produce, is essentially (or rather, co-essentially) Islamic.

There is general consensus that Llull was to some significant degree influenced by the great Islamic theologian al-Ghazālī (d. 1111 AD).[74] This is undeniably true, given that Llull's first written work, the *Compendium logicae Alguzelis*, is in part based upon some of al-Ghazālī's writings on logic.[75]

---

70   Avicenna, *Metaphysics of 'The Healing'* 8.6, trans. Michael E. Marmura (Provo: 2004).

71   Al-Ghazālī, *The Ninety-Nine Beautiful Names of God*, trans. David Burrell and Nazih Daher (Cambridge: 1992), 165.

72   For the notion of Llull's correlatives as a joining together of Christian and Islamic views, see Charles Lohr, "Ramon Llull and Thirteenth-Century Religious Dialogue," in *Diálogo filosófico-religioso entre Cristianismo, Judaísmo e Islamismo durante la Edad Media en la península Iberica* (Turnhout: 1994), 118–123.

73   See Fernando Domínguez Reboiras and Jordi Gayà Estelrich, "Life," in *Raimundus Lullus*, ROL Suppl. 2 (Turnhout: 2008), 60. On Llull's Arabisms, see Trías Mercant, "Arabismo e islamología en la obra de Ramón Llull," 449–450.

74   See Róbert Simon, "Remarks on Ramon Lull's Relation to Islam," *Acta Orientalia Academiae Scientiarum Hungaricae* 51 (1998): 21–29, esp. 24: "[Llull's] vast, though unusual and unscholastic erudition was rooted in the Classical Islamic *kalam* shaped by al-Ash'ari and mainly by the great al-Ghazali who was one of [Llull's] most important spiritual masters." See also J.N. Hillgarth, "The Attitudes of Ramon Llull and Alfonso X of Castile to Islam," in *Actas del V Congreso Internacional de Filosofía Medieval* (Madrid: 1979), 825–830.

75   For details of this work, see Fernando Domínguez Reboiras, "Works," in *Raimundus Lullus*, ROL Suppl. 2 (Turnhout: 2008), 135.

But does al-Ghazālī's influence on Llull's thought extend in more global and essential ways – and, if so, in what manners?

The path to an answer is indicated by one of al-Ghazālī's nicknames: "the Proof of Islam." This nickname does not so much mean that the miracle of al-Ghazālī's brilliant achievements stand as evidence in support of Islam; more pertinently, it stems from the fact that al-Ghazālī does not shy away from claiming that the articles of his faith can be *proven* by rational demonstration. This is precisely Llull's position with respect to the Christian faith. Al-Ghazālī, like the Asharite school of *kalam* from which he emerged, maintains that one can prove "the basic articles of Muslim religious belief without formal appeal to any premise or thesis that is taken from religious belief as such."[76] Regarding himself as one who "only accepts necessary truths" (like Llull's "necessary reasons"), al-Ghazālī has little respect for those (whom he calls "conformists" or "people of opinion") who think that citing authorities or the views of others is sufficient evidence in support of their positions.[77] Similarly embracing rationalism and very vehemently rejecting argumentation by recourse to the views of others, Llull in a general but very deep sense aligns himself with al-Ghazālī's brand of *kalam*.

Llull and al-Ghazālī recognize multiple methods of reasoning. Both, however, give a privileged place to one approach: reasoning grounded in reflection on the divine attributes, such as Llull's Dignities or al-Ghazālī's Names of God. Both are very careful to insist that the truths that one can attain through rational demonstration do not ever approach knowledge of God's essence. Rather, God's essence remains always above the grasp of human reason. Through reflecting, one can posit God's attributes and what those attributes must entail: God must be eternal, powerful, knowing, etc., and various truths must necessarily follow. But such knowledge does not amount to knowledge of God's essence. Both Llull and al-Ghazālī reserve a term for this unnamable essence, a "non-name" that involves (probably not coincidentally) the letter A. For Llull, this is the letter at the center of his Figure A, around which the letters B, C, D, E, F, G, H, I, K (each representing one of the nine Dignities) are arranged. In the Figure A, only the letter A is without name or definition, no doubt a way of referring to God's essence. For al-Ghazālī, God's "non-name" is *Allāh*. In his *The Ninety-Nine Beautiful Names of God*, al-Ghazālī begins his enumeration with the name *Allāh*, which, he says, is "indicative of the very being" of divinity and thus "does not need to be defined by something other than it, but rather the

---

76   Richard M. Frank, *Al-Ghazali and the Ash'arite School* (Durham, North Carolina: 1994), 5.

77   Al-Ghazālī, *The Rescuer from Error*, in *Medieval Islamic Philosophical Writings*, (ed.) Muhammad Ali Khalidi (Cambridge: 2005), 65.

others are defined by relation to it."[78] When we read in al-Ghazālī's text that *Allāh* "unites the attributes of divinity" and is the "subject of the attributes of lordship,"[79] it is difficult not to think of Llull's Figure A, in which the A (= al-Ghazālī's *Allāh*) is precisely that which *unites* and is the *subject of* the attributes (i.e., Dignities).[80]

Both Llull and al-Ghazālī were attacked for allowing autonomous human reason too much purchase on divine truth. They both defend themselves by making a distinction between knowing God and knowing things that pertain to God. Al-Ghazālī asserts both that one can know and that one cannot know God: "For I say: if one were to say: 'I know only God,' he would be right, and if he said: 'I do not know God,' he would be correct."[81] These two statements are not contradictory because they refer to two different kinds of knowing. First, we can have "knowledge that pertains to God – great and glorious – and [that] has for its object names derived from the attributes, which do not enter into the reality of the essence and its quiddity;" second, "knowing something is to know its essential reality and its quiddity, not the names derived from it."[82] Humans can know God in the manner of the first kind of knowing but not in the manner of the second. Llull defends himself against charges of heretical hyper-rationalism by making a distinction between knowing God through "apprehension" (grasping something in a partial and finite manner) and knowing God though "comprehension" (knowledge of a thing's essence): humans can use reason to attain the first but not the second kind of knowledge.[83]

Llull and al-Ghazālī also share in common a mistrust of religious faith in the sense of mere belief, the unthinking acceptance of hearsay and inherited dogmas. Al-Ghazālī dismisses one's simply accepting (without reasoned reflection) the religion of one's birth as servile conformism:

> The fetters of servile conformism fell away from me, and inherited beliefs lost their hold on me, when I was still young. For I saw that the children of Christians always grew up embracing Christianity, and the children of

---

78   Al-Ghazālī, *The Ninety-Nine Beautiful Names of God*, trans. David Burrell and Nazih Daher (Cambridge: 1992), 52.

79   Ibid., 51.

80   See Lohr, "The Islamic 'Beautiful Names of God' and the Lullian Art," 204.

81   Al-Ghazālī, *The Ninety-Nine Beautiful Names of God*, 36.

82   Ibid., 37.

83   Cf. *Disputa entre la Fe i l'Enteniment*, (eds.) Batalla and Fidora, 59 and 95; *Llibre de la disputa del clergue Pere i de Ramon, el fantàstic*, (ed.) Badia, 243; and *Declaratio Raimundi*, trans. Cécile Bonmariage and Michel Lambert, in *Lulle et la condemnation de 1277: La Déclaration de Raymond écrite sous forme de dialogue* (Louvain: 2006), 16.

Jews always grew up adhering to Judaism, and the children of Muslims always grew up following the religion of Islam.[84]

Al-Ghazālī restricts the use of logic (rational argumentation) to an elite group of learned intellectuals, who will no longer disagree if they follow the methods that he proposes.[85] As for "common people...the dull-witted" who "do not have [enough] intelligence to understand realities [truths]" – such people should be shielded from rational argumentation, since the Book and preaching alone will suffice for them.[86] Similarly, Llull sometimes represents inherited religious faith as a servile binding and as an accommodation for the weak intellects of the masses.[87]

5.5   Llull, the Philosophers, and Transcendence by Faith

Llull maintains an ambivalent relation to the great Islamic rationalist philosophers such as al-Farabi, Avicenna, and Averroes. On the one hand, he realizes that it is largely thanks to this tradition that there might exist one of the necessary preconditions for the success of the Art – namely, a sizeable number of powerful Muslim intellectuals inclined to interpret their religion according to the tenets of demonstrative reason. Llull's Muslim sage of the *Book of the Gentile and the Three Wise Men*, speaking of differing Islamic interpretations of Paradise, ranging from the strictly literalist to the philosophical, recognizes the danger posed to the faith by an unchecked impulse to rationalism:

> But there are others [i.e., the philosophers] among us who take this glory [i.e., Paradise] morally and interpret it spiritually, saying that Muhammad was speaking metaphorically to people who were backward and without understanding; and in order to inspire them with a love of God

---

84   Al-Ghazālī, *Deliverance from Error*, trans. R.J. McCarthy (Louisville: 1980), 55.

85   See Al-Ghazālī, "The Correct Balance," in *Deliverance from Error*, trans. R.J. McCarthy (Louisville: 1980), 271–272.

86   Ibid., 272.

87   See *Disputa entre la Fe i l'Enteniment*, (eds.) Batalla and Fidora, 92, where a personified Understanding (*Intellectus*) represents herself as "healthy and free" when understanding profound things but "bound" (*ligata*) when merely believing things; here Llull is clearly playing on an etymology of "religion" as *re-ligare* ("to bind fast"). Cf. ibid., 102–103, and 270–271, where *Intellectus* says that Faith is useful for ignorant people and those who cannot understand profound things. As so often in Llull's dialogues, one of the interlocutors clearly gives voice to Llull's own viewpoint; in this case the Llullian interlocutor is *Intellectus*, not Faith.

he recounted the above-mentioned glory. And therefore those who believe this say that in Paradise there will be no glory of eating or of lying
with women, nor of the other things mentioned above. And these men
are natural philosophers and great scholars, yet they are men who in
some ways do not follow too well the dictates of our religion, and this
is why we consider them as heretics, who have arrived at their heresy
by studying logic and natural science. And therefore it has been established among us that no man dare teach logic or natural science
publicly.[88]

Llull shares with the philosophers their high standard of certainty: truths must
be attained by demonstration and not merely given by opinion or authority.
And Llull wishes to exploit Arab philosophy's demand for demonstrative certainty in a way that will benefit Christianity and thus, in Llull's view, the world
as a whole.

On the other hand, Llull thought that Arabic Aristotelianism, while a useful
ally in his effort to destroy the Islamic faith, was also potentially deadly when
handled by Christians. Thus a substantial portion of Llull's writings, especially
in his later years, was directed against those philosophers in the Latin West
(the so-called Latin Averroists or Radical Aristotelians) who seemed to follow
the Arab philosophers in granting virtually complete autonomy to natural human reason unaided by faith.[89] Llull's chief complaint against Averroism was
its reticence or timidity regarding knowledge of entities existing above the natural, physical world – immaterial metaphysical entities such as angels and, of
course, God. Although in theory Arabic philosophy allowed for the possibility
of metaphysical knowledge (such knowledge was nothing less than "salvation"
in the true sense), in practice this possibility (and thus the very possibility of
salvation) was quietly denied. By limiting human knowledge to natural science (science that must always begin with premises attainable through sense
perception), Averroism, in Llull's view, leads to an improper separation of reason from faith, philosophy from theology, the human from the divine. The Art
overcomes this separation by providing principles common to all sciences,

88   *Book of the Gentile* 4.5, in *Doctor Illuminatus*, (ed.) Bonner, 160.
89   Llull's numerous anti-Averroist texts include the *Declaratio Raimundi*, a dialogue between
      Llull and a philosopher named Socrates, and the *Liber natalis pueri parvuli Christi Jesu*,
      (ed.) and trans. Luca Obertello (Florence: 1991). The *Breviculum* produced by Llull's Pari-
      sian devotees after his death includes fascinating miniatures depicting Llull's army sur-
      passing the armies of Averroes and Aristotle: on these illustrations, see *Llibre de la disputa
      del clergue Pere i de Ramon, el fantàstic*, ed. Badia, 93–101, and Pere Villalba i Varneda,
      Ramon Llull, escriptor i filòsof de la diferència (Barcelona: 2015).

including philosophy and theology, physics and metaphysics (which thus now share common ground). Llull also argues that Aristotelian methods of demonstration, which rely on arguments derived from sense-perception and based on knowledge of natural causes and effects, are surpassed by his new mode of demonstration *per aequiparantiam*, the premises of which are provided by reflection upon the equivalence or concordance of God's attributes (Dignities). Llull claims that his Art is better than Aristotelian philosophy and its most advanced Arabic development, Averroism, because it is grounded in and guaranteed by metaphysical truth.[90]

Llull insists that rationalist philosophy needs to be guided by faith and vice-versa.[91] This is not, of course, the mere faith (conformity to received opinion) that Llull accepts only as an unavoidable accommodation for the illiterate masses. But neither does faith for Llull function as it does for the Arabic philosophers or for Aquinas and the mainstream of Scholastic philosophy. Faith is not to be understood here in a modern sense as a subjective feeling or willed commitment. Rather, faith means an authoritative revelation, a set of crucial truths provided by one's religious scriptures and traditions. Llull, the Arab philosophers, and Aquinas all acknowledge the vital necessity of faith in this sense. But they differ widely on the purpose and nature of this faith. The question of this difference can best be posed as follows: what knowledge does faith (authoritative revelation) provide that natural human reason, left to its own resources, cannot attain? For the Arab philosophers, following al-Farabi, who established this as a fundamental principle of rational philosophy, the answer is, strictly speaking, nothing. The Qur'an provides representations, through images and symbols, of the same truths known by philosophers through human reason. Although Muhammad and other prophets may well receive truths instantly, in a flash of illumination, they receive nothing that cannot be fully worked out through the labor of philosophical study and nothing that does not harmonize with philosophy. For Aquinas, faith tells us truths – of the sort that cannot possibly ever be reached through philosophy – about things that we cannot understand (let alone demonstrate through "necessary reasons") until we enjoy the beatific vision of God in the afterlife. Such things are supernatural, metaphysical things that transcend the capacities of Aristotelian reasoning, which always starts with sense-perception of natural things. Aquinas, bracketing off the articles of faith from rational demonstration, promotes

---

90   See Ruiz Simon, *L'Art de Ramon Llull i la teoria escolàstica de la ciència*, 238–391, and Domínguez Reboiras, *Ramon Llull: El mejor libro del mundo*, 276–281.

91   Cf. *Disputa entre la Fe i l'Enteniment* 1.2.8, (eds.) Batalla and Fidora, 92, where Intellect tells Faith that "you are in me and I in you."

that very division of labor between philosophy and theology, the physical and the metaphysical, the human and the divine, that Llull vehemently opposes as Averroist.

For the Arab philosophers, faith does not transcend reason, while for Aquinas it does. Llull's position is different: faith motivates reason to transcend itself. But this fresh view gained by reason through its self-transcendence is itself a fully rational view. For faith merely provokes reason into asking whether those truths that it takes to be certain really are such. The result of reason's self-transcendence is not illumination concerning some transcendent realm above reason but rather a more truthful understanding of what accords with the rational. We can end up with intellection (true knowledge, science) of things that we once considered to be irrational or beyond reason's grasp. Transcendence, for Llull, is that point after which we now consider things to be rational that we previously considered contradictory to reason. Faith is that which pushes us to suppose possibilities; it challenges reason to check itself, to move beyond self-complacency. Reason without the challenges posed by faith would never fully develop its powers. Articles of faith are truths that one supposes, just for the sake of argument, could be true. The Art allows such suppositions (which appear to us as nothing more than authoritative opinions) to be put to the test of demonstrative truth. Some sets of suppositions, some faiths, will pass the test, while others will not. In putting suppositions to the test, reason will improve and transcend itself, finding some things to be rational, such as Trinity and Incarnation, that it previously had held to be irrational. Unlike the Arab philosophers, Llull does maintain that faith can provide something more than can be attained by philosophy alone. But unlike Aquinas, Llull maintains that this something more is itself philosophical. Faith will not contradict or exceed the grasp of a properly established system of human reasoning, namely Llull's Great Universal Art of Finding Truth.

Works Cited

Primary Works
Al-Ghazālī, *Deliverance from Error*, trans. R.J. McCarthy (Louisville: 1980).
Al-Ghazālī, *The Ninety-Nine Beautiful Names of God*, trans. David Burrell and Nazih Daher (Cambridge: 1992).
Al-Ghazālī, *The Rescuer from Error*, in *Medieval Islamic Philosophical Writings*, (ed.) Muhammad Ali Khalidi (Cambridge: 2005).
Avicenna, *The Metaphysics of "The Healing,"* trans. Michael E. Marmura (Provo: 2004).
Nahmanide, *La dispute de Barcelone*, trans. Éric Smilévitch and Luc Ferrier (Paris: 1984).

Primary Works: Llull

Book of the Gentile and the Three Wise Men, in *Doctor Illuminatus: A Ramon Llull Reader*, (ed.) and trans. Bonner, Anthony (Princeton: 1993), 73–172.

The Book of the Beasts, in *Doctor Illuminatus: A Ramon Llull Reader*, (ed.) and trans. Anthony Bonner (Princeton: 1993), 239–288.

Cent noms de Déu, in *Obras rimadas de Ramon Lull: escritas en idioma catalan-provenzal*, (ed.) Gelabert, P.J. (Palma: 1859), 176–304.

Declaratio Raimundi, trans. Cécile Bonmariage and Michel Lambert, in *Lulle et la condemnation de 1277: La Déclaration de Raymond écrite sous forme de dialogue* (Louvain: 2006).

Desconhort, ORL 19:219–254.

Disputatio fidei et intellectus, in *Disputatio fidei et intellectus/Disputa entre la Fe i l'Enteniment*, (eds.) and trans. Josep Batalla and Alexander Fidora (Turnhout: 2011).

Doctrina pueril, ORL 1:1–199.

Liber de acquisitione Terrae Sanctae, trans. Pere Llabrés, *Darrer llibre sobre la conquesta de Terra Santa* (Barcelona: 2002).

Liber de fine, ROL 9:249–291.

Liber de passagio, (eds.) Blanca Garí and Fernando Domínguez Reboiras, ROL 18: 255–353.

Liber disputationis Petri clerici et Raimundi sive Phantasticus, in *Llibre de la disputa del clergue Pere i de Ramon, el fantàstic. Llibre de la ciutat del món,* (ed.) and trans. Lola Badia (Santa Coloma de Queralt: 2008), 107–179.

Liber disputationis Raimundi christiani et Homeri saraceni, ROL 22:172–264.

Liber natalis pueri parvuli Christi Jesu, (ed.) and trans. Luca Obertello, *Il libro del natale/Il lamento della filosofia* (Florence: 1991).

Libre de meravelles, (ed.) Salvador Galmés, 4 vols. (Barcelona: 1931–34).

Llibre de contemplació: antologia, (ed.) Josep E. Rubio (Barcelona: 2009).

Llibre de la disputa del clergue Pere i de Ramon, el fantàstic. Llibre de la ciutat del món, (ed.) and trans. Lola Badia (Santa Coloma de Queralt: 2008).

Llibre de virtuts e de pecats, (ed.) Fernando Domínguez Reboiras, NEORL 1.

Rethorica nova, (ed.) and trans. Mark D. Johnston, *Ramon Llull's New Rhetoric: Text and Translation of Llull's* Rethorica Nova (Davis, Calif.: 1994).

Romanç d'Evast e Blaquerna, (eds.) Albert Soler and Joan Santanach, NEORL 8.

Vita coaetanea, in *Ramon Llull: A Contemporary Life,* trans. Anthony Bonner (Barcelona: 2010).

Secondary Works

Akasoy, Anna and Alexander Fidora, "Ibn Sabʿīn and Raimundus Lullus: The Question of the Arabic Sources of Lullus's Logic Revisited," in *Islamic Thought in the Middle Ages: Studies in Text, Transmission and Translation, in Honour of Hans Daiber* (Leiden: 2008), 433–458.

Bonner, Anthony, "La disputa interreligiosa, la solució enginyosa de Ramon Llull," in *Ramon Llull i l'islam: L'inici del diàleg,* (ed.) Maria Àngels Roque (Barcelona: 2008), 212–224.

Bonner, Anthony, "What Was Llull Up To?," in *Ramon Llull: From the Ars Magna to Artificial Intelligence,* (eds.) Alexander Fidora and Carles Sierra (Barcelona: 2011), 5–24.

Caputo, Nina, *Nahmanides in Medieval Catalonia: History, Community, and Messianism* (Notre Dame, Indiana: 2007).

Domínguez Reboiras, Fernando, *Ramon Llull: El mejor libro del mundo* (Barcelona: 2016).

Domínguez Reboiras, Fernando, "Works," in *Raimundus Lullus: An Introduction to his Life, Works, and Thought,* (eds.) Alexander Fidora and Josep E. Rubio, ROL Suppl. 2:125–242.

Domínguez Reboiras, Fernando and Jordi Gayà Estelrich, "Life," in *Raimundus Lullus: An Introduction to his Life, Works, and Thought,* (eds.) Alexander Fidora and Josep E. Rubio, ROL Suppl. 2:3–124.

Ensenyat, Gabriel, "Pacifisme i croada en Ramon Llull," in *Ramon Llull i l'islam: L'inici del diàleg,* (ed.) Maria Àngels Roque (Barcelona: 2008), 232–245.

Fidora, Alexander, "Combinatòria i reciprocitat: Una nota sobre la vigència de l'Art lul·liana," in *Ramon Llull i l'islam: L'inici del diàleg,* (ed.) Maria Àngels Roque (Barcelona: 2008), 196–205.

Fidora, Alexander, "From 'Manifying' to 'Pegasizing:' Ramon Llull's Theory of Definitions Between Arabic and Modern Logic," *Mirabilia* 7 (2007): 72–86.

Frank, Richard M., *Al-Ghazali and the Ash'arite School* (Durham, North Carolina: 1994).

Garcías Palou, Sebastian, *Ramon Llull y el Islam* (Palma: 1981).

Hillgarth, J.N., "The Attitudes of Ramon Llull and Alfonso X of Castile to Islam," in *Actas del V Congreso Internacional de Filosofía Medieval* (Madrid: 1979), 825–830.

Lohr, Charles, "The Islamic 'Beautiful Names of God' and the Lullian Art," in *Jews, Muslims, and Christians in and around the Crown of Aragon: Essays in Honour of Professor Elena Lourie,* (ed.) Harvey J. Hames (Leiden: 2004), 197–205.

Lohr, Charles, "Ramon Llull and Thirteenth-Century Religious Dialogue," in *Diálogo filosófico-religioso entre Cristianismo, Judaísmo e Islamismo durante la Edad Media en la península Iberica* (Turnhout: 1994), 117–129.

Mayer, Annemarie C., "Ramon Llull i el diàleg indispensable," in *Ramon Llull i l'islam: L'inici del diàleg,* (ed.) Maria Àngels Roque (Barcelona: 2008), 48–60.

Nederman, Cary J., *Worlds of Difference: European Discourses of Toleration c. 1100–c. 1550* (University Park, Penns.: 2000).

Porsia, Franco, *Progetti di Crociata: Il* De fine *di Raimondo Lullo* (Taranto: 2005).

Pring-Mill, Robert, "The Trinitarian World Picture of Ramon Lull," *Romanistisches Jahrbuch* 7 (1955–56): 229–256.

Raimundus Lullus: An Introduction to his Life, Works, and Thought, (eds.) Alexander Fidora and Josep E. Rubio, ROL Suppl. 2 (Turnhout: 2008).

Ramon Llull and Islam: the Beginning of Dialogue/Ramon Llull y el islam: el inicio del diálogo, (ed.) Maria Àngels Roque (Barcelona: 2008).

Ramon Llull i l'islam: L'inici del diàleg, (ed.) Maria Àngels Roque (Barcelona: 2008).

Romano, Marta M.M. and Óscar de la Cruz, "The Human Realm," in *Raimundus Lullus: An Introduction to His Life, Works, and Thought*, (eds.) Alexander Fidora and Josep E. Rubio, ROL Suppl. 2 (Turnhout: 2008), 413–459.

Rubio, Josep E. "Thought: The Art," in *Raimundus Lullus: An Introduction to His Life, Works, and Thought*, (eds.) Alexander Fidora and Josep E. Rubio, ROL Suppl. 2 (Turnhout: 2008), 243–311.

Ruiz Simon, Josep M., *L'Art de Ramon Llull i la teoria escolàstica de la ciència* (Barcelona: 1999).

Santanach, Joan, "Sobre el *Llibre del gentil i la coherència doctrinal de Ramon Llull*," in *Ramon Llull i l'islam: L'inici del diàleg*, (ed.) Maria Àngels Roque (Barcelona: 2008), 225–231.

Simon, Róbert, "Remarks on Ramon Lull's Relation to Islam," *Acta Orientalia Academiae Scientiarum Hungaricae* 51 (1998): 21–29.

Tolan, John V., *Saracens: Islam in the Medieval European Imagination* (New York: 2002).

Trías Mercant, Sebastián, "Arabismo e islamología en la obra de Ramón Llull," *La Ciudad de Dios* 28 (1995): 439–452.

Urvoy, Dominique, "Fins a quin punt el pensament de Ramon Llull va estar marcat per la seva relació amb l'islam," in *Ramon Llull i l'islam: L'inici del diàleg*, (ed.) Maria Àngels Roque (Barcelona: 2008), 29–47.

Urvoy, Dominique, *Penser l'Islam: Les présupposés islamiques de l'"Art" de Lull* (Paris: 1980).

Urvoy, Dominique, "Ramon Lull et l'Islam," *Islamochristiana* 7 (1981): 127–146.

Vega, Amador, "Ramon Llull: L'art d'inventar la veritat," in *Ramon Llull i l'islam: L'inici del diàleg*, (ed.) Maria Àngels Roque (Barcelona: 2008), 207–211.

Varneda, Pere Villalba i, *Ramon Llull, escriptor i filòsof de la diferència* (Barcelona: 2015).

Wolfson, H.A., "The Muslim Attributes and the Christian Trinity," *The Harvard Theological Review* 49 (1956): 1–18.

CHAPTER 6

Llull and Inter-Faith Dialogue

Annemarie C. Mayer

6.1 Procurator Infidelium

Did Ramon Llull rightly style himself as both an "advocate to the infidels" (*procurator infidelium*)[1] and an "Arabic Christian" (*christianus arabicus*)?[2] The experience of religious plurality was indeed with him from the cradle, as it were, in Majorca. Promptly upon his conversion, he deliberately chose the tasking of being an advocate to the infidels for his future life. Yet to what extent is Llull's theology, especially his doctrines and teachings on God, communicable to other religions? This chapter aims to discuss this question.

Llull was certainly not exaggerating when he wrote at the beginning of his early work, the *Libre del gentil e dels tres savis* [Book of the Gentile and the Three Wise Men], composed around 1274:

> Since for a long time we have had dealings with unbelievers and have heard their false opinions and errors; and in order that they may give praise to our Lord God and enter upon the path of eternal salvation, I ... hereby wish to exert myself to the utmost – trusting in the help of the Most High – by finding a new method and new reasons through which those in error might be shown the path to glory without end and the means of avoiding infinite suffering.[3]

As *procurator infidelium* Llull is concerned with the religious Other, and this not only regarding their earthly well-being but above all regarding their eternal

---

1 Cf. Llull, *Blaquerna* 61.4, ORL 9:211; *Disputatio fidelis et infidelis* Prol., MOG 4:377; as well as *Liber mirandarum demonstrationum*, MOG 2:341.

2 Cf. Llull, *Liber de fine* 1.2, ROL 9:256, and *Disputatio Raymundi Christiani et Hamar Saraceni* Prol., ROL 22:172.

3 *Libre del gentil e dels tres savis* Prol., NEORL 2:5–6: "Con ab los inffeels ajam participat lonch de temps, e ajam enteses lurs ffalses oppinions e errors, per ço que ells donen laor de nostre seynor Deus, e que vinguen a via de salut perdurable, yo ... me vull essforssar ab tots mos poders, conffiant en la ajuda del Altisme, a enssercar novella manera e novelles rahons per les quals poguessen esser endressats los errats a gloria qui no a ffi, e que ffugisen a inffinits trebals"; trans. Bonner, *SW* 1:110.

© KONINKLIJKE BRILL NV, LEIDEN, 2019 | DOI:10.1163/9789004379671_007

salvation. Today one cannot simply dismiss Llull's concept by pointing out that Llull's goal was to convert non-Christians and that his conclusions are therefore questionable:

> Even if he does not differ much from his contemporaries in terms of the object of his mission and the call to convert, yet he differed greatly with special regard to method, and as regards the depth of his knowledge about and his assessment of the otherness of the other.[4]

Moreover, conversion at that time was the universally accepted goal on all sides. This is in so far understandable and not to be rejected right away, as none of the representatives of any religion in those days could imagine that non-Christians, non-Jews or non-Muslims would be able to obtain eternal salvation. Seen from the perspective of the history of theology, any theologically justifiable openness in matters of soteriology was sadly lacking in those days. In Llull's time, therefore, any interreligious open-mindedness to dialogue would inevitably encounter the inexorable stumbling block of the unquestionable certainty that eternal damnation awaited all those who did not belong to one's own religion. Thus, Llull says of his gentile:

> While the gentile was worshiping our Lord God in this way, to his soul came remembrance of his land, of his father, of his mother and of the lack of faith in which they had died; and he remembered all the people living in that land who were on the path to eternal fire without realizing it, and on which they found themselves for the lack of grace.[5]

Neither the religions of his time nor Llull himself must be reproached for holding this conviction.

As a counterpoint to religious antagonism, Llull lays out his own unique vision of inter-faith dialogue; this can be found in the *Libre del gentil e dels tres*

---

4   *Libre del gentil e dels tres savis*, trans. Theodor Pindl, *Das Buch vom Heiden und den drei Weisen* (Stuttgart: 1998), 294–295: "Auch wenn er sich in der Zielsetzung, dem Missions- und Bekehrungsauftrag, von seinen Zeitgenossen nicht unterscheidet, so doch wesentlich in der Methode, der guten Kenntnis und der Bewertung der Andersheit des Anderen."

5   *Libre del gentil* 1. Epil., NEORL 2:44: "Dementre que lo gentil adorava en esta manera nostre seyner Deus, a sa anima vench remembrament de sa terra e de son pare e de sa mare, e de la error e de la inffidelitat en la qual eren morts; e membrá con tantes de gents qui eren en aquella térra e eren en via de ffoc perdurable, la qual via innoraven, e en la qual eren per deffalliment de gracia"; trans. Bonner, *SW* 1:147.

savis. Llull there cleverly has it described by one of the Wise Men of whom it remains undisclosed to which of the three religions he belongs:

> And just as there is only one God, Father, Creator, and Lord of everything that exists, so that all peoples could unite and become one people, and that people be on the path to salvation, under one faith and one religion, giving glory and praise to our Lord God. Think, gentlemen, ... of the harm that comes from men not belonging to a single sect, and of the good that would come from everyone being beneath one faith and one religion.[6]

But let us be clear, for Llull himself, this religion has a lot to do with Christianity and Llull's aim is not to establish belief in a general monotheistic religion.[7] However, precisely because he strives to spread *Christianity*, it is only reasonable for us to ask what place Llull ascribes to Islam and Judaism in achieving his vision.

To realize his vision, Llull developed, in his dialogues with non-Christians, his own method, which, he insisted, consisted of new arguments that would lead them thus upon the path of salvation, as in the Gentile's prayer, cited above. In other words, Llull was sure he had something new to offer, convinced as he was of its universal efficacy. Llull based his method on his vision of the unity of all peoples who, united in one faith, know, love, fear and honor God. This is the actual purpose of all human beings and all religions converge in this chief end "to love, know, fear, and serve God."[8] This note of worshipping God in common, irrespective of minor divergences of cultural tradition, echoes across Llull's works.

Converting other faiths through public disputation was part of the spirit of Llull's age: this ideal, for instance, formed the basis for founding the Dominican Order. It was in the final analysis based on the self-evidence of truth which emerges in all clarity from the close comparison of positions and the

---

6 Ibid. Prol., NEORL 2:11–12: "E que enaxí con es .i. Deu tan solament, pare e creador e seynor de quant es, que enaxí tots los pobles qui son s'unisen en esser .i. poble tan solament, e que aquell ffos en vía de salut, e que tuit ensemps aguessen .iª. ffe, .iª. lig, e donasen gloria e laor de nostre seyner Deus. Cogitáts, seynors –dix lo savi a sos compayons–, quants son los dans qui.s seguexen com los homens no an una secta tan solament, ni quants son los bens qui sserien si tuyt aviem .iª. ffe, .iª. lig"; trans. Bonner, *SW* 1:116.

7 This needs to be stated clearly against Boris Helmdach, "Das Relationale im Denken Ramon Llulls," Diplomarbeit Grund- und Integrativwissenschaftliche Fakultät Universität Wien (Vienna: 1994), 85.

8 *Libre del gentil* Prol. NEORL 2:11: "E la ffi es amar e conexer e tembre e sservir Deu"; trans. Bonner, *SW* 1:115.

balancing of arguments. What Llull regards as necessary for using public disputation successfully can be found clearly detailed in his first major work, the
Libre de contemplació. Pivotal is above all a good intention, not successful polemics. The goal of finding the truth should never be dispensed with and one
should preferably start arguing from common ground:

> Hence, in the beginning of a disputation, it must be established that one
> has a good intention and regard for the truth and that one agrees to concur
> with one's adversary about those things commonly accepted and be-
> lieved so that upon these one can base one's arguments and questions.[9]

To achieve this goal Llull focused on two interrelated and inseparable topics
that are like the two focal points of an ellipse, his concept of God's attributes
and the interreligious scope of his theology.

For this purpose, Llull needs to anchor the Christian particular teaching of
"in three persons" within the realm of the belief in one God which is common
to all three monotheistic religions. In order to achieve this he looks for already
existing similarities in the teaching on God across the three religions. Judaism,
Christianity, and Islam are "united in the belief in one God, one creator and
one rewarder. All three expressed this belief in the same language, namely the
language of Scholastic theology adapted from ancient Greek philosophy. …In
other words, in Llull's times, the discrepancies among the three religions resided on a common background, a *Weltbild* or *imago mundi* which was the same
for all."[10] Against this background, Llull states, what is of pivotal importance
for his doctrine of the Trinity, is that the doctrine of divine attributes forms the
common basis for all three religions.

---

9   *Libre de contemplació en Deu* 187.1, ORL 5:169: "On, en lo començament que hom disputa
     cové esser ordonat que hom aja bona entencio e que hom aja esguardament a veritat
     e que hom se concort a s avenga ab son aversari en aquelles coses qui son comuna-
     ment atorgades e creegudes per tal que en aquelles pusca hom fer sos arguments e ses
     demandes."

10   Eusebi Colomer i Pous, "Raimund Lulls Stellung zu den Andersgläubigen: Zwischen
     Zwie-und Streitgespräch," in *Religionsgespräche im Mittelalter*, (eds.) Bernard Lewis and
     Friedrich Niewöhner (Wiesbaden: 1992), 219: "sie waren alle drei Religionen, die auf einer
     Schrift fußten, der Bibel und dem Koran; alle drei vereinte der Glaube an einen Gott
     Schöpfer und Belohner und alle drei drückten diesen Glauben in der gleichen Sprache
     aus, d.h. jene der in scholastische Theologie umgewandelten griechischen Philosophie …
     Mit anderen Worten, zu Llulls Zeiten ergaben sich die Diskrepanzen innerhalb der drei
     Religionen auf einem gemeinsamen Hintergrund, einer *imago mundi*, die für alle gleich
     war."

6.2   Llull's Concept of the Divine Attributes

6.2.1   *Common Questions*

Llull chooses the attributes of God as his starting point, because their consideration raises issues that are common to all three monotheistic religions in his day.

Llull is steadfastly convinced that God can be known by a multitude of attributes. These attributes are no secret of His transcendent being. They are neither hidden nor totally unknowable, although God Himself is transcendent, for God has made the world and created the human being "in His image" (Gen. 1:26). So, when human beings look at God's creation and see how it is structured, they can draw conclusions about its Creator. By looking at the world and by using their reason and the intellectual facilities with which the Creator has endowed human beings, a human being contemplates God in turn. It is upon this basis that the *Libre de contemplació en Déu* is grounded.

Llull's list of attributes may be traced to Pseudo-Dionysius the Areopagite's *De divinis nominibus* as a classical Christian model, but the attributes of God were also widely discussed in other sources during Llull's epoch.[11] Most likely Llull would also have consulted Richard of Saint Victor, who observed that:

> It seems certain, then, that all people, whether educated or nay, by nature's hook or by her crook, are naturally persuaded by a *communis animi conceptio* to consider it undeniable that anything that is judged to be best, should be attributed to God without hesitation.[12]

Yet, predicating attributes of God, as natural as it may seem to Llull, is, from a theological point of view, not without problems: if the divine attributes were nothing else than human qualities in their absolutely highest intensified form, would this not invite the suspicion that here human attributes are projected into the Divine Being?

---

11   Cf. Dionysius Areopagita, *De Divinis Nominibus*, (ed.) B. R. Suchla (Berlin: 1990); cf. Isidore of Seville, *Sententiae* 1.1-4, (ed.) Pierre Cazier, Corpus Christianorum Series Latina 111 (Turnhout: 1998), 7–13.

12   Richard of St. Victor, *De Trinitate* 1.20, (ed.) Gaston Salet (Paris: 1999), 98: "Est itaque eruditis velut maxima propositio, est cunctis in commune velut communis animi conceptio Deo attribuere quidquid altius attingit humana aestimatio"; trans. Ruben Angelici, *On the Trinity* (Eugene, Oregon: 2011), 86. Hélène Merle, "Dignitas: signification philosophique et théologique de ce terme chez Lulle et ses predecesseurs médiévaux," *EL* 21 (1977): 184, reprises the earlier insistence of E. Longpré regarding Llull's familiarity with Richard's work and thought.

In addition, we must ask: can God ever possess attributes? What could be the basis on which finite human reason could reach at least a minimum of reliable knowledge about God's qualities? Can the one God possess a multitude of attributes? How should people logically reconcile such a multitude of attributes with the oneness and simplicity of God's being? Llull answers these and similar questions from the two premises that any predication that defines the Creator as a creature is false and that, furthermore: "The only legitimate discourse concerning the existence of God is that in which God's essence and His existence are predicated in such a way that they are identical."[13]

As every student of Scholasticism will know, orthodox medieval theologians tended to answer the basic question of whether God can ever have properties by applying the Aristotelian distinction between the "essence" of a "substance" and its "accidents." But even this distinction encounters cognitive and methodological challenges when applied to God, as the very term *essentia* can be ambiguous and problematic when predicated of God. The one and unique essence of God cannot be understood in the Aristotelian sense of a "single, individual substance" (πρώτη οὐσία), if "individual" here signifies an entity which can exist only in distinction from and in comparison with others. Likewise, God's nature cannot be reduced discursively to the status of a generic concept, Aristotle's "secondary being" (δεύτερα οὐσία) as this would open the door to the existence of a plurality of deities that would be subsumed under this genus.[14]

Considering the problem of the distinction between essence and accidents leads invariably to also dealing with the problem of the multiplicity of divine attributes. The main point of contention in this regard was whether the many attributes of God would have to be regarded as different from the unity of His being in order to avoid conceiving of God in the categories of "created being" and "creatureliness." Already the plurality of linguistic expression was regarded as pointing to a problem: that a human being needs to predicate many different characteristics of God, even if unable thus to capture the slightest bit of His essence, demonstrates the inadequacy of human categories of thought in naming God.[15] A further linguistic indicator of human inadequacy is the oscillation

---

13   Eberhard Jüngel, "Thesen zum Verhältnis von Existenz, Wesen und Eigenschaften Gottes," *Zeitschrift für Theologie und Kirche* 96 (1999): 407: "Gott entsprechende Rede von der Existenz Gottes ist nur solche Rede, die das Wesen Gottes und die Existenz Gottes als identische zur Sprache bringt."

14   Cf. Annemarie C. Mayer, *Drei Religionen – ein Gott? Ramon Llulls interreligiöse Diskussion der Eigenschaften Gottes* (Freiburg im Breisgau: 2008), 162–167.

15   Cf. David Burrell, "Beyond Idolatry: On 'Naming' the One – God," in *Finding God in All Things*, (ed.) Michael J. Himes (New York: 1996), 29: "our intellect, ascending from the

between the abstract and concrete terms when speaking about God. As Mark Johnson explains:

> We need to name him via an abstract name (e.g. goodness, truth, justice), in order to indicate that he does not enter into the composition of other things. But no sooner do we do that than we realize that abstract names in our experience cover the domain of things that don't subsist or have separate existence! So we are then compelled to name God with a concrete name (e.g. good, true, just) in order to insist that he does, indeed, enjoy a separate existence. But existing things in our experience that are good, true, and just are composed of many elements, are not essentially good, true, and just, and can therefore cease to be thus – something Christians could not tolerate in the case of God![16]

In order to be able, in view of this dilemma (which troubled not only Christians), to corroborate the conviction of the uncreated transcendence of the divine essence, a real difference between the attributes and the unity of the divine essence was claimed. The assumption of a real difference between God's essence and His attributes is not, however, compatible with the unity and simplicity of God. Therefore, the doctrine of God's attributes was accused of making God "complex" since a distinction between God and His respective attributes would necessarily be implied: "To affirm anything whatever of God is to imply that He is complex, for to affirm an attribute of Him, even one attribute, is to imply a distinction between God, to whom the attribute is attributed, and the attribute He is said to have."[17] Thus it is no longer guaranteed that God is fundamentally distinct from the world. And here the above-mentioned problem becomes difficult: what is the relation between God's essence and His attributes? Is there a real multiplicity and diversity of attributes in the essence of God, or is this merely the result of human thought?

The assumption that the divine attributes are only intellectually distinguishable, that their diversity is observable only in human perception due to the varied relations of God to the created world, while preserving the simplicity of God, also results necessarily in an *aporia*, or logical obstacle. For the consequence of holding the position that distinctions between the divine attributes are the result of human thought processes would be that, in the final

---

multiplicity of creatures to God, understands that there are many notions relating imperfectly to one God."

16   Mark Johnson, "Apophatic Theology's Cataphatic Dependencies," *The Thomist* 62 (1998): 531.

17   Alexander Broadie, "Maimonides and Aquinas on the Names of God," *Religious Studies* 23 (1987):159.

analysis, the essence of God would be some nondescript entity in which all and one would coincide. Although God's work in the world would stipulate the assumption that it was mediated via certain of His attributes, if these existed on a purely mental level, they would never meet His essence. This exclusive emphasis on simplicity would inexorably lead to the doctrine of the inexpressibility of the divine essence. For God would then be characterized not only as a sum of all perfections, but, by the same token, as featureless in the sense of without any property or quality.[18] Were the divine attributes to exist only in the human imagination, talk of God's essence would remain an empty idea. All these issues were hotly discussed not only among Christians, but by the spiritual leaders of all faiths.

Llull discussed the complex of questions pertaining to the classical doctrine of God outlined above in his *Libre de contemplació*, where he implicitly answers many of the wider issues associated with this. He is aware that his teaching concerning the divine attributes would otherwise not be able to sketch a coherent image of God. Llull summarizes his thoughts on the multiplicity of attributes, often used as a *prima facie* argument to counter the existence of a single divine essence, by making the following point:

> Though You, O Lord, are only one substance, even so this does not mean we must refrain from attributing to You many virtues and that we must not predicate of You many nobilities; for there are many powers in You, Lord, and these things may well be said of You.[19]

It is revealing that this quotation immediately follows a passage in which Llull bemoans the fate of the "wretched unbelievers whose beliefs are contrary to truth" (*mesquins infeels qui creen contra veritat*).[20] We learn from this that Llull's argument possesses a significant interreligious dimension, and one which was apparently aimed at the Mutazilite position and designed to counter the arguments adduced by Maimonides, whose vehemently defended "negative theology" in his *Guide for the Perplexed* was arguing a position diametrically opposed to that of Llull.[21]

---

18   Cf. Magnus Striet, *Offenbares Geheimnis: zur Kritik der negativen Theologie* (Regensburg: 2003), 88; cf. also Eberhard Jüngel, *Ganz werden* (Tübingen: 2003), 253 (thesis 1.31).

19   *Libre de contemplació* 9.28, ORL 2:45: "Jassía, Sènyer Deus, que vos siats una substancia tan solament, per tot assò no roman que nos no deyam atribuir a vos moltes virtuts e que no deyam dir de vos moltes noblees; car moltes vertuts ha en vos, Sènyer, e molt bé pot esser dit e entès de vos."

20   Ibid. 9.27, ORL 2:45.

21   Cf. Moses Maimonides, *The Guide for the Perplexed*, trans. Michael Friedländer (New York: 1904); cf. Mayer, *Drei Religionen*, 354–363.

Nevertheless Llull, though apparently deriving the attributes of God by logical deduction from consideration of finite characteristics, does not believe that these attributes may fully and ultimately be comprehended by the human being's insufficient endowments for "Nothing, Lord, is sufficient to recognize your whole goodness."[22] Yet, this is not due to any lack of the divine being or essence but is due rather to the natural limitations of human cognitive skills: "Even though your being is invisible to us in this world, because hidden from the five corporeal senses and so we cannot perceive or see it, nonetheless it does not follow that your being is untrue."[23]

Rather, for Llull, deriving the attributes of God from the properties of finite, created things is legitimate because God created everything. In creation God was and is not only equivocally, but also univocally (or at least by way of analogy) at work as its cause. That is, every created being carries God's traits, is a reflection of His being, and contains basic characteristics, the "likenesses of the first cause itself" (*similitudines ipsius primae causae*)[24] that constitute the similarities shared with the first cause itself; because, to put it bluntly, God does not lie. When He expresses himself in His creation, He expresses himself in it as He really is. His creation thus necessarily is modelled according to His image.

6.2.2   *Corresponding Answers*

So, as we have seen, Llull looked to other religions for common ground. But he could not find what he needed in all the various strands of Jewish and Muslim theological traditions. The Jewish speculative tradition on the whole, with a few notable exceptions like Avicebron, must be regarded as fiercely opposed to Llull's notion of divine attributes. The opposite is true of the Kabbalah, at least as regards its theosophical strand; Hames explains how:

> Lull's approach to conversion was based on the need to find principles common to members of the three monotheistic faiths, which could then be used as a basis for dialogue. The elaboration of these principles presupposes a knowledge of the other's faith, and given that Lull's

---

22   *Libre de contemplació* 19.6, ORL 2:93: "No es neguna cosa, Sènyer, que bast a conexer tota la vostra bonea."

23   Ibid. 23.13, ORL 2:114: "Jassía que lo vostre esser sia en est mon a nos inveible per raó dels .v. senys corporals a qui es amagat en so que noy podem atènyer a ell a veer; per tot assò no s seguex que vostre esser sia en falsetat."

24   Ramon Llull, *Declaratio Raymundi* 2, ROL 17:259. Cf. Jordi Gayà Estelrich, "Ramon Llull i l'Islam: 'Infideles sunt homines, sicut et nos'; 'Vós sou sant, Senyor Déu únic,'" in *Franciscanisme i Islam: Jornades d'Estudis Franciscans 2001* (Barcelona: 2002), 133.

intellectual milieu was the same as the Kabbalists', the possibility that their teachings made an impression on Lull's thought must be taken into account.[25]

Hames's assessment is certainly accurate and well-founded. Llull certainly was familiar with at least some teachings of the *Kabbalah*. But this does not mean that only these and these alone exerted an influence on Lullian thought with regard to Jewish theological concepts.

The same goes for Islam. Here not only Sufism but also the Ash'arite school, above all al-Ghazali, offered Llull a welcome opportunity to identify common ground.[26] Most likely, Llull had sufficient knowledge of Arabic to acquaint himself with a wide selection of Islamic philosophy and theology, thanks to nine years spent painstakingly studying the Arabic language—all because in Llull's opinion Islam forms more of a threat to the Christian faith than Judaism. By arguing that the Jews have been held in captivity (ever since the destruction of the Temple), the gentile in the *Libre del gentil* clearly and easily rejects conversion to Judaism. Yet, as regards conversion to Islam, financial or material benefits of a broader sense might be involved. This is why, if we were to introduce a ranking, Llull aims rather at applying his concept to Islam than to Judaism. At the same time, however, his striving for a three-way conversation needs to be emphasized.

Vis à vis the doctrine of attributes of the Ash'arite and Kabbalistic schools, Llull offers his own position, similarly based on the attributes of God. Llull's position stresses the fact that the attributes of God are properties of His nature, and the reasoning structures which Llull deploys show Christian, Islamic, and Jewish points of contact, with shared roots in Neoplatonism. This philosophical grounding serves to ensure the triumph of reason in his concept, combining logical coherence with the shortest route to salvation. Llull's approach is not attempting to foist or force Christianity upon non-Christians, rather it serves as an invitation to other religions to enter into dialogue in order to ascertain the truth upon common ground.

When facing a particular topic, Llull usually tended to begin by adopting a Christian perspective, before turning to alternative reasoning structures as ways of establishing common ground: "There is nothing wrong with deriving some statement or rule or recommendation from more than one source.

---

25   Harvey J. Hames, *The Art of Conversion: Christianity and Kabbalah in the Thirteenth Century* (Leiden: 2000), 2–3.

26   Cf. Walter Andreas Euler, *Unitas et Pax: Religionsvergleich bei Raimundus Lullus und Nikolaus von Kues* (Würzburg: 1990), 93.

There is no conflict or strain between the two principles."[27] Because the human psyche is so constituted that it rather accepts what it already knows, Llull sought to always find alternative logical structures wherever possible.[28] However, he never went so far as to incorporate alien doctrines into the Christian faith, and he never expected a complete match between contrasting religious doctrines, as any partial match was usually sufficient for Llull's purposes. Given these presuppositions, Llull's search for commonalities in the teachings of the three religions on the attributes of God resulted in his being at least partially successful.

6.3 The Interreligious Orientation of Llull's Theology

6.3.1 *The* Libre del Gentil e dels Tres Savis
Llull applied his specifically shaped doctrine of attributes both practically on itinerant preaching missions and theoretically in religious encounters conducted in fictional guise, as in the case of the *Libre del gentil e dels tres savis*, a work that provides a representative instance of Llull's negotiation of the question of religious "alterity." However, the book does not contain any interreligious dialogue in the modern sense of the word, but instead represents a conversation between three wise men, representatives of Judaism, Christianity, and Islam respectively, who together embark on the task to determine the *true* religion. The three meet to discuss this issue in an idealized *locus amoenus*, an idyllic grove far from the madding crowd. There they meet a lady named Intelligence (*Entallegencia*), personified Understanding.[29] By means of five trees she sets out for them pairs of concepts (signified by the leaves) providing a rational approach for their planned venture.[30] Once the lady bids them farewell, they

---

27 William A. Christian, "Studying Doctrines of Religious Communities," in *Inter-Religious Models and Criteria*, (ed.) James Kellenberger (Basingstoke: 1993), 149.

28 Cf. *Libre del gentil* Epil., NEORL 2:207; in relation to Nachmanides and the famous Barcelona Disputation of 1263, cf. Hans-Georg von Mutius, *Die christlich-jüdische Zwangsdisputation zu Barcelona, Nach dem hebräischen Protokoll des Moses Nachmanides* (Frankfurt: 1982), 151.

29 Cf. Roger Friedlein, *Der Dialog bei Ramon Llull: Literarische Gestaltung als apologetische Strategie* (Tübingen: 2004), 82, notes the term's equivalence to the Catalan word "understanding" (*enteniment*) that Llull uses elsewhere.

30 On the many possible Christian, Islamic, and Jewish antecedents for Llull's tree symbolism, cf. Gerschom Scholem, *Das Buch Bahir* (1923; repr. Darmstadt: 1970), 17; on the Tree of Porphyry, Aristotle, *Kategorien*, trans. Eugen Rolfes, 2nd. ed. (Hamburg: 1974), 5–34; on iconography, Johanna Flemming, "Baum, Bäume," in *Lexikon der christlichen Ikonographie*, Vol. 1, (ed.) Engelbert Kirschbaum (Rome: 1968), col. 266–267.

prepare to assault their theme with zeal, but the purpose of their meeting is thwarted by the arrival of the gentile, who driven by fear of death, has fallen into a deep existential crisis.

The three wise men try, united as one, to convince the gentile of the existence of God and of life after death. Once the wise men, pooling their wits, achieve this at the end of Book 1, the gentile, overwhelmed with joy, wants to join their "common" religion. Shamefaced, the three wise men are finally forced to admit that they each in fact pertain to three competing religions. Their disunity serves only to plunge the heathen into an even deeper existential crisis. Now no longer is it a matter concerning the fate of his present and ephemeral life on this miserable earth, it could easily become a question of the salvation of the gentile's eternal soul, should he make a mistake in his choice of the "true religion."

> [before]I had no fear of enduring infinite suffering after my death. But now I am sure that if I am not on the true path, every kind of punishment is waiting to torment my soul endlessly after I die.[31]

To save himself and others this fate, and to learn more about the faith of the wise men, the gentile wants the wise men to expedite the matter in his presence:

> And may it please you to teach me how, by the grace of God and by your doctrine, I may know and be able to lead to the path of salvation so many people who are on the path to eternal fire.[32]

Whereas earlier, in the first book, the reader had not been able to determine whether the Christian, the Muslim, or the Jew was actually speaking, the three have now become competitors. Each wants to win the gentile over as a follower of his respective religion and so they set out their core beliefs in a bid to win the gentile's adherence. The wise men agree to be constrained by the rules laid down for them by Lady Intelligence, employing the flowers of the five trees to guide them. This method guarantees for the wise men the quality of their arguments, for "whoever can, according to his belief, make the articles in

---

31 *Libre del gentil* 1. Epil., NEORL 2:45: "cor yo aprés ma mort no avia temor de sostenir treballs inffinits. Mas ara son segur que, si no son en via vera, que tota pena está – aparellada a turmentar la mia anima aprés ma mort perdurablament!;" trans. Bonner, *SW* 1:148.

32 Ibid., NEORL 2:44: "E placia-us enseynar a mi con, per gracia de Deu e per vostra doctrina, yo sapia e pusca endur a via saludable tantes de gents qui son en via de ffoc perdurable;" trans. Bonner, *SW* 1:148.

which he believes best accord with the flowers and with the conditions of the trees, will reveal and demonstrate that his belief is better than the others."[33] While one sage is discoursing upon his own religion, the remaining two are not allowed to interrupt. Only the gentile may ask questions. Each wise man begins with a prayer peculiar to his religion and then summarizes in a list those representative articles of his faith, which he wants to make the starting point of his argument. The Christian recites fourteen articles of his creed, the Jew names eight, the Muslim twelve.

The prayers quoted by Llull to represent the non-Christian monotheistic religions are intended to be realistic portrayals of prayer formulae found in the Jewish and Muslim faiths. The lists of articles of faith also contain *theologoumena* (statements of theological reflection on faith) indeed pertaining to these religions. Llull was fully aware of the fact that the conscious and even the unconscious violation of religious feelings is capable of mobilizing immense power. He made sure never to present Judaism or Islam in ways that would cause offense, respecting scrupulously the accuracy and the integrity of the religious identity of his counterpart in dialogue.

However, analysis of the behavior that the gentile displays in his responses to the interventions of the various wise men might lead one to identify a general opposition to the Muslim's viewpoint. At least in Book Four the gentile is portrayed as a "Christian in disguise." If the gentile's decision in the end is left to be figured out by the reader's imagination, this is because, as Llull explains in the epilogue, this forms part of his didactic strategy which conditions the whole work:

> This book constitutes a doctrine and method for enlightening clouded minds and awakening the great who sleep, and for entering into union with and getting to know strangers and friends, by asking what religion they think the gentile chose in order to find favor with God.[34]

As Colomer has observed: "beneath the appearance of a pleasant and elegant dialogue he produces a subtle apology for his thesis. If he refuses expressly to draw its conclusion, it is because he trusts the readers to draw

---

33   Ibid., NEORL 2:46: "qual que mills pusca, segons sa creensa, concordar los articles en que creu ab les fflors e ab les condicions dels arbres, aquell dará signifficança e demostració que sia en melor creenssa que los altres;" trans. Bonner, *SW* 1:149.

34   Ibid. Epil., NEORL 2:209: "lo qual libre es raó e manera a iluminar torbat enteniment, e a despertar los grans qui dormen, e a entrar en paria e en conexenssa de estranys e privats, demanant qual lig lur es semblant que·l gentil aja triada per eser agradable a Deu;" trans. Bonner, *SW* 1: 304.

it for themselves."[35] Within the fictitious framework the open ending is justified by the fact that the wise men want to continue their original project, the common search for the true religion, and that thus each may think that the gentile chose his religion. Because the framework of the dialogue establishes the same "conditions of discussing" for all the wise men; because it displays a friendly tone of coexistence and mutual respect as informing their discussion; and because it never reports the gentile's final decision, it bolsters the impression of an unbiased comparison of the religions at hand.[36] This impression is further reinforced by the equal treatment of the disputants' religions, even if this is only "implicitly conveyed through the stylistic devices of parallelism and mirroring."[37] In this way, Llull achieves the greatest possible objectivity in his exposition, while simultaneously bolstering his own unreserved conviction in Christianity. As Artus notes, "Llull did everything necessary to present his teachings and defense with great respect, objectivity, and impartiality, in so far as allowed by his firm conviction about the superiority and full truth of the Catholic religion."[38]

6.3.2   *The* Disputatio Raymundi Christiani et Hamar Saraceni

Let us then take a peek over Llull's shoulder, so to speak, by looking next at a "real" fragment of religious dialogue. "Real" needs to be bracketed, since this text represents not the independent transcript of a third party, but one of Llull's own *aide-mémoires*. In 1307, he undertook a mission trip to Bugia (Bejaia in Algeria today) and, standing on the market square, announced to all and sundry that he wanted to convert to Islam, if first someone could convince him using the incontrovertible grounds of reason. After several days of debate ending in

---

35   Eusebi Colomer i Pous, *El pensament als països catalans durant l'edat mitjana i el renaixement* (Barcelona: 1997), 148: "sota l'aparença d'un diàleg complaent i elegant duu a terme una apologia subtil de la seva tesi. Si refusa expressament de treure la conclusió, és perquè confia que el lector la traurà per ell mateix."

36   Cf. Anthony Bonner, "L'apologètica de Ramon Martí i Ramon Llull davant de l'Islam i del judaisme," in *El debat intercultural als segles XIII i XIV: Actes de les Primeres Jornades de Filosofia Catalana, Girona 25-27 d'abril del 1988*, (ed.) Marcel Salleras (Girona: 1989), 182, and Sarah Stroumsa, "Ibn al-Rāwandī's sū' adab al-mujādala: The Role of Bad Manners in Medieval Disputations," in *The Majlis: Interreligious Encounters in Medieval Islam*, (ed.) Hava Lazarus-Yafeh (Wiesbaden: 1999), 66–83.

37   Friedlein, *Dialog bei Ramon Llull*, 90: "implizit durch die parallelen Strukturen transportiert."

38   Walter W. Artus, "Judaísmo e Islamismo en la autobiografía y en algunos escritos de Raimundo Lulio," *Mediaevalia, Textos e Estúdios* 5–6 (1994): 203: "Raimundo hizo todo lo necesario para presentar esas enseñanzas y defensa[s] con gran respeto, objetividad e imparcialidad, tanto como se lo permitían sus firmes convicciones de la superioridad y verdad más completa de la religión católica."

fisticuffs, Llull went to prison. He was supplied with conversion literature and was visited daily by Hamar, a Muslim scholar sent to convert him. Llull asked for paper and pen and recorded the *Disputatio Raymundi christiani et Hamar saraceni*.[39] While discussing Llull's system of attributes, Hamar argues against the doctrine of the Trinity, by distinguishing between the conditions of being and the qualities.[40] He names eleven of the divine attributes: namely, Goodness, Greatness, Power, Wisdom, Will, Strength, Truth, Glory, Perfection, Justice, and Mercy.[41] However, they are neither determinations of the essence of God, nor accidents, because an accident always is imperfect and dependent on the essence it belongs to. Yet any imperfection would be incompatible with God's very being. So, to explain the relationship of these attributes to the essence of God, Hamar simply states that they are "rooted" in God. "Based on this understanding of God as rooted in the attributes, it follows that for Muslims God may neither be a trinity nor a human being."[42] Specifically, Hamar argues that there is no consubstantiality shared between the attributes and God. God's goodness, for example, is indeed rooted in the essence of God, but is not identical with God's essence; it rather is extrinsically aligned with it; it manifests itself as an active goodness, which, in turn, manifests the quality it represents outwards.[43] If we were to suppose that God's essence and His attributes were one, Hamar contends, then their effect would also be consubstantial with God. He explains this with the example of the sun. The sun does not engender any other suns, while yet producing heat. If God acted by a goodness consubstantial with His essence, He would only produce infinite goodness. There could be no evil. Empirically, however, we know that God brings forth a world distinct from His essence, where both good and evil find a place. Thus, it follows that God acts through a goodness that is to be distinguished from His essence:

---

39   *Disputatio Raymundi et Hamar*, ROL 22:159–264.

40   Cf. Annemarie Schimmel, "Raymundus Lullus und seine Auseinandersetzung mit dem Islam," *Eine Heilige Kirche* 27 (Munich: 1953–1954): 73, and Hans Daiber, "Raimundus Lullus in der Auseinandersetzung mit dem Islam: Eine philosophiegeschichtliche Analyse des Liber disputationis Raimundi Christiani et Homeri Saraceni," in *Juden, Christen und Muslime. Religionsdialoge im Mittelalter*, (eds.) Matthias Lutz-Bachmann and Alexander Fidora (Darmstadt: 2004), 137.

41   Cf. *Disputatio Raymundi et Hamar* 1.1, ROL 22:175: "Nos attribuimus Deo undecim qualitates. Quae sunt hae, uidelicet: (1) Bonitas, (2) Magnitudo, (3) Potestas, (4) Sapientia, (5) Voluntas, (6) Virtus, (7) Veritas, (8) Gloria, (9) Perfectio, (10) Iustitia, et (11) Misericordia." Cf. Siegfried Raeder, "Raimundus Lullus als Scholastiker in der Auseinandersetzung mit dem Islam," *Judaica* 52 (1996): 279.

42   Raeder, "Lullus als Scholastiker," 279–280: "Aus diesem Verständnis der in Gott wurzelnden Eigenschaften folgt für den Muslimen, daß Gott weder eine Dreiheit noch Mensch sein kann."

43   Cf. *Disputatio Raymundi et Hamar* 1.1.2, ROL 22:183. Cf. Daiber, "Raimundus Lullus in der Auseinandersetzung mit dem Islam," 136.

"thus it is proven, that God is not His goodness, and therefore He cannot be triune."[44] By this line of reasoning Hamar prepares the ground for his rejection of Christian teaching regarding the Trinity: in other words, "were God to bring forth a son out of something non-consubstantial with God's goodness, this son would differ substantially from God. He might be good only to the degree that He emanated from an attribute of God, but this goodness would be limited in extent because it does not directly emanate out of God's essence. The same is true of the Holy Spirit."[45] Yet since in God all the attributes reach their highest perfection, God Himself could not be a subject (*subiectum*) or bearer of an intradivinely produced limited good: "whence that goodness is not God; therefore it is partly good and partly not good."[46] So a Trinity *in God* is excluded.

The Islamic reasoning, as Llull reports it, depends primarily on the premise that it is not possible to create the Divine Persons of the Godhead, using properties not consubstantial with God. Here Lull perceptively observed that Islamic orthodoxy, as regards the question of God's relation to His attributes, avoids two extreme positions. The attributes of God were on the one hand considered to be real properties, but they are not classified as consubstantial with God; and on the other hand they are indeed rooted in God's essence, but are no *accidentia* of God. Because they avoid both extremes, God's attributes bring forth no being similar to Him in being, but only being-in-the-world or material reality.

However, for Llull God's attributes are indeed determining the divine essence and are active from eternity. Llull "makes it clear that the attributes of God are God's parameters of being, with which God in His whole being faces the world. His world-facingness is an expression of the Trinitarian, internal dynamics of the Divine Being and completes itself outwardly in the incarnation of God in man."[47] Yet God is not dependent on the world; rather, He actively faces it. Llull's counterargument, when given a contemporary formulation, means that creation is only one of God's "second order activities," for actually

---

44   *Disputatio Raymundi et Hamar* 1.1.2, ROL 22:183: "Probatum est, quod Deus non est sua bonitas, et ideo ipse non potest esse trinus."

45   Raeder, "Lullus als Scholastiker," 280: "Würde also Gott aus einer ihm nicht gleichwesentlichen [Gutheit] einen Sohn hervorbringen, so müßte sich dieser Sohn wesentlich von Gott unterscheiden. Er wäre zwar gut, sofern er aus einer Eigenschaft Gottes hervorginge, aber doch nur begrenzt gut, weil er nicht aus Gottes Wesen hervorginge. Entsprechendes gilt vom Heiligen Geist."

46   *Disputatio Raymundi et Hamar* 1.1.2, ROL 22:183: "postquam ipsa bonitas non est Deus; ergo partim est bona et partim non."

47   Raeder, "Lullus als Scholastiker," 287: "Raimundus Lullus will dagegen durch seine Auffassung der Eigenschaften Gottes als Wesensbestimmungen Gottes deutlich machen, daß Gott in seinem ganzen Wesen der Welt zugewandt ist. Seine Weltzugewandtheit ist Ausdruck der trinitarischen, inneren Dynamik des göttlichen Wesens und vollendet sich nach außen in der Menschwerdung Gottes."

the intrinsic action of the attributes as "first order activities" already presupposes the Trinity. Llull's opinion was not unique in his time. St. Bonaventure also classified the *diffusio in creaturam* as secondary.[48] A match between Llull and the Islamic position set out by Hamar may yet be achieved, however, "for both share the premise, that the essential goodness of God is really good only when it is active."[49]

Therefore, in Llull's eyes, the Islamic conception of the divine attributes seems so deficient because they do not assume that God's nature is already active in and of itself. Llull's verdict on Islamic theology, therefore, in his own words is:

> Muslims are men well educated in philosophy and fully rational, but of the essence of God and his attributes they possess too little knowledge. Therefore, in disputations, the Catholic should enable them to understand God and the activities of His intrinsic attributes; and from the said attributes, and from the statements that God is perfect and that His attributes possess an activity intrinsic to themselves, namely that his goodness makes good, his magnitude makes great and so on and so forth, they conclude that God is triune, and thus also from the extrinsic acts, which they have before them in created matter, from which follows the consequence that God became flesh.[50]

Llull continues: "And I held this type of disputation with them while I was in prison in Bugia, by making insoluble propositions for them and solving those that they made to me against the Holy Trinity and the Incarnation."[51]

---

48   Bonaventure, *Itinerarium mentis in Deum* 6.22, in *Opera omnia* 5 (Quarrachi: 1891), 310–311.

49   Daiber, "Raimundus Lullus in der Auseinandersetzung mit dem Islam," 137: "[d]enn beide vertreten im Grund genommen die Meinung, dass die wesenhafte Gutheit Gottes nur in ihrer aktiven Gestaltung wirklich gut ist."

50   Ramon Llull, *Liber de acquisitione Terrae Sanctae* 2.1, ed. Eugène Kamar, "Projet de Raymond Llull, *De acquisitione Terrae Sanctae*: Introduction et édition critique du texte," *Studia Orientalia Christiana* 6 (1961): 117: "Sarraceni sunt aliqui in philosophia bene litterati et sunt homines bene rationales, sed de Essentia Dei et dignitatibus suis parum sciunt. Idcirco Catholicus in disputationibus disponet ipsos ad intelligendum Deum et actus suarum dignitatum intrinsecos et ex dictis quod Deus sit perfectus et quod suae rationes habeant actus intrinsecos, videlicet, sua bonitas bonificare, sua magnitudo magnificare et coeterae consequentiae, concludunt quod Deus sit trinus et sic de actibus extensis, quos habent in creatis, ex quibus sequuntur consequentiae quod Deus est incarnatus." Cf. Jordi Gayà Estelrich, "Ramon Llull i l'Islam," 136, on the importance of this passage for Llull's theory of correlatives, Trinitarian model, and arguments for the illumination of faith that leads to confessing the Trinity.

51   *Liber de acquisitione Terrae Sanctae* 2.1, (ed.) Kamar, 117: "Et istum modum disputationis tenebam ego cum ipsis dum eram in carcere Bugiae, faciendo eis propositiones insolubiles et solvendo illas quas mihi faciebant contra Sanctam Trinitatem et Incarnationem."

6.4   God as Common Ground? Llull's Approach towards Dialogue

Llull was convinced throughout his life that if only Muslims and Jews were to understand the Trinity correctly, their conversion to Christianity would shortly follow: "But if they understood the Trinity as we believe it to exist in God, the force of reason, and the concordance of the flowers of the first tree along with its conditions, would make them see the truth of the Holy Trinity of our Lord God."[52] They refuse to exchange their own, uncertain faith for another, equally unprovable belief: "For the unbelievers say: we do not wish to abandon one faith for another, or one belief for another, but rather to abandon believing for understanding."[53] This theme occupies Llull in the episode of the king of Tunis, a story which turns up like a red thread running through Llull's oeuvre and which drew Llull's comment repeatedly.[54] A Christian missionary succeeds in convincing the king of Tunis of the falseness of his former faith; but when asked to provide a positive justification for Christianity, the missionary responds evasively that it is necessary to simply believe. It is not enough just to make an absurdity of other religions credible or even to drag them into ridicule; a better alternative must also be sustainable or defensible. Although a Christian missionary, in Llull's 13th-century view, must be able to demonstrate vociferously in what respects the Jewish and Muslim faiths be wrong or deficient, what is more important is that he must be able to represent his own faith convincingly and compassionately enough to members of other religions so that a dialogue may be entered into, in an atmosphere of discussion rather than hostility.

How right Llull was in his assessment is confirmed in view of the statements made by the spokesman of the Jewish community of Gerona, Moses ben Nahman, called Nachmanides or Bonastruc de Porta (1194–1270), in the famous Barcelona Disputation of 1263, held "not in order that the faith of Our Lord Jesus Christ, the certainty of which is never to be doubted, be disputed, […] but so that the truth of this very faith be made manifest for destroying the

---

52   *Libre del gentil* 3.2-4, NEORL 2:114–115: "Mas, si ells *entenien* la trinitat que nos creem esser en Deu, fforssa de rahó e concordanssa de les fflors del primer arbre e les condicions d'aquell los enclinaria a concebre veritat de la santa trinitat de nostre seyer Deus"; trans. Bonner, *SW* 1:217.

53   Llull, *Liber de demonstratione per aequiparantiam* Prol., ROL 9:222: "Quoniam infideles dicunt: Nolumus dimittere fidem pro fide aut credere pro credere; sed bene credere pro intelligere dimittemus."

54   The story recurs in Llull's *Blaquerna* 84, ORL 9:356–358; *Disputació de cinc savis*, (ed.) Josep Perarnau i Espelt, *Arxiu de Texts Catalans Antics* 5 (1986): 28–29; *Disputatio fidei et intellectus* 1.1, ROL 23:226; *Liber de convenientia fidei et intellectus* 3.1, MOG 4:574; *Liber de praedicatione* 2.B.1.26.2.1, ROL 4:104; and *Liber de fine* 1.5, ROL 9:267.

errors of the Jews and for removing the confidence [in their own faith] of many Jews."[55] When discussing the Trinity in disputation against the Dominican Paul Cristià (d. 1269), a recent convert from Judaism, Nachmanides insists that it is obvious that a person cannot believe what one does not know.[56] As Paul Cristià had previously claimed that even angels do not understand the Trinity, Nachmanides astutely reached the devastating conclusion that in such a case *even angels do not believe in the Trinity.*

Llull takes an approach explicitly attempting to learn from and to remedy the mistakes of Christian missionaries that have failed. From his decidedly Christian standpoint Llull does not depart from his own position nor does he make substantive concessions. On the contrary, he thought conceding counterproductive. For him watering down his own Christian belief is not the way; the other parties cannot be met halfway. For this would mean that the discussion could only skirt around peripheral issues; rather, Llull focused attention on the key elements of the Christian faith. With the doctrine of the Trinity Llull set his standards very high.

Llull's concern, like his contemporaries', focusses on the question of truth and the respective validity claims of religions. Yet, to use a modern theological classification, Llull is an "inclusivist," that is, he is not convinced of the validity of Christianity alone, but perceives of Christianity as maximally valid within a range of valuable alternatives. He does not believe that Christians exclusively may know, love, and serve God; but neither does he think that all religions are equally true.[57] This inclusivist attitude makes worthy of note the principles that Llull establishes for inter-faith dialogue. On a "methodological-formal level," or as "dialogue-etiquette," we come across guidelines such as "Unbelievers are human beings just like us" (*Infideles sunt homines sicut et nos*).[58] Eye-level

---

55   Thus in the Latin record of the disputation: Enrique Claudio Gribal, *Los judíos en Gerona* (Gerona: 1870), 66; repr. David Romano, *Per a una història de la Girona jueva*, Vol. 1 (Gerona: 1988), 92: "non ut fides Domini Jhesu Christi, quae propter sui certitudinem non est in disputatione ponenda ... sed ut ipsius fidei veritas manifesteretur propter destruendos Judeorum errores et ad tollendam confidentiam multorum Judeorum."

56   Nachmanides, *Vikuah* § 107, in *Judaism on Trial: Jewish-Christian Disputations in the Middle Ages*, (ed.) Hyam Maccoby (East Brunswick, New Jersey: 1982), 146. Cf. also Mutius, *Die christlich-jüdische Zwangsdisputation*, 23–301.

57   Cf. Hans Kessler, "Was macht Religionen pluralismusfähig (und authentisch)? Fragmente einer Theologie des religiösen Pluralismus – jenseits von *Dominus Iesus* und Pluralistischer Religionstheologie," in *Der eine Gott und die Welt der Religionen. Beiträge zu einer Theologie der Religionen und zum interreligiösen Dialog*, (ed.) Markus Witte (Würzburg: 2003), 303–304.

58   Llull, *Lectura super Artem inventivam et Tabulam generalem* Prol., MOG 5:360: "Ipsi infideles sunt homines, sicut et nos, et sunt de nostra natura."

encounters are only possible through dialogues conducted with this in mind. Only in this way can the substantial similarities between faiths be seen on closer inspection. Only thus can one reach the conclusion that what others do, think or believe is not bad in itself. This is because other faiths' search for God helps serve the common overarching goal, to love, praise, and honor God. In this way, Llull relies on reaching a mutual understanding by sharing information about one's own religion with members of other religions in a way that is non-threatening, in order to create a willingness to exchange ideas and foster dialogue. To the king of Sicily he suggested in July of 1312 the establishment of academic chairs to be held on a Christian-Muslim exchange basis.[59] The interlocutors of his fictitious dialogues combine an exquisite courtesy with the highest respect for each other, each trusting their counterparts upfront to be honest in their struggle to seek the truth.

More exciting than Llull's approach to the outer form of dialogue was its content, as I hope the example of Llull's teaching on the divine attributes has already partly shown. In terms of content, Llull recognized that there are certain principles that all religions must generally follow when engaging with the teachings of other religions. Within any one religion the principle of coherence prevails, i.e. a religion will always endeavor not to tolerate any obvious contradictions among its official teachings. Even when dealing with other religions the "coherence principle" always guides the search for a match, for example, between shared, compatible or at least comparable convictions. By bringing the principle of coherence to include their own as well as compatible teachings in other religions, it is possible to build on these or at least for them to serve as the objective basis of a comparison. Abstractly formulated, a religion always and invariably gathers its criteria for classification of other religions from its *own* sources. Yet this does not preclude agreement, or at least common ground, with the teachings and standards of other religions. For example, medieval Muslim theology never hesitated, when engaging dialectically with other religions, to follow the rule based on Sura 2:137: "Whatever agrees with the Koran is true, whatever contradicts it, is wrong."

When compared with this, Llull's approach stands out by its objective insistence upon adherence to strictly logical methodological criteria when assessing another religion, which he derives from common sense as well as specifically Christian presuppositions. As Llull explains:

It is proper for every wise man to hold to that faith which attributes to the eternal God, in whom all wise men of the world believe, the greatest

---

59   Cf. Llull, *Liber de participatione christianorum et saracenorum* Prol., ROL 16:246.

goodness, wisdom, virtue, truth, glory, perfection, etc., and all these things in the greatest equality and concordance. And most praiseworthy is that faith in God which places the greatest concordance or agreement between God, who is the highest and first cause, and His effect.[60]

The decisive point is that, in Llull's view, the specifically Christian criteria overlap contentwise with general logic, so that, as regards content, Llull can use Trinitarian theology, Christology, and soteriology as his standard, and, as regards form, he uses his rational method and the will to practice inter-faith dialogue.

6.4.1   Lullian Rational Method

What is meant by Llull's "rational method" or "method of ratiocination"? To explain this adequately, we must assume the premise that Llull was well aware that judgment regarding the competing truth claims of the monotheistic religions could never be adequately reached within just one religion. As philosopher of religion Markus Enders explains: "The judge of the conflicting truth claims of the monotheistic world religions needs to be independent of them and neutral and needs to possess such an authority as can be recognized by all three religions. These qualities that are sought for the deciding authority between the conflicting truth claims of the three monotheistic religions— namely the qualities of independence, neutrality, and universality or universal validity—are embodied only within the cognitive faculties of general human understanding and general human reason. Humans of course have these faculties at their disposal, so long as they make use of human language. Whatever this general means of human cognition ... recognizes as true, therefore, must be valid and binding to any human beings able to exercise their reason and judgment without undue hindrance. It follows from this that the natural faculty of human understanding and rational judgment, together with the factors determining reason, are the only appropriate tools with which to judge the disputes of world religions regarding the truth of their respective belief-systems"[61]

---

60   *Vita coaetanea* 26, ROL 8:290: "illam fidem tenere decet quemlibet sapientem, quae Deo aeterno, quem cuncti credunt mundi sapientes, attribuit maiorem bonitatem, sapientiam, uirtutem, ueritatem, gloriam et perfectionem et cetera huiusmodi; et haec omnia in maiori aequalitate et concordantia. Illa etiam fides de Deo laudabilior est, quae inter Deum, qui est summa et prima causa, et inter eius effectum maiorem ponit concordantiam seu conuenientiam"; trans. Anthony Bonner, *Ramon Llull: A Contemporary Life* (Barcelona & Woodbridge: 2010), 59.

61   Markus Enders, "Die Bedeutung der christlichen Philosophie der monotheistischen Weltreligionen im frühen Mittelalter für das interreligiöse Gespräch der Gegenwart," *Archa*

For this reason, the question of method acquires for Llull such poignancy. For, if the above is true, then instead of evidence from Scripture or reference to tradition, Llull deems sustainable the rational foundation on which he puts his religious dialogue, because it is not based on authoritative texts with contradicting passages; and thus no interpretative dilemmas could arise:

> And they even agreed among themselves that they would argue from reason, and not authority, since understanding is a primary act, true and necessarily pertaining to the intellect itself, and infallible, as long as it is correctly applied. From authorities however the intellect sometimes depends on belief, sometimes on understanding, which is why the meaning of authorities is subject to the mutability of opinions.[62]

Llull's position assumes that the authoritative texts are already hotly disputed and fallible within Christianity itself. Consequently, they were not a reliable common basis for dialogue with other faiths:

> And since we cannot agree by means of authorities, let us try to come to some agreement by means of demonstrative and necessary reasons.[63]
> ...

Verbi 7 (2010), 145–146: "Der Richter über die konfligierenden Wahrheitsansprüche der drei monotheistischen Weltreligionen muß von ihnen unabhängig und neutral sein und zudem eine solche Autorität besitzen, daß er von allen drei Religionen anerkannt werden kann. Diese für die Entscheidungsinstanz zwischen den Wahrheitsansprüchen der drei monotheistischen Weltreligionen gesuchten Eigenschaften der Unabhängigkeit bzw. Neutralität sowie der Allgemeingültigkeit besitzt aber nur das Erkenntnisvermögen des allgemeinen menschlichen Verstandes sowie der allgemeinen menschlichen Vernunft, über welche Menschen natürlicherweise und damit gleichermaßen verfügen, sofern sie von menschlicher Sprache Gebrauch machen. Was diese allgemein menschlichen Erkenntnisvermögen [...] als wahr anerkennen, muß daher für alle ihres Verstandes- und Vernunftgebrauchs fähigen menschlichen Wesen gültig und verbindlich sein. Nur das Verstandes- und Vernunfturteil und die sie bestimmenden Gründe sind daher der einzig geeignete Richter im Streit der Weltreligionen um die Wahrheit ihrer jeweiligen Glaubensauffassungen."

62   Ramon Llull, *Disputatio Raymundi et Averroistae* 1, ROL 7:9–10: "Et etiam conuenerunt inter se, quod disputarent per modum intelligendi, non per auctoritates, quoniam intelligere est actus primitiuus, uerus et necessarius ipsius intellectus, et infallibilis, dum est practicus. Per auctoritates autem intellectus quandoque uadit per credere, quandoque per intelligere, quia sensus auctoritatum patitur mutationem et opiniones."

63   *Libre del gentil* Prol., NEORL 2:12: "E pus per aucturitats no.ns podem avenir, que asajasem si.ns puriem avenir per rahons demostratives e necesaries"; trans. Bonner, *SW* 1:116.

a Christian and a Muslim disputed in turn by reasons, rather than by authorities, for they reject authorities, because of their diverse interpretations.[64]

The canonical books and texts on which the religions rely respectively cause and engender, in Llull's view, separation rather than unity. If Llull nevertheless occasionally refers to the Bible, the Church Fathers, or to notable theologians, he does so to provide evidence for the need to advance from believing to understanding:

> Blessed Augustine wrote a book for proving the Holy Trinity based on the merit of faith, which he was not against, because he was holy. Also Thomas Aquinas wrote a book *Against Gentiles*, who demand reasons, because they do not want to abandon believing for believing, but rather believing for understanding.[65]

Aquinas, for his part, held arguments from authority in theology as the most reasonable of all, and even warned against pursuing other manners of proof in matters of faith.[66] Indeed, Aquinas had recourse in the *Summa contra Gentiles* to rational arguments only when there was no alternative, for example, in the confrontation with Islam; however, he considers rational arguments to be inadequate for theological questions. Aquinas used a different approach with regard to the faith of the Hebrews, because he assumed that the Old Testament provided a meaningful common ground to engage with Judaism.[67] Llull rejected such changes in method, because faith-content is both, on the one

---

64   *Disputatio Raymundi et Hamar* 3, ROL 12:261: "quod christianus et Saracenus per rationes, et non per auctoritates, ad inuicem disputarent. Nam auctoritates calumniantur, ratione diuersarum expositionum." Cf. Bonner, "L'apologètica de Ramon Martí i Ramon Llull," 179.

65   *Liber de convenientia fidei et intellectus in obiecto* 1.2, MOG 4:572: "Beatus Augustinus fecit librum ad probandum divinam Trinitatem supposito merito fidei, contra quam fidem ipse non fuit, quia erat sanctus. Iterum (beatus) Thomas de Aquino fecit unum librum contra gentiles, qui requirunt rationes, quia nolunt dimittere credere pro credere, sed credere pro intelligere."

66   Cf. Thomas Aquinas, *Summa Theologiae* 1a.32.1 and 1a.1.8ad2.

67   Cf. Thomas Aquinas, *Summa contra gentiles* 1.2.4. Cf. Matthias Lutz-Bachmann, "Rationalität und Religion: Der Beitrag des Thomas von Aquin zu einer rationalen Grundlegung des Religionsdialogs in der *Summa contra gentiles*," in *Juden, Christen und Muslime: Religionsdialoge im Mittelalter*, (ed.) Matthias Lutz-Bachmann and Alexander Fidora (Darmstadt: 2004), 114–116, and Ramon Llull, *Liber predicationis contra iudeos*, (ed.) José M. Millás Vallicrosa (Madrid and Barcelona: 1957), 71ff.

hand, discovered and developed rationally, and, on the other, it is revealed by God Himself. Llull thus replaced Aquinas's tenet "partly accessible to reason and partly through revelation"[68] with one which reads "both accessible to reason and through revelation."[69] In this reason-based approach, Llull considered himself to be backed up by Aquinas.

For Llull, there is no realm of Christian faith completely closed to reason and accessible to faith alone. This also applies to the doctrine that certain attributes or divine virtues belong to God, who has revealed His name (as in Ex. 3.14), His patience and mercy (as in Ex. 34.6-7), and His innermost essence that manifests "love" (as in 1 John 4.8). Llull severely restricts the Christian position, insofar as it derives its list of basic attributes from only rational arguments, and this as attributes that logically cannot be conceived of otherwise. With this conviction he is committed to the Christian tradition in the wake of Anselm of Canterbury. As we have already noted above, Llull abandoned arguments from authority derived from Christian revelation for ones based on and accessible via the natural exercise of reason: "Unbelievers do not stand for Christian authorities, but they do stand for reasons" (*Infideles non stant ad auctoritates fidelium, et tamen stant ad rationes*).[70]

His missionary experience taught Llull that adherents of other faiths, in spite of many doubts and uncertainties, hardly ever leave their faith and convert to Christianity, unless they are thoroughly convinced by evidence of the truth of the Christian faith. He therefore formulated the maxim "they will not abandon belief for belief, but belief for understanding" (*nolunt dimittere credere pro credere sed credere pro intelligere*).[71] According to Llull, people want to understand why Christianity is a better religion for them, why its tenets of faith are more plausible. If Christianity were merely a question of belief, this would leave little space for arguing why a non-Christian should convert to Christianity. Were it God's will that the articles of faith be in their nature incapable of proof, as Ramon Martí declares,[72] then God Himself would be guilty of the damnation of non-Christians. "Since such a wrong in God is impossible, it

---

68   *Summa Theologiae* 1a.1.1.

69   Raeder, "Lullus als Scholastiker," 285.

70   *Liber de demonstratione per aequiparantiam* Prol.4, ROL 9:221.

71   *Liber de convenientia fidei et intellectus in obiecto* 1.2, MOG 4:572; *Blaquerna* 84.5, ORL 9:326; *Liber super Psalmum Quicumque vult* Prol.2, MOG 4:348; *Disputació de cinc savis* Prol., (ed.) Perarnau i Espelt, 29; *Liber de fine*, ROL 9:267–268.

72   Cf. Ramon Martí, *Pugio fidei adversus Mauros et Judaeos* 1.13, § 11 (1687; repr. Farnborough: 1967), 229: "the Articles of Faith cannot be proven demonstratively" (*articula autem fidei demonstrative probari non possunt*).

follows that the most Holy Trinity must be demonstrable,"[73] i.e. explainable in a logically consistent manner. A rational proof can neither be replaced by subjective certainty, nor by appealing to authority.[74] Ergo Llull seeks to convince his addressees on rational grounds.[75]

On this basis, for Llull the faith of the so-called infidels is faith nevertheless. Yet faith as such is characterized or defined by not doubting. Faith can therefore be directed toward the path of truth or toward the path of error, since "faith can be wrong or right, but reason is always right;"[76] reason knows, albeit only discursively, yet it is able to check its assumptions critically. With interreligious sensitivity, Llull does not assume that what is happening in other religions is idolatry or mere paganism; Llull still considered this an instantiation of religious faith, albeit of faith that is in error and to whom it is one's duty, as a rational thinker, to help out of this error through appropriate explanation. This is why Llull presents his religious dialogue on a rational basis. In order for rational argumentation to be able to reach into questions of faith, belief and reason cannot contradict one another. For Llull, faith is the indispensable basis for a proper knowledge and understanding in matters of religion, but it is a necessary, not a sufficient condition for understanding. For Llull faith and reason converge, forming but two moments of a single process. As Colomer explains it: "Reason rests on faith and faith rides upon reason. At heart, this is surely a special version of Anselm's *fides quaerens intellectum*."[77]

6.4.2   *What Is New in Llull's Approach?*

Using the attributes of God for an encounter of religions is certainly neither new nor unique. Yet the method developed by Llull is both, in that it neither proceeds according to the pattern of affirming one's identity through differentiation, nor does it simply pursue persuasion as its goal, but is, as we have already discussed, based on convincing through *rationes necessariae*.[78] The

---

73   *Disputatio fidei et intellectus* 1.5, MOG 4:482: "et quia talis injuria in Deo est impossibilis, sequitur igitur, quod beatissima Trinitas sit demonstrabilis."

74   Cf. *Libre de contemplació* 154.6, ORL 4:323.

75   Cf. Vittorio Hösle, "Einführung in die *Logica nova*," in Ramon Llull, *Logica nova*, (ed.) Charles Lohr (Hamburg: 1985), LXIII.

76   *Libre de contemplació* 154.4 and 154.7, ORL 4:323–324: "Fe és cosa qui pot ésser en veritat o falsetat ...; e raó, Senyer, null temps no està si no en veritat."

77   Eusebi Colomer i Pous, "El problema de la relació fe-raó en Ramon Llull: proposta de solució," in *Actes del Simposi Internacional de Filosofia de l'Edat Mitjana* (*Vic-Girona, 11-16 d'abril del 1993*) (Vic: 1996), 17: "la raó recolza sobre la fe i la fe cavalca sobre al raó. En el fons, es tracta segurament d'una versió peculiar de fides quaerens intellectum de sant Anselm."

78   Cf. Hames, *Art of Conversion*, 9, on the uniqueness of Llull's method vs. those of the Mendicants.

two more common missionary strategies of Dominican and Franciscan friars, deploying arguments *ex auctoritate* and relying on rhetorical tricks of persuasion, are vehemently rejected by Llull.

Llull was interested in a veritable "tria-log" among the three monotheistic faiths. Even if in the course of his life Llull developed an unquenchable focus on Islam, because this seemed more of a challenge, Judaism remained a constant travel companion. What was exciting and original in Llull's approach was exactly his refusal to leave anything out, proceeding instead with a rigorous "tria-logic," and on this basis striving for co-operation between religions. He does this, however, not primarily as a quest for justice and peace, although these are implied in Llull's search for one "true religion" (*vera religio*) that makes possible unity and peace among peoples: rather, Llull is concerned first and foremost with saving souls irrespective of their religious background.

Llull understood how to link, on the one hand, comparable religious teachings with, on the other hand, the compatibility of the religions themselves. The truth of the one God is the common condition that Llull posits for this task. The attributes are the pragmatic starting points of Llull's missionary praxis. Llull based himself on and benefited from the real historical exchange of religious ideas between learned men and women of various faiths and geographical locations; Llull intentionally prepares the ground so that in actual fact they can find common starting points for each other's teachings. This might be a deliberately engineered "horizon-fusion," to employ Gadamer's notion that in "the process of understanding there takes place a real fusing of horizons."[79] Llull himself used such a fusion of horizons for countering misunderstandings or the lack of understanding of the Christian religion.

Thus, the theory of Herman Beck must be questioned, for it considers Llull a model for today's interreligious dialogue only with regard to formal, not to substantive aspects.[80] Llull's "inclusivism" involved a limited "principle of charity," in the sense described by Donaldson.[81] This was why Llull became so engaged with the topic of pure hermeneutics, based, for him, on the irrefutable axiom that some of the statements of other religions must have a true propositional

---

79   Hans Georg Gadamer, *Truth and Method* (London: 1975), 273.
80   Cf. Herman L. Beck, "Ramon Llull's Approach to Islam: A Change from Dialogue to Refutation?" in *Für die Freiheit verantwortlich*, (ed.) Jan Jans (Freiburg: 2004), 147.
81   Cf. Donald Davidson, *Inquiries into Truth and Interpretation* (Oxford: 1984), XVII: "it counsels us quite generally to prefer theories of interpretation that minimize disagreement ... But minimizing disagreement, or maximizing agreement, is a confused ideal. The aim of interpretation is not agreement but understanding. My point has always been that understanding can be secured only by interpreting in a way that makes for the right sort of agreement. The 'right sort,' however, is no easier to specify than to say what constitutes a good reason for holding a particular belief."

content, meaning that their teachings are thus correct, but only in so far as they can also be derived or deduced from Christian teaching. Out of this limitation arise both Llull's ambivalence toward the value of other religions as well as the notion of "surpassing" by including. While the faith of "infidels" is yet "faith," this faith is outdone by Christian faith, "for no faith can, by not believing in the Trinity, be greater than the faith which believes that God is one person who begets another infinitely in Goodness, Greatness, Eternity, etc., and that from both there proceeds another person infinitely in Goodness, Greatness, Eternity, etc."[82] Little wonder then that Llull had to accept setbacks and failures in pursuit of inter-faith dialogue.

Works Cited

Primary Works

Thomas Aquinas, *Summa contra gentiles*, trans. Karl Albrecht and Paulus Engelhardt (Darmstadt: 1993).

Thomas Aquinas, *Summa Theologiae*, in *Thomae Aquinatis Opera Omnia, cum hypertextibus in CD-ROM*, (ed.) Robert Busa (Mailand: 1996).

Aristotle, *Kategorien*, trans. Eugen Rolfes, 2nd. ed. (Hamburg: 1974).

Bonaventure, *Itinerarium mentis in Deum*, in *Opera omnia* 5 (Quarrachi: 1891), 293–316.

Dionysius Areopagita, *De Divinis Nominibus*, Corpus Dionysiacum 1, (ed.) Beate Regina Suchla (Berlin: 1990).

Gribal, Enrique Claudio, *Los judíos en Gerona* (Gerona: 1870).

Isidore of Seville, *Sententiae*, (ed.) Pierre Cazier, Corpus Christianorum Series Latina 111 (Turnhout: 1998).

Moses Maimonides, *The Guide for the Perplexed*, trans. Michael Friedländer (New York: 1904).

Martí, Ramon, *Pugio fidei adversus Mauros et Judaeos* (1687; repr. Farnborough: 1967).

Nachmanides (Bonastruc de Porta), *Vikuah*, in *Judaism on Trial: Jewish-Christian Disputations in the Middle Ages*, (ed.) Hyam Maccoby (East Brunswick: 1982), 102–146.

Richard of Saint Victor, *De Trinitate*, (ed.) and trans. Gaston Salet (Paris: 1999).

Richard of Saint Victor, *On the Trinity*, trans. by Ruben Angelici (Eugene, Oregon: 2011).

Romano, David, *Per a una història de la Girona jueva*, Vol. 1 (Gerona: 1988).

---

82   *Libre del gentil* 3.2-4.17, NEORL 2:104–105: "Cor nulla ffe no pot eser major en descreure trinitat, que la ffe qui creu que en Deu sia .iª. persona qui engenre altra persona inffinidament en bonea, granea, eternitat, etc., e que d'amdós isca altra persona inffinidament en bonea, granea, eternitat, etc.;" trans. Bonner, *SW* 1:207–208.

Primary Works: Llull

Blaquerna [*Libre de Blanquerna*], ORL 9.

Declaratio Raymundi, ROL 17:219–402.

Disputació de cinc savis, (ed.) Josep Perarnau i Espelt, *Arxiu de Texts Antics Catalans* 5 (1986): 7–229.

Disputatio fidei et intellectus, ROL 23:213–279.

Disputatio fidelis et infidelis, MOG 4:377–429 (text 6, sep. pag.).

Disputatio Raymundi christiani et Hamar saraceni, ROL 22:159–264.

Disputatio Raymundi et Averroistae, ROL 7:1–17.

Lectura super Artem inventivam et Tabulam generalem, MOG 5:359–716 (text 5, sep. pag.).

Liber de acquisitione Terrae Sanctae, (ed.) Eugène Kamar, "Projet de Raymond Llull *De acquisitione Terrae Sanctae*: Introduction et édition critique du texte," *Studia Orientalia Christiana* 6 (1961): 103–131.

Liber de convenientia fidei et intellectus, MOG 4:571–575 (text 11, sep. pag.).

Liber de demonstratione per aequiparantiam, ROL 9:201–231.

Liber de fine, ROL 9:233–291.

Liber de participatione christianorum et saracenorum, ROL 16:237–260.

Liber de praedicatione, ROL 3–4.

Liber mirandarum demonstrationum, MOG 2:177–420 (text 5, sep. pag.).

Liber predicationis contra judeos, (ed.) José M. Millás Vallicrosa (Madrid and Barcelona: 1957).

Liber super Psalmum Quicumque vult, MOG 4:347–376 (text 5, sep. pag.).

Libre de contemplació en Deu, ORL 2–8.

Libre del gentil e dels tres savis, NEORL 2.

Libre del gentil e dels tres savis, trans. Pindl, Theodor, *Das Buch vom Heiden und den drei Weisen* (Stuttgart: 1998).

Logica nova, (ed.) Charles Lohr (Hamburg: 1985).

Vita coaetanea, ROL 8:259–309.

Vita coaetanea, trans. Bonner, Anthony, *Ramon Llull: A Contemporary Life* (Barcelona & Woodbridge: 2010).

Secondary Works

Artus, Walter W., "Judaísmo e Islamismo en la autobiografía y en algunos escritos de Raimundo Lulio," *Mediaevalia Textos e Estúdios* 5–6 (1994): 191–203.

Beck, Herman L., "Ramon Llull's Approach to Islam: A Change from Dialogue to Refutation?" in *Für die Freiheit verantwortlich*, (ed.) Jan Jans (Freiburg: 2004), 135–147.

Bonner, Anthony, "L'apologètica de Ramon Martí i Ramon Llull davant de l'Islam i del judaisme," in *El debat intercultural als segles XIII i XIV: Actes de les Primeres*

Jornades de Filosofia Catalana, Girona 25–27 d'abril del 1988, (ed.) Marcel Salleras (Girona: 1989), 171–185.

Broadie, Alexander, "Maimonides and Aquinas on the Names of God," *Religious Studies* 23 (1987): 157–170.

Burrell, David, "Beyond Idolatry: On 'Naming' the One – God," in *Finding God in All Things*, (ed.) Michael J. Himes (New York: 1996), 28–37.

Christian, William A., "Studying Doctrines of Religious Communities," in *Inter-Religious Models and Criteria*, (ed.) James Kellenberger (Basingstoke: 1993), 135–150.

Eusebi Colomer i Pous, *El pensament als països catalans durant l'edat mitjana i el renaixement* (Barcelona: 1997).

Eusebi Colomer i Pous, "El problema de la relació fe-raó en Ramon Llull: proposta de solució," in *Actes del Simposi Internacional de Filosofia de l'Edat Mitjana (Vic-Girona, 11-16 d'abril del 1993)* (Vic: 1996), 11–20.

Eusebi Colomer i Pous, "Raimund Lulls Stellung zu den Andersgläubigen: Zwischen Zwie-und Streitgespräch," in *Religionsgespräche im Mittelalter*, (eds.) Bernard Lewis and Friedrich Niewöhner (Wiesbaden: 1992), 217–236.

Daiber, Hans, "Raimundus Lullus in der Auseinandersetzung mit dem Islam: Eine philosophiegeschichtliche Analyse des Liber disputationis Raimundi Christiani et Homeri Saraceni," in *Juden, Christen und Muslime. Religionsdialoge im Mittelalter*, (eds.) Matthias Lutz-Bachmann and Alexander Fidora (Darmstadt: 2004), 136–172.

Davidson, Donald, *Inquiries into Truth and Interpretation* (Oxford: 1984).

Enders, Markus, "Die Bedeutung der christlichen Philosophie der monotheistischen Weltreligionen im frühen Mittelalter für das interreligiöse Gespräch der Gegenwart," *Archa Verbi* 7 (2010), 143–165.

Euler, Walter Andreas, Unitas et Pax: *Religionsvergleich bei Raimundus Lullus und Nikolaus von Kues* (Würzburg: 1990).

Flemming, Johanna, "Baum, Bäume," in *Lexikon der christlichen Ikonographie*, Vol. 1, (ed.) Engelbert Kirschbaum (Rome: 1968), col. 266–267.

Friedlein, Roger, *Der Dialog bei Ramon Llull: Literarische Gestaltung als apologetische Strategie* (Tübingen: 2004).

Gadamer, Hans Georg, *Truth and Method*, trans. Joel Weinsheimer and Donald G. Marshall (London: 1975).

Gayà Estelrich, Jordi, "Ramon Llull i l'Islam: 'Infideles sunt homines, sicut et nos'; 'Vós sou sant, Senyor Déu únic,'" in *Franciscanisme i Islam: Jornades d'Estudis Franciscans 2001* (Barcelona: 2002), 115–143.

Hames, Harvey J., *The Art of Conversion: Christianity and Kabbalah in the Thirteenth Century* (Leiden: 2000).

Helmdach, Boris, "Das Relationale im Denken Ramon Llulls," Diplomarbeit Grund- und Integrativwissenschaftliche Fakultät Universität Wien (Vienna: 1994).

Hösle, Vittorio, "Einführung in die *Logica nova*," in Ramon Llull, *Logica nova*, (ed.) Charles Lohr (Hamburg: 1985), IX–XCIV.

Johnson, Mark, "Apophatic Theology's Cataphatic Dependencies," *The Thomist* 62 (1998): 519–531.

Jüngel, Eberhard, *Ganz werden* (Tübingen: 2003).

Jüngel, Eberhard, "Thesen zum Verhältnis von Existenz, Wesen und Eigenschaften Gottes," *Zeitschrift für Theologie und Kirche* 96 (1999): 405–423.

Kamar, Eugène, "Projet de Raymond Llull *De acquisitione Terrae Sanctae*: Introduction et édition critique du texte," *Studia Orientalia Cristiana Collectanea* 6 (1961): 103–131.

Kessler, Hans, "Was macht Religionen pluralismusfähig (und authentisch)? Fragmente einer Theologie des religiösen Pluralismus – jenseits von *Dominus Iesus* und Pluralistischer Religionstheologie," in *Der eine Gott und die Welt der Religionen: Beiträge zu einer Theologie der Religionen und zum interreligiösen Dialog*, (ed.) Markus Witte (Würzburg: 2003), 277–314.

Lutz-Bachmann, Matthias, "Rationalität und Religion: Der Beitrag des Thomas von Aquin zu einer rationalen Grundlegung des Religionsdialogs in der *Summa contra gentiles*," in *Juden, Christen und Muslime: Religionsdialoge im Mittelalter*, (eds.) Matthias Lutz-Bachmann and Alexander Fidora (Darmstadt: 2004), 96–118.

Mayer, Annemarie C., *Drei Religionen – ein Gott? Ramon Llulls interreligiöse Diskussion der Eigenschaften Gottes* (Freiburg im Breisgau: 2008).

Merle, Hélène, "Dignitas: signification philosophique et théologique de ce terme chez Lulle et ses predecesseurs médiévaux," *EL* 21 (1977): 173–193.

Mutius, Hans-Georg von, *Die christlich-jüdische Zwangsdisputation zu Barcelona, Nach dem hebräischen Protokoll des Moses Nachmanides* (Frankfurt: 1982).

Raeder, Siegfried, "Raimundus Lullus als Scholastiker in der Auseinandersetzung mit dem Islam," *Judaica* 52 (1996): 271–288.

Schimmel, Annemarie, "Raymundus Lullus und seine Auseinandersetzung mit dem Islam," *Eine Heilige Kirche* 27 (Munich: 1953–1954): 64–76.

Scholem, Gerschom, *Das Buch Bahir* (1923; repr. Darmstadt: 1970).

Striet, Magnus, *Offenbares Geheimnis: zur Kritik der negativen Theologie* (Regensburg: 2003).

Stroumsa, Sarah, "Ibn al-Rāwandī's *sū' adab al-mujādala*: The Role of Bad Manners in Medieval Disputations," in *The Majils: Interreligious Encounters in Medieval Islam*, (ed.) Hava Lazarus-Yafeh (Wiesbaden: 1999), 66–83.

CHAPTER 7

Ramon Llull's Crusade Treatises

Pamela Beattie

> Ah! When will the lover boast of dying for his beloved? And when will the
> beloved see the lover languishing for love of him?
>
> Book of the Lover and the Beloved[1]

Although Llull's treatises on crusade can justifiably be considered "minor"
in comparison to his Great Art and his better known philosophical, literary,
and mystical works, they are nevertheless significant. Close attention to Llull's
ideas about crusading reveals that they are firmly grounded in the specific
goals he embraced upon the occasion of his "conversion" and to which the autobiographical *Vita Coaetanea* testifies retrospectively; namely to "give up his
life and soul for the sake of [Christ's] love and honor," to do so "carrying out the
task of converting to His worship and service the Saracens who in such numbers surrounded the Christians on all sides," and to accomplish this by writing
"a book, the best in the world, against the errors of the unbelievers" and to
procure the establishment of missionary schools.[2] Indeed, Llull's crusade texts
can be understood as specific applications of the basic tenets which underpin
his Art and emerge from his post-conversion attempts to realize and, literally,
to embody these goals. Consequently, careful reading of Llull's writings about
crusade indicates the general religious preoccupations behind his life's work.
Such a study also provides an avenue through which historians of the crusades
and late medieval religious culture can explore the internalization and appro-
priation of crusade ideology by the educated laity of Llull's time.

It is clear that the subjects of evangelization and crusading were consistently
on Llull's mind and connected to the promotion of his Art because references
to these topics permeate his works. The autobiographical poems *Lo desconhort*
and *Cant de Ramon* offer compelling testimony about the degree to which Llull

---

1 *Book of the Lover and the Beloved*, para. 5, trans. Eve Bonner, in Anthony Bonner, *Doctor Illuminatus: A Ramon Llull Reader* (Princeton: 1993), 190; for the original Catalan see *Romanç
   d'Evast e Blaquerna*, NEORL 8:430.
2 *Vita coaetanea*, ROL 8:259–309; Bonner, *Ramon Llull: A Contemporary Life* (Barcelona: 2010),
   provides a facing-page English translation; for the conversion story, see 32–37.

was invested in garnering support for these proposals.[3] His most significant vernacular books, such as *Libre de contemplació, Romanç d'Evast e Blaquerna,* and *Libre del gentil e dels tres savis,* discuss peaceful dialogue with unbelievers, crusading, and church reform in the broadest sense. Indeed, these topics provide the focus of the entire fourth book of *Romanç d'Evast e Blaquerna.* Not all these works supported crusading unequivocally.[4] Still, they demonstrate how thoroughly evangelization, crusading, and even church reform were entangled in Llull's mind and integrated into his thought. And, Llull also wrote a small number of works in which he specifically addressed the subject of the recovery of the Holy Land, starting with the *Liber de passagio* of 1292 and ending with a memorandum on the subject for the Council of Vienne in 1311. With the exception of the *Liber de fine* of 1305, these treatises were relatively short. Their titles and prologues advertise the specificity of their subject but their contents prove that for Llull, crusading was inseparable from issues connected to evangelization of unbelievers and Church reform. In each text Llull discusses missionary strategies and the spiritual benefits of crusading alongside traditional aspects of crusade planning and military strategy. Additionally, each treatise responds to contemporary political and religious issues. Taken together then, these texts simultaneously reveal Llull's unique perspective and provide a glimpse into the complexities of late 13th-century crusade ideology. It is upon these particular texts that this essay places it focus.[5]

---

3 For example, *Lo desconhort* 24, cites Llull's treatise *Lo Passatge* (the *Liber de passagio*), which he claims clearly shows how the Holy Sepulchre can be recovered; *Lo desconhort/Der desconhort,* (ed.) and trans. Johannes and Vittorio Hösle (Munich: 1998), 72. The much shorter *Cant de Ramon,* ORL 19:255–260, contains an equally passionate lament about his apparent failure to gain support.

4 For example, *Libre contra antichrist* 3.2, "Of wars and battles" (*De guerres e de batalles*), NEORL 3:158–160; Latin *Liber contra antichristum,* ROL 36:122–124; echoes of these criticisms appear already in *Libre de contemplació* 112, ORL 4:59. *Romanç d'Evast e Blaquerna* 78–95, NEORL 8:342–418, on the apostolic life, voices both support for and criticism of crusading. In the *Libre del gentil e dels tres savis* 4.4.2, NEORL 2:167–168, Llull's Saracen argues that Muslim control of the Holy Land is proof of the truth of the Qur'an and the error of Christians and Jews. Another reflection of Llull's ambiguity about crusade can be found in *Libre de meravelles* 1.12, trans. Bonner, *SW* 2:715, where Felix "wonders" that the Christians have "put up with the situation [of Saracens possessing the Holy Land] for such a long time," to which the hermit Blaquerna responds with an anecdote in which a sultan expresses wonder that Christians use the methods of Mohammed, namely physical force, to try to recapture the Holy Land. On this anecdote, repeated in *Romanç d'Evast e Blaquerna* 80, the *Ars notatoria,* and the *Liber de Sancta Maria,* see Bonner, *SW* 2:715, n. 60.

5 Llull's crusade treatises are: *Liber de passagio,* ROL 28:255–353; *Petitio Raimundi pro conuersione infidelium ad Coelestinum V papam* and *Petitio Raimundi pro conuersione infidelium ad Bonifatium VIII papam,* ROL 35:403–437, which contains facing-page critical editions of

The late thirteenth and early fourteenth centuries saw what could arguably be described as an explosion of crusade treatises. They contained, in various combinations, elements of crusade sermons, historical narrative, advice about organization and financing, and suggestions about military strategy. The texts could be short and epistolary in nature or much longer and more historical. They could be didactic or exhortatory. Some were unsolicited. Each text responded to specific historical circumstances or political and economic opportunities. Llull was one of the most prolific writers of these texts, like his contemporaries composing works of various lengths sometimes "on spec" and sometimes, as in the case of his memorandum for the Council of Vienne, in response to calls for advice.[6] A brief summary and analysis of the first of Llull's crusade proposals, and its comparison to subsequent works, evinces the remarkable consistency of their basic contours as well as Llull's flexibility in detail and responsiveness to circumstance. An important benefit of such a study is that it also allows us to gauge the extent to which Llull's texts can help us understand the history of the reception and dissemination of contemporary crusading discourse.

Llull's earliest "recovery treatise," the *Liber de passagio,* was most probably written in response to Pope Nicholas IV's appeal for advice concerning the Holy Land and is comprised of two texts which could be read independently of each other. The first very short text, sometimes described as an *epistola,* is *Quomodo terra sancta recuperari potest.* The second is a slightly lengthier memorandum called *Tractatus de modo convertendi infideles.*[7] The coupling of

---

the letters; a Catalan version of the letter to Celestine V, edited by Josep Pernarnau, "Un text català de Ramon Llull desconegut: la 'Petició de Ramon al papa Celestí V per la conversió dels infidels,' edició i estudi," *Arxiu de Textos Catalans Antics* 1 (1982): 9–46; *Liber de fine,* ROL 9:249–291; *Liber de acquisitione Terrae Sanctae,* (ed.) E. Longpré, *Criterion* 3 (1927): 265–278, and by E. Kamar, Studia Orientalia Christiana 6 (1961): 103–131; for this essay I consulted Paris, Bibliothèque Nationale, Lat. 15450, fols. 544v-47v. In addition, Llull promotes mission and crusade in his recommendations to the Council of Vienne, "Ordinationes decem quas Raimundus intendit praesentare in Concilio generale," included as Section 6 of his *Liber de ente quod simpliciter est per se et propter se existens et agens* ROL 8:179–245.

6   On the proliferation of "recovery treatises" as an important feature of the crusading movement after 1291, see Norman Housley, *The Later Crusades from Lyon to Alcazar 1274–1580* (Oxford: 2001), 23ff. Anthony Leopold, *How to Recover the Holy Land: The Crusade Proposals of the Late Thirteenth and Early Fourteenth Centuries* (Aldershot: 2000), surveys and compares almost thirty treatises written between the pontificate of Nicholas IV and the beginning of the Hundred Years War. Still one of the best surveys of Llull's ideas in historical context is J.N. Hillgarth, *RLL,* updated in *Ramon Llull i el naixement del Lul·lisme* (Barcelona: 1998).

7   See the excellent introduction to the *Liber de passagio* by Fernando Domínguez Reboiras, ROL 28:257–331, and his "La idea de cruzada en el 'Liber de Passagio' de Ramón Llull," *Patristica et mediaevalia* 25 (2004): 45–74. The manuscript history of the text makes it clear

these two texts, one primarily focused on the recovery of the Holy Land and one on the conversion of unbelievers, shows how Llull's crusading theory was inextricably intertwined with issues of evangelization even in the manuscript history of his works. In addition, despite the indications of the titles, Llull discusses both subjects in both parts of the *Liber de passagio*.[8]

Llull begins *Quomodo terra sancta recuperari potest* (hereafter *Quomodo terra sancta*) with merely the briefest of invocations: "God, in your virtue, let it be shown here how the Holy Land can be recovered,"[9] and proceeds to address in equally summary fashion some important aspects of crusade planning. These include unification of the military orders, leadership, education of missionaries, strategies for evangelization, the relationship between the Latin and Greek churches, finances, the advantages that the Muslims have over the Christians

---

that the two parts did circulate independently of one another. See Domínguez Reboiras, ROL 28:316–322; cf. Sebastián Garcías Palou, "Sobre la identificacion del 'Libre del passatge,'" *EL* 16 (1972): 216–230.

8   It is possible to consider the dichotomy between mission and crusade as more of a contemporary problem than a medieval one. See: Berthold Altaner, "Glaubenszwang und Glaubensfreiheit in der Missionstheorie des Raymundus Lullus: Ein Beitrag zur Geschichte der Toleranz," *Historisches Jahrbuch* 48 (1928): 586–610; Pamela Beattie, "'Pro exaltation sanctae fidei catholicae': Mission and Crusade in the writings of Ramon Llull," in Larry J. Simon (ed.), *Iberia and the Mediterranean World of the Middle Ages: Studies in Honor of Robert I. Burns S.J.*, 2 vols. (Leiden: 1995), 1:113–129; Gabriel Ensenyat, "Pacifisme i croada en Ramon Llull," in Maria-Àngels Roque (ed.), *Ramon Llull i l'Islam: L'inici del diàleg* (Barcelona: 2008), 232–245; Franco Cardini, *Studi sulla storia e sull'idea di crociata* (Rome: 1993); E.R. Daniel, *The Franciscan Concept of Mission in the High Middle Ages* (Lexington, Kentucky: 1975); Benjamin Z. Kedar, *Crusade and Mission: European Approaches Toward the Muslims* (Princeton: 1984), especially his section on "The Many Opinions of Ramon Llull," 189–197; Paul Rousset, "La Croisade obstacle à la mission," *Nova et vetera* 57 (1982): 133–142; Steven Runciman, "The Decline of the Crusading Idea," in *Relazioni del Congresso Internazionale di Scienze Storiche*, vol. 3: *Storia del medioevo* (Florence: 1995), 637–652; Ramon Sugranyes de Franch, *Raymond Lulle, Docteur des Missions* (Schönick-Beckenried: 1954). Josep Perarnau i Espelt, "Consideracions sobre el tema 'Missió i Croada en Ramon Llull,'" *Arxiu de Textos Catalans Antics* 22 (2003): 561–578, analyzes Llull's *Libre de contemplació* 346, which he sees as Llull's first synthesis of the theme of mission and crusade. Perarnau also reviews a number of works focused primarily on Llull's missionary ideas: Jordi Gayà Estelrich, "Ramon Llull, il suo impegno missionario," *Analecta TOR* 32 (2001): 379–388; "Ramon Llull i l'Islam: 'Infideles sunt homines, sicut nos'," in *"Vós sou sant, Senyor Déu únic": Franciscanisme i Islam* (Barcelona: 2002), 115–143; *Raimondo Lullo: Una teologia per la missione* (Milan: 2002); and Llull, *Darrer llibre sobre la conquesta de Terra Santa*, intr. Jordi Gayà Estelrich, trans. Pere Llabrés (Barcelona: 2002). Robin Vose, *Dominicans, Muslims and Jews in the Medieval Crown of Aragon* (Cambridge: 2009) does not specifically discuss crusading or the *reconquista*, but his important book clarifies the complex nature of interfaith contacts in the medieval Crown of Aragon.

9   *Quomodo terra sancta* 2.1-2, ROL 28:328. For a useful and concise discussion, see Charles-Emmanuel Dufourcq, "La Méditerranée et le Christianisme: Cadre géopolitique et économique de l'apostolat missionaire de Ramon Llull," *EL* 24 (1980): 5–22.

in warfare, and the great benefit to the Church and Christendom that would accrue if Llull's plans were to be followed. Although he does not discuss any one of these subjects at length, taken together they demonstrate Llull's systematic and structural way of thinking, in which a number of individual provisions and actions are intricately related to each other in subordination to a greater goal, in this case the unification of all believers in their proper state of knowing and loving God.[10] This kind of systematic organization and interest in the relationship between the parts and the whole is, of course, characteristic of Llull's age. Llull's Art is the most obvious example of this structured or organized approach to knowledge. However, although other contemporary theorists give comparable advice on some of the topics Llull addresses, his range of crusade topics is unparalleled, and no other theorist combines crusade and evangelization in the same deliberate and insistent way that he does.[11]

The *Quomodo terra sancta* is also a good example of how Llull was able to harness contemporary concerns in the service of his own unique goals. In August 1291, Pope Nicholas IV published two bulls soliciting advice about the recovery of the Holy Land in which he also requested recommendations concerning the military orders.[12] Probably in response to this request, Llull's first, emphatic, piece of advice in *Quomodo terra sancta* expresses his conviction that all the military orders ought to be unified into a single "Order of the Holy Spirit."[13] Some of Llull's contemporaries also advocated the unification

10   On this greater goal, see Marta M.M. Romano and Óscar de la Cruz, "The Human Realm," in *Raimundus Lullus: An Introduction to his Life, Works and Thought*, (eds.) Alexander Fidora and Josep E. Rubio, ROL Suppl. 2:399–402 and 413–414.

11   Leopold, *How to Recover the Holy Land*, compares in detail contemporary treatises on topics ranging from preparations for crusading to routes for the crusading armies.

12   *Dirum amaritudinis* (August 13, 1291) and *Dura nimis* (August 18, 1291); see *Registres de Nicolas IV*, (ed.) E. Langlois (Paris: 1886–91), nos. 6791-5, and Leopold, *How to Recover the Holy* Land, 16–24. Domínguez Reboiras discusses Nicholas IV as the recipient for Llull's *Liber de passagio* in ROL 28:292–303, and in "Nicolás IV, destinatario del 'Liber de passagio,' y Ramon Llull," *SL* 44 (2004): 3–15. On crusade proposals from Nicholas' pontificate, see also Sylvia Schein, *Fideles Crucis: The Papacy, the West, and the Recovery of the Holy Land 1274–1314* (Oxford:1991) and Housley, *The Later Crusades*, 7–30. On Nicholas IV's general interest in the east, see James D. Ryan, "Nicholas IV and the Evolution of the Eastern Missionary Effort," *Archivum Historiae Pontificiae* 19 (1981): 79–96.

13   For the history of the military orders in general see the numerous publications by A.J. Forey, especially *The Military Orders from the Twelfth to the Early Fourteenth Centuries* (Toronto: 1992) and *Military Orders and Crusades* (Aldershot: 1994). Of specific relevance is his "The Military Orders in the Crusading Proposals of the Late-thirteenth and Early-fourteenth Centuries," *Traditio* 36 (1980): 317–345, and "The Military Orders and the Conversion of Muslims in the Twelfth and Thirteenth Centuries," *Journal of Medieval History* 28 (2002): 1–22.

of the military orders, most notably Pierre Dubois.[14] However, Llull's proposal for a unified military order had some unique elements. For example, he proposed that the leader of this order should be some strong and devout king, either without a wife or willing to put her aside. Llull insisted that such a person existed.[15] This *magister* should be accompanied on campaign by a cardinal legate, in whose hands the finances, particularly the crusading tithes, could securely rest. Llull's proposal recognized the organizational and strategic problems inherent in the very enterprise of crusading and tried to unify both ecclesiastical and temporal leaders in the service of a good that he saw as transcending personal and even institutional ambitions; successful crusading required participation and leadership from both segments of society. In his suggestion that the *magister* cooperate with a papal legate who should control the crusading tithes, Llull acknowledged the concerns of critics who complained about the misappropriation of crusade funds, suggesting an organizational structure designed to make it more difficult for leaders to divert such monies for other, often personal and dynastic, ends.[16] His advocacy of a naval campaign along the coastline of Lesser Armenia (Cilicia) and a naval embargo against the Muslims reflects the development of new military strategy after the fall of Acre in 1291, naval advantages western Europeans had over their Muslim enemies, and perpetual prohibitions against trade with the enemy, particularly in war materials.[17] The idea of a trade embargo against the Muslims, especially with respect to war material, was a consistent concern of crusade planners even before the fall of Acre and according to the *Consitutiones pro Zelo Fidei*, the measures promulgated for aid of the Holy Land at the Second Council of Lyons, those who supplied the Saracens with such materials would be excommunicated and lose their property.[18]

---

14   "De recuperatione Terre Sancte," (ed.) and trans. W. Brandt, *The Recovery of the Holy Land* (New York: 1956). On the support of provincial councils called by Nicholas IV to merge the orders, see Leopold, *How to Recover the Holy Land*, 19–20.

15   *Quomodo terra sancta*, ROL 28:329–330. For a possible identification of this candidate, see Garcías Palou, "El candidato de Ramon Llull para el cargo de 'Maestre General de la Orden Militar del Espíritu Santo,'" *EL* 16 (1972): 63–77. On Llull's connections with Frederick III and Sicily, see Alessandro Musco and Marta M.M. Romano (eds.), *Il Mediterraneo del '300: Raimondo Lullo e Federico III d'Aragona, re di Sicilia: Omaggio a Fernando Domínguez Reiboiras* (Turnhout: 2008).

16   *Quomodo terra sancta*, ROL 28:330.

17   Ibid., ROL 28:328.

18   See Heinrich Finke, *Konzilienstudien zur Geschichte des 13. Jahrhunderts* (Münster: 1891), 113–116; the Lyons decree appears in Housley (ed. and trans.), *Documents on the Later Crusades, 1274–1580* (New York: 1996), 16–20. See also Schein, *Fideles crucis*, 36–41, and, for the increased significance of a naval blockade after the fall of Acre, 79–83.

An essential component of Llull's proposal is his promotion of parallel military and missionary campaigns. Although Llull did not here articulate the precise relationship between the *magister* of the unified military order and the individual leaders of these other campaigns, he insisted that these leaders too should be of exemplary character. Llull argued that the missionary campaign should be led by a master in theology spearheading an army of holy and devoted men who have studied the languages of the unbelievers and schismatics, who are knowledgeable in the fields of theology and philosophy and who, most importantly, have such devotion that they are willing to die for God and to preach the word of God throughout the whole world. These are consistent characteristics of Llull's missionaries throughout his works and connected with the foundation of Llull's missionary monastery of Miramar on Majorca.[19] If the sailors have galleys (and presumably other military technology) at their disposal, the missionaries should be armed with "necessary reasons" contained in books which have been sent to them. Llull's discussion of intellectual (or spiritual) combat dependent on "necessary reasons," like his discussion of leadership and the unification of the military orders, boiled extremely complex issues down to their bare essentials. He also alluded to contemporary controversies surrounding the use of reason in apologetics. Crucial to Llull's methodology is his conviction that Christian doctrines can be proven rationally and so in this treatise, as in others, he unabashedly asserts that his "necessary reasons" are so powerful that they can both destroy the objections that unbelievers have to the Christian faith as well as create "positions" that unbelievers cannot, in turn, defeat.[20] He was convinced that if the Saracens knew what Christians really believed about the Trinity and the Incarnation, they would recognize the truth in Christian doctrine. Llull was confident that his well-educated missionaries could overcome what he perceived to be the major stumbling block to conversion, namely ineffective communication. If Christian doctrine were adequately conveyed to educated Muslims (who, Llull seemed to think, did not really believe in the faith of Muhammad anyway), their conversion would be inevitable.[21] Thus, even in this short treatise, Llull tied his "necessary reasons" to the rationale for the crusade and to what he imagined as its successful outcome, namely conversion and unity.[22]

---

19   *Quomodo terra sancta*, ROL 28:328–329. See Sebastián Garcías Palou, *El Miramar de Ramon Llull* (Palma: 1977); for relevant documents, see Jocelyn N. Hillgarth (ed.), *Diplomatari Lul·lià* (Barcelona: 2001).

20   Ibid., ROL 28:329.

21   Ibid., ROL 28:329.

22   On Llull's "necessary reasons," see Bonner, *AL,* 12–18, and Josep Enric Rubio, "Thought: the Art," in *Raimundus Lullus*, ROL Suppl. 2:243–249. On dialogue and rational disputation

In the *Quomodo terra sancta,* Muslim conversion was somewhat contingent upon reconciliation between Catholics and schismatic Christians of various kinds. Indeed, it seems that Llull imagined the process of conversion as a chain reaction: destruction of the schism through the unification of all Christians would ensure that the Tartars could more easily come to the Catholic faith, especially since they were people "without law."[23] Only Jews, Christians and Muslims, people of the book, have a "law" in the religious sense. Once the Tartars converted, then the Muslims could be destroyed. One event follows the other like a line of toppling dominos, all accomplished easily. Llull's tone is urgent; he cautioned that if the Tartars converted to Islam rather than to Christianity, "all of Christendom will be in great danger."[24] He reiterated this idea at the end of his proposal, warning that if his recommendations were not followed, the Tartars and Muslim would acquire the territories of the Greeks, become neighbors of the Latins, and thus present a great danger.[25] None of the crusade proposals contemporary with the *Liber de passagio* share Llull's suggestion for parallel military and missionary campaigns. However, even here he reflects contemporary preoccupations, ranging from the scholastic (necessary reasons) to the practical (the race to convert the Mongols and heal the schism with the Greek church).

Llull acknowledged that Muslims had some advantages over the Christians, particularly with respect to weapons and organization. In his treatise he expressed admiration for their hierarchical military discipline but argued that their advantages could be overcome if the Church would follow his advice. And so, in the conclusion to his proposal, Llull spelled out the benefits that would accrue to Christendom if his advice were followed, arguing that his plan was "easy" (*leuis*), "possible" (*possibilis*) and "very loveable" (*multum amabilis*) on account of God's honor. Implementation of Llull's plans would both allow church leaders to provide a good example for the laity, inspiring them to great

---

in Llull's work, see Roger Friedlein, *Der Dialog bei Ramon Llull: literarische Gestaltung als apologetische Strategie* (Tubingen: 2004); and Harvey J. Hames, *The Art of Conversion: Christianity and Kabbalah in the Thirteenth Century* (Leiden: 2000).

23 *Quomodo terra sancta,* ROL 28:329. On Llull and the Tartars, see Albert Soler i Llompart, "El 'Liber super Psalmum Quicumque' de Ramon Llull i l'opció pels tartars," *SL* 32 (1992): 3–29. On the Tartars as potential allies, see Peter Jackson, "Hülegü Khan and the Christians: the Making of a Myth," in Peter Edbury and Jonathan Phillips (eds.), *The Experience of Crusading,* vol. 2, *Defining the Crusader Kingdom* (Cambridge: 2003), 196–213; Leopold, *How to Recover the Holy Land,* 111–119; and Sylvia Schein, "*Gesta Dei per Mongolos* 1300: the Genesis of a Non-event," *English Historical Review* 95 (1979): 805–819.

24 *Quomodo terra sancta,* ROL 28:329: "in magno periculo erit tota christianitas."

25 Ibid., ROL 28:331.

good, and would be of great utility to Christendom.[26] In an implied response to those critics who saw the fall of Acre as an expression of God's judgment on Christendom, Llull declared that if the Church did what it should, "God will infuse its efforts with grace and blessing, the manner and devotion through which the Church was exalted through the holy martyrs shall return, and infidels will be converted to the way of truth through the outpouring of their blood."[27] Previously, Llull had hinted that he understood missionary efforts to be an embodiment of the apostolic ideal; here, the allusions become explicit.

The *Quomodo terra sancta* contains a succinct statement of Llull's keys ideas about crusading and connects them to both theoretical and practical issues currently under discussion at the secular and ecclesiastical courts of Europe. It is also exemplary of the unique characteristics of Llull's crusading proposals, chief of which is his inability to discuss military campaigns against unbelievers without concurrently promoting missionary campaigns. Furthermore, both efforts must be understood in the context of the Llull's broader aim, which is to bring the world to its proper end or goal. In this great "business" (*negotium*), Christians of all kinds have a role to play. The consistent concern for the idea of lay vocation, which is evident in many of Llull's writings, is also apparent here. Llull's subsequent crusade proposals, including the second part of the *Liber de passagio* follow essentially the same outline even when they vary slightly in detail, reflecting his response to contemporary events and subsequent adjustment or adaptation of his plans.

The precise relationship between the two parts of the *Liber de passagio* is somewhat unclear. As we have seen, the *Quomodo terra sancta*, dated 1292 in Rome, is a distilled text: it has no addressee and proceeds immediately to the recommendation that the pope and cardinals should unify the military orders. The second, undated part, the *Tractatus de modo convertendi infideles*, is lengthier and more detailed; it is specifically addressed to the pope and his cardinals, with a prologue. Internal evidence suggests that the epistle (*epistola*), or first part of the *Liber de passagio* was written after the second part, the treatise (*tractatus*), by way of introduction, and, more importantly, to address the particular interests and aspirations of the current pope, Nicholas IV, as noted above.[28]

---

26 Ibid., ROL 28:331.

27 Ibid.: "Et, quia ecclesia faceret debitum et posse suum, Deus influeret gratiam et benedictionem negotio praedicto, et rediret modus et deuotio, per quam Ecclesia exaltata fuit per sanctos uiros martires, qui per effusionem sui sanguinis infideles conuertebant ad uiam ueritatis."

28 It was not Llull's consistent habit to record the date and place of composition of his works until 1294. On the relationship between the two parts of the *Liber de passagio*, see

Comparison of the two parts of the *Liber de passagio* is instructive. As the title indicates, Llull's primary emphasis in the *Tractatus* is on the conversion of unbelievers and the reconciliation of all Christians into one church. Thus, of the six parts of the treatise, in the first two sections Llull rather briefly addressed organization and strategies for campaigns at sea (where Christians had a clear advantage) and campaigns at land (which were more complicated by virtue of multiple fronts and varied opponents). In the remaining sections, Llull expanded upon and offered a rationale for his proposals for a missionary campaign, explained why infidels could not be converted through some other method, and, with a rather nice analogy to form and matter, suggested how his proposals could be financed.[29] The structure of the memorandum receives ideological underpinnings in a brief passage at the end of the prologue, where Llull explained that he "proceeds in the way he does, with hope and confidence, because his treatment of the subject corresponds to the nature of the disposition of lands, sea, and the status of the peoples, according to the nature of the powers of the soul, and especially according to the nature of the divine dignities and their virtues."[30] In other words, this treatise corresponds to the basic ideals and method of Llull's Art.

An example of specific differences between the two parts of the *Liber de passagio* can be seen in Llull's plans for military organization and leadership. Possibly in an effort to accommodate (or even capitalize upon) the maritime ambitions of specific European leaders, Llull suggested that that three admirals could divide the Mediterranean into three naval theaters of war. Instead of calling for a unified military order, he argued that deleterious effects of conflict between the military orders could be alleviated by sending each to campaign on a different front, claiming that the more distant each order was from the other, the more each order could prosper in harmony and love.[31] Somewhat startling is Llull's suggestion in the *Tractatus* that the land expedition to Greece should be led by the pope himself, accompanied by a king and the masters of the Templars, Hospitallers, and Teutonic Knights. He argued first that this plan

---

Domínguez Reboiras, ROL 28:307–308 and 316–322. On Llull's flexibility regarding contemporary politics, see Hillgarth, RLL 307–308 and 318–319.

29   *Tractatus de modo convertendi infideles* 6, ROL 28:352.

30   Ibid., ROL 28:336: "Modum, quem in isto tractatu tenemus, consistit secundum naturam dispositionis terrarum, maris ac status gentium; ac etiam secundum naturam potentiarum animae, et maxime secundum diuinas dignitates et naturam et uirtutem earum. In quarum spe et confidentia procedimus."

31   Ibid., ROL 28:339. This passage is the main evidence for believing that Llull wrote this part of the *Liber de passagio* before the *epistola* (*Quomodo terra sancta*), which clearly supports Nicholas IV's promotion of a unified military order.

corresponded to the theory of the Church's "two swords," spiritual and corporeal. Second, he claimed that it was appropriate for the pope to have greater zeal for the exaltation of the faith than for anything else. Third, he declared that by participating in the campaign, the pope would set a good example for prelates and princes, inspiring many to take up the cross.[32] In effect, the pope's role in this treatise is comparable to the one Llull envisioned for the commander of the missionary campaign in the *epistola*. The pope's evangelical endeavors should focus on the Greeks who would be warned that, if they refused to submit to the spiritual sword (*gladium spirituale*), it would be necessary to subdue them with the corporeal sword (*gladium corporale*). Llull's dependence on the "two-swords" terminology is noteworthy in light of contemporary canonistic discussions about the legitimacy of non-Christian political authority and the implications of those discussions for missionary and crusading activities.[33] Llull tends to distinguish between "schismatics," "unbelievers," and "pagans," thus falling more into the camp of Innocent IV than that of Hostiensis and 13th-century decretalists on the topic. Like many contemporaries, Llull understood reconciliation between Rome and Constantinople to be essential for the success of any crusading endeavors. He was also realistic enough to realize that this was a long-term project, advising that successive popes should continue these measures until "until the proposal shall be completed."[34] As additional arguments in support of his proposals, he explains that the enterprise is connected to the "public good" (*publica utilitas*) and is even relevant to the responsibilities of the Roman Emperor.[35]

The fulcrum for Llull's ideas in both parts of the *Liber de passagio* is his promotion of evangelization. His missionary plans are explicated at much greater length in the *Tractatus*, whose structure accentuates their centrality. Only the first two, relatively brief, sections of the *Tractatus* focus on the tactical and organizational aspects of crusading. The remaining four parts of the treatise, its bulk, treat evangelical matters. Although a detailed discussion of Llull's

---

32   Ibid., 2, ROL 28:337–338.

33   Pierre de la Palude's *Tractatus de potestate papae*, (ed.) P.T. Stella (Zurich: 1966) of c. 1316 also asserts complete papal authority over crusading; passages are translated in Housley, *Documents*, 49–50. For canonical questions surrounding mission and crusade see James Muldoon, *Popes, Lawyers and Infidels: The Church and the Non-Christian World 1250–1550* (Philadelphia: 1979), especially Chapters 1–4, and Kedar, *Crusade and Mission*, especially Chapter 5. Llull relates the two swords to Emperor Constantine in his 1311 treatise *Liber disputationis Petri clerici et Raimundi sive Phantasticus* 5, ROL 16:28.

34   *Tractatus de modo convertendi infideles* 2, ROL 28:338: "Si tamen uita unius Papae ad propositum non sufficiat, ipsius successor secundum modum praedictum procedat et sic successiue quousque propositum compleatur."

35   Ibid., ROL 28:340.

missionary proposals is beyond the scope of this essay, a few points are relevant for understanding Llull's crusading plans. First, although missionaries
could certainly exercise their vocation apart from the crusade, it appears to
be inconceivable to Llull that crusaders should campaign without concurrent
evangelical efforts. Second, although Llull recognizes the diversity amongst
groups of non-Catholics who comprise the audience for his missionaries, his
fundamental approach to each group is undifferentiated. It is grounded in education and focuses on the establishment of missionary colleges (*studia*) in
which suitable holy men could be instructed in the necessary languages and
cultural characteristics of their intended audience. These learned men of good
moral character were also supposed to study Llull's Art and his "necessary reasons." Thirdly, specific details of the missionary plans provide evidence that
Llull was responding to his contemporary political, cultural, and ideological
context. For example, in the *Tractatus,* Llull incorporated contemporary aspirations for a Mongol-Christian alliance into his plans. He also seems to make
a direct reference to the fall of Acre, using the event to elicit an emotional
response and thus support of his plans. Llull explains that since the Tartars are
"simple men" (*homines rudes*), they may be enticed to convert to Islam by Muslim promises of pleasures in the next life, which include "women, and food,
and many other sensual things."[36]

In Parts 4 and 5 of the *Tractatus*, Llull outlined the theoretical and ideological foundations for his plans. These help explain how and why Llull linked
crusading to evangelization and vice versa. It is remarkable how many contemporary religious and theological issues Llull alluded to in this discussion. He
touched on ontology; the nature of God's being; the relationship between God's
essence and his divine attributes; the ways in which loving and knowing God,
or engaging in contemplation, allow us to participate in God in the mystical
sense; the ideals of the apostolic church and the *imitatio Christi*; and concepts
of the public good. Although Llull did include traditional arguments in support
of crusading (such as his claim that Muslim occupation of formerly Christian
lands makes crusading just), most of the reasons he elucidated in support of
his plans are related to his central idea about the end for which God created
mankind, namely to love and serve God. He believed that Christians had a
moral responsibility to participate in activities which would achieve this end;
they have been blessed with gifts and talents which range from the mundane

---

36   Ibid., 4.3, ROL 28:345: "feminas, et comestiones, et potum et multa alia sensibilia sicut in
      lege eorum continetur." For the reference to Acre, see Ibid., 4.4, ROL 28:346. Vose, *Domini-
      cans, Muslims and Jews*, 21–59, provides important context for Llull's specific missionary
      ideas, especially vis à vis Dominican ideology.

(superiority at sea) to the spiritual (superiority in faith), all of which should be employed in God's service. Llull argued that simply participation alone would contribute to the public good, regardless of any success in converting unbelievers. For example, kings, counts, barons and others could leave behind their wars and other worldly ambitions and instead fight against the infidel. The resulting peace and harmony in Christian lands would be a blessing.[37]

Llull supported his convictions with recourse to his Art.[38] The *Tractatus* is noteworthy as an application of a new version of Llull's Art, developed in the *Ars inventiua ueritatis* of 1290. He used his Dignities to argue that it was offensive for Christians to do little good when they could do great good (the Will of Christians should be equal to their Power and Wisdom). He discussed his ideas about primary and secondary intentions as they related to philosophical concepts of substance, accidents and being. He maintained that worldly honors, luxuries, and longevity were blessings bestowed through the second intention; prioritizing them above knowing and loving God subverted both the first and the second intention of humankind. Is it any wonder that the world is in a bad state, asked Llull. The analogy of a sick man on his deathbed explains how he saw the world (sick with sin). The only remedy would be for the pope, his curia, and other brave men to follow a plan so great and lofty that the whole world would return to the way of truth. Of course, such a plan is outlined in Llull's treatise.[39] In Part 5 of the treatise, Llull argued on the basis of the philosophical principles of form and matter that his methods were, in fact, the only way to convert unbelievers. Using his Relative Principles, he expressed his conviction that his plans best accorded with the divine dignities. For example, with respect to crusading, based on Llull's Relative Principles of Beginning, Middle, and End, he insisted on the necessity of reunion with the Greeks before the conquest of the Holy Land, which is very distant from the Latins.[40] It is somewhat ironic that, in a treatise that supports crusading in its first two parts, Llull's application of his Principles of Concordance and Contrariety in this part led him to an emphatic statement that peaceful disputation with infidels accords more with the divine dignities than fighting against them

---

37   *Tractatus de modo convertendi infideles* 4, ROL 28:344–348, offers ten reasons (among many possible ones) to explain why his proposals should be followed.

38   See Rubio's explanation of this stage of the Art in Chapter 4 of this volume.

39   *Tractatus de modo convertendi infideles* 4.10, ROL 28:348: "Oportet, ergo, quod summus pontifex et fratres eius et alii uiri ualentes ordinent ita magnam et altam ordinationem quod totus mundus in uia ueritatis deueniat, ita quod magnitudo multo magis sit infusa in bono quam in malo, et in scientia quam in ignorantia et in vero quam in falso; et sic de aliis. Haec autem fieri potest secundum praedictam ordinationem."

40   Ibid., 5.2, ROL 28:349.

with the *gladio corporali* to seize their lands and killing them.[41] Application of these same principles emphasized the need for harmony amongst Christians as a prerequisite for the conversion of unbelievers and enhanced the desirability of reconciliation between the Latins and Greeks.[42] And finally, making an analogy between the persons of the Holy Trinity on the one hand and clergy and laity on the other, Llull used his Principle of Concordance to explain why both clerics and laymen should carry out the respective responsibilities allotted to them in his plan.[43] In the last section of the *Tractatus*, Llull returned to his analogy of form and matter to discuss funding for his proposals and argued that the church should contribute a tenth of ecclesiastical goods annually until the things he has proposed are accomplished, because it does not accord with the divine dignities that its form (his plans) should be deficient in matter (funding).[44] The application of the principles of his Art to his proposals for evangelization and crusading has enormous implications for understanding Llull's ideas about vocation, ecclesiology, and the role of the laity in Christian society. It also points to the centrality of the concepts of unity and order in all aspects of Llull's thought.

Between them, the two texts that comprise the *Liber de passagio* contain most elements of Llull's crusade and missionary ideology and good examples of the strategies by which he imagined his goals could be achieved. Differences between the two texts can be explained by audience and circumstances of composition. Llull, correctly saw Nicholas IV as someone who shared his interests in evangelization. As a Franciscan, Nicholas may also have been sympathetic to Llull's vision of a reformed Christendom and the ideals of *imitatio Christi*, which he promoted both in his writings and in his own actions. This particular treatise also responded to the news of the fall of Acre, the pope's requests for advice on mounting a new crusade, recognition of the strategic importance of reconciliation between the Latin and Greek churches, optimism surrounding the possible conversion of the Tartars and Mongols to Christianity, and the growing sense of urgency surrounding all these issues. Llull's subsequent crusade treatises reveal a mounting sense of urgency, as well as continued attention to questions of audience and historical circumstance.

Shortly after completing the *Liber de passagio*, Llull experienced a spiritual crisis. He apparently was torn between what he seemed to see (at least temporarily) as the competing claims of his vocation (*imitatio Christi* through

---

41   Ibid., 5.3, ROL 28:349.
42   See Ibid., 5.6 and 5.9, ROL 28:350 and 351.
43   Ibid., 5.10, ROL 28:352.
44   Ibid., 6, ROL 28:352–353.

missionary activity) and the promulgation of his Art. But by September 1293, Llull was in Tunis, apparently following his own advice from the *Liber de passagio*, by engaging in missionary activity and religious disputation using the methods of his Art.[45] Llull's trip to Tunis was unsuccessful; his ideas for achieving the conversion of Muslims through the conversion of their sovereigns and religious leaders seem to have been based more upon "old-fashioned" tactics than on a firm grasp of the realities of the practical religious pluralism which obtained in the North African states of his time, or of the complex cultural and political circumstances of the relationships between the Hafsids and the Catalans.[46] His failure in Tunis, as well as subsequent contacts with the Muslims in Lucera in 1294 and stories of Christian conversions to Islam there, may have stimulated a resumption of his efforts to gain audience for his ideas about both evangelization and crusading. Thus he addressed short crusade petitions to Celestine V and Boniface VIII in quick succession.[47] Although these *petitiones* share the same basic structure and contents as the *Liber de passagio*, the attentive reader can discern a notable shift in emphasis, although not in basic tactics, especially in the text addressed to Celestine V, whose personal

45   *Vita coaetanea* 4–7, ROL 8:283–289, and the commentary of Hillgarth, *RLL* 21–23. For Vose, *Dominicans, Muslims and Jews*, 33, this event shows how thinkers such as Bacon and Llull represent "different branches of an extreme tendency advocating universal proselytism through reason." There were exceptions, whose examples were not followed to any great extent by the Dominican Order as an institution.

46   The mendicants had a historical presence in Tunis. See John V. Tolan, "Taking Gratian to Africa: Raymond de Penyafort's Legal Advice to the Dominicans and Franciscans in Tunis (1234)," in Adnan A. Husain and K.E. Fleming (eds.), *A Faithful Sea: The Religious Cultures of the Mediterranean, 1200–1700* (Oxford: 2007), 45–63. The fundamental study of Catalan relations with the Maghrib remains Charles-Emmanuel Dufourcq, *L'Espagne catalane et le Maghrib aux XIIIe et XIVe siècles: de la bataille de Las Navas de Tolosa (1212) à l'avènement du sultan mérinide Abou-l-Hasan (1331)* (Paris: 1966). See also Jamil M. Abun-Nasr, *A History of the Maghrib in the Islamic Period* (Cambridge: 1987), esp. 125 on Llull. Vose, *Dominicans, Muslims and Jews*, 222–249, persuasively challenges some of the traditionally held views about missionary efforts in the Maghrib, and shows how entangled these efforts were with political and diplomatic goals, something that Llull's crusade treatises demonstrate that he recognized all too well.

47   On Llull and Lucera, see Fernando Domínguez Reboiras and Jordi Gayà Estelrich, "Life," in *Raimundus Lullus*, ROL Suppl. 2:79–80, and, Hillgarth, *Diplomatari Lul·lià*, 66. On Lucera and crusading ideas, see: Christopher T. Maier, "Crusade and Rhetoric against the Muslim Colony of Lucera: Eudes of Châteauroux's 'Sermones de Rebellione Sarracenorum Lucheri in Apulia," *Journal of Medieval History* 21 (1995): 343–385; Karla Mallette, "Insularity: A Literary History of Muslim Lucera," in Adnan A. Husain and K.E. Fleming (eds.), *A Faithful Sea: The Religious Cultures of the Mediterranean, 1200–1700* (Oxford: 2007), 27–46; and Julie Taylor, *Muslims in Medieval Italy: The Colony at Lucera* (Lanham, Maryland: 2003).

character and interests, even more than those of Nicholas IV, would suggest an affinity with Llull and receptivity to his spiritual ideas.[48]

There is a noteworthy coincidence between Celestine V's own biography and the career of Llull's saintly, but fictional, Pope Blaquerna, who in Book Four of the *Romanç d'Evast e Blaquerna* extensively promotes proposals similar to Llull's own and eventually retires from the papacy to become a hermit. What is important for our purposes is that Llull's treatment of the subject in his vernacular and didactic novel is evidence of how thoroughly he considered sponsorship and direction of evangelization and crusading to be the responsibility of the papal curia.[49]

Llull's shift in emphasis is evident in his vocabulary, rhetorical style, and choice of examples, all of which evoke increased urgency. His plans are framed by a distinctive sense of historical time. For example, he continued to stress the idea of competition with Muslims in the work of conversion but raised the specter of losing that contest by reminding the pope about the numerical superiority of unbelievers over Christians. He referred to the decrepitude of the world, giving the impression that Christendom was running out of time. Llull's urgency may partially be explained by personal frustration, but one can also discern a general influence of the Spiritual Franciscans and their view of history in Llull's short *petitio*, as well as in his emphasis on personal responsibility.[50] Interestingly, Llull's theoretical terminology in this *petitio* also shifts from appealing to the "spiritual and corporeal *swords*" of the Church to its "spiritual and corporeal *treasure*."[51] Llull's language reflects emerging ideas about individual spirituality and penance. Theories about indulgences developed in the

---

48   Perarnau i Espelt, "Un text català de Ramon Llull desconegut," 17–22, compares this *petitio* to the *Liber de passagio*.

49   See Sebastián Garcías Palou, "El papa 'Blanquerna' de Ramon Llull y Celestino V," *EL* 20 (1976): 71–86.

50   See David Burr, *The Spiritual Franciscans: From Protest to Persecution in the Century after St. Francis* (State College, Pennsylvania: 2001). On apocalyptic ideas connected to Celestine V see, Bernard McGinn, "Angel Pope and Papal Antichrist," *Church History* 47 (1978): 155–173; on contemporary eschatalogical ideas, my introduction to Llull's *Liber contra Antichristum*, ROL 36:3–43; on Llull's concept of history, Romano and Cruz, "The Human Realm," in *Raimundus Lullus*, ROL Suppl. 2:432–438. On Llull and the mendicants in general, see Fernando Domínguez Reboiras, "Raimundo Lulio y el Ideal Mendicante: Afinidades y Divergencias," in Fernando Domínguez Reboiras, R. Imbach, T. Pindl, and P. Walter (eds.), *Aristotelica et Lulliana magistro doctissimo Charles H. Lohr septuagesimum annum feliciter agenti dedicata* (Steenbergen and The Hague: 1995), 377–413, and Antonio Oliver, "El beato Ramón Llull en sus relaciones con la Escuela Franciscana de los siglos XIII–XIV," *EL* 9 (1965): 55–70, 145–165; 10 (1966): 47–55; 11 (1967): 89–119; and 13 (1969): 51–65.

51   *Petició de Ramon al papa Celestí V*, (ed.) Perarnau i Espelt, 32–33.

context of crusade ideology, especially in connection to the redemption of crusading vows. New ideas about purgatory associated with the second Council of Lyons were beginning to circulate more broadly. Llull's *petitio* uses the contemporary spiritual language of treasures, debts, and payments.[52] The change in language, increased sense of urgency and focus on the responsibility of individual Christians could all be rooted in Llull's spiritual and psychological crisis described in the *Vita coaetanea*, which presented him as wracked with worry about eternal damnation.[53] All of this may help to explain the more pastoral approach Llull took in this *petitio* in which his ideas appear to be supported more by references to the traditional catechism than to the principles of his own Art.[54] Finally, the aura of the Holy Spirit pervades the treatise; by explicitly associating the Holy Spirit with the election of Celestine v to the papacy, Llull implied that papal authority to use the spiritual and corporeal treasure of the Church to support the work of bringing all those in error into the light of truth was also bestowed by the Holy Spirit. By extension then, Llull associated that same inspiration with his own proposals.[55] At the conclusion of this short text, Llull reiterated the link between his proposals, the end for which God created man, and the need for Christians to follow the example of Christ, the apostles, and the martyrs.[56]

Llull's petition to Celestine was dated in Naples, 1294. The following year, Llull addressed an almost identical *petitio* to Boniface VIII, his *Petitio Raimundi pro conversione infidelium ad Bonifatium VIII papam*.[57] In both *petitiones*, as in

---

52   The classic study of canon law in crusading remains James Brundage, *Medieval Canon Law and the Crusader* (London: 1969). Penny J. Cole, *The Preaching of the Crusades to the Holy Land, 1095–1270* (Cambridge, Mass.: 1991), 142–176, demonstrates persuasively the close interrelationship between crusade theology and medieval ideas of penance. John W. Baldwin, "From the Ordeal to Confession: In Search of Lay Religion in Early Thirteenth-Century France," in Peter Biller and A.J. Minnis (ed.), *Handling Sin: Confession in the Middle Ages* (York: 1998), 191–209, uses an exploration of vernacular romances to show how deeply ingrained these ideas of penance were in 13th-century social milieus such as Llull's.

53   *Vita coaetanea* 4 and 5, ROL 8:285–289, refer explicitly to damnation and penitential sorrow. For similar language in the petition to Celestine v see *Petició a Celestí v*, (ed.) Perarnau i Espelt, 31. This concern with damnation is even more apparent in the *Liber de fine*, analyzed below.

54   See, for example, the opening paragraph of the *Petició a Celestí v*, (ed.) Perarnau i Espelt, 29–32, and especially Perarnau's notes to this text in the apparatus.

55   Ibid., 31. The presence of the Holy Spirit, like Llull's concerns about judgment and damnation, intensified in the *Liber de fine*, written about ten years later.

56   Ibid., 43.

57   This text also appears in A.S. Atiya, *The Crusade in the Later Middle Ages* (London: 1938): 487–489.

the *Liber de passagio*, intended for Nicholas IV, Llull emphasized that the pope and his curia should assume the responsibility for these plans as spiritual leaders of the body of Christ. Together the three texts provide ample evidence that Llull believed crusading was only one possible strategy for bringing the world to its appointed end. It is significant that he prioritized the "spiritual treasure" and inter-religious dialogue in all three texts. But it is also meaningful that he does not engage in any extensive justification of the "corporeal treasure" in these texts either. His acceptance of crusading must be understood as related to his confidence that all Christians can embody the apostolic life according to their individual vocations.[58] This helps to explain Llull's emphasis on the benefits of his plans for the public good and their connection to the spiritual and institutional reform of the Church, also apparent in these texts. For example, he argued that the worst symptom of the bad state of the world is the passivity of Christians. Perhaps responding to recriminations surrounding the fall of Acre, Llull noted that Christians had lost their lands and the courage they once showed against the Muslims. He tried to rally Christians and their leaders and inspire them anew by reminding them of the great good they could accomplish by following his plans. Clerics especially should participate in order to be exemplars and promoters of the public good—which Llull equated to the will of God for the right order of society.[59] Additionally, Llull's willingness to be flexible in the details of his plans for crusade depending on his particular audience suggests that another reason why he may have supported crusading was in order to gain support for his missionary plans.

Llull's appeals to the papal curia yielded neither obvious nor immediate results. He lamented this failure, expressing his disappointment in subsequent works including the prologue to *Arbor scientiae* and his remarkable poem *Lo desconhort*. It is not surprising then, that when Llull resumed his promotion of crusading in the *De fine* of 1305, by far his lengthiest and most thorough treatment of the subject, he appealed to a broader audience, even incorporating the ambitions of James II of Aragon into his plans.[60] The title of this book seems deliberately ambiguous, referring both to the "end" for which man was created, possibly imminent eschatological matters, and Llull's final efforts to achieve his goals. As in his previous works promoting crusading, the most important

---

58   This idea appears in many of Llull's vernacular and Latin texts; see Óscar de la Cruz on
      "Man and Society," in *Raimundus Lullus*, ROL Suppl. 2:413–432.

59   As very succinctly explained in *Petició a Celestí* 5, (ed.) Perarnau i Espelt, 40–43.

60   Franco Porsia, *Progetti di Crociata: Il* De fine *di Raimondo Lullo* (Toronto: 2005), discusses
      other texts in which Llull mentions crusading in the period between 1295 and 1305, including *Lo desconhort* and *Cant de Ramon*, with an appendix containing a range of texts
      translated into Italian, which have bearing on the issues discussed by Llull in the *De fine*.

theme of *De fine* is not the military expedition which Llull advocated in the text, but rather preaching to non-Christians.[61] The treatise recapitulated the plans for evangelization and crusade contained in Llull's earlier texts, both expanding on and clarifying some aspects but also offering some variations in response to the changed audience and historical circumstances. The organization of *De fine* is more systematic and thus it more deliberately expresses the complex relationship between mission and crusade that existed in Llull's thought. The ordering of the three parts of the treatise is indicative of the relationship between peaceful (if not uncoerced) methods of evangelization and direct warfare. After a substantial prologue, Llull discusses first interreligious dialogue; second, plans for crusading; and third, the exaltation of the intellect. Within this structure, even the distinction on warfare contains a section dedicated to preaching.[62]

The prologue to *De fine* is important because it establishes an ideological frame of reference for Llull's more specific proposals. Ideas that were merely hinted at in his earlier texts now are made more explicit. At least three characteristics of Llull's treatment of the topic here should be noted. First is the increased urgency of his tone, apparent in his focus on the bad state of the world, his description of Christians as a beleaguered minority, and his lamentation that, to the shame of the heavenly curia, infidels continue to possess the Holy Land. The exhortatory quality of the prologue is unmistakable and Llull's rhetoric echoes that of crusade sermons.[63] However, Llull's inclusion of autobiographical details similar to those voiced in *Lo desconhort* and *Cant de Ramon,* and his expression of personal frustration, gave his urgent tone the ring of authenticity. We should remember that by 1305, Llull was far from being a young man. In the intervening years between his *petitio* to Boniface VIII and this treatise, he had travelled extensively. Llull's language in *De fine* reflects an awareness of the complexity of the world beyond the borders of Christendom that was born of personal experience. Llull spent time in Majorca where he received permission from James II of Aragon to preach in mosques and synagogues.[64] By 1301, when James II of Majorca transferred the properties

---

61   See Fernando Domínguez Reboiras, "Works," in *Raimundus Lullus,* ROL Suppl. 2:190.

62   *De fine,* ROL 11:249–291. The modern Catalan translation by P. Llabrés and J. Gayà Estelrich (Barcelona: 2002) has a helpful introduction.

63   See my "Crusading and the Penitential Life: James of Vitry's Crusade Sermon Models and Llull's *De fine,*" *SL* 54 (2014): 33–66. For a general introduction to preaching the crusades see Cole, *The Preaching of the Crusades*; Christoph T. Maier, *Preaching the Crusades: Mendicant Friars and the Cross in the Thirteenth Century* (Cambridge: 1994) and *Crusade Propaganda and Ideology: Model Sermons for the Preaching of the Cross* (Cambridge: 2000).

64   For the documents, see Hillgarth, *Diplomatari lul·lià,* 71–72.

of Miramar to the monastery of La Real, it was clear that Llull's dreams for his missionary college were over.[65] The most significant personal experience of Llull's was likely his journey to the east upon hearing the news of Ghazan Khan's campaign against Syria. Llull travelled to Cyprus and Asia Minor, during which time he apparently was well received by Jacques de Molay, the Grand Master of the Temple, and he possibly even made it to Jerusalem.[66]

Moreover, the ephemeral dream of converting the Mongols and joining with them in a military alliance against the Muslims had passed.[67] By this point in his life, Llull already had written well over one hundred works and, although the development of various versions of his Art can certainly be seen as the fruition of his desire to "write the best book possible," it would be hard to argue that he had enjoyed more than limited success in accomplishing the goals he had embraced at his conversion.[68]

Thus, besides being urgent, Llull's tone in the prologue is weary. He emphasized that he personally had strived to follow the precepts of the Gospel. That his plans had not been realized was due to the fact that the "the public good has no friends" rather than to his own lack of effort. This book was to be his last word on the subject (*libellus iste Finis omnium erit dictus*). He asserted that on Judgment Day, the judge would recognize that Llull had done all he could do "in this matter" (*in isto negotium*); he could not say how those who failed to act on his proposals would fare.[69] The prologue concluded with a rhetorical flourish reminiscent of ancient prophets: "he who has ears to hear, let him hear what I said, and may it fervently with fear of Judgment Day impress his understanding."[70] By referring to the bad state of the world and the Last Judgment, Llull placed a good deal of moral pressure upon his audience. He increased this pressure by claiming that his proposals would benefit the

---

65   Ibid., 73. For an overview of the context for such efforts, see Vose, *Dominicans, Muslims and Jews in the Medieval Crown of Aragon*, 104–115 and 155–164.

66   See Jordi Gayà Estelrich, "Ramon Llull en Oriente (1301–1302)," *SL* 37 (1997): 25–78. For this period in Llull's life, see *Vita coaetanea* 8, ROL 8:294–296; on the Tartars and the conversion of "Cassanus" to Islam, see his *De fine* 1.5, ROL 9:266–269.

67   On the complexities of Christian-Mongol-Muslim relationships, see David Bundy, "The Syriac and Armenian Christian Responses to the Islamification of the Mongols," in John Victor V. Tolan (ed.), *Medieval Christian Perceptions of Islam: A Book of Essays* (New York: 1996), 33–53; and J.S. Boyle, "The Il-Khans of Persia and the Princes of Europe," *Central Asiatic Journal* 20 (1976): 25–40.

68   This pessimistic assessment, themes of his *Lo desconhort* and *Cant de Ramon*, also appears in the *Vita coaetanea* 8, ROL 8:293–295.

69   *De fine* Prol., ROL 9:251.

70   Ibid., 252: "qui habet aures audiendi, audiat hoc, quod dixi, et feruenter in terrore magni iudicii suum imprimat intellectum."

individual as well as the collective good. He reminded readers that time was running out and implied that in this context effort was ultimately more important than tangible results, especially when it came to following gospel precepts. Thus, besides exuding a sense of urgency and weariness, *De fine* conveyed pastoral concerns, reflective of the spiritual sensibilities of an educated layman influenced by mendicant ideals. During time spent in Genoa and Montpellier prior to writing *De fine*, Llull wrote his substantial work on preaching, *Liber de praedicatione,* to which he refers in this treatise. Although the urgency Llull displayed may be reminiscent more specifically of the Spiritual Franciscans, Llull's other pastoral preoccupations reflected general mendicant concerns. For Llull also held out hope: if the religious and secular leaders of Christendom would embrace his proposals, with the aid of God's grace, the universe could be returned to a good state and united in one Catholic flock.[71] The prologue thus served to contextualize Llull's plans for mission and crusade, emphatically connecting them with his overall vision of the good order of the world. Personal responsibility and the communal good were unified in Llull's proposals, and he claimed that the actions he advocated would result in a unity that reflected Divine Unity. The way that Llull connected the proposals contained within *De fine* to his unique way of thinking about the good order of the universe and ideals of the "renovation of the world" (*renovatio mundi*) in this prologue went beyond traditional crusade rhetoric.

The details of these plans expanded on the ideas Llull articulated in the prologue. For example, with respect to their urgency, in the first distinction, *De disputatione infidelium*, Llull betrayed his awareness of a specific eschatological timeframe when he contrasted his own era with the age of the early church, in which the Catholic Faith began by way of preaching and increased by way of sanctity, blood, and labor. Why, he asked, is the church not growing in our time? Llull's response: "Because we do not have the martyrs, nor the laborers with the fervent desire of sanctity."[72] He urged the papal curia to "Begin for God, begin. For death will come, and thousands of years have passed, in which there was no better plan."[73] In the same section, Llull's pastoral approach is evident when he linked the two swords theory to the heart of the Christian life by quoting well known gospel precepts ("He who is not with

---

71   *De fine* Prol., ROL 9:250.

72   Ibid.1.1, ROL 9:254: "Quia non habemus martyres, neque laborantes cum feruenti desiderio de sanctitate."

73   Ibid 1.1 ROL 9:254: "Incipite pro Deo, incipite. Nam mors uenit, et mille anni sunt iam praeteriti seu elapsi, in quibus melius negotium isto inceptum non fuit." Later, in the section on preaching to the Tartars, Llull also emphasized the passage of time and the inactivity of the Church: *De fine* 1.5, ROL 9:268–269.

me is against me" and "Love the Lord, your God, with all your heart").[74] The advice for missionaries advanced here explicitly drew upon Llull's personal experience and referred to books that he had written in Arabic and Latin. The many references to his own books contained in *De fine* is testimony to Llull's confidence in his Art.[75] Repeatedly he focused on commonalities of belief between Catholics and other groups and the efficacy of his books to clear up misunderstandings. There is also a literary and homiletic flair to this section: Llull included stories and personal anecdotes to buttress his arguments.[76]

Similar examples of the urgent, autobiographical, and pastoral qualities of this text appear in the second distinction of the treatise, "On waging war" (*De modo bellandi*), which Llull organized into seven parts, addressing subjects ranging from the general (the recovery of the Holy Land is desirable for angels who are in paradise and for saints, and also for Latins) to the very specific (such as the preferred colors for the habits and insignia of the members of a unified military order).[77] All three qualities can be discerned in his plans for the leadership of the crusade. Although Llull believed that the curia should have ultimate responsibility over both the spiritual and corporeal swords, he expanded on his innovative idea of delegating immediate control over the latter to a *Bellator Rex*, who would lead a single, unified military order and who

---

74   Ibid.1.1, ROL 9:255.

75   Ibid., 1.1 and 1.2, ROL 9:254 and 256. Llull cites a number of his writings in this section, including his *Liber de demonstratione per aequiparantiam* (Montpellier, 1305), *Liber de praedicatione* (Montpellier, 1304), the section of his *Ars amativa boni* entitled *Liber de Deo et Iesu Christo* (Majorca, 1300), *Disputatio fidei et intellectus* (Montpellier, 1303), and *Liber de ascensu et descensu intellectus* (Montpellier, 1305). He gives a different list of nine texts for creating arguments to persuade Jews to convert in *De fine* 1.3, ROL 9:259; for the Gentiles, in Section 1.4, ROL 9:260 and 262, where he refers to the *Liber de passagio*; and for the Tartars, Section 1.5, ROL 9:267–268. He also refers readers to his own texts for advice about leadership of the crusading armies, particularly in terms of how the *Bellator Rex* should behave: ibid., 2.2, ROL 9:275. Section 2.6 (on preaching), ROL 9:282–283, again mentions his own works as well as the *Liber alchindi* and *Liber teliph*; on these rare citations of non-Lullian texts, see Thomas E. Burman, "The Influence of the 'Apology of Al-Kindi' and *Contrarietas Alfolica* on Ramon Lull's Late Religious Polemics, 1305–1313," *Mediaeval Studies* 53 (1991): 197–228. Finally, the third distinction contains a catalogue of Llull's works which he deems useful for the enterprises laid out in this treatise (3. Prol., ROL 9:285–286).

76   Especially in Section 1.5 on the Tartars, where he cited again a well-known anecdote about Ramon Martí; Hames, *Art of Conversion,* 8–9, discusses this story. See also Eusebio Colomer, "Ramon Llull y Ramon Martí," *EL* 28 (1988): 1–37, and Vose, *Dominicans, Muslims and Jews*, 239–242.

77   *De fine* 2, ROL 9:269–285, at 269. Section 2.2, ROL 9:273–275, specifies the recommended garb and appearance of the unified military order.

would receive the Kingdom of Jerusalem to rule.[78] Llull connected good leadership with successful fund-raising, both necessary for the success of his plans. Some of Llull's contemporaries also voiced concerns about misuse and embezzlement of crusade tithes. But Llull was more adamant than other theorists about linking these plans to the general well-being of Christendom, noting that there were many who desired to suffer death for Jesus Christ and that his plans would give them confidence to contribute financially or even join the crusading army. He mentioned specifically secular knights, burghers, and other "lay men of the people" (*homines saeculares et populares*).[79] Llull's suggestions for a *Bellator Rex* were in keeping with his ideas about clerical and lay involvement in the reform of Christendom and realization of the proper "end" of the world through mission and crusade. Specific aspects of Llull's plans may well have been idealistic and unrealizable, but it is difficult to argue that they were not based on a fairly shrewd assessment of human motivations.[80] Llull's use of apocalyptic-sounding rhetoric was unmistakable when he wrote about evading the horrible punishments of hell and contrasted the splendors of St. Peter's in Rome with the devastation of the Holy Land, so ravaged that "everywhere serpents lay in small crannies" (*multi serpentes in cauernulis commorantur*).[81] Thus personal experience, concerns about the spiritual well-being of Christians, and apocalyptic allusions all combined to lend urgency and an unusual character to the proposals about leadership and finance articulated in *De fine*.

Llull's plans in *De fine* were designed to appeal to his particular audience, especially James II of Aragon, the conduit through whom this treatise would reach Clement V.[82] Most notably, Llull promoted Spain as the best theatre of warfare for the crusading armies.[83] Such a plan can be seen as aligned with

---

78   Ibid., 2.1, ROL 9:270. On the significance of the *Bellator Rex* in Llull's political views, see Hillgarth, *RLL* 64–69. Leopold, *How to Recover the Holy Land*, 65–69, reviews contemporary questions of leadership and organization in this period, though without citing Llull's *Bellator Rex*.

79   *De fine* 2.1, ROL 9:272.

80   On Llull's idealism, see Jocelyn N. Hillgarth, "Ramon Llull et l'Utopie," *EL* 25 (1981–83): 175–185.

81   *De fine* 2.1, ROL 9: 272–273.

82   See Domínguez Reboiras and Gayà Estelrich, *Raimundus Lullus*, ROL Suppl. 2:98–100, and Llull, *Liber disputationis Raimundi christiani et Homeri saraceni*, ROL 22:264. On Llull's strategies for disseminating this work, see Lola Badia, Joan Santanach, and Albert Soler i Llompart (eds.), *Ramon Llull as a Vernacular Writer: Communicating a New Kind of Knowledge* (Woodbridge: 2016), 203–209.

83   *De fine* 2.3, ROL 9:276–277, offers five possible routes for the crusading armies: by land via Constantinople, Asia Minor and Syria; by sea via Rashid (Rosetta) and Alexandria; by sea via Cyprus and Armenia; via Tunis (referring to St. Louis IX's ill-fated expedition); and via Spain to the Barbary Coast, Ceuta, Tunis, Egypt, and the Holy Land.

the ambitions of the Aragonese court at the time. It is even possible that Llull envisioned James himself taking up the office of *Bellator Rex*, although he was not then strictly speaking the designated "king's son" (*regis filius*). Certain prophetic, apocalyptic, and messianic ideas circulating at the time connected the crown of Aragon with the acquisition of Jerusalem and the end of the world; perhaps Llull echoed these notions.[84] More importantly for crusade historians, it firmly situates the Iberian reconquest in the context of crusading while also making it clear that the ultimate goal for the crusading armies, no matter what the route, was the Holy Land.[85] Other details of Llull's plans for warfare also reflect contemporary concerns. For example, even if his call for unification of military orders was hardly unique, his discussion of the symbolic meaning of the colors and fabrics that he advocated for the habits and insignia of the new order was more unusual.[86] Also unusual was his recommendation that the *Bellator Rex*, and all the participants in the military campaign, should consult his books for advice in developing the moral rectitude, right intention, and knowledge necessary for the success of the crusading armies.[87] The section on "Craftsmen" (*De mechanicis*), detailing methods for acquiring and organizing supplies of all kinds, supported Llull's conviction that every participant has a specific vocation which can contribute to the success of the crusading army.[88]

---

84 On eschatology and crusading, see Norman Housley, "The Eschatological Imperative: Messianism and Holy War in Europe, 1260–1556," in P. Schäfer and M.R. Cohen (eds.), *Toward the Millennium: Messianic Expectations from the Bible to Waco* (Leiden: 1998), 123–150; on prophecy, Marjorie Reeves, *The Influence of Prophecy in the Later Middle Ages: A Study in Joachimism* (Oxford: 1969), and Robert Lerner, *The Powers of Prophecy: The Cedar of Lebanon Vision from the Mongol Onslaught to the Dawn of the Enlightenment* (Berkeley: 1983); on apocalypticism, David Burr, *Olivi's Peaceable Kingdom: A Reading of the Apocalypse Commentary* (Philadelphia: 1993), 27–62. The figure most associated with messianic prophecies regarding the kings of Aragon was Llull's contemporary, Arnau de Vilanova: see José Guadalajara Medina, *El Anticristo en la España medieval* (Madrid: 2004), 57–65; Harold Lee, Marjorie Reeves, and Giulio Silano, *Western Mediterranean Prophecy: The School of Joachim of Fiore and the Fourteenth-Century Breviloquium* (Toronto: 1989), 27–60; and José Pou y Martí, *Visionarios, beguinos y fraticelos catalanes (siglos XIII–XV)* (Vich: 1930).

85 On Llull's relations with the Aragonese court, see Hillgarth, *Diplomatari Lul·lià*, 74–76. On crusading and the Iberian reconquest, see: Peter Lock, *The Routledge Companion to the Crusades* (New York: 2006): 205–213; Norman Housley, *Contesting the Crusades*, (Oxford: 2006) 1–23, 99–109, and 122–132; and Joseph F. O'Callaghan, *Reconquest and Crusade in Medieval Spain* (Philadephia: 2003).

86 *De fine* 2.2, ROL 9:273–275.

87 *De fine* 2.2, ROL 9:275, cites Llull's *Ars consilii* and "other vernacular works that we have written, which would be good for the soldiers' morals" (*alios libros fecimus in uulgari, qui boni essent suis militibus propter mores*), and identifies these as his *Doctrina pueril*, *Blaquerna*, *Libre de meravelles*, etc.

88 *De fine* 2.7, ROL 9:284–285; cf. ibid., 2.6, ROL 9:282.

The connection between crusading success and moral rectitude was strengthened in the section on preaching. Llull argued that the brothers of the military order should hear sermons about the theological and moral virtues and vices (through Llull's book *De praedicatione*). They should also be instructed in the precautions of warfare against the infidel (for this Llull recommends both his *Ars generalis* and *Liber de consilio*); the preachers accompanying the crusading army should also ensure that masses would be sung, confessions heard, and the Divine Office prayed—in short, that all the liturgical and sacramental requirements of the faithful would be met. Llull's implication was that without such measures, success would be uncertain.[89] In this section of the treatise, Llull cemented the relationship between crusading and missionary efforts when he advised that clerics learned in foreign languages, especially Arabic, should accompany the *Bellator Rex*. They would be able to engage in religious disputations with captives, at least proving to them that Mohammed was not a true prophet, if not converting them to Christianity. The clerics could also serve as emissaries to Muslim leaders, both encouraging them to convert and threatening them with a perpetual military and missionary campaign. Llull even suggested that these "religious Arabs" (*religiosos arabicos*) could serve as spies and be sent on reconnaissance missions. And finally, in a suggestion reflecting contemporary mendicant efforts, Llull advised that clerics be sent throughout Christian lands to increase devotion and support for the work of the *Bellator Rex*.[90] The work of evangelization and crusading were presented as beneficial for Christians and infidels alike.

In the final distinction of the treatise, "On Elevating the Intellect" (*De exaltatione intellectus*), Llull returned to the themes of the prologue. He provided a brief catalogue of his own works on the basic principles and foundations of the Art and examples of its application to specific topics. These books would demonstrate the manner in which the Art could quickly destroy all the errors in the world and bring it to a good and true state. The intellectual enlightenment achieved through the study of the Art would contribute to the aim of *De fine* itself, namely to bring the world to its created end. Llull concluded *De fine* with the same sort of autobiographical lament with which he started, reverting to a prophetic tone, connecting his Art to his proposals for mission and crusade, and tying all of them to the public utility and good.[91] As he did in his *petitio* to Celestine v, Llull invoked the power of the Holy Spirit and implied that those who sinned against the public and common good (*bonum publicum*

---

89   Ibid., 2.6, ROL 9:282.
90   Ibid., 2.6, ROL 9:283–284.
91   Ibid., 3.2, ROL 9:289–290.

et commune) by ignoring his proposals, sinned against the Holy Spirit itself. He supported his contentions with references to the gospels.[92] Attention to Llull's proposals would bring about an end to heresy and dissent, lead to the exaltation of the holy faith through support offered to the *Bellator Rex*, and bring about peace and harmony between princes and prelates, their communities, and their people.[93]

Llull intended *De fine* to be his last word on the subject. In it he expanded on his previous ideas, using an autobiographical framework which made his calls for action more urgent. This text evokes a distinct sense of historical time and draws a more obvious connection between Llull's proposals and the work of the Holy Spirit. The relationship between mission and crusade is more clearly articulated in this text, as is their connection to the public good and the end for which man was created. In practical terms, *De fine* is more systematic and detailed than Llull's other works on the subject, incorporating contemporary aspects of crusade planning and, most likely, appropriating the ambitions of the Aragonese curia for its own purposes.[94]

As it turned out, by 1309, circumstances had changed again, and so Llull wrote one more text devoted to the subject. Just as the ideological contours and specific proposals of *De fine* were shaped by Llull's personal experiences and current events, his *Liber de acquistione Terrae Sanctae* of 1309 was responsive to circumstance and opportunity.[95] In the intervening years, Llull, again frustrated at the lack of support for his proposals from the papal curia, left Europe for an unsuccessful missionary trip to Bougie, where he was incarcerated for blasphemy. Upon his release, he sailed for Genoa but was shipwrecked and ended up in Pisa instead. For the next several years, Llull travelled extensively between Italy and France, possibly engaged in James II's negotiations for a North African crusade. The author of the *Vita* reports that, during this time, Llull received both written and monetary support from the citizens of Pisa and Genoa, including especially devout women, towards the recovery of the Holy Land. Besides meeting with the pope during this period, Llull may also have

---

92   Ibid., "De fine huius libri," ROL 9:290.

93   Ibid., ROL 9:290.

94   Hillgarth, *RLL* 65, thus calls *De fine* Llull's most important work on the crusade. Cf. Tomaž Mastnak, *Crusading Peace: Christendom, the Muslim World, and Western Political Order* (Berkeley: 2002), 216–228.

95   Citations below are from the only surviving manuscript, *Electorium*, Paris B.N. lat 15450, ff. 544vb-547va, which combines it with Llull's *petitiones* to Boniface VIII and the Council of Vienne under the rubric *Procuratio recuperationis terre sancte et infidelium conversio et mori pro fide Christi.*

met with Philip IV in Poitiers in the summer of 1308.[96] It should not surprise us that Llull seized this opportunity to promote his plans for mission and crusade in another short treatise.[97]

Most elements of Llull's plans in *De acquisitione Terrae Sanctae* are similar to those in his earlier texts. However, the organizing principal of this treatise is unique, focusing on the three gifts of the Holy Spirit required for the acquisition of the Holy Land: wisdom, power, and love. In a very brief prologue, Llull mentioned that he was offering these plans because he desired the public good and spoke the truth. He declared that his conscience would not permit him to remain silent and that he must do all he could for the project in order to avoid hypocrisy and perpetual infernal punishment.[98] He also reported that he had already presented Clement V with a book on this subject, but that he had modified his plans in light of the suppression of the Templars.[99] What we have already known to be true about Llull's approach to the subject is confirmed by his own words. However, his underlying concerns remained consistent. He continued to express his belief that the acquisition of the Holy Land was related to the embodiment of Christian virtues, especially as they related to the Holy Spirit; he tied this enterprise to the public good; he eagerly and personally promoted these proposals in order to avoid both deficiency in moral virtue and the pains of hell; and he looked to the papal curia for leadership of his multi-pronged campaign. In the three parts of this treatise, he explained how to achieve victory through arms and through preaching, and recounted *exempla* for avoiding the threats facing beleaguered Christendom.

The section on crusading contained several important features, among which is Llull's emphasis on the significance of Christian military experience in Spain. He listed this experience as one of the six general advantages that Christians had against the Muslims.[100] Another important feature is Llull's renewal of support for a crusading campaign through Constantinople, referring

---

96   See *Vita coaetanea* 9.36–10.43, ROL 8:297–302, for Llull's itinerary during this period, which Bonner calls "a tremendous simplification of Llull's travels and labors," *Doctor Illuminatus: A Ramon Llull Reader* (Princeton: 1985), 38, n. 115. See also Domínguez Reboiras and Gayà Estelrich, *Raimundus Lullus*, ROL Suppl. 2:105–106, and Hillgarth, *Diplomatari Lul·lià*, 77–79. On Genoese women supporting crusade plans, see James M. Powell, "The Role of Women in the Fifth Crusade," in *The Crusades, the Kingdom of Sicily, and the Mediterranean* (Aldershot: 2007), 294–301.

97   On Llull's relations with the French court at this time, see Hillgarth, RLL 83–129; Schein, *Fideles Crucis*, 206–208; and Housley, *The Avignon Papacy and the Crusades, 1305–1378* (Oxford:1986), 9–17 and 243–244.

98   *Liber de acquistione Terrae Sanctae* Prol., f. 544vb.

99   Ibid., f. 544vb: 219–238.

100   *Liber de acquistione Terrae Sanctae* 1.1.5, f. 545ra.

specifically to the plans of Charles of Valois and Fulk of Villaret, Master of the Hospitallers.[101] Llull goes on to explain how the acquisition of Constantinople will lead to victory over the Mamluks through Armenia, Antioch, Syria, Alexandria, Damietta, and Raycet. Previously, Llull had rejected this route as too difficult, although he supported it in the earlier *Liber de passagio*.[102]

Llull did not abandon the Spanish crusade, although he did make it a second option in this treatise. He suggested that the four Iberian kings could work together to capture Granada and explained how the conquest of Granada must precede the conquest of Ceuta. Thence, crusading armies could acquire the North African kingdoms of Morocco, Tunis, Bougie, and so on—all the way to Egypt. Llull also argued that the pope and cardinals should support financially the campaign to acquire Ceuta.[103]

The kings to whom Llull is referring could be James II of Majorca, James II of Aragon, Ferdinand IV of Castile, and Frederick III of Sicily, all of whom had interests of one kind or another in North Africa. James II of Aragon, in particular, was unhappy about the proposed Hospitaller expedition, which was to be based on Cyprus and Rhodes, and in fact, his objections were quite reasonable and sound. It is worth noting that even in the previous section on the route through Constantinope, Llull advises using the island of Raycet (otherwise known as Rosetta or Rashid) as a naval base, rather than Cyprus or Rhodes. This can be seen as evidence that he maintained some independence from both French and Aragonese royal houses in his proposals for crusading. The argument for financial support suggests that campaigning against Muslims in Spain was not automatically considered to be crusading.

Llull's discussion of the unification of the military orders into a single great crusading army was also significant and contained slight variations from his previous proposals. Whereas in *Liber de passagio* Llull had considered a strong and devoted king without a wife as a candidate for leading the military order, and in *De fine* he suggested that the son of a king would make a good leader, here he argued that the leader should come from within the order since sons would not necessarily be as devoted to the Holy Land as their fathers had been and since the fathers were also interested in acquiring the Holy Land for their sons.[104] Llull's attention to practical details in connection to the military orders is also evidence that he was aware of conversations and negotiations taking

---

101   *Liber de acquisitione Terrae Sanctae* 1.2, f. 545rb.

102   See *De fine* 2.3.1, ROL 9:276. On contemporary crusading proposals and the aspirations of the French curia, see Housley, *The Later Crusades,* 25–30; on the Catalans in Greece, ibid., 161–165; and on the Templars and Hospitallers in this period, ibid., 204–217.

103   *Liber de acquisitione Terrae Sanctae* 1.3, f. 545rb-545vb.

104   *Liber de acquisitione Terrae Sanctae* 1.4, f. 545vb.

place in high political circles. Thus, he suggested that the master of the new military order should be a feudatory of the pope and advised that the Order of the Templars be destroyed and their goods transferred to the Master General of the new order. He concluded that these matters should all be confirmed at the Council of Vienne.[105]

None of Llull's treatises on crusading would be complete without a presentation of his proposals for the establishment of missionary schools and reaffirmation of the connection between the apostolic life, willingness to die for love of Christ, and successful missionary efforts. Llull provided this in the second and third distinctions of his *Liber de acquisitione Terrae Sanctae*. These parts of the treatise also revealed the influence of contemporary events. In particular, the second distinction "On preaching" (*De praedicandi*) reflected Llull's recent experiences in Bougie.[106] For example, Llull recounted that Muslims argued that Christian loss of the Holy Land was God's punishment for their failure to recognize the Qur'an as the true law of God. Lull's response was conventional: Christians had lost their lands because they were deficient in wisdom, power and charity; in other words, they had failed to live up to the demands of their own sacred scriptures.[107]

The final distinction of this short treatise is divided into two parts. The first, on *exempla*, provided anecdotal evidence proving why Llull's Art and his "necessary reasons" were, in fact, necessary. The second, on "dangers" (*pericula*), provided equally anecdotal examples of the dangers to Christendom, which could be evaded only through the realization of Llull's plans for mission and crusade.[108] Most of the examples pertain to inter-religious dialogue but several relate more specifically to crusading. For example, Llull identified the first

---

105   Ibid., 1.4, f. 545vb-546ra. On suppressing the Templars, see Malcolm Barber, *The Trial of the Templars* (Cambridge: 1993).

106   *Liber de acquisitione Terrae Sanctae* 2.2, f. 546ra-546va. Llull's subsequent discussion in this section reflects the discussions he must have had with Muslim interlocutors, especially about the Qu'ran. Cf. his *Liber disputationis Raimundi christiani et Homeri saraceni*, ROL 22:172–264.

107   *Liber de acquisitione Terrae Sanctae* 2.2, f. 546va. The phrase commonly used to explain Christian losses in the Holy Land from the time of St. Bernard of Clairvaux and the failures of the Second Crusade is "due to our sins" (*nostris peccatis exigentibus*). Humbert of Romans addressed this question in *De praedicatione sanctae crucis* (Nuremburg: 1495) f. 2v-3r. See Edward T. Brett, *Humbert of Romans: His Life and Views of Thirteenth-Century Society* (Toronto: 1984), 176–194, and Elizabeth Siberry, *Criticism of Crusading 1095–1274* (Oxford: 1985), 69–108.

108   *Liber de acquisitione Terrae Sanctae* 3.1, f. 547ra-547rb. These *exempla* include again the well-known story about Raymond Martí, and other anecdotes used in Llull's other writings.

danger threatening the "little ship of St. Peter" (*navicula Sancti Petri*) as the affair of the Templars, using the great damage caused by Templar affair as the basis for his recommendation, in the first distinction of the treatise, that their order be suppressed.[109] Equally relevant is Llull's reminder of the tremendous military success of the Tartars, which if it should continue, could seriously endanger Christian efforts to recover the Holy Land, especially in light of the fact that one of the three great Tartar rulers had already converted to Islam.[110] In essence, the *exempla* and *pericula* of the third distinction were meant to persuade the curia to support the plans for crusade and missions that Llull had set out in the previous two distinctions. Perhaps more than any of his previous works, the *Liber de acquisitione Terrae Sanctae* shows that Llull's proposals for mission and crusade were both subordinate to his greater goal of bringing peace and unity to the world in order that all men may love and serve God.

Llull intended for Clement v to present the *Liber de acquisitione Terrae Sanctae*, or at least the ideas contained therein, at the upcoming general church council at Vienne.[111] In fact, in a short *petitio* specifically addressed to the council, Llull reiterated much of its contents. With stirring admonitory rhetoric, Llull warned the council members that if they should fail to undertake what he advised, it would have been better if the council had never met at all.[112] Llull's first recommendation to the Council was for the support of missionary colleges (*studia*). Next, he recommended that the military orders be unified but then divided into two parts, one campaigning towards the acquisition of the Holy Land via Constantinople and the other via Spain.[113] His third and fourth recommendations firmly tied the financing of the passage (*passagium*) to issues of church reform, specifically to excess clerical wealth and the holding of multiple prebends. Here he also recommended that if the Templar order were to be destroyed, their goods should be transferred to the unified military order that he had advocated. He firmly warned against handing these goods over to princes or clerics, since they are already wealthy enough; rather the

---

109   Ibid., 3.2, f. 547rb. Llull's use of the phrase *navicula Sancti Petri* is significant in light of the sense of eschatological urgency that is evident in his crusading proposals because it appears in versions of the "Vision of Tripoli," an apocalyptic vision of the fate of the Holy Land and the conversion of the Muslims which was popular around 1300; see Schein, *Fideles Crucis*, 68–71, 117–119, and 134.

110   *Liber de acquisitione Terrae Sanctae* 3.2, f. 547va.

111   Ibid., 3.2, f. 547va.

112   For Llull's ten proposals to the council, with its fiery invocation and concluding admonitions, see *Liber de ente quod simpliciter est per se et propter se existens et agens*, "Ordinationes decem quas Raimundus intendit praesentare in Concilio generali," ROL 8:179–145.

113   In effect, a merging of his advice in previous treatises; see ibid., 6.2, ROL 8:240.

wealth should be distributed for the service of the Holy Land.[114] The remaining recommendations to the general council expressed concerns ranging from the color of clerical robes, laymen wearing clerical tonsures, and the problems of usury, to mandates about the types of philosophy which should be avoided, preaching to Jews and Muslims on their holy days and the reform of the fields of law and medicine.[115] Did Llull's proposals achieve long-awaited success at the council? Several later texts intimate that Llull himself thought they did. Both his *Liber de locutione angelorum* and *Liber de participatione christiano-rum et sarracenorum* imply that he had influenced the Council's decisions to establish language schools and to support crusading by turning over the goods of the Templars to the Hospitallers.[116] However, after the Council of Vienne, Llull addressed the energies of his final years to his plans for peaceful inter-religious dialogue, and he abandoned his promotion of crusade. This may have been the result of his disillusionment with, among other things, the debacle of the Templars and the failure of any of the rulers to whom his plans were directed to engage in successful campaigning.[117]

Over the course of about two decades, Llull wrote a handful of treatises specifically aimed at garnering papal support for what really amounted to his plans for helping the world achieve the goal for which it was created: namely, to love and serve God. Other texts written by Llull made it clear that armed confrontation and military campaigns were not necessarily his preferred means for achieving this goal. However, Llull's willingness to accept crusading as a legitimate vocation in which one could embody at least some of the spiritual

---

114   Ibid., 6.3-4, ROL 8:240–242.

115   Goals reduced to three in his *Liber disputationis Petri et Raimundi sive Phantasticus* Prol., ROL 16:14: the establishment of missionary *studia*, unification of military orders for the recovery of the Holy Land, and extirpation of the errors of the Averroists. He summarized the same goals in a contemporary text that he dedicated to Philip IV, *Liber natalis*, ROL 6:69–70.

116   Llull also wrote about the council in his poem *Del consili*, ORL 20:253–288; cf. *Vita coaeta-nea* 11, ROL 8:302–303. On Llull and the Council of Vienne, see: Domínguez Reboiras and Gayà, *Raimundus Lullus: An Introduction*, 112–117. For Llull's own assessment of his success, see *Liber de locutione angelorum* Prol., ROL 16:216, and *Liber de particpatione chris-tianorum et saracenorum* Prol., ROL 16:246. For the decisions of the Council of Vienne, see Ewald Müller, *Das Konzil von Vienne, 1311–1312, seine Quellen und seine Geschichte* (Münster: 1934); Berthold Altaner, "Raymundus Lullus und der Sprachenkanon (can. 11) des Konzils von Vienne," *Historisches Jahrbuch* 53 (1933): 190–219; and Sebastián Garcías Palou, "Ramon Llull ante la convocación del Concilio de Vienne," *Estudios Franciscanos* 76 (1975): 343–358.

117   On these failures, see: Housley, *The Later Crusades*, 28–31, 211–220, and 277–278; on the failure of Iberian rulers to eliminate Granada, see Schein, *Fideles crucis*, 239–257.

values of the gospels, particularly the desire to suffer for Christ, suggests that he was influenced by the medieval culture of crusade, and by crusade sermons and histories in particular. His proposals are not those of a specialist but convey the basic knowledge that a layman of his social class and education could have been expected to acquire throughout his travels and from his known contacts. Even if some of the details of Llull's plans were unrealistic or impractical, they often reflected the hopes and aspirations of the very audience to whom the treatises were addressed. That he unrelentingly attached plans for evangelization to his proposals for military campaigns against unbelievers and that he consistently reminded his readers of the spiritual benefit of supporting or participating in his proposals, reminds us that he was not approaching the subject as a traditional courtier, curialist or policy maker. Instead, he offered these proposals from his own unique perspective as a layman who had undergone a radical conversion experience and who, as a result of that experience, had dedicated his life to the service of Christ. This is the source of the underlying consistency in the treatises. It is also the reason why the study of these treatises is so important for scholars of the crusades and missions of the later medieval period. Their significance rests not so much in the specific details of the military plans they offer, but rather in the way they give voice to the penetration of certain aspects of crusade ideology and lay spirituality amongst those members of western Christian society whose individual voices are not regularly heard.

Works Cited

Primary Works

Dubois, Pierre, "De recuperatione Terre Sancte," (ed.) and trans. Walther I. Brandt, *The Recovery of the Holy Land* (New York: 1956).

Humbert of Romans, *De praedicatione sanctae crucis* (Nuremberg: 1495).

Nicholas IV, Pope, *Registres de Nicolas IV*, (ed.) Ernest Langlois, 2 vols. (Paris: 1886–91).

Pierre de la Palude, *Tractatus de potestate papae*, (ed.) P.T. Stella (Zürich: 1966).

Primary Works: Llull

Arbor scientiae, ROL 24–26.

Ars amativa boni, ROL 29:1–432.

Ars notatoria, (ed.) and trans. Jordi Gayà Estelrich (Madrid: 1978).

Book of the Lover and the Beloved, trans. Eve Bonner, in Anthony Bonner (ed.), *Doctor Illuminatus: A Ramon Llull Reader* (Princeton: 1993), 173–238.

Cant de Ramon, (ed.) Salvador Galmés, ORL 19: 255–260.

Del consili, ORL 20:253–288.

Disputatio fidei et intellectus, ROL 23:213–279.

Doctor Illuminatus: A Ramon Llull Reader, (ed.) and trans. Anthony Bonner (Princeton: 1985).

Doctrina pueril, NEORL 7.

Liber contra antichristum, (ed.) Pamela Beattie, ROL 36:1–124.

Liber de acquisitione Terrae Sanctae, Paris, Bibliothèque Nationale, Lat. 15450, fols. 544v-547v.

Liber de acquisitione Terrae Sanctae, (ed.) Éphrem Longpré, *Criterion* 3 (1927): 265–278

Liber de acquisitione Terrae Sanctae, (ed.) Eugène Kamar, *Studia Orientalia Christiana* 6 (1961): 102–131.

Liber de acquisitione Terrae Sanctae, trans. Pere Llabrés, *Darrer llibre sobre la conquesta de Terra Santa* (Barcelona: 2002).

Liber de ascensu et descensu intellectus, ROL 9:20–199.

Liber de consilio, ROL 10:119–235.

Liber de demonstratione per aequiparantiam, ROL 9:216–232.

Liber de ente quod simpliciter est per se et propter se existens et agens, ROL 8:179–245.

Liber de fine, ROL 9:249–291.

Liber de fine, trans. Pere Llabrés and Jordi Gayà Estelrich (Barcelona: 2002).

Liber de locutione angelorum, ROL 16:215–236.

Liber de passagio, (ed.) Fernando Domínguez Reboiras, ROL 28:257–353.

Liber de praedicatione, ROL 3 and 4.

Liber de participatione christianorum et saracenorum, (eds.) Antoni Oliver and Michel Senellart, ROL 16:245–260.

Liber de Sancta Maria, (ed.) Blanca Garí, ROL 28:1–241.

Liber disputationis Petri clerici et Raimundi sive Phantasticus, ROL 16:13–30.

Liber disputationis Raimundi christiani et Homeri saraceni, ROL 22:172–264.

Liber natalis pueri paruuli Christi Jesu, ROL 7:168–177.

Libre contra anticrist, (ed.) Gret Schib, NEORL 3:103–160.

Libre de contemplació en Déu, ORL 2–8.

Libre de meravelles, NEORL 10 and 13.

Libre de meravelles, trans. Anthony Bonner, SW 2:647–1105.

Libre del gentil e dels tres savis, NEORL 2.

Lo desconhort/Der desconhort, (ed.) and trans. Johannes and Vittorio Hösle (Munich: 1998).

Petició de Ramon al papa Celestí V per la conversió dels infidels, (ed.) Josep Perarnau i Espelt, "Un text català de Ramon Llull desconegut: la 'Petició de Ramon al Papa Celestí V per a la conversió dels ifidels', edició i estudi," *Arxiu de Textos Catalans Antics* 1 (1982): 9–46.

Petitio Raimundi pro conuersione infidelium ad Coelestinum V papam and *Petitio Raimundi pro conuersione infidelium ad Bonifatium VIII papam*, (ed.) Viola Tenge-Wolf, ROL 35:403–437.

Quomodo terra sancta recuperari potest, ROL 28:325–331.

Ramon Llull: A Contemporary Life, trans. Anthony Bonner (Barcelona: 2010).

Romanç d'Evast e Blaquerna, (eds.) Albert Soler and Joan Santanach, NEORL 8.

Tractatus de modo convertendi infideles, ROL 28:333–352.

Vita coaetanea, ROL 8:259–309.

Secondary Works

Abun-Nasr, Jamil M., *A History of the Maghrib in the Islamic Period* (Cambridge: 1987).

Altaner, Berthold, "Glaubenszwang und Glaubensfreiheit in der Missionstheorie des Raymundus Lullus: Ein Beitrag zur Geschichte der Toleranz," *Historisches Jahrbuch* 48 (1928): 586–610.

Altaner, Berthold, "Raymundus Lullus und der Sprachenkanon (can. 11) des Konzils von Vienne," *Historisches Jahrbuch* 53 (1933): 190–219.

Atiya, A.S., *The Crusade in the Later Middle Ages* (London: 1938).

Badia, Lola, Joan Santanach, and Albert Soler (eds.), *Ramon Llull as a Vernacular Writer: Communicating a New Kind of Knowledge* (Woodbridge: 2016).

Baldwin, John W., "From the Ordeal to Confession: In Search of Lay Religion in Thirteenth-Century France," in Peter Biller and Alastair J. Minnis (eds.), *Handling Sin: Confession in the Middle Ages* (York: 2013), 191–209.

Barber, Malcolm, *The Trial of the Templars* (Cambridge: 1993).

Beattie, Pamela, "'Pro exaltatione sanctae fidei catholicae': Mission and Crusade in the Writings of Ramon Llull," in Larry J. Simon (ed.), *Iberia and the Mediterranean World of the Middle Ages: Studies in Honor of Robert I. Burns S.J.*, 2 vols. (Leiden: 1995), 1:113–129.

Beattie, Pamela, "Crusading and the Penitential Life: James of Vitry's Crusade Sermon Models and Llull's *De fine*," *SL* 54 (2014): 33–66.

Biller, Peter and Alastair J. Minnis (eds.), *Handling Sin: Confession in the Middle Ages* (York: 2013).

Boyle, John Andrew, "The Il-Khans of Persia and the Princes of Europe," *Central Asiatic Journal* 20 (1976): 25–40.

Brett, Edward T., *Humbert of Romans: His Life and Views of Thirteenth-Century Society* (Toronto: 1984).

Brundage, James, *Medieval Canon Law and the Crusader* (London: 1969).

Bundy, David, "The Syriac and Armenian Christian Responses to the Islamification of the Mongols," in John V. Tolan (ed.), *Medieval Christian Perceptions of Islam: A Book of Essays* (New York: 1996), 33–53.

Burman, Thomas E., "The Influence of the 'Apology of Al-Kindî' and *Contrarietas Alfolica* on Ramon Lull's Late Religious Polemics, 1305–1313," *Mediaeval Studies* 53 (1991): 197–228.

Burr, David, *Olivi's Peaceable Kingdom: A Reading of the Apocalypse Commentary* (Philadelphia: 1993).

Burr, David, *The Spiritual Franciscans: From Protest to Persecution in the Century after St. Francis* (State College, Pennsylvania: 2001).

Cardini, Franco, *Studi sulla storia e sull'idea di crociata* (Rome: 1993).

Cole, Penny J., *The Preaching of the Crusades to the Holy Land 1095–1270* (Cambridge, Mass.: 1991).

Colomer, Eusebio, "Ramon Llull y Ramon Martí," *EL* 28 (1988): 1–37.

Daniel, E. Randolph, *The Franciscan Concept of Mission in the High Middle Ages* (Lexington, Kentucky: 1975).

Domínguez Reiboras, Fernando, "La idea de cruzada en el 'Liber de passagio' de Ramón Llull," *Patristica et medaevalia* 25 (2004): 45–74.

Domínguez Reiboras, Fernando, "Nicolás IV, destinatario del 'Liber de passagio,' y Ramon Llull," *SL* 44 (2004): 3–15.

Domínguez Reiboras, Fernando, "Raimundo Lulio y el ideal mendicante: Afinidades y divergencias," in Fernando Domínguez Reboiras, R. Imbach, T. Pindl, and P. Walter (eds.), *Aristotelica et Lulliana magistro doctissimo Charles H. Lohr septuagesimum annum feliciter agenti dedicata*, Instrumenta Patristica XXVI (Steenbergen and The Hague: 1995), 377–413.

Dufourcq, Charles-Emmanuel, "La Méditerranée et le Christianisme: Cadre géopolitique et économique de l'apostolat missionnaire de Ramon Llull," *EL* 24 (1980): 5–22.

Dufourcq, Charles-Emmanuel, *L'Espagne catalane et le Maghrib aux XIIIe et XXIVe siècles: de la bataille de Las Navas de Tolosa (1212) à l'avènement du sultan mérinide Abou-l-Hasan (1331)* (Paris: 1966).

Ensenyat, Gabriel, "Pacifisme i croada en Ramon Llull," in Maria-Àngels Roque (ed.), *Ramon Llull i l'Islam: L'inici del diàleg* (Barcelona: 2008), 232–245.

Finke, Heinrich, *Konzilienstudien zur Geschichte des 13. Jahrhunderts* (Münster, 1891).

Forey, Alan J., *Military Orders and Crusades* (Aldershot: 1994).

Forey, Alan J., *The Military Orders from the Twelfth to the Early Fourteenth Centuries* (Toronto: 1992).

Forey, Alan J., "The Military Orders and the Conversion of Muslims in the Twelfth and Thirteenth Centuries," *Journal of Medieval History* 28 (2002): 1–22.

Forey, Alan J., "The Military Orders in the Crusading Proposals of the Late-thirteenth and Early-fourteenth Centuries," *Traditio* 36 (1980): 317–345.

Freidlein, Roger, *Der Dialog bei Ramon Llull: literarische Gestaltung als apologetische Strategie* (Tübingen: 2004).

Friedlein, Roger, *Der Dialog bei Ramon Llull: literarische Gestaltung als apologetische Strategie* (Tubingen: 2004)

Garcías Palou, Sebastián, "El candidato de Ramon Llull para el cargo de 'Maestre General de la Orden Militar del Espíritu Santo,'" *EL* 16 (1972a): 63–77.

Garcías Palou, Sebastián, "El papa 'Blanquerna' de Ramon Llull y Celestino V," *EL* 20 (1976): 71–86.

Garcías Palou, Sebastián, *El Miramar de Ramon Llull* (Palma: 1977).

Garcías Palou, Sebastián, "Ramon Llull ante la convocación del concilio de Vienne," *Estudios Franciscanos* 76 (1975): 343–358.

Garcías Palou, Sebastián, "Sobre la identificacion del 'Libre del Passatge,'" *EL* 16 (1972b): 216–230.

Garcías Palou, Sebastián, "Sobre la identificacion del 'Libre del passatge,'" *EL* 16 (1972): 216–230.

Gayà Estelrich, Jordi, "Ramon Llull, il suo impegno missionario," *Analecta TOR* 32 (2001):379–388.

Gayà Estelrich, Jordi, "Ramon Llull en Oriente (1301–1302)," *SL* 37 (1997): 25–78.

Gayà Estelrich, Jordi, "Ramon Llull i l'Islam: 'Infideles sunt homines, sicut et nos,'" in *'Vós sou sant Senyor Déu únic': Franciscanisme i Islam* (Barcelona: 2002), 115–143.

Gayà Estelrich, Jordi, *"Raimondo Lullo: Una teologia per la missione"* (Milan: 2002).

Guadalajara Medina, José, *El anticristo en la España medieval* (Madrid: 2004).

Hames, Harvey J., *The Art of Conversion: Christianity and Kabbalah in the Thirteenth Century* (Leiden: 2000).

Hillgarth, Jocelyn N. (ed.), *Diplomatari Lul.lià* (Barcelona: 2001).

Hillgarth, Jocelyn N., "Ramon Llull et l'utopie," *EL* 25 (1981–83): 175–185.

Hillgarth, Jocelyn N., *Ramon Llull i el Naixement del Lul.lisme* (Barcelona: 1998).

Housley, Norman, *The Avignon Papacy and the Crusades, 1305–1378* (Oxford: 1986).

Housley, Norman, *Contesting the Crusades* (Oxford: 2006).

Housley, Norman, *Crusading and Warfare in Medieval and Renaissance Europe* (Ashgate: 2001).

Housley, Norman (ed.) and trans, *Documents on the Later Crusades, 1274–1580* (New York: 1996).

Housley, Norman, "The Eschatological Imperative: Messianism and Holy War in Europe, 1260–1556," in Peter Schäffer and Mark R. Cohen (eds.), *Toward the Millennium: Messianic Expectations from the Bible to Waco* (Leiden: 1998), 123–150.

Housley, Norman, *The Later Crusades from Lyon to Alcazar 1274–1580* (Oxford: 1992).

Jackson, Peter, "Hülegü Khan and the Christians: The Making of a Myth," in Peter J. Edbury and Jonathan Phillips (eds.), *The Experience of Crusading*, vol. 2, *Defining the Crusader Kingdom* (Cambridge: 2003), 196–213.

Kedar, Benjamin Z., *Crusade and Mission: European Approaches Toward the Muslims* (Princeton: 1984).

Lee, Harold, Marjorie Reeves, and Giulio Silano, *Western Mediterranean Prophecy: The School of Joachim of Fiore and the Fourteenth-Century Breviloquium* (Toronto: 1989).

Leopold, Antony, *How to Recover the Holy Land: The Crusade Proposals of the Late Thirteenth and Early Fourteenth Centuries* (Aldershot: 2000).

Lerner, Robert, *The Powers of Prophecy: The Cedar of Lebanon Vision from the Mongol Onslaught to the Dawn of the Enlightenment* (Berkeley: 1983).

Lock, Peter, *The Routledge Companion to the Crusades* (New York: 2006).

Maier, Christoph T., *Crusade Propaganda and Ideology: Model Sermons for the Preaching of the Cross* (Cambridge: 2000).

Maier, Christoph T., "Crusade and Rhetoric against the Muslim Colony of Lucera: Eudes of Châteauroux's 'Sermones de Rebellione Sarracenorum Lucheri in Apulia,'" *Journal of Medieval History* 21 (1995): 343–385.

Maier, Christoph T., *Preaching the Crusades: Mendicant Friars and the Cross in the Thirteenth Century* (Cambridge: 1994).

Mallette, Karla, "Insularity: A Literary History of Muslim Lucera," in Adnan A. Husain and K.E. Fleming (ed.), *A Faithful Sea: The Religious Cultures of the Mediterranean, 1200–1700* (Oxford: 2007), 27–46.

Mastnak, Tomaž, *Crusading Peace: Christendom, the Muslim World, and the Western Political Order* (Berkeley: 2002).

McGinn, Bernard, "Angel Pope and Papal Antichrist," *Church History* 47 (1978): 155–173.

Muldoon, James, *Popes, Lawyers and Infidels: The Church and the Non-Christian World 1250–1550* (Philadelphia: 1979).

Müller, Ewald, *Das Konzil von Vienne, 1311–1312, seine Quellen und seine Geschichte* (Münster: 1934).

Musco, Alessandro and Marta M.M. Romano (eds), *Il Mediterraneo del '300: Raimondo Lullo e Federico III d'Aragona, re di Sicilia: Omaggio a Fernando Domínguez Reiboiras* (Turnhout: 2008).

O'Callaghan, Joseph F., *Reconquest and Crusade in Medieval Spain* (Philadelphia: 2003).

Oliver, Antonio, "El beato Ramón Llull en sus relaciones con la Escuela Franciscana de los siglos XIII–XIV," *EL* 9 (1965): 55–70, 145–165; 10 (1966): 47–55; 11 (1967): 89–119; 13 (1969): 51–65.

Perarnau i Espelt, Josep, "Consideracions sobre el tema 'Missió i Croada en Ramon Llull,'" *Arxiu de Textos Catalans Antics* 22 (2003): 561–578.

Porsia, Franco, *Progetti di Crociata: Il* De fine *di Raimondo Lullo* (Toronto: 2005).

Pou y Martí, José, *Visionarios, beguinos y fraticelos catalanes (siglos XIII-XV)* (Vich: 1930).

Powell, James M., "The Role of Women in the Fifth Crusade," in *The Crusades, the Kingdom of Sicily, and the Mediterranean* (Aldershot: 2007), 294–301.

Raimundus Lullus: An Introduction to his Life, Works, and Thought, (eds.) Fidora, Alexander and Joseph E. Rubio, ROL Suppl. 2 (Turnhout: 2008).

Reeves, Marjorie, *The Influence of Prophecy in the Later Middle Ages: A Study in Joachimism* (Oxford: 1969).

Rousett, Paul, "La Croisade obstacle à la mission," *Nova et Vetera* 57 (1982): 133–142.

Runciman, Steven, "The Decline of the Crusading Idea," *Relazioni del Congresso Internazionale di Scienze Storiche*, vol. 3, *Storia del medioevo* (Florence: 1995): 637–652.

Ryan, James D., "Nicholas IV and the Evolution of the Eastern Missionary Effort," *Archivum Historiae Pontificiae* 19 (1981): 79–96.

Schein, Sylvia, *Fideles Crucis: The Papacy, the West, and the Recovery of the Holy Land 1274–1314* (Oxford: 1991).

Schein, Sylvia, *"Gesta Dei per Mongolos* 1300: The Genesis of a Non-event," *English Historical Review* 95 (1979):805–819.

Siberry, Elizabeth, *Criticism of Crusading 1095–1274* (Oxford: 1985).

Soler i Llompart, Albert, "El 'Liber super Psalmum Quicumque' de Ramon Llull i l'opció pels tartars," *SL* 32 (1992): 3–29.

Ramon Sugranyes de Franch, *Raymond Lulle, Docteur des Missions* (Schönick-Beckenried: 1954).

Taylor, Julie, *Muslims in Medieval Italy: The Colony at Lucera* (Lanham, MD: 2003).

Tolan, John V., "Taking Gratian to Africa: Raymond de Penyafort's Legal Advice to the Dominicans and Franciscans in Tunis (1234)," in Adnan A. Husain and Katherine Elizabeth Fleming (eds.), *A Faithful Sea: The Religious Cultures of the Mediterranean, 1200–1700* (Oxford: 2007), 45–63.

Vose, Robin, *Dominicans, Muslims and Jews in the Medieval Crown of Aragon* (Cambridge: 2009).

PART 3

Llull as Vernacular Writer

∵

CHAPTER 8

Ephemeral Stories: Llull and Medieval Exemplary Literature

José Aragüés Aldaz

8.1 Introduction: Lullian Exemplary Literature: An Overview

The oeuvre of Ramon Llull abounds in stories, fables, comparisons and other short didactic forms, all susceptible of inclusion under the label of *exempla*. Attention to this literature has been a constant in Lullian scholarship and has enjoyed a notable surge in recent years. While we still lack an overall analysis of this author's *exempla*, there is no lack of attempts to define the genre, or of approaches to its aesthetic and rhetorical principles.[1] Most common are studies focused on the presence of exemplary forms in specific works. This presence has been traced in his *Blaquerna*, completed in 1283,[2] the first great novel of Llull's Quaternary Phase (1274–1289), and in particular sections of his second great novel from this period, the *Libre de meravelles* [Book of Marvels] written

---

1 For introductions to Lullian *exempla*, see: Guillermo Colom Ferrá, "Ramon Llull y los orígenes de la literatura catalana [8]," *EL* 16 (1972): 37–47; Lola Badia, "No cal que tragats exempli dels romans," in *Miscel·lània Pere Bohigas* 1, Estudis de Llengua i Literatura Catalanes 3 (Barcelona: 1981), 87–94; Lola Badia and Anthony Bonner, *Ramón Llull: Vida, pensamiento y obra literaria* (Barcelona: 1993), 109–117 and 140–155; Mark D. Johnston, *ER* 100–116; José Aragüés Aldaz, "*Exempla inquirere et invenire*: Fundamentos retóricos para un análisis de las formas breves lulianas," in *La literatura en la época de Sancho IV: Actas del Congreso Internacional "La literatura en la época de Sancho IV" (Alcalá de Henares, del 21 al 24 de febrero de 1994)*, (eds.) Carlos Alvar and José Manuel Lucía Megías (Alcalá de Henares: 1996), 289–311; Eugènia Gisbert, "*Metaforice loquendo*: de l'analogia a la metàfora en els *Començaments de medicina* de Ramon Llull," *SL* 44 (2004): 17–52; Rubén Luzón Díaz, "Una aproximación a la noción de *exemplum* en la obra luliana, seguida de un breve comentario en los *exempla* del capítulo 62 del *Llibre de meravelles*," *Revista de lenguas y literaturas catalana, gallega y vasca* 12 (2006): 253–276; Anthony Bonner, *L'Art i la lògica de Ramon Llull: Manual d'ús*, trans. H. Lamuela (Barcelona and Palma: 2012), 293–302; and Lola Badia, Joan Santanach and Albert Soler, "Ramon Llull," in *Historia de la Literatura Catalana*, (ed.) À. Broch (Barcelona: 2013), 1:400–403. Xavier Bonillo Hoyos, "Catálogo de ejemplos lulianos," *Magníficat* 2 (2015): 55–127 offers a useful catalog of Lullian *exempla*; José Aragüés Aldaz, *Ramon Llull y la literatura ejemplar* (Alicante: 2016) provides a more detailed version of the analyses in this chapter.

2 Miguel Arbona Piza, "Los *exemplis* en el *Llibre de Evast e Blanquerna*," *EL* 20 (1976): 53–70.

between 1287–1289.[3] A very rich bibliography exists especially for the seventh, well-known section of the latter text, known as the *Libre de les bèsties* [Book of Beasts], a text consisting of "stories within a story" and subjected to analysis for decades.[4] We also have noteworthy studies of the two great compilations of *exempla* from Llull's Ternary Phase (1290–1308): the *Arbre exemplifical* [Exemplary Tree] (the penultimate book of the encyclopedic *Arbre de sciencia* [Tree of Knowledge], composed in 1296,[5] and the section of "beautiful *exempla*" (*pulcra exempla*) included in Llull's *Rhetorica nova* of 1301.[6] Finally, there also exist studies of those forms that favor exemplary expression, such as Marian miracles, whose peculiarities have been explored in two texts from different eras of Llull's career: the *Libre d'Ave Maria* [Book of Ave Maria] (included in *Blaquerna*) and the *Libre de sancta Maria* [Book of Saint Mary] (1290–92?),[7] composed in his Ternary Phase. In short, much is known. But there remains much to know, because nothing is more constant in the oeuvre of Blessed Ramon than his recourse to these short forms, present from his foundational *Libre de contemplació* [Book of Contemplation](1273–1274?), composed before the formulation of his Great Art, to the sermons composed on Majorca during 1312–1313, in the period after the finished Art.

For the reader interested in the medieval *exemplum*, a first glance at Llull's production can be provocative, yet disconcerting. It is true that Llull displays

3 Mark D. Johnston, "Exemplary Reading in Ramon Llull's *Llibre de meravelles*," *Forum for Modern Language Studies* 28 (1992): 235–250; Josep-Antoni Ysern, "*Exempla* i estructures exemplars en el primer llibre del *Fèlix*," *SL* 39 (1999): 25–54; Xavier Bonillo Hoyos, "Els exemples del paradís i de l'infern del *Llibre de meravelles* de Ramon Llull," *SL* 44 (2004): 53–78; "L'estructura dels llibres del Paradís i de l'Infern al *Fèlix* de Ramon Llull," in *Actes de les Jornades Internacionals Lullianes: Ramon Llull al S. XXI* (Palma: 2004), (ed.) Maria Isabel Ripoll (Palma and Barcelona: 2005), 217–233; and *Literatura al "Llibre de meravelles"* (Barcelona: 2008), 98–107.

4 Barry Taylor, "Some Complexities of the *Exemplum* in Ramon Llull's *Llibre de les bèsties*," *The Modern Language Review* 90 (1995): 646–658.

5 Lluís Cabré, Marcel Ortín and Josep Pujol, "'Coneixer e haver moralitats bones:' L'ús de la literatura en l'*Arbre exemplifical* de Ramon Llull," *EL* 28 (1988): 139–167; Albert G. Hauf, "Sobre l'*Arbor exemplificalis*," in *Arbor Scientiae: Der Baum des Wissens von Ramon Llull (Akten des Internationalen Kongresses aus Anlaß des 40-jährigen Jubiläums des Raimundus-Lullus-Instituts der Universität Freiburg i. Br.)*, (eds.) Fernando Domínguez Reboiras, Pere Villalba Varneda and Peter Walter (Turnhout: 2002), 303–342; Robert D.F. Pring-Mill, "Els *recontaments* de l'*Arbre Exemplifical* de Ramon Llull: la transmutació de la ciència en literatura," in *Estudis sobre Ramon Llull (1956–1978)* (Montserrat and Barcelona: 1991), 307–317.

6 Ramon Llull, *Retòrica nova*, (eds.) Josep Batalla, Lluís Cabré and Marcel Ortín (Turnhout and Santa Coloma de Queralt: 2006), 68–71.

7 Paule Bétérous, "Ramon Llull et le renouvellement du thème des miracles Mariaux au XIIIe siècle," *Cultura Neolatina* 38 (1978): 37–47; David J. Viera, "*Exempla* in the *Libre de Sancta Maria* and Traditional Medieval Marian Miracles," *Catalan Review* 4 (1990): 221–231.

some respect for the traditional terminology of this genre, demonstrates knowledge of its essential forms, and utilizes some themes and arguments disseminated in exemplary compendia of his era. But this is only the point of departure for creating a corpus of material that is, for the most part, completely new. Within traditional generic (and some much more novel) models lie hidden hundreds of highly original, at times even surprising, stories. This approach contrasts with the practice of many contemporary writers, so often limited to reiterating narratives already consolidated in the literature or oral media of their milieu. As with the sermons or novels of this author, any analysis of the Lullian *exemplum* must begin, in effect, by recognizing its "alterity."[8]

The reasons for this singularity are obvious. For Blessed Ramon, exemplary literature is not simply a vehicle for expounding norms of behavior. It is, above all, an instrument for disseminating the principles of his new Art, and thus a means for explicating the structure of the universe. It is not, then, just any means. Exemplary forms possess an obvious analogical dimension, thanks to their ability to illustrate spiritual ideas through comparison with the natural and human worlds, and analogy is precisely the foundation of the design of the cosmos in the thought of this author, faithful to the principles of "divine exemplarism," that is to say, to the idea that the Creation reproduces, in each and all of its levels, the very form of the Creator.

In this sense, there are many details of the Art that necessarily reinforce the possibility (and even the necessity) of assiduously using exemplary literature. Among them, the confidence placed, during Llull's Quaternary Phase, in a very concrete analogical procedure for the demonstration of reality, the so-called "elemental exemplarism." According to this procedure, analysis of the modes of interaction among the four elements allows establishing a complex combinatory pattern, which illuminates analogically the activity of the other spheres of Creation. That labor of illumination alone would justify Ramon Llull's invention of a new exemplary form, the so-called "metaphor" (*matafora*). Needless to say, his variety bears only a very tangential relation with the canonical forms of exemplary literature in his era: in its most advanced formulation (proposed in the *Començaments de medicina* [Principles of Medicine], written between 1274–1283), the Lullian "metaphor" accords the appearance of an *exemplum* to what clearly constitutes a rigorous intellective and demonstrational mechanism, established as an indispensable element in the functioning

---

8   Lola Badia, "La literatura alternativa de Ramon Llull: tres mostres," in *Actes del VII Congrés de l'Associació Hispànica de Literatura Medieval* (*Castelló de la Plana, 22–26 de setembre de 1997*), (eds.) Santiago Fortuño Llorens and Tomàs Martínez Romero (Castelló de la Plana: 1999), 1:11–32, offers a clear discussion of this "alterity."

of his Art. Ramon Llull does appreciate the value of other, more modest and conventional, exemplary forms, granting them considerable space in his oeuvre. The majority of Llull's *exempla* constitute, in effect, a valuable didactic aid, a literary recourse that makes concrete his theoretical assumptions, following the common function of the genre in every era. None the less, even in his most humble stories and similes there is latent some transcendent conception of the analogy defined by divine exemplarism. The *exempla* of Ramon Llull do not simply explain "metaphorically" spiritual realities from natural ones. On the contrary, they presuppose the existence of a real connection between them.

Such a transposition of advanced principles of exemplarism into exemplary literature was not common in the Middle Ages. In fact, Llull's stories often acquire unusual complexity, demanding from the reader enormous exegetical effort, sometimes guided by the author himself. Thanks precisely to this complexity, correlations become a suitable instrument for meditating on all Creation and, in that way, for contemplating the Creator. From this derives an aesthetic value that goes far beyond the decorative pleasure and utility traditionally associated with the genre. In the case of the Lullian *exemplum*, delight results from successfully deciphering its transcendent meaning; beauty, from the power of the genre to translate, through words, the lovely design of Creation.

Ramon Llull grants to the *exemplum*, in effect, an ambitious goal, imposing on it at the same time some inviolable limits: his associations are limited to translating into literary language the philosophical presuppositions of his Art, following strict, rigorous correlations. For this purpose, exemplary literature can of course pursue the most diverse formal pathways. Llull's writings manage to include the simplest similes deduced from the natural and human worlds, as well as the most complex comparisons (the most extreme in difficulty being the afore-mentioned *mataforas* from the *Començaments de medicina*). On the other hand, he must forego almost completely the brief narrative form most common in the homiletic and didactic literature of his era: the historical or true *exemplum*. The discovery of valid arguments to illustrate the principles of his Art is only possible by appealing to the far freer and more flexible realm of the imagination. Hence the Lullian oeuvre is filled with fictional tales, even though the concrete aspects of these display a certain oscillation over the course of time. This oscillation is dictated perhaps less by any evolution in the tastes of their author than by the requirements and specific character of the successive texts in which he inserts these *exempla*.

In the two novels already mentioned from his Quaternary phase (*Blaquerna* and the *Libre de meravelles*), their intercalated stories fit into two generic molds already well-established in literary tradition: the animal fable and the verisimilar *exemplum* (story featuring human characters). Examples of both models (some taken directly from oriental sources) co-exist within the plot involving animals in the *Libre de les bèsties*. But it is the verisimilar *exemplum* of his own making that clearly dominates the enormous fictional richness of the rest of the *Libre de meravelles* (and somewhat more modestly of *Blaquerna*), accommodated to the scheme, always plausible, that supports the plot in each work. In Llull's Ternary Phase, his writings adopt a new, somewhat more daring, exemplary modality. Their protagonists become personifications corresponding to the most diverse objects or natural beings (a sword, a shield, a rose, or a pepper) and to the abstract realities that appear in the theoretical pages of his Art (the Divine Dignities, the faculties of the soul, or even verbal tenses). These strange stories, which we might call "artful" because inspired by the methods of Llull's Art, flourish in the *Arbre exemplifical*, a repertory of brief forms created in order to recount, through a more accessible lense, the theoretical contents of the great *Arbre de sciencia*. The discovery of this new exemplary modality is, as it were, the happy result of a specific need and a certain apparent desire to explore new horizons of this genre. None the less, it does not imply any loss of confidence for Llull regarding the fable or the verisimilar story. Both genres also have a prominent presence in the *Arbre exemplifical*, and will continue to co-exist with the "artful" stories in the section of *pulcra exempla* already cited from the *Rhetorica nova*. The interest of this latter repertory is, moreover, considerable, since its contents present a kind of compromise between Llull's peculiar presuppositions and the expectations of readers undoubtedly accustomed to rather more conventional exemplary literature. Perhaps to aid this desire for accommodation, the *Rhetorica nova* offers Llull's most deliberate attempts to establish a minimal taxonomy for the genre and a strict application of its terminology, employed more loosely (although not, as we will see, wholly at random) in his earlier work.

In the trajectory that leads from the two novels of Llull's Quaternary phase to these later repertories, exemplary literature in time consolidates its place in the Lullian oeuvre. A glance at those novels allows us to observe the sense of this evolution. If *Blaquerna* is essentially a narrative occasionally adorned with *exempla*, the *Libre de meravelles* demonstrates the inversion of this scheme, by making its dialogued plot barely a foundation for sustaining an infinitely rich and varied mass of stories. The transition to Llull's Ternary Phase, on the other hand, imposes on expansion of the genre some theoretical obstacles, whose consequences are not easy to evaluate. The shift in the "analogical paradigm" that sustained the Art (that is, the replacement of "elemental exemplarism" with a new model for explaining reality, based on his theory of "correlatives") could presumably have caused some decline in use of the Lullian *matafora* (at least in so far as it was conceived in the early *Començaments de medicina*). Neither his shift in paradigm nor his abandonment of the novel appears to have affected substantially the rest of the exemplary forms practiced by Blessed Ramon. On the contrary, perhaps the clearest consequence of Llull's abandonment of the novel is his investment of his literary vocation in the genre of *exempla*. In the *Arbre exemplifical* and *Rhetorica nova*, comparative passages appear juxtaposed without respect for any narrative frame. The *exemplum* has at last become an essential, if not unique, tool for the literary expression of Llull's Art that he had sought from its beginnings.[9]

Llull projects his own narrative vocation onto the protagonists of his novels, expressing his esteem for the genre by making them narrate a myriad of *exempla*. As voiced by these protagonists, stories become an efficient medium for transmitting instruction and for dialectical debate. The stories themselves thus end up establishing among themselves a kind of "dialogue:" in a thread of conversational avatars, one *exemplum* can complete, contextualize, or refute the meaning of another. Moreover, any of the characters that appears in these stories (whether a human, an animal, or an object) can introduce a new story, and thus generate a cascading multiplication of narrative levels, full of echoes and specular reflections, with a trace of *mise en abŷme* that can surprise. Of course there is no lack of precedents in medieval literature for the dialogued deployment of stories or the successive subordination of narrative levels. But this narrative artifice truly attains, above all in the *Libre de meravelles*, remarkable beauty and an air of irreality. There is in fact, no definitive analysis of the literary techniques and procedures deployed in this novel (or in *Blaquerna*) that would reorient somewhat the existing scholarly attention accorded to the very short (and much more conventional) *Libre de les bèsties*. Obviously, these strategies have much less impact in the two major repertories from Llull's Quaternary phase, but this is a topic that also demands more detailed analysis. There is no lack of instances of the narrative subordination of stories in the *Arbre exemplifical*, and certainly nothing seems left to chance in the structure of this text or in the section of *pulcra exempla* from the *Rhetorica nova*. The arrangement alone of material in both texts, determined by two different journeys through the levels of being, constitute a useful summary of the Lullian conception of the design of Creation.

The exemplary literature of Llull is the child of an enormous effort of experimentation. There are, as we have said, very few *exempla* employed by Blessed Ramon with a prior existence. Most of these passages are fruits of

---

9   See Badia, "Literatura alternativa," 12.

his imagination, *ad hoc* creations, whose arguments take form following the specific needs of the context in which they occur. Unlike traditional stories repeated again and again, the life of most Lullian stories begins and ends in a single discursive moment, which lends to them at times the sense of a fleeting, ephemeral construction. The creation of these stories thus seems to owe something to the combinatory skill established as the axis of Llull's writing and thought. There are many Lullian stories created from the mix and slight modification of a relatively limited cast of characters, scenes, and situations. This quasi-mechanical generation of stories makes some of them seem mere simulacra or narrative "hypotheses," capable of reformulation again and again in order to generate new narratives, as real (or unreal) as those before. Of course this may have to do with the simple sensation or impression caused by the contrast between this endless parade of associations and the conventions of a storytelling tradition based on a much more compact and limited body of narratives. Yet it is also true that Llull's stories do not lack examples of narrative "inconsistency:" as we will see, a particular story may seem to arise simply to include within itself another story (to the point that the resolution of this "frame-tale" is absent or lacks any sense), while other stories display a provisional or unstable plot, as if they lacked a definitive or univocal argument for all their possible audiences within the world of the novelistic fiction itself.

Once again, we should not exaggerate the number or the implications of these cases of apparent narrative incoherence. If they demonstrate anything, it is simply the versatility of a genre conceived by Llull as a "language," as simply a conventional means of illustrating reality (and therefore conveniently adaptable in the course of narration). In every case, this assumed adaptability must be seen in relation to another, indisputable fact: the exemplary literature of Ramon Llull constitutes a corpus that is ultimately provisional and incomplete. The stories included in the *Arbre exemplifical* are conceived, in effect, simply as samples of the entire universe of comparisons that a full exemplification of the contents of the *Arbre de sciencia* could come to produce. The stories in this work and those from the *Rhetorica nova* explicitly offer narrative models or patterns, which readers should imitate in order to fabricate their own repertoire of stories or *exempla*, adapted to their own specific needs. Both texts thus propose a true "art of creating *exempla*," inviting those readers to participate in the work of literary experimentation initiated by Llull. Complete mastery of this work requires, in any case, other forays into the extensive oeuvre of the author: for example, consulting the theoretical precepts on analogy and exemplarity scattered in his various writings (from the early *Començaments de medicina* to his final treatises on preaching), or even reading his novels. Reflections by their protagonists on exemplary literature (such as their commentaries on the true

meaning of some connections or their objections to the *exempla* presented
by other characters) not only help to interpret correctly the keys to Lullian
thought, but above all, show to readers a path for conceiving their own stories
and for including them properly in their own discourse, whether public or private, oral or written. Viewed thus, Lullian storytelling displays a truly "meta-
exemplary" dimension, which reveals clearly the "reflexive distance" adopted
by Llull regarding this genre and thus underscores unmistakably the singularity of his narrative production within the panorama of medieval literature.

8.2   Exemplary Literature and Divine Exemplarism in the Middle Ages

8.2.1   *Varieties of Exemplary Literature*
Discussion of medieval exemplarism requires considering a whole mass of
theoretical concepts and textual currents. As we know, the exemplarist inspiration of the Lullian oeuvre is sustained in large measure through the intelligent
harmonization of two of those concepts and currents: divine exemplarism,
philosophical and theological in nature, and the somewhat more accessible literature of *exempla*. Regarding the latter, the medieval West witnessed in the 13th
and 14th centuries the convergence of a plethora of traditions.[10] Some of these
shared a preference for the historical or true *exemplum*. This model embraces,
in effect, two somewhat diverse forms: the "homiletic *exemplum*" designed
for preaching, and the so-called "rhetorical *exemplum*" with a more obviously
historiographical application.[11] The origins of the latter remit to Greco-Roman
Antiquity, and its essential model was the *Facta et dicta memorabilia* of Valerius
Maximus, which recounts the heroic and virtuous actions of many more or
less famous personages. This work enjoyed wide circulation in the Middle Ages
and was translated into several languages, including, among others, Catalan

---

10   María Jesús Lacarra (ed.), *Cuento y novela corta en España: 1. Edad Media* (Barcelona:
      2010), 25–41.
11   The vast bibliography on the collections of *exempla* includes: Jean Thiebaut Welter,
      L'Exemplum dans la littérature religieuse et didactique du Moyen Âge (Paris and Toulouse:
      1927); Jacques Le Goff, Claude Brémond, and Jean-Claude Schmitt (ed.), *L'exemplum*,
      Typologie des sources du Moyen Age Occidental 40 (Louvain: 1982); Peter Von Moos,
      Geschichte als Topik: Das rhetorische Exemplum von der Antike zur Neuzeit und die his-
      toriae *in "Policraticus" Johanns von Salisbury* (Hildesheim: 1988); Jacques Berlioz and
      Marie Anne Polo de Beaulieu, "Les prologues des recueils d'*exempla* (XIIIᵉ–XVᵉ siècles):
      Une grille d'analyse," in *La predicazione dei Frati dalla metà del '200 alla fine del '300: Atti
      del XXII Convegno Internazionale, Assisi, 13–15 ottobre 1994* (Spoleto: 1995), 268–299; and
      Jacques Berlioz and Marie Anne Polo de Beaulieu (ed.), *Les* Exempla *médiévaux: Nouvelles
      perspectives* (Paris: 1998).

and Castilian. Its classical contents inspired other new works that confirm the importance of the rhetorical *exemplum* in the learned culture of the era, such as the *Gesta Romanorum* and treatises by John of Wales and John of Salisbury. However, its presence in preaching was more modest. Imposition in the 13th century of a new model of sermonizing (the so-called "thematic sermon") fostered the composition of numerous tools to aid preachers, among which the collections of homiletic *exempla* occupied a central place. Compiling material from biblical and hagiographical sources along with every kind of moral anecdote (stories illustrating the rewards and punishment received, here or in the hereafter, by typically anonymous characters), these collections, redacted in Latin by Cistercians, Franciscans, and Dominicans, circulated widely throughout the West, eventually with vernacular translations. In the Catalan sphere, the 14th century saw the compilation of a massive *Recull d'exemples i miracles* [Collection of *Exempla* and Miracles], a version of the *Alphabetum narrationum* of Arnold of Liège.[12] The presence of the historical *exemplum* (whether rhetorical or homiletic) in the Catalan sphere is likewise evident in other diverse works, from the sermons of Francesc Eiximenis and Vincent Ferrer to translations of the French *Somme le Roi*, the *De vitis patrum* (Catalan *Libre d'exemples de Sants Pares*) and the *De ludo scachorum* of Jacques de Cessolis (Catalan *Libre de bones costumes dels homens*). By the end of the Middle Ages, the historical *exemplum* had effectively invaded almost all domains of written and oral discourse, establishing itself as an indispensable instrument for the transmission of any moral instruction.

Another narrative form linked, though somewhat problematically, to the *exempla* comprises hagiographic and Marian miracle stories. Various authors insist on distinguishing *exempla* and miracles, given the inimitable character of miraculous deeds, although some miracle stories certainly do offer models of behavior worthy of imitation among devotees of a saint or of the Virgin. Compilations of Marian miracles in fact illustrate both their filiation with exemplary literature and their undeniable specificity: many of these stories find a place in collections of homiletic *exempla*, but collections exclusively of miracles in Latin also enjoyed growing popularity after the 11th century and, somewhat later, translation into the vernacular languages. The best-known are from the 13th century: collections in Castilian by Berceo, in Galician-Portuguese by Alfonso X, and in French by Coinci.[13] From the end of this century or the

---

12   Arnau de Lieja, *Recull d'exemples i miracles ordenat per alfabet,* (ed.) Josep-Antoni Ysern (Barcelona: 2004).

13   Juan Carlos Bayo, "Las colecciones universales de milagros de la Virgen hasta Gonzalo de Berceo," *Bulletin of Hispanic Studies* 81 (2004): 854–871.

beginning of the 14th date the Catalan prose *Miracles de la Verge Maria* [Miracles of the Virgin Mary], slightly after the two Marian works of Llull mentioned already.[14]

Exempla and miracles coexist in the sermon with a third brief form, the simile. Unlike the narrative character of these genres, the simile is descriptive in function: it illustrates an abstract reality by comparing it atemporally with some aspect of human or natural activity. Despite its frequent use, it did not attract compilations comparable to those of the other genres, although the *Summa de exemplis et similitudines* of Giovanni di San Gimignano, written between 1300 and 1310, certainly enjoyed wide fame throughout the West.

Less common in the sermon, but certainly popular in other spheres are the two narrative forms found so frequently in Llull's writings: the animal fable and the verisimilar *exemplum* featuring human characters. The former entered medieval literature in various ways. The first was the Greco-Roman fable tradition, whose origins were associated with the legendary figure of Aesop. This material enjoyed wide diffusion in the Middle Ages, thanks especially to its use in teaching rhetoric and grammar, although the medieval era also produced some original works, such as the *Narrationes* of Odo of Cheriton or the famous *Roman de Renart*, the animal epic with some traces in Llull's *Libre de les bèsties*. All these texts coexisted with others from a second fabulary tradition, apparently much better known to Blessed Ramon: oriental tales. This tradition, in which fables mix easily with verisimilar stories, brought to the West a new way of storytelling, based on subordination of its tales to a more or less complex narrative frame. In the Iberian Peninsula, various oriental tales appear in the 12th-century *Disciplina clericalis*, composed in Latin by the converted Jew Petrus Alfonsi and widely circulated in later centuries. Equally popular, though more complex, is the transmission of several works of oriental origin: *Kalila wa-Dimna, Sendebar,* and *Barlaam et Josaphat*. The first of these – which clearly influences the main plot and the corpus of stories in Llull's *Libre de les bèsties* – has its origins in the Indian *Panchatantra*, as passed via Persia and the Arab world to the West through various channels. A Castilian translation, commissioned by the future king Alfonso X, appeared in the mid-13th century, although the work was known in Europe from a Latin translation, based on a Hebrew

---

14   *Miracles de la Verge Maria: Col·lecció del segle XIV*, (ed.) Pere Bohigas (Barcelona: 1956); *Miracles de la verge Maria: Un "mariale" lleidatà*, (ed.) Antoni Maria Parramon (Lerida: 1976); and Bétérous, "Ramon Llull et le renouvellement," 37–38. Carme Arronis Llopis, "Els miracles marians en *La vida de la verge Maria* de Miquel Peres," in *Actas del XIII Congreso Internacional de la Asociación Hispánica de Literatura Medieval*, (eds.) J.M. Fradejas Rueda et al. (Valladolid: 2010), 389–406, analyzes the later tradition of this genre in Catalan literature.

version, by John of Capua between 1273 and 1305, with the title *Directorium humanae vitae*; Raimon de Béziers also produced another version of the *Kalila*, influenced by the Castilian translation of the 13th century. Much more limited are traces in the Lullian oeuvre of the *Sendebar*. This work of uncertain origin circulated in two independent streams. The first, Oriental, stream corresponds to an Arabic text and its Castilian translation from the mid-13th century. But its dissemination in the West occurred chiefly through a stream of Latin versions, such as the 12th-century *Historia septem sapientium Romae* or the *Dolopathos*, by John of Alta Silva. From the former work derives a French translation in the same century and a Catalan version of the 13th century.[15] Finally, Llull's novels seem to offer some echoes of the third influential Oriental work, *Barlaam et Josaphat*, which was originally composed in India, then translated into Arabic and Greek, with Latin versions made from the latter. Thanks to this process of transmission, what began simply as a biography of Buddha spawned an account of two supposedly Christian saints, widely circulated in East and West: the first Latin version appeared in Constantinople in 1048; other versions were incorporated, in the 13th century, in the *Speculum historiale* of Vincent of Beauvais and in the *Legenda aurea* of Jacobus de Voragine, thus assuring wide diffusion in the West. In the Catalan sphere, their legend appears included in the *Flors Sanctorum romançat* (based on the *Legenda aurea*) from the late 13th century. Somewhat earlier, the Barcelona Jew Abraham ben Šemuel ibn Hasday composed a Hebrew version.[16] In effect, in the Iberian Peninsula Jewish and Muslim communities had enjoyed access to many Oriental texts, such as the *Thousand and One Nights,* since at least the 10th century. These communities produced a rich body of stories, dispersed in many kinds of texts: historical and philosophical works, travel narratives, and the literature of *adab* (miscellanies that offer certain norms of conduct of a practical nature, and related to the *māqāmat,* stories that weave diverse adventures around a major character). The result was an abundance of genres, whose knowledge by Ramon Llull is today difficult to assess.[17]

---

15   On the Catalan version, see: Edward J. Neugaard, "Les col·leccions de *exempla* en la literatura catalana medieval," in *Josep Maria Solá-Solé. Homage. Homenaje. Homatge (miscelánea de estudios de amigos y discípulos)*, (eds.) A. Torres-Alcalá, V. Agüera and N.B. Smith, 2 vols. (Barcelona: 1984), 1:165–168; and Miriam Cabré and Anton M. Espadaler, "La narrativa en vers," in *Historia de la Literatura Catalana*, (ed.) À. Broch (Barcelona: 2013), 1:367–369.

16   Tessa Calders i Artís, "El *Blanquerna* de Llull i el Príncep de Hasday," *Miscelánea de Estudios Árabes y Hebraicos: Sección de Hebreo* 60 (2011): 67–98.

17   Rameline E. Marsan, *Itinéraire espagnol du conte medieval (VIIIᵉ–XVᵉ siècles)* (Paris: 1974).

These were not, of course, the only exemplary genres available in this era. Didactic literature also incorporates allegorical narrative *exempla* and complex comparisons (some very far in tone from the sermon similes mentioned above). On the other hand, oral transmission was the natural channel for the dissemination of innumerable popular stories, in constant osmosis with those circulated in writing. All these genres and channels filter, in greater or lesser degrees, the "taste for telling" that ultimately leads from exemplary literature to the literary story, and from there to the *novella*. Minimizing didacticism, complicating plots, and multiplying narrative detail constitute the keys to this development, and its critical stages in the works of Don Juan Manuel, Chaucer and Boccaccio. Ramon Llull's storytelling, somewhat earlier and rather less investigated, offers a different example of the same effort at experimentation, and the same "taste for telling."

8.2.2 *Illustration, Persuasion, and Ornament: The Functions of the Genre*

Medieval literature offered its readers not only an enormous wealth of *exempla*, but also a preceptive method for the genre, based on a rich convergence of traditions. In their reflections on exemplary literature, classical preceptists had already proposed three complementary functions for the *exemplum*: (1) as a resource for persuasion; (2) as a didactic tool for the exposition or demonstration of abstract concepts; and (3) as a means to ornament discourse. The latter function derives from the status of the *exemplum* as a rhetorical *figura*, thanks to which it appears sometimes as a "figure of thought" and sometimes as a "trope." The first two functions derive, on the other hand, from appreciation of the *exemplum* as a "proof," that is, from its capacity to demonstrate the suitability of a particular behavior (recalled from a similar past deed, real or fictitious) or to corroborate the truth of a general rule or law (cited from a particular case or through comparison with another, analogous general rule).

Its probative value, contextualized more precisely below, appears recognized already in the works of Aristotle, Cicero, or Quintilian, which conceive the *paradeigma* or *exemplum* as an especially effective means of persuasion in deliberative oratory. This function obviously seems better suited to the historical *exemplum* than to fictitious ones or to similes. Quintilian thus appears to limit the function of these latter forms to the mere metaphorical illustration of abstract realities, and Cicero therefore links the exploitation of these forms to elegance of style and to pleasure, in works such as *Brutus* and *Orator*. In his *De oratore*, he defines the *exemplum* and simile as *figurae sententiarum*, the same classification found in the *Rhetorica ad Herennium* and *Institutio oratoria* of Quintilian. Oddly, late Antique grammarians such as Donatus and Diomedes shift these devices to the somewhat more elite category of tropes, associating them with the more elegant metaphor.[18]

In the 13th and 14th centuries, knowledge of the tenets of ancient grammar and rhetoric was of course undeniable, as evidenced by the circulation of many of the texts cited and the filtering of their ideas through medieval treatises on these disciplines or through new preceptive guides for the arts of poetry, letter-writing, and preaching in this era. In all of these spheres, the *exemplum* maintains its triple value as persuasion, illustration, and pleasure, though certainly with some interesting innovations. New grammatical treatises like the *Doctrinale* of Alexander de Villa Dei and the *Graecismus* of Evrard de Bethune, adopted as textbooks in 13th-century universities, repeat the classification of the *exemplum* as a trope, but illustrate this function with biblical examples. The dominant influence of the *Rhetorica ad Herennium* in medieval rhetoric maintains the interpretation of the *exemplum* as a figure of thought. This same interpretation appears in the arts of poetry of the 12th and 13th centuries, somewhat surprisingly, given their origins in grammatical doctrine: the treatises by Geoffrey of Vinsauf, Evrard de Bethune, and John of Garland classify the *exemplum* and comparisons among the figures of thought recommended for the "simple ornament" (*ornatus facilis*) of a poem, thus sanctioning their utility within a specific literary genre.

Advice from the classical rhetoricians about using *exempla* in prologs appears adapted in all three major medieval arts of discourse: the *artes poetriae* recommend the *exemplum* as a device for the "artful" beginning of a poem; the *artes dictaminis* make the *exemplum* a mode of introduction in epistles; and the *artes praedicandi* acknowledge its value in the introduction of a sermon. For example, the 14th-century sermon theorist Henry of Hesse asserts that the insertion of *exempla* in the *prothema* of a sermon is characteristic of modern homiletic style, although the older and ancient styles also admitted the use of similes and allegories. In the same period, Robert of Basevorn and Alfonso d'Alprão note the option of using *exempla* in another introductory section (the *introductio thematis*), as does Martín de Córdoba in the 15th century, recommending that sermons begin with comparisons, hagiographical *exempla* or "lovely fictions" (allegories that obviously recall the tenor of many Lullian *exempla*). This was not the only role prescribed in homiletics for exemplary material, which also possessed an obvious value in developing a sermon (that is, in its *amplificatio* or *prosecutio*), as is clear from the treatises of Robert

---

18   Marsh H. McCall, *Ancient Rhetorical Theories of Simile and Comparison* (Cambridge, Mass.: 1969); Bennett J. Price, "*Paradeigma* and *Exemplum* in Ancient Rhetorical Theory," Ph.D. dissertation, University of California (Berkeley: 1975).

of Basevorn, Richard of Thetford or the Catalan Francesc Eiximenis. In their texts, the dual utility of *exempla* for beginning or amplifying a sermon combines with the three other functions (demonstration, illustration, ornamentation) already recognized by classical and medieval preceptists.[19] These define very well a scheme of techniques familiar to Ramon Llull, though of course necessarily redirected in his theoretical recommendations and in the use of exemplary literature in his writings.

8.2.3   A "Lesser" Proof: Scope and Audiences

Theorists treating the *exemplum* defend its demonstrative function just as insistently as they contextualize its use. Their wavering collocation of the genre is comprehensible in the light of Aristotelian theory regarding the "hierarchy of argumentation," in which the *exemplum* or *paradigma* is a kind of comparative proof proper to the realm of rhetoric, and thus subordinate to the enthymeme, or "intrinsic" argumentation. The more rigorous realm of logic or dialectic demands, on the other hand, use of (comparative) induction or (intrinsic) syllogisms, both conclusive or "necessary" forms of argument, instead of the simply "probable" *exemplum* and enthymeme.

The comparative and rhetorical character of the *exemplum* thus imposes a dual limitation on this genre: one from its irrelevance in the realm of logic and the other from its subordination to intrinsic reasoning as a means of understanding reality. But these same limitations suggest as well the reasons for its success.[20] Its restriction to rhetorical discourse also acknowledges its persuasive value in civic oratory and the contexts associated with this, but even more importantly for the Middle Ages, in the exhortation to virtue. For this purpose, the superiority of the *exemplum* requires expression with conviction and without limits, in support of the famous dictum "actions speak louder than words" (*magis movent exempla quam verba*). This truism embraces multiple levels of meaning, all predicated on the superiority of deeds to words. These could range from the importance of a preacher's own behavior (the *exemplum* of his life) in fostering virtue to the efficacy, for the same purpose, of recalling real events (historical *exempla*) rather than fictitious ones. But they could also appeal to the persuasive power of any historical or fictional account or even a simile

---

19   José Aragüés Aldaz, *"Deus concionator:" Mundo predicado y retórica del "exemplum" en los Siglos de Oro* (Amsterdam: 1999), 181–204, summarizes medieval doctrines on this genre. Similarly, Welter, *L'Exemplum*, 66–82; and Le Goff, Brémond, and Schmitt, *L'Exemplum*, 43–57 and 145–164. On the rhetorical *exemplum*, see Jean-Yves Tilliette, "L'*exemplum* rhétorique: questions de définition," and Peter Von Moos, "L'*exemplum* et les *exempla* des prêcheurs," in Jacques Berlioz and Marie Anne Polo de Beaulieu (ed.), *Les Exempla médiévaux: Nouvelles perspectives* (Paris: 1998), 43–65 and 67–82.

20   Aragüés Aldaz, *"Deus concionator,"* 67–86.

(an *exemplum*, in the broad sense) over any subtle or sophisticated argumentation. This power clearly involves the concrete and accessible quality of the genre. For Humbert de Romans, stories are "easily understood by the intellect, impressed firmly in memory, and heard with delight by many."[21] The simplicity of *exempla*, their mnemonic force, and their ability to provoke pleasure are, in effect, the advantages recognized in every era by the preceptists and compilers of this little genre, who do not hesitate to ponder its capacity for evoking visual images or for moving emotions from admiration to pathos. Taken as a whole, these advantages reflect the perfect match of exemplary literature to the needs of the three powers of the soul (memory, intellect, and will). At the same time, they explain its utility for instructing uneducated audiences, such as those "simple" people (*vulgus et simplices*) whom Giovanni di San Gimignano cites in the preface to his famous collection of similes.[22] The appeal of this genre to the humblest levels of society obviously cannot be exaggerated, because the *exemplum* also served much more demanding audiences, especially in the realm of rhetoric, and in all the literary modes supported by that art, whether for pleasure (the novel) or for instruction (the sermon), yet still far removed from the exalted speculations of philosophy or theology. The latter disciplines had developed a concept of analogy and exemplarity – divine exemplarism – that was far more transcendent and ambitious, and with which exemplary literature maintained, even in the best cases, only a tangential connection.

8.2.4   *Exemplary Literature and Divine Exemplarism: Divergences*

Exemplarism is, as is well known, a premise common to all creationist philosophies in the medieval West, supported by several complementary concepts. First, the conception of Creation as a reflection of God, a lovely image full of theophanies or manifestations of divinity, offered to humankind for its interpretation. Second, the perception in the universe of an orderly hierarchy of being, descending from the angels to the most humble beings, but reproducing, though with increasing imperfection, the divine exemplar. From all this derives a definition of human nature as a world in miniature (a microcosmos) and an understanding of all existence as a perfect system of correspondences (that is, analogies) between spiritual and material realities.

The origins of some of these ideas remit to the Bible (beginning with Gen. 1.26, "Let us make man in our likeness") and to the earliest patristic commentaries on Creation (the so-called hexameral literature). It is equally obvious that, in its later formulations, divine exemplarism also displays an unequivocally

---

21   Cited in J. Th. Welter, *L'exemplum*, 72: "Narraciones ... et exempla facilius in intellectu capiuntur et memorie firmius imprimiuntur et a multis libencius audiuntur."
22   Ioannes de Sancto Geminiano, *Universum praedicabile* (Cologne: 1679), 2.

Platonic conception of the cosmos. The harmonious structure of the universe, the "participation" of the material world with an ideal realm, and the gradation of beings are Platonic concepts that, as filtered through Neoplatonism, pervade medieval Christian thought. The works of Saint Augustine and the Pseudo-Dionysius (clearly echoed in Lullian thought) mark two essential phases in the transmission of these principles, adopted by many thinkers of the 12th century (from Saint Anselm to Hugh of St. Victor), and ultimately elaborated by Aquinas, Bonaventure, and other scholastic authorities.[23]

The work of all these authors established a conception of exemplarism very different from that presented in the exemplary literature of the era. Their language reveals the magnitude of this gap, in the use of some deceptively common terms. The looseness surrounding the utilization of words such as *exemplum* and "likeness" in the literary compilations of brief genres contrasts with the rigor imposed in employing these and similar terms among the theologians. This rigor appears in endless qualifications, sometimes reluctantly, as when Bonaventure distinguishes true "likenesses" from those that are merely "vestiges" or "images" of divinity, or considers two possible terms for designating earthly realities, depending on whether they involve simply "passive" copies of the divine exemplar (*exemplata*) or "active" models for human contemplation (*exemplaria*). He resolves this quandary in favor of the first term, undoubtedly because it corresponds best to the actual assumptions of his overall scheme.[24]

Exemplary literature and divine exemplarism constitute two very different discourses, just as their audiences are different, which explains their scant interaction in the medieval era. For this reason, perhaps the literary form most suitable to the principles treated by the theologians is the natural simile, a form that allows (at least in theory) exploration of the analogies between the material and spiritual realms of Creation. For this same reason, some principles of divine exemplarism could tacitly support use of this concrete genre in contemporary sermonizing and didactic literature. However, this generally

---

23   Leo Spitzer, *L'armonia del mondo: Storia semantica di un'idea* (Bologna: 1967); Johann Auer, *El mundo, creación de Dios*, in *Curso de Teología Dogmática*, (eds.) Johann Auer and Josef Ratzinger, Vol. 3 (Barcelona: 1979); and Hans Urs Von Balthasar, *Gloria: Una estética teológica* (Madrid: 1986) are among the many accounts of these developments. On their role in Llull's work, see Robert D.F. Pring-Mill, "El microcosmos lul·lià," in *Estudis sobre Ramon Llull (1956–1978)* (Barcelona: 1991), 53–85.

24   José Aragüés Aldaz, "Fronteras estéticas de la analogía medieval: Del adorno retórico a la belleza del Verbo," *Revista Española de Filosofía Medieval* 6 (1999): 157–174; cf. Bonaventure, *Itinerarium mentis ad Deum* 2.12, *Obras de San Buenaventura*, (eds.) L. Amorós et al., 6 vols. (Madrid: 1955), 1:588–589.

involves only a vague influence, since these similes rarely serve a real heuristic or intellective intention.

On the other hand, recourse to comparative forms is hardly lacking in the writings of scholastic authorities, most especially in the work of Bonaventure. However, his examples explore reflections of divine activity not only in nature, but also in human language and knowledge, thus anticipating the focus of some of Llull's most advanced "metaphors." For example, Bonaventure asserts that every object generates a likeness of itself perceptible to the senses, symbolizing thus the eternal generation of the *Verbum*, an "image" of the eternal Father, and of His salvific Incarnation. In his *Itinerarium mentis ad Deum* and other writings, human intellection is not only a means for investigating divine being, but also perhaps its most complete metaphor. Founded on principles of divine exemplarism, theological discourse always prefers exploring these and other sublime analogies, limiting the simple natural simile to a very restricted space, and refusing any place to the other forms of exemplary literature, such as the fable or story. At least until Ramon Llull, whose work in this regard presents a felicitous innovation, and a clear exception.[25]

8.3   Theoretical Foundations: Exemplary Literature and the Lullian Art

8.3.1   *Exemplary Literature and Divine Exemplarism: Intersection*
The oeuvre of Ramon Llull offers a transparent space of intersection between divine exemplarism and exemplary literature, perhaps the fullest and most surprising from the entire medieval era. The convergence of these traditions in his work is certainly not coincidental or sporadic. Rather, this phenomenon results from profound theoretical convictions and constitutes the natural outcome of the dual intention that guides the writing of Blessed Ramon: that is, the desire to base his Art on appropriate theological foundations and the need to disseminate it among an audience not accustomed to such an elevated level of discourse.

For this second purpose (dissemination of his thought), he makes use of exemplary literature. Some episodes of *Blaquerna* present this literature as a tool for instructing the most humble, but it was familiar to all those audiences to which Llull directed his missionary and catechetical efforts: for Jews and Muslims (for whom the *exemplum* was a common means of transmitting

---

25   José Aragüés Aldaz, "*Falses semblances*: Ejemplarismo divino y literatura ejemplar a la luz de Ramón Llull," in *Actas del VIII Congreso de la Asociación Hispánica de Literatura Medieval (Santander, del 22 al 26 de septiembre de 1999)* (Santander: 2000), 1:175–184.

knowledge), for the bourgeoisie of Majorca and Montepellier, and for the demanding members of the Faculty of Arts at Paris, whose early schooling would have included Aesopian fables.[26]

Divine exemplarism, for its part, offered to these demanding academic readers a familiar language and, at the same time, provided Lullian thought a dual ontological and heuristic foundation: that is, a key to the mode of real being (*modus essendi*) and a method to understanding it (*modus intelligendi*). Llull thus owes to divine exemplarism his harmonious conception of the universe, based on a belief in the perfect analogical correspondence between all its levels, and between these and the divine exemplar that they ultimately reproduce. And he owes to exemplarism as well his essential mechanism for exploring the universe, based on the constant navigation of its analogical pathways. From his *Libre de contemplació* to his last learned writings, he conceives perceptible reality as a "sign" of intellectual reality and of divine truth, following these same pathways. Thanks to this cosmic symbolism, all creatures "signify and demonstrate" God to the human mind.[27]

8.3.2   *The Lullian Art and Metaphor*

Of course, divine exemplarism acquires in Llull's oeuvre very specific characteristics, derived from its adaptation to the complex structure of his Art, and also involves diverse manifestations in the course of development over time of its original theoretical structure. In his Quaternary Phase, exemplarist principles crystalize in a specific demonstrational method, which Frances Yates

---

26   *Blaquerna* 2.66, (eds.) Soler and Santanach, NEORL 8:303. See Badia and Bonner, *Ramón Llull*, 109–129, and Arbona Piza, "Los exemplis," 60.

27   *Doctrina pueril* 68, (ed.) Joan Santanach i Suñol, NEORL 7:176: "all creatures signify and demonstrate God to human understanding" ("totes creatures signifiquen e demostren Deus a la humanal intelligencia"); compare *Libre de contemplació* 2.29.169, (eds.) Antoni Sancho and Miquel Arbona, in *OE* 2:482–486, and similar passages discussed by Bonner, *L'Art i la lògica*, 293–298. On Llull's analogical exemplarism, see Pring-Mill, "El microcosmos lul·lià" and "L'estructura analògica de l'Art luliana," in *Estudis sobre Ramon Llull (1956–1978)* (Barcelona: 1991), 241–252; Mark D. Johnston, "The Semblance of Significance: Language and Exemplarism in the 'Art' of Ramon Llull," Ph.D. dissertation, The Johns Hopkins University (Baltimore: 1978), 37–44; Michela Pereira, "El concepte de natura en el context de les obres científiques de Ramon Llull," *Randa* 19 (1988): 57–67; Josep Maria Ruiz Simón, "De la naturalesa com a mescla a l'art de mesclar (sobre la fonamentació cosmològica de les arts lul·lianes)," *Randa* 19 (1988): 69–99, and *L'Art de Ramon Llull i la teoria escolàstica de la ciència* (Barcelona: 1999); Manuel Bauçà Ochogavia, *L'exemplarisme de Ramon Llull* (Palma: 1989); Gisbert, "*Metaphorice loquendo*," 29–37; and Josep E. Rubio, "Thought: The Art" and "The Natural Realm," in *Raimundus Lullus: An Introduction to his Life, Works and Thought*, (eds.) Alexander Fidora and Josep E. Rubio (Turnhout: 2008), 243–310 and 311–362.

labeled "elemental exemplarism."[28] According to this method, the analysis of the relationships between the four elements provides a combinatory pattern that the Art converts into a paradigm for the allegorical explication of any theological, moral, or learned question.

Elemental exemplarism permeates much of Llull's exemplary literature but finds the vehicle best suited to its expression in the novel and demanding comparative category of the Lullian *matafora*. As noted already, the essential text for understanding the sense of this category is the *Començaments de medicina* (1274–1283). This work is one of four born from applying the first version of his Art (the *Ars compendiosa inveniendi veritatem* of ca. 1274) to various other academic disciplines (the other three works treat theology, philosophy, and law). Starting from the traditional principles of medicine, the work seeks to shed new light on them by explaining them, as Llull says, "artfully and metaphorically" (*artificialment et mataforicalment*). The meaning of this dual expression is complicated. Basically, Llull proposes the solution for an urgent problem of his era (the compounding and proofing of simple medications), by systematizing ways to mix their elements according to his combinatory method. The latter is thus an "artful" model, and so harmonized with the preliminary rules of his Art. It is also "metaphorical" in two different senses. First, because it employs language codified according to the peculiar nomenclature of Llull's Art. Second, because it is constructed on a combinatory pattern for the analogical illumination of every material and spiritual realm of reality. That illumination finds expression through the *matafora*, a concept to which Llull devotes the final chapter of this work.[29] After defining the term in the conventional way ("signifying one thing through another"), he exemplifies it through a series of passages, which explore the analogical correspondences between different medical, natural, moral, and theological questions, all illuminated through the abstract and universal system of his Art. For example, various passages develop the analogical implications of complex concepts associated with the processes of material generation and corruption, such as the "seventh simple point" (*lo.vii. punt simple*), related metaphorically to the seven days of the week, the Incarnation, the Holy Trinity, "and many other things lengthy to tell" (*et moltes d'altres coses que serien longes a recomptar*). This final chapter therefore treats matters as diverse as eating and fasting, poisons and laxative herbs, the hours

---

28 Frances A. Yates, "The Art of Ramon Llull: An approach to it through Lull's Theory of the Elements," *Journal of the Warburg and Courtauld Institutes* 17 (1954): 115–173.

29 Gisbert, "*Metaforice loquendo*," 25–29 and 37–45, analyzes this concept of *matafora* and its antecedents in theology and exegesis; see also Ruiz Simón, "De la naturalesa com a mescla," 75–76, and Bonner, *L'Art i la lògica*, 63–66 and 293–300.

of the day and night, the seasons of the year, justice and law, the dangers of vanity, and the superiority of Christ's nature above all others.[30]

Only the bearings of the Art allow the mind to navigate safely the realms of knowledge. Thus the *Començaments de medicina* exceed the boundaries of their apparent purpose (explaining medical science) in order to become a guide for studying all other disciplines: "we treat metaphor in this art, so that it will be a method for uplifting the mind in this discipline and in other disciplines, since through metaphor the mind is empowered to understand, because it considers different species at one time."[31] In this sense, the metaphorical exposition of medicine is only one possibility within a symbolic reading of all aspects of reality. The text thus strives not only to offer a handful of more or less suggestive analogies, but also represents these analogies as samples or models for guiding a reader in learning strategies of analogical demonstration, that is, in mastery of Llull's Art as a "metaphor" that makes sense of every realm of Creation. Seen thus, the comparisons included in this work anticipate, very early, the paradigmatic or "meta-exemplary" dimension achieved in so many other manifestations of Lullian literature.

Created as an expression of elemental exemplarism, metaphor occupies a central place in the demonstrational mechanism of Llull's Art throughout his Quaternary Phase. However, elemental exemplarism plays a more modest role in the next, Ternary, phase of Lullian thought. Beginning with his *Ars inventiva veritatis* (1290), Ramon Llull proposes a new explanatory model of reality, based on re-establishing the function of the Divine Dignities and on application of his new theory of "correlatives." It is unnecessary to explore here the details of this new foundation, explained fully in chapter four of this volume, but is simply sufficient to recall that, following this new paradigm, the likenesses of the nine Dignities constitute not only the ontological foundations (*principia essendi*) of all Creation, but also the indispensable means of understanding it (*principia cognoscendi*). Knowledge arises from observing the immanence of these likenesses in each and every level of the universe, and so renders largely unnecessary recourse to the model of the four elements for allegorical comprehension of higher realities.[32]

---

30   *Començaments de medicina* 10, (ed.) Lola Badia, NEORL 5:104–114; see also parts 1 and 6, (ed.) Badia, NEORL 5:47–50, 88–91 and 100–101.

31   *Començaments de medicina* 1, (ed.) Badia, NEORL 5:48–49: "de matafora tractam en esta art, per tal que sia art a exalsar l'enteniment en esta art et en altres artz, cor per matafora s'apodera l'enteniment a entendre, per so cor en .i. temps se gira sobre diverses especies."

32   Ruiz Simón, "De la naturalesa com a mescla," 90, reviews this foundational role of divine likenesses; Badia and Bonner, *Ramon Llull*, 92, note the corresponding decline in recourse to metaphorical techniques.

The Ternary Phase thus reinforces the analogical design of Creation at the same time that it displaces the use of metaphorical techniques for explicating its structure. Elemental exemplarism remains, but as an alternative method of demonstration, which evidently implies a corresponding decline in the use of metaphor. But this is a matter to analyze carefully. The *Ars inventiva veritatis* recommends use of this device, linking it still to the expression of elemental exemplarism. Moreover, it is possible that Llull began extending his initial conception of it, in order to make it a form able to assume new functions. This is what the later *Liber de lumine* (1303) appears to suggest. This text starts from a very concrete reference (the light of a candle) in order to illustrate analogically the operation of the Art in all levels of reality. That is, it operates "artfully and metaphorically" (*artificialiter ac metaphorice*), as Llull recalls, repeating the same phrase used in his *Començaments de medicina*. The latter section of the *Liber de lumine* tours various spheres of reality (beginning with God, the angels, and heaven) by means of the usual series of questions or problems (*quaestiones*), which the reader must solve based on the theory of Llull's Art applied to the light of a candle in the previous sections.[33] However, a vast gulf separates the advanced *mataforas* of the *Començaments de medicina* from the comparisons in the *Liber de lumine*, which are much simpler and subjected to the later postulates of his Art, from the *Tabula Generalis* (1293–1294) and *Ars compendiosa* (1299). It is impossible to know, therefore, whether Llull regards these comparisons as true *mataforas* or, on the other hand, they constitute a less precise type of exemplary literature. In effect, Llull appears to avoid applying the term "metaphor" to them, preferring instead the generic terms *exemplum* and *similitudo* ("likeness") already established in the tradition of that literature.

8.3.3   *The Lullian Art and Exemplary Literature*

As a result, it is not easy to define the limits of Lullian "metaphor" and so to fix exactly its relationship to the other exemplary forms that Llull employs. The *Art demostrativa* and the *Ars inventiva veritatis* allude collectively to the persuasive force of "metaphors, likenesses, and *exempla*" (*metàfores e semblances e exemplis*; *exempla, similia vel metaphoras*).[34] The terms *exemplum* and "likeness" often possess equivalent meaning in Llull's works, applicable to any comparative passage employed in his discourse. It is possible that in these two texts

---

33   *Liber de lumine*, (ed.) Jordi Gayà Estelrich, ROL 20:36–62.

34   Gisbert, "*Metaphorice loquendo*," 25, notes the relevance of *Art demostrativa* 3.10; cf. *Obres selectes de Ramon Llull* (1232–1316), (ed.) Anthony Bonner, 2 vols. (Palma: 1989), 1:388; see also the *Ars inventiva veritatis* 3.7, MOG 5:45.

the term "metaphor" offers a similar meaning, in which case the series just quoted would be limited to presenting a triad of synonyms. However, it is also clear that this term has no basis in the tradition of exemplary literature, which is why, in Llull's case, it almost always seems to define a very specific (and demanding) category situated within the upper limits of that literature.

Hence, the *mataforas* of the *Començaments de medicina* possess at least three distinctive traits: their novelty, their theoretical sophistication, and their subjection to principles of elemental exemplarism. The rest of Llull's exemplary literature displays more flexible and conventional features. Most of that literature consists of forms with an obvious traditional heritage (stories, fables, similes), easily recognizable by any contemporary reader as *exempla* (though obviously without denying the radical originality of much of their content). The complexity of these forms varies enormously in degree: exegetical difficulty is the norm in many passages, but there is no lack of easy comparisons and stories with very simple plots. In regard to their reading, many Lullian *exempla* constitute channels (even in his Ternary Phase) for expressing the elemental exemplarism that permeates his *mataforas*. However, this is not their only function. These *exempla* can also presuppose the theoretical foundations from the second phase of his Art, such as investigating the presence of divine likenesses in material beings, in order to illustrate analogically their configuration in spiritual reality. They likewise can assist generally in a more conventional illumination of any learned, theological, or moral issue that appears in Llull's writings.

The presence of exemplary literature is a constant throughout all Llull's oeuvre and should be considered one more sign of the quest for analogy that guides his thought. In fact, that literature not only coexists with divine exemplarism in Lullian texts but is in some ways its natural projection. The very multiplicity of meanings that the word "likeness" displays in his writings favors such a close connection. Leaving aside the cognitive sense of the term ("likenesses" are the images of perceived objects in the human imagination), it defines as well the echoes of divinity deployed in Creation, the analogies existing between any of its beings, and of course the rhetorical or literary genre that enables their oral or written expression. An obvious thread of continuity exists among these meanings, which at times seem superimposed in Lullian discourse.[35] In the *Libre de meravelles*, for example, the protagonist asks a prince, a student of philosophy, how one candle can light another without diminishing its own flame. The prince expounds the relevant arguments, but his master reprimands him for failing to respond "through likeness" (*per semblança*).

---

35   Johnston, "Semblance of Significance," 19–77.

The phrase may simply allude to the need for "metaphorical" illustration in the prince's response, but it possesses a more transcendent sense. He does explain various comparisons, such as parents who produce a child without diminishing their own being, a tree that sprouts without damaging itself, and Christians who convert unbelievers without losing their faith. These examples are not coincidental, but rather occasions arranged by God "for providing some likeness" (*per tal que donen alguna semblança*) of the generation of His Son without any loss.[36] Seen thus, many of Ramon Llull's *exempla* do not seek to create a corpus of clever analogies, but instead claim to reveal them.

8.3.4   *A Lesser Proof? Demonstration in the Lullian Art*

Ramon Llull grants to exemplary literature a central place in his oeuvre while imposing on it certain obligations. Its manifestations appear subject to the thematic limits set by his Art, and their design governed by infinitely more rigorous criteria than those guiding the creation of stories and similes in other authors of his era. Given the need to translate exactly a precedent universal harmony, the labor of finding these *exempla* (the *ars inveniendi exempla*) cannot be a facile or, obviously, random task.

The commitment to this rigor supports the high value attributed by Llull to exemplary literature for demonstrating the "truth" of his Art. Numerous passages in his work insist on the genre's probative capability, far superior to that conceded in traditional rhetoric. In the *Ars demostrativa*, Llull declares, though without going further, the aptness of using *exempla* in disputation, assigning to metaphors and likenesses the ability to "answer questions" (*soure questions*) in the realms of instruction or polemical debate.[37] This new role for the *exemplum* will also appear reflected in the peculiar reformulation of the Aristotelian hierarchy of argumentation that Llull proposes. He was surely familiar with the doctrine of the four types of proof (syllogism, induction, enthymeme, and *exemplum*) from the *Summulae logicae* of Petrus Hispanus. Echoes of that doctrine appear in texts widely separated in time, such as his *Compendium logicae Algazelis* of 1271–1272 and his *Lectura Artis* of 1304. The latter instance consists of a mere enumeration, in which there is no trace, at least explicitly, of the dual opposition between these proofs (dialectical versus rhetorical, intrinsic versus comparative) that makes the *exemplum*, in Aristotle's opinion,

---

36   *Libre de meravelles* 4.20, in *Libre de meravelles: Volum I* (*Llibres I–VII*), (eds.) Lola Badia, Xavier Bonillo, Eugènia Gisbert, and Montserrat Lluch, NEORL 10:170.

37   Jordi Rubió i Balaguer, "Alguns aspects de l'obra literària de Ramon Llull," in *Ramon Llull i el lul·lisme*, Obres de Jordi Rubió i Balaguer, Vol. 3 (Barcelona: 1985), 290; Pring-Mill, "L'estructura analògica de l'Art luliana," 250–251.

the least of all these. Even though the four Aristotelian types do appear in later texts, this classification does not seem the one adopted with most conviction by Llull.

In his very important *Ars inventiva veritatis*, Llull proposes another division, more relevant to understanding the place of exemplary literature in his oeuvre: he establishes an opposition beween "strict demonstrations" (*demonstrationes propriae*) and those based "on likeness" (*demonstrationes similitudinariae*). The former include three types: from causes, from effects, and "from equivalence" (*per equiparantiam*), the third invented by Llull in opposition to the first two Aristotelian types, and ultimately linked with the *exemplum*, as we will see. Overall, the type that best matches the genre of exemplary literature is demonstration "from likeness," since this is achieved, literally, through "*exempla*, similitudes, or metaphors." Here, Llull echoes various familiar rhetorical concepts, such as the need to avoid metaphors that obscure an issue or do not correctly suit it, while assuming the argumentational superiority of strict proofs. Demonstration achieved "from likeness" thus seems simply to prepare or guide the mind toward those others. He reinforces this idea in a later passage, stating that demonstration achieved "from likeness" lacks "necessity." Yet this passage none the less introduces an important innovation, by admitting the possibility that some comparative forms (perhaps alluding above all to his demanding *mataforas*) might exceed this subsidiary function in order to become "strict" proofs based on equivalence (*per equiparantiam*): "metaphors do not imply necessity, but rather conformity (*convenientia*) and if they imply necessity, they can form part of strict proof, in the category of equivalence (*ad speciem equiparantiae*)."[38] As we have said, this last category constitutes a new type, destined by Llull to proving the Articles of Faith, and therefore appears situated at the summit of the hierarchy of arguments that he advocates as a departure from Aristotelian doctrine. The possibility that exemplary literature (or, at least, his *matafora*) sometimes merges with that type of proof lends it an absolutely exceptional status in historical debate about the genre. Thanks to that status, we can understand the real functioning of the *exemplum* in Lullian thought, and also its distance from what remains, for so many other authorities, simply a form of persuasion directed to uneducated audiences.[39]

---

38   *Ars inventiva veritatis* 3.7, MOG 5:45: "Et sciendum est, quod metaphorae non inferunt necessitatem, sed convenientiam, & si inferant necessitatem, transeunt in propriam demonstrationem ad speciem aequiparantiae." See also *Lectura Artis, quae intitulata est brevis practica Tabulae Generalis*, (ed.) Jordi Gayà Estelrich, ROL 20:421–423.

39   Bonner, *L'Art i la lògica*, 298–302, provides an excellent analysis of Lullian categories of argumentation, though without considering the scant demonstrative value traditionally accorded to the genre, which requires further study to appreciate the novelty of

8.3.5   *Traditional Purposes*

Demonstration through Llull's Art, in the context of theological disputation or argumentation, constitutes an essential function of the Lullian *exemplum*, but he also recognizes for the genre other more conventional purposes. In his *Rhetorica nova*, Llull explains its capacity for ornamentation and its value for beginning or amplifying any discourse, assuming thus some of the roles attributed to exemplary literature in classical and medieval treatises. Still, none of his explanations about this role attain the density or interest expressed at the beginning of his *Arbre exemplifical*:

> And from the *exempla* that we will provide, one can have instruction for knowing both material and spiritual hidden truths, for preaching, for good mores, and for comfort and friendship with other people. And even more, one can have from them a universal means of understanding many things pleasing to understand and to hear.[40]

This passage thus exceeds the tenor of traditional rhetorical commentaries and proposes a true pragmatics for the genre. The passage affirms the utility of *exempla* read privately in collections or presented orally, whether in sermons or in the more intimate context of friendly conversation. In all these realms, the *exemplum* becomes a means for knowing material and spiritual realities, a purpose that includes the above-cited theological demonstration through Llull's Art, but also exceeds it, achieving as well a more personal dimension through private meditation, as we will see. However, this genre is also a vehicle for transmitting moral instruction and a means for seeking delight, not only in the pleasing character of its content, but likewise in the intellectual exercise of revealing a metaphorical meaning. It is not difficult to perceive here the echo of the triple purpose attributed to exemplary literature by theorists: moral persuasion, illustration, and ornamentation. None the less, this passage insinuates, still more forcefully, surpassing or even transgressing those purposes, given the place that the genre occupies in Llull's oeuvre.

---

demonstration *per equiparantiam*. See also Jordi Pardo Pastor, "Filosofía y teología de Ramón Llull: la *Demonstratio per aequiparantiam*," *Revista Española de Filosofía Medieval* 9 (2002): 265–274. Johnston, *ER* 112, analyzes other echoes in Llull's oeuvre of this appreciation of the *exemplum* as a form of proof.

40   *Arbre de ciència* 15. Prolog, (eds.) Joaquim Carreras i Artau and Tomàs Carreras i Artau, *OE* 1:799: "e per los exemplis que darem pot hom haver doctrina a conèixer los secrets naturals e sobre natura, e a preïcar e a haver moralitats bones e solaç e amistat de les gents. E encara, en pot hom haver universal hàbit a entendre moltes coses plaents a entendre e plaents a oïr."

8.3.6   *From Moral Persuasion to Illustration*

In his *Liber de modo naturali intelligendi*, Llull explains how one understands the essence of the vices and virtues. A moderate person observes how someone overcome by gluttony eats and drinks, and how this vice causes lies, sickness, and a miserable death. A humble person sees how no one desires to befriend the proud, engrossed in labor, anguish, and pain. A chaste person, finally, contrasts the benefits associated with that virtue (such as preserving marriage) to the evils of lust, which would be too many to tell.[41] It is impossible not to recall, from these simple reflections, the point of departure of so many Lullian stories, which recreate, within a literary mold, the same teachings that daily life offered to the medieval reader.

Of course, moralizing interpretation was the most prevalent framework of all exemplary literature in Llull's era. None the less, that interpretation almost always appears in Lullian *exempla* subordinated (and ultimately, juxtaposed) to the essential goal of such passages: understanding the principles of his Art, and through them, the structure of Creation. For example, in the *Libre de meravelles* and *Arbre exemplifical*, the illustration of the elemental or vegetal realm occurs through some stories with human protagonists, whose plots recreate virtuous or contemptible behaviors. The moral instruction in these stories is logically unequivocal, but that instruction never overshadows their main lesson, which is ontological in character, and so also emphasizes their distance from the *exempla* used by preachers.[42] Moreover, both works devote, in their journey through the levels of creation, some pages specifically to the realm of the vices and virtues: the *Libre de meravelles*, in its eighth section on humankind, and the *Arbre exemplifical*, in its section devoted to reviewing the contents of the *Arbre moral*. Once again, the stories from these pages illustrate consequences from the whole range of praiseworthy or sinful behaviors. But this illustration is only one more expression of the intention that guides both collections: the orderly explication of all aspects, material or spiritual, in Creation.

In the case of Blessed Ramon, that illustration takes on unique features. Traditionally, exemplary literature made use of natural reality and human activity to shed light on spiritual concepts, following a kind of upward trajectory, inductive in nature, by the mind. In Llull's work, however, the short forms can take their subject matter either from material or spiritual beings, and the method of illumination can also operate downward (deductively), explaining

---

41   *Liber de modo naturali intelligendi* 7, (ed.) Helmut Riedlinger, ROL 6:204–209.

42   Bonillo Hoyos, "Els exemples," 59, 60, 63, 65, 74, considers the originality of those that he labels, quite rightly, *nova exempla*.

the essence of natural beings from the divine form itself. Founded on the analogical principles of his Art, the *exemplum* thus constitutes a true "heuristic" recourse, that is to say, "a means of making explicit those relationships in the levels of being that would otherwise remain hidden."[43] Without a doubt, the most obvious signs of the singularity of Lullian *exempla* is its redeployment from the realm of moral persuasion (which was traditionally mostly natural) to that of understanding both reality and the Art that explains it. Of course, properly considered, that understanding initiates the true moral path of all humans, according to Llull's doctrine of "first intention," toward knowing God through Creation.

8.3.7 *Allegorical Difficulty and the Ascent of the Mind*

Exempla constitute not only tools for uncovering the analogical keys of reality but are also an essential recourse for recalling them. The *Libre de meravelles* recognizes them as such when it affirms the power of likenesses to acquire "knowledge" and to exalt the soul for "remembering, understanding, and desiring." The latter phrase also reveals the adecuation of *exempla* to the three powers of the soul, which the *Començaments de medicina* also assigns to the *matafora*.[44] Neither that suitability nor claims for the mnemotechnical qualities of the genre were new, but in Llull's case they constitute a theoretical basis for making *exempla* resources for meditation as well. Consideration of exemplary texts can constitute the point of departure for a deliberate and profound meditation on the lessons of Creation, which is surely what the already-cited prolog to the *Arbre exemplifical* suggests when it mentions the utility of this genre for acquiring a "universal means of understanding."

Comprehending the universe (that is, the exegesis of the "book of creatures") demands true mastery of exemplary methods. Indeed, it is their advances in this mastery that allow the protagonists of Llull's novels to become truly wise. And, as we will see, this same process of mastery is projected in specular fashion upon the readers, schooling them in managing strategies of exemplarity. Mastering Lullian *exempla* is of course no easy task. His exemplary passages illuminate numerous points of his Art, but by the same measure, understanding these passages requires a certain familiarity with its principles. The analogies established between different planes of reality are truly subtle,

---

43   Luzón Díaz, "Una aproximación," 258–259: "un medio para hacer explícitas aquellas relaciones de la escala del ser que, de otro modo, permanecerían ocultas."

44   *Libre de meravelles* "De la fi del libre," in *Obres selectes de Ramon Llull (1232–1316),* (ed.) Anthony Bonner, 2 vols. (Palma: 1989), 2: 391; *Començaments de medicina* 1.5, (ed.) Badia, NEORL 5:48–49.

if not enigmatic, as are the relationships between the narrative subject matter and the allegorical lesson that it shrouds. Llull's esteem for difficulty has been compared to the Augustinian and Thomistic justifications for the obscurity of some biblical passages and, I suspect, probably owes something to the use of parables in the Gospels, and many Lullian stories do appear accompanied by an exposition of their meaning, just as do the parables of Christ.[45] Yet, there are many other Lullian passages that, despite their complexity, remain suspended within his discourse without any explanation, thus complicating their comprehension by the reader.[46] Llull himself is aware of this difficulty, since indeed his own characters often request clarification about the meaning of *exempla* expounded by their interlocutors. They even show their confusion about stories seemingly devoid of meaning, as in the often-cited query from the protagonist of the *Libre de meravelles* to a hermit: "Sir ... your *exempla* amaze me, because it seems that they have nothing to do with the purpose of what I ask you." The passage is highly revealing, above all, because the hermit's answer clarifies the rationale for allegorical obscurity, directed always to promoting the "ascent of the mind:"

> "Dear friend," said the hermit, "I offer you these likenesses deliberately, so that your mind will rise in understanding, because where a likeness is most obscure, the mind grasps more highly what that likeness comprehends."[47]

This ascent of the mind seems one with all analogical reasoning, that is, with that turn of the mind that "considers different species at one time" (*en .i. temps*

---

45   See Taylor, "Some complexities," 654–656, who applies as well to Llull's *exempla* the commonplace scheme of the "four senses of Scripture."

46   Arbona Piza, "Los exemplis," 59.

47   *Libre de meravelles* 2.14, (eds.) Badia et al., NEORL 10:149: "Senyer –dix Felix al sant hermità-, molt me maravell de vostros eximplis, cor vijares m'es que no facen res al proposit de que yo us deman. Bell amich –dix l'ermitá-, scientment vos faç aytals semblançes per ço que vostre enteniment exalçets ha entendre, cor on pus escura es la semblança, pus altament enten l'enteniment que aquella semblança enten." Arbona Piza, "Los exemplis," 70; Badia, "Literatura alternativa," 16; Hauf, "Sobre l'*Arbor exemplificalis*," 311; Luzón Díaz, "Una aproximación," 259; Taylor, "Some complexities," 653–654; and Llúcia Martín Pascual, "'On pus escura és la semblança, pus altament entén l'enteniment qui aquella semblança entén:' Ramon Llull i el didactisme cientifico-teològic del *Llibre de meravelles*," *Randa* 50 (2002): 25–39, are among the many analyses of this passage and of the difficulty of Lullian *exempla* in general. Johnston, *SL* 77–79, and *ER* 52–55, offer a detailed analysis, in the context of Llull's theories of intellection, with references to medieval precedents for the esteem of obscurity.

se gira sobre diverses especies) as suggested already in the *Començaments de medicina*.[48] Yet, it evidently must be multiplied in those passages that demand a complex exegesis, as in the *mataforas* of the latter work or those "likenesses of high exposition" suggested by the *Libre de meravelles* in a later passage.

Of course, the ultimate goal of the mind's ascent is devout contemplation of the Creator. In this sense, the protagonist of *Blaquerna* recalls the "words of love and short *exempla*" (in reality, proverbs) of Muslim sufis, forms always requiring exegesis, which makes them elevate simultaneously the mind and devotion. The *Libre de contemplació* already develops this value of allegorical discourse for contemplation and prayer, inspired by that "moral exposition which is called *rams* in the Arabic language" (*esposició moral la qual és apella-da en lengua aràbica "rams"*).[49] In light of all this, one understands the spiritual and mystical connotations of all the images of "ascent" employed by Ramon Llull to suggest the intellective process of exemplary literature. These images do not simply allude (not even principally) to the intellectual or heuristic height of the truths known thanks to *exempla*, but indicate the place of these truths in the loving and affective trajectory that leads the soul to its Creator.

8.3.8   *Delight and Verbal Aesthetic*

The prolog to the *Arbre exemplifical* suggested the capacity of an *exemplum* to transmit "many things pleasing to understand and to hear." This work thus associates the act of understanding *exempla* with what we might consider a dual pleasure, in so far as understanding the beautiful analogical design of the universe follows from the delight derived from the allegorical deciphering of a passage. For its part, the concluding mention of "things pleasing to hear" may be appealing, in a much more modest way, to the actual ludic and pleasurable dimensions of the plots in some stories, that is, to the delight found in the simple act of telling and hearing stories, which that prolog invokes when referring to the capacity of the genre to promote comfort and friendship with other people. In this respect, Lullian exemplary literature does engage the tradition that extends from oriental storytelling to the narratives of Chaucer, Boccaccio, or Don Juan Manuel, although it does so with undeniably unique features: fundamentally, the subordination of delight to didacticism and, based on this,

---

48   *Començaments de medicina* 1.5, (ed.) Badia, NEORL 5:48–49.

49   *Libre de contemplació* 352.7, (eds.) Sancho and Arbona, *OE* 2:1181. On this passage, see: Colom Ferrá, "Ramon Llull y los orígenes," 42, and Badia, Santanach, and Soler, "Ramon Llull," 408–410. Compare also *Blaquerna* 99, (eds.) Soler and Santanach, NEORL 8:426–427. See also Díaz, "Una aproximación," 263, and Jaume Medina, "Oscuridad y elevación del entendimiento en la obra de Ramon Llull," *Revista de Lenguas y Literaturas Catalana, Gallega y Vasca* 14 (2009): 255–259, on the concept of elevating the mind in Llull's works.

the sacrifice of all ornamental detail in favor of the precise communication (though sometimes cryptic) of the transcendent message in its passages.[50] The guidelines that direct the composition of Lullian *exempla* are the same that govern his entire work. Ramon Llull, far from writing "literature," simply adopts literary expression in order to communicate truth.[51]

Thanks only to these premises can we grasp something implied throughout Llull's work, namely the value accorded to the *exemplum* as a means for adorning discourse. Traditional rhetoric and grammar unanimously recognized this value, making the *exemplum*, in those arts, a "figure of thought" and sometimes a trope. It is obvious that Llull knew these traditions, and so we see the special place that the genre occupies among the expressive recourses in his *Rhetorica nova*. However, it is also evident that the value of Lullian *exempla* as ornament has little to do with these traditional tenets. Their value results, in effect, from his peculiar concept of style, specifically, as traced in the path of that "homology between the discursive and metaphysical orders" upon which Blessed Ramon bases all beauty in human discourse.[52] The Lullian short genres aspire only to translating, in their rhetorical simplicity, the nuances of divine beauty unfolded throughout the universe, apart from and prior to any discursive manipulation. It is this aesthetic reading of Creation that infuses every passage, endowing them of course with a transcendent beauty, but minimizing

50   Hauf, "Sobre l'*Arbor exemplificalis*," 322–331, analyzes the *Arbre exemplifical* in this regard, noting the distance between the stories of Llull and those of Boccaccio and Chaucer, among others. Llúcia Martín Pascual, "Huella del *Calila e Dimna* en la literatura catalana medieval," in *Énoncés sapientiels et littérature exemplaire: une intertextualité complexe*, (ed.) M.S. Ortola (Nancy: 2013), 93, and Josep A. Grimalt, "Notes sobre les fonts del *Llibre de les bèsties* de Ramon Llull," *Randa*, 48 (2002): 39, also observe the same tendency toward didacticism and lack of ornament in Llull's versions of stories from *Kalila wa-Dimna*.

51   On this aspect of Llull's work, see: Jordi Rubió i Balaguer, "L'expressió literària de Ramon Llull," in *Ramon Llull i el lul·lisme*, Obres de Jordi Rubió i Balaguer 3 (Barcelona: 1985), 300–314; Lola Badia, "Ramon Llull i la tradició literària," *EL* 28 (1988): 121–128, and "Literature as an 'ancilla artis': the transformation of science into literature according to Robert Pring-Mill and Ramon Llull," *Hispanic Research Journal* 10 (2009): 18–28; and Pring-Mill, "Els recontaments," 314–317.

52   *Ramon Llull's New Rhetoric: Text and Translation of Llull's "Rethorica Nova,"* (ed.) Mark D. Johnston (Davis, Calif.: 1994), xxii. On the general relationship between language, beauty, and exemplary forms, see: Mark D. Johnston, "*Affatus*: Natural Science as Moral Theology," *EL* 30 (1990): 3–30 and 139–159; Josep E. Rubio, "L'estètica en Ramon Llull: una qüestió epistemològica," *Tesserae* 2 (1996): 73–80; Ignasi Roviró i Alemany, "De la bellesa sensible a la font de la bellesa: la bellesa en Ramon Llull," in *Actes del Simposi Internacional de Filosofia de l'Edat Mitjana: Vic-Girona, 11–16 d'abril de 1993* (Vic: 1996), 389–395; Johnston, *ER* 83–116; and Luzón Díaz, "Una aproximación," 264–265.

at the same time the possibility of any other aesthetic esteem. The section on beautiful *exempla* in the *Rhetorica nova* begins by alluding to the rhetorical value of various divine *exempla*: the display of likenesses of the Trinity in creatures, in the Incarnation, and in the Passion of Christ. These *exempla* possess an intrinsic beauty, and only that beauty adorns the words of a speaker and in turn, penetrates "the imagination, memory, and intellect of the listeners." In short, an *exemplum* is beautiful only in so far as it constitutes the translation of an innately beautiful reality.[53]

8.4   Plots, Forms, Contexts: Exemplary Material for Creating a Corpus

8.4.1   *A New Exemplary Literature*

Apart from any other consideration, the originality of Llull's exemplary writing is apparent in a simple, but rather unusual, fact: most of the *exempla* that appear in Llull's writings are his own creations. In this sense, we could say that his writings subvert the usual relationship between *exempla* and their discursive context. Many authors do incorporate traditional (usually anonymous) *exempla* in their own discourses, adding ultimately some personal details. In the case of Ramon Llull, the requirements of his works end up generating an exclusive corpus of narratives, definitively linked with the name of their author. The originality of Llull's Art requires this new literature, just as it demands a new logic, a new medicine, or a new astronomy. Just as occurs with the treatises devoted to these genres, the exemplary literature of Blessed Ramon is deliberately alternative, to the point of constituting a kind of *contrafactum*, an inversion of their readings.[54]

Of course, this does not mean that some stories from other sources do not appear in the Lullian oeuvre. The most obvious case, and most studied by critics, involves the contents of his *Libre de les bèsties*. Nine or ten of its stories already appear in *Kalila wa-Dimna*, while others derive from *Sendebar* and the *1001 Nights*. There are several other stories from other sources in other texts by Llull. None the less, these examples seem little more than exceptions in the immense Lullian corpus. The *Libre de les bèsties* itself includes numerous original stories, and these dominate almost completely the narrative flow of the

---

53   *Rhetorica nova* 2.4.1–3, (ed.) Johnston, 15–16.

54   Badia, "La literatura alternativa," 11–14; Bonner, *L'Art i la lògica*, 332–336; and Badia, Santanach, and Soler, "Ramon Llull," 395–409, all address the profound significance of this deliberate alternative.

Libre de meravelles, as before in *Blaquerna* and later in the *Arbre exemplifical* and *Rhetorica nova*.

8.4.2   *The Inspiration for the "Original"* Exempla

The division of the Lullian exemplary corpus into two main sections—one represented by those few stories from other sources and one corresponding to his very many original stories—can serve as a simple point of departure for understanding the quantitative importance of the latter in Llull's work. But such a division runs the risk of simplifying to excess the relationship of Llull's stories with tradition, and this, essentially, for two reasons. First, because (as we will see later regarding an Oriental fable) the traditional narratives cited undergo an obvious manipulation through incorporation into the texts of Blessed Ramon, where they appear without any mention of their provenance. Second, because the stories that we confidently classify as "original" at times reproduce ancient literary motifs, combining them and giving them a new look that ultimately obscures their origins.

A good example of the latter appears in the story of the "evil astrologer" included in the *Arbre exemplifical*.[55] This tale tells the story of a king, upset and sick because an astrologer had foretold his death within the year. To improve his state of mind, another king sends him, as a gift, a maiden who nourishes herself with poison. The astrologer cannot believe that this is possible, since it contradicts his learning and also because the maiden was born under the sign of Aries, with a hot and moist complexion, the opposite of the poison. Having verified this marvel, the king realizes that astrology is not always right, which offers him some small comfort. In the end, his predicament is only resolved thanks to the intervention of a wise knight, who realizes that the astrologer is plotting the death of the king with his false prophecy. The knight asks the astrologer if he knows the time of his own death, and immediately beheads him in order to demonstrate the error of his predictions. All this suggests that we are faced with an original Lullian story. But, as Lola Badia has shown, its novelty results from the fusion of two independent traditional motifs. The theme of soothsayers unable to foresee their own death is as old as the *Aeneid*. The legend of the poison maiden appears in the famous "Letter of Aristotle to Alexander the Great," disseminated in the West after the 12th century in *Placides et Timeo*. There, an enemy king presents Alexander the Great with a maiden nourished on poison, who kills anyone who kisses her. Aristotle uncovers the deception

---

55   *Arbre de ciència* 15.3.10, (eds.) Carreras i Artau and Carreras i Artau, *OE* 1:814. Badia, "La
       literatura alternativa," 17–21; Marsan, *Itinéraire espagnol*, 38; and Cabré, Ortín, and Pujol,
       "'Coneixer e haver moralitats bones,'" 154–157, offer useful analyses of the story.

and saves the king, who beheads the unwelcome maiden. Llull seems to have adapted this legend to create his story. But, curiously, he displaces the motif of conspiracy against the king (and the punishment for that conspiracy) onto the figure of the astrologer. The mention of the maiden loses the negative connotations found in its original, embedding itself in the main plot (concerning the false prophecy) with secondary functions: demonstrating to the king the inability of astrology to explain all phenomena and, perhaps also, demonstrating to the student of Lullian science the ignorance of the astrologer himself, since the sign of Aries is not "hot and moist," as he claims, but rather hot and dry.

8.4.3   Levels of Imitation

Without a doubt, identifying this type of partial debt constitutes a challenge to Lullian scholarship. The trail, more or less deep, of traditional motifs can be traced in various stories from the *Arbre exemplifical* or the *Libre de meravelles*, and extends as well to other Lullian genres, such as his miracles of the Virgin. It is true that, in contrast with the desire for historicity that the genre traditionally displays, most of Lull's miracle stories are decidedly fictitious and original. But, for this same reason, they are enormously interesting for understanding a question related to Llull's manipulation of sources, namely the existence of very diverse levels in his exploitation of traditional material (and therefore, in the degree of originality of Llull's own passages).

Some of the miracles that appear in the *Libre d'Ave Maria* display a slight debt to contemporary literature. Such is the case with the last of this series, in which a monk, the preacher *Ora pro nobis*, finds in a cave a shepherd living with a woman kidnapped from her husband. The monk tells them a "specular" *exemplum*, in which a certain shepherd, living in sin with a woman, dreams of how the Virgin records in a book the woman's name along with all those for whom she will pray to God, but omits the name of the shepherd. After hearing this *exemplum*, the shepherd repents and does penance, while the woman returns to her home, trusting in the Virgin, and accompanied by the monk. They soon find her husband, asleep beneath a tree, and armed for vengeance. The husband dreams that they hang him for murder, and that a horrible demon snatches his soul, protected by Mary. After this dream (again, "specular"), he awakens and hears *Ora pro nobis* from the monk and his wife, kneeling before him. Finally, the husband pardons his wife, and both live in chastity for the remainder of their days.[56] The miracle displays a certain convergence of Marian and hagiographic motifs. The book written by the Virgin obviously relates to the Book of Life containing the names of the elect. Supernatural visions, for

---

56   *Blaquerna*, 2.66, (eds.) Soler and Santanach, NEORL 8:300–303.

their part, are commonplace in collections of *exempla* as well as in Marian miracle stories, which also include frequently the motif of the dispute over a soul between demons and angels. Yet, despite all this, it seems absolutely impossible to find a specific source or any story really similar, overall, to this Lullian miracle.

Another story, better known to medieval readers, appears as an episode of the *Libre d'Ave Maria* that recounts how a shortage of wheat affects abbot Blaquerna's monastery to the point of endangering its charity for the poor.[57] Blaquerna visits the farm, tended by a brother devoted to Our Lady. He offers to provide wheat for the monastery throughout the year, placing his trust in Mary. The brother sends all the wheat in his silo to the abbot, and greets the Virgin with *Ave María, gratia plena*. At first the silo remains empty, prompting his doubts, but soon it miraculously refills, and subsequently satisfies all the needs of the monastery. Later, Blaquerna discovers the monk's special devotion to the phrase *Gratia plena*, and orders construction of a cell with this name to honor the Virgin. The traditional inspiration of this chapter is not difficult to discern: the miracle of the replenished wheat appears in the 6th-century *De gloria martyrum* of Gregory of Tours, from which it passes into numerous Latin and vernacular collections.[58] The story appears highly modified in Llull's text, which includes no trace of the original beneficiaries of the event (monks of a monastery in Jerusalem, ordered built by the Virgin over a synagogue sold to the apostles), ascribes it instead to various fictional characters, and utilizes it to illustrate symbolically the meaning of a phrase from the *Ave Maria*. However, readers of the *Libre d'Ave Maria* would see that Llull's story was inspired by a specific miracle, well-known in the Marian literature of the era.

The debt to a specific miracle is even closer in a passage incorporated by Llull into his *Arbre exemplifical*. Following an allusion to the concept of hope, Ramon introduces a miracle story, set in England, about a young man who seeks to go on pilgrimage to a famous shrine of the Virgin, but his mother is opposed, fearing that the relatives of a knight killed by her husband might take vengeance on their son. The young man rebukes his mother for her lack of hope and undertakes his journey, commended by her to the care of Our Lady. At a stop on the way, enemies seize him, cut off his hands, and pluck out his eyes. The young man manages to reach the shrine and, coming before the Virgin, imagines that his mother has failed in her hope. But his suspicion is unfounded: upon hearing news of the horrible attack, his mother refuses to

---

57   *Blaquerna*, 2.62, (eds.) Soler and Santanach, NEORL 8:283–285.
58   Bétérous, "Ramon Llull et le renouvellement," 44.

believe it, trusting in the protection of Mary. Finally, she travels to the shrine, where she finds her son uninjured, as she had expected.[59]

This story clearly recalls the plot from one of the *Cantigas de Santa Maria* of Alfonso X the Wise, which recounts a miracle, known from oral sources, that features a mother and her son, though set in France. In it, the young man sets out on pilgrimage to the sanctuary of Our Lady of "Albeza," located in Catalonia (or perhaps in Aragon), though without mention of the mother's fear of their enemies. On his journey, enemies seize him and one of them plucks out his eyes and cuts off his hands. Nonetheless, other pilgrims manage to carry him to the sanctuary, trusting that Mary will heal him there. In this case, the news leaves the mother very troubled, "turned blacker than pitch or coal" (*mais ca pez / tornou negra nen que carvon*), but she goes to Albeza and begs God to heal her son. Finally, the Virgin restores his hands and causes him to grow lovely little new eyes, "like those of a partridge" (*come de perdiz*).[60]

Of course there are obvious differences between the *cantiga* of Alfonso X and Llull's miracle story. Besides the enigmatic geographic relocation of the incident, Ramon Llull performs other subtle transformations in the story, designed to emphasize the conflict between hope and despair that justifies its insertion in his text. In these modifications, Llull disregards the emphasis on historicity that the miracle displayed in the tradition, redirecting its plot into the realm of fiction. Yet nonetheless, the miracle still remains perfectly recognizable. Any reader could perceive its obligatory debt to a source, oral or written, connected in some way with the *cantiga* of Alfonso X. Only with difficulty can we accept this Lullian passage as an "original" miracle tale. In all honesty, we must recognize that it moves in a vague realm, which obviously lacks absolute respect for sources, but is still not the realm of creating *ad hoc* a new plot.[61]

It is precisely the disparity that Llull displays in manipulating his sources that betrays the insufficiency of a simple opposition between stories from others and his own stories within his work. In this respect, it seems much more appropriate to propose a kind of gradation, which ranges from exploiting a handful of traditional fables and miracle stories (always presented with some

---

59   *Arbre de ciència* 15.3.13, (eds.) Carreras i Artau and Carreras i Artau, *OE* 1:815–816.

60   Alfonso X el Sabio, *Cantigas de Santa Maria* 146, (ed.) Walter Mettman, 3 vols. (Madrid: 1986–1989), 2:127–130.

61   Ysern, "*Exempla* i estructures exemplars," 49, indicates the impossibility of finding in medieval *exempla* collections exact sources for the stories of the *Libre de les meravelles*, while offering a suggestive number of parallels and partial echoes. Marsan, *Itinéraire espagnol*, 200–203, 215–217, 220–221, 245–248, 361–362, 379–382, 388–394, 411, and 461–464, merits attention from Lullian scholarship in this regard for placing many of Llull's stories in relation to similar narratives from diverse traditions.

variations) to creating a much greater number of passages almost without precedents (or with very vague antecedents): a gradation, in any case, that includes infinite intermediate stages, in which his and others' elements fuse in variable proportions, and without apparent awareness of their difference. If one tenet guides the redaction of each and every Lullian story, it is, in effect, creative freedom. The writings of Ramon Llull are not faithful slaves of received texts, nor do they serve a gratuitous (and also anachronistic) quest for originality. The imagination of their author moves between both extremes with complete ease, unafraid to utilize known motifs and plots, and never hesitating to transform them according to his whim.

8.4.4 *Variations on a Fable*
Another sign of this freedom in treating material is the different appearance that the same plot can take on in different Lullian texts. Not infrequent, in fact, is the repetition of some *exempla* in texts distant in time. The best-known of these recounts the failed attempt by a Christian preacher to convert a sultan, an anecdote with historical resonances repeated on at least seven occasions by Llull; we will return to it later. For now, it may prove more useful to stop along the route among Llull's texts at one of the stories derived from *Kalila wa-Dimna*: the fable of the monkeys, the firefly, and the bird. The evolution of this fable allows us to understand well Llull's process of rewriting exemplary material, as well as the previously noted liberty that guides his adaptation of stories obviously derived from other sources. This story figures in four of the author's works, scattered across two decades: *Blaquerna* (completed in 1283), the *Libre de les bèsties* (definitely prior to 1287–1289), the *Arbre exemplifical* (1295–1296), and the *Rhetorica nova* (1301).[62]

In the version from *Kalila wa-Dimna*, a troupe of monkeys tries to build a bonfire on a firefly, confusing it with an actual fire. A bird seeks to advise the monkeys of their error. This prompts the intervention of another character, which is a man in the Arabic version most widely circulated and in its Castilian translation, but one of the monkeys in the Latin translation of John of Capua and in the ancient Indian *Panchatantra*. This man (or monkey) attempts to dissuade the bird from its pious intention. The bird nonetheless approaches

---

62 *Blaquerna* 2.52, (eds.) Soler and Santanach, NEORL 8:245; *Libre de les bèsties*, in *Libre de meravelles* 7.42; (eds.) Badia et al., NEORL 10:263; *Arbre exemplifical*, in *Arbre de ciència* 15.3.8, (eds.) Carreras i Artau and Carreras i Artau, *OE* 1:813; *Rhetorica nova* 2.4.13, (ed.) Johnston, 21. Armand Llinarès, "Les singes, le ver luisant et l'oiseau: Note sur l'utilisation répétée d'une même fable dans l'oeuvre de Lulle," *Romania* 108 (1987): 97–106, and Hauf, "Sobre l' *Arbor exemplificalis*," 314–319, offer relevant analyses.

thc monkeys who, annoyed by its advice, kill it. The fable thus teaches the risk of attempting to correct those who accept no advice: a lesson summarized in the unfortunate end of the well-intentioned bird, but perhaps also insinuated in "specular" fashion in its own behavior, since it ignored the prudent advice of the man (or other monkey). The match with the framework story of *Kalila wa-Dimna* is perfect: the fable is narrated by Kalila, the prudent jackal, to Dimna, the ambitious jackal, to lament the scant impact that the former's warnings have had on the latter. Of course, this effort seems to have little effect on the obstinate Dimna, thus repeating, within the framework story, the universal value of its lesson.

This specific narrative frame disappears in Llull's texts. In the *Rhetorica nova* the story appears on its own. In the rest of his works it appears always spoken by characters, although their identities vary enormously, along with the intention for which the fable is told and the consequences of that telling in the framework story. In the *Arbre exemplifical*, the fable forms part of a series of linked *exempla*, and is recounted by an executioner, in response to a story told by a king, although it is difficult to determine its ultimate meaning in this context. Its function is much more transparent in *Blaquerna*, where the squire who serves Narpan (an evil and unruly knight), recounts the story to the protagonist, the virtuous Blaquerna, so that the latter will cease attempting to reform the behavior of their master. But the fable, true to its purpose and lesson, has no effect: Blaquerna, trusting in his spiritual weapons, refuses the advice of the squire and continues in his mission. In the *Libre de les bèsties*, the story appears in the mouth of a rooster, who expresses before the lion, the king of beasts, his fear about the excessive responsibility implied in becoming a member of his royal council. This time the story does bear consequences, although these are contrary to what its teller expects: the fable provokes the ire of the lion, who understands that it compares his behavior to that of the stubborn monkeys, and the clever fox exploits that ire in order to execute the rooster. Thanks to the latter's unjust death, the framing story not only confirms the validity of the fable's lesson, but also constitutes an almost exact echo of its plot.

Equally interesting are the variations that these same texts offer in their presentations of the story. To begin with, there exists a series of details shared by all four Lullian versions, but unknown in the best-known versions of *Kalila wa-Dimna* (the Arabic, the Castilian, or the Latin by John of Capua). These details are, essentially, the specification of a limited number of monkeys, the identification of the species of the protagonist bird, and the replacement of the wise counselor (man or monkey) with a second bird:

	Kalila / Directorium	Blaquerna	Libre de les bèsties	Arbre exemplifical	Rhetorica nova
Obstinate characters	Group of monkeys	Two monkeys	One monkey	Two monkeys	Two monkeys
First advisor	A bird	A parrot	A parrot	A dove	A dove
Second advisor	A bird or monkey	A crow	A crow	A magpie	A crow
Consequences	Killed	Killed	Killed	Killed and eaten	Killed and eaten

It is likely that Ramon Llull introduced these modifications in the first of his versions (included in *Blaquerna*), and that the three later redactions emanated from it. However, I would not reject other solutions. One should remember that the second text, with regard to chronology (the *Libre de les bèsties*), displays a much greater overall debt to *Kalila wa-Dimna*, since it includes eight or nine stories from the latter work. The insertion of these materials in the *Libre de les bèsties* poses numerous problems. Hence it is possible, in the specific case of the fable of "The monkeys, the firefly, and the bird," that Ramon Llull abandoned the version present in the oriental collection in order to use the version of the very different story that he himself had prepared in *Blaquerna*. However, it would not be incongruous to consider the existence of a text prior to *Blaquerna*, where the fable existed with the established modifications, a text composed by someone else or by Ramon Llull, and used as the source both for this story alone in *Blaquerna* and for the group of oriental materials utilized in the *Libre de les bèsties*.

Apart from this, collation of the four Lullian versions of the story allows recognition of various individual differences, which are further testimony to the expository freedom that we noted originally. For example, the well-meaning counselor is a parrot in the case of the first two works (*Blaquerna* and the *Libre de les bèsties*), but in the *Arbre exemplifical* and somewhat later in the *Rhetorica nova* they come to be a dove. This suggests, I believe, the existence of a special filiation between these two works, corroborated through another fact: in both, the monkeys end up eating the unfortunate protagonist, a detail without equivalent in either the original Oriental version or in Llull's first versions. Other variants conform somewhat less to the supposed linear temporality of these four versions. For example, the character who attempts to dissuade the bird (a crow in *Blaquerna* and in the *Libre de les bèsties*) is replaced in the *Arbre exemplifical* by a magpie (*garsa*), but the *Rhetorica nova* does not repeat this innovation, returning instead to assigning this role to the crow. We cannot know the reasons for this "relapse" to the contents from the two earlier versions of the story. In this light, the version from the *Rhetorica nova* constitutes a kind of transition (at least formal, if not chronological) between the redaction in the *Libre de les bèsties* and that from the *Arbre exemplifical*, the latter a version that, despite its date, appears the most removed from the others. It is probably unnecessary to draw more inferences from this handful of variants. The intertextuality of Lullian works is indeed a very complex matter. We do not know, in fact, to what degree Llull worked from his previous versions of the story or relied on his memory for each of its new expositions. All that is really certain is that none of these four works displays a literal, exact copy of a previous version.

Llull's redaction of exemplary literature seems to rest in an easy balance between expressive stability and creative freedom. On the one hand, the purpose of his stories appears absolutely determined by the interests and theoretical assumptions of his Art. On the other, their themes and plots display unlimited variety. In this respect, the specific redaction of these passages allows no subjection to the authority of a received text, whether someone else's or even his own. Contemporary stories thus appear as a simple point of departure for creating a rigorously "new" exemplary corpus, one surprising not only for the daring in some of its plots, but also for the very magnitude of its material dimensions. Through Llull's writings parade hundreds and hundreds of stories and analogies, the product of a feverish creativity maintained throughout his literary production. That activity also appears projected upon Llull's own characters: the protagonists of his novels, and even those of his own stories, become tellers (and implicitly, authors) of unusual *exempla*. The generative mechanism for new passages is thus reinforced from within his fictions, in a specular process that ultimately and inevitably involves the reader. Llull's readers are, in effect, invited to create their own exemplary repertories. For this task, Llull's stories stand as models, but also as source material, capable of re-creation and adaptation by his readers, just as their author did with *exempla* drawn from other sources.

8.5   Forms: Typology and Terminology

Thanks to the modeling function described above, readers of Llull's exemplary literature find there a guide to the types of genres that they can adopt in creating their own material: an implicit typology of exemplary forms, shaped by Llull over several decades of practice and effort. This typology does not strictly coincide with that which dominates exemplary production in his era, where, as we have seen, there coexists forms like the historical *exemplum*, the Marian or hagiographical miracle story, the verisimilar story, the animal fable, and the comparison. These forms are only the foundation upon which Llull erects a far more audacious literature. Many Lullian passages do seem to correspond to the conventions of some of these categories, but many also exceed them, posing for scholars a taxonomic challenge. Thus, any attempt to classify this complex corpus is necessarily inadequate and perhaps unfair. Still, I think that, for purely didactic reasons and as a basis for further considerations, it can be useful to distinguish in Llull's exemplary literature several basic narrative forms: the verisimilar *exemplum*, the Marian miracle (both fictitious and verisimilar in Llull's peculiar formulation), the animal fable, and the "artful" *exemplum*. To these we should add comparative and descriptive forms (that is, those lacking a narrative plot), which range from simple similes, based on human or natural activities, to more ambitious comparisons, developed from the theory of the elements and the strict principles of his Art, the latter forms attaining an extreme degree of complexity in the *matafora* analyzed already.

8.5.1   *Forgetting History*

Be this as it may, the first and most striking impression made by review of Llull's exemplary corpus is the evidence of a lack: the nearly absolute absence of historical *exempla*. This is rather surprising given the importance attained by this genre in contemporary literature and preaching. Indeed, in this tradition the term *exemplum* resolves its general meaning into a more limited definition, one reserved for designating exclusively the narration of true events.[63] The latter definition has become widespread in some modern scholarship, leading critics to exaggerate wrongly the "exceptionality" of Lull's own fictitious *exempla*.[64] In any case, Llull himself seems to acknowledge the importance of the historical *exemplum*. In *Blaquerna*, he recounts the case of a messenger who joins a group of pilgrims to Santiago, telling them "*exempla* … stories from

---

63   Le Goff, Brémond, and Schmitt, *L'exemplum*, 38, offer the best-known modern definition of *exemplum* in this limited sense, with reference chiefly to the *exempla* collections of the era: "a brief story presented as true and intended for insertion into a discourse – generally a sermon – to persuade an audience through a useful lesson" ("un récit bref donné comme véridique et destiné à être inséré dans un discours – en général un sermon – pour convaincre un auditoire par une leçon salutaire").

64   Badia and Bonner, *Ramón Llull*, 118–119, along with Ysern, "*Exempla* i estructures exemplars," 26, note the disparity between this modern definition and Llull's "ahistorical" *exempla*, although this disparity is due chiefly to the highly limited character of the modern definition.

the Old and New Testament ... and the deeds of the apostles and of emperors taken from chronicles" (*exemplis ... stories del Vell Testament e del Novell ... fets qui son passats dels apostols e dels emperadors segons que son scrits en les croniques*); his *Articuli fidei christianae* mentions the "books and deeds of the Romans" (*libris et gestis Romanorum*); finally, the *Rhetorica nova* recalls the utility of memorizing "the deeds of those glorious men ... that are constantly recited so that their examples will be imitated" (*gesta gloriosorum virorum qui ... ad hoc continue recitantur ut eorum imitentur exempla*).[65] The latter text also includes historical *exempla* concerning Alexander the Great and an unnamed emperor. We already know that the *Rhetorica nova* is an exceptional work, given its openness to those exemplary genres most familiar to its readers. But apart from this concession, classical anecdotes do not seem to suit Llull's tastes, nor do biblical stories. In the absence of a systematic search, the inventory of these in Llull's oeuvre seems limited to brief allusions to the virtues of John the Baptist, Mary, Christ, or the apostles. All these stand alongside those *exempla* from the *Rhetorica nova* that recount the Passion and death of Christ, which perhaps again express a kind of concession to his readers.

Apart from these, some Lullian stories certainly possess a historical background, although this seems deliberately blurred, to the point that these passages become hidden within Llull's own inventions. A passage from the *Disputatio fidei et intellectus*, for example, reproduces the well-known story of the encounter between Saint Augustine, engrossed in trying to understand the mystery of the Holy Trinity, and a child struggling to send all the water in the sea through a hole. This passage constitutes a brief incursion by Llull into the realm of hagiographical *exempla*, but its appearance confirms the strange relationship between its author and this genre: the passage does not name the saint and the sea becomes "a great river" (*unum magnum flumen*).[66] There is no better proof of Llull's distance from the standards that governed citation of historical *exempla* in his era. The same text displays, as it happens, an identical profile in another *exemplum*, mentioned above. In it, a Christian convinces a Saracen king of the error of his religion, but cannot demonstrate to him with necessary reasons the truth of the Christian faith, provoking the king's ire. This *exemplum* reproduces a true anecdote (the failed attempt to convert a sultan by a Dominican, sometimes identified as Ramon Martí), but the absence of precise details in Llull's account brings it closer to the realm of a fictional story.

---

65   *Blaquerna* 4.88, (eds.) Soler and Santanach, NEORL 8:397–398; *Articuli fidei christianae* (Strasburg: 1651), 956; *Rhetorica nova* 3.1.3., (ed.) Johnston, 35. Colom Ferrá, 40–41, and Rubió i Balaguer, "Alguns aspects," 294–295, analyze these passages.

66   *Disputatio fidei et intellectus* 1.8, (ed.) Walter Euler, ROL 23:233.

As we noted, Llull tells this same story in six other texts. In the *Libre de mera-velles* the story appears as a "likeness" (*semblança*), a name also accorded there to made-up stories. In *Blaquerna*, the anecdote is integrated into development of its novelesque fiction, included by the "historical" sultan himself in a letter addressed to the "fictitious" protagonist, now Pope Blaquerna.[67]

It is not easy to establish a single reason for this Lullian distancing from "history." Some have insisted on his dislike for stories from Roman history, evident in the prolog to his *Libre de sancta Maria*. There, the allegorical character Praise recalls the Romans' love for the common good as a model for the new Christianity. But these words are countered by Prayer, who demystifies the value of the *exemplum*, saying "it is unnecessary for you to cite the example of the Romans" (*No cal que tragats exempli dels romans*), recalling that the same love moves the Tatars, a people "without faith, laws or learning" (*sens fe e sens lei e no han ciència*).[68] The rejection of ancient *exempla* has been linked to Llull's "anti-classicism,"[69] but should doubtless be understood in the broader context of Llull's rejection of "authorities" (*auctoritates*) as a recourse of argumentation: authorities are susceptible to arbitrary and improper use (as in the case of the *exemplum* of the Romans cited by Praise) and are worthless in the face of the objective, universal, and unquestionable character of Llull's Art.[70]

In any case, there is no lack of more practical reasons for Llull's preference for fictitious types of exemplarity. In contrast with the limited number of plots provided by historical materials, fictional stories offer infinite possibilities for finding the arguments suited to any occasion (something recognized long

---

67   *Libre de meravelles* 1.7, (eds.) Badia et al., NEORL 10:117–118; *Blaquerna* 4.84, (eds.) Soler and Santanach, NEORL 8:379; compare *Disputatio fidei et intellectus* 1.1, (ed.) Euler, ROL 23:226. Bonner, *Obres selectes*, 1:60 and 1:94, discusses Llull's mentions of this anecdote, as does Harvey Hames, "Through Ramon Llull's Looking Glass: What was the thirteenth-Century Dominican mission really about?" in *Ramon Llull i el lul·lisme: pensament i llenguatge. Actes de les jornades en homenatge a J.N. Hillgarth i A. Bonner*, (eds.) M.I. Ripoll and M. Tortella (Palma: 2012), 51–74. Bonner, *L'Art i la lògica*, 15, notes Ruiz Simon's assertion that the protagonist of this event could not be Ramon Martí (as Longpré proposed), but rather was André de Longjumeau. Rubió i Balaguer, "Alguns aspects," 291–292, and Luzón Díaz, "Una aproximación," 260–261, discuss Llull's rejection of hagiography.

68   *Libre de sancta Maria* Prol.16, (ed.) Andreu Caimari, *OE* 1:1157.

69   Badia, "'No cal que tragats exempli dels romans,'" and Badia and Bonner, *Ramón Llull*, 121, offer excellent analyses of this anti-classicism and of this passage.

70   Badia, "Literatura alternativa," 16, and Johnston, *ER* 114, suggest how this conception of Llull's Art as the only authority explains: his scant citation of Holy Scripture, of Patristic or Scholastic authorities, and of Greek or Arab authors; his rejection of hagiography as scarcely authoritative for non-Christian audiences; and his characteristic "ahistorical" descriptions of reality.

before by Aristotle).[71] In this respect, Llull's aspiration to endow these forms with a complex metaphorical reading also finds a more inviting context (and a more defined tradition) in invented *exempla*: here, it is precisely the quest for a determined allegorical meaning that determines the definitive configuration of their composition, molding each and every detail of their arguments.

8.5.2   *A Verisimilar Universe*

In large measure, the space traditionally accorded to historical *exempla* is occupied in Llull's work by verisimilar *exempla*, that is, by narratives of fictional events featuring human beings (kings, nobles, merchants, bishops, monks, hermits), set in the spaces both real and symbolic (the court, the city, the wilderness) where a good many medieval novels take place. Verisimilar *exempla* are not lacking in *Blaquerna*, in the compilations from his Ternary Phase, or in his Marian works; they practically monopolize the narrative flow in the *Libre de meravelles*, with the exception of the *Libre de les bèsties*, where the genre alternates with the fable. Some of the stories from the *Libre de les bèsties* are clearly inspired by Oriental tales, which must constitute, moreover, one point of reference for Llull's theoretical conception of the genre. It was not, of course, the only one. The oriental collections seem to favor too frequently stories about cunning and deception (especially in marital life), and these are not the primary focus of Llull's verisimilar *exempla*. As mentioned already, their complex allegorical projection undoubtedly owes much to the practice of Gospel parables. As for their plots and protagonists, as well as for the gallery of virtues and vices that they illustrate, these stories seem to reproduce above all the tone of historical *exempla*. Perhaps aware of the preeminence that the latter enjoyed within the panorama of contemporary literature, Llull devises a parallel fictitious universe, in the end still recognizable to his readers. He begins with a few structural elements, often employed in historical *exempla* (stories of loyalty and treason among lords and vassals, the dialectic between the quest for virtue and the quest for honors and wealth), molding and combining them to produce a huge corpus of narratives, one with minimal variations in plot, but sufficient for adaptation to the specific context where they appear and to the interpretation (often complicated) that they seek to impart.

8.5.3   *Imagined Miracles*

Marian miracle stories enjoy a more modest presence in the work of Ramon Llull. The contexts most favorable to this genre are the *Libre d'Ave Maria* and the lengthy *Libre de sancta Maria*, while it occasionally appears as well in other

---

71   *Rhetoric* 2.21 1393–1394.

works, such as the *Arbre exemplifical.* (The role of Mary in Lullian discourse is necessarily related to the importance of the Incarnation, which is critical to both his religious apologetic for unbelievers and to his notions of likeness.)[72] In all these writings, the Lullian miracle story assumes its own new contours, which distance it enormously from the conventions of the genre. The poetics of medieval miracle stories consists, as is well known, in the defense of the historicity of the events presented. These passages abound in signs of authenticity and, in their Latin versions, appear subjected to an extraordinarily faithful transmission of their literal text; vernacular translations reproduce more freely these literal contents, but always with a respect for the history constantly invoked in their sources. By contrast, Ramon Llull imposes on the genre an unprecedented departure, by offering a whole gallery of imagined miracles, although these might be inspired, in a more or less remote way, by some traditional motifs. All these passages are integrated into the special literary universe that supports these works: in the *Libre d'Ave Maria,* for example, Llull manages to transform the novelesque characters that parade through this work into beneficiaries of intervention by Our Lady. The *Libre de sancta Maria* offers in turn a different structure, but equally distant from conventions of the genre. Here the miracle stories appear narrated by its characters comprise the framing dialogue of the text, in order to illustrate complex theoretical issues, related to Llull's doctrine of "first and second intentions," that is, the need for all people to conduct their affairs according to the true intention of their creation, loving and praising God, rather than according to other secondary purposes. Thanks to this subordination to Llull's theory of "intentions," the material in this work adopts a more elevated intellectual tenor than traditional miracle stories. They consist of "theological" miracle stories, in which the absence of spatial and temporal details accentuates their character as simply "hypothetical cases" invented solely for the reader's reflection (although this does not prevent two of these examples from being incorporated into a conventional collection of miracle stories in the 15th century). Their intellectual tenor also distances them from the miracle stories that comprise the *Libre d'Ave Maria,* but this perhaps matters least. What is important to note is that in both texts, Llull manages to elaborate, using traditional materials, an entire series of new miracle stories. Obviously, these miracles are presented as mere literary fictions that imitate and replace historical truth, in the same terms with which their verisimilar stories seek to replace and copy the similarly historical material

---

72   Robert D. Hughes, "Speculum, Similitude and Signification: the Incarnation as Exemplary and Proportional Sign in the Arts of Ramon Llull," *SL* 45–46 (2005–2006): 3–37.

disseminated in contemporary *exempla* collections. *Exempla* and miracle stories share, in effect, conventions of verisimilar narration (in a Christian sense, of course, that accepts occasional divine interventions), despite the unavoidable distance that separates the two genres in their traditional postures: thus, while the creation of human examples typical of the verisimilar *exemplum* was a constant in storytelling of the era, the manipulation of miracles about the Virgin Mary, their "invention" by any author, must have seemed, in the eyes of their readers, a truly daring novelty.[73]

8.5.4   *A Universe of Fables*

In Lullian texts, the world of verisimilar fiction lives harmoniously with the world of animal fables, just as in Oriental collections of stories. As we know, one of these collections, *Kalila wa-Dimna,* is the source for several of the fables of the *Libre de les bèsties.* But this brief text also includes original fables by Llull, just as *Blaquerna* does before, and the *Arbre exemplifical* and the *Rhetorica nova* do later. All these passages (his own and others') observe the conventions of the genre established in the Oriental tradition and in Aesopic literature. In a fable, animals possess some human capabilities (especially speech) and assume diverse social and moral behaviors, according to the diversity of traditionally defined roles. However, none of this prevents the genre from adopting, in the work of Blessed Ramon, some unique features: upon entering Llull's writings, the Oriental narratives lose many embellishments, which noticeably obscure their moral lessons. This, of course, minimizes the distance between stories from other sources and Llull's original fables, and so from other exemplary genres included in his work.[74]

8.5.5   *A Lullian Universe*

Many Lullian stories do not have human or animal protagonists, but rather, the characters in these narratives are personifications corresponding to the most diverse realities treated in the theoretical pages of Llull's Art: realities

---

73   Aragüés Aldaz, *Ramón Llull y la literatura ejemplar*, offers a more detailed analysis. See also, especially: Bétérous, "Ramon Llull et le renouvellement;" Viera, "*Exempla* in the *Libre de Sancta Maria*;" Joan Santanach i Suñol, "Dos exemples de Ramon Llull inclosos en un recull de miracles," *Randa* 55 (2005): 7–13; and David Barnett, "The Sources of a Fifteenth-Century Catalan Collection of Marian Miracle Stories," in *"Gaude Virgo Gloriosa:" Marian Miracle Literature in the Iberian Peninsula and France in the Middle Ages,* (eds.) J.C. Conde and E. Gatland (London: 2011), 116–118.

74   Llúcia Martín Pascual, "Algunes consideracions sobre la relació entre les faules del *Llibre de les Bèsties* de Ramon Llull i l'original oriental," *Catalan Review* 11 (1997): 92–93, and Taylor, "Some Complexities," 657–658, analyze this aspect.

drawn from both the eternal world of God and from the material and spiritual realms of Creation. The words and deeds of these characters, determined by their interactions in the universe and by their respective positions in the scale of being, present us with a new – and above all, profoundly harmonious and coherent – exemplary mode. The most conventional characters in these stories are probably personifications of the vices, virtues, and spiritual faculties (Justice, Mercy, Greed, Wrath, Memory, Understanding, and so forth), that is, of entities with known precedents in medieval allegorical literature. However, in Llull's case these acquire new features, thanks to their specific functions in his complex theological system. These characters coexist in his stories with other logical and theological entities, again universal in nature, but bearing a precise meaning within the architecture of his Art. Such is the case with his Divine Dignities, his Correlatives, and other essential concepts (Goodness, Eternity, Truth, Difference, Contrarity, Beginning, End, Generation, Corruption, etc.). As a result, Llull's stories ultimately personify all manner of abstractions: the square, the circle, the triangle, the past, present, and future, day and night, speech, vision, hearing, etc. These are uncommon in exemplary literature of his era, but integral to the explication of Creation proposed by Llull, which also requires other more material characters. Among these are objects traditionally endowed (or not) with symbolic value (the sword, the shield, the crown, the oven), just as are any beings in all levels of Creation. There are beings drawn from the celestial and sublunary realms, surprising as protagonists in a story: Lord Saturn, Lord Aries, the sun, gold, the emerald, the rose, the pumpkin, lettuce, and even the cold-sore.

The nature of these characters definitely exceeds traditional usage in this genre in favor of establishing Llull's own original, fictive, and even extravagant, universe. It is clear that the plots in these narratives resemble those of verisimilar stories or fables (with examples of friendship and hatred, loyalty and treason, vice and virtue), just as all these share with fables the recourse to personification. But it is perhaps precisely the "humanization" of these unusual entities that enhances their air of unreality, signaling clearly the singularity of their invention within the vast panorama of medieval story.[75] A term like "fable" therefore seems rather inadequate for these stories featuring the four elements, or plants and stones, just as the traditional concept of the allegorical *exemplum* cannot account for the function and meaning of stories featuring

---

75   Badia, "Literatura alternativa," 16–17, and Luzón Díaz, "Una aproximación," 261 examine these consequences of Llull's personifications. Hauf, "Sobre l'*Arbor exemplificalis*," 324–325, provides an exhaustive listing of these characters (and their "humanized" behaviors) in the *Arbre exemplifical*.

the Divine Dignities and the Correlative Principles. On the other hand, such Lullian *exempla* seem designed according to these principles and seem to demand a common name, which would recognize their profound coherence, based on Llull's theoretical principles. For this reason, the most appropriate name is probably that of the "artful" *exemplum*, as proposed already, but understood as "artful" because, even if all types of *exempla* in Llull's work pertain to illustrating his Art, in the case of the singular stories under consideration it is his own Art that generates, almost mechanically, an entire universe of narrative plots.

In this respect, the "artful" *exemplum* always arises from a specific context: in the text of the *Arbre exemplifical*, from illustrating the theoretical contents of the *Arbre de sciencia*. Still, Llull obviously anticipated some of its most unusual stories in *Blaquerna* (for example, the debate between the palm, pine, and fig trees) and in the *Libre de meravelles* (the allegorical story featuring Wisdom, Madness, Love, and Devotion), and this genre also appears notably in the later *Rhetorica nova*, a text guided, as we will explain later, by an effort to anthologize and to integrate every type of exemplary form.

8.5.6   *On the Margins of Narration: From Simile to Metaphor*
The Lullian oeuvre also brings together other exemplary forms distinguished by their lack of narrative action. Such is the case with the simile, dedicated to illustrating an abstract concept based on some natural quality or on an aspect of human activity. In general, these similes have a conventional tone that combines their simplicity with an obvious effort at ornamentation, and so are different from other comparative passages employed according to more demanding theoretical assumptions. Among these are the various comparisons intended to explore in detail both the affinities and the differences among beings. These include, of course, the *mataforas* from the *Començaments de medicina*, based on rigorous application of elemental exemplarism. Despite the huge distance between these diverse forms, all of them exhibit Ramon Llull's unshakeable faith in analogy as a tool for comprehending Creation. Its presence is therefore traceable from his first writings to his late sermons but may seem somewhat obscured in his novels (and definitively eclipsed in the *Arbre exemplifical*), thanks to the preponderance of exemplary narratives in these texts. Similes nonetheless return with vigor in the *Rhetorica nova*, where they display a more conventional appearance, by drawing some of their arguments from bestiary and lapidary literature. This is hardly surprising. In the *Rhetorica nova*, the presence of the simile reveals again not simply Llull's enthusiasm for this genre, but also a tribute to the place that it occupies in the encyclopedic literature of his era.

8.5.7   *Terminological Freedom*

The typology presented here should be understood as a provisional paradigm. There obviously exist many unclear boundaries between these genres, just as there exist passages that seem to exceed them and so deserve a new label. Still, despite these limitations, simply listing these categories allows us to understand the skillful balance between tradition and innovation that supports Lullian exemplary literature. Llull both accepts and refuses points of reference for traditional genres, in so far as he respects some basic forms (such as the simile or fable), subtly oscillates between one and another (such as the verisimilar story, inflected with plots from the historical *exemplum*, or such as the Marian miracle stories, conceived as a fictional *contrapunctum* to the traditional miracles circulating in his era), and proposes a largely new genre (the "artful" story, based on converting the principles of his Art into literature). Taken together, the genres preferred by Llull manifest an obvious partisan position in favor of some of the basic uses of exemplarity defined in contemporary rhetorical theory, to the detriment of others: fiction over history, allegorical over literal interpretation, and illustrating abstract realities over simply exhorting to virtue. In light of these three preferences, we can understand his abandonment of the historical *exemplum*, traditionally limited to the literal presentation of an exclusively moral lesson.

Llull's knowledge of the principles of exemplarity (and their free adaptation for his literary purposes) can be appreciated as well in the realm of terminology, which is worth reviewing in detail. In his era, terms such as *exemplum* and similitude display an obvious debt to rhetorical theory. To begin with, the two terms (along with some others, such as *comparabile* or *homoeosis*, the latter of grammatical origins) can be understood as synonyms, used indifferently to define any brief comparison deployed within any oral or written discourse. Of course, contemporary theorists exploit other more specific terms in order to delimit each of the forms included in this very broad genre. Thus, rhetorical and grammatical treatises provide various more or less familiar names to recognize the specificity of the historical *exemplum* (*historiae narratio, historia certa*), of the fabulous (*fabella, apologatio, apologus*), and of the verisimilar *exemplum* (*exemplum verisimile*), as well as of the comparison or simile (*collatio*). The problem, recognized by classical and later theorists, is that this parceling out of the exemplary territory typically involves as well use of the two major terms of exemplarity (*exemplum* and *similitudo*), conceived not as synonyms, but rather as the respective designations of two different forms. Their distinction is a commonplace in rhetorical treatises, to the point of appearing often in the concise formula "the difference between an *exemplum* and a similitude is ..." (*inter exemplum et similitudinem hoc interest ...*). Very often, this formula attempts to divide the entire range of exemplary literature into two great opposing categories. We need not exert ourselves in understanding the disputes generated by this attempt; it is sufficient to recall that the boundary between the *exemplum* and the similitude underwent vast shifts. Since Quintilian, it was common to assign the name *exemplum* to all exemplary forms of narrative character (whether historical, verisimilar, or fictional), reserving the name *similitudo* for descriptive or atemporal comparisons (that is, *collationes*). This is not, however, the only solution to the problem, even though many recent studies, aware or not of its origins, have based on it their own definitions of both categories. Other ancient authors in fact restrict the term *exemplum* exclusively to narrating historical events (as we indicated above), while extending *similitudo* to all other forms (narrative or descriptive). There are also those who assign the latter term to any form endowed with metaphorical or allegorical meaning, in contrast to the *exemplum* always directed toward the literal presentation of paradigms of virtue. As will become clear, the existence of these divergent views makes it impossible to assign univocally many exemplary forms (the verisimilar *exemplum* and the fable, to begin with) to one category or another, given their alternating participation in the characteristics assigned to both.

In addition, this proliferation of criteria opposing the *exemplum* and the similitude is not completely unjustified. The dissemination of the two solutions cited above, to the detriment of that given by Quintilian, may be motivated within Christian culture as an attempt to confirm the precision of biblical terminology: in the Gospels, the Greek term *parabola*, traditionally translated into Latin as *similitudo*, designates the passages employed by Christ in his preaching, which can be both narrative and descriptive, but are always in fact fictional and metaphorical.[76] Curiously, and perhaps not completely by coincidence, the features of Gospel parables are exactly those that underlie the exemplary paradigm adopted by Llull: his *exempla* are narrative or descriptive, as we have seen, but almost always metaphorical and non-historical.

In any case, Llull's position regarding these exemplary forms is alien to the terminological hair-splitting cited above. The use in his texts of Latin terms such as *exemplum* and *similitudo*, along with their vernacular equivalents (*exempli*, *eximpli* or *exemple*, on the one hand, and *semblança*, on the other) is in fact very loose, though without becoming really erratic or aleatory. These terms often occur together in his work without a specific value, although perhaps with a tangential relationship to rhetorical usage, as in the phrases

---

76   Aragüés Aldaz, "Deus concionator," 23–66.

"give an example" or "exemplify" (*donar exempli* or *exemplificar*).[77] When employed as technical rhetorical terms, *exemplum* and *similitudo* are simply synonyms, and appear endowed with a generic value, capable of embracing all forms of comparison. This broad definition (common traditionally, as noted already), is what the term *exemplum* clearly invokes in the title of the *Arbre exemplifical* and in the subtitle *pulcra exempla* from the *Rhetorica nova*. In Llull's two novels, the Catalan terms *exempli* and *semblança* also possess this generic value, alternating without conflict as synonymous expressions. The first of these terms seems to predominate in *Blaquerna*, although the second is not uncommon, and both, ultimately, can serve to designate the same passage in the text. This happens also in the *Libre de meravelles*, which perhaps displays a slight statistical advantage for the term *semblança*.[78]

Even so, the *Libre de meravelles* hides within itself an even more surprising terminological usage, apparently unnoticed by scholars. The alternation between the two terms breaks off practically in the middle of the seventh section, the celebrated *Libre de les bèsties*, where the Catalan term *exempli* clearly overwhelms *semblança*, which almost disappears in this section. Of course we should recall the relative autonomy of this little work (perhaps composed previously) within the totality of the novel, but the reasons for this sudden shift in terminology surely lie elsewhere, perhaps in the origins of the narratives included here. Thus, where the passages of Llull's own invention appear unlabeled in the *Libre de les bèsties,* or under the vague designation of "similitude" (*semblança*) or *exemplum* (*exempli*), the latter term is applied almost invariably to name the stories taken from Oriental sources. The use of the term *exempli* in this little work thus seems to reflect Llull's awareness of the presence of these stories in the literature of his era, and the predominance of this term (or its equivalent from other languages) in the collections that disseminated them. Once the *Libre de les bèsties* ends, the novel resumes its habitual usage, that is, it is filled with verisimilar stories of Llull's own invention, gathered without distinction under either of the two main terms that run throughout the history of exemplarity: *exemplum* or similitude.

---

77   For example, *Libre d'intenció* 5.27, (ed.) Galmés, ORL 18:59. Arbona Piza, "Los exemplis," 56, discusses the variant spellings of exempli.

78   *Libre de meravelles* 2.14, (eds.) Badia et al., NEORL 10:149, and *Blaquerna* 30, (eds.) Soler and Santanach, NEORL 8:260–261, illustrate the dual application of these terms to the same passage. Arbona Piza, "Los exemplis," 56 and 60; Rubió i Balaguer, "Alguns aspects," 290, and Pring-Mill, "Els recontaments," 310, stress the equivalent use of these terms.

8.5.8   *Lullian Taxonomies*

Besides these uses of terminology, Ramon Llull includes in his works other reflections regarding exemplary literature, which help us to understand his vision of the external and internal boundaries of the genre. In the *Rhetorica nova*, Llull proposes an interesting classification of the passages included in the section titled "beautiful exempla" (*pulcra exempla*): "Beautiful *exempla*," he states, "arise from two subject matters, since they deal either with natural or moral affairs" (*pulcra exempla sunt ex duplici materia, quia vel sunt de rebus naturalibus aut de rebus moralibus*). For their part, "natural affairs are either spiritual (like God and the angels) or corporeal (like the heavens, earth, and animals)," (*res autem naturales, aut sunt spirituales – ut deus et angeli – aut corporales – ut celum, terra, et animalia*) while "moral affairs are also twofold, since they deal either with virtues, or by contrast, with vices and sins" (*similiter res morales sunt duplices, quia aut virtutes aut sunt econtra vicia et peccata*).[79] Llull's taxonomy recalls the tenor of other more or less contemporary classifications, but despite its simplicity and perfect symmetry, readers might find difficult its application to the passages included in the section on *pulcra exempla.* If the distinction between natural and moral affairs refers exclusively to the plot or content of the passages, then perhaps only five of these (examples of Christ's passion and of a hypocritical bishop, along with three animal fables) pertain to the second category, since they seem to be the only ones offering stories about praiseworthy or blameworthy behavior. The rest of the passages instead take for their subjects the structure of Creation, whether treated in comparisons to the natural world or in more complex passages based on principles from Llull's Art. On the other hand, if we decide to apply Llull's taxonomy not to the subject, but to the intention or lesson of these stories, then we must consider practically all of the passages in this section to be "moral" *exempla*, with the exception of its first two, which seek to explain in general terms the "natural" design of all creatures in the image and likeness of God.[80]

With regard to Llull's conception of the boundaries of genre of the *exemplum*, it is also worth considering the contents of the *Arbre exemplifical*, the most copious repertory of *exempla* that he provides in his Ternary Phase. As it happens, many of the nearly 450 illustrative passages included in this text are simply proverbs. These constitute Llull's first major contribution to the genre of proverbs, although his interest in sententious and aphoristic forms is evident already in 1290, coinciding with his overhaul of the demonstrative

---

79   *Rhetorica nova* 2.4.0, (ed.) Johnston, 14.

80   Johnston, *ER* 306–307, notes some similarity between Llull's scheme and that proposed by John of Garland in his *Parisiana Poetria*.

methods of his Art. In 1296, the year of completion of the *Arbre de sciencia*, Llull brings forth his first compilation of proverbs alone, the *Proverbis de Ramon*, followed by the selection of proverbs in his *Rhetorica nova* and the compilation *Mil proverbis* [Thousand Proverbs], still from his Ternary Phase, and finally the collection *Proverbis d'ensenyament* [Proverbs of Instruction], from the post-Art phase in his work.[81] The very rich development of this genre in the *Arbre exemplifical* evidently represents the fruit of a true literary "discovery" by Llull, announced in the prologue to this text, where he asserts his intention to divide its *exempla* into two parts, "namely, into stories and proverbs" (*recontaments e proverbis*).[82]

This presentation of the proverb as a "part" (or better, "type") of *exemplum* is as ambiguous as it is fundamentally disconcerting. Rhetorical tradition had established a clear boundary between these two genres, and Llull's awareness of that boundary in fact underlies his separate presentation of both genres in their respective chapters from the *Rhetorica nova*. This awareness appears as well within the *Arbre exemplifical*: in this text, the series of proverbs always bear a heading with this term, while its stories do not appear with the title "tales" (*recontaments*), but instead directly under the term *exempla* (*exemplis*), which tacitly assumes the more restricted conventional use of this name.

Of course there is no lack of precedents for conflating these genres and the terminology of each form. In Arabic and Hebrew, the terms *mathal* and *māshal* designated without distinction any kind of brief didactic passage: similes, stories, proverbs, or famous sayings. Likewise, in the West, the term *exemplum* and its vernacular equivalents could occasionally designate a saying or proverb, as occurs in numerous texts of wisdom literature (many of Oriental derivation),[83] in some 13th-century copies of the *Disciplina clericalis*,[84] or in the oeuvre of Don Juan Manuel. In the 14th century, Francesc Eiximenis very specifically gave the term "brief *exempla*" (*exemplis breus*) to proverbial sayings, in order to distinguish them from *exempla* in the strict sense. Finally,

---

81   See Francesc Tous Prieto, "La forma proverbi en l'obra de Ramon Llull: Una aproximació," M.A. thesis, Universitat de Barcelona-Universitat Autònoma de Barcelona (Barcelona: 2010) and "Breus proposicions que contenen molta sentència: els proverbis lul·lians i les 'formes sentencioses,'" *SL* 51 (2011): 77–98. Hauf, "Sobre l'*Arbor exemplificalis*," 308, analyzes the placement of proverbs in the *Arbre exemplifical*.

82   *Arbre de ciència* 15. Prol., (eds.) Carreras i Artau and Carreras i Artau, *OE* 1:799: "los exemplis que proposam donar volem departir en dues parts, ço és a saber, en recontaments e proverbis."

83   As in *El Libro de los Doze Sabios*, ch. 30, (ed.) John K. Walsh, Anejos del *BRAE* 29 (Madrid: 1975), 102.

84   Le Goff, Brémond, and Schmitt, *L'exemplum*, 55.

Llull himself refers, in his *Blaquerna,* to certain proverbial forms employed by Muslim sufis with the label "short *exempla*" (*exemplis abreujats*).[85] This broad terminological usage, combined with Llull's usual laxity in deploying technical vocabulary, suffices to justify assimilating proverbs and *exempla*, two genres often combined in contemporary literature and ultimately directed, in Llull's oeuvre, to the single goal of illustrating his Art.[86]

Nonetheless, it is possible that the design of the *Arbre exemplifical* offers additional reasons for the convergence of these two genres. First, we should not forget that some series of proverbs appear in the text inside of various tales told by their protagonists. The section on branches illustrates this well: it offers fourteen stories, usually presented as *exempla*, but with the second, third, and seventh labeled as "proverbs" (*proverbis*).[87] The latter three offer, nevertheless, a structure similar to the others, including narrative activity that could legitimately qualify them as tales. Their only real difference consists in their inclusion of a series of proverbs, placed in the mouths of characters or, in the last case, written on the door of a palace as rules that should govern the behavior of a monarch.

The integration of proverbs within this text – that is, their presentation as an exemplary form – may also have originated in another way, related to the possibility of reading them as the seed or as the condensation of a complete tale. Rhetorical doctrine had already established this "reversibility" between *exempla* and sententious forms, understood as different expressions of the same lesson. The very first of the *exempla* in the *Arbre exemplifical* confirms this. At the beginning of this passage, Ramon states a proverb: "Fire wants its heat to be good in water so that its goodness be very strong, and so water told air to remember its weakness" (*Lo foc vol que la sua calor sia bona en l'aigua per ço que la sua bonea haja gran virtut; e per ço dix l'aigua a l'àer que la membràs en la sua malaltia*). When his interlocutor cannot grasp the meaning of the proverb, Ramon explains it, precisely through a tale, in which air lies suffering from its love for fire and from the dryness caused by fire. Water suggests that air draw near to it, but air prefers to suffer in pain rather than to betray its like and beloved. This gloss by Ramon in the form of a story illustrates the generic

---

85   Hauf, "Sobre l'*Arbor exemplificalis*," 307 and 310, reviews the usage of Don Juan Manuel, Eiximenis, and Llull's *Blaquerna* 5.99, (eds.) Soler and Santanach, NEORL 8:426–427.

86   Luzón Díaz, "Una aproximación," 259–260, analyzes this laxity, noting details from Rubió i Balaguer, "Alguns aspects," 290; Ysern, "*Exempla* i estructures exemplars," 48; and Hauf, "Sobre l'*Arbor exemplificalis*," 307.

87   *Arbre de ciència* 15.4, (eds.) Carreras i Artau and Carreras i Artau, *OE* 1:817–826.

essence of the proverb, conceived thus as the minimal statement capable of replacing and in some way substituting for a story or tale.[88]

In light of this opening passage, one might imagine that Llull conceives the *exemplum* as something formed by combining a tale or story and a proverb. The very ambiguity of the prolog, where Llull speaks of dividing the text's *exempla* in two "parts," might suggest this, but it is not necessary to go so far: stories and proverbs do appear as two alternative exemplary modes, though potentially affiliated.[89] In this respect, the duality of the first *exemplum* in the *Arbre exemplifical* is exceptional and, arguably, deliberately exceptional. Llull surely seeks only to demonstrate from the outset of his text the nature of these two exemplary genres, and the close relationship that they can embrace. Subsequently, both genres usually appear on their own.

None of this prevents the text from displaying some signs of their genetic relationship. Many Lullian proverbs exhibit, for example, the form of a dialogue among several characters, thanks to an initial dramatic illusion. Only the brevity of these passages qualifies them as proverbs, since their content differs little from any tale or story in the text. The respective deployment of *exempla* and proverbs for expounding Llull's Art ultimately results in minimizing their generic boundaries. This thematic and formal affinity between *exempla* and proverbs thus favors their joint compilation in the work, and their conception as two possible varieties of *exempla*. By the end of the *Arbre exemplifical*, its reader realizes what Ramon Llull has demonstrated in the first of its passages: many of the proverbs can be read as the kernels of tales or stories, and many of the tales or stories can likewise be converted easily into proverbs. The text tacitly invites traversing the path from one form to the other, as one more facet from the exercise of the exemplary strategies proposed to the reader in the prologue. Toward this end, the *Arbre exemplifical* suggests the sensation of an incomplete text, of a repertory *in fieri*.

8.6   Exemplary Metamorphoses: Discursive Contexts and the Evolution of the Lullian Exemplum

8.6.1   *The Insertion of Passages*
If anything characterizes medieval exemplary literature, it is its protean character and capacity for adaptation to the most diverse discursive con-

---

88   *Arbre de ciència* 15.1, (eds.) Carreras i Artau and Carreras i Artau, *OE* 1:799; see also the analysis by Pring-Mill, "Els recontaments," 309–317.

89   Cabré, Ortín, and Pujol, "'Coneixer e haver moralitats bones,'" 140–141.

texts. The means of inserting *exempla* into texts are thus almost innumerable. Ramon Llull practices many of these, although scholars have perhaps not noticed sufficiently their variety and the familiarity with contemporary literature that this reveals.

Medieval collections of historical *exempla* (both rhetorical and homiletic), typically juxtapose passages, grouping them in large thematic chapters (corresponding to the vices and virtues or other moral and philosophical concepts) and ordering them either alphabetically or logically (according to some system of similar or opposing themes). The two major compilations created by Ramon Llull (the very extensive *Arbre exemplifical* and the brief selection of *pulcra exempla* from the *Rhetorica nova*) reproduce this scheme, at the same time that they depart from it, thanks to the nature of their contents (which largely consist of fictional *exempla*) and to their peculiar arrangement, dictated by various routes through the hierarchy of Creation. Other Lullian series of *exempla*, like the *mataforas* that comprise the final chapter of the *Començaments de medicina*, present a scheme far removed from this compilatory tradition.

In the medieval era, historical *exempla* also occur subordinated within a discourse, appearing occasionally to illustrate some theoretical question. This occurs in didactic texts from many diverse disciplines, but of course in sermons, typically adorned (perhaps more in oral delivery than in writing) with this brief genre. Tracing this "discontinuous" or "occasional" appearance of *exempla* in the works of Ramon Llull would be an endless labor. Passages of this type abound both in his later homiletic works (although most of them correspond there to simpler types of comparison) and in his legal and medical treatises. The sections of "questions" (*qüestions, quaestiones*), examples or problems provided for a reader's practice, that typically conclude the theoretical expositions of Llull's Art yield, in this respect, more than a few surprises. These sections again offer a refuge for series of *exempla* (like the analogies that conclude the *Liber de lumine*) and intermittently display incipient forms of a story. Examples that merit special notice in this regard are the questions proffered in Llull's works on law, sometimes posed about hypothetical situations invested with a certain narrative element. Of course, for this Blessed Ramon benefits from the long tradition of a genre (the "legal case") teeming with connections to medieval storytelling.

The many modes of medieval fiction provide very diverse models for the insertion of narratives. Some appear juxtaposed in a manner similar to that from collections of historical *exempla*, although with a much freer arrangement, as in Aesopic texts or, to a certain degree, in the *Disciplina clericalis*. Others appear in discontinuous fashion, subordinated within texts more complex in nature. Hence, stories occasionally adorn the speeches of the protagonists in some novels, a scheme that Ramon Llull especially adopts in *Blaquerna*. Contemporary stories develop some more daring narrative purposes, based on a curious balance between the weight of the *exempla* and the narrative frame that encloses them. This clearly occurs in texts such as *Kalila wa-Dimna* or *Sendebar*, where the stories ultimately modulate the development of the actual outcome of the main story. Among Llull's writings, the *Libre de meravelles* comes relatively close to this scheme. It would thus be unfair to see this work as a novel sprinkled with stories, like *Blaquerna*: the numerous stories in the *Libre de meravelles* not only adorn its debates, but also define and construct its plot, guiding the intellectual journey of its young protagonist, Fèlix. The influence of these schemes is even more evident still in the *Libre de les bèsties*, the section of the novel that inherits, as we have seen, part of the plot of *Kalila wa-Dimna* and so all the force that intercalated stories bear in that work. These stories define not only the intentions of their animal protagonists, but also their fortunes and fate in the lion's court. This debt to oriental storytelling can also explain the practice, in the entire *Libre de meravelles*, in *Blaquerna*, and in the *Arbre exemplifical*, of some complex techniques for successively subordinating new stories (the so-called method of "Russian dolls" or "Chinese boxes"), which he undoubtedly would have known from *Kalila wa-Dimna*.

Certain other medieval narrative techniques for inserting stories also have more modest echoes in Llull's work. The so-called process of *enfilage* (weaving or braiding) of stories, in which these succeed one another (that is, coordinated, unlike the schemes for juxtaposition and subordination mentioned already), shaping the plot in a work of fiction. The *Libre d'Ave Maria*, woven from a stream of events occurring in the monastery of abbot Blaquerna, loosely reproduces this scheme. But traces of it also occur at various points in *Blaquerna* and the *Libre de meravelles*.[90] In both novels, some episodes from the main story constitute brief exemplary scenes, as stories "staged" by their characters for teaching others. These "eye-witness" *exempla* complement, at a higher narrative level, the lessons recounted by these same characters. These passages imply not only an expansion of the novel's possible exemplary readings but assume as well acceptance of another purpose for these brief forms: they are

---

90   Viktor Shklovski, *Sobre la prosa literaria* (Barcelona: 1971), 119–124, discusses these modes
      of inserting stories and narrative strategies in medieval storytelling. María Pilar Palomo,
      La novela cortesana (Barcelona: 1976), 33–44; Ventura De la Torre Rodríguez, "El relato
      intercalado en la *Historia de los siete sabios de Roma*," in *El relato intercalado*, (eds.)
      M. Smerdou Altolaguirre and M. Bonsoms (Madrid: 1992), 67–75; and María Jesús Lacarra,
      Cuentística medieval en España: los orígenes (Zaragoza: 1979), 47–75, review the Hispanic
      tradition.

not only subordinate to the main plot of the work, but also to a large degree construct it in successive vignettes.[91]

Likewise, some scenes of obvious literary inspiration occasionally appear inserted at the beginning of Llull's theoretical writings. This happens in the *Libre de l'orde de cavalleria* and various works of theological debate, inaugurated often by the meeting of several characters in an idyllic setting, as in the *Libre del gentil i dels tres savis*, *Disputatio fidei et intellectus*, or the *Phantasticus*.[92] Of course, these scenes bear only a tangential relationship to the exemplary forms that occupy us here, but both one and the other constitute a haven for the constant literary enterprise of their author, once he has abandoned his major novelizing projects.

Study of the mechanisms for inserting stories, and certainly of the discursive contexts in which they appear, remains an incomplete chapter in scholarship on Blessed Ramon. It is surely necessary, since it is clear that the choice of a particular type of exemplary literature conditions (and in turn is conditioned by) the nature of each context. The path of development of Lullian *exempla* is thus also the history of the works that enclose it.[93]

8.6.2   *Early Works: The Passion for Comparison*

Thus, Llull's first forays into the territory of exemplary literature seem to correspond with the use of brief comparisons in the heart of his theoretical discourse. These forms can be found in the monumental *Libre de contemplació* (1273–1274?), a text preceding Llull's Art that includes the seeds of many of his future philosophical and literary positions. It is a comprehensive encyclopedia, carefully structured with numerical symbolism, and based on an analogical conception of the cosmos, the symbolic reading of the "Book of Creation." This text does include some complex allegorical constructions. Overall, however, it draws inspiration from simple similes and comparisons, following Llull's broad stylistic preference for parallel and dual constructions. These comparisons abound especially in the beginning of the text's third book, devoted to all the exemplary lessons available from observation of the natural world and from human occupations (clergy, princes, physicians, sailors, minstrels, painters, etc.) Despite their brevity, these passages transcend their esthetic function

---

91   Badia, Santanach, and Soler, "Ramon Llull," 433–435, analyze examples.

92   Colom Ferrá, "Ramon Llull y los orígenes," 39–40, and Rubió i Balaguer, "Alguns aspects," 292–293, discuss these examples. Roger Friedlein, *El diàleg en Ramon Llull: l'expressió literària com a estratègia apologètica* (Barcelona and Palma: 2011) offers a global analysis of Lullian dialogue.

93   Aragüés Aldaz, *Ramón Llull y la literatura ejemplar*, offers more detailed treatment of the following review of Lullian exemplary literature.

in order to insinuate tentatively the profound harmony that exists among all levels of Creation.

The recourse to comparison is also one of the rhetorical keys to the *Libre de l'orde de cavalleria* (1274–1276), written at the beginning of Llull's Quaternary Phase. This recourse embraces none the less forms and purposes that are ultimately very diverse. Many passages collate the practice of knighthood with other professions in medieval society, especially the clergy, who become a mirror for knights. These comparisons accord a precise and transcendent meaning to the principles and duties of knighthood, but many of them certainly lack the metaphorical distance and expressive purpose that seem essential to rhetorical similes.[94]

A more suggestive conception of exemplary literature appears in the contemporary *Doctrina pueril* (1274–1276), destined by Llull for educating his own son (and by extension, any young audience) in the fundamentals of Christian belief and other areas of knowledge. As a theoretical precept, it recommends providing "beautiful *exempla*" at the beginning of a speech, if one wishes to "speak rhetorically" (*Si tu, fils, vols parlar per retorica, dona bels aximplis de beles cozes al comensament de tes paraules*),[95] His desire to provide a text accessible to non-expert readers fills it with this type of exemplary passages, such as some very brief Gospel *conmemorationes* (regarding the poverty of Christ, Mary, and the apostles), as well as a considerable range of similes. These generally consist of simple, even naive, comparisons drawn from daily life, but still endowed always with unmistakable plasticity. For example, the body of Christ bled out in the Passion and Crucifixion is comparable to a "jar so broken that it could not hold even a drop of wine" (*enaxí con empola qui es ten forment trencada que no y pot romanir gens de vi*).[96] These passages thus popularize some of Llull's essential principles and seem to proliferate especially in certain chapters of the work. For example, in the chapter dedicated to Understanding or in the chapter devoted to the Sixth Beatitude. The latter abounds in comparisons between the material and spiritual worlds, while also implicating, in an increasingly profound way, the son whom the text addresses, by inviting him to consider the feelings of his own mother: "Beloved son, if your mother delights in seeing you, who are mortal and come from nothing ... how much more you

---

94   Mario Ruffini, "Lo stile del Lullo nel *Libre del Orde de Cavaylerie*," *EL* 3 (1959): 51–52, notes that these passages more properly pertain to the so-called *comparatio per collationem* rather than to the *similitudo* in a strict sense.

95   *Doctrina pueril* 78, (eds.) Joan Santanach i Suñol, NEORL 7:191. See also Jordi Rubió i Balaguer, "La *Rhetorica Nova* de Ramon Llull," in *Ramon Llull i el lul·lisme*, Obres de Jordi Rubió i Balaguer 3 (Barcelona: 1985), 208.

96   *Doctrina pueril* 8, (ed.) Santanach, NEORL 7:34–35.

should delight in seeing God, the Father and Lord of all that is" (*Amable fil, si la tua mare ha gran delit en veer tu, qui est mortal e est vengut de no-re (...) quant mes tu pots aver major pler en veer Deu, qui es par·e senyor de tot quant es*).[97] In this way, the text attains a familiar, almost intimate, tone, in keeping with this simple and tender use of similes. However, this kind of familiar reference also acquires a somewhat more transcendent meaning in the chapters on the Joys of the Virgin, where Llull invites his son to imagine his own crucifixion and resurrection, and then the reactions of his mother – converted into another Mary – in those circumstances.[98]

Greater complexity, and with a higher theoretical import, appears in another text from the same era, the *Libre dels àngels* (1276–1283?). Various similes appear in this work, illustrating the condition of the angels – both good and bad – with the properties of the sun and fire, or directly, of the four elements. The most interesting passages are surely those that illustrate the speech and conversation (*lucució*) of angels with images derived from human speech (an issue related to Llull's theory of *affatus*). Just as an evil person speaks with someone equally evil in order to express evil intentions, and both agree to do something wrong, so the bad angels communicate spiritually in order to realize evil deeds. Similarly, just as people cannot speak to each other without hearing themselves (or employing sign language), so the soul and an angel cannot communicate unless the latter comes very close to the former.[99] The sophistication of some of these comparisons belongs to a very different context than that represented by the simple similes from the *Doctrina pueril* or the *Libre de l'orde de cavalleria*. They are now very close to the transcendent conception of analogy reflected in the *Començaments de medicina*, where, as we have seen, Ramon Llull designs a new exemplary form, the *matafora*, capable of translating the complex principles of elemental exemplarism in an exact and rigorous way.

8.6.3   *Under the Sign of the Novel*: Blaquerna

Elemental exemplarism also permeates other exemplary forms, from simple comparisons to passages endowed with more or less developed narrative action. However, the emergence of the latter types cannot be separated from Llull's novelizing experiments. The choice of the novel and the recourse to these exemplary forms are products of the same literary vocation, of the same esteem for imagination and writing fiction.

---

97   Ibid. 42, (ed.) Santanach, NEORL 7:108.
98   Ibid. 48, (ed.) Santanach, NEORL 7:122.
99   *Libre dels àngels* 2.4 and 6.2, (eds.) Miquel Tous Gayà and Rafel Ginard Bauçà, ORL 21:334–342 and 374.

The first of these novels is the *Romanç d'Evast e Blaquerna*, at once a "sermon-novel," mirror of society, and Christian utopia, a work that demonstrates the fertile adaptation of very diverse readings and literary traditions. It embraces many motifs from the chivalric novel, applied in a plot with obvious hagiographical features. The use of exemplary forms thus constitutes one more projection of the exemplary nature that the novel as a whole displays, while demonstrating neatly, at the same time, the place that these short forms have found in oral culture and in religious writings throughout the 13th century. In this respect, the number of passages that allude to the use of *exempla* and comparisons by a wide range of characters is very significant. Most of these *exempla* do not appear in the novel, but it is not difficult to guess the features that Llull imagines for them, if we consider the character of his own *exempla* that he includes in the novel.

The exemplary discourse in *Blaquerna* still manifests considerable respect for the conventions of the genre. The text does include some brief exemplary mentions of historical events, usually from the Gospel. Still, as we know, the narrative flow of this work appears dominated by the fable and the verisimilar *exemplum*. The work includes at least five fables. With the exception of the fable about the monkeys and the firefly, which we have already considered, the rest of these fables seem to be the author's own compositions, though clearly preserving traditional traits. Verisimilar *exempla* are somewhat more abundant, although this model includes the most diverse examples, some of which seem to reproduce themes and arguments of oriental origin (and so closer to those of fables). Story-like features appear in the tale of the blind man, pursuing a rabbit, but led off a cliff by his own guide-dog,[100] or that of a man who drowned rather than travel five days to find a safe route across water.[101] On the other hand, some stories seem created by Llull in imitation of plots from collections of historical *exempla*, such as those that revolve around the opposition between Christian virtue and sin. In *Blaquerna* the recourse to verisimilar *exempla* provides an excellent compromise for reconciling Llull's enthusiasm for novelty with respect for traditional exemplary literature. The themes and plots in these stories would not have seemed strange to a reader familiar with contemporary collections of historical *exempla* or other anecdotes. Moreover, it is obvious that precisely this kind of *exemplum* fits most naturally in the context of a Lullian novel, constructed upon a verisimilar plot.

---

100   *Blaquerna* 2.54, (eds.) Soler and Santanach, NEORL 8:253.
101   Ibid. 4.87, (eds.) Soler and Santanach, NEORL 8:390.

8.6.4   *The Verisimilar* Exemplum *and Dialog: The* Libre de meravelles

Fèlix or the *Libre de meravelles* constitutes Llull's most deliberate foray into this world of verisimilar fiction. As in *Blaquerna*, that world defines the main plot of the novel, now somewhat more schematic, by focusing on the learning process of its protagonist, Fèlix, in a series of dialogues. Most of the stories incorporated into that plot correspond in turn to the model of the verisimilar *exemplum*. Nonetheless, in the *Libre de meravelles*, these stories occupy a central place, constructed with the rhetorical tool most often used by its characters to show the structure of reality. No fewer than five hundred stories enhance the dialogued plot of the work.[102] In this regard, the composition of the novel reveals an unprecedented creative effort.

The presence of these stories, moreover, constitutes only one more among the various facets of exemplarity in the text. It is not just a matter of *exempla* contributing to explicate metaphorically the structure of Creation, but rather the universe itself constitutes, at all levels, reflections of its Creator. Seen thus, the *Libre de meravelles* is both a novel and a peculiar kind of encyclopedia.[103] The lessons learned by Fèlix unfold in ten books corresponding to God, the angels, heaven, the four elements, plants, stones, animals, humans, paradise, and hell. The text traverses the various levels of existence. Throughout this journey, the education of Fèlix occurs through conversation: with the exception of the seventh book (the *Libre de les bèsties*) the text proffers a series of dialogues between its hero and the wise men encountered along his journey. At the end of his journey, Fèlix shares with them his accrued wisdom.

The text thus appears to pour out in its discourse, in a quest for wisdom, and in fulfillment of that quest. This context enables the circulation or interchange of *exempla* between Fèlix and his interlocutors. He occasionally poses questions about Creation throughout the narrative, but more often, it is the wise men who proffer their answers or illustrate them through stories. This exchange of information is not always simple or linear in nature. Many of the *exempla* are difficult to interpret, and the dialogues are full of doubts and requests for clarification, contextualization, or correction. Some of the stories therefore serve to clarify a previous story; others simply to justify a personal view, a position in a debate. Thus, if its plot is what justifies the appearance

---

102 Bonillo Hoyos, *Literatura al "Llibre de Meravelles,"* 107–128, offers a highly useful list of the exempla in the text.

103 Bonillo Hoyos, *Literatura al "Llibre de Meravelles,"* 37–50; Martín Pascual, "Algunes consideracions," 27; and Luzón Díaz, "Una aproximación," 265–266, analyze the dual novelistic and encyclopedic dimension of the text. Fernando Domínguez Reboiras, "Una lectura del *Llibre de meravelles* como *ars praedicandi,*" *Caplletra* 43 (2007): 131–160, reads it as a manual of preaching.

of the intercalated stories, the latter frequently appear to guide that plot, demanding responses from its characters, and the introduction of new stories. All of which clearly serves to confirm the central role of exemplary literature in the narrative construction of the novel.

Any reader would, in effect, perceive the presence of these stories as the chief literary contribution of this text. At times, the *Libre de meravelles* in fact appears to consist simply of a narrative repertory, built up almost entirely from verisimilar *exempla*, or even apparently relying on just one book (the *Libre de les bèsties*), which accentuates its autonomy within the work as a whole. The stories in the *Libre de meravelles* are populated with kings (often wise men) and knights (not always virtuous), with monks and hermits, with townspeople and philosophers. Some of their stories seem directly derived from Oriental sources, like the story of the king and the false alchemist, already present in the Arabic work of Al-Yawbarī a century before Llull, and later enjoying considerable popularity. Likewise the story of the blind man who recovers a thousand coins with another thousand that he does not have, a story related to known oriental moral fables about safeguarding treasure, documented early in Arabic tradition and later disseminated widely, both orally and in writing.[104] Still, many *exempla* from the *Libre de meravelles* best recall the tone of anecdotes from contemporary collections of historical *exempla*. Scholars have connected stories from the first book with *exempla* in the *Dialogus Miraculorum* or the *Alphabetum narrationum* of Arnold of Liège, and more broadly, other sections of the novel with other contemporary texts. Llull's debts to these works are, in any case, always partial. They reveal both his knowledge of that literature, and his definitive advances over it.[105] Building upon the foundation of collections of historical *exempla*, Llull devises a parallel repertory of fictional anecdotes, an original collection of verisimilar *exempla*.

The *Libre de meravelles* also shares with these collections of historical *exempla* a decided moral intention. Still, we should not forget that the didacticism of Llull's text appears guided once more by his theory of "first intention," and therefore that these moral teachings are only comprehensible within the framework of a more ambitious program, that of illustrating all features of

---

104   Marsan, *Itinéraire espagnol*, 388–394 and 461–464, analyzes both of these; on the second, see José Luis Agúndez García, "Cuentos populares andaluces (XXII)," *Revista de Folklore* 326 (2008): 60–72, and Fernando de la Granja, "Nunca más perro al molino," *Al-Andalus* 39 (1974): 431–442.

105   Ysern, "*Exempla* i estructures exemplars," analyzes these in the first book of the text, and Bonillo, *Literatura al "Llibre de Meravelles,"* 98–107, in other sections. Giuseppe E. Sansone, "Ramon Llull narratore," *Revista de Filología Española* 43 (1960): 86, emphasizes the distance between Llull's version and those in contemporary compilations.

Creation as means for knowing God. Toward this end, the stories recounted by the wise men in Llull's novel always treat human events, though often doing so to explain metaphorically the nature of angels, animals, plants, or stones. This lends to the text a strange, paradoxical tenor, which inverts contemporary exemplary conventions. Medieval readers were accustomed to understanding the moral and social conflicts that afflict humans through comparisons made to the natural world, through *exempla* taken from the spectacle of Creation. The *Libre de meravelles* proposes the opposite approach: metaphorically illustrating all levels of existence through dramatization of the most diverse situations involving humans.

8.6.5   *The Realm of the Fable: The* Libre de les bèsties

The *Libre de les bèsties*, the seventh of the books constituting the *Libre de meravelles*, possesses an exceptional character, for many reasons. Modern scholars have often suggested the possibility of the text's composition prior to the rest of the encyclopedic novel and its subsequent interpolation into it.[106] Whatever the circumstances of its composition, what remains indisputable is the enormous distance between the overall purpose of the *Libre de meravelles* and that of this little work, which fuses social criticism with political utopia to construct a guide to good government. This sense of autonomy is confirmed by examining its narrative methods. The basic structure of the *Libre de meravelles* actually breaks down in the *Libre de les bèsties*. The protagonist, Fèlix, appears only at the outset of this strange section, becoming thereafter a mere spectator of this long fable featuring animal characters. It recounts the efforts of the animals to choose a king (the lion), the election of a series of counselors (among which the ox plays a leading role), and the plotting by a fox seeking power (Na Renart), who is ultimately executed. All these animals occupy, in some way, the space reserved to Fèlix and his masters in the rest of the *Libre de meravelles*, assuming all of their abilities: the capacity for reflection (which allows them to share some of the best-known principles of Lullian thought),[107] the constant recourse to dialogue, and the incorporation of a whole gallery of stories that, conceived as a means of debate and of transmitting instruction, enhance the exemplary value of the book with further nuances of meaning.

---

106   See, among others, *Le livre des bêtes*, (ed.) Armand Llinarès, 12–16, but compare the opinion of John Dagenais, "New Considerations on the Date and Composition of Llull's *Libre de les bèsties*," in *Actes del Segon Col·loqui d'Estudis Catalans a Nord-Amèrica* (Yale, 1979) (Barcelona: 1982), 132–135.

107   Grimalt, "Notes sobre les fonts," 41, notes that the protagonist, Na Renart, mentions Llull's doctrine of "first intention;" cf. *Libre de meravelles* 7.37, (eds.) Badia et al., NEORL 10:223.

The animal plot of the *Libre de les bèsties* does not simply interrupt the narrative thread that the *Libre de meravelles* maintains before and after this section, but also effectively rejects what has been its founding principle: verisimilitude. This seeming betrayal also affects the other intercalated stories, given the presence among them of numerous fables. Along with these fables, the *Libre de les bèsties* includes a considerable number of *exempla* featuring human characters, whose presence in the mouths of animals clearly assumes a curious "inversion of reality." However, it cannot be said that events in which animals converse or tell stories would have seemed strange to Llull's readers. On the contrary, many of them would have found in these events a world more familiar than the one that fills other passages from the *Libre de meravelles*. The *Libre de les bèsties* simply reproduces a literary model well-known in its era, though born centuries before in the East.

This undisguised debt to oriental storytelling constitutes one final indication of the distance between this text and the other sections of the *Libre de meravelles*. The general plot of the *Libre de les bèsties* constitutes, as we know, an adaptation of the organizing story from an Arabic collection of tales, *Kalila wa-Dimna*. Many of the stories intercalated in Llull's little text also clearly constitute adaptations of stories from Oriental sources. One verisimilar tale seems based on part of the main plot of *Sendebar*. Another story has its origin in the *Thousand and One Nights*. Nine or ten of its stories appear, with more or less variation, in *Kalila wa-Dimna,* but only one of these constitutes a verisimilar story. The remaining stories correspond instead to the model of the fable or, at least, feature animal protagonists, although on occasion these appear endowed with human powers, such as speech. It is more difficult to identify which specific versions of these oriental stories Blessed Ramon manipulates in the composition of his text. With regard to *Kalila wa-Dimna*, Llull may have had access to the Arabic original, to the Latin translation by John of Capua, or (less probably) to the Castilian version produced under the auspices of Alfonso X. In any case, and as indicated already, it seems necessary to suppose that the appearance of material from *Kalila wa-Dimna* in the *Libre de les bèsties* was the product of an intermediary text, from which would have derived as well one of the fables in *Blaquerna* (the monkey and the firefly). That text may well have been a modified translation of *Kalila wa-Dimna*, or a miscellany of Oriental material (as some scholars have suggested), from the hand of Llull or another.[108]

---

108   Llinarès (ed.), *Le livre des bêtes*, 19, suggests such an intermediary compilation. See also, regarding the doubt about the version of *Kalila wa-Dimna* closest to Llull's text: Llinarès, "Les singes, le ver luisant et l'oiseau," 98–99; Martín Pascual, "Algunes consideracions,"

In addition, to stories of oriental provenance Llull also joins no lesser number of original *exempla*, fifteen in all, among which figure eleven verisimilar
exempla, three fables, and one allegorical story. Despite its mix of original and
non-original *exempla*, the *Libre de les bèsties* displays an absolutely uniform
and harmonious tone, the fruit of a kind of formal and thematic convergence
between one passage and another.

8.6.6   *New Paths: The* Arbre Exemplifical

The onset of the Ternary Phase of Llull's Art in 1290 establishes a new context for his exemplary literature. As indicated at the outset of this study, it
is difficult to evaluate exactly the consequences of this shift. Obviously, the
replacement of elemental exemplarism by his "intrinsic" demonstrative model
(born from application of his theory of "correlatives") necessarily implies some
displacement of analogical and metaphorical methods. But we have seen that
elemental exemplarism continues to thrive as an alternative method of illustration, in support of which Ramon Llull recommends the use of metaphors
and other comparative devices in the founding text of his Ternary Phase, the
Ars inventiva veritatis. Moreover, exemplary literature is also able to accept
the new tenets of his Art, just as it is able to continue supporting in general
the clarification and dissemination of any scientific or ethical subject treated
by Llull.

At the same time, the Ternary Phase witnesses a change in orientation in the
writings of Blessed Ramon, resulting in abandonment of his novelizing experiments, with a few exceptions, such as the "Vagaries of Love" (*Accidents d'amor*),
a sentimental story included in the later *Arbre de filosofia d'amor*.[109] But this
abandonment does not seem to have occasioned an immediate decline in
his production of *exempla*. To the contrary, the latter remains one of the only
arenas in which Llull can pursue his taste for literature, forcing acknowledge-
ment of an obvious paradox: if composing novels has enabled the emergence
of the Lullian *exemplum*, their rejection favors its consolidation as an essential
recourse for disseminating in literature the tenets of his thought, something
that becomes evident above all in the *Arbre exemplifical*, composed in his Ternary Phase. The evolution of Llull's writing surely needs reinterpretation in the
light of this increasing faith in the value of the exemplary genre. This evolution
is a quest for the literary expression best-suited to his Art: an expression that
has its first attempts in the comparisons from the *Libre de contemplació*, which

---

101–106; Martín Pascual, "Huella del *Calila e Dimna*," 85–86; Grimalt, "Notes sobre les
fonts," 42–45; and Hauf, "Sobre l' *Arbor exemplificalis*," 314–315.

109   Badia, Santanach, and Soler, "Ramon Llull," 403, 465.

is consolidated in the fables and stories of *Blaquerna* and in the far more numerous examples from the *Libre de meravelles*, but that only attains maturity
in the new stories of the *Arbre exemplifical*. Badia has insightfully observed
that attributing to Llull a rejection of "literature" in his Ternary Phase rests
upon a rigid conception of this term, a concept anachronistic and incapable
of comprehending the "literary" dimension of Llull's writing and the role that
exemplary forms play in it. Designed as an efficient means for the "transmuta-
tion of knowledge into literature," the *exempla* of the *Arbre exemplifical* effectively constitute the definitive locus of convergence between "knowledge and
its pleasing expression" intended by Llull from the beginning.[110]

The *Arbre exemplifical* and the *Arbre qüestional* constitute the two final
books of the *Arbre de sciencia*. Their purpose is to restate, through their respective series of brief forms, the theoretical precepts of the fourteen prior books
of this work, which, for their part, attempt to offer a comprehensive review of
all knowledge and, at the same time, to render more accessible the principles
of Llull's Art expounded in the *Tabula generalis* of 1293–1294. The instruction
provided in the *exempla* of the *Arbre exemplifical* therefore displays a much
closer connection with the principles of the Lullian Art, while also adopting
the innovations of its Ternary Phase, though still with a notable presence of
elementary exemplarism from its previous phase. The narrative foundation of
these passages also takes on a new appearance: although the *Arbre exemplifical*
certainly includes examples of narrative genres already employed by Llull
(fables, miracle stories, and verisimilar *exempla*), the text essentially relies on
"artful" *exempla*, created by personifying the gallery of beings found in every
material and spiritual level of reality. In addition, these passages adopt without differentiation the form of stories and proverbs, marking thus the onset
of Llull's interest in the latter genre, of great importance in his later writings.

Overall, the most significant innovation in the *Arbre exemplifical* is perhaps its structure: in this text passages appear simply juxtaposed, without
any novelizing frame, while also independent of the content that they illustrate. Conceived as an exclusive collection of brief genres, the text nonetheless
does not constitute simply an appendix for facilitating comprehension of the
teachings in the *Arbre de sciencia*: rather, it displays the character of a true
instrumentum, a useful repertory of material suitable for readers to employ in
their own discourses. Still, none of this should imply that its overall design

---

110   Pring-Mill, "Els recontaments," 307–317; Badia, "Literatura alternativa,"12; Cabré, Ortín,
       and Pujol, "'Coneixer e haver moralitats bones';" Hauf, "Sobre l' *Arbor exemplificalis*;" and
       Badia, Santanach, and Soler, "Ramon Llull," 459–464.

lacks interest: its procession of *exempla* offers an orderly tour of the analogical structure of the universe, a systematic re-reading of the "Book of Creation."

8.6.7   *A Look Back: The* Rhetorica Nova

Five years after writing the *Arbre exemplifical*, Ramon Llull offers a new repertory consisting only of *exempla*: the section of twenty-four *pulcra exempla* from the *Rhetorica nova*. Once again, these passages appear here juxtaposed, independent of any fictional frame. And, as in the case of the *Arbre exemplifical*, the exemplary material from the *Rhetorica nova* comprises an orderly survey of Creation, but with the notable difference that the very complex itinerary, in ascending order, from the *Arbre*, here gives way to a brief and simple tour of the scale of being, in descending order.

The *exempla* from this text display, moreover, a kind of compromise or attempt at reconciliation between defending Llull's own proposals (realized from the long maturation of his literary production and largely unavoidable) and a concession (much more obvious than in his earlier works) to the conventions of the genre and to the expectations of readers familiar with this type of literature. This collection includes, in effect, samples of Llull's successive efforts and attempts in the world of exemplary forms. It thus collects various passages created to support his Art, whether by reproducing his theory of divine likenesses or by exploring anew the elemental exemplarism found in his work almost from its very beginning. This collection also presents a verisimilar *exemplum* (about a hypocritical bishop),[111] like those adorning his novels, as well as three fables: two derived from *Kalila wa-Dimna* and already found in his *Libre de les bèsties* ("The crane and the crab" and "The monkey, the firefly, and the bird") and a third that recalls the main plot of the latter work (the fox conspires to join the council of the lion, the king of beasts, despite the reservations of other characters).[112] The three fables, on their own, symbolize to perfection the intersection of storytelling tradition and Llull's exemplary schemes.

However, as we have said, this text also concedes space to other varieties much more frequent in contemporary sermons. Seen thus, one must recognize the enormous quantitative importance of the text's similes concerning nature (half of the twenty-four examples) and above all, that many of them display a character very different from that found in Llull's earlier works. Indeed, the appearance of these similes in the *Rhetorica nova* seems to have resulted, in more than one instance, from consultation of popular bestiaries and lapidaries. Equally significant is the space conceded in this section, even if limited, to

---

111   *Rhetorica nova* 2.4.6, (ed.) Johnston, 17.
112   Ibid. 2.4.11–13, (ed.) Johnston, 18–21.

the historical *exemplum*, through its mention of the Passion and Crucifixion of Christ as a model for virtuous people. This Christological lesson is undeniably essential to Llull's thought, but its inclusion in this collection (alongside other classical *exempla* in other sections of the work) perhaps indicates his awareness of the prominence of this genre in the tastes of his readers. Definitively, the discursive context of the *Rhetorica nova*, conceived as a general art of discourse, does not dictate Llull's choice of a single exemplary model, but rather of the genre's openness to all of its forms and possible applications.

8.6.8   *Treatises and Sermons: Exemplary Forms in the Later Work*

Shortly after writing the *Rhetorica nova*, Ramon Llull brought forth the truly analogical monument that is the *Liber de lumine* (1303). Still, many more of his works from this era continue demonstrating the value of the exemplary genre for illustrating and adorning. Mid-way between the verisimilar story and the allegorical story stands the chapter devoted to the "Honor of Love" (*De les honors d'amor*) in the *Arbre de filosofia d'amor* [Tree of the Philosophy of Love] of 1298, a text created to make more accessible, by means of narrative, the contents of the *Art amativa*, a mystical version, in turn, of the *Ars inventiva veritatis* of 1290.[113] Neither is exemplary literature lacking in theological debates, such as the *Disputatio fidei et intellectus* (1303). In this work, Faith and Reason, duly personified, attempt to defend their respective arguments through stories, some already used in Llull's other works, transferring to a separate narrative level the same dispute that sustains the text's frame story.[114] Among the more interesting are Llull's juridical works such as the *Ars de iure* (1304) or the *Ars brevis de inventione iuris* (1308). These texts include diverse similes and comparisons but provide a much more accommodating space for brief forms in their final sections, dedicated to *quaestiones*, that is, to examples of practical cases. As we know, these practical cases maintained a productive relationship with storytelling throughout the medieval juridical tradition. In many of the cases from Llull's texts, there appear the same characters and conflicts that inspired the verisimilar *exempla* of the *Libre de meravelles*. Compared to the latter, the *quaestiones* from the *Ars de iure* seem true *exempla* in miniature, although perhaps the reverse perspective might be more appropriate: we know that many of the earlier Lullian stories are nothing more than literary adaptations of sophisticated legal and theological cases.[115]

---

113   *Arbre de filosofia d'amor* 6.3, (ed.) Salvador Galmès, ORL 18:197–204.

114   *Disputatio fidei et intellectus* 1.1, 1.5 and 1.8, (ed.) Euler, ROL 23:226, 231, 233.

115   *Ars de iure* 2.2.A-B, (ed.) Jordi Gayà Estelrich, ROL 20:157, 160, and 162; *Ars brevis de inventione iuris*, (ed.) Aloisius Madre, ROL 12:274, 281, 301–302, and 347–351. See Colom Ferrá, "Ramon Llull y los orígenes," 40.

Llull's treatises on sermons confirm, in a theoretical domain, the acknowledged value of the exemplary genre in contemporary preaching. The *Liber de
praedicatione* (1304) recommends beginning a sermon by means "of a metaphor, proverb, or *exemplum*" (*per metaphora vel per proverbium vel exemplum*)
and illustrates this precept with a lengthy story, adapted from the *Arbre exemplifical*.[116] The *Liber de praedicatione* includes, moreover, a *corpus* of one hundred sermons, presented as homiletic models, capable of application ad hoc
as needed by individual preachers. A quick review of these hundred sermons
reveals how far Llull's homiletics also resorts to linking comparative forms
and analogical reflections, not always rigorously grounded in his Art. Finally, exemplary literature also makes an appearance in the *Summa sermonum*,
which includes the corpus of homiletic and catechetic material composed by
Blessed Ramon on Majorca in 1212–1213, that is, in the post-Art phase of his
career.[117] It is true that the examples appearing in these texts now demonstrate
Llull's neglect of exemplary forms developed as narratives, in favor of assiduously employing more obviously simple forms that are essentially similes. It
is useless to seek in these sermons the humor of the fable or the imaginative
daring of Llull's "artful" stories. Llull's gradual abandonment of fiction during
his Ternary Phase ultimately led him to discard these two exemplary genres.
The trajectory of Llull's literary production, his quest for a formula of expression, ultimately "denatures" his own exemplary literature, reducing it to its
most profitable types, or perhaps simply to those most comprehensible to his
audience. In these late writings, little seems to remain of that "taste for telling"
distilled into the *Libre de meravelles* or the *Arbre exemplifical*.[118]

8.7   Narrative Artifices: Specular Play

8.7.1   *The Plot and Its Stories*
Ramon Llull's production of *exempla* offers an ample space for narrative
experimentation, both with respect to the internal design of their sequenc-
es and with respect to their "specular" relationship with the discursive frame
that surrounds them. All of this is evident in a special (though of course not

---

116   *Liber de praedicatione* 2.A.1.3, (ed.) Abraham Soria Flores, ROL 31:399.
117   See Lola Badia, "*Raimundi Lulli Opera Latina*, XV: Ramon Llull i la predicació," *Llengua &
        Literatura* 3 (1988–1989): 574–575.
118   Badia and Bonner, *Ramón Llull*, 202; Bonner, *L'Art i la lògica*, 297; and Tous Prieto, "La
        forma proverbi," 28, all discuss the relative decline of exemplary literature in Llull's post-
        Art Phase, parallel to his abandonment of other forms such as metaphor.

exclusive) way in his novels. A glance at the *Libre de meravelles* discussed above is sufficient. The novel takes shape, as we have seen, through successive encounters between its protagonist and various wise men, from whose dialogs arise hundreds of stories. The structure of these becomes very diverse, although they fundamentally obey two possible models: many take the form of an anecdote (that is, a sequence of actions and conflicts, ultimately resolved), while others are limited to reporting a very brief dialogue between two characters (frequently, a master and his disciple).

In the first model, the plot of the anecdote answers, in metaphorical fashion, the problem posed in the frame story. This happens, for example, in a tale told by a hermit in response to Fèlix's amazement that the world could have been created from nothing. In the story, a king sends a knight to fight at another court. Shortly afterwards, a maiden visits the king and reports the knight's victory. The news, received with enormous joy, is actually an invention of the maiden. The moral of the story is obvious: if the king can rejoice about something that was nothing and non-existent, with far more reason was God able to make the world from nothing.[119] The simplicity of this example should not, however, deceive us. Interpretation of the stories can sometimes pose enormous difficulty, usually as a result of the distance that exists between the literal and allegorical levels of a story. It can also be due to a kind of lack of symmetry between the two levels. Obvious cases are those stories with a lesson inferred not from their complete plots, but rather from some aspect of the plot that is perhaps tangential or apparently secondary. There are in fact numerous Lullian *exempla* that require an "oblique" reading for their exegesis, just as there are also many that, far from offering the solution for a problem, serve only to suggest some keys for Fèlix (and the reader) to find the solution on their own.[120]

The *exempla* corresponding to our second model (a brief dialogue between a master and his disciple) are rather diverse. Many of these *exempla* reproduce with absolute symmetry the same situation as the frame story in which they occur: a question from Fèlix to one of his masters prompts the latter's narration of a dialogue story. Even more: at times, a question from Fèlix himself reappears, literally, in the mouth of the disciple in the story, so that the master's response to this answers precisely the question of the novel's hero. The absolute simplicity of these very brief stories, which display a certain underutilization of the recourses of exemplarity, has perhaps not attracted sufficient

---

119   *Libre de meravelles* 50.6, (eds.) Badia et al., NEORL 10:108.

120   Jordi Gayà Estelrich, "Sobre algunes estructures literaries del *Llibre de meravelles*," *Randa* 10 (1980): 67–68.

emphasis. These stories generally appear naked, with a minimal degree of narrativity, and therefore lack as well any metaphorical value. Their only purpose seems to be displacing, into another narrative level, an answer that could have been offered directly. The characters in these stories are little more than masks, behind which the reader perceives in a transparent way, the voices of the protagonists from the frame story. Apart from this modest function, these characters (and their stories) have no reason to exist.

This shift, into an anecdote, of the problem under consideration in the frame story does sometimes occur with more sophistication. Fèlix asks, in a passage from the first book, how the apostles, so few in number, could convert so many people. Blaquerna answers him with a story: a student of philosophy marvels that one spark of fire is enough to burn as much wood as one wishes, a problem that his master explicates with a very relevant image, that of the apostles who were able to convert masses because inflamed by divinely inspired grace.[121] Thanks to the latter phrase, the story offers a literal and absolutely exact response to the question posed by Fèlix in the frame story, but it does so through a curious circumlocution, since the image of the apostles is, within the level of the story, an ingenious metaphor for illustrating its central issue, the power of fire. Of course this circumlocution is not pointless: both Fèlix and the novel's readers can reverse that metaphor in order to discover within the image of fire a precious comparison to the matter of real interest to them, namely the miraculous missionary effort of the disciples of Christ. There is no lack, in the *Libre de meravelles*, of stories with exegesis that requires a simple reversal or exchange of its literal and allegorical elements. These passages fill the novel with inverted reflections between the frame story and the narrative levels subordinated to it, and thus enable introduction of the allegorizing so desired by its author.

This allegorizing can also color more suggestively these dialogue stories. Toward the end of book three, Fèlix asks a shepherd why the sun seems larger in the morning than at noon. The shepherd tells a story in which a philosopher strolls through a lovely garden after eating in order to promote digestion; there a student asks him the same question posed by Fèlix, and the philosopher explains how morning vapors, thick and undigested because not yet purged by the heat of the sun itself, distort the shape of the sun in the morning. Once again, the answer to Fèlix's question appears explicitly in the mouth of a character from a story, this time without the analogical inversion found in the previous example. The allegorical dimension of the philosopher's story necessarily arises from its own plot, a plot certainly thin, though in no way

---

121   *Libre de meravelles* 1.12, (eds.) Badia et al., NEORL 10:138.

gratuitous. The philosopher's initial stroll seeking agreeable digestion constitutes a metaphorical referent for illuminating the central question of the tale
and its frame story: the undigested quality of morning airs and the need for the
sun to purify them.[122] By means of a very slight complication in their plots, dialogued *exempla* can approximate the anecdotal tales of the first model, with
which they often mix and fuse in the course of the novel.

8.7.2   *The Story-within-a-story*

The *exempla* from the *Libre de meravelles* can also attain a much more complex
structure, since any of their characters can become, in turn, the narrator of
a new story. Ramon Llull manipulates this recourse with complete freedom,
which permits the indefinite multiplication of narrative levels in the novel. As
a result, the text is full of specular correspondences and echoes, which affirm
the careful experimental labor invested in its composition.

Each of the stories introduced successively in the novel seeks, in general
lines, to offer the literal or metaphorical answer for a question posed in the
immediately preceding narrative level. When these levels multiply, they can
give rise once more to a curious play of identities and differences between
the respective lessons of each successively intercalated story. This process can
nonetheless become considerably sophisticated, to the point of permitting one
single story to answer various different questions, posed in successive levels of
narration. For example, in the third book, Fèlix formulates for his interlocutor,
a shepherd, this question: "Sir, why is the moon larger at some times than at
others?" (*Senyer, per que la luna es major en un temps que en altre?*). The shepherd initially marvels at this treatment as "sir" (*senyer*), but then understands
that it corresponds to his wisdom, rather than to his appearance or sumptuous
dress. From this point, the shepherd's purpose becomes dual: illustrating the
recently posed issue of vanity, and at the same time, answering Fèlix's question
about the moon. He therefore offers an *exemplum*, which recounts the efforts
of a woman to adorn herself and so appear more beautiful, and her husband's
opposition to this behavior. However, this *exemplum* includes a new story, told
by the husband to his wife and friends, in which the sun one day shines with
full splendor upon the moon, which becomes vainly proud, and so the sun
decides to conceal its light, placing the earth between itself and the moon.
This short tale serves to warn the vain woman in the surrounding story and
sheds light, in passing, on the problem posed in the frame story (Fèlix's question about the varying size of the moon).[123] Stories like these constitute the

---

122   Ibid. 3.18, (eds.) Badia et al., NEORL 10:161–162.
123   Ibid. 3.18, (eds.) Badia et al., NEORL 10:162–163. See Taylor, "Some complexities," 649.

best example of Llull's ability to manipulate recourses of exemplarity. The very brief intercalated story discussed above ties together and answers the questions posed in two preceding levels of narration, establishing thus a "dialogue" between both levels, upon which it depends not only for its narrative subordination, but also for the ultimate design of its plot.

8.7.3   *Mise en Abŷme*

Llull's procedures for inserting narratives can also display much more audacious contours. In this respect, one of the most eloquent and delightful chapters in the *Libre de meravelles*, from its fifth book, concerns the decay of trees. Here, two dependent narrative levels, consisting of intercalated examples, are subordinated to the frame story. In the latter, Félix and his interlocutor, a solitary philosopher, observe how a man cuts down a beautiful, but unfruitful, tree. Shortly afterwards they observe a second tree, with many limbs broken from the weight of numerous fruits. Fèlix asks how a tree can cause its own destruction, and the philosopher responds with his first story, about two brothers who display opposing behaviors. One brother is a bishop, handsome but incapable of fulfilling his duties, like the tree without fruit. The other brother is a knight, who works day and night to maintain justice in a city, to the point of endangering his health, like the tree with fruit. One day, a madman rebukes the bishop for behaving so differently than his brother, which prompts the intervention of a wise cleric, who introduces the second story. The latter establishes, on the one hand, subtle connections with the rural setting of the frame story, and, on the other, with the story of the bishop and his brother in which it occurs. It describes a vineyard that includes two apple trees, one beautiful but sterile, and the other weighted down with fruit. The two trees obviously symbolize the two brothers in the first story, but also recall (or, simply are) the two trees from the frame story. Their reappearance at this deep level within the narrative evokes an obvious surprise, which the story extends by presenting the owner of the vineyard as he orders the removal of the first apple tree (something that ultimately occurs in the frame story). The circular (and potentially infinite) nature of this *mise en abŷme* prompts a paradoxical impression on the reader, a strange sensation of irreality. The story thus constructs a narrative mechanism that truly manipulates the boundaries of verisimilitude in a kind of illusionist game, in what constitutes a felicitous transgression of the techniques most common in story-telling of his era.[124]

---

124   *Libre de meravelles* 5.31, (eds.) Badia et al., NEORL 10:197–199. The echoes among the three narrative levels do not end here, as the chapter introduces several more *exempla* and digressions. Badia, Santanach, and Soler, "Ramon Llull," 453–455, offer an excellent

The play of mirrors between the narrative level of the story and that of frame story also takes on very ingenious contours in one of the first scenes from the *Libre de les bèsties*. There, the bear, the leopard, and the lynx, unable to decide between the lion and the horse as their future king, request postponement of the election. The fox, supporting the lion, tells a story in which the canons of a church must choose a bishop but, unable to agree, elect instead a man of weak and lewd character. Faced with this situation, one canon offers a brief reflection, in which the characters, surprisingly, are the animals from the frame story: according to the canon, if the lion ends up as king without support from the bear, the lynx, and the leopard in its election, the lion will despise them. On the other hand, if the horse wins election, but the lion offends him, he cannot defend himself from the lion. The minimal fable told by the canon apparently seeks to illustrate metaphorically the dilemma posed in his church by the unworthy bishop, but the reality is just the opposite: the story of the new bishop is, at best, a vehicle for illustrating metaphorically the risks of electing a bad king in the frame story. It could even be something simpler: a mere narrative illusion (a true mirror-image) astutely devised by the fox in order to offer its literal opinion about the ideal king. Thanks to this story within a story, and by means of a double metaphorical "turn," the words of the fox return precisely to the same point as the beginning of its speech (an explicit defense of the lion). The latter is the only issue of interest for advancing the narrative: we learn nothing about the subsequent condition of the church that needed a bishop (the story is effectively incomplete), but the bear, the lynx, and the leopard decide, after hearing the fox, to support election of the proposed candidate as their king.[125] Despite the brevity of this passage, it is impossible not to recognize in it an echo of the careful artifice apparent elsewhere in the *Libre de meravelles*. The exact reappearance of the animals who are main characters of the plot within a lower narrative level – the reflection offered by a human character from a story invented by one of the animals – is indeed surprising. It confronts us once more with a paradoxical circularity, with the vertigo of an impossible *mise en abŷme*, thanks to its transgression of narrative logic as slight as it is ingenious.

---

analysis of the theological, moral, and natural scientific contents of the story. For the concept of "mise en abŷme," see Lucien Dällenbach, *Le récit spéculaire: Essai sur la mise en abŷme* (Paris: 1977).

125   *Libre de meravelles* 7.37, (eds.) Badia et al., NEORL 10:234.

8.7.4   *Irreality*

The sensation of irreality in Lullian exemplary literature can occur in other ways, for example, through the actual narrative substance of some passages. This is especially apparent in the *Arbre exemplifical*. The mere presence of "artful" stories situates us within an absolutely odd atmosphere, which manifests fully Llull's attempt to manipulate and to transgress the boundaries of the exemplary genre. Having broken with all the conventions of traditional storytelling, the "artful" *exemplum* at times offers the appearance of a simple verbal construct or artifice.

The irreality of such stories is apparent even more notably in those cases where entities from the Lullian Art (the vices and virtues, the four elements, the faculties of the soul) engage in dialog within a story, becoming thus narrators of a verisimilar story with human protagonists. Examples of this authentic "inversion of reality" are abundant. The tenth section of the chapter on roots in the *Arbre exemplifical* includes, for example, a story featuring two knights litigating over ownership of a castle. They both bribe the judge, one with a thousand florins and the other only a hundred. Their king, learning of the matter, inquires in his council about the cause of the dispute. A wise man realizes that the knight with a hundred florins was the legitimate owner of the castle and therefore did not want to spend an excessive amount on what belonged to him by right. This true *exemplum* of Solomonic judgement rightly belongs to the lovely panoply of verisimilar stories provided by Llull in this and other works. However, in this case, it is narrated by the allegorical character Dryness in order to excuse its intervention as judge in a dispute between the Rose and the Pepper, opposing one another in an argument over the respective merits of Water and Fire.[126]

The *Arbre exemplifical* houses the most daring and most conventional *exempla*, combining them variously thanks to its obvious proliferation of narrative levels. This text thus opens considerable space for exercising the exemplary strategies already practiced in the *Libre de meravelles*, filling them with specular play and echoes. Especially interesting, in this regard, are certain passages, like the one crafted in the *exemplum* for the branch of Sensation. This story begins with a plot typical of an animal fable, in which a young rat tells her mother of her wish to befriend a kitten playing with a feather, supposing that the kitten would be too young to know the "contrarity" between their respective species. Thanks to this friendship, thinks the young rat, the kitten would not harm it when grown older. The mother responds with a verisimilar story. In it, a burgher kills a knight, and seeks to restore peace among their friends

---

126   *Arbre de ciència* 15.1, (eds.) Carreras i Artau and Carreras i Artau, *OE* 1:802.

by marrying his daughter to the son of the victim; at this point, the wife of the burgher offers a fable, featuring a horse and a lion. These two decide to go on pilgrimage, but at the last moment the horse decides not to go, given the risk of being devoured by the lion if it finds itself without food. The fable causes the burgher to reflect, and he decides not to marry his daughter, remembering that knights are arrogant and "do not forgive offenses" (*no perdonen a fellonia*).[127] This lengthy passage ends here, without explaining clearly the resolution of the story that initiated it (the young rat and her mother). Such an explanation of course becomes absolutely unnecessary, since the outcome of the fable appears tacitly reflected (and anticipated) in the two stories subordinated within its plot. These three levels of narration essentially reproduce the same story. This multiplication, potentially endless, of one same plot, is the best example of the experimental nature so often displayed in Llull's *exempla*.

8.8   Narrative Virtuality

8.8.1   *Provisional Stories*

Ramon Llull's zeal for experimentation, and the sense of irreality that his plots and narrative structures generate, are inseparable from another feature, mentioned initially in these pages: this is the provisional, almost ephemeral air that some of the stories display inside his works. Most of the stories from the Lullian novels are fictions created *ex professo* in order to illuminate specific questions in a particular moment. This appears to be the function that they serve "within" their fictions. We should not, therefore, imagine that Llull's characters have heard and memorized these stories in any moment prior to their appearance in the novel: instead, their originality invites us to accept them as the products of his imagination, or perhaps better, of his talent for improvisation.

The existence of these passages begins and ends in a single expression, and that sensation of fugacity becomes even more acute in the case of a work such as the *Libre de meravelles*, as we consider the immense proportions of its exemplary corpus, the dizzying parade of hundreds of stories in the course of its ten books. The very nature of these stories reinforces this impression. A good number of them, as we know, are constructed from a limited number of human scenarios, conflicts, and archetypes, combined in a thousand different ways. This combinatory exercise can be see as well in the *Arbre exemplifical*. There, the generation of many passages obeys, without disguise, an almost mechanical procedure, yielding the orderly construction of narrative plots based on the

---

127   *Arbre de ciència* 15.3.3, (eds.) Carreras i Artau and Carreras i Artau, *OE* 1:810.

systematic reproduction of the relationships among the beings presented in the *Arbre de sciencia*. There, just as in the *Libre de meravelles*, some stories take on the appearance of mere narrative hypotheses, created to be reformulated over and over, giving rise to new narrative constructions, each as provisional as the one before.

In the *Libre de meravelles*, one story can actually serve two different purposes in two different moments. In the eighth book, addressing the sin of sloth, the hermit who speaks with Fèlix introduces the case of a hospital ruined by the neglect of its administrators and by the inaction of the local bishop and his chapter, to whom a wealthy founder had entrusted its care. This is almost exactly the point of departure for an *exemplum* told by the same hermit in the tenth book, dedicated to the punishments of hell, but in this case the story is much more complex. The story initially begins by recounting the ruin of the hospital due to the neglect of a (single) administrator and of the bishop entrusted with this care. At first, this prompts Fèlix to reflect on the possible eternal condemnation of the bishop, which is the theme of the chapter. However, after this initial reflection, which would seem to end the story, it concludes with two more episodes, without clearly indicating whether the narrator of these additions is the hermit or Fèlix himself (as the syntax of the passage seems to suggest).[128] The first of these added episodes tells the story of a cleric who, after extinguishing a fire during the night, is unable to rise and attend to a dying man, thus causing his eternal damnation. Even more surprising is the second episode, in which the bishop from the beginning of the story reappears to rebuke the lazy cleric for neglecting the dying man, while the cleric scolds the bishop for neglecting the ruin of the hospital. The latter story establishes a convenient connection between the core of the original *exemplum* and its strange continuation. Above all, however, it affirms the open, provisional character of its plot. The story told by the hermit in the eighth book lacks a fixed ending and if, as it appears, the narrator of its continuation in the tenth book is Fèlix, neither can it be regarded as the property of a single author.

The provisionality of Llull's stories is more than a vague impression: it has clear narrative consequences and calls into question the laws that govern the discursive logic of his stories. In extreme cases, the stories from the *Libre de meravelles* can adopt an almost virtual, simply illusory air. In the first book, Fèlix asks why there are no prophets in the present day, and the answer from Blaquerna consists exclusively of a story: a king sends messengers throughout

---

128   *Libre de meravelles* 10.121, (ed.) Bonner, *Obres selectes*, 2:387–388, where the latter favors
         this possibility, as does Bonillo Hoyos, "Els exemples," 66–68. Compare *Libre de meravelles*
         8.72, (ed.) Bonner, *Obres selectes*, 2:240, for the first version of the story.

his realm, charged with announcing assembly of a court for honoring his son, for knighting him, and for ceding to him the crown. Once the court is over, the messengers' work is done. The allegorical correspondence of the king, his son, and the messengers with God, Christ, and the prophets is so obvious that Fèlix requires no explanation. Shortly afterwards, Fèlix in fact continues pursuing some questions about the matter, but with exclusive reference to the characters in the story. In one of these, Fèlix asks why the messengers died before the court took place, a question obviously relevant to the prophets, dead before the coming of Christ, but unrelated to Blaquerna's story, in which they simply end their mission after the court assembly, and so are alive both before and after the event. This slight discrepancy betrays the true meaning of this *exemplum* for Fèlix (and for Ramon Llull as well): it is not simply a univocal and immutable literary element, but rather a flexible fiction, capable of reformulation in the evolving course of the requirements of a conversation. The characters in the story likewise lack individuality: they are simply "names" for designating, in a transparent metaphor, the beings of true importance in this conversation from the frame story. The initial story is little more than a pretext, a point of departure for advancing the dialogue, and as such susceptible to betrayal.[129]

8.8.2   *Meta-exemplarity*

The versatility of Lullian stories, their apparently "open" character, is surely the most obvious sign of the "dual" purpose that guides the proposition of these stories in his work. The *exempla* of Ramon Llull seek not only to illuminate metaphorically, for his readers, the principles of his Art or the design of the universe: above all, they aspire to train the reader in manipulating the tools of analogy, that is, in the task of interpreting and elaborating *exempla*.

All this becomes evident in the *Arbre exemplifical*. The structure of this text reflects (in some respect "inverted") the design of the *Arbre de sciencia*. As we know, the latter offers a review of all knowledge by means of fourteen books or thematic "trees" (from the elements to God) each divided in turn into seven sections (roots, trunk, limbs, branches, leaves, flowers, and fruits). The *Arbre exemplifical* is organized into these same seven sections, each capable in turn of division into fourteen parts, one for each of the trees in the encyclopedia. But this final scheme of divisions remains unrealized, since Llull does not develop all of its possible parts nor all of the theoretical possibilities that each part implicates. Llull's focus and desire for brevity make the contents of the *Arbre exemplifical* only a small sample of the material that a full "exemplification of the Art" might yield, as his prologue explicitly indicates, but nonetheless

---

129   *Libre de meravelles* 1.11, (eds.) Badia et al., NEORL 10:134.

a valuable sample for readers to "find new proverbs and new stories, and to extend their knowledge through the vast contents of this Tree" (*doctrina darem com hom se pusca haver a atrobar novells proverbis e novells recontaments, e estendre son enteniment per la gran matèria d'aquest arbre*).[130] In this respect, the incomplete nature of the *Arbre exemplifical* seems not so much a lack, as an invitation for readers to participate in reflection and in their own metaphorical dissemination of Llull's Art, conceived thus as an open and incomplete endeavor.

That value of Lullian exemplary literature as a model or "paradigm" for the invention of new *exempla* by the reader appears as well in other texts, such as the *Liber de lumine*. This work offers, in effect, a set of exercises designed to guide the mind in the techniques of analogical reflection, and constitutes as well, according to its colophon, an instrument to serve preachers, since it "teaches how to extract and apply likenesses for a purpose, as is obvious from the light of a candle and from those things said thanks to it" (*docet extrahere et applicare similitudines ad propositum, ut patet in lumine candelae et in eis, quae per ipsam dicta sunt*).[131]

Nonetheless, it is in the examples from the *Rhetorica nova* where this kind of "meta-exemplarity" appears with the greatest clarity and determination. There, the section on *pulcra exempla* is framed by two commentaries, almost identical, that establish the preferred reading of the passages offered in this light. At the beginning of the series, Llull declares that it seeks to provide the instruction necessary for a speaker to learn how "to take *exempla* and apply them duly ordered in his words" (*exempla sumere et ad verba sua ordine debito applicare*), inserting them "in appropriate places" (*in locis congruentibus*).[132] The *exempla* proposed, Llull reiterates in concluding this section, provide instruction for anyone to "grant splendour to discourse by narrating beautiful *exempla* and applying them to a suitable purpose" (*conferre decorem narrando pulcra exempla, et ipsa fini verborum cui conveniunt applicando*). In short, they offer, more than a mass of instructions, a true method for "seeking and finding *exempla*" (*exempla inquirere et invenire*).[133]

8.8.3 *Training in Exemplarity*

The meta-exemplary condition of Llull's stories does not affect only the series or repertories of *exempla* included in his theoretical writings. In some fashion,

---

130   *Arbre de ciència* 15. Prol., (eds.) Carreras i Artau and Carreras i Artau, *OE* 1:799.
131   *Liber de lumine* 3, (ed.) Gayà Estelrich, 62.
132   *Rhetorica nova* 2.4.0, (ed.) Johnston, 14.
133   Ibid. 2.4.25, (ed.) Johnston, 24.

it is projected upon the *exempla* that adorn his works of fiction, and perhaps only in this light does the design of the *Libre de meravelles* become comprehensible. Both a novel and an encyclopedia, this work seems founded upon the concept of exemplarity, because it not only attempts to make its stories contribute to explaining metaphorically the structure of Creation, but, on the contrary, in this work the universe itself constitutes, in all its levels, an "exemplary" reflection of its Creator. The text thus combines two successive and complementary processes of analogical reading, the ontological and the rhetorical, displaying its hero's training in their respective techniques, and, at the same time, offering to the reader a model for undertaking both tasks: investigating the likenesses of God in the world and their joyous communication by means of ingenious stories.

This irresistible analogical vocation appears at many points in the text. In a passage from the fourth book, mentioned above, a student of philosophy hears the teachings of his master about the four elements and systematically repeats the lesson "through similitude" (*per semblança*). In response to Fèlix's question about how one candle can ignite another without decreasing its light, the student abandons this method of exposition and responds literally. As we have seen, this abandonment of the metaphorical method prompts the master's harsh rebuke.[134] The tacit agreement to use exemplary forms finally becomes explicit: exemplarity is definitely a language or, better, *the* language of the *Libre de meravelles*.

The entire novel is devoted to teaching Fèlix the use of this language. Fèlix's entire training is founded on a succession of "heard" and "lived" *exempla*. The context of this training makes full sense of the constant clarifications of his masters about the precise interpretation of their stories, and of the doubts about the correspondence of some likenesses to the matter at hand. But that training also involves a whole series of specular mechanisms, facilitated through the obvious multiplication of narrative levels. Numerous *exempla* therefore reproduce the "gradated" interplay among the stories that define the framing plot of the novel, demonstrating to Fèlix an exact mirror of the training that he undergoes. This mirror surely extends to the readers, who find in the doubts and progress of the novel's characters (above all, Fèlix himself) a dramatized version of the same initiation in the techniques of exemplarity that they must undertake.[135]

Training in exemplarity thus results from a slow process, which the novel itself carefully unfolds. It is enough to compare Fèlix's initial, somewhat amazed

---

134   *Libre de meravelles* 4.20, (eds.) Badia et al., NEORL 10:170.
135   Ysern, "*Exempla* i estructures exemplars," 41–42; Johnston, "Exemplary Reading," 237–245.

and passive, response to the stories of his masters, with the command of storytelling that he demonstrates toward the end of the fourth book. However, the definitive command of this exemplary ability only appears with the teachings of the hermit, his last master, in the final three books of the work. With him, Fèlix becomes accustomed "to understanding one likeness from another" (*entendre un semblant per altre*) and to expounding its deeper meaning.[136] Only after being "well taught" (*bé adoctrinat*) is the hero able to reverse the most common terms from a dialogue of the frame story, moving from the role of student to that of teacher and becoming, above all, a narrator of similitudes. This occurs in the epilogue to the work, where he arrives at a very distinguished abbey and devotes himself to telling "*exempla* and marvels" (*dels eximplis e de les meravelles*) to its monks, then taking their habit and committing himself to travel the world recounting the *Libre de meravelles*. Death overtakes him before he can do so, but shortly afterwards, another saintly monk who has memorized these *exempla* and marvels assumes his mission. Under the name of the "second Fèlix" (*Segon Fèlix*), this monk travels the world, disseminating the *Libre de meravelles*, "and extending it, according to the marvels that he found" (*e muntiplicà aquell, segons les meravelles que atrobava*).[137] Exemplarity is thus conceived as an infinite chain, as a storehouse of memory that holds old *exempla* and adds new similitudes to them. Almost virtually, the itinerary and the contents of the *Libre de meravelles* are projected beyond the final lines of the novel, negating any possibility of its end. Thanks to this open ending, the spectacle of Creation offers itself to the eyes of its readers as an unending book of *exempla*, as a true "book of marvels."

Works Cited

Primary Works

Alfonso X, Rey de Castilla, *Cantigas de Santa María*, (ed.) Walter Mettmann, 3 vols. (Madrid: 1986–1989).

Aristotle, *Retórica*, (ed.) A. Tovar (Madrid: 1971).

Arnau de Lieja, *Recull d'exemples i miracles ordenat per alfabet*, (ed.) Josep-Antoni Ysern (Barcelona: 2004).

Bonaventure, *Itinerarium mentis ad Deum*, in *Obras de San Buenaventura*, (eds.) León Amorós et al., 6 vols. (Madrid: 1955), 1:543–633.

Ioannes de Sancto Geminiano, *Universum praedicabile* (Cologne: 1679).

---

136   *Libre de meravelles* 8.100 and 9.121; (ed.) Bonner, *Obres selectes*, 2:326 and 387.

137   Ibid. "De la fi del libre," (ed.) Bonner, *Obres selectes*, 2:391–332.

El Libro de los Doce Sabios, (ed.) John K. Walsh, Anejos del *BRAE* 29 (Madrid: 1975).

Miracles de la Verge Maria: Col·lecció del segle XIV, (ed.) Pere Bohigas (Barcelona: 1956).

Miracles de la verge Maria: Un "mariale" lleidatà, (ed.) Antoni Maria Parramon (Lerida: 1976).

Primary Works: Llull

Arbre de ciència, (eds.) Joaquim Carreras i Artau and Tomàs Carreras i Artau, *OE* 1:555–1046.

Arbre de filosofia d'amor, (ed.) Salvador Galmès, ORL 18:67–227.

Ars brevis de inventione iuris, (ed.) Aloisius Madre, ROL 12:257–389.

Ars compendiosa inveniendi veritatem, MOG 1:433–473.

Ars compendiosa, (ed.) Carmelo Ottaviano, *L' "Ars compendiosa" de R. Lulle, avec une étude sur la bibliographie et le fond Ambrosien de Lulle*, Études de Philosophie Médiévale 12 (París: 1930), 105–161.

Ars de iure, (ed.) Jordi Gayà Estelrich, ROL 20:119–177.

Ars generalis ultima, (ed.) Aloisius Madre, ROL 14.

Ars inventiva veritatis, MOG 5:1–211.

Art amativa, (ed.) Salvador Galmès, ORL 17:1–388.

Art demostrativa, (ed.) Anthony Bonner, *Obres selectes de Ramon Llull (1232–1316)*, 2 vols. (Palma: 1989), 1:273–521.

Articuli fidei christianae, in *Opera omnia* (Strasburg: 1651), 917–967.

Començaments de medicina, (ed.) Lola Badia, NEORL 5:35–114.

Compendium logicae Algazelis, (ed.) Charles Lohr, "Raimundus Lullus' *Compendium Logicae Algazelis*: Quellen, Lehre und Stellung in der Geschichte der Logik," Ph.D. Thesis, Albert Ludwig University of Freiburg (Freiburg im Breisgau: 1967).

Disputatio fidei et intellectus, (ed.) Walter Euler, ROL 23:213–279.

Doctrina pueril, (ed.) Joan Santanach i Suñol, NEORL 7.

Lectura Artis, quae intitulata est brevis practica Tabulae Generalis, (ed.) Jordi Gayà Estelrich, ROL 20:335–438.

Liber de lumine, (ed.) Jordi Gayà Estelrich, ROL 20:1–62.

Liber de modo naturali intelligendi, (ed.) Helmut Riedlinger, ROL 6:177–223.

Liber de praedicatione, (ed.) Abraham Soria Flores, 2 vols., ROL 3–4.

Libre de Sancta Maria, (ed.) Andreu Caimari, in *OE* 1:1155–1242.

Libre del orde de cavallería, (ed.) M. Obrador y Bennassar, ORL 1:201–247.

Le livre des bêtes: Version française du XVe siècle, (ed.) Armand Llinarès (Paris: 1964).

Libre d'Ave Maria, in *Romanç d'Evast e Blaquerna*, (eds.) Albert Soler and Joan Santanach, NEORL 8:279–304.

Libre de contemplació en Déu, (ed.) Antoni Sancho y Miquel Arbona, *OE* 2:85–1269.

Libre de les bèsties, in *Llibre de meravelles: Volum I (Llibres I–VII)*, (eds.) Lola Badia, Xavier Bonillo, Eugènia Gisbert, and Montserrat Lluch, NEORL 10:221–269.

Libre de meravelles: Volum I (*Llibres I–VII*), (eds.) Lola Badia, Xavier Bonillo, Eugènia Gisbert, and Montserrat Lluch, NEORL 10.

Libre de meravelles, (ed.) Anthony Bonner, in *Obres selectes de Ramon Llull (1232–1316),* 2 vols. (Palma: 1989), 2:7–393.

Libre del gentil, (ed.) Anthony Bonner, *Obres selectes de Ramon Llull (1232–1316),* 2 vols. (Palma: 1989), 1:89–271.

Libre dels àngels, (ed.) Miquel Tous Gayà i Rafel Ginard Bauçà, ORL 21:305–375.

Libre d'intenció, (ed.) Salvador Galmés, ORL 18:1–66.

Mil proverbis, (ed.) Salvador Galmès, ORL 14:325–372.

Obres selectes de Ramon Llull (1232–1316), (ed.) Anthony Bonner, 2 vols. (Palma: 1989).

Phantasticus, (eds.) Antoni Oliver, Michel Senellart and Fernando Domínguez, ROL 16:1–30.

Proverbis d'ensenyament, (ed.) Salvador Galmès, ORL 14:373–389.

Proverbis de Ramon, (ed.) Salvador Galmès, ORL 14:1–324.

Retòrica nova, (eds.) Josep Batalla, Lluís Cabré, and Marcel Ortín (Turnhout and Santa Coloma de Queralt: 2006).

Rhetorica Nova, in *Ramon Llull's New Rhetoric: Text and Translation of Llull's "Rethorica Nova,"* (ed.) Mark D. Johnston, (Davis, Calif.: 1994).

Romanç d'Evast e Blaquerna, (eds.) Albert Soler and Joan Santanach, NEORL 8.

Summa sermonum in civitate Maioricensi annis mcccxii-mcccxiii composita, (ed.) Fernando Domínguez Reboiras y Abraham Soria Flores, ROL 15.

Tabula generalis, (ed.) Viola Tenge-Wolf, ROL 27.

Secondary Works

Agúndez García, José Luis, "Cuentos populares andaluces (XXII)," *Revista de Folklore* 326 (2008): 60–72.

Aragüés Aldaz, José, *"Deus concionator:" Mundo predicado y retórica del "exemplum" en los Siglos de Oro* (Amsterdam: 1999).

Aragüés Aldaz, José, *"Exempla inquirere et invenire:* Fundamentos retóricos para un análisis de las formas breves lulianas," in *La literatura en la época de Sancho IV: Actas del Congreso Internacional "La literatura en la época de Sancho IV" (Alcalá de Henares, del 21 al 24 de febrero de 1994),* (eds.) Carlos Alvar and José Manuel Lucía Megías (Alcalá de Henares: 1996), 289–311.

Aragüés Aldaz, José, *"Falses semblances:* Ejemplarismo divino y literatura ejemplar a la luz de Ramón Llull," in *Actas del VIII Congreso de la Asociación Hispánica de Literatura Medieval (Santander, del 22 al 26 de septiembre de 1999),* 2 vols. (Santander: 2000), 1:175–184.

Aragüés Aldaz, José, "Fronteras estéticas de la analogía medieval: Del adorno retórico a la belleza del Verbo," *Revista Española de Filosofía Medieval* 6 (1999): 157–174.

Aragüés Aldaz, José, *Ramon Llull y la literatura ejemplar* (Alicante: 2016).

Arbona Piza, Miguel, "Los *exemplis* en el *Llibre de Evast e Blanquerna*," *EL* 20 (1976): 53–70.

Arronis Llopis, Carme, "Els miracles marians en *La vida de la verge Maria* de Miquel Peres," in *Actas del XIII Congreso Internacional de la Asociación Hispánica de Literatura Medieval*, (ed.) J.M. Fradejas Rueda et al. (Valladolid: 2010), 389–406.

Auer, Johann, *El mundo, creación de Dios*, in Johann Auer and Josef Ratzinger (ed.), *Curso de Teología Dogmática*, vol. 3 (Barcelona: 1979).

Badia, Lola, "La literatura alternativa de Ramon Llull: tres mostres," in *Actes del VII Congrés de l'Associació Hispànica de Literatura Medieval* (*Castelló de la Plana, 22–26 de setembre de 1997*), (eds.) Santiago Fortuño Llorens and Tomàs Martínez Romero, 3 vols. (Castelló de la Plana: 1999), 1:11–32.

Badia, Lola, "Literature as an 'ancilla artis': the transformation of science into literature according to Robert Pring-Mill and Ramon Llull," *Hispanic Research Journal* 10 (2009): 18–28.

Badia, Lola, "*No cal que tragats exempli dels romans*," in *Miscel·lània Pere Bohigas* 1, Estudis de Llengua i Literatura Catalanes 3 (Barcelona: 1981), 87–94.

Badia, Lola, "*Raimundi Lulli Opera Latina, XV*: Ramon Llull i la predicació," *Llengua & Literatura* 3 (1988–1989): 563–575.

Badia, Lola, "Ramon Llull i la tradició literària," *EL* 28 (1988): 121–138.

Badia, Lola and Anthony Bonner, *Ramón Llull: Vida, pensamiento y obra literaria*, (Barcelona: 1993).

Badia, Lola, Joan Santanach and Albert Soler, "Ramon Llull," in *Historia de la Literatura Catalana 1, Literatura medieval (1): Dels orígens al segle XIV*, (ed.) Lola Badia (Barcelona: 2013), 377–476.

Barnett, David, "The Sources of a Fifteenth-Century Catalan Collection of Marian Miracle Stories," in *Gaude Virgo Gloriosa: Marian Miracle Literature in the Iberian Peninsula and France in the Middle Ages*, (eds.) J.C. Conde and E. Gatland (London: 2011), 107–125.

Bauçà Ochogavia, Manuel, *L'exemplarisme de Ramon Llull* (Palma: 1989).

Bayo, Juan Carlos, "Las colecciones universales de milagros de la Virgen hasta Gonzalo de Berceo," *Bulletin of Hispanic Studies* 81 (2004): 854–871.

Berlioz, Jacques and Marie Anne Polo de Beaulieu (eds.), *Les Exempla médiévaux: Nouvelles perspectives* (Paris: 1998).

Berlioz, Jacques and Marie Anne Polo de Beaulieu, "Les prologues des recueils d'*exempla* (XIIIe–XVe siècles): Une grille d'analyse," in *La predicazione dei Frati dalla metà del '200 alla fine del '300: Atti del XXII Convegno Internazionale, Assisi, 13–15 ottobre 1994* (Spoleto: 1995), 268–299.

Bétérous, Paule, "Ramon Llull et le renouvellement du thème des miracles Mariaux au XIIIe siècle," *Cultura Neolatina* 38 (1978): 37–47.

Bonillo Hoyos, Xavier, "Catálogo de ejemplos lulianos," *Magníficat* 2 (2015): 55–127.

Bonillo Hoyos, Xavier, "Els exemples del paradís i de l'infern del *Llibre de meravelles* de Ramon Llull," *SL* 44 (2004): 53–78.

Bonillo Hoyos, Xavier, "L'estructura dels llibres del Paradís i de l'Infern al Fèlix de Ramon Llull," in *Actes de les Jornades Internacionals Lullianes. Ramon Llull al S. XXI (Palma, 2004)*, (ed.) Maria Isabel Ripoll (Palma and Barcelona: 2005), 217–233.

Bonillo Hoyos, Xavier, *Literatura al "Llibre de Meravelles"* (Barcelona: 2008).

Bonner, Anthony, *L'Art i la lògica de Ramon Llull: Manual d'ús*, trans. H. Lamuela (Barcelona and Palma: 2012).

Cabré, Lluís, Marcel Ortin, and Josep Pujol, "'Coneixer e haver moralitats bones:' L'ús de la literatura en l'*Arbre exemplifical* de Ramon Llull," *EL* 28 (1988): 139–167.

Cabré, Miriam and M. Espadaler Anton, "La narrativa en vers," in *Historia de la Literatura Catalana* 1: *Literatura medieval (1): Dels orígens al segle XIV*, dir. Lola Badia (Barcelona: 2013), 297–372.

Calders i Artís, Tessa, "El *Blanquerna* de Llull i el *Príncep* de Hasday," *Miscelánea de Estudios Árabes y Hebraico: Sección de Hebreo* 60 (2011): 67–98.

Colom Ferrá, Guillermo, "Ramon Llull y los orígenes de la literatura catalana [8]," *EL* 16 (1972): 37–47.

Dagenais, John, "New Considerations on the Date and Composition of Llull's *Libre de les bèsties*," in *Actes del Segon Col·loqui d'Estudis Catalans a Nord-Amèrica (Yale, 1979)* (Barcelona: 1982), 131–139.

Dällenbach, Lucien, *Le récit spéculaire: Essai sur la mise en abŷme* (Paris: 1977).

De la Granja, Fernando, "Nunca más perro al molino," *Al-Andalus* 39 (1974): 431–442.

De la Torre Rodríguez, Ventura, "El relato intercalado en la *Historia de los siete sabios de Roma*," in *El relato intercalado*, (eds.) M. Smerdou Altolaguirre and M. Bonsoms (Madrid: 1992), 67–75.

Domínguez Reboiras, Fernando, "Una lectura del *Llibre de meravelles* como *ars praedicandi*," *Caplletra* 43 (2007): 131–160.

Friedlein, Roger, *El diàleg en Ramon Llull: l'expressió literària com a estratègia apologètica* (Barcelona and Palma: 2011).

Gayà Estelrich, Jordi, "Sobre algunes estructures literaries del *Llibre de meravelles*," *Randa* 10 (1980): 63–69.

Gisbert, Eugènia, "*Metaforice loquendo*: de l'analogia a la metàfora en els *Començaments de medicina* de Ramon Llull," *SL* 44 (2004): 17–52.

Grimalt, Josep A., "Notes sobre les fonts del *Llibre de les bèsties* de Ramon Llull," *Randa*, 48 (2002): 37–46.

Hames, Harvey, "Through Ramon Llull's Looking Glass: What was the thirteenth-Century Dominican mission really about?," in *Ramon Llull i el lul·lisme: pensament i llenguatge: Actes de les jornades en homenatge a J.N. Hillgarth i A. Bonner*, (eds.) M.I. Ripoll and M. Tortella (Palma: 2012), 51–74.

Hauf, Albert G., "Sobre l'*Arbor exemplificalis*," in *Arbor Scientiae: Der Baum des Wissens von Ramon Llull (Akten des Internationalen Kongresses aus Anlaß des 40-jährigen*

Jubiläums des Raimundus-Lullus-Instituts der Universität Freiburg i. Br.), (eds.) Fernando Domínguez Reboiras, Pere Villalba Varneda, and Peter Walter (Brepols: 2002), 303–342.

Hughes, Robert D., "Speculum, Similitude and Signification: the Incarnation as Exemplary and Proportionale Sign in the Arts of Ramon Llull," *SL* 45–46 (2005–2006): 3–37.

Johnston, Mark D., "*Affatus:* Natural Science as Moral Theology," *EL* 30 (1990): 3–30 and 139–159.

Johnston, Mark D., "Exemplary Reading in Ramon Llull's *Llibre de meravelles,*" *Forum for Modern Language Studies* 28 (1992): 235–250.

Johnston, Mark D., "The Semblance of Signifiance. Language and Exemplarism in the 'Art' of Ramon Llull. With the text of the 'Rhetorica nova' from Paris B.N. Ms. Lat. 6443C." Ph.D. dissertation, The Johns Hopkins University (Baltimore: 1978).

Lacarra, María Jesús, *Cuentística medieval en España: los orígenes* (Zaragoza: 1979).

Lacarra, María Jesús (ed.), *Cuento y novela corta en España 1: Edad Media* (Barcelona: 2010).

Le Goff, Jacques, Claude Brémond, and Jean-Claude Schmitt, *L'exemplum* (Louvain: 1982).

Llinarès, Armand, "Les singes, le ver luisant et l'oiseau: Note sur l'utilisation répétée d'une même fable dans l'oeuvre de Lulle," *Romania* 108 (1987): 97–106.

Luzón Díaz, Rubén, "Una aproximación a la noción de *exemplum* en la obra luliana, seguida de un breve comentario en los *exempla* del capítulo 62 del *Llibre de meravelles,*" *Revista de lenguas y literaturas catalana, gallega y vasca* 12 (2006): 253–276.

Marsan, Rameline E., *Itinéraire espagnol du conte medieval (VIIIᵉ–XVᵉ siècles)* (Paris: 1974).

Martín Pascual, Llúcia, "Algunes consideracions sobre la relació entre les faules del *Llibre de les Bèsties* de Ramon Llull i l'original oriental," *Catalan Review* 11 (1997): 83–112.

Martín Pascual, Llúcia, "Huella del *Calila e Dimna* en la literatura catalana medieval," in *Énoncés sapientiels et littérature exemplaire: une intertextualité complexe,* (ed.) M.S. Ortola (Nancy: 2013), 81–99.

Martín Pascual, Llúcia, "'On pus escura és la semblança, pus altament entén l'enteniment qui aquella semblança entén': Ramon Llull i el didactisme cientifico-teològic del *Llibre de meravelles,*" *Randa* 50 (2002): 25–39.

McCall, Marsh H., *Ancient Rhetorical Theories of Simile and Comparison* (Cambridge, Mass.: 1969).

Medina, Jaume, "Oscuridad y elevación del entendimiento en la obra de Ramon Llull," *Revista de Lenguas y Literaturas Catalana, Gallega y Vasca* 14 (2009): 253–259.

Neugaard, Edward J., "Les col·leccions de *exempla* en la literatura catalana medieval," in *Josep Maria Solá-Solé. Homage. Homenaje. Homatge (miscelánea de estudios de amigos y discípulos*), (eds.) A. Torres-Alcalá, V. Agüera and N.B. Smith, 2 vols. (Barcelona: 1984), 1:165–168.

Palomo, María Pilar, *La novela cortesana* (Barcelona: 1976).

Pastor, Jordi Pardo, "Filosofía y teología de Ramón Llull: la *Demonstratio per aequiparantiam*," *Revista Española de Filosofía Medieval* 9 (2002): 265–274.

Pereira, Michela, "El concepte de natura en el context de les obres científiques de Ramon Llull," *Randa* 19 (1988): 57–67.

Price, Bennett J., "Paradeigma and Exemplum in Ancient Rhetorical Theory," Ph.D. dissertation, University of California (Berkeley: 1975).

Pring-Mill, Robert D.F, "L'estructura analògica de l'Art luliana," in *Estudis sobre Ramon Llull (1956–1978)* (Barcelona: 1991), 241–252.

Pring-Mill, Robert D.F, "El microcosmos lul·lià," in *Estudis sobre Ramon Llull (1956–1978)* (Barcelona: 1991), 31–112.

Pring-Mill, Robert D.F, "Els *recontaments* de l'*Arbre Exemplifical* de Ramon Llull: la transmutació de la ciència en literatura," in *Estudis sobre Ramon Llull (1956–1978)* (Barcelona: 1991), 307–317.

Roviró i Alemany, Ignasi, "De la bellesa sensible a la font de la bellesa: la bellesa en Ramon Llull," in *Actes del Simposi Internacional de Filosofia de l'Edat Mitjana: Vic-Girona, 11–16 d'abril de 1993* (Vic: 1996), 389–395.

Rubio, Josep Enric, "L'estètica en Ramon Llull: una qüestió epistemològica," *Tesserae* 2 (1996): 73–80.

Rubio, Josep Enric, "The Natural Realm," in *Raimundus Lullus: An Introduction to his Life, Works and Thought*, (ed.) Alexander Fidora and J.E. Rubio (Turnhout: 2008), 311–362.

Rubio, Josep Enric, "Thought: The Art," in *Raimundus Lullus: An Introduction to his Life, Works and Thought*, (eds.) Alexander Fidora and J.E. Rubio (Turnhout: 2008), 243–310.

Rubió, Jordi, "Alguns aspects de l'obra literària de Ramon Llull," in *Ramon Llull i el lul·lisme*, Obres de Jordi Rubió i Balaguer 3 (Barcelona; 1985), 248–299.

Rubió, Jordi, "L'expressió literària de Ramon Llull," in *Ramon Llull i el lul·lisme*, Obres de Jordi Rubió i Balaguer 3 (Barcelona; 1985), 300–314.

Rubió, Jordi, "La *Rhetorica Nova* de Ramon Llull," in *Ramon Llull i el lul·lisme*, Obres de Jordi Rubió i Balaguer 3 (Barcelona; 1985), 202–233.

Ruffini, Mario, "Lo stile del Lullo nel *Libre del Orde de Cavaylerie*," *EL* 3 (1959): 37–52.

Ruiz Simón, Josep Maria, *L'Art de Ramon Llull i la teoria escolàstica de la ciència* (Barcelona: 1999).

Ruiz Simón, Josep Maria, "De la naturalesa com a mescla a l'art de mesclar (sobre la fonamentació cosmològica de les arts lul·lianes)," *Randa* 19 (1988): 69–99.

Sansone, Giuseppe E., "Ramon Llull narratore," *Revista de Filología Española* 43 (1960): 81–96.

Santanach i Suñol, Joan, "Dos exemples de Ramon Llull inclosos en un recull de miracles," *Randa* 55 (2005): 7–13.

Sklovski, Viktor, *Sobre la prosa literaria* (Barcelona: 1971).

Spitzer, Leo, *L'armonia del mondo: Storia semantica di un'idea* (Bolonia: 1967).

Taylor, Barry, "Some Complexities of the *Exemplum* in Ramon Llull's *Llibre de les bèsties*," *The Modern Language Review* 90 (1995): 646–658.

Tilliette, Jean-Yves, "L'*exemplum* rhétorique: questions de définition," in *Les* Exempla *médiévaux: Nouvelles perspectives*, ed. Jacques Berlioz and Marie Anne Polo de Beaulieu (Paris: 1998), 43–65.

Tous Prieto, Francesc, "Breus proposicions que contenen molta sentència: els proverbis lul·lians i les 'formes sentencioses'," *SL* 51 (2011): 77–98.

Tous Prieto, Francesc, "La forma proverbi en l'obra de Ramon Llull: una aproximació," M.A. Thesis, Universitat de Barcelona-Universitat Autònoma de Barcelona (Barcelona: 2010).

Viera, David J., "Exempla in the *Libre de Sancta Maria* and Traditional Medieval Marian Miracles," *Catalan Review* 4 (1990): 221–231.

Von Balthasar, Hans Urs, *Gloria: Una estética teológica* (Madrid: 1986).

Von Moos, Peter, "L'*exemplum* et les *exempla* des prêcheurs," in *Les* Exempla *médiévaux: Nouvelles perspectives*, ed. Jacques Berlioz and Marie Anne Polo de Beaulieu (Paris: 1998), 67–82.

Von Moos, Peter, *Geschichte als Topik: Das rhetorische Exemplum von der Antike zur Neuzeit und die* historiae *im "Policraticus" Johanns von Salisbury* (Hildesheim: 1988).

Welter, Jean Thiebaut, *L'Exemplum dans la littérature religieuse et didactique du Moyen Âge* (Paris and Toulouse: 1927).

Yates, Frances A., "The Art of Ramon Llull: An approach to it through Lull's Theory of the Elements," *Journal of the Warburg and Courtauld Institutes* 17 (1954): 115–173.

Ysern, Josep-Antoni, "*Exempla* i estructures exemplars en el primer llibre del *Fèlix*," *SL* 39 (1999): 25–54.

CHAPTER 9

Narrative Structure and Cultural Significance in the Novels of Ramon Llull

Alexander W. Ibarz

9.1 Introduction

Ramon Llull is a novelist of primary importance to the evolution of the Western canon. The precedent of Llull's two "spiritual romances," *Blaquerna* and the *Libre de meravelles*,[1] is such that without him a "best-seller" of chivalric romance like the *Tirant lo Blanc* of Joanot Martorell is scarcely imaginable. Without the latter Cervantes might not have been so gentle with the genre of chivalric romance, and so the cultural significance of Llull in the Western canon must be fairly obvious to anyone acquainted with the issues involved. This fact was intuited over fifty years ago by Frank Pierce, who termed *Blaquerna* an "imaginative autobiography." Pierce observed "that this novel of adventures can be regarded ... as his *Don Quixote*," concluding that Llull,

> has given us a piece of novelistic realism that transcends the collections of *exempla* ... for originality, subtlety and total achievement. The present writer, at least, regards his *Blanquerna* as one of our great novels and feels that the time is now ripe for a re-appraisal and a renewed interest from our "post-realistic" age.[2]

Still, when Elena Rossi returned to assess the novel's significance in 1990, she concluded that "the extraordinary power of Llull's writing in *Blanquerna*" constitutes a "unique and largely unexamined contribution to the modern narrative genre."[3] The availability now of a reliable critical edition significantly

---

1 All subsequent references cite: *Romanç d'Evast e Blaquerna*, (eds.) Albert Soler and Joan Santanach, NEORL 8; *Libre de meravelles*, (ed.) Salvador Galmés, 4 vols. (Barcelona: 1931–34).

2 Frank Pierce, "Some notes on Llull's Mediaeval Novel," *Quaderni Ibero-Americani* 17 (1955): 49 and 51. Pierce's teacher, Allison Peers, went even further in "Ramon Lull and the World of Today," *Hispania*, 11 (1928): 467: "For it is not conceivable that, while a spark of love for God remains in a human soul, Ramon's sublime hymns of love can be forgotten."

3 Elena Rossi, "Ramon Llull as novelist: the visionary realism of *Blanquerna*," *Catalan Review* 4 (1990): 297.

aids scholarship on this text, and there is a growing body of secondary literature that critics cannot now ignore.[4]

One major reason for Ramon Llull's importance is his exploitation of analogy as a narrative device. Llull is of course well-known for the central role that
analogy plays in his idiosyncratic philosophical system, the Great Art.[5] He also
composed numerous works of literature based on that figure of thought, which
makes them of central interest to a wide range of scholars. Especially noteworthy is the composition of his works within a lively dialogical space that included both Christian readers familiar with the Occitan troubadour tradition,
which was Llull's native vernacular poetic idiom, and Muslim audiences familiar with the techniques of sufi literature, which Llull famously cites as models
in his writings. Modern scholars of course continue to speculate about the relative debt of his analogical techniques to both the troubadours and the sufis.

Ramon Llull was, I believe, affiliated to the troubadour tradition in a way
more pervasive than is usually accepted.[6] This argument of course presents
some problems, which I approach below with the due caution, while focusing
on Llull's development of literary structure. For those interested in exploring
this question, Oriana Scarpati's major study provides an exhaustive account
of analogy in Old Occitan lyric; fascinatingly, she argues that authors of the
artes poetriae tended to exclude the simile or comparison from their works
on ideological grounds.[7] Robert Archer has also shown comprehensively how
later troubadours perpetuated this figure of thought: its strongest exponent
was Ausias March, the last troubadour of the Catalano-Occitan tradition.[8]

Our understanding of Llull's self-proclaimed familiarity with sufi practices has also advanced significantly thanks to modern scholarship on his

---

4 Caroline A. Jewers, *Chivalric Fiction and the History of the Novel* (Gainesville, Florida: 2001)
and Harold Bloom, *The Western Canon: The Books and School of the Ages* (New York: 1994), are
unfortunate examples of studies that neglect Llull's significance.

5 Thanks especially to the pioneering studies of Robert D.F. Pring-Mill, "The Analogical Structure of the Lullian Art," in *Islamic Philosophy and the Classical Tradition: Essays presented by
his friends and pupils to Richard Walzer on his seventieth birthday*, (eds.) S.M. Stern, A. Hourani, and V. Brown (Columbia, S. Carolina: 1972), 315–326; and "The Trinitarian World-Picture of
Ramón Lull," *Romanistisches Jahrbuch* 7 (1955–56): 229–256.

6 Alexander W. Ibarz, "Ausias March and the Troubadour Question," Ph.D. Dissertation, University of Cambridge (Cambridge: 2005).

7 Oriana Scarpati, *Retorica del trobar: Le comparazioni nella lirica occitana* (Rome: 2008), 31.

8 Robert Archer, *The Pervasive Image: The Role of Analogy in the Poetry of Ausiàs March* (Amsterdam: 1985). See also Pere Ramírez i Molas, *La poesia d'Ausiàs March: anàlisi textual, cronologia i elements filosòfics* (Basel: 1970). Full study of Llull's influence on March remains a
desideratum in this field.

engagement with Islamic culture,[9] though we remain far from a consensus on Llull's intentionality, and thereby his cultural significance, when citing sufi models.

While this essay recognizes, following many modern critics, the importance of both the troubadours and the sufis as a type of literary influence, their identification as sources of Llull's technique is an unhelpful simplification for two reasons. First, because it is fully subordinated to Llull's other interests, and thus diminishes their cultural significance. Second, because it risks obscuring the historical context of Lullian speech acts as a living discourse in a society both literate and oral in nature, addressed to audiences living in cultures of "mixed orality."

For example, no satisfactory explanation has been forwarded with regard to such a key question as Llull's place within the broad spectrum of mendicant evangelizing initiatives.[10] Insistence upon his evangelical message rather than upon his novelistic form has tended to obscure the forest for the trees. While the importance of Llull's evangelism is not in question, reduction of Llull's literary efforts to expressions of missionary zeal is to privilege a static, transnational discourse at the expense of explaining what is culturally specific. All authors, in every cultural epoch, face a different social context, against which – and only against it – the specific nature and tenor of their unique interventions may be gauged. The classic formulation of the view I subscribe to here, regarding the "re-purposing" of a tradition as a response to an adaptive context, albeit in the rather different framework of speech act theory, is to be found in Skinner's seminal essay.[11] That an aspiring lay missionary and preacher like Ramon Llull should contemplate writing a work of fiction in the first place is enough to alert us that the form of the discourse requires as much attention as its sources, if its cultural significance is to be explained. A work of fiction is as far as one can go from a sermon with regard to discourse type: a sermonizer can tell

9   Álvaro Galmés de Fuentes, *Ramón Llull y la tradición árabe* (Barcelona: 1999) offers an introduction to the Sufi view of courtly love and its relevance to Llull. Dominique Urvoy, *Penser l'Islam: les présupposés islamiques de l'Art' de Lull* (Paris: 1980) remains the best overall study of the debt of Llull's system to Islamic thought.

10   Mark D. Johnston, *ER* goes a long way towards filling this gap. Albert Soler, "Espiritualitat i Cultura: els laics i l'accés al saber a final del segle XIII a la corona d'Aragó," *SL* 38 (1998): 18–19, notes especially the difference in outlook even between Llull and his close associate Arnau de Vilanova, Llull being far more optimistic in the appropriateness of speculative philosophy as a topic of interest to laymen.

11   Quentin Skinner, "Meaning and Understanding in the History of Ideas," *History and Theory* 8 (1969): 3–53.

stories but cannot call himself a storyteller; whereas a novelist can give sermons, but cannot call himself a sermonizer. The perils of dealing reductive-
ly with Llull's sources are clear when a scholar claims that "My purpose is to
show that Llull's own needs as a missionary determine the evolution of his
arts of preaching towards the composition of an exemplary novel-sermon in
Blanquerna."[12] The argument that Llull might have thought that a story could
contain sermons is one thing; *Tirant lo Blanc*, for example, instantiates such
a novel type. However, to propose that a novel can in some way be commen-
surate with the discursive genre of a sermon is treading on thin ice. Even the
most didactic of novels, by virtue of its representation of multiple discourses
via the presence of multiple characters, evades the subjugating power of its
didactic moral and opens up a space of coexistence for multiple points of view.

My reservation on this point is also applicable more widely to those who,
like J.-A. Ysern, take for granted that "zeal for converting the infidels through
necessary reasons informs Ramon Llull's entire immense oeuvre, infusing it
with an eminently didactic character."[13] Even as sensitive a scholar as Martí
de Riquer was hardly more careful to avoid this fallacy, the source of much
subsequent imprecision:

> In *Blaquerna*, then, Llull deliberately intends to offer something similar
> to a novel, although subjugated to a mass of instruction and of moral and
> mystical experiences that it now expounds within a narrative plot.[14]

One might object that it is not the novelistic form which is subject to its
content, but vice versa. The absurd concept of the "novel-sermon" ignores this
distinction, together with a whole series of details concerning the intended audience of the work, the delivery of the story, and the novelist's intention. Or, to
put it another way: "It seems to me that one must study this work for what it is,
instead of asking that it were something very different,"[15] meaning that Llull's

12   Roberto González-Casanovas, "Llull's Blanquerna and the Art of Preaching: The Evolution
     Towards the Novel-Sermon," *Catalan Review* 4 (1990): 233; cf. also his *La novela ejemplar de
     Ramón Llull: interpretaciones literarias de la misión* (Gijón:1998).

13   Josep-Antoni Ysern, "Exempla I estructures exemplars en el primer llibre del *Fèlix*," SL 39
     (1999): 25: "El deler de convertir els infidels a força de raons necessàries informa tota la
     immensa obrada de Ramon Liull, bo i infonent-li un caràcter eminentment didàctic."

14   Martí de Riquer, *Història de la literatura catalana*, vol. 1 (Barcelona: 1964), 270: "Hi ha,
     doncs, al *Blanquerna*, per voluntat del mateix Llull, la intenció d'oferir alguna cosa sem-
     blant a la novel·la, encara que subjectada a un conjunt d'ensenyaments i d'experiencies
     morals i místiques que ara exposa dins una trama narrativa."

15   Robert D.F. Pring-Mill, "Bibliografía," EL 3 (1958): 342: "Me parece que habría que estudi-
     arse la obra por lo que es, en lugar de pedir que fuese cosa bien distinta."

work should be viewed as a single object, in which vernacular and Latin, storytelling and philosophy, function together and not independently. This does not, *contra scriptum*, justify making what Llull writes subject to an intention external of one reasonably to be deduced from reading the text.

If the Lullian system and literary output share an intentionality, an explication of Llull's novels cannot subordinate both to an extra-textual intention of Llull to sermonize. If he wrote a fiction, it follows that his intention was to fictionalize.[16] Lola Badia has observed accurately that Llull inherits the Occitan prose tradition of *Barlaam e Josaphat*, to which he is indebted for the quality of his prose as well as its structuring devices.[17] It is unclear what prevents scholars from championing the Lullian novel as a component of the novel genre with a role in the Western tradition, nor why there is a recent movement to distance Llull from the concept of literature altogether, a provocative move the repercussions of which are yet to be determined:

> It must be very clear that [Llull's] inclusion in histories of Catalan language and literature is the result of an academic construction that must be reformulated according to subsequent scholarly contributions, introducing thus corrections that imply proof that Llull's vernacular work has a more practical and functional motivation, and not just esthetic and symbolic.[18]

In light of all this, Johnston is surely right to draw our attention to the historically specific cultural repercussions of Llull's status as a layman; in *The Evangelical Rhetoric*, he judges as flawed both the desire to view Llull "as the singularly inspired creator of a unique intellectual system," and the other dominant tendency of recent scholarship, to regard him "as a great Scholastic thinker on a par with Bonaventure, Aquinas, or Duns Scotus."[19] These arguments dehistoricize

---

16 Anthony J. Close, "Don Quixote and the 'Intentionalist Fallacy,'" in *On Literary Intention. Critical Essays*, (ed.) D. Newton-De Molina (Edinburgh:1976), 174–193, expresses the common-sense solution followed here concerning the "intentional fallacy."

17 Lola Badia, "La novel·la espiritual de *Barlaam i Josafat* en el rerafons de la literatura lul·liana," in *Teoria i pràctica de la literatura en Llull* (Barcelona:1992), 97–120.

18 Lola Badia et al., "La llengua i la literatua de Ramon Llull: llocs comuns, malentesos i propostes," *Els Marges* 87 (2009): 85: "Cal tenir molt clar que la seva inclusió [sc. de Ramon Llull] en les històries de la llengua i de la literatura catalanes és fruit d'una construcció acadèmica que s'ha de reformular d'acord amb les successives aportacions de la crítica filològica, introduint, doncs, les correccions que implica haver comprovat que l'obra en vulgar de Llull té una motivació més pràctica i funcional que no pas estètica i simbòlica."

19 Johnston, *ER* 185. Mark D. Johnston, *Ramon Llull's New Rhetoric: Text and Translation of Llull's* Rethorica Nova (Davis, Calif.: 1994), details how Rhetoric formed an important part of Llull's teaching interests.

Llull and prevent us from explaining adequately the nature of Llull's contribution within his cultural milieu:

> Llull's work manifests a constant tension between his Great Art and Scholastic *curricula* and between his evangelical plans and Church policy on missions. On the one hand, he offers his system as a divinely inspired alternative to the flawed human sophistications of the schools. On the other hand, he often begins or ends his writings with invitations for their correction by Church and university authorities.[20]

As Johnston notes, Llull challenges the Church to correct him, a superb piece of lay posturing, which needs to be understood as part of a wider lay movement (and *ergo* of indigenous and not transnational formation): "Llull's dual goals of contemplation and self-expression foster consciousness of a personal and a social as well as a literary subjectivity."[21]

Llull has proven so resistant to this type of argument for so long in part because of his ambiguous relation to contemporary narrative conventions, noted by Rossi as a central problem: "One is tempted to use the adjective 'revolutionary' in describing Blanquerna, although there was nothing similar in the literature before it against which to rebel."[22] And yet Llull's novelistic works cannot be ignored, if the subsequent tradition is to be adequately explained. The problem of sources has proved to be something of an alluring honey-trap in Lullian studies, making it possible, for instance, to describe the *Libre de les bèsties* as "a collection of some twenty-eight apologues or *exempla* intercalated as 'Book Seven' in the *Llibre de meravelles*."[23] This makes what is a structurally cohesive story (with a function as part of the larger work) sound like an encyclopedic bestiary. Corominas observed that "Llull is a rich quarry of materials for the study of the literary and social phenomenon of *joglaria* or minstrelsy,"[24] although Llull's value lies not only as a source of information, but in his mode of storytelling itself.

A large component of my argument has already been laid out by others and there will be no need for me to rehearse it. The importance of literary

---

20   *ER* 187.

21   *ER* 189.

22   Rossi, "Ramon Llull as novelist," 280.

23   Edward J. Neugaard, "The Sources of the Folk Tales in Ramon Llull's *Llibre de les bèsties*," *Journal of American Folklore* 84 (1971): 333.

24   Joan Corominas, "The *joglar a lo diví* in the life and work of Ramon Llull," *Catalan Review* 4 (1990): 179.

structure for pedagogical purposes has been recognized as innovative with regard to Llull's *exempla*. Ysern's cogent analysis shows how Llull departs from
contemporary practice:[25]

> His *exempla* are always presented as problems. More than a synthetic
> summary of a doctrine – as in traditional sermons – they are spurs to
> thought, which require a minimum of attention – sometimes much
> more than a minimum – and are a point of departure more often than
> a point of arrival. Saint Vicent Ferrer subordinated *exempla* to doctrine.
> He expounded and developed the theme of his sermon and, as support,
> deployed *exempla*. Llull takes these as a point of departure for arriving at
> doctrine.[26]

Ysern's useful definition of the Lullian *exemplum* as one employing "concentric exemplary structures" finally confirms what scholars have long suspected,
namely that Llull's exemplary structures mirror the working of his Art.[27] Llull's
spiritual interpretation of logic, as explained by Johnston, employs the same
structures in its *figurae*.[28] The best representation of this in Llull's narrative
might well be the structural devices that aid the establishment of concentric,
as well as contiguous, cognitive schemata. Repetition is a traditional narrative technique for establishing a concentric or circular structure, whereas
juxtaposition is a traditional technique for establishing comparisons through
contiguity (the metonymic or syntagmatic mode). Llull uses the traditional
narrative structural devices known to him. In addition, he experiments with
structures unknown to his contemporaries, some of which later novelists adopt

---

25   J.-A. Ysern, "*Exempla* i estructures exemplars en el primer llibre del Fènix," *SL* 39 (1999): 47.

26   Ysern, "*Exempla* i estructures exemplars," 47: "Per això els seus *exempla* es presenten
      sempre com a problemes. Més que ser el resum sintètic d'una doctrina – com en els ser-
      mons tradicionals – son esperons per a pensar, que exigeixen un mínim d'atenció – de
      vegades molt mes que un mínim – i que són un punt de partença més aviat que no pas
      un punt d'arribada. S. Vicent Ferrer subordinava els *exempla* a la doctrina. Exposava i de-
      senvolupava el tema del seu sermó i, com a auxili, disseminava els *exempla*. Llull, parteix
      d'aquests per a arribar a la doctrina."

27   Xavier Bonillo Hoyos, "Els exemples del paradis i de l'infern del *Llibre de meravelles* de
      Ramon Llull," *SL* 44 (2004): 75: "Llull seems to create *exempla* to serve his needs and the
      system of his own Art" ("Llull sembla crear els exempla en funcio de les seves necessitats
      i del sistema de la propia *Ars*"); cf. Barry Taylor, "Some Complexities of the 'Exemplum'
      in Ramon Llull's 'Llibre de les bèsties,'" *The Modern Language Review* 90 (1995): 649: "A
      development of the 'Chinese box' is the technique which I term 'circularity,' and which I
      believe may be distinctive of Llull."

28   Cf. Johnston, *SL passim*.

(as in *Tirant lo Blanc*), and some of which remain unique to Llull, such as his method of "analogical stylized dialogue," which serves to establish transitions between the ontological levels of the narrative: from the discourse world of author and reader to the embedded stories-within-stories, as well as between the literal and the allegorical.

It follows that investigation of Llull's narrative structure in the traditional manner might also make some contribution to wider debates regarding how narrative structure allows the reader to comprehend meaning which is produced cumulatively, from the interplay of connected *exempla* and explicatory discourse, and from the novel *qua* novel. With this in mind, this essay seeks the restitution of Llull's place as a novelist within the tradition of the novel. Stefano Cingolani's words on Bernat Metge resonate here for Llull: "As in a puzzle of Chinese boxes, they exist only within the whole [sc. literary tradition], since inside the last one, we may find nothing."[29]

Finally, as Tzvetan Todorov once observed of the Grail cycle, we might say that Llull's stories grab our attention, not as much by hooking us on what happens next, but by showing us, *mutatis mutandis*, the true nature of the Grail.[30] For this reason, their structure is particularly worthy of our attention. If Llull is both "an essential phase in our understanding of Western thought"[31] and traditionally held to be "the patriarch of Catalan literature,"[32] then his presence remains as vital to the field of culture as it is to the domain of thought. This essay studies Llull's two major works of fiction, the *Blaquerna* (1276–1283), and the *Fèlix* or *Libre de Meravelles* (1287–1289), that are representative of the novel as a genre in order to exemplify the way his storytelling engages the culture that he inhabits.[33] In this way I hope to show that, although most of Llull's novels deal with Church culture, he is able to bring his layman's point of view to bear on many realms of spirit. This, I suggest, is only possible thanks to the discursive space of the novel. In order to make this point, it is necessary first to examine the way Llull constructs an acute social critique of the Church.

---

29   Stefano Cingolani, *El somni d'una cultura: "Lo Somni" de Bernat Metge* (Barcelona: 2002), 278: "Com en un joc de caixes xineses, l'existència és en el conjunt [sc. de la tradició literària], ja que, a l'interior de l'última, potser no hi trobaríem res."

30   Tzvetan Todorov, *Poétique de la prose* (Paris, 1971), 73.

31   Yves Pélicier, "Un gran catalan du XIIIme siècle: Raymond Lulle," *Revue de Psychologie des Peuples*, 25.2 (1970): 196: "une étape essentielle pour notre connaissance de la pensée occidentale."

32   E. Allison Peers, "Ramon Lull and the World of Today," *Hispania*, 11 (1928): 464; Xavier Bonillo Hoyos, *Literatura al "Llibre de Meravelles"* (Barcelona, 2008), 13.

33   On the date of *Blaquerna*, see *Romanç d'Evast e Blaquerna*, (eds.) Soler and Santanach, pp. 24–30. On the date of the *Libre de meravelles*, see: *Libre de Meravelles, Volum 1: Llibres I–VII*, (ed.) Lola Badia (Palma: 2011), 23–27.

Llull's novels are of wider cultural significance than is suggested by those who forward them as an example of universal sermonizing. So, when I focus on the birth of the hero as a framing device, the novel's social realism, or the use of irony and understatement to achieve narratorial distance, these critical exercises are not ends in themselves, but are intended rather to test Llull's apology of lay culture. This perspective will, I hope, provide objectively measurable ways of approaching an otherwise difficult and inaccessible realm.

9.2 Libre d'Evast e Blaquerna

Blaquerna is an early prototype *Bildungsroman*, in the tradition of popular folk-tales like *Li Contes del Graal.* As in that romance, the genetic origin of the hero performs a central role in Llull's creation.[34] But, unlike Perceval, Blaquerna can escape his genetic destiny. This primary inversion of the genre's basic structure serves to open up a dialogical space in which the competing demands of lay and ecclesiastical cultures are placed in tension. The main narrative device used to negotiate this opposition is the guardianship of lineage through the institution of marriage. The thematic importance of the topic resonates throughout the novel, which is concerned with a layman's participation in religious life against his will as a propaedeutic to his ultimate liberation from worldly affairs (including the temporal aspect of the Church) in the life of the lay hermit, which Blaquerna finally achieves after he relinquishes the Papacy. Therefore it is necessary to outline how Llull privileges the hero's family history at the outset of the novel to appreciate what the narrative purpose of this is, and what effects it engenders in terms of social realism and narrative voice, two of the features of novelistic discourse which enable the reader to determine Llull's contribution to lay culture (in his development of the novel genre).

At the start of the novel, Blaquerna's father Evast is struggling to determine how his life may best serve God: the decision he has to take is whether it is better to join the religious estate, or remain a layman, defined by Llull as the

---

34 Chrétien de Troyes, *Perceval or The Story of the Grail*, lines 408–15, trans. Ruth Harwood Cline (Athens, Georgia: 1985), p. 14: "I had expected / sweet son, that you could be protected / so perfectly from chivalry / that you would never hear or see / one thing about it, for by right, / dear son, you would have been a knight, / if God had let your father and other / friends live to raise you;" (ed.) Keith Busby, *Roman de Perceval ou le Conte du Graal* (Tübingen: 1993), pp. 17–18: "Biax dols fix, de chevalerie / vos quidoie si bien garder / que ja n'en oïssiez parler / ne que ja nul n'en veïssiez. / Chevaliers estre deüssiez, / biax fix, se Damedieu pleüst, / qui vostre pere vos eüt / gardé et vos autres amis."

"Order of Matrimony" (*orde de matrimoni*).[35] Three things incline Evast not to take a religious career. He is from a noble lineage, he is its principal heir, and it can only be perpetuated if he continues to maintain it. The need to continue to administer his wealth provides a social good, because he will continue his father's tradition of distributing wealth in the community, through his charitable foundations. This requires him to marry. The marriage he asks his parents to arrange is described as a model of lay spirituality, and a number of things are remarkable about the way Llull introduces the theme. First of all, the decisions that Evast takes are his own, and the narrator makes it explicit that he is not responding to societal or parental pressure: "When Evast had duly considered and meditated upon [the matter]."[36] His wife, Aloma, is chosen as the ideal candidate, because she has been well educated, is of good character and has administrative experience: "The good lady oversaw and maintained her mother's household [well]."[37] At this point, Llull counters the reader's expectations when he juxtaposes the excitement in the city the wedding inspires, with the ceremony itself: "The whole city looked forward to the Wedding Day."[38] The excitement suggests that because of the family's wealth and status, the wedding will be an occasion for great festivities. But in order to dedicate the marriage to God, Evast holds a a simple ceremony "with few people" (*amb poques persones*), and the wedding day is spent in prayer and in charitable deeds for the city poor.[39]

The desire of Evast and Aloma to sanctify their own marriage sacrament is reminiscent of certain hagiographical devotions in Catalonia and the Midi around before Llull and continued long after him. Stories of chaste marriages, such as the one about Saint Elzear de Sabran, which continued to inspire marital vows of chastity to gain blessings before a child was conceived or to practice after sufficient heirs were sired. At the close of the 14th century, this story inspired Pere March's and Leonor de Ripoll's choice of name for their son, Ausias (derived from "Elzear"), who was sired late in his father's life after a period of self-imposed chastity, resulting from or anticipating the death in maturity of his heir, Joan March.[40] Neither was it uncommon for women who

---

35   *Blaquerna* 1.1, (eds.) Soler and Santanach, NEORL 8:89. The textual tradition is fragmentary, and neither the Catalan base manuscript (*A*) or the Occitan manuscript (*P*) preserve the opening chapters, which has been reconstructed by the editors in modern Catalan from a Latin source.

36   Ibid.: "Quan Evast hagué concebut i deliberat en la seva voluntat."

37   Ibid., NEORL 8:90: "aquella dona era molt bona i regia i manava tota la casa de sa mare."

38   Ibid.: "Gran fou la fama per tota la ciutat del dia de les bodes."

39   Ibid.

40   Ferran Garcia Oliver, *En la vida d'Ausiàs March* (Valencia: 1998), 49, 53; Germà Colon Domènech, "El nom de fonts del poeta Ausias March," *Boletín de la Sociedad Castellonense de Cultura* 46 (1970): 161–214.

had produced children to enter monastic orders, a practice as common among Christians as it had been in the Albigensian communities of the Languedoc: "We find there precisely this ancient Midi tradition ... which saw wealthy widows consecrate themselves to God and even to wear a religious habit within their own home, in the absence of any nearby convent."[41] Thus *Blaquerna's* opening does not place undue stress upon the credulity of its audience. Llull does not open his story in a mythical land, but in a contemporary setting that might have struck readers as unfamiliar, yet not unknown. A reader might well identify with Aloma's horror at her son's desire to become a hermit, so the narrative complication would certainly have grabbed a lay audience's attention with questions of marriage and inheritances, an area in which Llull displays careful courtesy as well as experience. Llull's wife Blanca Picany had to seek legal authority to manage her estate in 1276, after Llull relinquished his responsibilities in pursuit of the *vita contemplativa* which, like his hero Blaquerna, he had so much sought after his mid-life spiritual crisis.[42]

On the face of it, Llull represents exemplary models of lay piety. Indeed the tone is almost one of hagiography, as Evast and Aloma's virtues are extolled as paradigms of behavior. But Llull's purpose in preceding the introduction of Blaquerna by anticipating his father's spiritual struggle – which will be repeated in Blaquerna when he comes of marrying age – exposes a dialogical significance stemming from Llull's lack of dogmatism, which has so far attracted little attention. Llull achieves this novelistic sensibility by laying aside the genre of hagiography in the pursuit of a more satisfying literary structure with which to bring his world alive. Blaquerna's subsequent opposition to his mother thus opens up an ironic novelistic space in which each person legitimately presents their own viewpoint as unique, and which the novelist works hard to refrain from judging or condemning. This respect for subjective difference has consequences for the way Llull deploys the novel as a discursive space.

For example, Llull uses hyperbole to push to their natural conclusion the consequences of a marriage devoted to God. Blaquerna's birth was miraculous because the parents struggled to have children until God rewarded their patience. Blaquerna was a child *destined* to seek spiritual perfection, destined to serve God, and this provokes familial and social tension, which Llull explores in detail. The inversion of hagiography is also demonstrated when Aloma

---

41 Anne Brenon, *Les femmes cathares* (Paris: 2004), 130: "Nous retrouvons là, précisément, cette ancienne tradition méridionale ... et qui voyait de hautes veuves se consacrer à Dieu et même revêtir l'habit religieux dans leur propre maison, faute d'établissement féminin à proximité."

42 Jocelyn N. Hillgarth, *Diplomatari lul·lià: documents relatius a Ramon Llull i a la seva família*, trans. L. Cifuentes (Barcelona: 2001), 36.

becomes her son's narrative opponent. Blaquerna discusses his decision to adopt the life of a hermit with his parents, and both give him advice to the contrary, although Evast's reaction is more sympathetic than his mother's. Evast provides common sense advice of the type "practice being penitent and living a strict life among us, before going away into the wilderness."[43] Aloma fears the disastrous consequences in the social order of her son's departure. She is subsequently portrayed as an interfering matchmaker, who places temptation in the way of her son through the prospect of marriage to an attractive girl.[44] This contrasts with her saintly persona as depicted in the opening chapter. Interestingly, though, Llull remains objective (thus indicating the novel form's inherent dialogicity) because Evast's decision to marry was extolled as legitimate in the opening chapter. So rather than attempting to privilege one decision over the other, Llull would seem to be placing the two decisions in juxtaposition in order to achieve a structural effect, whereby neither decision is discounted *a priori* from being morally valid. He is also, by implication, ironizing his hero, by making his rashness seem, in comparison with the common sense of his father, indicative of youthful naivety, thus also providing a wide scope for humor later in the novel. The way that Natana's proposal of marriage is handled provides a particularly striking instance of Llull's social engagement, one which requires a narrator capable of manipulating the narratorial voice through understatement.

For example, the declaration of the chapter heading, "How Natana tempted Blaquerna" ("De la temptació que Natana féu a Blaquerna"), provides a piece of understatement, because Natana is described in terms which contemporaries would recognize as instantiating cultural values of femininity: "Natana, so beautiful as she was, with prudence, devotion and a great show of love, addressed Blaquerna as follows."[45] Llull is not interested here in discussing the doctrine of temptation, so much as providing a courteous portrayal of Blaquerna's female opponents and showing them to act according to socially legitimate propositions (and which Llull's audience could legitimately identify with). First, Aloma, troubled by her son's decision to jump ship, confides her troubles to her friend, Nastàsia. Nastàsia seeks to honor her duty of friendship and attempts to matchmake Blaquerna with her daughter Natana. The actions of each in this subterfuge are morally blameless and the result provides a funny

---

43   *Blaquerna* 1.5, (eds.) Soler and Santanach, NEORL 8:108: "assaja enfre nos a fer penitencia e aspra vida, ans que vajes en los lochs agrests."
44   *Blaquerna* 1.6.
45   *Blaquerna* 1.6, (eds.) Soler and Santanach, NEORL 8:112: "Bella era Natana i prudentment i devotament i amb semblança de gran amor digué a Blaquerna aquestes paraules."

portrait of what one imagines might have been a common scenario then as now. From the start of this original novel, one is not faced with straightforward hagiography or devotional literature, and this stance shows us that Llull respects the individual desires of the three women Aloma, Nastàsia, and Natana.

The penetration of this irony from the level of the episode into the fabric of the novel is evinced through the reappearance of Natana, who now serves to mirror Blaquerna, much to the dismay of her mother. The reader is led to believe for a moment that Natana has shared in a short courtly romance and one might think that she plots to win Blaquerna; instead we find Blaquerna's words provide an example to follow:

> When Blaquerna had left Natana, day after day was Natana troubled by Blaquerna's parting words; and she thought [often] of the Passion of Jesus Christ and of the martyrdoms endured in this World by Saints Catherine and Eulalia and the Magdalene for the love of God.[46]

Blanquerna's deeds remind her of her own lay devotion to popular models of female sainthood. By analogy – Llull's preferred *modus operandi* – Blanquerna has disinterestedly influenced his admirer. This model will be repeated whenever Blaquerna influences others through his spiritual apostolate. The dramatic irony results from the fact that Natana was intended to marry Blaquerna and ends up following his example *not* to marry. In doing so, Llull is not opposing marriage and religious worship, so much as placing the two in dialogue. The dialogical component (only revealed structurally by juxtaposition with Evast's example) is that Llull is not against parents arranging marriages, as we have seen; he does seem, however, to be against forced marriages; he wants parents to arrange marriages in accordance with the desire for sons and daughters to seek marriages in the service of God.

That Llull could hold this view suggests he was writing in a cultural context open to the spirit of lay education. After all, Natana chooses to enter a monastic order *against her mother's wishes*. This is not so much a lesson about the necessity for young girls to take holy orders (for example, should their parents want them to). The ironic subtext is Llull's reversal of the usual scenario, whereby a parent might place a child in a monastery. So Llull's point would seem rather to be about the right of the girl to do so should she reach the inescapable

---

46   *Blaquerna* 2.19, (eds.) Soler and Santanach, NEORL 8:145: "Depuys que Blaquerna fo partit de Natana, fo Nathana en gran pensament tots jorns de les paraules que li hac dites Blaquerna; e cogitava en la passió de Jesuchrist e en los treballs e la mort de santa Catherina, santa Eulalia, santa Magdalena, que sostengren per la amor de Deu en est mon."

conclusion that this is the right thing to do. To reach this decision Natana is guided by the first part of the soul, Memory (exemplified by her remembering Blanquerna, through whom she remembers God), and she proves the harmony of Reason with Will through demonstrable argument. Natana has passed her first course in dialectic. Natana also possesses an education in courtly manners, which makes her something of a *trobairitz*, able to deploy *argumentatio per analogiam*, based on the hyperbolic analogies of troubadour discourse. To paraphrase the dialogue: "Isn't she worthy to be the wife of a king?" she asks, appealing both to courtly convention and to her mother's pride, and "isn't Jesus the greatest lord she could marry, and so shouldn't she marry him?"[47] Nastàsia responds over the next days by attempting to interest her daughter in the idea of a worldly marriage in order to protect the inheritance. In the end, we are left with Nastàsia insomniac, threatening to disinherit her daughter, but Natana, in cahoots with the abbess of her chosen asylum, enters holy orders while her mother is at Mass, leaving a servant to inform her mother of a *fait accompli*. Conscious of the capacity of Natana and Aloma to appeal to a female audience, Llull includes Natana's tale as a story-within-a-story that resonates concentrically with the wider narrative. Blaquerna rises through the ecclesiastical establishment in a way which Natana's rise to abbess anticipates.[48] This achievement is all the more remarkable because a realistic setting is used to negotiate lay cultural discourses with more sympathy than satire.

Hyperbole and understatement contribute to a certain carnivalesque dialogism in Llull's novel, which is accompanied by realism. Together these key elements of the novel genre distance the narrator from his protagonist. The inevitable result is a pervasive irony, from which the protagonist, equitably, is not immune.

Blaquerna's naivety is ironized by the postponement of his declared objective – to adopt the life of a hermit – by forcing him into positions where the correct decision to solve the challenge of each episode squarely contradicts his objective to become a hermit, thereby plunging him deeper and deeper into temporal affairs. The greater irony is the one that results from the fact that Blaquerna's virtue allows him to reform structures which in reality are not amenable of reform. This structure enables Llull to achieve a number of goals which, taken individually, are pedagogical, and taken together perform a narratorial service of wider cultural significance. No one should wish to dispute the self-evident truth that *Blaquerna* is a novel which is remarkable for

---

47   *Blaquerna* 2.19, (eds.) Soler and Santanach, NEORL 8:146: "Jesuchrist es lo millor e·ll pus bell e·ll pus savi e·ll pus amable que negun home qui hanc fos."

48   *Blaquerna* 2.41.

its spiritual exemplarity, its adherence to and pedagogical explanation of the Great Art, and for its social realism. Yet it is the latter feature which has been most neglected by critics. Realism is a component which, together with narrative structure, serves wider purposes. It is here that we can pursue the study of Llull's cultural significance as an author of the *poësis*, of *historiae fictae* or narrative fictions defined in ancient literary theory.

It will be objected that the concept of "narrative structure" is one alien to all medieval accounts of rhetoric, because the classical and medieval poetic treatises did not deal with the basic components of storytelling which relied on an implicit knowledge of rhetoric. The latter was such an elementary part of the curriculum, that it was either taken for granted or its purview was misinterpreted, because the *Prima Rhetorica* was restricted to the three classes of oratory as defined by Cicero, following Aristotle, in his *De Inventione*.[49] Be this as it may, the modern notion of literary structure is subsumable within the traditional rhetorical category of *dispositio*, and therefore may be applied without anachronism, if we accept that a medieval author intended his work to be laid out in a way that enhanced its meaning.

The structural perspective does not necessarily need to contradict the declared structuring principles with which Llull prefaces his work, such as the symbolic statement in *Blaquerna's* preface that the work is divided into five books, mirroring the five wounds of Christ. Such divisions may reflect doctrine, but they do not reflect the narrative structure. So, for example, the fact that Chapters 61–66 of the second book each bear as their title a verse from the *Ave Maria*, is a doctrinal correspondence that resonates with the Marian sub-themes of the chapters, but it does not affect how the story unfolds in terms of *dispositio*. Llull's realism, by way of contrast, exercises a far more pervasive structural function in this regard. I will argue in the remainder of this section that realism is used in order to make his societal critique a means of defending lay cultural values and integrating them within a spiritual discourse which seeks to defend them against admonishment from ecclesiastical sources, and that in this lies Llull's cultural significance, in so far as it can be determined through features of novelistic discourse loosely considered to perform structural functions. The object of Llull's irony is the Church, because his hero is a layman, uninterested in the ecclesiastical estate and seeking to be a hermit, yet he finds himself having to sort out all kinds of problems in the ecclesiastical world.

For example, in Chapter 63 "Dominus Tecum," the third verse of the *Ave Maria* is mirrored in the chapter when Blaquerna's greeting "Dominus Tecum" is muffled by a peasant, digging a vineyard with his wide-bladed hoe (*càvec*). The

---

49   Cicero, *De inventione* 1.7, (ed.) H.M. Hubbell (Cambridge, Mass.: 1949), 19–20.

allegorical, exegetical context, reminiscent as it is of Llull's use of *exempla*, is offset by the strictly narrative components, which, curiously, are those very elements which provide verisimilitude or realism to the episode, by lending it an unexpected tenor reminiscent of what the Russian formalists once called "defamiliarization." So, the hero Blaquerna, who at this point in the novel has been elected abbot, sets out to resolve a conflict arisen between the monastery and a peasant who has started working on a vineyard belonging to the monastery farm. The situation exemplifies the novel's realism. Blaquerna's first attempts to greet the peasant fall on deaf ears. Blaquerna decides that he will "kneel before the peasant and greet him with devout humility so that his greeting would be filled with the power of virtue."[50] The action of the abbot Blaquerna towards the peasant strikes the reader as unfamiliar. Paradoxically, as well as defamiliarizing the context, it enhances verisimilitude. And Llull reinforces this impression explicitly, by reporting the perspective of the cellarer (a leading monastic official) who accompanies the abbot. The cellarer serves as Blaquerna's dialectical opponent throughout Book Two: "The cellarer reprimanded the abbot vehemently, saying that he brought the good name of the monastery into disrepute by honoring the peasant so."[51] Blaquerna's actions on spiritual grounds, rather than in accordance with social *mores*, through humility, serve verisimilitude, by making Blaquerna unique (i.e. willing to ignore convention where appropriate). This uniqueness, in turn, reminds the reader of the social context in a way which otherwise would not have been so apparent. Blaquerna's uniqueness also serves to push against the allegorical component of the narrative.

Llull is quite alone in medieval literature for depending on the whole upon realistic narrative scenarios, notable for their ordinariness. Events in Book Two, for example, are not merely plausible, they actively promote a stark sense of realism, for which there are few precursors in the Western canon. A modern reader might not be struck by Llull's realism because several things distract from the impression, such as the doctrinal component, the lack of description, paradigmatic characterization, intensely abstract or minimal use of narrative indices, the exaggerated (yet exemplary) naivety of the protagonist, and, most importantly, our exposure to novels which take for granted half a millennium of subsequent developments in narrative techniques, including a sophistication in the tools of language for representing consciousness. Some commentators

---

50   *Blaquerna* 2.63, (eds.) Soler and Santanach, NEORL 8:289: "que s'agenollás al pagés e que·l saludás ab devoció e ab humilitat per tal que en la salutació vengués virtut."

51   Ibid.: "Lo cellerer représ fortment l'abat dient que tot lo monestir era avilat en la honor que ell fahia al pages."

clearly view Llull's realism as a byproduct of his exemplarity and relate it to his missionary or sermonizing tendencies. One must object, however, that if Llull's realism is narratively significant, its functions go beyond the sphere of the *dispositio* of the sermon genre and properly enter the more dialogical space of literary fiction. If this is so, as I argue, the repercussions may be worth pursuing further.

The realistic elements become more apparent in Chapter 52 of Book Two, when Blaquerna sets out to seek Narpan, the false penitent, and this picaresque episode brings Blaquerna into contact with monastic life, resulting in a conflict of interests which gives increased prominence to representing social reality as a key theme of the novel. The fact that narrative structure itself becomes more sophisticated indicates that it serves a purpose which is tied to the greater demands made on the narrator as a result of attempting to lend his work verisimilitude. This emergent novelistic consciousness presupposes a wider sense of narrative technique than episodic structure allows of itself. Chapter 53 "On Perseverance" refers to spiritual teachings which are diversely interpreted by the abbot and by the protagonist. Blaquerna thinks he should persevere in his original quest to lead a *vita contemplativa*, whereas for the abbot perseverance means subordinating the development of the virtues to the wider needs of society, which in this case, means that Blaquerna should join the society of his monastery, an argument supported by the prior, *pace* Blaquerna's objections. The exchange is left unresolved, and the decision Blaquerna takes in the following Chapter 54 "On Obedience" reflects the fruit of the protagonist's meditation of the question, which evinces that the chapters are not self-contained doctrinal units as much as they develop into something which is more than episodic, as the parts serve a developing whole, with discursive consequences. The importance of narrative structure to Llull's novel is patent, then, because only developments in the narrative – events in the life experience of the protagonist – determine Blaquerna's response to life in an emotionally engaged way. Let us examine how Blaquerna's decision to join the monastery demonstrates this.

Blaquerna remains skeptical at the beginning of Chapter 54 as to the wisdom of joining the monastery and is willing to argue with the cellarer and the sacristan. Experience – which Llull can only show in a novel form – teaches Blaquerna when he consoles a dying man, plagued with doubt about the sacraments, by reigniting the man's belief. This shows Blaquerna the truth, that he should put his knowledge to use in helping people. In a manner typical of Llull's psychological realism, Blaquerna requires more time to consider a matter as grave as taking holy orders. Llull's decision to pursue the question across another chapter reveals narrative ambition and a desire to make narrative structures reflect real processes. So, he makes the narrative experiential rather than schematic. Over several days, Blaquerna ponders the teaching received and finally resolves, after much starlit meditation before dawn, that his literacy, knowledge and his dexterity in the Lullian Art mean that he cannot pursue his own enlightenment selfishly, but must share it where it is needed, in society. This socially engaged coming of age by the protagonist-in-search-of-illumination represents a subsumption of pedagogical purpose within known types of narrative structure, because it allows the narrator to distance himself from the viewpoint of the protagonist. The separation of the narratorial voice underscores the sense of realism and also allows the author to criticize society obliquely.

Let us examine the textual methods of Llull's narrator to achieve the effect of narratorial distance (an achievement given the limited materials with which he had to work), in the following passage:

> Blaquerna taught the sciences and the Art according to the procedure stated above. And one day the abbot and the prior and the cellarer were in the abbot's chambers and spoke with Blaquerna about his students. The cellarer said to the abbot that he suspected that a time would come when they would be scorned by Blaquerna's pupils, since knowledge is surely an occasion for vanity and pride, because of which those lacking knowledge are scorned. So the cellarer advised the abbot that they abolish the school, especially because of the school's great cost.[52]

The decision to narrate in *oratio obliqua* achieves a number of objectives with rapidity. The method distances narratorial viewpoint from that of the protagonist, by demonstrating an awareness of the social opposition around educational reform more widely – and not just Llull's pedagogical involvement with his Art, the benefits of which Blaquerna extols at the end of Chapter 53. By using the quotative modality of the subjunctive after a reporting clause or indirect speech, indicating that the speaker is not responsible for the truth-validity of the discourse spoken, the narrator is automatically at a distance and conveys his non-committal attitude to the propositional content of the utterance itself, thereby opening up the novelistic space to irony. This narrator is

---

52   *Blaquerna* 2.57, (eds.) Soler and Santanach, NEORL 8:262: "Blaquerna mostrá les sciencies e la art segons l'ordenament demunt dit. L'abat e·l prior e·ll cellerer staven .i. jorn en la cambra del abat e parlaven de Blaquerna e de sos escolans. Lo cellerer dix a l'abat e al prior que ell duptava que temps vengués que ells fossen menyspreats per los scolans de Blaquerna, con sia cosa que sciencia sia occasió de vanagloria e ergull, per la qual son menyspreats aquells qui no han sciença. E per açò lo çellerer conselá a l'abat e al prior que destruysen l'estudi, e majorment per la gran messió que levava l'estudi."

not like the personal narrator who appears earlier (and occasionally later on), as in this passage:

> You have seen how Blaquerna adored God in the Thirteen Articles, and how Evast adored God in His essence and virtues, and how Aloma begged Our Lady Mary for her son Blaquerna; hence, the great affection and love that they had in their prayer matched their words. And so it behooves us to love God and His works so strongly that the soul and words agree when entreating God.[53]

The increasing withdrawal of the presence of a personalized omniscient narrator to an impersonal one is only possible once Llull has gained confidence in the relative autonomy of his characters to provide the exemplary models he is seeking to propagate within vernacular culture. It is relevant to the development of the history of the Western novel.

The withdrawal of the narrator from adopting an overtly moralizing discourse is a discovery that Llull appears to have made in the course of redacting the *Blaquerna*, but it is a technique which allows greater technical dexterity in the achievement of Llull's missionary objectives, by developing a multi-layered narrative world, in which several narrative techniques combine to produce the effect of realism which Llull discovers in this novel. Chapter 57 exemplifies this simple but effective narratorial method, characterized by its use of narratorial description mainly for the representation of consciousness from an omniscient perspective, including the ability to tell once what happened many times, or narrative compression, for example: "Oftentimes the Prior had imagined and secretly coveted succeeding the abbot after his death."[54] Psychological realism is essential, because without the similitude to reality, readers wouldn't be convinced by the solutions proposed by the Art to the moral dilemmas posed by the novel. After providing information on what characters are thinking, the narrator obviously describes their actions, and he represents their dialogue in a highly stylized manner, wherein the characters frequently use *exempla*, with the contents of conversations reported indirectly. Nonetheless, Llull is careful

---

53   *Blaquerna* 2.40, (eds.) Soler and Santanach. NEORL 8:200–201: "Entés havets con Blaquerna aorava Deu en los .xiii. articles, ni com Evast adorava Deu en essencia e en vertuts, ni con Aloma pregava per son fill Blaquerna nostra dona santa Maria; on, la gran afecció e amor que havien en lur oració s'acordava ab les paraules. E per açó cové que nosaltres amem tant fortment Deu e ses obres que·l anima e les paraules se concorden a pregar Deu."

54   *Blaquerna* 2.57, (eds.) Soler and Santanach, NEORL 8:262: "Moltes vegades s'esdevench que·l prior havia ymaginat e considerat e desirat con fos abat aprés la mort del abat."

in his first novel not to display over-reliance on the stylized dialogue form, with its demands on analogical reasoning skills, which Llull strives to introduce gently. So, in Chapter 57, direct speech is restricted to two short *exempla*, which are intersected by a new line of narrative development. The arrival of two friars from another monastic order allows Llull to demonstrate within the narrative space what was only resolved implicitly via *exempla*. That Llull is organizing his *dispositio* narratively and not rhetorically is proven when he suspends discussion between the abbot and the prior – the cause of the latter's depression being his secret ambition to win the abbacy for himself – and introduces two friars who come with theological questions (a reprise of the previous chapter), which are brought to Blanquerna's brightest student to answer. The interlude serves to prove the ill-founded nature of the cellarer's earlier suspicions (having educated monks instead enhances the reputation of the monastery in the wider world), and serves to lend narrative dynamism to the chapter, when the abbot picks up the thread of his discussion with the prior, and the prior realizes the vanity of his aspirations to become abbot.

Blaquerna has to be convinced, at each new juncture of his ascent in the ecclesiastical hierarchy, of the inadequacy of all other candidates before he will begrudgingly grant his consent to accept his new election. This repetitive structure instances a narrative technique which transcends episodes, affecting the dialogical meaning of the novel, by emphasizing its unity of form and content. Blaquerna is also tempted on his ascent, so that his virtue matches his responsibilities at each stage of the process. The novelty of this form of exemplarity is that it depends on instantiating the inner states of the protagonist. The abstract way in which Blaquerna is guided in his moral decisions through objective or demonstrable proofs balances psychological realism against Llull's realistic depiction of external reality (albeit abstracted in time and place, etc.), and it is thanks to this that Llull manages to enact performatively a three-way conversation in the novel between a naive, disinterested and morally blameless practitioner of his Art, society, and the audience.

This allows Llull to effect what could not have been done directly, to wit, Llull performs in *Blaquerna* a penetrating novelistic social critique. Having a character disinterested entirely in the sins of society allows the author to lift a mirror to society in the way that anyone else would be unable to do, including the narrator. In turn the ironic space of the novel inverts situations which appear to be quite inoffensive. From these apparently inauspicious surroundings, Blaquerna's unexpected and hyperbolic reactions achieve the rest, producing a situational comedy that is not dependent on the narrator's overt explication for its moral to be clear to the reader, a type of novelistic procedure unknown to sermon writers.

For example, Chapter 58 begins with the abbot and the cellarer taking Blaquerna on a visit to the monastery's farms, in recompense for his hard work teaching the novice monks, "so that he could take some time off to relax."[55] And the narrator continues, innocuously mentioning some food items which the two monks pack in their picnic: "The abbot and the cellarer were carrying salted fish and sauces and other things."[56] The way that the narrator only mentions "fish and sauces and other things" does not draw the reader's attention to any impropriety of diet (no mention is made of it being a fasting day, and the monks carry fish, not meat); and so it comes as some surprise that these foodstuffs elicit Blaquerna's admonishment; the latter requests that his benefactors "lay aside things contrary to a simple life and akin to a worldly one."[57] The humor Llull elicits depends on understatement, and this narratorial stance, serves to enhance situational comedy, which develops momentum as conflict between Blaquerna and the cellarer reaches a crescendo with the cellarer's whipping.

The comedy is accompanied – to avoid the descent into slapstick – by a Lullian concern with mental states rather than personal attacks (Llull's *constitutio* is, as far as possible, *generalis*). The rhetorical type of the Lullian novel thus evinces a mild form of Menippean satire, and this vision might explain the topsy-turvy world he is able to create, which participates in some aspects of the carnivalesque: the temporary inversion of the social order in a way recalls Bakhtin's description of the medieval "Feast of Fools," although it is checked by Blaquerna's Apollonian spirit.[58] Like the bishops who wander through Sherwood Forest to be robbed by the merry outlaws, the bishop whom Blaquerna and his monks encounter in Chapter 58,

> went upon his merry way, before him a much-loved nephew, accompanied by a host of hunting companions with goshawks, kestrels, falcons and various breeds of dog. The bishop bid the abbot and his entourage to join them and together they entered the city to dine with the bishop.[59]

---

55 *Blaquerna* 2.58, (eds.) Soler and Santanach, NEORL 8:266: "per ço que hagués alcun recreament a sa persona."

56 Ibid.: "l'abat e·ll cellerer agren peix salat e salses e d'altres coses que portassen."

57 Ibid.: "lexasen aquelles coses qui son contraries a aspra vida e semblans a vida activa."

58 Mikhail Bakhtin, *Rabelais and His World*, trans. Hélène Iswolsky (Bloomington, Indiana: 1984), 77–79.

59 *Blaquerna* 2.58, (eds.) Soler and Santanach, NEORL 8:267: "s'anava deportant, e devant si anava un nebot que molt amava, lo qual anava ab gran re de companyons qui caçaven e portaven auztors, esparvers, falcons, e menaven cans de diversses maneres. Aquel bisbe

Llull paints a jolly hunting scene, without apportioning either praise or blame *ad hominem* (thus avoiding a *constitutio conjecturalis*). The mention of "a much-loved nephew" brings to mind the serious problem of nepotism in the high clerical advancement of extended families and favorites, often featuring nephews (as John XXII later practiced), which led to clashes with the Spiritual Franciscans and other proponents of mendicant poverty during Llull's own lifetime. The bishop represents aristocratic virtues, as his merry company is also a generous one. Blaquerna's reaction to the prelate's pomp strains the bounds of courtesy. Llull's hero frames his discourse from the courtly perspective, by inserting his critique within the frame of minstrelsy – an appropriate fictional space of social critique – by first requesting permission to be the bishop's *jongleur*. Still, the criticism of the bishop's lavish feasting and extravagant entourage does not go down well, and the narrator allows an ambiguity in the bishop's reaction:

> Blaquerna wept. The bishop and everyone else were greatly embarrassed; and the abbot and the cellarer were most displeased with Blaquerna for reprimanding the bishop with such vehemence.[60]

Is the bishop ashamed for his own faults or for Blaquerna's uncourtly display of what onlookers might confuse with puerile emotion (even when it is the result of sincere devotion)? One may note that the narrator restricts himself to a report of the characters' reactions, leaving some play for the reader to interpret the situation. Blaquerna's companions are not at all pleased by his lack of gratitude and good manners. Narratorial distance from the protagonist is evinced by his allowance for the fact that his protagonist's reaction is exaggerated, and this allows the element of social critique to pass through the avenue of good humor. This method of hyperbolic criticism from the earnest Blaquerna creates a dissonance between the object of criticism and the discourse of Blaquerna's moral critique. The scene ends incongruously, when Blaquerna's apparently implacable stubbornness wins a change of heart from the monks, indicating that it was Llull's intention to ironize monasticism and the Church more widely, from within the safety of novelistic dialogicity.

When the cellarer invites a popular monk from a rival monastery to join his own order, and earns himself a torrent of abuse from Blaquerna for the sin of

---

  convidá l'abat ab sos companyons e ensemps entraren-se·n en la çiutat aquel dia e menjaren ab lo bisbe."

60 Ibid.: "Plorá Blaquerna. Molt agren gran vergonya lo bisbe e tots los altres; e·l abat e·ll cellerer agren gran desplaer de Blaquerna con reprenia lo bisbe tant fortment."

envy, Llull's teaching on envy is serious – it corresponds to his Art; but peda-gogical seriousness is not reflected in the narrative content. The doctrine is serious, but the narrative vehicle is funny and consequently more memorable. Innocuous, if puerile, conversations between monks in which "each praised his own Order so highly that he denigrated the other,"[61] are reported matter-of-factly. The cellarer – whose role in the monastic context has to do with pro-visioning and acquisition – makes some harmless comments about purchasing a farm. The normality of the conversation, vouchsafed by the abbot's question "whether the treasurer had enough money to buy the place,"[62] elicits an an-gry response from Blaquerna. On his return to the monastery, Blaquerna not only defends himself against the accusation brought against him by the abbot "since he was so rude to the bishop who had been so generous to them,"[63] but manages to get the better of the cellarer and Blaquerna has him disciplined. The lighthearted yet realistic setting in which this occurs, contrasts with the hypersensitive and naive hero, whose righteous anger has been exaggerated against a fairly innocuous context. This results in a contrast between the object of criticism and the method of criticism, which suggests parody. It is not clear whether Blaquerna's ironization is a distraction from the strangeness of the Church's representation, which behaves in ways which are entirely contrary to expectation, and therefore indicative in turn of an ironization.

If the humor of the piece derives from Blaquerna's inability to accept the world as it is, this spiritual necessity is the root of the novel's ironic stance. Blaquerna changes his world in exaggerated ways, solving the problems he encounters in every level of the Church and rising through the ecclesiastical hierarchy until he is elected Pope. The irony of this absurd career serves to crit-icize society in a way that frequently inverts its own implicit propositions. For example, the bishop whom Blaquerna castigates turns out to be, not a repre-sentative of the corrupt clergy at all, but a most gentle soul who later decides to join the abbot when he retires to a farm, and spend his autumn days in gentle conversation, like uncle Toby in Tristram Shandy.

Llull uses this vehicle in order to make a set of serious explanations about the nature of virtue and power concordant with his moralizing logic. So, when Blaquerna is elected abbot, Llull shows power is servanthood, and no one who is sane should seek more than is given, for in doing so they sin against them-selves, humanity and God. Blaquerna encapsulates Llull's politics when he has Prudence (also one of the four cardinal virtues in Llull's contemplative art)

---

61   Ibid.: "cascú loava tant son orde que dehia mal de l'altre orde."
62   Ibid., NEORL 8:268: "si lo tresorer tenia tants diners que poguesen comprar aquel loch."
63   Ibid.: "con représ tan fortment lo bisbe qui·ls havia covidats."

state that "these [virtues] are great for governing an individual, but they are stronger when they are put in the service of governing the many, and this is why Justice and Merit find greater power in me than before,"[64] that is, now that Blaquerna is responsible for the virtue of others. The young Blaquerna was in no way a threatening figure when he held no power, and was free to criticize whom he chose. But as Blaquerna moves up the hierarchy, he changes his critique into an active reform of the social institutions he can now change radically.

Blaquerna as bishop encapsulates the spirit of the eight Gospel beatitudes, using them to structure his reform program in the same way that they provide Llull with his chapter headings.[65] And Blaquerna's literal-mindedness – a major discursive distraction, which distances him from Llull – transmits spiritual messages in ways that are not devoid of situational comedy, and thus better allow the author to make his point. The very notion of a bishop assigning, in fulfilment of the second beatitude, a canon with "the duty of meekness ... who should preach meekness and be meek so that his sermons be more truthful,"[66] is certainly contrary to everyday experience, meekness being a spiritual quality that is not usually literalized or made so concrete as to be capable of becoming an office. In other words, humor arises from the narrative tension opposing *reductio ad allegoriam.* When Llull places the different officers, created by bishop Blaquerna, in conflict, they behave in a manner contrary to the Art. So, if ideally virtues – human or divine – participate co-essentially and cannot contradict one another, the contrary result produces an ironic humor, where Llull appears to be satirizing too simplistic interpretations of the Gospels by some of his fellow mendicants:

> It came to pass that one day the Archdeacon's majordomo had bought meat, chickens, partridges; and the Canon of the Poor went with a multitude of paupers along the street and met the archdeacon's majordomo, accompanied by two men carrying meat. The canon and the paupers cried out: "Stop thief! Stop thief! The archdeacon's stealing meat from

---

64   *Blaquerna* 2.60, (eds.) Soler and Santanach, p. 277: "Gran son ... en governar una persona, mas molt major so en governar moltes persones; e per açó justicia e merit se cové mills ab mi que fer no sulia." Cicero, *De inventione*, 2.53.159–160, (ed.) Hubbell, p. 326, is the *locus classicus* for the classification of the cardinal virtues as political qualities.

65   Matt. 5:3–12 becomes Chapter 69, "On poverty," Chapter 70 "On meekness," Chapter 71 "On mourning," Chapter 72 "On affliction," Chapter 73 "On mercy," Chapter 74 "On cleanness" (of heart), Chapter 75 "On peace," and Chapter 76 "On persecution."

66   *Blaquerna* 3.70, (eds.) Soler and Santanach, NEORL 8:313: "ufici de suavetat ... lo qual degués prehicar suavetat e suau fos per ço que sos sermons ne fossen pus vertaders."

the Poor [of Christ]!" The majordomo was scandalized and irate, and the archdeacon more so when the Majordomo told him. So angry was the Archdeacon that he wanted to do violence to the Canon of the Poor, but the Canon of Meekness reminded him that Our Lord Jesus Christ remained meek on the Cross.[67]

Funnily mnemonic passages like this also demonstrate the central premise of the Art. One virtue alone, taken to extremes, is dangerous, if not supported by others in concord. So, while Llull frames the story within the narrative world of the central story, it is also capable of an allegorical reading, suggesting that the tension between the two is important to Llull, and itself productive of meaning. Llull does not appear to want to subordinate one meaning to the other, or to arrange them hierarchically.

The literalization of the beatitudes, as offices of Blaquerna's canonry, allows him to pass witness on topics that would be difficult for a moralizing sermonizer to discuss, without condemning them, as when Llull writes sensitively on prostitution:

> On the outskirts of the town lived the prostitutes. One day it came to pass that the Canon of Tears was passing by and he saw there a multitude of those women and he sat down next to them and started to say: "I want to weep over the sins of these women, who sell themselves to devils for a denier. The wide world isn't worth the price of a single soul, yet each gives her soul for a denier to the devil! It behooves me to weep since the ruler does not stop women making men sin in this place. My eyes weep for there is no one to ensure these women need not do this work."[68]

---

67   Ibid.: "Sdevench-se un jorn que lo mayordom de l'artiacha ach comprada carn, gallines, perdius; e lo canonge de pobrea anava ab gran re de pobres per la carrera e encontrá·s ab lo majordome de l'artiacha, qui venia ab .ii. homens carregats de carn. Lo canonge e·ls pobres cridaren: 'A ladres! A ladres! Que l'artiacha embla la carn als pobres de Jesucrisst!' Molt fo scandalitzat e hirat lo majordome e pus fortment ne fo hirat l'artiacha, al qual ho dix lo majordome. Tant fortment fo irat l'artiacha que ell volch ferir lo canonge de pobretat, mas lo canonge de suavetat li remembrá con nostre senyor Jesucrist fo ssuau en la creu."

68   *Blaquerna* 3.71, (eds.) Soler and Santanach, NEORL 8:318: "A l'entrant de la çiutat estaven fembres de bordel. Un jorn s'esdevench que·l canonge de plors passava per aquel loch he viu gran re d'aquelles fembres e asech-se costa elles e començà a dir aquestes paraules: 'Plorar vull los peccats d'aquestes fembres, que·s venen als demonis per un diner. Tot lo mon no val una anima e cascuna dona sa anima per un diner al demoni! A plorar me cové con lo princep no veda que en aquest loch aquestes fembres qui fan peccar los homens no

This attitude is concordant with what Trías Mercant has observed of Llull's *Libre de meravelles*: "Llull's ethics is not a morality of punishment, but rather of persuasion and of love. 'It is true that justice punishes thieves,' he writes in *Blaquerna*, but this is not the moral solution."[69] Blaquerna's canon is a passive witness to the injustice of prostitution, as a matter beyond the jurisdiction of canon law. And though he does pay lip service to the misogynistic view of prostitution as an instance of Eve's temptation, he tacitly relocates the discourse as a problem of lay culture (and so not exclusively a theological problem) within the sphere of secular jurisdiction. Llull's prostitute is a victim who requires help, not condemnation, "to ensure these poor women need not do this work." *De facto* Blaquerna's canon opposes condemnation of prostitution, by sitting in the company of these women, as *women*, not as prostitutes. Here Llull defines the prostitutes as "poor women," rather than with the usual Lullian phrase "fallen woman" (*foylla fembra*).

The narrative world of *Blaquerna* is a mature and well-rounded one. Narration is not subordinate to an *idée fixe* or interpreted from a particular ideological position. Humanity is laid bare for what it is. A spirit of compassion renders what is due unto Caesar, respecting the institutions both of the laity (represented by the monarchy) and of the Church, while lifting a mirror to those areas which might be improved. What is curious is that Llull manages to achieve his social critique while remaining sympathetic to all the representatives of medieval society. His description of the papal court, for example, is both realistic and affectionate; a far cry from the more discourteous attacks of the Franciscan Spirituals upon the institution itself. And, while Llull—like his protagonist—was disinterested in temporal ambition, he never challenges the basis of temporal authority, a satisfying and spiritually enlightened position upon which to construct a societal critique. This does not mean that there is not an underlying anticlericalism associated with Llull's posturing in the novel, as I have attempted to argue.

The value of structure in allowing Llull to make a culturally-determined intervention, to act as a moralizing agent within, not against, lay culture, may appear to function within *Blaquerna*, which sets out to teach the *Art* to a lay audience by poking fun at the Church, affectionately and not without sympathy. But "the distinctive traits of the novel genre, that suit much of the *Romanç*

---

estien. Ploren mos hulls con no es en esta çiutat qui precur que aquestes pobres fembres no aguesen aquest ofici.'"

69   Sebastián Trías Mercant, "La ética luliana en el *Fèlix de les meravelles*," EL 13 (1969): 121: "La ética de Llull no es una moral de castigos, sino de convencimiento y de amor. 'Es verdad que la justicia castiga a los ladrones,' escribirá en el *Blanquerna*; pero no es ésta la solución moral."

d'Evast e Blaquerna, do not define the *Fèlix* or *Llibre de meravelles*."[70] With this in mind we can now face Llull's other major work of fiction.

9.3 The *Libre de Meravelles:* "Felix Qui Potuit Rerum Cognoscere Causas"

The *Libre de Meravelles* (or *Fèlix*) is divided into ten books of unequal length that mirror the earlier *Libre de contemplació* (ca. 1274). Its principal axes, to borrow Rubio's definition, are transcendence and immanence,[71] and the book practices both ascents (from the four elements to man, from man to God) and descents (from God to man, from man to the four elements) in order to make patent the analogical structures permeating the universe, viewed dynamically and teleologically. So, as in the *Libre de contemplació*, the titles of the books in the *Libre de meravelles* give a rough impression of this external structure.

From these chapter headings, it would not have been apparent to a medieval reader perusing a *Meravelles* manuscript that they had traffic with a fiction. The title resembles the genus of *mirabilia*, which peaked in the 14th century, with demand for encyclopedic works by authors like Bartholomaeus Anglicus and Brunetto Latini, pseudo-historical works containing marvelous elements like the *Pseudo-Turpin*, miraculous hagiographies, mythical or fantastic works, and exotic travel writing like Marco Polo's, a genre which overlapped with nostalgic narratives of the Holy Land and the crusades, by authors such as Caesarius of Heisterbach and Marino Sanudo the Elder. A reader attracted by such topics might well be disappointed by Llull. His book was not for a general audience but presupposes some familiarity with his teachings or earlier vernacular writings.

There is a vertical descent from God to Hell, which explains the placement of Hell after Paradise in Book Nine, and reinforces the basic dual structure of Llull's logic as a process of "affirmation" and "negation,"[72] which deploys the three species of argument and demonstration outlined by Llull's *Ars demonstrativa*, as *argumentatio per aequiparantiam*. The latter is a method unique to the Lullian system, involving correlation of co-essential essences or, as Llull defines it, "demonstration ... from equal things, like demonstrating that God cannot sin, because his *Potestas* is one same essence with his *Voluntas*," a form

---

70   Badia et al., "La llengua i la literatura," 27: "els trets distintius del gènere novel·la, que escauen en gran part al *Romanç d'Evast e Blaquerna*, no defineixen el *Fèlix* o *Llibre de meravelles*."

71   Josep E. Rubio, *Les bases del pensament de Ramon Llull* (Barcelona: 1997), 30–31.

72   Johnston, SL 84.

of argumentation which works across all the levels of being, and which is supported by the traditional Aristotelian demonstrations *propter quid* (proof of
effect from cause) and *quia* (demonstration of cause from effect).[73]

Llull begins the *Libre de meravelles* with the first of the ten questions that
medieval students studied as the ten Aristotelian categories.[74] Thus, *Utrum?*
corresponds to the chapter heading "Whether God exists" (*Si Déus és*) and to
Aristotle's category of being (*ens* or *res*), an appropriate introductory question
for a course in Llull's Art, granted that he had only just exemplified it in his *Ars
demonstrativa* (ca. 1283).[75] The novel opens with Felix's temptation to disbe-
lieve in God, which places him in the position of doubt, a necessary condition
for anyone to be in, according to Llull, if they are to be susceptible either to
disbelief, or its opposite, belief, either of which places the soul in a state of
receptivity to demonstrable reason. Johnston argues that this is a *sine qua non*
of Llull's Art as a method capable of providing proofs based both on supposi-
tion and on demonstration.[76] Of the distinctions or conditions which allow
the eventual establishment of "affirmation" or "negation" (Figures Y and Z in
the Lullian Art) with regard to a question posed, Llull accepts the distinctions
of "possibility, impossibility, doubt and certitude," leading him to recommend
doubt as preferable to conviction of the impossibility of a given proposition in
cases like the existence of God or a doctrine based on revelation.[77]

In the first chapter of the *Libre de meravelles*, Llull's bold move, in having his
protagonist fall into doubt about God's existence, provides us with an example
of the Lullian narrative art, worth exploring in some detail because without explanation it might otherwise strike the reader as idiosyncratic or even
strange. We should first recall how the first episode unfolds. Felix comes across
a shepherdess in a context redolent of the topic and discourse of the troubadour pastourelle, but which quickly departs from the *locus amoenus* of lyric or
pastoral. The "brave shepherdess" (*azalta pastora*) is depicted as a firm servant
of God who demonstrates her bravery by chasing a wolf who steals one of her
lambs. When the brave heroine is killed by the wolf, the protagonist "marvels"
(*mervavella*), meaning he "wonders" or "doubts:"

> So that, to his great marvel, Felix fell into thought concerning what he
> had witnessed, and he brought to mind the words the shepherdess had

---

73   Johnston, *SL* 114–117.
74   Ibid., 25. Cf. the later diagram of the *Arbor Naturalis et Logicalis* from Llull's *Logica Nova*
of 1303; ibid., 158.
75   Bonner, *AL* 80.
76   Johnston, *SL* 84.
77   Cf. *Logica del Gatzel*, ll. 658–667, ORL 19:28–29; cf. Johnston, *SL* 85.

spoken about God, on which she set so great store. While Felix thought on this he marveled that God had not helped the shepherdess, since she trusted in Him so. Thus he fell into temptation and doubted in God, and came to the opinion that God did not exist, for it seemed to him that if God existed, he would have helped the shepherdess.[78]

Felix wanders in this state until night, when he is given shelter by a hermit, to whom he confesses his state of incomprehension. The hermit replies by means of an allegorical tale, later called a "likeness" (*semblança*) or *exemplum* (*eximpli*), which provides one of the main structural narrative devices of the whole work. The subject of the similitude is a king upon whose throne there was a man's arm sculpted in stone holding a sword piercing a heart (a red jewel). In the fairytale kingdom which Llull's hermit uses for his tale, a great serpent destroys the king's palace, and with it the meaning of the analogy is lost, until a "holy man" (*sant home*) rediscovers years later the ruin, and after much thought rediscovers the meaning of the *figura*. By using the Art, the hermit succeeds in moving Felix from doubt to curiosity.

Llull's argument juxtaposes three narrative levels, which *per aequiparantiam* he unfolds to reveal the answer to Felix's question. The first story represents the Virtue (belief in God) and Bravery of the shepherdess; these correspond both to the sword of God's justice (in the allegory) and to the Love (*Voluntas*) of the King (which represents the *Voluntas* of God). In turn, a new answer space is created for Felix, as he learns that God did not allow the girl to die as an unjust act (conceived of in terms of her removal from the world, her lack being considered evil), but rather as a change of categorical space, by showing that the shepherdess's evil fate is only relatively so, because the "love and justice" (*caritas e justícia*) which fueled both her bravery and her faith in God earned her glory in the Divine Presence, and serves as an example to remain strong in the face of temptation.

As explained by Bonillo Hoyos,[79] the second section of the first book begins in Chapter 7, when Felix has accepted the teaching concerning the nature of God, and sets out again into the forest in order to continue his quest in search of marvels. Chapter 7 mirrors the structure already analyzed in Chapter 1.

---

78 *Libre de meravelles* 1.1, (ed.) Galmés, 1:28: "Sí que, a gran meravella, entrà Fèlix en pensament de ço que vist havia, e membrà les paraules que la pastora li havia dites de Déu, en què tan fort se confiava. Dementre que Fèlix en açò cogitava e·s meravellava de Déu, qui a la pastora no hac ajudat, pus que en ell se confiava, caech en gran temptació, e dubtà en Déu, e ach opinió que Déu no fos res, car semblant li fo que si Déus fos res, que a la pastora ajudàs."

79 *Literatura al "Llibre de Meravelles,"* 56–57.

Narrative events are used to set up a psychological conflict in the protagonist. The passage is worth quoting in full:

> While Felix marveled thus, a fallen woman passed by. She rode a palfrey, dressed in finery, and was on her way to visit a prelate, who had sent her the palfrey with one of his priests. Felix rose to his feet when he saw the fallen woman and greeted her. The palfrey on entering the water started and the fallen woman fell into the water; but Felix and the priest accompanying the woman went to her aid and removed her from the water. The fallen woman wept and wailed greatly at her wet clothes, and swore and cursed Felix, as it was Felix rising to his feet that had startled her mount and caused her to fall. Felix marveled at how the fallen woman swore at him, for he had not risen meaning for her to fall in the water; and since he had saved her life he marveled at how she swore, the ungrateful woman. The priest in turn marveled at Felix's patience, who sang the woman's blessings all the while she swore at him.[80]

The narrative technique Llull uses here is quite typical. The narrator appears to adopt a "matter-of-fact" style, which once subsequent events unfold, turns out to withhold narrative information, and therefore manipulate point of view to suspend the interpretation of events. The reader only knows marginally more about the "fallen woman" (*foylla fembra*) than Felix. The reader has been informed that the woman is travelling in the company of a cleric having been sent for by a bishop. The lewdness of the topic elicits, however, no comment from the narrator. It is postponed, mirroring Felix's point of view. Llull seems more concerned with the characterization and dramatization of the situation to parody the chivalric romance.

Felix, ignorant of the lady's profession, behaves as a hero should, rescuing a lady fallen from her horse (also a mnemonic metaphor of her fallen state,

---

80   Ibid. 1.7, (ed.) Galmés, 1:77–78: "Dementre que Fèlix en axí se meravellava, .Iª. folla fembra passava per aquell loch hon Fèlix stava. Aquella fembra era cavalcant en .I. paleffrè; molt bé era vestida; a .I. prelat anava, lo qual li hac tremès per .I. seu clergue lo paleffrè en què cavalcava. Fèlix se levà con viu prop de si la folla fembra, la qual saludà. Lo paleffrè qui era entrat en l'agygua se squivà, e la folla fembra caech en la aygua, la qual mullà tots sos vestiments e fóra negade en la aygua; mas Fèlix e el clergua qui anava amb la fembra li ajudaren e la trasqueren de la aygua. Aquella folla fembra plorà e planyia molt forment com havia mullats sos vestiments, e blastomà e maldix Fèlix, cor per son levar s'era squivat son palefrè, e ella era caüda en la aygua. Fèlix se meravellà de la folla fembra com lo blastomava, pus que ell no·s levà per entenció que ella caygués en la aygua; e, car la havia storta de morir, meravellà's car lo blastomava e no li'n havie grat. Molt se meravellà lo clergua de la paciència de Fèlix, lo qual beneí la fembra dementre que ella lo blastomava."

i.e. one which would serve a student of the Art to remember the story). The arbitrary and fickle response the "lady" deals up to Felix, dumbfounds the protagonist, and this silence is formally presented as the viewpoint of the narrator (here an omniscient one). Llull filters his narratorial viewpoint (deceitfully, as it will transpire) through the view of the accompanying cleric, by displaying Felix's virtuous patience as it is interpreted by the priest. That the shocked Felix may not in fact be exercising the virtue of patience to contrast anger is suggested when he loses his patience and gets angry with the prostitute. Llull hereby shows that he has not yet exhausted the humorous possibilities of the episode. Felix inquires of the cleric what their business is, and finally knows as much as the reader; Llull saves his joke for now: "'My lord,' said the priest, 'she is going to visit a prelate, who has sent me as a courier so that he may sin with her.'"[81] Felix righteously expresses his anger (the sin for which ironically the cleric had thought to praise him), to which the cleric, dolefully attempts to explain:

> My lord ... the prelate who you marvel at is a great lord, and he is a man who loves this wench very well, with whom he has sinned for ages; and for this reason, and so that my lord reward me, I remain his most humble servant.[82]

Cleric-procurors of harlots who lack the discretion to hide the sins of their episcopal paymasters would obviously have gotten a laugh out of a lay audience. Llull's parodic intention and ironic use of the narratorial techniques available to him, shows that Felix's lack of self-control and "courteous comportment" (*capteniment*) makes his "sermon" fall upon deaf ears – the woman promptly departs shouting a string of abuse at Felix, which Llull's modesty and sense of rhetorical decorum prevent him from sharing with posterity. Felix's bad example to himself (he should restrain his anger through patience) is compounded by that of the harlot and the imbricated clerical hierarchy. Together these bad examples lead to a loss of spiritual control in the unhappy protagonist, whose moral weakness reaches its lowest ebb, causing him to doubt Christ's teaching because it is not reflected in the practice of a corrupt Church. The structural problem Llull creates, is that he needs to lead the protagonist from a state of

---

81   Ibid. 1.7, (ed.) Galmés, 1:78: "Sènyer – dix lo clerga –, a .I. prelat va, lo qual li ha tremès mi per missatge, per tal que puscha peccar ab ella."

82   Ibid. 1.7, (ed.) Galmés, 1:78–79: "Sènyer ... aquell prelat de qui vós vos meravellats, ha molt gran renda e senyoria, e és hom qui molt ama aquesta folla fembra, ab la qual ha peccat molt longament; e, per ço que a mi provescha de alcun beniffici, són obedient a tot son manament."

doubt to one of belief, by teaching him that the corruption of the Church does not falsify Christ's teachings.

The arrival of a grief-torn mother renders Llull's solution of the narrative problem – delivering Felix to his next master, Blaquerna – more verisimilar. In accordance with the doctrine of similitudes underpinning the Art, Llull cross-es Felix's path with a woman seeking Blaquerna's guidance. She who knows more than Felix: enough to know that she needs healing, but not enough to prevent her disbelief. She becomes Felix's Virgil, an intermediate guide, that he might continue on his quest in spite of his fallen state. Indeed, Felix falls a second time, much to his own consternation, when he lusts after his guide *en route* to the hermit Blanquerna. The second half of the chapter resolves these temptations by explaining their causes through the exchange of analogies.

Just as we can countenance the epistolary novel as a legitimate form, so too we can accept one in which stylized *exempla* substituting for dialogue as one that is none the less novelistic. One of the tales told in this mode has special significance for a lay audience, because it shows us Llull's often-simplified po-sition on courtly love. In it an attractive maiden (*donzella*), described in terms a lay audience would identify with as "most coveted for carnal pleasure" (*molt cobejada per lo carnal delit*) is proud of her chastity, but becomes angered when her enemies spread false rumors about her lack of it. Anger – as it was for Felix – conquers her chastity, because she placed too much store by it, and did not fortify it with the theological or cardinal virtues, or other ones such as *patientia*, and so leads her – as it did Felix – to consider sleeping with the knight who so chivalrously had been paying her service. Tormented by her fail-ure, she sought the advice of a wise man and his advice accords with righteous and courteous comportment: "The holy man asked the maiden to forgive the man, asking her to love him in her heart, so that she might have patience and fortitude, and not be vainglorious of her virginity."[83]

The terms of the advice, I think, are deliberately left vague, not to attract un-warranted attention to the courtly persona which he here adopts, which some less cosmopolitan critics of lay culture, like Francesc Eiximenis, might well have frowned at. A perfectly legitimate interpretation of the wise man's advice is that the maiden should correspond her noble knight's love, albeit chastely, and that not giving herself airs about her chastity – vainglory – does not ex-clude the prospect of the knight's marrying the maiden at some future date, and thus resolving the matter both courteously and within the accepted social restraints. The story, as a moral explanation of Felix's condition, is indicative

---

83   Ibid. 1.7, (ed.) Galmés, 1:87: "Lo sant hom dix a la donzella que perdonàs a aquell hom, e que en son cor lo amàs, per tal que hagués paciència e fortitut, e que no·s donàs vana glòria de sa virginitat."

of Llull's method of not tackling problems head on, but tangentially, and yet in ways which are appropriate to the problems of the querent. Felix is like the girl, both because of his anger, and because he is a young person for whom courtly love doctrines (*Fin' Amor*) are appropriate for regulating the sexual drive. The wise man's counsel for the maiden accords with a righteous interpretation of *Fin'Amor*, which is, one would imagine, the way it was socially interpreted in medieval society, when it was not being unfairly condemned. Llull shows here that he retained his allegiance to courtly love (akin to the *Futuwah* of the Sufi knights), if practiced in socially acceptable ways.

Llull's interest in these matters and cognizance of the importance of lay society in resolving them for itself is manifest in some of his stories that are interpreted literally, rather than analogically. For example, in one case a woman who was too fond of her own beauty became aware of her own fault, through the beneficent influence of her plainer friend:

> The lady fair thought on her wealth, both her beauty and her riches, and thought on the ugliness of the other lady and the goodness that was hers; and in this way she realized her error, against both her husband and herself.[84]

Llull's lay remit as a courtly and more broadly a social author, albeit with a penetratingly spiritual agenda, might lead one to doubt the interpretation of the *Vita coaetanea* often too simplistically asserted by critics. A question which has not received attention is the extent to which the widespread view concerning Llull's spiritual conversion is supported. Did Llull's conversion really entail a rejection of his courtly cultural heritage? The text says:

> Ramon, senescal of the table of the king of Mallorca, while still a young man was given over too much to composing vain lyrics or songs and other worldly lascivities one night was sitting next to his bed, ready to dictate and write in his vernacular a song about a certain lady, who then he desired with a fatuous love. While he was about to write the said song, looking to his right he saw our Lord Jesus Christ as if he were hanging from the cross.[85]

---

84   Ibid. 6.34, (ed.) Galmés, 2:67: "La dona bella considerà en la sua granea, la qual havia en bellesa e en riquesa, e considerà en la legesa de la dona e en la bonesa que havia; per la qual consideració hac conexença de felliment, que feya contre son marit e contre si mateixa."

85   *Vita coaetanea* 1.2, (ed.) Hermogenes Harada, ROL 8:272–273: "Raimundus senescallus mensae regis Maioricarum, dum iuuenis adhuc in uanis cantilenis seu carminibus componendis et aliis lasciuiis saeculi deditus esset nimis, sedebat nocte quadam iuxta lectum

Rubio draws attention to "writing" and "love," both of which change the nature of their "intentionality" after the conversion, when Llull rejected "profane and 'foolish' writing" (*escriptura profana i "folla"*).[86] That Llull dictated the *Vita* to the Carthusian monks outside Paris justifies the conclusion Rubio draws that the object of his affection was erroneous from the old man's point of view: "a beloved once esteemed; a love subjected to temporal change, situational, a sinful passion that sickens the mental faculties of the individual."[87] But is this confession tantamount to a rejection of lay literature *tout court*? Is it not rather a rejection of a young man's lack of sincerity in writing his poetry, and indulging in a relationship that was not sincere (*fatuus*)? The question is one which can only be answered by recourse to the intentionality of his extant work as a contemporary audience might have interpreted it. In my view, with regard to the passage cited, it is culturally significant even here that Llull maintains the question deliberately open, with the presence of the adverb "overly" (*nimis*) indicative of a relativity in Llull's view: the young man (his former self) has taken his passion too far. In light of the fact that Llull was already married to Blanca Picany and had two children at this point in his career, it seems legitimate to assume this would have colored Llull's own view of his former self. These indications seem more relevant than a rejection of lay literature, or even, of courtly love poetry and its role within lay society. In support of this view we may adduce that Llull resisted, long after his "intellectual revelation" on Mount Randa in 1274, to betray his condition as a layman, even to adopt tertiary orders, which he only did so on the recommendation of a personal revelation as late as 1299.

The way Llull adapts this background cultural discourse, which he infuses into his novel for the needs of laymen, is by constructing an argument which is largely implicit and *e contrario*. Were Llull interested in condemning the sexual *mores* of his lay brethren, he would have adopted the anti-courtly stance of ecclesiastics. But Llull is careful not to condemn courtly love or troubadour poetry *per se*.[88] Against this view, some scholars insist on quoting Llull's frequent

---

suum, paratus ad dictandum et scribendum in suo uulgari unam cantilenam de quadam domina, quam tunc amore fatuo diligebat. Dum igitur cantilenam praedictam inciperet scribere, respiciens a dextris uidit Dominum Iesum Christum tanquam pendentem in cruce;" cf. Rubio, *Les bases del pensament*, 20–21.

86   Rubio, *Les bases del pensament*, 21.

87   Ibid.: "una enamorada llavors estimada; un amor sotmès als canvis temporals, conjuntural, una passió pecaminosa que emmalalteix les facultats anímiques de l'individu."

88   Still useful are Manuel de Montoliu, "Ramon Llull, trobador," *Estudis Universitaris Catalans* 21 (1936): 363–398; Dieter Reichardt, "Ramon Llull, trovador: A propósito de un estudio de Manuel de Montoliu," *SL* 7 (1963): 75–78; Nathaniel B. Smith, "Ramon Llull, trobador exalçat," *Hispanófila* 26 (1982): 1–7. A major study of this central topic is still lacking; cf. Johnston, *ER* 25, 55, 86–89, 112, 137, 150, and 213.

condemnations of villainous and mercantile jongleurs, but this does not signify a rejection of the troubadour tradition. Condemnation of jongleury was an old topic in troubadour poetry.[89] *Joglars* were held in low esteem by aristocratic troubadours, and Llull does nothing more than repeat such scornful commonplaces. If Llull's literary praxis was a natural extension of troubadour ideas of literary practice, Llull's relation to the troubadour tradition ought perhaps to be taken more seriously than it is at present.

It is beyond the scope of this essay to go too deeply into this topic, but a number of anticlerical traditions in troubadour poetry serve to contextualize Llull's own intervention in this arena. A generation before Llull, in poems he may well have heard and in a context still understood by his contemporaries, as it had to do with a past in living memory, the troubadour writers of the anticlerical *sirventes* reflected deep concern and anger against the Church's prosecution of the Albigensian War, leading Guilhem Figueira to claim that the Papal See was the seat of the Antichrist. Peire Cardenal extended this to all priests, whom he called killers dressed up as shepherds.[90] Evidently, this anticlerical anger was appropriate to a society in the midst of trauma, in which troubadours were attempting to rally support and mobilize resistance to the invaders. After the Treaty of the Pyrenees (1258), the region's fate was sealed, and the moment for direct critique passed. Authors, like Llull, who still felt unhappy with the state of the Church, never again dressed their discourse in the terms of the troubadour *sirventes*. And yet, one cannot help but notice allusions to the old troubadour anticlerical values when, for example, Llull has a pilgrim condemn the Church's representatives, albeit in milder terms and adapted to a new context: "While the pilgrim stood there, he saw two priests entering the Church talking about sex, a topic which delighted them and entertained them at length."[91] The non-specific nature of the criticism, which could refer to any kind of sexual gossip or tittle-tattle (or worse), would hardly be worth noting, were it not for the fact that Llull associates the priests' inappropriate behaviour with the topic of the apostolic succession. Of course, Llull

---

89   Famous examples include: Guillem de Berguedà, "Cantarey mentre m'estau," in *Les poesies de Guillem de Berguedà*, (ed.) Martí de Riquer (Barcelona: 1996), 126; Peire Vidal, "Tant an ben dig del marques," in *Peire Vidal: poesie,* (ed.) D'Arco Silvio Avalle, 2 vols. (Milan and Naples: 1960), 2:107; and the anonymous "Ges al meu grat non sui joglar," in Vincenzo De Bartholomaeis, *Poesie provenzali storiche relative all'Italia,* 2 vols. (Rome: 1931), 2:301–303.

90   Francesco Zambon, *Paratge: Els trobadors i la croada contra els càtars* (Barcelona: 1998), 100 and 108.

91   *Libre de meravelles* 1.12, (ed.) Galmés, 1:127: "Dementre que aquest palegrí enaxí stava, ell viu entrar en la sgleya .ii. capellans qui de les coses corporals perlaven, en les quals peraules se alegraven e stigueren longament."

does not adopt the mode of troubadour invective, but has his pilgrim say to the pornographic priests:

> My lord priests, you [must] know that after the death of Jesus Christ the Holy Church was entrusted to Saint Peter, and that after the death of Saint Peter until now many apostles have successively been Pastors of the Holy Church.[92]

There is nothing overtly suspect about the content of the assertion, but the relation of the apostolic succession to the activity of the priests is indicative of an association frequently made by so-called heretics, when they questioned the legitimacy of papal authority.

For Llull, even the heretic (only mentioned once in an *exemplum*) is more righteous than many of the Church's representatives:

> In a city there was a heretic who did great mortification to his body. He lived in that city in such a way that no one knew that he was a heretic. It happened one day that he met in the street a canon who was very finely dressed and rode a lovely palfrey. The heretic pondered the harsh life that he led and the wealth in which the canon lived. And in his ponderings, he marveled greatly, then spoke these words: "Oh, wretch, what does it avail you to fast in poverty, entreat God poorly clothed, sleep badly, and be scorned by others, when this canon, vain, proud, rich, and blessed, lives in this world in a nobler and more honored church than yours? ... Fool, become a Christian, for it seems that there is more virtue in the Christian faith than in yours."[93]

---

92   Ibid.: "Senyors capellans, vosaltres sabets que aprés la mort de Jhesuxrist fo comanade la santa Sgleya en guarda de sant Pere, e aprés la mort de sant Pere tro ara ha haüts molts apòstols que successivament són estats pastors de santa Sgleya."

93   Ibid. 5.32, (ed.) Galmés, 2:58–59: "En una ciutat havia .I. heretge que feya gran afflicció de son cors. Aquell heretge stava en aquella ciutat en tal manera, que null hom no sabia que ell fos heretge. Esdevench-se .I. die que ell encontrà en la via .I. canonge qui era molt noblament vestit, e cavalcava en .I. bell paleffrè. Molt considerà lo heretge en la aspra vida que ell feya, e·n les benanançes en què el canonge vivia. Stant lo heretge en aytals consideracions, meravellà's fortment, e dix aquestes paraules: 'Oy, las, caytiu! que·t val dejunar ne paupertat, pregar Déu ne mal vestit, mal jaser ne star menyspreat enfre les gents, pus que aquest canonge, ab vanitats e argull, riqueses e benanançes, està en lo món en pus noble sgleya e pus honrada que la tua? ... Foll, fé't crestià; car par que major virtut sia en la fels xristians que en la tua.'"

In spite of the ironic and anticlerical humor with which the tale is told – which would even have pleased any heretics among Llull's audience – the moral of the tale, according to Llull, is that the virtue of the heretic (which he has had to hide because of his erroneous choice of religion) better enables him to fulfil the better potential virtue of the Catholic Church by his conversion to the True Faith. Heretics, Llull seems to be saying, should convert in order to make the Church a better one. Another interpretation would be that Llull is acknowledging their continuing presence, hidden, within the heart of his own society. Llull presents his discourse as apolitical. But the fact that he mentions the topic at all is worthy of attention. Frances Yates thought the story "astonishing."[94] Yet, the prominent role given to shepherds and peasants makes one think that it is among them that genuine apostles are to be found in Llull's world: in Book Three Felix turns to a shepherd as his master, albeit a shepherd who had once studied natural philosophy. So, although these stories are subject to a symbolic interpretation (as illustrations of demonstrable truths concordant with Llull's Art), they also have cultural significance in themselves. They are polysemic, and their lesser, or literal meaning, is the one that carries significance for determining Llull's cultural attitudes. It is thanks to Llull's skill in blending this "indicial information"[95] into his narrative that the effect, which is cumulative, can be felt.

This cumulative feeling of having contact with a teaching both profound and unorthodox is partly the effect of a tension arising from Llull's juxtaposition of narrative with the representation of a course in the Art. Here Llull's number symbolism provides correspondences so central to his overall meaning, that they need to be explained, because they subsequently re-emerge as part of the narrative.

The microcosm-macrocosm structure in which both worlds reflect one another in a unity of hierarchical creation leads Llull to favor the elements as the building blocks of the microcosm, because their number, four, is a prime factor of the sixteen Divine Dignities, and the four degrees of each element combine to produce sixteen degrees. Llull uses the Pythagorean number symbolism associated with the degrees of the elements, so that he discusses the four elements in the fourth book, and because the sum of the constituents of four (1, 2, 3, 4) produces 10, it would not seem out of keeping with Llull's Neoplatonism to view his division of the *Libre de meravelles* into ten books as expressive of

---

94   Frances Yates, "The Art of Ramon Lull: An Approach to it through Lull's Theory of the Elements," *Journal of the Warburg and Courtauld Institutes* 17 (1954): 138.

95   In the sense defined by Roland Barthes, "Introduction à l'analyse structurale des récits," *Communications* 8 (1966): 1–27.

the pervasiveness of elemental theory in his cosmic vision.[96] Each of the four humors is composed of ten degrees, beginning with an element in the fourth degree and descending. The elements are also, as Yates explained, reflected in the division of the planets into triads of earth, fire, air and water signs.[97]

Llull avoids boring his audience with a detailed outline of the role of the elements and their degrees in his cosmogony in the *Libre de meravelles*, but chooses rather to exemplify the role of the elements analogically, as an aid to remembering, understanding and loving the power of Divine Grace for leading men away from sin and ignorance and towards knowledge of God through the principles of his Art. Llull's attempt to do this in a novelistic discourse is emblematic of the value and structural difficulty of certain parts of the novel, and the following is worth recalling as an illustration of these points:

> The philosopher said that elemental generation occurs when it engenders itself in some composite thing, just as fire engenders a pepper grain, through participation in its hot nature, thus attaining the complexion of a dry, humid and cold nature, while [also] participating in the cold and humidity of earth, in the humidity and heat of the air, and in the humidity and cold of water.[98]

What Llull means is that each element, when it is the predominant element in a compound, presents itself in the fourth degree in that substance; that is not to say that the other elements are not present as well: thus the adjacent clockwise element is present in the third degree because that element influences the substance most significantly. The one that is opposite diagonally is present in the second degree (i.e. one element or degree removed) and the one that is furthest clockwise (i.e. adjacent anti-clockwise) is present least, because influence flows anti-clockwise, and so it is three degrees removed or distant.

As Llull has just explained in a previous passage, pepper is a compounded element, comprising four degrees, with fire in the fourth (giving heat as its primary quality), earth in the third (giving dryness as its primary quality), air in the

---

96   Robert D.F. Pring-Mill, *Estudis sobre Ramon Llull* (Barcelona: 1991), 137; the tetrad or "set of four," represented for Pythagoras the harmony of the spheres, and for Plato a relation to the decad structuring the *Anima Mundi* (*Timaeus* 35B).

97   Yates, "The Art of Ramon Lull."

98   *Libre de meravelles*, 4.20, (ed.) Galmés, 2:11: "Lo phisoloff dix que generació de element és con engendre si mateix en alcuna cosa elementade, axí com lo foch, qui engendrant lo gran del pebre, engendre, sots complecció de calda natura, complecció de secha, humida e freda natura, corrumpent en la terra complecció freda e humida; en l'aer, complecció humida e calda; e en l'aygua, complecció humida e freda."

second (with moisture as its primary quality) and water in the first (coldness being its primary quality). Each element affects the one adjacent to it by lending it its primary quality, which becomes the secondary property of the adjacent element (so air receives its hotness from fire as its secondary property).[99] Each element also receives a secondary property (so fire receives dryness from earth). Thanks to this active/passive component a circular motion of influence affecting each element is produced, the contrariness of elements (i.e. fire and water, earth and air, meaning these elements cannot directly participate in each other), is overcome indirectly. This influence is referred to as "corruption" or "perversion" by Llull and has far-reaching consequences for Llull's Art with regard to the operations of its Figure S (the Subject viewed as the faculties of the soul viewed individually and compositely).[100] The relevance of all this is explained in the *Libre de meravelles* by the Philosopher's student in the following terms:

> When the philosopher had explained the generation and corruption of elements with the example of the pepper grain, the king's son repeated the lesson with the following analogy: "Justice wanted to engender charity in a sinner, in whom Offence resided; Justice moved the Memory of the man to remember, and his Understanding to understand, and his will to love God's charity. Wisdom lent the way of knowing to Justice so that she could move the Memory to remember, and the Understanding to understand, and the Will to love. And it came to pass that Offence opposed Justice, and Ignorance opposed Wisdom; but Fortitude helped Justice, and Temperance Wisdom, thanks to which Offence, Ignorance, Frailty and Gluttony were defeated, and Charity was engendered, in which there remained Justice, Wisdom, *Fortitudo* and Temperance."[101]

---

99   Ibid. 4.19, (ed.) Galmés, 2:10. Cf. Bonner, *AL* 59, for a diagram of these relationships.

100   Rubio, *Les bases del pensament*, 126–146.

101   *Libre de meravelles* 4.20, (ed.) Galmés, 2:11–12: "Can lo phisolop hac significade la generació e la corrupció dels elaments en lo gran del pebre, lo fill del rey repetí la liçó per esta semblança:- Justícia volch engendrar caritat en .I. hom peccador, en lo qual era injúria; la justícia moch la memòria d'aquell hom a menbrar, e l'enteniment a entendre, e la volentat a amar la caritat de Déu. Saviesa donà la manera de conèxer a la justícia per la qual mogués la memòria a menbrar, e l'anteniment a entendre, e la volentat a amar. Esdevench-se que injúria contrestà a la justícia, e ignorància a la saviesa; mas *fortitudo* ajudà a la justícia, e trempança a la saviesa, per la qual ajude foren vençudes injúria, ignorància, frevoltat e gola, e fo engendrada caritat, en la qual stigueren justícia, saviesa, *fortitudo* e trempança."

In his *Ars compendiosa inveniendi veritatem*, Llull explains the process of "perversion" in the soul that is caused by doubt:

> When D [the Will] is stronger than B [Memory] C [Intellect], then E [the composite soul DBC] is perverted in N [the composite soul of KLM, where K is a memory forgetting, L is an intellect ignoring and M is loving or hating].[102]

This also functions, as he explains in this passage, in the inverse direction (moral ascent rather than descent). So, in the case of a man whose sin is caused by anger (*ira* or here *injúria*), it cannot be directly influenced by charity, because anger is the opposite of love (see the Figure V). This state of being is contrary to God's Justice (one of the 16 dignities of the Figure A), and a "relative opposite" of Wisdom (*Sapientia*) in Figure X, which seeks to ignite in man charity. By analogy with the elements this can be achieved indirectly, as Llull says, with the help of Wisdom, the relative opposite of Justice (*Justitia*). If through Wisdom, knowledge of Justice can be learned, the perverted state of man's soul in which remembering and understanding are functioning only potentially as forgetting and misunderstanding, leading to love of sin, can be altered to ascend from the state of the composite soul in N back to E. Because opposites on the elemental level contrast (i.e. fire and water), so do Justice and Charity, Wisdom and Ignorance. If indirect influence of opposites is possible among the elements, so too on the moral level. So that if another contiguous virtue like Fortitude (*Fortitudo*) imparts its influence upon Justice, this is enough to overpower Justice's contrary, just as the cardinal virtue Temperance (*Temperantia*) may influence Wisdom to overcome its contrary, Ignorance. Thus an equal number of cardinal virtues, combined, can overthrow an equal number of cardinal vices, but only if they act in concert.

This teaching perhaps explains some of what is strange in Llull's *ars narrativa*. In the same way that Llull teaches us that virtues alone are weak, but in combination strong, so he habitually places *exempla* together in groups of three or more; sometimes, as we have illustrated, building on each other, sometimes explaining related points of a larger question. This approach is elemental in so far as the way that the moralizing logic works is equivalent to the way that elements exert their influence only in combination. In turn, this belief perhaps explains why Llull is keen to explore the dialogical space of the novel, as its ability to represent multiple points of view seems to Llull more

---

102   *Ars compendiosa inveniendi veritatem* 2.1.13, MOG 1:448: "Quando D est fortius quam B C, tunc E pervertitur in N." Cf. Rubio, *Les bases del pensament*, 146, for analysis.

powerful than the restricted point of view of a direct statement of his doctrine. Llull's choice of *exempla* rarely concerns directly his immediate topic, but can exemplify it tangentially or *e contrario*, as if Llull often thinks that either an oppositional or contiguous approach to a topic can prove more effective. If this view derives from elemental theory (and medicine), which showed Llull that all the elements are present in varying degrees and that their relation is a structural one that can be represented on the narrative level, it would follow that a concentric exemplarity of Llull's analogies cannot be divorced from the wider narrative and that they legitimately form part of the novelistic discourse in which Llull placed them. As we have seen, this is because characters in the narrative learn lessons or teach them via the examples, and the interaction between the stories and the *exempla* is itself functional according to elemental theory, which shows Llull that moral states are equally susceptible to change through influence. Llull's use of *exempla* as part of the narrative texture itself shows that detaching them from it can lead to a misapprehension of the relation pertaining between literal and metaphorical, which is not always clear, as in the following example.

The philosopher's student mentioned above is presented as the eldest son of a king who was introduced as a kind of Platonic Philosopher-King and whose worth is not determined by his generic status, but by the measure of his moral worth. Kingship here is measured according to humility. When greeted reverently by Felix at the start of Book Four (in Chapter 18), he wonders why Felix adopts a reverential attitude towards him. Felix replies with a tale of a proud king criticized by a pilgrim for not playing his role in the recovery of Jerusalem, thus showing two things: first, that the king is humble, and second, that Felix is worthy enough to recognize his humility. This allows the reader, *e contrario*, by comparison of the king in the narrative with the king in the *exemplum,* to conclude that: (1) the recovery of Jerusalem is meant metaphorically (neglect of duty) and not literally; (2) the King is not one of the six criticized by the pilgrim (because he fulfills his duty). The purpose of the tale hereby emerges by comparison with the literal narrative, in which Felix explains that his reverence is due to the king educating his children in God's honor, and so elicits honor. Irony results from the contrast of metaphorical and literal meanings. Unlike the pilgrim, Felix is not concerned with crusading policy, but with education, an intentionality which might be seen to resonate with Llull's own priorities.

This suspicion finds support in the narrative background for Book Four on the elements, which outlines Llull's view of education from the monarchic perspective. It transpires that a queen appears to be criticized for preferring her younger to her elder son. She prefers chivalry to natural philosophy as an education suitable for a young prince. Although one science is hierarchically

superior to the other in the chain of being, both are needed to function in harmony, just as the elements are co-essential to the functioning of higher levels.
So, in contrast with the literal interpretation of Felix's preference for natural
sciences, Llull's exposition of the complementarity of both disciplines apparently explains *theoria* and *praxis* as two sides of the same coin. From this it
follows that Llull's lay philosophy is not placed in opposition to monarchy or
to the chivalric arts, but that he exalts them equally. In turn this suggests that
Llull's vision of monarchy is faithful to the aristocratic and meritocratic ethos
of the cultural circles of Llull's own training.

And this leads me to suppose that Llull's moralizing exemplarity does not
position him *a priori* against troubadours *per se*, but rather against insincere
ones. Llull's novelistic exemplarity, like Plato's teaching on banishing the poets
(which Llull of course did not have access to, but which he repeats, as it were,
sympathetically) leads him to the simple, yet cogent position, that at all the
levels of creation – and in particular in human society – "like engenders like,"
poor examples breed poor social behavior and good examples multiply by the
same mechanism. This suggests that Llull's intention in adopting an exemplary
discourse is not necessarily to subordinate it to a religious perspective alien to
lay culture, but rather to adapt his own spiritual illumination to support existing lay cultural practices, while performing a critique of ecclesiastical institutions. So, whereas Felix's teacher in the court was leading by the best example,
according to the precepts of natural philosophy, in the service of lay monarchy,
Llull's guide into the realm of flora in Book Five is the best example of his kind,
a natural philosopher who has left the city behind him to pursue his meditation
on the natural world in the company of the mountains and the stars.

Once again Felix leads us into the happy space of the *locus amoenus* of pastoral genres, in which knight-philosophers address their pupils as "fair friends"
(*bells amichs*) and in which the stories they tell one another hold a mirror to
reality. So, for example, Felix first learns of the philosopher-knight from an encounter with his lamenting squire, who complains to him that his lord has left
him to meditate in the mountains. In his company Felix's sense of marvel will
unfold at the "significance that plants give of their creator" (*significança que
les plantes donen de lur creador*).[103] The knight has left the city because "a time
has come upon us in which so many are the sins afflicting the world that a man
may well wonder how any man can do anything which is pleasing or agreeable
to God."[104] This suggests that the multiplication of bad examples provides the

---

103   *Libre de meravelles*, 5.Prol., (ed.) Galmés, 2:40.
104   Ibid., (ed.) Galmés, 2:42: "en temps som venguts, que tants de deffelliments se fan en lo
       món, que a meravellar-nos cové con algun hom fa neguna cosa qui sia a Déu plasent ni
       agradable."

raison d'être for Llull's own diversion into the mountainous space of narrative as a means of a more popular engagement with those same social concerns that populate the dialogue between the philosopher and Felix in Book Five, a concern that Felix raises explicitly. He asks: who has chosen better, the son of a bourgeois who studied theology and then chose to become a hermit, or the one who stayed in the city to teach the people to love God?

Llull leaves both choices open as equally valid. Man's freedom of choice, or in the medieval scheme, man's free will, is a sacrosanct part of the divine order. The argument unfolds in a number of ways, some of which are structured for resonance. The correlative of applying theological doctrine onto the sphere of society produces an argument of cultural tolerance and social libertarianism. This is the product of absolute moral values, as in the Gospels: "Either make the tree good, and its fruit good; or make the tree bad, and its fruit bad; for the tree is known by its fruit."[105] Llull's moral absolutism is central to the hyperbolic world-view of the troubadours which Llull also inhabits, as when Marcabru condemns "false seeds" (*falsa semensa*).[106] Llull recalls this in the structural tree metaphor of Book Five.

The tree metaphor, which occupies Chapter 31, is prompted by the sight of a man cutting down a large and beautiful tree. Felix asks why the tree needed to be cut, and it leads to a series of metaphorical stories; the first about the avarice of a wealthy banker (*cambiador*) who refused to give "a single dime" (*.i. diner*) in alms. It occurred to the man who was refused that it would be better if the banker were dead, as his death would put into circulation the money he was hoarding. Shortly after, God cut short the banker's life, and much good ensued. God, in other words, had cut down a bad tree, because trees are not good if they do not produce fruit. This definition of humanity as performing a function beyond itself, rather than being an end in itself, is elaborated in two *exempla*, the first about two brothers. One is a "bisbe ... molt bell de persona e havia moltes letres" who nonetheless served no other purpose because, as Llull says, "that bishop cared nothing for the ultimate purpose of being a bishop, and so produced no fruit."[107] Llull contrasts the bishops with his brother, an

---

105 Matt. 12:33.

106 Marcabru, "Ges l'estornels no·n s'ublida," ll. 71–77, in *Marcabru: A Critical Edition*, (eds.) Simon Gaunt, Ruth Harvey, Linda Paterson, and John Marshall (Cambridge: 2000), p. 358. Cf. Alexander W. Ibarz, "Ausiàs March i l'ús especial de la hipèrbole dels clàssics occitans," *La Catalogna in Europa, l'Europa in Catalogna: Transiti, passaggi, traduzioni : Associazione italiana di studi catalani: Atti del IX Congresso internazionale* (*Venezia, 14–16 febbraio 2008*) (Naples: 2008), s.p.

107 *Libre de meravelles*, 5.31, (ed.) Galmés, 2:51: "bisbe ... molt bell de persona e havia moltes letres ... aquell bisbe no curava de la final entenció per què era bisbe, e no feya negun fruyt."

"urban knight" (*veger de la ciutat*) who worked day and night fulfilling his duty to the crown, "a labor that wore down and destroyed his being" (*per lo qual treball confonia e corrumpia sa persona*). The knight died younger than the bishop, who by his lifestyle tried to extend his life. A certain "madman" (*foll*) – perhaps so-called because he criticized a bishop – accused the prelate of being less like a servant of Jesus Christ than his brother "who, for the sake of saving his people, preferred to labor in this world" (*qui per son poble a salvar volch en aquest món treballar*). In this case, Llull complicates the structure usually operating between metaphor and literal story.

Llull frames the story-within-a-story as if it were an allegorical explanation of a literal act (a man cutting down a tree). In fact, the converse is true, the literal story, the act of cutting down a tree, is the real metaphor of the chapter. Llull's deceptive framing device alerts the reader to the typical Lullian form of irony, which is deployed to make the story-within-a-story sometimes more important (as literal truth) than the metaphor it apparently serves. More rarely, as in this case, the narrative level serves to provide an interpretative metaphor by which to judge the *exempla* as literally true. What we have, then, in such cases is allegiance to lay culture coupled with spiritual condemnation of the corrupt tree of the Church. This sentiment is compounded when Llull ends the chapter with more anticlerical invective masquerading as metaphor, when he poses a rhetorical question which requires no answer: which is least true to the order he is supposed to serve, the layman who enjoys sleeping with a "fallen woman" (*folla fembra*) or the cleric who seeks to prevent the man from sleeping with the woman, because he secretly desires to do the same thing? Llull is condemning the Church's vow of celibacy as a greater sin because of its hypocrisy. For this reason, Llull not only cannot answer his question, but relies on narrative structure to fill in the gaps that open discourse cannot fill, although the construction of Chapter 31 furnishes the lay reader with all she needs to know in order to reach her own conclusion.

Llull's preternatural foresight as a narrative artist seems therefore to derive in part from his spiritual program, given that he needs to say more than one thing at the same time in order to realize his co-essential vision. One example is particularly memorable in order to illustrate the care with which Llull can make two opposing meanings depend on two narrative levels. This is the case already mentioned (from Chapter Seven of Book One) where the king who allows his bailiff (*batlle*) to go unpunished is criticized by the knight. The knight is only wrong from the perspective of allegory, which serves to explain that God does not interfere in temporal justice because he has granted men free will. Within the literal story of which the knight is part – that is, in terms of a real temporal king – the knight has a point. A king cannot allow his representatives to dishonor his office. These categorical distinctions between the correct interpretation of the literal story and its allegorical meaning is something that Llull pays special attention to. Llull's lay remit, then, is to make the case that spiritual salvation is a question pertaining to the sphere of spiritual education; the only sphere of temporal justice with validity is the office of the temporal ruler or king. His position seems to be that we should not attempt to confuse temporal and spiritual justice, by attempting to govern spiritual states by opening windows into men's souls. Llull's position, then, is implicitly anticlerical, because it follows from his argument that the true Church is not a temporal, but a spiritual, institution. In Book Five he condemns those who would try to corrupt temporal authority.[108]

The outcome of this strategic and context-specific deployment (because it only applies to Llull's society) of the theological doctrine of free will to the political sphere is remarkable, because it implicitly condemns those who seek to punish sins (and by extension beliefs) – rather than crimes – and thus fail to apply the Gospels' distinctions between man's justice, capable of punishing crimes, and God's justice, which punishes sins.[109] Llull implicitly rejects the Church's position, which sought to regulate man's spiritual life as if it were capable of submitting human beliefs to temporal justice, when beliefs and crimes pertain to two separate spheres, and the spiritual realm is only subject to God's justice. Llull's position suggests that he thought the Church guilty of abusing secular power (perhaps by actively using ecclesiastical authorities to persecute people for their beliefs, but having secular authority execute the sentences). If this is correct, it might explain why Llull seeks to bolster lay confidence in temporal authority as a response to the formation of a persecuting society, by seeking to restrict temporal authority to the field of secular justice. In Llull's fictional space, it behooves students like Felix who fall into temptation to seek the teaching of hermits and shepherds and philosophers, and one might even get the impression that they prefer the solitude of the woods, far from inquisitors.

And this brings us to Book Seven (Chapters 37–43) of the *Libre de meravelles*, known as the *Libre de les bèsties*. Chapter nine from this volume analyzes in detail the *Libre de les bèsties*. Its relevance to the present essay is that it has so often been studied as a work considered to be independent. I do not consider it "anomalous ... as critics have often pointed out and that this separateness is marked by two discontinuities in the text."[110] The discourse of the fox appears

---

108   Ibid. 5.30, (ed.) Galmés, 2:47, for example.
109   E.g. Matt. 22:21; Luke 6:37; John 8:7.
110   Taylor, "Some Complexities," 648.

to mirror the kind of discourse we have come to be familiar with between Felix and his various masters. The fox, after all, provides reasoned discourse based on demonstrative reasons amply illustrated with recourse to the same types of likenesses (*semblances*) or *exempla* (*eximplis*) habitually employed, by characters in the novel, in place of dialogue. The only difference is intention. The fox's intention is not sincere, and her use of the analogical Art is entirely subordinate to her own self-serving interest. Book Seven appears to provide an antidote to exemplary discourse. As an inverted reflection of the *Libre de meravelles*, what is sincere in the rest of the book becomes insincere in Book Seven, for here we are reminded that discourse can and frequently is manipulated in society. In this regard it is telling, that in contrast to the rest of the *Libre de meravelles*, almost all of the "likenesses" (*semblances*) in Book Seven, and certainly all those told by the fox, are false, because they are intended to deceive. Many of the parables (*semblances*) told by other animals are also false because they are based on false premises, resulting from false belief in the discourse of the fox. For Llull, sincerity in discourse reflects Will (*Voluntas*), emanating from the heart.[111] This is implicit in Llull's preference for translating *voluntas* with the verb "to love" (*amar*), but it is curious that he does not specifically mention the importance of the heart as the physical and spiritual location of love, at least not in *Blaquerna* or the *Libre de meravelles*. Perhaps he thinks this is obvious and so not worth mentioning. Although a simple example, it illustrates the oral nature of the *opera aperta*: the heart as the seat of love is a basic concept that Llull shares with the troubadours. Or perhaps Llull doesn't mention it in order not to break with the formal definition of the Augustinian soul, which appears to have left the doctrine unexplained. In any case, without a sincere intention, man is worse than the beasts, who lack higher reason, because humans misuse their God-given faculty. So we may conclude that the *Libre de les bèsties* is not a separate "novel about beasts," in so much as its meaning depends on contrasting the intentionality of analogies wrongly used against their proper use elsewhere in the *Libre de meravelles*. To this extent, it is about carnivorous men who insincerely deceive the naive herbivores of this world. What man becomes if he is not careful – worse than the beasts – is only explained positively in Book Eight, the structural heart of the novel, in which all the varied strands of Llull's rich fictional world are tied together. It is enough here to end this survey, by looking briefly at some of the societal representations in Book Eight that are of greatest significance for the present argument.

---

111   Avicenna, *A Treatise on the Canon of Medicine of Avicenna*, (ed.) O.C. Gruner (New York: 1970), 140 and 143, explains the place of the heart in the compound soul.

Llull's representation of kings and kingship serves a variety of functions within the narrative, and one ought to be skeptical of any attempt to quantify their positive and negative associations, or to draw any conclusions from this. On balance, we would have to accept a simplification for this to be feasible, namely that the literal content of the *exempla* can serve as an ancillary confirmation of Ramon Llull's political theory. A further simplification is needed, to accept that the king's *persona* occupies the central position. Our task may be aided by a comparison of kings and prelates, both of which Llull considers representatives of temporal authority.

The highest ecclesiastical office represented in Book Eight is the archbishop, although quantitatively, bishops are more common, and so both categories may be subsumed under the broader genus of "prelate," as the equivalent of "prince" (within which Llull includes kings). Asymmetrically, Llull's four positive references to the figure of the emperor are not matched by references to a pope; none the less, the positive treatment of the former indicates Ghibelline sympathies in keeping with Barcelona's foreign policy in this period. Positive references to kings occur in roughly half the total number of 78 mentions: if the sum of those kings who are virtuous (28) is added to the number of kings who undergo positive transformation in the course of an *exemplum* (12), they total 40, against 36 instances of corrupt or unrepentantly sinful monarchs, a fair and balanced proportion. The statistics are provided from tabulation of characters mentioned as individuals across 323 *exempla* in the edition used of Book Eight. The subjective component of classification as "positive" or "negative" transformations has been minimized as far as possible but cannot be excluded entirely in all cases; uncertain cases are treated as "neutral."[112]

Llull's ideal monarch is one who understands (as *Blaquerna* teaches in regard to the ecclesiastical estate) that greater power entails greater servanthood, and it is a lesson taught repeatedly. So for example, a hermit who meets a king in the desert recognizes a king's virtue by asking the question "can great wealth defeat envy?" to which the wise king replies: "human desire is greater when it defeats envy in greatness, than when it defeats it in smallness."[113] Llull's spiritual logic applied to the institution of monarchy supports the institution. Just as it is not the office of the prelate which is corrupt, but rather the sinful occupant, so it is not the office of kingship which is in itself productive of the

---

112   Bonillo Hoyos, *Literatura al "Llibre de Meravelles,"* 113–128, has inspired the approach adopted here, although the *exempla* counted are fewer than those tabulated by Bonillo Hoyos.

113   *Libre de meravelles* 8.74, (ed.) Galmés, 4:6: "umà desir era pus forts quant vens enveya en granea, que quant la vens en poquea."

corruption of power. To this end, Llull's political theory teaches that the king's subjects (*poble*) owe their allegiance to both good and bad kings, although Llull teaches that God wants kings to be good: "God wanted the Prince to be good, so that he might be loved by his peoples,"[114] because in this way, as he says in this passage and elsewhere, a good king better enables the whole of society to function to its maximum potential "that greatness might reside in every degree [of the social order]" (*que hi sia granea en cascun dels graus*).[115] However, as Llull's bourgeois would-be tyrannicide learns in Chapter 75 of Book Eight, bad kings need to be endured as a test of man's patience (passivity or suffering) in loyal servanthood. Here the bourgeois discovers that, although he is right to be angry at a bad lord (righteous anger), he must be patient not to entertain the madness of acting on his anger to the detriment of his natural lord's right to rule. The social perils of bad kingship, which Llull is encouraging the bourgeois to combat by more spiritual means, are revealed when negative exemplarity effects a trickledown effect "and the intention of all the king's judges, municipal representatives, and officials converged to follow the example of the king."[116] A corrupt intention among those in political power causes a multiplication of sin in the lower orders.

The "people" (*poble*) assume an active role only in eight *exempla*, in four of which they take an oppositional role towards the king. In advising kings on how to deal with their subjects, Llull's Art comes out well from a comparison with Machiavellian political theory: comparison reveals Llull to be neither naive nor unaware of the needs of *Realpolitik*, as the following passage instantiates, when an emperor asks a king for advice:

> There was a king who was wont to presume a man to be bad before he met him; ...first he tempted him before placing his trust in him; and if he was bad, he would make him fear him; if he proved himself to be good, he would make him love him.[117]

It is better for a ruler to be loved than to be feared, but it is legitimate to employ fear where there is no possibility of inspiring love. In this way, Llull both

---

114   Ibid. 4.98, (ed.) Galmés, 4:164: "Déus volch que príncep sia bo, per ço que sia amat per ses gents."
115   Ibid. 8.107, (ed.) Galmés, 4:220.
116   Ibid. 8.107, (ed.) Galmés, 4:221: "e en aquella entenció del rey se convertia tota le entenció de sos vaguers, batles, jutges e officials."
117   Ibid. 8.111, (ed.) Galmés, 4:247: "Era .i. príncep qui havia manera que tot hom, ans que·l conegués, presumia que fos hom mal; ...ell lo temptava primerament, ans que en ell se fias; e si era mal, faye's a ell tembre; si era bo, feya's a ell amar."

anticipates Machiavelli and provides a more satisfying account of the role of human nature in the body politic than was apparently available in 15th-century Florence. Even good kings can suffer the disloyalty of ungrateful subjects, and just as virtue is earned by enduring a cruel king, the opposite is also the case. What is true of kings is also true of other lords (and allegorically of all estates), so that a people who struggle overmuch to increase their liberties and privileges (*franqueses*) inappropriately cause damage not only to their lords, but to themselves.[118]

The aristocracy is hardly ever represented in the *exempla*: only four counts (*comtes*), one countess (*comtessa*), one marquis (*marquès*), and one baron (*baró*) appear. The minor aristocracy, representing Llull's own background, are frequently mentioned in small roles, and they are on the whole positively or neutrally assessed (10 positive exemplars, 7 negative, 4 transform to virtuous conduct and 16 appear neutral). They appear fighting, where their virtue is associated with their justice in victory or their patience in defeat.[119] Their role is morally neutral on the literal level, either because they perform the role of bystanders or because they perform some other neutral function, such as the example of the "the lightweight knight" (*cavaller leuger*), who could jump higher than anyone else.[120] Their squires, however, are almost always devious (in 5 out of 7 cases), and this perhaps reflects a social stereotype of squirely mischief and ambitions of social climbing, although their numbers are too low to determine this quantitatively. More probably, Llull thinks of squires as exemplifying betrayal of a lord, for the simple reason that the most common lords in daily contact with people were from the cavalier class. One example breaks the abstractness of context when Llull refers to a Templar squire who becomes "jealous, proud, anger-prone, and died in sin" (*enveyós, erguyllós, mal yrós, e morí en peccat*).[121] This may reflect popular discontent with the Order in the period leading up to its dissolution, before the loss of Acre in 1291 signaled the accelerating decline of the Levantine ideal. In one case, Llull leaves a question unanswered, when a bishop refuses to answer a knight. In this *exemplum*, a knight reveals in confession that he cannot afford to repay money that he has taken from one of his peasants; the bishop imposes as penance repayment of the money, but the knight replies with a question of his own:

---

118   Ibid. 8.72, (ed.) Galmés, 3:163–169 and 8.74, (ed.) Galmés, 4:78–79.
119   Ibid. 8.94, (ed.) Galmés, 4:141.
120   Ibid. 8.97, (ed.) Galmés, 4:157.
121   Ibid. 8.97, (ed.) Galmés, 4:160.

Lord bishop, I beg you to tell me who is more at fault, whether I who refuses to repay the thousand sous, or you who could donate a thousand sous for love of God, but refuse to do so, and from the treasure that you have acquired you refuse to do the good that you might with it.[122]

This leads us again to the question of Llull's anticlericalism, which would have made his stories more popular among a lay audience, given his tendency to be more lenient on laymen than on the clerical establishment. Llull's indulgence of kings and greater stringency on bishops can be explained by his basic idea that a cleric's office makes him closer to God, and therefore his responsibility to honor his office is greater than that of a layman. Perhaps this is sufficient explanation, given the fact that his whole *oeuvre* teaches the obligation of everyone to honor God as far as their place in society allows; the lower the social position, the less is necessary to secure a place in heaven. However, there seems to be a legitimate argument for viewing Llull's more positive treatment of kings than prelates as indicative of the thinly veiled anticlerical vein in Llull's outlook, already suggested. I can find no other reason to explain the great imbalance between six positive exemplars of bishops out of a total of 35, and that 24 of these are represented as being irreparably lost to sin, while only two are represented as capable of positive transformation.

The picture grows comparatively worse when one considers that some of the kings considered as negative exemplars are guilty of no more than negligence of their duties, by enjoying a game of chess or a hunting expedition. The main foundation of Llull's anticlericalism seems to have to do with the vow of celibacy, which he hardly mentions as a sin of monarchs. Llull goes to great pains to contrast laymen's indulgence of the sin of lust (*luxuria*) with its treatment among the clergy, as in these cases: the "false confessor" (*fals confessor*) who seduces a "good woman" (*bona dona*) by convincing her that sex is not a sin;[123] "the maiden sinned with a priest who spent all day singing the Mass to the lady;"[124] "the priest then realized the sin of lust into which he had fallen;"[125] "a burgher had an attractive wife, whom he discovered one day fornicating with

---

122   Ibid. 8.103, (ed.) Galmés, 4:200: "Sènyer bisbe, prech-vos que·m digats qui fa major faylliment, ho jo qui no vuyll haver volentat ne contrecció dels .M. sols, o vós qui poríets donar .M. sols, per amor de Déu, e no·ls volets donar, ne d'aquell thresaur que tenits ajustat no volets fer lo bé que fer ne poríets."

123   Ibid. 8.60, (ed.) Galmés, 3:88–89.

124   Ibid. 8.78, (ed.) Galmés, 4:33: "aquella donzella hac peccat ab .i. clerga que tot dia cantava la missa a la dona."

125   Ibid. 8.81, (ed.) Galmés, 4:56: "lo clergue hac adonchs consciència del peccat de luxúria en lo qual era."

a priest;"[126] "there once was a priest who kept a harlot at home with whom he sinned;"[127] "when he had heard many women confess the sin of lust, the holy man was tempted by carnal pleasure;"[128] "this bishop was mean, proud, slothful and lustful ... [and] was ruining the purpose for which he was a bishop;"[129] "the hermit said to Felix that a bishop had sex with a prostitute;"[130] and, "it came to pass that [a priest] became corrupt and had sex with a prostitute."[131]

Luxuria may not be the sin that afflicts clergy the most. Their avarice (a sin resulting from Llull's implication that they are wrongly embroiled in temporal affairs) is more frequently mentioned, but their corruption through lustfulness is far more memorable, as in the story of a prelate who, while considering the beauty of the mass, "remembered a lady he had loved very much and with whom he had sinned at length."[132] As we have seen, it is not the only time that Llull makes the image more memorable through the conjunction of opposites, by associating sex and the sacrament of the mass. By way of contrast, Llull's kings are rarely associated with lust, and when they are, they are treated with more dignity.

So, there is the case of the society which marvels at the lack of concern with the business of government, demonstrated by their king, but his fault is his escapism, an excessive predilection for hunting,[133] and this stereotypical criticism resonates across several *exempla*, making it structurally significant. For example, in Chapter 67 Llull implicitly associates "foolishness" (*follia*) not with hunting *per se* but with a king who hunts alone while neglecting the greatness of the royal personage; this is implicitly the same king who risked staying alone with the peasant of the son he executed.[134] In another case, hunting is a cipher of the neglect of duty (applicable allegorically to everyman): "you are the king,

---

126 Ibid. 8.94, (ed.) Galmés, 4:138–139: ".i. burgues havia bella muller, la qual atrobà un .i. jorn ab .i. clergue en peccat de fornicació."

127 Ibid. 8.103, (ed.) Galmés, 4:196: "era un prevera qui en sa casa tenia una foylla fembra ab qui peccava."

128 Ibid. 8.103, (ed.) Galmés, 4:201: "hoydes moltes fembres que a ell se confessaven del peccat de luxúria. Aquell sant hom fo molt temptat del delit carnal."

129 Ibid. 8.107, (ed.) Galmés, 4:220: "Aquell bisbe era hom havar, erguyllós, accidiós e luxuriós' ... destrouia la entenció per que era bisbe."

130 Ibid. 8.113, (ed.) Galmés, 4:258: "L'ermità dix a Fèlix que .i. bisba féu peccat de luxúria ab .iª. foylla fembre."

131 Ibid. 8.94, (ed.) Galmés, 4:140: "esdevench-se que ell [sc. .i. clergue] se corrumpé e peccà ab .iª. foylla fembra."

132 Ibid. 8.93, (ed.) Galmés, 4:134: "adonchs remenbrà .iª. dona que molt avia amada e ab qui havia longament peccat."

133 Ibid. 8.99, (ed.) Galmés, 4:174.

134 Ibid. 8.67, (ed.) Galmés, 3:130.

but you do not respect your office, for you do things contrary to it,"[135] Llull concludes. The association of neglectful kings with hunting is akin to the use of the
game of chess to depict a prince and prelate wasting time,[136] and so can hardly
be used to conclude that Llull was against hunting or enjoying oneself in sport
per se. Llull's Felix, one recalls, enjoys "sport" (*deport*) in the company of the
philosopher.[137] Llull's criticism seems more to do with a lack of proper mod-
eration (*mezura*), resulting in neglect, rather than with a prohibitive attitude
to leisure itself. The story of the king who stole a knight's woman is remarkable
as an exception, and for its lack of insistence on the aspect of lust, but instead
on the abuse of power.[138] In the only other example of a lustful king, the latter's behavior towards a countess is reminiscent of a courtly *requête d'amour*,
although Llull describes it with his standard euphemism for sex: "he sought
foolishness from her" (*demená-la de foyllia*). The countess replies courteously,
and the chastity of the lady leaves the king's lust unrequited.[139]

In short, one cannot but be struck by two quantitative facts about Llull's
exemplary discourse in the *Libre de meravelles*. First, it is heavily weighted towards the representation of lay culture: of a total of 481 characters examined
(excluding social groups or characters with little protagonism), 392 of these
(about 75%) pertain to the laity (all sectors of society), of which 112 (about
29%) are featured as irremediably lost to sin. These data are indicative of Llull's
positive pedagogical approach, given the fact that the percentages in his *exempla* far exceed those that he states to be the norm (only 1 in 100 or 1000 is virtuous, he says). Too much need not be made of the statistics per se, although,
even granting the fact that they could be made less approximate and more
precise, what would remain largely unchanged is the comparative ratio of the
clergy: they comprise approximately 15% of the characters in Llull's *exempla*,
but 46 out of the 89 counted (52%) are viewed as irremediably lost to sin. The
condition of the Church apparently leads Llull to view it as inevitably condu-
cive to sinfulness. For a lay preacher like Llull, this leads one to assume that the
possibility of Llull's veiled anticlericalism is worthy of further study.

The dialogue form, which dominates Book Eight more than any other, means
that narrative structure is both absent and dominant in the stories within the
dialogue. The result is cumulative, a non-linear structure which depends for
its impact on repetition and resonance, associations transcending a single

---

135   Ibid. 8.85, (ed.) Galmés, 4:84: "tu estas rey, mas no estas en offici de rey, ans estas ab coses
       dessemblants a rey."
136   Ibid. 8.90, (ed.) Galmés, 4:112.
137   Ibid. 3.31, (ed.) Galmés, 2:48.
138   Ibid. 3.71, (ed.) Galmés, 3:160.
139   Ibid. 4.88, (ed.) Galmés, 4:100.

exemplum. As I have tried to show, the effect is not restricted to a particular metaphorical function in the moralizing discourse of the individual chapter, but rather exerts non-linearly a resonance across stories which is culturally significant.

9.4   Conclusion

The present contribution to the study of Llull's narrative structure has sought to outline its role in determining his engagement with contemporary culture. Llull's *Weltbild* shares a remarkable resemblance to that of the troubadours. In common with the troubadours, Llull supports the legitimacy of lay culture un-equivocally. Like the troubadours, he also supports the legitimacy of the monarchy as the supreme political institution. His program of spiritual education is also a program of social reform, an aspect it distributes, like troubadour poetry, alongside an agenda of humor and social entertainment. It is also anti-clerical to a degree that requires narrative structure of an ingeniously complex kind to disguise, in order for it to be palatable both to the fanatics and to the "the initi-ated" (*entenents*) of courtly society. In this, Llull's narrative discourse is framed as a response to the formation of a persecuting society by the Church, which was attempting in this period, and had been doing so since the Albigensian War, to use secular authority illegitimately to justify repression. The repression of the Church is felt by Llull to impinge negatively on what we would now call the sphere of lay culture.

   Perhaps more provocatively, Frances Yates once asked whether Llull's copy of Eriugena's *De divisione naturae* was not one "which had escaped destruc-tion in the Albigensian wars? In other words, did the influence of the banned book still linger in the south, so that Lull might have come across it in his own world?"[140] Her answer is worth recalling here in full:

> The young Prince James of Mallorca with whom Lull was brought up at the Mallorcan court, married in 1275 a lady called Esclarmonde, sister to a Count of Foix. This lady belonged to the same family and bore the same name as the most famous of the aristocratic female "Perfects," Esclar-mone, Princess of Foix, whose castle of Montségur was the last strong-hold of the Albigenses. Since, therefore, there were contacts between the Mallorcan court and the courts of the French Languedoc, formerly

---

140   Frances Yates, "Ramon Lull and John Scotus Erigena," *Journal of the Warburg and Cour-tauld Institutes* 23 (1960): 37.

hot-beds of the heresy, it is possible that in the southern court of Mallorca the influence of the sacred book still lingered, so that even in his troubadour days, as a courtier, Lull might have met with it. Moreover, the town of Montpellier, beyond the Pyrenees, belonged to the rulers of Mallorca, and Lull often visited it, and through his interest in medicine, might have talked with the doctors there, studied their books. The Cathars were noted for their practice of some curious form of medicine. Was this based, like Lull's medicine, on an astrological adaptation of Scotism and did the influence of it linger in Montpellier? [...] I am not, of course, suggesting that Lull was a Cathar heretic, but that the Cathar heretics, or secretly unconvinced converts from the heresy, might have been yet another class of people – besides Arabs and Jews – to whom the Art was addressed, setting out to prove to them from their own book, and perhaps by methods similar to theirs, that their heresy was false and the Catholic religion true.[141]

No doubt Llull was a Neoplatonist. His Neoplatonism would eventually lead to suspicion from the Church. Examination of the narrative structure of Llull's novels is enough to show that Llull's antagonism to the Church is only thinly veiled by his overt statements. From this it follows that Llull's affiliation to Neoplatonism is greater than his affiliation to a Church that he considered temporally corrupt. Whether Llull redirected the Neoplatonism of Catharism, whether his *Weltbild* was formed independently of Catharism, or whether he received some complementary spiritual teaching which is not of Catholic provenance, and the acceptance of which would contradict Llull's alleged Catholicism, is hard to demonstrate. Like the Cathars, Llull, is tolerant of the established Church but, unlike pre-Albigensian Cathars, he is willing to work alongside it. None the less, to ignore the main avenues for Neoplatonism of the type channeled so uniquely by Llull, and yet to claim that Llull was a representative of orthodox Catholic culture would be, if not simply erroneous, at least an oversimplification of his unorthodox pedagogical style. Yates's statement is thus suggestive of a possible link with Catharism and her ultimate negation of it in favor of orthodox Catholicism rings untrue. The dominance in Llull's novels of the figure of the lay hermit as the arbiter of all matters spiritual suggests that Llull's hermit might well represent an alternative to the Roman Church and, to this extent, represent Cathar hermit types, then taking refuge in the Pyrenees and documented further south in areas like Montsant (Tarragona), where evidence of their cave dwellings are still visible to this day.

---

141   Ibid. 37–38.

Llull's allegiance to the royal house of Majorca, and to the Aragonese federation more widely, is part of his spiritual lay mission. The only historical person mentioned by name in Llull's novels is his benefactor, King James of Majorca:

> It just so happened that in the Synod there was a priest from the island in the sea, called Majorca; and he told the Bishop in the presence of everyone that that island belongs to a noble and wise king, called James, King of Majorca.[142]

This personal flattery is so rare in Llull that it constitutes an exception demonstrative of the author's cultural allegiance as a spiritual author whose mission tolerates the Church, but finds its true home in lay culture, with the monarch its highest representative.

This sense is compounded by the structure of *Blaquerna* as a novel, which rejects the papacy as the highest representative of God on earth, because above the pope in the Lullian hierarchy of Book Five is the figure of the hermit, whose illumination mirrors that of the sufi saints (as the *Libre d'Amic e Amat* testifies). The other main avenue of Neoplatonism available to Llull, of course, is the sufi tradition, which Llull specifically refers to as an avenue of direct influence in his storytelling in *Blaquerna*:

> While Blaquerna was thinking in this manner, he remembered how once when he was pope a Muslim told him that Muslims have some religious men amidst the other ones, and that those ones who are the most esteemed among them are some people who are called "Sufis."[143]

The throw-away line "once when he was pope" must strike any reader as somewhat ironic, even if the papacy was not always a lifetime appointment in the Middle Ages. Kinkade once suggested that Llull's point of contact with the Sufis may have been their redaction of *Kalila*.[144] Positing a literary dependence

---

142 *Blaquerna*, 2.65, (eds.) Soler and Santanach, NEORL 8:296–297: "Ventura e cas fo que en aquel senet ach un clergue qui era de una illa sobre mar, la qual es apellada Mallorques; e recomptá al bisbe en presencia de tots que aquella illa es de un noble rey savi, lo qual es apellat en Jacme rey de Mallorques."

143 *Blaquerna*, 5.99, (eds.) Soler and Santanach, NEORL 8:426: "Dementre considerava en esta manera Blaquerna, el remembrá con una vegada con era apostoli li recomtá .i. sserray que los serrayns an alcuns homens religiosos enfre los altres, e aquells qui son mes preats enfre ells son unes gents qui han nom 'sufies.'"

144 Richard P. Kinkade, "Arabic Mysticism and the *Libro de buen amor*," in *Estudios literarios de hispanistas norteamericanos dedicados a Helmut Hatzfeld con motivo de su 80 aniversario*, (eds.) Josep M. Solà-Solé et al. (Barcelona: 1974), 51–70.

for doctrines on a writer so imbricated in (mixed) orality seems overly restrictive. Llull represents a confluence of forms of Neoplatonism that demonstrably stand outside the Christian textual tradition as it has been defined by Catholic dogma. This is why Llull has always been excluded from the history of Western philosophy. Nor can he at present be made to fit into it either, as long as the Art itself is not adequately explained as a functioning system. Until then, Llull's reaction to the Western tradition can only be partially measured.

My argument will have been worthwhile only if it has shown that Llull's dialogical engagement with lay culture stemmed from an environment towards which he was not antagonistic and that, moreover, his system itself was sympathetic to lay life as a category of human culture of transcendent value. From his early *Libre de contemplació* (1274), through both the Quaternary and Ternary Phases of his Great Art and their various subject-specific applications, Llull's work remains focused entirely on one driving passion – the perfection of his system, viewed as a universal structure of thought. In comparison to these achievements, Llull's literary works may seem almost unworthy of notice. Nothing is further from the truth. Llull's fictional prose works offer the closest thing Llull came to writing in terms of a logocentric discourse, defined Platonically as a self-standing discourse, or one in which form and content coalesce to become mutually self-supporting. An analysis of their structure shows that the philosopher spent a good deal of time in composing them, and that their literary structure was of significance to his pedagogical project more widely. It certainly seems significant to me that Llull appears to have spent more time on his two literary works than he spent in the composition of most of his philosophical works. This is a curious state of affairs for a philosopher. Perhaps then Llull, far less even than Plato – and unlike many in the intervening canon – did not fully acknowledge an absolute separation between his works of fiction and his works of philosophy. And this is the case I have attempted to state, through an analysis of aspects of literary structure in both novels, in order to argue that these structural components embody the cultural significance of Llull's declared and undeclared intentions.

Works Cited

Primary Works

Avicenna, *A Treatise on the Canon of Medicine of Avicenna*, (ed.) O. Cameron Gruner (New York: 1970).

De Bartholomaeis, Vincenzo (ed.), *Poesie provenzali storiche relative all'Italia* (Roma: 1931).

Chrétien de Troyes, *Perceval or The Story of the Grail*, trans. Ruth Harwood Cline (Athens, Georgia: 1985).

Chrétien de Troyes, *Le Roman de Perceval ou le Conte du Graal,* (ed.) Keith Busby (Tübingen: 1993).

Cicero, *De inventione*, (ed.) H.M. Hubbell (Cambridge, Mass.: 1949).

Guillem de Berguedà, *Les poesies de Guillem de Berguedà*, (ed.) Martí de Riquer (Barcelona: 1996).

Hillgarth, Jocelyn N. (ed.), *Diplomatari lul·lià: documents relatius a Ramon Llull i a la seva família*, trans. L. Cifuentes (Barcelona: 2001).

Marcabru, *Marcabru: A Critical Edition*, (eds.) Simon Gaunt, Ruth Harvey, Linda Paterson, and John Marshall (Cambridge: 2000).

Vidal, Peire, *Peire Vidal: poesie,* (ed.) D'Arco Silvio Avalle, 2 vols. (Milan and Naples: 1960).

Primary Works: Llull

Ars compendiosa inueniendi ueritatem, MOG 1:433–473 (text 7, sep. pag.).

Libre de meravelles, (ed.) Salvador Galmés, 4 vols. (Barcelona: 1931–34).

Libre de meravelles, Volum 1: Llibres I–VII, (ed.) Lola Badia (Palma: 2011).

Rhetorica nova, in *Ramon Llull's New Rhetoric: Text and Translation of Llull's* Rethorica Nova, (ed.) Mark D. Johnston (Davis, Calif.: 1994).

Romanç d'Evast e Blaquerna, (eds.) Albert Soler and Joan Santanach, NEORL 8.

Vita coaetanea, (ed.) Hermogenes Harada, ROL 8:259–309.

Secondary Works

Archer, Robert, *The Pervasive Image: The Role of Analogy in the Poetry of Ausiàs March* (Amsterdam: 1985).

Badia, Lola, "La novel·la espiritual de *Barlaam i Josafat* en el rerafons de la literatura lul·liana," in *Teoria i pràctica de la literatura en Llull* (Barcelona: 1992), 97–120.

Badia, Lola et al., "La llengua i la literatua de Ramon Llull: llocs comuns, malentesos i propostes," *Els Marges* 87 (2009): 73–90.

Bakhtin, Mikhail, *Rabelais and His World*, trans. Hélène Iswolsky (Bloomington, Indiana: 1984).

Barthes, Roland, "Introduction à l'analyse structurale des récits," *Communications* 8 (1966): 1–27.

Bloom, Harold, *The Western Canon: The Books and School of the Ages* (New York: 1994).

Bonillo Hoyos, Xavier, *Literatura al "Llibre de Meravelles"* (Barcelona: 2008).

Bonillo Hoyos, Xavier, "Els exemples del paradis i de l'infern del *Llibre de meravelles* de Ramon Llull," *SL* 44 (2004): 53–78.

Brenon, Anne, *Les femmes cathares* (Paris: 2004).

Cingolani, Stefano Maria, *El somni d'una cultura: "Lo Somni" de Bernat Metge* (Barcelona: 2002).

Close, Anthony J., "Don Quixote and the 'Intentionalist Fallacy,'" in *On Literary Intention: Critical Essays,* (ed.) D. Newton-De Molina (Edinburgh: 1976), 174–193.

Colon Domènech, Germà, "El nom de fonts del poeta Ausias March," *Boletín de la Sociedad Castellonense de Cultura* 46 (1970): 161–214.

Corominas, Joan, "The *joglar a lo diví* in the life and work of Ramon Llull," *Catalan Review* 4 (1990): 179–200.

Crawford, Lawrence, "Viktor Shklovskij: *Différance* in Defamiliarization," *Comparative Literature* 36 (1984): 209–219.

Galmés de Fuentes, Álvaro, *Ramón Llull y la tradición árabe* (Barcelona: 1999).

Garcia Oliver, Ferran, *En la vida d'Ausiàs March* (Valencia: 1998).

González-Casanovas, Roberto, *La novela ejemplar de Ramón Llull: interpretaciones literarias de la misión* (Gijón: 1998).

González-Casanovas, Roberto, "Llull's Blanquerna and the Art of Preaching: The Evolution Towards the Novel-Sermon," *Catalan Review* 4 (1990): 233–262.

Ibarz, Alexander W., "Ausias March and the Troubadour Question," Ph.D. Dissertation, University of Cambridge (Cambridge: 2005).

Ibarz, Alexander W., "Ausiàs March i l'ús especial de la hipèrbole dels clàssics occitans," in *La Catalogna in Europa, l'Europa in Catalogna: Transiti, passaggi, traduzioni; Atti del IX Congresso internazionale della Associazione italiana di studi catalani (Venezia, 14–16 febbraio 2008)* (Naples: 2008), s.p.

Jewers, Caroline A., *Chivalric Fiction and the History of the Novel* (Gainesville, Florida: 2001).

Kinkade, Richard P., "Arabic Mysticism and the *Libro de buen amor*,"in *Estudios literarios de hispanistas norteamericanos dedicados a Helmut Hatzfeld con motivo de su 80 aniversario,* (eds.) Josep M. Solà-Solé et al. (Barcelona: 1974), 51–70.

Montoliu, Manuel de, "Ramon Llull, trobador," *Estudis Universitaris Catalans* 21 (1936): 363–398.

Neugaard, Edward J., "The Sources of the Folk Tales in Ramon Llull's *Llibre de les bèsties*," *Journal of American Folklore* 84 (1971): 333–337.

Peers, E. Allison, "Ramon Lull and the World of Today," *Hispania*, 11 (1928): 459–467.

Pélicier, Yves, "Un gran catalan du XIIIme siècle: Raymond Lulle," *Revue de Psychologie des Peuples*, 25.2 (1970): 190–196.

Pierce, Frank, "Some notes on Llull's Mediaeval Novel," *Quaderni Ibero-Americani* 17 (1955): 49–51.

Pring-Mill, Robert D. F., "The Analogical Structure of the Lullian Art," in *Islamic Philosophy and the Classical Tradition: Essays presented by his friends and pupils to Richard Walzer on his seventieth birthday,* (eds.) S.M. Stern, A. Hourani, and V. Brown (Columbia, S. Carolina: 1972), 315–326.

Pring-Mill, Robert D. F., "Bibliografía," *EL* 3 (1958): 342.

Pring-Mill, Robert D. F., *Estudis sobre Ramon Llull* (Barcelona: 1991).

Pring-Mill, Robert D. F., "The Trinitarian World-Picture of Ramón Lull," *Romanistisches Jahrbuch* 7 (1955–56): 229–256.

Ramírez i Molas, Pere, *La poesia d'Ausiàs March: anàlisi textual, cronologia i elements filosòfics* (Basel: 1970).

Reichardt, Dieter, "Ramon Llull, trovador: A propósito de un estudio de Manuel de Montoliu," *SL* 7 (1963): 75–78.

Riquer, Martí de, *Història de la literatura catalana*, vol. 1 (Barcelona: 1964).

Rossi, Elena, "Ramon Llull as novelist: the visionary realism of *Blanquerna*," *Catalan Review*, 4 (1990): 279–297.

Rubio, Josep E., *Les bases del pensament de Ramon Llull* (Barcelona: 1997).

Scarpati, Oriana, *Retorica del trobar: Le comparazioni nella lirica occitana* (Rome: 2008).

Skinner, Quentin, "Meaning and Understanding in the History of Ideas," *History and Theory* 8 (1969): 3–53.

Smith, Nathaniel B., "Ramon Llull, trobador exalçat," *Hispanófila* 26 (1982): 1–7.

Soler, Albert, "Espiritualitat i Cultura: els laics i l'accés al saber a final del segle XIII a la corona d'Aragó," *SL* 38 (1998): 3–36.

Taylor, Barry, "Some Complexities of the 'Exemplum' in Ramon Llull's *Llibre de les bèsties*," *Modern Language Review* 90 (1995): 646–658.

Todorov, Tzvetan, *Poétique de la prose* (Paris: 1971).

Trías Mercant, Sebastián, "La ética luliana en el *Fèlix de les meravelles*," *EL* 13 (1969): 113–132 and 114 (1970): 133–152.

Urvoy, Dominique, *Penser l'Islam: les présupposés islamiques de l'Art' de Lull* (Paris: 1980).

Yates, Frances, "The Art of Ramon Lull: An Approach to it through Lull's Theory of the Elements," *Journal of the Warburg and Courtauld Institutes* 17 (1954): 115–174.

Yates, Frances, "Ramon Lull and John Scotus Erigena," *Journal of the Warburg and Courtauld Institute* 23 (1960): 1–44.

Ysern, Josep-Antoni, "Exempla I estructures exemplars en el primer llibre del *Fèlix*," *SL* 39 (1999): 25–54.

Zambon, Francesco, *Paratge: Els trobadors i la croada contra els càtars* (Barcelona: 1998).

CHAPTER 10

Ramon Llull as Encyclopedist

Mary Franklin-Brown

10.1 Introduction

Ramon Llull is not the first name that springs to mind when one thinks of the "Century of Encyclopedias."[1] Thomas of Cantimpré, Vincent of Beauvais and Bartholomeus Anglicus are well known for their encyclopedic compendia.[2] Thomas's *De natura rerum* (1228), Vincent's *Speculum maius* (1240–65), and Bartholomeus's *De proprietatibus rerum* (1230–1240) circulated in hundreds of copies throughout Europe in the later Middle Ages. Compared to them, the encyclopedic texts that Llull wrote in the last three decades of the 13th century – the *Libre de contemplació* [Book of Contemplation], the *Doctrina pueril* [Instruction for Children], the *Libre de meravelles* [Book of Marvels], and the *Arbre de sciència* [Tree of Knowledge] – found only a limited readership.[3] Even

---

1 Émile Mâle, *L'Art religieux du XIIIe siècle en France: Étude sur l'iconographie du Moyen Âge et sur ses sources d'inspiration*, 7th ed. (Paris: 1931), 23; Jacques Le Goff, "Pourquoi le XIIIe siècle a-t-il été plus particulièrement un siècle d'encyclopédisme?," in *L'Enciclopedismo medievale: Atti del convegno "L'enciclopedismo medievale," San Gimignano 8–10 ottobre 1992*, (ed.) Michelangelo Picone (Ravenna: 1994), 34. Helpful general studies of medieval encyclopedism are: Mary Franklin-Brown, *Reading the World: Encyclopedic Writing in the Scholastic Age* (Chicago: 2012); Maria Teresa Fumagalli, *Le Enciclopedie dell'occidente medioevale* (Turin: 1981); Christel Meier, "Grundzüge der mittelalterlichen Enzyklopädik: Zu Inhalten, Formen und Funktionen einer problematischen Gattung," in *Literatur und Laienbildung im Spätmittelalter und in der Reformationszeit*, (eds.) Ludger Grenzmann and Karl Stackmann (Stuttgart, 1984), 467–503, and "Über den Zusammenhang von Erkenntnistheorie und enzyklopädischem Ordo in Mittelalter und Früher Neuzeit," *Frühmittelalterliche Studien* 36 (2002): 171–192; Monique Paulmier-Foucart and Marie-Christine Duchenne, *Vincent de Beauvais et le grand miroir du monde* (Turnhout: 2004); Bernard Ribémont, *De natura rerum: Études sur les encyclopédies médiévales* (Orléans: 1995), *Les Origines des encyclopédies médiévales: D'Isidore de Séville aux Carolingiens* (Paris: 2001), and *Littérature et encyclopédies du Moyen Age* (Orléans: 2002).

2 Vincent of Beauvais, *Speculum quadruplex sive Speculum maius*, 4 vols. (1624; repr. Graz: 1965); Bartholomaeus Anglicus *De proprietatibus rerum: De genuinis rerum coelestium, terrestrium et inferarum proprietatibus libri XVIII* (1601; facsimile, Frankfurt: 1964); Thomas of Cantimpré, *De naturis rerum*, (ed.) Helmut Boese, one volume to date (Berlin and New York: 1973.

3 Ramon Llull, *Libre de contemplació*, (eds.) Antoni Sancho and Miquel Arbona, *OE* 2:83–1269; *Doctrina pueril*, (ed.) Joan Santanach i Suñol, NEORL 7; *Fèlix o el Libre de meravelles*, (ed.) Anthony Bonner, *Obres selectes de Ramon Llull (1232–1316)*, 2 vols. (Palma: 1989), 2:7–393; *Arbre*

© KONINKLIJKE BRILL NV, LEIDEN, 2019 | DOI:10.1163/9789004379671_011

by the more modest standards of Llull's *œuvre* they were not his most popular works: 20 medieval manuscripts survive of the *Libre de contemplació*, 19 of the *Doctrina Pueril*, 13 of the *Libre de meravelles*, and 23 of the *Arbre de sciència*, compared to 36 of the *Ars generalis ultima* and 61 of the *Ars brevis*. Nonetheless, certain of Llull's encyclopedic texts proved the most popular of his *œuvre* among vernacular readers. Judging by the numbers of manuscripts, the only vernacular work that exceeded the diffusion of the *Libre de contemplació* and the *Doctrina pueril* was the *Libre de l'orde de cavalleria,* due to the popularity of its French translation, not the Catalan original.[4] Although taxonomically-minded critics have debated whether texts such as the *Arbre de sciència* are really encyclopedias,[5] their relation to the encyclopedic movement becomes clear when the problem of genre is approached through the lens of medieval encyclopedic practices rather than modern paradigms. Many of their apparent eccentricities derive from an original synthesis of traditional materials and practices. Thus, as Lola Badia has observed, Llull's novelty as an encyclopedist derives from the principals of "newness" or "modernity" in literature of the twelfth and thirteenth centuries: a recombination of familiar materials.[6] Llull engaged repeatedly in experimentation and innovation within the encyclo-pedic mode, suggesting long and deep reflection on the purposes, limitations, and internal contradictions of scholastic encyclopedism. He fully deserves to be ranked among the most significant encyclopedic practitioners of the 13th century.

This chapter opens with a brief introduction to the methods and varieties of medieval encyclopedism, followed by an overview of strategies for describing and analyzing these texts. Then, employing these strategies, I discuss each of Llull's encyclopedic texts in turn, indicating its continuities and discontinui-ties with other texts of the period. Although I begin with the *Doctrina pueril*, as the text that is the least innovative and addresses the most elementary level of learning, I otherwise treat the texts in chronological order. The discussion is not perfectly balanced, however. I devote more time to the early, massive,

---

de sciència, *OE* 1:547–1046. Unless otherwise indicated, all quotations and page references are from these editions.

4   Numbers taken from Base de Dades Ramon Llull, <http://orbita.bib.ub.edu/llull/obres.asp>, and include all manuscripts and fragments from before 1500. See also Anthony Bonner, "Es-tadístiques sobre la recepció de l'obra de Ramon Llull," *SL* 43 (2003): 83–92.

5   Ramon Llull, *Arbor scientiae*, (ed.) Pere Villalba Varneda, ROL 24:5*–9*.

6   Lola Badia, "The *Arbor scientiae*: A 'New' Encyclopedia in the Thirteenth-Century Occitan-Catalan Cultural Context," in *Arbor scientiae: Der Baum des Wissens von Ramon Lull,* (eds.) Fernando Domínguez Reboiras, Pere Villalba Varneda, and Peter Walter (Turnhout: 2002), 1–19; Lola Badia, *Teoria i practica de la literatura en Ramon Llull* (Barcelona: 1992); Lola Badia and Anthony Bonner, *Ramon Llull: Vida, pensamiento y obra literaria* (Barcelona: 1992).

and influential *Libre de contemplació*, which has less often entered into discussions of Llull's encyclopedism, than to the *Libre de meravelles* and the *Arbre de sciència*, which have been discussed extensively elsewhere. The *Libre de contemplació* merits attention because it contains the seeds of the later texts: as Llull claims, "this work ... is the demonstration and figure of many others."[7] It represents a decisive moment in Llull's reinvention of scholastic encyclopedism, allowing us to measure the distance he assumed with regards to his predecessors and to establish a point of comparison for the *Libre de meravelles* and the *Arbre de sciència*.

10.2   Medieval Encyclopedism

Encyclopedism, defined broadly as a movement to compile, organize, and promulgate knowledge, existed long before the word "encyclopedia" was coined in the Renaissance, and we have inherited a number of recognizably encyclopedic texts from the premodern world.[8] In the Middle Ages, encyclopedias were principally compilations.[9] The practice stretches back to Antiquity: in the 1st century A.D., Pliny the Elder's *Naturalis historia* gathered and translated Greek writing on the subject. When in the 7th century Isidore of Seville wrote his *Etymologiae*, the dominant encyclopedia of the early Middle Ages, he borrowed from Pliny, often paraphrasing or quoting verbatim. In his *Speculum naturale*, Vincent of Beauvais quoted Isidore, revisited Pliny for passages that Isidore had not used, and then juxtaposed this material with the latest writings of Albert the Great. Some of Vincent's quotations contradicted each other, but this mattered less than the bare fact that he had quoted from such a wealth of accepted authorities. The paradigm of knowledge was *textual*; the practice of citation and the authority of the source more important than the verifiability or coherence of the information.

One consequence of the textual paradigm of knowledge in the Middle Ages is the emphasis on language and exegesis, even in encyclopedias. What sets the *Etymologiae* apart from the *Naturalis historia* is Isidore's interest in the connection between words and things. Christian writers believed the natural

---

7   *Libre de contemplació* 365.30, *OE* 2:1251: "aquesta obra ... és demonstració e figura a moltes altres obres." Unless otherwise indicated, all translations are my own.

8   Robert L. Fowler, "Encyclopaedias: Definitions and Theoretical Problems," in *Pre-modern Encyclopedic Texts: Proceedings of the Second COMERS Congress, Groningen, 1–4 July 1996,* (ed.) Peter Binkley (Leiden: 1997), 3–29.

9   Franklin-Brown, *Reading the World,* 33–91, offers more extensive notes and references on this question.

world to be another revelation to man, requiring both literal and spiritual commentary, just as Scripture did. As for pagan writers of astronomy, natural history, medicine, and so on, their texts too required commentary. Vincent cited from these commentaries in an encyclopedia whose own organization followed that of the Bible, providing an extended commentary on Scripture. This explains why, even during high scholasticism, library catalogues still classed encyclopedias as works related to the Bible.[10] The exegetical impulse shaped these compilations in another way as well. They were intended as a resource for clergy preparing sermons, providing them a selection of examples from which to draw spiritual meaning for their flocks.[11] For this reason, medieval encyclopedias' information about the world is often framed by an incipient spiritual exegesis: in the *De proprietatibus rerum*, a program of moralizing glosses appears in many manuscripts; in the *Speculum maius*, two *florilegia* concerning exegesis provide bookends for the material on natural history.[12]

Scripture was not the only possible order for an encyclopedia: Bartholomeus relied upon the ontological hierarchy elaborated by Pseudo-Dionysus, while Brunetto Latini employed for the *Tresor* (1260–66) an ancient schema of the disciplines.[13] The essential thing was that there be an order (preferably taken from some authoritative text), setting encyclopedic *florilegia* apart from personal or eccentric collections of extracts. As the advent of scholasticism renewed learning and libraries swelled with new or rediscovered texts, order allowed individuals to locate the material they needed.[14] The individual codex was transformed by innovations such as chapter divisions, running headings, concordances and indices.[15] The scholastic emphasis on division and

---

10   Gilbert Dahan, "Encyclopédies et exégèse de la Bible aux XIIe et XIIIe siècles," *Cahiers de recherches médiévales (XIIIe–XVe s.)* 6 (1999): 19–40.

11   Jacques Berlioz and Marie-Anne Polo de Beaulieu, "Les Recueils d'*exempla* et la diffusion de l'encyclopédisme médiéval," in *L'Enciclopedismo medievale: Atti del convegno "L'enciclopedismo medievale," San Gimignano 8–10 ottobre 1992*, (ed.) Michelangelo Picone (Ravenna: 1994), 179–212.

12   Heinz Meyer, *Die Enzyklopädie des Bartholomäus Anglicus: Untersuchungen zur Überlieferungs- und Rezeptionsgeschichte von De Proprietatibus Rerum* (Munich: 2000), 205–223, 283–296; Vincent of Beauvais, *Speculum maius*, vol. 1, lib. 1, cap. 10–15 and lib. 29, cap. 3–33, cols. 26–31 and 2063–87.

13   Brunetto Latini, *Li Livres dou tresor*, (eds.) Spurgeon Baldwin and Paul Barrette (Tempe: Ariz.: 2003).

14   Donatella Nebbiai-Dalla Guarda, "Classifications et classements," in *Histoire des bibliothèques françaises: Les Bibliothèques médiévales, du VIe siècle à 1530*, (ed.) André Vernet (Paris: 1989), 373–393.

15   Malcom B. Parkes, "The Influence of the Concepts of *Ordinatio* and *Compilatio* on the Development of the Book," in *Medieval Learning and Literature: Essays Presented to Richard William Hunt*, (eds.) J.J.G. Alexander and M.T. Gibson (Oxford: 1976), 115–141; and Richard

subdivision as a mode of analysis transformed the sermon into an intricately structured genre and gave shape to a complex new literary form, the *summa*.[16] Encyclopedists exploited many of these developments. Yet the results were never wholly successful. The diversity of the material that the scholastics had inherited resisted neat schemes of classification. The hand-copying of texts and the expense of books encouraged an ongoing, intentional revision of encyclopedias as well as the accidental loss or garbling of their material.

In the 13th century, encyclopedic Latin *florilegia* were largely the work of mendicant friars. Encyclopedism harmonized well with the scholastic love of learning, its mania for order, and the mendicants' project of education and preaching. The affinity between encyclopedism and scholasticism also helps explain why the period has left us a number of Latin texts encyclopedic in scope, order, or pedagogical purpose but distinct from the *florilegia*.[17] Such are the *didascalica*, introductions to philosophy that explain the relations between the disciplines, set out methodologies, or recommend a particular course of reading. The best known today is Hugh of St. Victor's *Didascalicon* (late 1120s), but the genre continued to flourish in the 13th century, with texts such as Robert Kilwardby's *De ortu scientiarum* (ca. 1250).[18] At the same time, scholastics such as Albert the Great (the *Doctor universalis*) and Roger Bacon (the *Doctor mirabilis*) were completing intellectual projects that ranged across all the disciplines. While these projects involved quotation and commentary on authoritative texts, the two thinkers submitted received opinion to critique and advanced their own arguments, producing texts that were more unified in tone and idea, and more explicitly *authored*, than the *florilegia*. Some of the individual texts in these series were titled *summae*, like the great theological

---

H. and Mary A. Rouse, "Concordances et Index," in *Mise en page et mise en texte du livre manuscrit*, (eds.) Henri-Jean Martin and Jean Vezin (Paris: 1990), 219–228.

16   Siegfried Wenzel, "The Arts of Preaching," in *The Cambridge History of Literary Criticism, Vol. 2, The Middle Ages*, (eds.) Alastair Minnis and Ian Johnson (Cambridge: 2005), 84–96, offers a good overview of the possible relation between increasingly complex encyclopedic organization and the branching structures of the scholastic sermon, which remains to be studied.

17   Franklin-Brown, *Reading the World*, 9–11, 68–72, 78, and 319–320; Robert Bultot, Léopold Genicot, et al., *Les Genres littéraires dans les sources théologiques et philosophiques médiévales: Définition, critique et exploitation: Actes du Colloque internationale de Louvain-la-Neuve 25–27 mai 1981* (Louvain-la-Neuve: 1982); and Olga Weijers, *Le Maniement du savoir: Pratiques intellectuelles à l'époque des premières universités (XIIIe–XIVe siècles)* (Turnhout: 1996) are especially helpful for the genres of scholastic intellectual life.

18   Hugh of St. Victor, *Didascalicon*, (ed.) Charles Henry Buttimer (Washington, D.C.: 1939); trans. Jerome Taylor, *The* Didascalicon *of Hugh of Saint Victor: A Medieval Guide to the Arts* (New York: 1961); Robert Kilwardby, *De ortu scientiarum*, (ed.) Albert G. Judy (London: 1976).

summae of Alexander of Hales (ca.1230–1245) and Thomas Aquinas (1265–74). The term designates a complete, structured presentation of the knowledge in a particular field, offering solutions to problems and controversies that have arisen. Within its narrower parameters, this genre could also be considered encyclopedic.

Into this constellation of encyclopedic genres, vernacular texts began to emerge: in Occitan with Peire de Corbian's incomplete *Tezaurs* (ca. 1225), then in French with two popular encyclopedias, Gossuin de Metz's *Image du monde* (1246) and Brunetto Latini's *Tresor*, and finally in Catalan, with the vernacular versions of Ramon Llull's *Libre de contemplació* and *Doctrina pueril*. Usually more basic than the Latin compendia, vernacular encyclopedias nonetheless made knowledge of the arts and the world available to individuals, especially lay people, with a poor grasp of Latin. Translations between the vernaculars were common from the earliest days: Gossuin's text was translated into English; Latini's into Italian, Catalan, and Castilian; Llull's *Doctrina* into Occitan and French. The act of writing an encyclopedia in the vernacular also seemed to encourage literary innovation. We shall see that Llull's encyclopedias, likely to be read directly by those in need of spiritual edification rather than interpreted to them by a preacher, offer their own spiritualizing interpretations of information about the universe.

Likewise, Matfre Ermengaud's *Breviari d'amor* (1288), the most successful encyclopedia in Occitan, frames such knowledge with spiritual exegesis. With its heavy use of troubadour lyric, the *Breviari* exemplifies the new hybrid encyclopedias of the last decades of the century, which fuse encyclopedic material and methods with established courtly genres in order to appeal to a broader lay readership, delighting even while instructing (to adapt Horace's *dictum*, well known in the period). The entire *Breviari* is in verse, and Matfre exploits the Occitan pun between "vers" (verse) and "vers" (true) to make a strong truth claim for his form.[19] In fact, verse encyclopedias were common in the vernacular: Peire de Corbian's *Tezaurs* had been in verse, as had a second recension of Gossouin's *Image du monde*. Llull wrote all his encyclopedic texts in prose, but he exploited syntactic structures more common to vernacular verse and – especially in the Catalan version of the *Arbre de sciència* (1295–96) – the parallelisms and *adnominatio* of Latin sermons as well as occasional rhyme.[20] Surely the pleasures afforded by Llull's style derive part of their justification from

---

19   Adrian Armstrong, Sarah Kay, et al., *Knowing Poetry: Verse in Medieval France from the "Rose" to the Rhétoriqueurs* (Ithaca: 2011), esp. 5–9 and 101–134.

20   Jordi Rubió i Balaguer, "Sobre la prosa rimada en R.L.," in *Estudios dedicados a Menéndez Pidal,* Vol. 5 (Madrid: 1954), 307–318; Wenzel, "The Arts of Preaching," 87.

Horace's commonplace about the purpose of "poetry." Moreover, Llull's *Libre de meravelles*, written at the nearly the same date as the *Breviari*, is also generically hybrid, offering both a quest romance and an encyclopedic vision of the world. Like two poetic masterpieces of the same period, Jean de Meun's continuation of the *Roman de la Rose* (ca. 1269–76) and Dante's *Commedia* (ca. 1308–21), the *Libre de meravelles* offers a fictionalized meditation on encyclopedic ideals.

10.3   Approaches to the Corpus

The proliferation of titles in the previous section suggests that the encyclopedic *corpus* of the scholastic period is large, and some scholars would concur. Based upon the scope of their projects, Maria Teresa Fumagalli has included Albert the Great's and Roger Bacon's *œuvres*, as well as Hugh of St. Victor's *Didascalicon*, in her influential studies of medieval encyclopedism. Fumagalli distinguishes between a "static" encyclopedia on the model of the *De proprietatibus rerum*, whose purpose is to gather existing material on topics without investigating its significance or attempting to transform knowledge, and a "projectual" or "dynamic" encyclopedia on the model of the *œuvres* of the *Doctor Universalis* and *Doctor Mirabilis*. The latter encyclopedism investigates and transforms even as it draws upon the intellectual heritage.[21] Fumagalli's broad understanding of encyclopedism allows her to include the writers whose work was most eccentric relative to the encyclopedic *florilegium*, and here, beside Albert the Great and Roger Bacon, Ramon Llull takes his place. Llull not only wrote individual texts of encyclopedic scope but also produced an *œuvre* spanning the disciplines, reforming them according to a new method of thought.[22]

We therefore need this notion of a dynamic encyclopedism when studying Llull. However, we must also keep in mind that, because the "encyclopedia" as a single generic category did not exist in the Middle Ages, modern scholars have worked with shifting notions of the encyclopedic *corpus*, producing different accounts of the movement.[23] Fumagalli's is one of the most expansive, but that scope comes at the cost of neglecting significant formal differences between texts. If we define encyclopedism in the way that I suggested in the previous

---

21   Fumagalli, *Le Enciclopedie*, 9–10, and "Premessa," *Rivista di storia della filosofia*, n.s. 1 (1985): 3–4. Anna Sigrídur Arnar, *Encyclopedism from Pliny to Borges* (Chicago: 1990), 1, groups encyclopedias with theological *summae*, which Fumagalli does not discuss.

22   Fumagalli, *Le Enciclopedie*, 44 and 48.

23   Fumagalli, *Le Enciclopedie*, and Ribémont, *De natura rerum*, offer starkly contrasting views of medieval encyclopedism derived from different ways of delimiting the *corpus*.

section, then the generic terms that medieval writers did employ – *flores* (for the collection of extracts that we now call a *florilegium*), *speculum, didasca-licon, summa,* and (in vernacular letters) *image, tresor, roman* – can identify texts that share an encyclopedic ambition. Nonetheless, it is often possible to distinguish them as genres. By preserving these historical categories, we can describe Llull's texts and their innovations with more precision.

In addition, I have elsewhere suggested a new binary of descriptors, based upon the hermeneutic that each text privileges.[24] In the Middle Ages, theologians distinguished literal and spiritual modes of exegesis. The literal mode explicated visible and, by extension, historical truth. The spiritual mode (subdivided into moral, allegorical, and anagogical modes) connected the letter of the text to some referent other than the one most immediately evident, thus assigning a spiritual meaning.[25] Medieval encyclopedists, as exegetes of the world, could emphasize one mode or the other. They could not justify their projects purely in terms of a literal exposition of the world, which would make them guilty of *curiositas*, a vice. Vincent makes it clear that the creatures he describes must be interpreted spiritually as signs of God's greatness and munificence.[26] But he leaves that work to the reader, limiting himself to a literal exegesis of the universe and history. Because the *Speculum maius* offers a broad treatment of the objects in the world, but rarely subjects them to a spiritual exegesis that would connect them to other levels of meaning, I have termed this kind of encyclopedia "horizontal." "Vertical" encyclopedias, on the other hand, place an emphasis upon spiritual exegesis, and most of Llull's texts fall into this category.

Medieval genres and the heuristic distinctions between static and dynamic, horizontal and vertical, encyclopedism allow us to plot Llull's position relative to the other encyclopedists of his day. But a more thorough study of Llull's encyclopedism must move beyond the analysis of textual form and exegetical mode to take account of the text's material realization, of the *book*, and of the relation it entertains with its author or first-person subject and with its implied and historical readers. The first topic arises because scholastic encyclopedias, like any reference books, were conceived as physical objects whose characteristics had to suit their function. Hence the emphasis upon the order

---

24 Franklin-Brown, *Reading the World*, 94.

25 Henri de Lubac, *Exégèse médiévale: Les Quatre Sens de l'Ecriture*, 4 vols. (Paris: 1959) and Beryl Smalley, *The Study of the Bible in the Middle Ages*, 2nd ed. (Notre Dame, Ind.: 1964) are the classic studies of medieval exegesis.

26 Vincent of Beauvais, *Speculum maius*, "Prologus," cap. 18, trans. Monique Paulmier-Foucart, in Monique Paulmier-Foucart and Marie-Christine Duchenne, "Prologue au *Speculum maius*," in *Vincent de Beauvais et le grand miroir du monde* (Turnhout: 2004), 168–170.

of these texts; hence also Vincent's comments in the preface to the *Speculum maius* concerning the layout of its pages, the placement of rubrics, and the creation of tables.[27] Many vernacular encyclopedias call for diagrams or illustrations, often lavishly produced in luxury volumes for wealthy patrons later in the texts' transmission. Ironically, the author of one of the encyclopedias most frequently transmitted in this way, Gossuin de Metz, expressed concern about the physical beauty of books, which could distract even clerics from the value of their contents.[28] From Ramon Llull I know of no surviving directions for the design of his encyclopedias. However, his exploitation of figures and volvelles elsewhere makes it clear that he had given thought to the materiality and technology of the codex. If we read his encyclopedic texts closely, we catch glimmers of a meditation on the use and misuse of the physical book – a meditation that results in encyclopedic innovations.

Likewise, Llull's approach to authorship/authority and to the role of the reader can be productively studied in relation to contemporary literature. Alastair Minnis has connected the evolution of academic prologs in the scholastic period to changing attitudes toward authority and authorship, a greater interest in the human authors of Scripture, including their role as ethical example.[29] Scholars such as Sarah Kay and Michel Zink have traced the concurrent development of a new literary subjectivity in vernacular lyric and narrative.[30] However, Vincent declined the title of *auctor* in favor of *compilator*, an empowering gesture of humility by which he could excuse both his presumption in including topics that he had not formally studied and his failure to reconcile different authorities with each other.[31] For his part, Ramon Llull made the most of the exemplary role of the first-person subject and eventually came to affirm his authorship of texts of all kinds, in a

---

27   Ibid., cap. 3, 151–152. cf. Paulmier-Foucart's description of Vincent's organizational practices, *Vincent de Beauvais et le grand miroir*, 37–40.

28   Gossouin de Metz, *L'Image du monde de Maître Gossouin: Rédaction en prose*, (ed.) O.H. Prior (Lausanne: 1913), 74. Chantal Connochie-Bourgne, "Quelques Aspects de la réception d'une œuvre encyclopédique au Moyen Âge: Les Cas de l'*Image du monde*," *Littérales* 21 (1997): 221–244, analyzes the illustration of this encyclopedia.

29   Alastair Minnis, *Medieval Theory of Authorship: Scholastic Literary Attitudes in the Later Middle Ages*, 2nd ed. (Philadelphia: 1988), 103–112.

30   Sarah Kay, *Subjectivity in Troubadour Poetry* (Cambridge: 1990); Michel Zink, *La Subjectivité littéraire: Autour du siècle de saint Louis* (Paris: 1985).

31   Vincent of Beauvais, *Speculum maius*, "Prologus," cap. 7–8, 156–158. Parkes, "Influence of the Concepts," and Alastair J. Minnis, "Late Medieval Discussions of *Compilatio* and the Rôle of the *Compilator*," *Beiträge zur Geschichte der Deutschen Sprache und Literatur* 101 (1979): 385–421, treat the question of Vincent's authorship, and provide insight into encyclopedic authorship of the period more generally.

self-authorizing gesture that responded to the concerns that had troubled Vincent.[32] At the same time, Llull showed great sensitivity to the process of reading by which others would make sense of his texts. Recent scholarship on medieval literary criticism has found a similar sensitivity in the writings of Bacon and his contemporaries, who, inspired by Horace and the Averroistic version of Aristotle's *Poetics*, were thinking about the way poetic and rhetorical texts influence the imagination and moral impulses of readers.[33] Llull eventually combined these two – the authorial subject as moral example and the readerly subject who responds – in the critical fiction of the second Fèlix, the reader as encyclopedist.[34]

10.4   Llull's *Doctrina Pueril*

Llull wrote the *Doctrina pueril* after a decade of study on Majorca, a period that culminated with a visit to Montpellier around 1275, at the summons of Prince James of Aragon, and then a return to the island in the following year for the founding of Miramar.[35] Unlike Llull's later texts, this one does not give a precise date and place of composition, but internal evidence places it between 1274 and 1276.[36] By this time, Llull had completed the *Libre de contemplació*, the *Ars compendiosa inveniendi veritatem* (the first version of his Art), and the *Art abreujada d'atrobar veritat*. These texts hover in the background of the *Doctrina pueril*,

---

32   Lola Badia, "Ramon Llull: Autor i personatge," in *Aristotelica et Lulliana: magistro doctissimo Charles H. Lohr septuagesimum annum feliciter agenti dedicata*, (eds.) Fernando Domínguez Reboiras et al. (The Hague: 1995), 355–375, and Anthony Bonner, "Ramon Llull: Autor, autoritat i illuminat," in *Actes de l'onzè col·loqui internacional de llengua i literatura catalanes, Palma, Mallorca, 8–12 de setembre de 1998*, (eds.) Joan Mas et al. (Barcelona: 1998), 35–60, treat Llull's creation of himself as "author and character."

33   Gilbert Dahan, "Notes et textes sur la poétique au Moyen Âge," *Archives d'histoire doctrinale et littéraire du Moyen Age* 47 (1981): 171–239; Vincent Gillespie, "From the Twelfth Century to *ca.* 1450," in *The Cambridge History of Literary Criticism, Vol. 2, The Middle Ages*, (eds.) Alastair Minnis and Ian Johnson (Cambridge: 2005), 145–235.

34   Franklin-Brown, *Reading the World*, 263–300, offers a fuller discussion of this subject.

35   Armand Llinarès, "Algunos aspectos de la educación en la *Doctrina pueril* de Ramón Llull," *EL* 11 (1967): 201–209; Robert D. F. Pring-Mill, "La *Doctrina pueril*: conreu i transmissió d'una cultura," in *Estudis sobre Ramon Llull*, (eds.) Lola Badia and Albert Soler (Barcelona: 1991), 319–331; and Joan Santanach i Suñol, "'Cové que hom fassa aprendre a son fill los .xiiii. articles:' La *Doctrina pueril* com a tractat catequètic," in *Literatura i cultura a la corona d'Aragó (s. XIII–XV): Actes del III Col·loqui "Problemes i mètodes de literatura catalana antiga," Universitat de Girona, 5–8 de juliol del 2000*, (eds.) Lola Badia et al. (Barcelona: 2002), 419–430.

36   *Doctrina pueril*, (ed.) Joan Santanach i Suñol, NEORL 7:xxxi–xxxiii.

but their intricacies and innovations throw into relief the *Doctrina*'s elementary and traditional nature. Addressed to a "son" who may be as much rhetorical as historical figure, the prologue promises that the text will give him the general knowledge he needs before beginning specialized studies. Such an uninitiated readership explains the *Doctrina*'s vernacularity: Llull wrote the original in Catalan and may have initiated the translations into Occitan and French (he also initiated a Latin translation, which had little diffusion).

The first 70 of the *Doctrina*'s 100 chapters respond to the need to better instruct the Christian laity in the fundamentals of their religion. This need was expressed by churchmen many times during the period; Joan Santanach, the *Doctrina*'s most recent editor, draws particular attention to the call by the 1274 Council of Lyon for an *opusculum* instructing the ignorant in these matters.[37] Llull's text was one of several manuals of this type from the last quarter of the 13th century. Most widely known are the anonymous *Miroir du monde*, probably of the 1270s, and Lawrence of Orléan's *Somme le roi*, written in 1279 at the request of Philip III "the Bold" of France.[38] A comparison between this last and the *Doctrina pueril* is instructive, for the two differ in their rhetoric and the breadth of their content. Both writers adopt a conversational tone, full of apostrophes to the imagined reader. But Lawrence amplifies his text with *exempla* and the description of visual figures; the treatise on the vices (cap. 31–39) is organized according to the shape of the Beast of the Apocalypse, while that on the virtues (cap. 50–59) describes a Garden of Virtues with trees, fountains, and damsels, each of whom represents one of the topics covered. In contrast, Llull offers Spartan chapters, but the *Doctrina pueril* covers far more topics. Like the *Somme*, its religious sections explain the articles of the faith, the ten commandments, and the virtues and vices, but also review the seven sacraments, the seven joys of Mary, and the different religions or "laws" (the law of nature, the old law, and the new law, with additional chapters on Muslims and "gentiles"), which Lawrence does not cover.

Once this material is concluded, the *Doctrina* becomes a different kind of text: a *didascalicon*, presenting an overview of all the disciplines and domains of knowledge that a beginning learner could encounter. Thus it fulfills the promise of the prolog through a genre change. The two parts are not formally divided (for example, into separate volumes), and Llull does not articulate the relation between them. Santanach i Suñol suggests that the material on the arts belongs here because not only faith, but also knowledge can play a role

---

37   Ibid., xxxiv.
38   *Le Miroir du monde*, (ed.) Félix Chavannes (Lausanne: 1845); Laurent, *La Somme le roi par Frère Laurent*, (eds.) Édith Brayer and Anne-Françoise Leurquin-Labie (Paris: 2008).

in attaining salvation.[39] Traditionally, didascalical literature had presented the arts within the framework of the human being's faith and quest to attain salvation; as Hugh of St. Victor had put it, "we are restored through instruction" (*reparamur ... per doctrinam*).[40] There is also a close affinity between treatises on the virtues and vices and encyclopedic literature: the earliest version of Vincent's *Speculum maius* included just such a treatise, and the virtues and vices form the bulk of the ethical content at the center of Latini's *Tresor*, which had been written just a decade before the *Doctrina*.[41] Despite these implicit connections, the intellectual structure of the *Doctrina* remains inchoate, exemplifying the difficulty all encyclopedists faced: how to absorb a series of distinct lists into a larger structure comprehensible to readers and – ideally – significant in its own right. The *Libre de meravelles* and *Arbre de sciència* will offer two different solutions to this problem.

The didascalical portion of the *Doctrina* is at first glance traditional. The liberal arts appear in the usual order, followed by theology, law, natural philosophy, and medicine. After medicine come the mechanical arts (agriculture, smithery, and so on), which Hugh and Vincent had likewise discussed. Nonetheless, there are some idiosyncrasies here. In the *Doctrina*, as in his other writings, Llull cites specific authorities rarely, yet the long Chapter 77 on natural philosophy ends with an introduction to Aristotle's *œuvre*. The Stagirite is mostly absent from Llull's other writings. His presence here and the length of the chapter on natural philosophy are all the more surprising because the chapters on other disciplines indicate considerable tension between the necessity of giving a traditional overview of the arts and Llull's own opinions about what kinds of learning merit time. After describing the *quadrivium*, he discourages the reader from pursuing astronomy, arithmetic, or geometry, the first because it lends itself to abuses, and the last two because the effort they require interferes with devotion. He also expresses ambivalence about civil law.[42] In other encyclopedic texts, Llull will resolve this tension by framing a traditional discipline in such a way that its spiritual significance is paramount, by radically reformulating it in terms of his Art, or by omitting it entirely. In the *Doctrina*, faithful to its *didascalical* paradigm, he makes no such moves. However, he exploits the conventions of the *didascalicon* to direct students to his other writings, where the arts will appear in a different light. His own books,

---

39   Santanach i Suñol, "Cové qu hom fassa apendre," 424.
40   *Didascalicon* 1.1, (ed.) Buttimer, 6; trans. Taylor, 47.
41   Paulmier-Foucart, *Vincent de Beauvais*, 59–62; Latini, *Tresor*, (eds.) Baldwin and Barrette, xx.
42   *Doctrina pueril* 74.43–48, 76.27–30, NEORL 7:194, 198.

including an "*Art d'atrobar veritat*" (either the *Art abreujada d'atrobar veritat* or a Catalan version of the *Ars compendiosa inveniendi veritatem*) and the *Libre de contemplació*, appear beside the titles of established authorities as texts the student should go on to read.[43]

The *Doctrina* also distinguishes itself from other *didascalica* by presenting the roles of various groups of people in the larger social order – an interest that Llull manifests in all of his encyclopedic texts as well as in the *Libre de l'orde de cavalleria* and the *Libre de Blaquerna*.[44] Chapter 79 of the *Doctrina* on the mechanical arts contains little about the arts themselves, their materials and techniques, but a great deal about the artists, the necessity of their work to the larger economy and that of their household. This treatment of the mechanical arts provides a transition to Chapters 80–82 on rulers, the clergy, and the hermetic and monastic lives. Here a supplementary chapter on the knighthood will appear in the French and Latin translations, added perhaps by Llull himself.[45] As an encyclopedist, Llull is more concerned with the order of humanity than with the order of nature or the order of the disciplines. In this way, he can be compared to his close contemporaries Brunetto Latini (whose ultimate interest is the proper government of the city-state) and Matfre Ermengaud (concerned with right relationships among human beings and between the human being and God). Such social or interpersonal preoccupations distinguish the vernacular encyclopedism of the second half of the "Century of Encyclopedias."

10.5   The *Libre de Contemplació en Déu*

The *Doctrina pueril* and the *Libre de contemplació* represent opposite ends of the spectrum of Llull's encyclopedic writing. The former is the closest thing to a static and horizontal encyclopedia that Llull ever wrote. The latter is strongly dynamic and vertical. Linguistically, the *Libre de contemplació* cannot simply be categorized according to the Latin-vernacular binary, because Llull first wrote it – on Majorca, a few years before the *Doctrina pueril* – in the Arabic language he had taken such pains to learn. This version has been lost. The subsequent Catalan version proved Llull's most frequently copied of any genre in

---

43   Ibid., 83.66–71, 87.46–48, 91.99–101, 100.57, NEORL 7:225, 240, 256, 284.

44   Marta M.M. Romano and Óscar de la Cruz, "The Human Realm," in *Raimundus Lullus: An Introduction to his Life, Works and Thought*, (eds.) Alexander Fidora and Josep E. Rubio (Turnhout: 2008), 363–459, offer a good overview of Llull's understanding of the human being and human society.

45   *Doctrina pueril*, NEORL 7:xliv, 287–294.

the language. Because of its length, however, it was rarely transmitted complete. A Latin translation enjoyed more modest circulation.[46]

The *Libre de contemplació* occupies 1161 pages in the modern edition of the *Obres essencials*, as compared to 486 for the *Arbre de sciència* and 190 for the *Libre de meravelles*. The mid-point of the *Libre de contemplació*, as calculated by page numbers rather than chapters, occurs at the beginning of Chapter 230, which begins the distinction on sensual and intellectual things; Llull's comments about the contents and purpose of the book are placed at the end of that chapter.[47] Llull claims that the book is composed "of theological and natural knowledge" (*de ciència teological et de ciència natural*). The Catalan term *sciència* invites comparison to the *Arbre de sciència*, but by translating *sciència* and *scientia* as "knowledge" or, elsewhere, "discipline," I wish to avoid the epistemological and disciplinary denotations of the word "science" in contemporary English. The translation "knowledge" emphasizes the etymological connection of the medieval term to the act of knowing by a thinking subject – a connection that was particularly important to Llull.[48] He states that the work was written and should be contemplated for the glory of God. In a description of the book in its concluding chapter, he further elaborates upon its contents and purposes, arranging them into hierarchies. According to this account, the *Libre de contemplació* provides knowledge, but that knowledge is of God, and the creatures are merely signifiers for God's virtues, which are signifiers for God. Thus natural knowledge is subordinated to theological knowledge.[49] More importantly, the book has higher purposes than mere knowledge. It makes possible a virtuous life, filled with praise and gratitude to God. Finally, it helps the reader perceive God by every power of the human soul: "this book is good for imagining and remembering and understanding and loving you [God]."[50]

---

46   Martí de Riquer, *Història de la literatura catalana*, vol. 1 (Barcelona, 1964), 256–269, remains an excellent introduction to the *Libre de contemplació*. Jordi Gayà, "Significación y demostración en el *Libre de Contemplació* de Ramon Llull," in *Aristotelica et Lulliana: magistro doctissimo Charles H. Lohr septuagesimum annum feliciter agenti dedicata*, (eds.) Fernando Domínguez Reboiras et al. (The Hague: 1995), 477–499, is especially helpful on the text's hermeneutic and its relation to the Art.

47   *Libre de contemplació* 230.30, *OE* 2:686.

48   Mariken Teeuwen, *The Vocabulary of Intellectual Life in the Middle Ages* (Turnhout: 2003), 358–360, reviews the medieval use of *scientia*.

49   Josep Enric Rubio, "The Natural Realm," in *Raimundus Lullus: An Introduction to his Life, Works and Thought*, (eds.) Alexander Fidora and Josep E. Rubio (Turnhout: 2008), 311–362, reviews the relation between natural and theological knowledge in Llull's thought.

50   *Libre de contemplació* 366.5, *OE* 2:1252: "aquest libre és bo a imaginar e a membrar e a entendre e a amar vós."

These goals alone do not distinguish the *Libre de contemplació* from encyclopedias such as the *De proprietatibus rerum* of Bartholomaeus Anglicus or Vincent of Beauvais's *Speculum maius*. Reflection upon God's greatness, which ought to engage all the powers of the soul and result in praise, gratitude, and a virtuous life, is also the *raison d'être* for the Latin *florilegia*. The difference between the *Libre de contemplació* and these *florilegia* lies not in its ultimate purpose but in its execution. Llull does not presuppose that a priest will interpret the contents of the *Libre de contemplació* for his flock; destined to be read directly by those it seeks to reform, the book must make every lesson explicit. Llull anticipates that readers will be hermits or monks or laymen who have withdrawn from the world.[51] At the same time, Llull rarely quotes anything. The lack of quotation distinguishes the *Libre de contemplació*, as well as the subsequent *Libre de meravelles* and *Arbre de sciència*, not only from earlier encyclopedic *compendia*, but also from treatises and *summae* of the period. It likely derives from Llull's interest in mission and his awareness that the texts Christians accept as authorities are not authoritative for Jews and Muslims, so it is counterproductive to cite them.[52] That the *Libre de contemplació* was a component of Llull's missionary project is clear from the fact that he first wrote it in Arabic.

Impersonal third-person discourse about a topic is also rare in this text. Taking a page from Augustine's *Confessions*, Llull makes readers eavesdroppers on his own devotions, establishing the first-person speaker as an exemplary man in need of understanding and reform. The encyclopedic materials are folded into a prayer of praise to God that is apportioned out to a year-long period, with a chapter of thirty verses for each day. This textual year is divided into five books, to reflect the five wounds of Christ, and into 40 distinctions, representing Christ's 40 days of fasting in the desert. The distribution of the distinctions through the individual books and of the verses through the individual chapters is also significant; with the exception of the largest division, into three volumes of one or two books each, every unit of the intricate structure of the *Libre de contemplació* bears an explicit symbolic meaning.[53]

Volume One contains two books, the first on God, the second on Creation as God's action in the world. Thus far, the structure follows that of many earlier encyclopedias. In the second book, we find the first discussion of the universe and the human being: distinction ten, on creation, including the firmament, the elements, metals, plants, animals, and angels; and distinction eleven,

51 *Libre de contemplació* 366.21, *OE* 2:1256.
52 Anthony Bonner, *AL* 12–14.
53 *Libre de contemplació*, Prol.3–14, *OE* 2:107.

on God's ordering of the world, which principally treats God's design of the human person, then the Incarnation, the Passion, Redemption, Judgment, and the world to come. These distinctions do communicate some basics of medieval science, psychology, and theology, but Llull employs rhetorical, exegetical, and homiletic practices to transform the traditional encyclopedic materials. Parallel grammatical structures appear everywhere, and *amplificatio* is rampant. Most chapters begin with an apostrophe to God, then continue with second-person narration of his actions. The process by which fallen humans may derive knowledge of God from the world is demonstrated through numerous analogies, in which glimmer traces of Llull's paradigm of divine virtues. Thus the spiritual interpretation of objects in the world, which in horizontal encyclopedias is relegated to a frame, is in the *Libre de contemplació* integrated into every chapter.

Volume Two, occupied entirely by book three, is devoted to the processes by which humans perceive, think about, and react to their world. Although such material has already been dispersed unannounced through volume one, the emphasis has shifted, from God's work to our perception, as the succession of rubrics indicates. The chiastic structure reflects the discursive situation: volume one is devoted to the addressee, volume two to the addressor. But while the rubrics of volume two might announce a subtle discourse on medieval psychology, distinction 24, on vision, which opens the volume, offers an extended exercise in moral exegesis, treating some of the same orders of creation that appeared in volume one, then the social order. Individual creatures make cameo appearances (the ant, the lion, the vulture, the bee), and at these moments Llull's interpretation recalls that of bestiaries, relating characteristics of the creature to our spiritual lives, but it is briefer, based upon a characteristic that can be sketched in a single verse.

How, one may ask, is this about vision? The answer comes in the final chapter of the distinction, which explains the limitations of physical vision and the necessity of employing spiritual vision to see "spiritual things" (*coses espirituals*).[54] Llull offers several analogies for spiritual vision: the clarity of glass or water, which allows things within or beyond them to be represented on their surface, and the mirror, on whose surface appears whatever stands before it.[55] The mirror analogy is frequent in the *Libre de contemplació*, linking this text to the literary tradition of moral treatises and encyclopedias. Yet Llull employs it in more than one way.[56] Later, in distinction 39 on consciousness,

---

54   *Libre de contemplació* 124.6, *OE* 2:372.

55   Ibid., 124.7, *OE* 2:372.

56   Ritamary Bradley, "Backgrounds of the Title *Speculum* in Medieval Literature," *Speculum* 29 (1954): 100–115; Franklin-Brown, *Reading the World*, 271–280; and Einar Már Jónsson,

he uses mirrors to represent initial physical vision, which serves as a "ladder and demonstration" (*escala e demostració*) by which we may know intellectual things. The distortions that mirrors can cause thus represent the dangers inherent in our perception of "sensual things:" "for since they are disordered and disturbed in their disposition and ordering, they deceive in the demonstration that they provide of intellectual things."[57] It is this concern about physical perception that leads Llull to neglect literal exegesis, which he calls "sensual" in favor of spiritual or "intellectual" interpretation, as he explains in distinction 28, devoted to thought.[58]

In this way, volume two of the *Libre de contemplació* elaborates the epistemology and hermeneutics that underpinned the encyclopedia of volume one. The treatment of epistemology and hermeneutics in an encyclopedia is nearly unprecedented – before Llull, only Vincent of Beauvais had included such material. The difference between the two is that Vincent inserted these subject matters into an infinitely expanding text that he could never complete. More disciplined, Llull set fixed bounds for the *Libre de contemplació*, which obliged him to omit a great deal of natural history, all of the liberal arts, and all of human history. Yet he opened a central place for the *method* of knowing.

Like volume two, volume three revisits the material that preceded it, but it is devoted to metaphysics and doctrine (book four) and then love and prayer (book five). This review of previous material through new optics we will see again in the final books of the *Arbre de sciència*. Volume three anticipates the *Arbre de sciència* in another way as well, for Llull here introduces his first series of tree figures, which structure the six distinctions of book four. Compared to the trees that Llull will elaborate in later texts, those of the *Libre de contemplació* are rudimentary devices. The Tree of the Cross accompanying distinction 36, on faith and reason, is of course cruciform, but the other trees exhibit a series of nodes on their trunk, each node corresponding to a chapter. The nodes have two or four branches attached to them, representing approaches to the topic of each chapter; for most of the figures the labels for the branches are the same for each node. There is virtually no description of the trees, whose presence the text signals solely through the rubrics for the distinctions and the first or last verse of each distinction, though a verse in the distinction on faith and reason makes an analogy between the signifying function of the mirror

---

Le Miroir: Naissance d'un genre littéraire (Paris: 1995) review the mirror trope and related genres.

57   *Libre de contemplació* 169.1–2, *OE* 2:483: "com elles són desordonades e destorbades en lur disposició e ordonació, adoncs menten en la demostració que donen a home de la coses intel·lectuals."

58   *Libre de contemplació* 155.20–21, *OE* 2:448.

(a traditional figure for the encyclopedia) and that of the tree.[59] Nonetheless, these early trees represent a stunning structural experiment: freeing the text from the traditional list organization of encyclopedias that has governed the first two books, they introduce a second dimension, creating a matrix that allows him to structure material not easily broken down into simple lists. Probably inspired by the power of the combinatory figures that he had introduced in his Art, Llull is reintroducing complex diagrammatic structures to encyclopedic writing. Schemas of the disciplines were common in *didascalica* and trees of virtues and vices in catechetic manuals, but newly invented diagrams or graphic figures had not been used to organize encyclopedic compilations since Lambert of St. Omer's Romanesque picture encyclopedia, the *Liber floridus* (ca. 1125).

Llull's structural innovations indicate that he gave thought to the *shape* of this vast text. That he also thought about its transmission in a physical book is clear from its final chapter. Here Llull plays feely upon the vocabulary of medieval books and writing, but he employs it in such a way that the physical experience of the book – like our physical perception of the world – is subordinated to a higher form of contemplation. For instance, he plays upon ambiguity in use of the Catalan preposition "a" ("to" or "for") with verb infinitives: "This book, Lord, is so good that it is good to (*bo a*) see, to hear, to smell, to taste, to sense, for thinking, for perceiving, and for having awareness, subtlety, and resolve."[60] Not until we reach the later verbs does it become clear that the formulation "good to" with an infinitive does not mean that the book is "good to see" but rather "good for seeing" something else. And after reading volume two we can no longer take literally the terms for the senses. Hence, as it circulates, the *Libre de contemplació* will come into the "hands" of readers,[61] who may draw profit and pleasure from it in one of four ways. A reader may read it straight through over the course of a year, enjoying the novelty of new reasonings. Someone who already knows the book may read haphazardly, wandering from one "verse" or "paragraph" or "chapter" to another, drawing from it what he or she needs at the moment, pleased to find one "flower" (as in medieval *flores*) and then another. Alternatively, such a reader may return only to the table of rubrics, using them as a memory aid and taking pleasure from "abridgement of the sensual figure" (*l'abreujament de la figura sensual*).[62] Finally, the

---

59 *Libre de contemplació* 238.6, *OE* 2:712.
60 *Libre de contemplació* 366.6, *OE* 2:1252: "Tan és bo, Sènyer, aquest libre, que ell és bo a veer, e a oir, e a odorar, e a gustar, e a sentir, e a cogitar, e a apercebre, e a haver consciència, e subtilea, e animositat."
61 Ibid., 366.27, *OE* 2:1257.
62 Ibid., 366.20, *OE* 2:1255.

reader may return to the book solely in the mind, and this "intellectual contemplation is the highest form of profit and pleasure."[63] At the moment when Llull offers us the clearest image of his book, he argues that our goal should be ultimately to set the codex aside.

A similar sleight of hand occurs with regards to Llull's authorship of both the *Doctrina pueril* and the *Libre de contemplació*: a *mise en scène* of the author that simultaneously conceals his identity. The prologue to the *Doctrina* introduces its author in the third person as a "poor, sinful man, scorned by people, culpable, wretched, and unworthy to have his name written in this book."[64] In the last verse of the prologue to the *Libre de contemplació*, we read:

> I am not worthy to have my name written in the work, nor to have it attributed to me; therefore I banish and omit my name from this work, and I attribute and give it to you, Lord, who are our lord God.[65]

Both prologues, written within a few years of each other, exploit the humility trope to raise this anonymous writer up as a moral example for his readers. Both present this man in a filial relationship that is also literary; the author of the *Doctrina pueril* writes a book for his son to read, while God the Father inspires his "son" to write the *Libre de contemplació*. The fusion of filial and literary relationships will return in Llull's later encyclopedic prologues, although the human beings involved will acquire more precise (though not necessarily more real) identities as Llull seeks credentials as an author of books.

10.6   The *Libre de Meravelles*

Llull wrote the *Libre de meravelles* or *Fèlix* more than a decade after the *Libre de contemplació* and *Doctrina pueril*.[66] He seems to have spent much of the intervening time in Montpellier. He completed there a number of books devoted to his Art, including an encyclopedic series of texts demonstrating

---

63   Ibid., 366. 20, *OE* 2:1255: "l'entel·lectual contemplació és sobirana a donar profit e plaer."
64   *Doctrina pueril*, Prologue, lines 11–13, NEORL 7:9: "hom pobre, peccador, menyspreat de les gens, colpable, mesquí, indigna que [son] nom ssia escrit en aquest libra."
65   *Libre de contemplació*, Prolog.30, *OE* 2:108: "Jo no som digne que en esta obra mon nom sia escrit, ne que a mi sia atribuïda esta obra; per què jo mon nom exil e delesc d'esta obra, e ella, Sènyer, atribuesc e dó a vós, qui sóts nostre senyor Déus."
66   Riquer, *Història de la literatura catalana*, 1:293–316; and, more recently, Xavier Bonillo Hoyos, *Literatura al "Llibre de meravelles" de Ramon Llull* (Barcelona: 2008) and Franklin-Brown, *Reading the World*, 33–56, 289–301.

its applicability to the disciplines of theology, philosophy, law, and medicine, about which I will say more in the next section. More relevant to the *Libre de meravelles* are the appealing imaginative texts that Llull had written in this period: the *Libre del gentil e dels tres savis* and the *Libre d'Evast e d'Aloma e de Blaquerna*. In 1287, he made his first trip to Rome to seek (unsuccessfully) the foundation of more monasteries on the model of Miramar, and in 1288 he traveled to Paris to promote his Art at the University and to seek the support of King Philip IV the Fair for his evangelical projects. There he remained until 1289, forming acquaintances with Parisian intellectuals and possibly members of the court, and writing the *Fèlix*.

Although he may already have encountered such texts in Majorca, Llull's time in Montpellier and Paris would have given him ample access to the courtly narrative writing of the French tradition. The Arabic and Castilian traditions of the *Calila e Dimna* animal fables clearly inspired his treatment of the beasts in the *Fèlix*, but so did the fox protagonist of a similar French text, the *Roman de Renart*.[67] Also influential in the period was the prose Arthurian cycle known as the Vulgate or the *Lancelot-Graal*, filled with wandering knights and hermits conveniently placed to interpret their dreams to them. And just a decade before Llull's arrival in Paris, Jean de Meun had published his continuation of the *Roman de la Rose*, in which a limited and unreliable narrator-lover dramatizes the disordering effects of desire on the human ability to understand the world. All three texts fall within the genre of romance. Llull, the great synthesizer, had tried his hand at this form with the *Blaquerna*, creating something like a quest romance with spiritual ends. He seems to have been satisfied enough with the result to fuse the genre with the encyclopedia in *Fèlix*. The elaboration of a fictional subject in the *Roman de la Rose* may also have suggested to a writer as interested in psychology as Llull that he could take the exemplary encyclopedist figure of the *Libre de contemplació* in new directions. The synthesis of diverse currents of vernacular literature accomplished in the *Fèlix* may explain why this encyclopedia-romance was translated into more vernacular languages (Italian, French, and Castilian) in the Middle Ages than any of his other texts, but never into Latin.

The *Libre de meravelles* has two over-arching organizational principles. In the table of rubrics we see an encyclopedia dealing first with the spiritual realm (God, the angels) and the highest levels of the heavens (the empyrean and the firmament), then the material realm (the elements, plants, metals, and beasts), then the human person (the faculties of the soul, the senses, the virtues and vices, the components of spiritual life), and finally that person's two possible destinations, paradise and hell. The order is not ontological, but

---

67   Riquer, *Història de la literatura catalana*, 1:312–316.

biblical and narrative: if we skip the creation of the heavenly bodies on the fourth day and that of the fish and fowl on the fifth, this is the order of Genesis 1, followed by a glance at Revelation. Llull thus gives us a lacunary version of Vincent of Beauvais's order for the *Speculum naturale*. But whereas the narrative quality of Vincent's order is submerged under the mass of *flores* that make up the *Speculum maius*, Llull draws attention to narrative form by superposing upon the order of Genesis 1 the fictional quest of his protagonist, Fèlix, who has set out to see the wonders of the world.

Fèlix sees many things he does not understand, but like Arthurian knights he regularly encounters hermits who interpret his experiences. This narrative structure allows Llull to separate his initial perception of the world from its interpretation, drawing attention to the fact that perception alone is never adequate. He then assigns interpretation, which had been carried out by the single speaker of the *Libre de contemplació*, to a succession of figures who derive authority not only from their exemplary lives, but also from the exegetical role that they play in the romance tradition. Overlapping with the romance paradigm, dialogues on theology, natural philosophy, or hagiography – such as Honorius Augustodunensis's *Elucidarium* (before 1098), William of Conches's *Dragmaticon Philosophiae* (ca. 1147–49) and Caesarius of Heisterbach's *Dialogus miraculorum* (before 1238) – likewise establish an authoritative teacher or philosopher figure. The dialoguised encyclopedia form appears in French in the 13th-century translations of the *Elucidarium*, then in the 1290s with a new text, the *Livre de Sydrac*. In the *Libre de meravelles*, the character of the hermit alternates with that of the "philosopher" – or rather, the two roles are one and the same. Within this structure, Llull can offer readers more complex objects for interpretation than he was able to do within the atomized structure of the *Libre de contemplació*. A comparison of Chapter 108 (on the vision of beasts) in that earlier encyclopedia to book seven of the *Fèlix* shows that the simple observations about animal behavior in the earlier text have now metamorphosed into fables in which the beasts think, speak, and interact like members of human society. Riquer has observed that this "book of the beasts" is really about humans and constitutes a political and sociological allegory;[68] in this way book seven doubles as a presentation of the human orders.

Fèlix's experiences elsewhere in the text are more difficult to interpret – thoroughly obscure, they would make no sense without the exegesis of the hermit. Thus the *Libre de meravelles* introduces into medieval encyclopedism the element of obscurity, a literary practice that had long sustained other genres (from spiritual exegesis of the Bible to the lyric of the *trobar clus*) but would

---

68   Riquer, *Història de la literatura catalana*, 1:299.

seem inimical to the encyclopedic purpose of disseminating knowledge as widely as possible.[69] Helpfully, a hermit explains the value of obscurity to Fèlix when discussing the prophets: "there where the prophets spoke most obscurely of the advent of Jesus Christ, the human understanding has more occasion to exalt in subtleness, and in seeking the works that God possesses in himself and outside himself."[70] It is impossible to take obscure prophecies literally, and so the reader is forced to exercise his or her intelligence in the search for a spiritual meaning. An encyclopedia that incorporates obscurity thus protects readers from the *curiositas* regarding physical objects or historical events that had concerned Vincent of Beauvais. According to Llull's aesthetics, obscure formulations also render language beautiful and capable of momentarily sating the desires of the soul, for they are new and strange, qualities that he had lauded in the *Libre de contemplació*.[71] Together, newness and strangeness are the qualities that Llull attributes to the marvel in the *Libre de meravelles*.[72] Through the marvel, the encyclopedia, often the most conservative of texts because of its purpose of transmitting already existing knowledge, comes in Llull's work to accommodate the sort of rhetorical modernity vaunted by the poets and poeticians of the time. It fulfills its evangelical purpose of transforming the vision of its reader and converting his or her understanding.

This intense exercise of the mind involves assuming a certain distance from the text immediately before one's eyes – just as the ideal readers of the *Libre de contemplació* had to set the book aside and turn its meaning over in their minds. It may seem paradoxical, then, that the *Libre de meravelles* contains the lengthy description of another encyclopedia, the *Libre de plasent visió*, in all its physical beauty. Toward the middle of the *Fèlix* – that is, in Chapter 57 "On the Pleasure of Hearing" from book eight "On Man" – a hermit tells Fèlix of another philosopher-hermit, who created a marvelous book of figures depicting cosmology, the natural world, and human history. The beauty of the book afforded physical pleasure, while spiritual pleasure was derived from its utility

---

69   Jan M. Ziolkowski, "Theories of Obscurity in the Latin Tradition," *Mediaevalia* 19 (1996): 101–170. Riquer, *Història de la literatura catalana*, 1:345–350, offers an overview of Llull's theories of language and exploitation of obscurity. Jordi Rubió, "L'Expressió literària en l'obra lul·liana," in *OE* 1:85–110, provides a sensitive description of Llull's literary practices and style. Lola Badia, "The *Arbor scientiae*," 14–18, has compared the obscurity of passages in this text's "Arbor exemplificalis" to the style of the Catalan troubadour Cerverí de Girona.

70   *Fèlix o el Libre de meravelles* 1.11, (ed.) Bonner, 60: "on plus fortment los profetes parlaven escurament de l'aveniment de Jesucrist, pus ocasionat és lo humanal enteniment a exalçar si mateix en subtilitat, e en cercar les obres que Déus ha en si mateix e fora si mateix."

71   *Libre de contemplació* 359.26, *OE* 2:1218.

72   *Libre de meravelles* 8.115, (ed.) Bonner, 366–369; see Bonillo Hoyos, *Literatura*, 22–37.

for contemplation: "seeing with spiritual eyes" (*veser ab ulls esperitals*).[73] Upon his death, the hermit-encyclopedist bequeathed the book to a pious king, who then abdicated his throne and founded a monastery in which he could study the *Libre de plasent visió* with the brothers. On his own deathbed, the king asked his son to live in the same way, suggesting that the encyclopedia would be passed down from monastic father to royal son in perpetuity. Recognizing that the hermit-philosopher could be a representation of Llull himself, early scholars considered this passage testimony to the fact that Llull had created another encyclopedia, which had been lost. Bonner has since debunked the theory of the lost encyclopedia.[74] But the passage is in fact another *exemplum* – for the writing and reading of encyclopedias. It describes the kind of compilation that had absorbed Vincent's life, as well as the more Lullian practice of representing objects through "figures" (a polysemous term that does not necessarily have to indicate graphic illustrations), and the meditative reading that both encyclopedists demanded for their books. While the title of this imaginary work emphasizes vision and the long description cites the beauty of the book, the *exemplum* is placed in the chapter on hearing, rather than sight, befitting a book that is only described, never seen. Such a representation of the physical book renders it even less tangible than the references to books in the final chapter of the *Libre de contemplació*.

As in the *Libre de contemplació*, the allusion to the book in the middle of the text is linked to the initial and final passages. The prolog and epilog to the *Libre de meravelles* introduce and conclude yet another *exemplum* of the encyclopedia. According to the prolog, a man in a foreign land, marveling how little people know and love God, writes the *Libre de meravelles*. He sends his son Fèlix (whose name initially seems only to indicate the felicity of a devout life) out into the world to discover its marvels and devote his life to knowing and loving God. At the end of the book, Fèlix comes upon a monastery, where he recounts the *Libre de meravelles* to the monks. Preparing to set out and tell his story to others, he falls ill and dies, but a monk reflecting on his death observes another marvel that Fèlix had not recounted in his book. He adds the new marvel, then assumes Fèlix's name and office as a wanderer in search of marvels. The abbot ordains that a monk of their community will always hold the office and name of Fèlix (the *paronomasia* with *fènix* now becomes significant). The first encyclopedist, then, (the father) cedes the office to his son, who cedes it to a reader/listener willing to assume his name and task of compiling the encyclopedia,

---

73   *Libre de meravelles* 8.58, (ed.) Bonner, 196.

74   *Libre de meravelles*, (ed.) Miquel Batllori, *OE* 1:510, n. 38; Anthony Bonner, "Notes de bibliografia i cronologia lul·lianes," *EL* 24 (1980): 71–86.

and so a cycle begins. The devout encyclopedist and the devout reader are one and the same, responding to the ethical imperative of loving God more fully by better understanding the world he created.

10.7   The *Arbre de Sciència*

After the *Fèlix*, nearly another decade passed before Llull attempted his final encyclopedic text. The intervening period was tumultuous, with the news of the fall of Acre in 1291, Llull's fruitless attempts to gain papal support for his project of mission and crusade, his spiritual crisis in Genoa, and his first unsuccessful mission to North Africa. In 1295, back in Rome, Llull commenced the *Arbre de sciència*, which he would publish in both Latin and Catalan. The former proved his most widely diffused encyclopedia among Latin readers; the latter, whose literary qualities are much appreciated today, seems to have had little circulation in the Middle Ages.[75]

This final encyclopedia constitutes a synthesis not only of elements from his earlier encyclopedias, but also of the innovations in his other writings during the previous decade. These texts suggest a new awareness of the difficulties that the Art posed and a determination to address them: several books consisting of questions and answers, a new streamlined version of the Art itself, and more texts demonstrating the application of the Art to individual disciplines. His writing in this period also manifests a growing willingness to identify himself as an author and authority with a biography of his own and academic credentials. His unwillingness to base his method of finding truth upon texts traditionally accepted as authoritative – whose evangelical rationale was clear – had exposed the Art to considerable doubt from the very Christians whom he needed to support his missionary projects. Bonner has suggested that Llull's elaboration of an authorial persona was an attempt to compensate for the absence of other *auctoritates* from his writings. Thus the appearance of his first "signed" text, the *Cent noms de Déu* (probably 1288), where he identified himself as "I, Ramon Llull, unworthy" (*Yo, Ramon Luyl, indigne*). In 1289 he sent to the Doge of Venice a manuscript whose dedication began "I, master Ramon Llull, Catalan" (*Ego, magister Raymundus Lul, cathalanus*).[76] In 1292, Llull began to attach colophons to his writings with the place and date of their composition. And in 1295, he penned the *Desconhort*, a versified

---

75   Franklin-Brown, *Reading the World*, 129–179.

76   *Cent noms de Deu*, ORL 1:79; Venice, Biblioteca Nazionale Marciana lat. VI.200 (2757); see Bonner, "Ramon Llull," 42–43.

dialogue between "Ramon" and a hermit in which the former decries the indifference of Christian leaders to his projects.[77]

We have seen that the prologue to the *Fèlix* creates the fiction of an exemplary encyclopedist/reader. The prologue to the *Arbre* likewise exploits literary tropes (an orchard, an encounter), and these spaces and events are no less stylized or exemplary, but the encyclopedist does not assume a fictional or symbolic name. He is "Ramon," weeping beneath a beautiful tree, where he continues his "distress" (*desconhort*). A monk who finds him there requests that he write "a book general to all disciplines that can be easily understood and through which the General Art may also be understood, for it is too difficult to understand."[78] The *Arbre de sciència* is thus inscribed in the autobiography that Llull began with the *Desconhort* and will continue in the *Vita* that he will dictate to a Carthusian colleague at Paris in 1311. At the same time, the notion that a "book general to all disciplines" can make the Art comprehensible ties the encyclopedia to Llull's method of finding truth to a degree that none of his previous encyclopedias had been. Within the fiction of this prologue, the interest that the Art has solicited and the difficulties it presents justify this new assay of encyclopedism, and Ramon's authority as author of the Art qualifies him for the task, despite his unconventional scholarly background and the fact that, in his own words, "my books are little appreciated, and many people take me for a fool."[79]

It is curious that the prologue to the *Arbre de sciència* makes no mention of Llull's earlier effort to demonstrate the Art's relevance to all the advanced disciplines, in the four *libri principiorum* (for theology, philosophy, law, and medicine), written in Montpellier sometime between 1274 and 1283. The *libri principiorum* showed how this combinatorial method, based upon figures, could be used as a new and superior approach to each discipline. When the fictional monk of the *Arbre* cites the lack of a book general to all disciplines that would help explain the Art, his comments may be taken as a tacit admission on Llull's part that the earlier series of texts had not served, perhaps because they were too difficult for many readers, or perhaps because they constituted a series of books rather than a single work. Yet the idea of elaborating the use of the Art through a commentary upon a sequence of figures can help us understand one of the most remarkable qualities of the *Arbre de sciència*: Llull's last encyclopedia is structured entirely according to a sequence of figures that he has invented, so that he plays the double role of *auctoritas* (and that two

---

77   *Desconhort, OE* 1:1308–1328.

78   *Arbre de ciència* Prol., *OE* 1:555: "un libre general a totes ciències qui leugerament se pogués entendre, e per lo qual hom pogués entendre la sua *Art general* que feta havia, car trop era subtil a entendre."

79   Ibid., Prologue, 1:555: "mos libres són poc presats, ans vos dic que molts hòmens me tenen per fat."

times over, as author of the Art and creator of the figures) and exegete. The "endo-referential" quality that Bonner has identified in the Art is also present in the *Arbre*.[80]

The style of the *Arbre de sciència* is more expansive and accessible than that of *libri principiorum*, free of the alphabetical code that renders his texts on the Art so obscure. The figures of this text are trees, rather than graphs or matrices, a more gracious form with a distinguished cultural pedigree – from the literary trope of the individual sitting beneath a tree, to the trees of virtues and vices in spiritual manuals, to the tree of Jesse in manuscript illumination and stained glass. Llull had been experimenting with the arboreal form fitfully since the *Libre de contemplació*. He opened the *Libre del gentil* with a series of tree-matrices. Trees had not been among the figures of the Art itself, but he introduced a hybrid tree-matrix in the *Liber principiorum medicinae*. Although there is no way to prove influence, I have suggested elsewhere that the increasing complexity of these trees could have resulted from Llull's encounter, during his wide travels, with the trees of Lambert of Saint-Omer's *Liber floridus*, Joachim of Fiore's *Figurae* (late 12th century), or Matfre Ermengaud's *Breviari d'amor*.[81] Particularly significant, to my mind, is the way that Lambert and Joachim place trees whose forms mirror each other across the opening of a book, an innovation that might have suggested to Llull a more intellectually satisfying way to connect multiple trees than the orchard arrangement that he used in the *Libre del Gentil*. However, no literary precedent approaches the complexity of the trees Llull created for the *Arbre de sciència*.

Each tree structures a book of the text; the close correlation between the form of the tree and the textual organization also sets the *Arbre de sciència* apart from the *Libre de contemplació*. All trees have the divine dignities and relative principles of the Art for their roots, demonstrating the utility of the Art in the study of every discipline or aspect of Creation. Above the roots, however, each tree is arranged differently, according to the inherent structure of the subject in question. The trunk represents something peculiar to the subject, but generally speaking the branches express the powers of a particular level of being; the boughs its operations, the leaves its accidents, the flowers its instruments, and the fruits its effects.

Beginning with the elements, the sequence of trees and topics reflects an ascent from the material to the spiritual, following the general paradigm of the *scala creaturarum*. However, Llull dilates this structure at the level of the human being – the microcosm of the entire created world – with a sequence of books relative to knowledge and ethics. Another way to understand

---

80   Bonner, *AL* 14.
81   Franklin-Brown, *Reading the World*, 137–154.

the sequence is as an example of medieval anthropology and psychology: hence trees devoted to the vegetative power, the sensitive, and the imaginative (books two through four). A "human tree" (*arbre humanal*) follows as book five, dealing not only with the body but also with the powers of memory, understanding, and will (which constitute the tree's "spiritual" branches) and with the arts (in the descriptions of the leaves we encounter the mechanical and liberal arts, law, medicine, philosophy, and theology). A moral tree (book six) sets out the virtues and vices, while imperial and apostolic trees treat human government (books seven through eight). We have seen much of this content already in the *Doctrina pueril*, but the lists that there formed a disjointed series here assume places within a structure that indicates their role in human life. Much later in the text, after trees devoted to the celestial realm, the angels, the saints, the Virgin, Jesus Christ, and God (books nine through fourteen), Llull adds two final books that revisit the material in the earlier ones through new optics: the tree of *exempla* (book 15) and the tree of questions (book 16). The chapter by Aragüés Aldaz in this volume has already shown the importance of *exempla* to Llull's encyclopedic writing, and here is where Llull indulges in rhymed prose and even occasional verse, amplifying the literary pleasures of his text. The tree of questions, which occupies a full 200 of the text's 500 pages in the modern edition of *Obres essencials*, reflects Llull's long habit of inserting heuristic questions at the end of his books.

Despite the fictional monk's request for a book that is easy to understand, and despite the elegance of Llull's Catalan prose, the *Arbre de sciència* poses considerable challenges to readers. Its 200 pages of questions are only the most obvious. More subtle is the problem of the representation of the trees and the connections between them. Manuscript illustrators and early modern printers frequently attempted to sketch the trees, and their lack of success indicates to what degree figures of this complexity resist graphic realization.[82] The singular title *Arbre* appears to contradict the sequence of 16 trees, yet Llull either describes a relation between individual trees that is impossible to visualize, or neglects to state how the trees might be attached to each other. Such difficulties can be best understood in relation to Llull's earlier ambivalence about the attractions of physical books and his celebration of obscurity. They indicate a subtle but powerful response to the dangers of *curiositas*. The *Arbre de sciència* resists the kind of illustration that would make it into a luxury book like so many other vernacular encyclopedias of the time, admired but not read, while

---

82   The Latin edition of the *Arbor scientiae* by Villalba Varneda provides generous reproductions sufficient to recognize the problem; see also Franklin-Brown, *Reading the World*, 166–175.

the obscure relation between the trees forces readers to set the book aside and reflect on the analogies that unite creation.

10.8   Ramon Llull as Encyclopedist

Llull's encyclopedic experiments afford us great insight into scholastic encyclopedism while showing the new directions in which the movement could be pushed. In pursuit of the goal of reaching the largest possible audience, Llull set his sights not only on lay readers, but also on Muslim ones. Paradoxically, this goal – which was merely an extension of the educational aims of encyclopedists such as Vincent of Beauvais or Matfre Ermengaud – obliged Llull to eschew the compilational method of his predecessors, because it presupposed agreement about what texts constituted authorities. Nonetheless, his encyclopedias remained exegetical, emphasizing the process by which we must interpret creation as a sign of God, while also offering Llull's own invented figures as the objects of exegesis. The exegesis of combinatory figures is only one of the ways he found to resolve the organizational difficulties with which scholastic encyclopedists struggled; he also borrowed the narrative structure of vernacular romance. The clear – if surprising – organization of his later encyclopedias renders it easy to locate specific passages in these books, another goal of the encyclopedic movement. Nonetheless, his treatments of the physical book challenge readers to move beyond their initial perception, avoiding the *curiositas* that would lead them to collect books for their beauty or become distracted by the sight and variety of objects in the world. Obscurity forces readers to engage in the spiritual interpretation modeled for them by the appealing *exemplum* of the encyclopedist. A space opens for the reader to share in his intellectual work.

Works Cited

Primary Works
Alexander of Hales, Jean de la Rochelle, et al., *Summa theologica* (Venice: 1575).
Alighieri, Dante, *The Divine Comedy*, (ed.) Charles Singleton, 3 vols. (Princeton: 1970–73).
Aquinas, Thomas, *Opera omnia,* 7 vols., (eds.) Roberto Busa et al. (Stuttgart: 1980).
Augustine, *Confessiones,* (ed.) M. Skutella, trans. E. Tréhorel and G. Bouissou, 2nd. ed., 2 vols. (Paris: 1992).
Bartholomaeus Anglicus, *De proprietatibus rerum: De genuinis rerum coelestium, terrestrium et inferarum proprietatibus libri XVIII* (1601; facsimile, Frankfurt: 1964).

Caesarius of Heisterbach, *Dialogus miraculorum*, (eds.) and trans. Horst Schneider and Nikolaus Nösges, 5 vols. (Turnhout: 2009).

Corbian, Peire de, "Le *Thezaur* de Peire de Corbian," (eds.) A. Jeanroy and G. Bertoni, *Annales du Midi* 23 (1911): 289–305 and 451–471.

Calila e Dimna, (eds.) J.M. Cacho Blecua and M.J. Lacarra (Madrid: 1984).

Ermengaud, Matfre, *Breviari d'amor*, (ed.) Peter Ricketts, 4 vols. to date (London, Turnhout, and Leiden: 1976–2004).

Gossouin de Metz, *L'Image du monde de Maître Gossouin: Rédaction en prose*, (ed.) O.H. Prior (Lausanne: 1913).

Honorius Augustodunensis, *Elucidarium* (Milan: 1493).

Hugh of St. Victor, *Didascalicon*, trans. Jerome Taylor, *The* Didascalicon *of Hugh of Saint Victor: A Medieval Guide to the Arts* (New York: 1961).

Hugh of St. Victor, *Didascalicon de studio legendi*, (ed.) Charles Henry Buttimer (Washington, DC: 1939).

Isidore of Seville, *Etymologiarum sive originum libri XX*, (ed.) W. M. Lindsay, 2 vols. (Oxford: 1989–91).

Joachim of Fiore, *Figurae*, in Marjorie Reeves and Beatrice Hirsch-Reich, *The Figurae of Joachim of Fiore* (Oxford: 1972).

Kilwardby, Robert, *De ortu scientiarum*, (ed.) Albert G. Judy (London: 1976).

Lambert of St. Omer, *Liber floridus, codex autographus bibliothecae universitatis gandavensis*, (ed.) Albert Derolez (Ghent: 1968).

Latini, Brunetto, *Li Livres dou tresor*, (eds.) Spurgeon Baldwin and Paul Barrette (Tempe: 2003).

Lawrence of Orléans, *La Somme le roi par Frère Laurent*, (eds.) Édith Brayer and Anne-Françoise Leurquin-Labie (Paris: 2008).

Livre de Sydrac, (ed.) Ernstpeter Ruhe, *Livre de la fontaine de toutes sciences* (Weisbaden: 2000).

Le Miroir du monde, (ed.) Félix Chavannes (Lausanne: 1845).

Lorris, Guillaume de and Jean de Meun, *Le Roman de la Rose*, (ed.) Félix Lecoy, 3 vols. (Paris: 1970).

Pliny the Elder, *Naturalis historiae libri XXXVII*, (eds.) Ludwig von Jan and Karl Friedrich Theodor Mayhoff (Stuttgart: 1967–70).

Pseudo-Dionysius, *Ecclesiastical Hierarchy*, trans. Thomas Campbell (Washington, D.C.: 1981).

La Queste del saint Graal, (ed.) Albert Pauphilet (Paris: 1923).

Le Roman de Lancelot en prose, (ed.) Alexandre Micha, 9 vols. (Geneva: 1978–83.).

Le Roman de Renart, (eds.) Armand Strubel, Roger Bellon, Dominique Boutet, and Sylvie Lefèvre (Paris: 1998).

Thomas of Cantimpré, *De naturis rerum*, (ed.) Helmut Boese, one volume to date (Berlin and New York: 1973).

Vincent of Beauvais, *Speculum quadruplex sive Speculum maius*, 4 vols. (1624; repr. Graz: 1965).

Vincent of Beauvais, "Prologue au *Speculum maius*," trans. Monique Paulmier-Foucart, in Monique Paulmier-Foucart and Marie-Christine Duchenne, *Vincent de Beauvais et le grand miroir du monde* (Turnhout: 2004), 147–170.

William of Conches, *Dragmaticon Philosophiae*, (eds.) I. Ronca, L. Badia, and J. Pujol (Turnhout: 1997).

Primary Works: Llull

Arbor scientiae, (eds.) Pere Villalba Varneda, 3 vols., ROL 24–26.

Arbre de sciència, (eds.) Tomàs Carreras i Artau and Joaquim Carreras i Artau, *OE*, 1:547–1046.

Ars brevis, (ed.) Alexander Fidora (Tesina: 1999).

Ars compendiosa inveniendi veritatem, MOG 1:1–41.

Ars generalis ultima, (ed.) Alois Madre, ROL 14.

Cent noms de Déu, ORL 19:75–170.

Desconhort, (ed.) Josep Romeu i Figueras, *OE* 1:1308–1328.

Doctrina pueril, (ed.) Joan Santanach i Suñol, NEORL 7.

Fèlix o el Libre de meravelles, (ed.) Anthony Bonner, *Obres selectes de Ramon Llull (1232–1316)*, 2 vols. (Palma: 1989), 2:7–393.

Liber principiorum medicinae, (ed.) María Asunción Sánchez Manzano in *Quattuor libri principiorum*, ROL 31:413–560.

Libre d'Evast e d'Aloma e de Blaquerna, (ed.) Joan Pons i Marquès, *OE* 1:111–307.

Libre de contemplació, (eds.) Antoni Sancho and Miquel Arbona, *OE* 2:83–1269.

Libre del Gentil e dels tres Savis, (ed.) Anthony Bonner, NEORL 2.

Libre de l'orde de cavalleria, (ed.) Pere Bohigas, *OE* 1:513–545.

Obres selectes de Ramon Llull (1232–1316), (ed.) Anthony Bonner, 2 vols. (Palma: 1989).

Venice, Biblioteca Nazionale Marciana lat. VI.200 (2757).

Secondary Works

Armstrong, Adrian, Sarah Kay, et al., *Knowing Poetry: Verse in Medieval France from the "Rose" to the Rhétoriqueurs* (Ithaca: 2011).

Arnar, Anna Sigrídur, *Encyclopedism from Pliny to Borges* (Chicago: 1990).

Badia, Lola, "The *Arbor scientiae*: A 'New' Encyclopedia in the Thirteenth-Century Occitan-Catalan Cultural Context," in *Arbor scientiae: Der Baum des Wissens von Ramon Lull*, (eds.) Fernando Domínguez Reboiras, Pere Villalba Varneda, and Peter Walter (Turnhout: 2002), 1–19.

Badia, Lola, "Ramon Llull: Autor i personatge," in *Aristotelica et Lulliana: magistro doctissimo Charles H. Lohr septuagesimum annum feliciter agenti dedicata*, (eds.) Fernando Domínguez Reboiras et al. (The Hague: 1995), 355–375.

Badia, Lola, *Teoria i practica de la literatura en Ramon Llull* (Barcelona: 1992).

Badia, Lola and Anthony Bonner, *Ramon Llull: Vida, pensamiento y obra literaria* (Barcelona: 1992).

Berlioz, Jacques and Marie-Anne Polo de Beaulieu, "Les Recueils d'*exempla* et la diffusion de l'encyclopédisme médiéval," in *L'Enciclopedismo medievale: Atti del convegno "L'enciclopedismo medievale," San Gimignano 8–10 ottobre 1992*, (ed.) Michelangelo Picone (Ravenna: 1994), 179–212.

Bonillo Hoyos, Xavier, *Literatura al "Llibre de meravelles" de Ramon Llull* (Barcelona: 2008).

Bonner, Anthony, "Estadístiques sobre la recepció de l'obra de Ramon Llull," *SL* 43 (2003): 83–92.

Bonner, Anthony, "Notes de bibliografia i cronologia lul·lianes," *EL* 24 (1980): 71–86.

Bonner, Anthony, "Ramon Llull: Autor, autoritat i illuminat," in *Actes de l'onzè col·loqui internacional de llengua i literatura catalanes, Palma, Mallorca, 8–12 de setembre de 1998*, (eds.) Joan Mas et al. (Barcelona: 1998), 35–60.

Bradley, Ritamary, "Backgrounds of the Title *Speculum* in Medieval Literature," *Speculum* 29 (1954): 100–115.

Bultot, Robert, Léopold Genicot, et al., *Les Genres littéraires dans les sources théologiques et philosophiques médiévales: Définition, critique et exploitation: Actes du Colloque internationale de Louvain-la-Neuve 25–27 mai 1981* (Louvain-la-Neuve: 1982).

Connochie-Bourgne, Chantal, "Quelques Aspects de la réception d'une œuvre encyclopédique au Moyen Âge: Les Cas de l'*Image du monde*," *Littérales* 21 (1997): 221–244.

Dahan, Gilbert, "Encyclopédies et exégèse de la Bible aux XIIe et XIII e siècles," *Cahiers de recherches médiévales (XIIIe–XVe s.)* 6 (1999): 19–40.

Dahan, Gilbert, "Notes et textes sur la poétique au Moyen Âge," *Archives d'histoire doctrinale et littéraire du Moyen Age* 47 (1981): 171–239.

Domínguez Reboiras, Fernando, Pere Villalba Varneda, and Peter Walter, (eds.), *Arbor scientiae: Der Baum des Wissens von Ramon Lull, Akten des Internationalen Kongresses aus Anlaß des 40-jährigen Jubiläums des Raimundus-Lullus-Instituts der Universität Freiburg i. Br.* (Turnhout: 2002).

Fowler, Robert L., "Encyclopaedias: Definitions and Theoretical Problems," in *Premodern Encyclopedic Texts: Proceedings of the Second COMERS Congress, Groningen, 1–4 July 1996*, (ed.) Peter Binkley (Leiden: 1997), 3–29.

Franklin-Brown, Mary, *Reading the World: Encyclopedic Writing in the Scholastic Age* (Chicago: 2012).

Fumagalli, Maria Teresa, *Le Enciclopedie dell'occidente medioevale* (Turin: 1981).

Fumagalli, Maria Teresa, "Premessa," *Rivista di storia della filosofia*, n.s. 1 (1985): 3–4.

Gayà, Jordi, "Significación y demostración en el *Libre de Contemplació* de Ramon Llull," in *Aristotelica et Lulliana: magistro doctissimo Charles H. Lohr septuagesimum annum feliciter agenti dedicata*, (eds.) Fernando Domínguez Reboiras et al. (The Hague: 1995), 477–499.

Gillespie, Vincent, "From the Twelfth Century to *c.* 1450," in *The Cambridge History of Literary Criticism, Vol. 2, The Middle Ages*, (eds.) Alastair Minnis and Ian Johnson (Cambridge: 2005), 145–235.

Jónsson, Einar Már, *Le Miroir: Naissance d'un genre littéraire* (Paris: 1995).

Kay, Sarah, *Subjectivity in Troubadour Poetry* (Cambridge: 1990).

Le Goff, Jacques, "Pourquoi le XIIIe siècle a-t-il été plus particulièrement un siècle d'encyclopédisme?" in *L'Enciclopedismo medievale: Atti del convegno "L'enciclopedismo medievale," San Gimignano 8–10 ottobre 1992*, (ed.) Michelangelo Picone (Ravenna: 1994), 23–40.

Llinarès, Armand, "Algunos aspectos de la educación en la *Doctrina pueril* de Ramón Llull," *EL* 11 (1967): 201–209.

Llinarès, Armand, "Esprit encyclopédique et volonté de système chez Rayond Lulle," in *L'Encyclopédisme: Actes du colloque de Caen, 12–16 janvier 1987*, (ed.) Annie Becq (Paris: 1991), 449–458.

Lubac, Henri de, *Exégèse médiévale: Les Quatre Sens de l'Ecriture*, 4 vols. (Paris: 1959).

Mâle, Émile, *L'Art religieux du XIIIe siècle en France: Étude sur l'iconographie du Moyen Âge et sur ses sources d'inspiration*, 7th ed. (Paris: 1931).

Meier, Christel, "Grundzüge der mittelalterlichen Enzyklopädik: Zu Inhalten, Formen und Funktionen einer problematischen Gattung," in *Literatur und Laienbildung im Spätmittelalter und in der Reformationszeit*, (eds.) Ludger Grenzmann and Karl Stackmann (Stuttgart, 1984), 467–503.

Meier, Christel, "Über den Zusammenhang von Erkenntnistheorie und enzyklopädischem Ordo in Mittelalter und Früher Neuzeit," *Frühmittelalterliche Studien* 36 (2002): 171–192.

Meyer, Heinz, *Die Enzyklopädie des Bartholomäus Anglicus: Untersuchungen zur Überlieferungs- und Rezeptionsgeschichte von De Proprietatibus Rerum* (Munich: 2000).

Minnis, Alastair, *Medieval Theory of Authorship: Scholastic Literary Attitudes in the Later Middle Ages*, 2nd ed. (Philadelphia: 1988).

Minnis, Alastair, "Late Medieval Discussions of *Compilatio* and the Role of the *Compilator*," *Beiträge zur Geschichte der Deutschen Sprache und Literatur* 101 (1979): 385–421.

Nebbiai-Dalla Guarda, Donatella, "Classifications et classements," in *Histoire des bibliothèques françaises: Les Bibliothèques médiévales, du VIe siècle à 1530*, (ed.) André Vernet (Paris: 1989), 373–393.

Parkes, Malcom B., "The Influence of the Concepts of *Ordinatio* and *Compilatio* on the Development of the Book," in *Medieval Learning and Literature: Essays Presented to Richard William Hunt*, (eds.) J.J.G. Alexander and M.T. Gibson (Oxford: 1976), 115–141.

Paulmier-Foucart, Monique and Marie-Christine Duchenne, *Vincent de Beauvais et le grand miroir du monde* (Turnhout: 2004).

Pring-Mill, Robert, "La *Doctrina pueril*: conreu i transmissió d'una cultura," in *Estudis sobre Ramon Llull*, (eds.) Lola Badia and Albert Soler (Barcelona: 1991), 319–331.

Ribémont, Bernard, *De natura rerum: Études sur les encyclopédies médiévales* (Orléans: 1995).

Ribémont, Bernard, *Littérature et encyclopédies du Moyen Age* (Orléans: 2002).

Ribémont, Bernard, *Les Origines des encyclopédies médiévales: D'Isidore de Séville aux Carolingiens* (Paris: 2001).

Richard, H. and Mary A. Rouse, "Concordances et Index," in *Mise en page et mise en texte du livre manuscrit*, (eds.) Henri-Jean Martin and Jean Vezin (Paris: 1990), 219–228.

Riquer, Martí de, *Història de la literatura catalana*, vol. 1 (Barcelona: 1964).

Romano, Marta M.M. and Óscar de la Cruz, "The Human Realm," in *Raimundus Lullus: An Introduction to his Life, Works and Thought*, (eds.) Alexander Fidora and Josep E. Rubio (Turnhout: 2008), 363–459.

Rubio, Josep Enric, "The Natural Realm," in *Raimundus Lullus: An Introduction to his Life, Works and Thought*, (eds.) Alexander Fidora and Josep E. Rubio (Turnhout: 2008), 311–362.

Rubió i Balaguer, Jordi, "L'Expressió literària en l'obra lul·liana," in *OE*, 1:85–110.

Rubió i Balaguer, Jordi, "Sobre la prosa rimada en R.L.," *Estudios dedicados a Menéndez Pidal*, vol. 5 (Madrid: 1954), 307–318.

Santanach i Suñol, Joan, "'Cové que hom fassa aprendre a son fill los .xiiii. articles': La *Doctrina pueril* com a tractat catequètic," in *Literatura i cultura a la corona d'Aragó (s. XIII–XV): Actes del III Col·loqui "Problemes i mètodes de literatura catalana antiga," Universitat de Girona, 5–8 de juliol del 2000*, (eds.) Lola Badia et al. (Barcelona: 2002), 419–430.

Smalley, Beryl, *The Study of the Bible in the Middle Ages*, 2nd ed. (Notre Dame, Indiana: 1964).

Teeuwen, Mariken, *The Vocabulary of Intellectual Life in the Middle Ages* (Turnhout: 2003).

Weijers, Olga, *Le Maniement du savoir: Pratiques intellectuelles à l'époque des premières universités (XIIIe–XIVe siècles)* (Turnhout: 1996).

Wenzel, Siegfried, "The Arts of Preaching," in *The Cambridge History of Literary Criticism, Vol. 2, The Middle Ages*, (eds.) Alastair Minnis and Ian Johnson (Cambridge: 2005), 84–96.

Zink, Michel, *La Subjectivité littéraire: Autour du siècle de saint Louis* (Paris: 1985).

Ziolkowski, Jan M., "Theories of Obscurity in the Latin Tradition," *Mediaevalia* 19 (1996): 101–170.

PART 4

Renaissance and Modern Lullism

∵

CHAPTER 11

Lullism among French and Spanish Humanists of the Early 16th Century

Linda Báez Rubí

11.1 Introduction

During the 16th century, the legacy of Ramon Llull's thought undergoes considerable transformation within the new currents of humanist thought. The characteristic features of early 16th-century Lullism can only be understood within the context of the ideological inclinations and encyclopedic culture of two specific groups – composed of philosophers, theologians, and printers – that joined forces to set in motion the pro-Lullian editorial activity that would reach all the way to the lands of the New World.

Several historical events and social circumstances became increasingly important at the dawn of the 16th century: the Turkish advance obviously threatened the frontiers of Christendom, while a moral and religious crisis plunged the institutions of the Church into an internal schism. The restoration of a primitive Church more aligned with the evangelical and apostolic tenets of reforming movements, from the *devotio moderna* to the Observant Franciscans, emerged in the Iberian Peninsula as a political project derived from the pressure applied by social movements opposed to the opulence and disfunction of ecclesiastical institutions.[1] At the same time, the discovery of the New World posed new questions about both relationships with European economic power and the goals of Christian missionizing. This stage of colonizing and "civilizing" lands overseas opened, especially in the realm of the Church's work, new horizons and promising opportunities for achieving the conversion and evangelization that had suffered so many defeats in the Arab world. Within this context appeared two groups of "humanist theologians" with Lullist interests, one gathered around the Frenchman Jacques Lefèvre d'Étaples (Iacobus Faber Stapulensis, 1460?–1536) and another around the

---

1 Melquíades Andrés, *Historia de la mística de la Edad de Oro en España y América* (Madrid: 1994), analyzes comprehensively these aspects of this era.

Spanish Cardinal Francisco Jiménez de Cisneros (1436–1517).[2] Their combined efforts constituted a project devoted especially to the introduction of new didactic methods, the dissemination of knowledge, the promotion of Catholic ideals imbued with a mystical sensibility, the renewal of rhetoric as an instrument of persuasion, and the development of a Neoplatonic Christian theology.[3] In this environment, the fascinating multifaceted figure of Ramon Llull, writer, theologian, and philosopher, presented to the eyes of his admirers a panoply of possibilities for incorporation within and across many fields of knowledge as well as religious life.[4] It is essential to recognize that both of these humanist groups responsible for the printing of Lullian and pseudo-Lullian texts, despite the obvious differences among them,[5] proposed, defended, and spread a conception of the Lullian Art that emphasized its utility in converting unbelievers, unifying the Church, and universalizing the Christian faith. Within this ideology, conversion involved a dual application: within the realm of an active life it shaped missionary exercises of evangelism and preaching; within the realm of a contemplative life, devoted to attaining experience of the divine in solitude, it found expression in eremetic practices, in a religious piety characterized by interior reflection and a quest for knowledge of the divine within human existence that favored meditation and mystical experiences, as well as the development of a spiritual anthropology.

11.2   Jacques Lefèvre d'Étaples and His Lullian Publishing Activity

Jacques Lefèvre d'Étaples,[6] a professor in the Faculty of Arts at Paris and in the College of Cardinal Lemoine, devoted himself early in his intellectual career

---

2   Briefly outlined by Marcel Bataillon, *Erasmo y España: Estudios sobre la historia espiritual del siglo XVI*, trans. Antonio Alatorre, 2nd ed. (Mexico: 1966), 52–60; Joaquín Carreras i Artau and Tomás Carreras i Artau, *Historia de la filosofía española*, 2 vols. (Madrid: 1939–1943), 2: 251–257.

3   Cesare Vasoli, *Civitas mundi: Studi sulla cultura del cinquecento* (Rome: 1996); Yelena Mazour-Matusevich, *Le siècle d'or de la mystique française: un autre regard: étude de la littérature spiri-tuelle de Jean Gerson (1363–1429) à Jacques Lefèvre d'Étaples (1450?–1537)* (Milan: 2004).

4   Cesare Vasoli, *L' enciclopedismo del Seicento* (Naples: 1978); Paolo Rossi, *Clavis universalis: arti della mnemoniche e logica combinatoria da Lullo a Leibniz* (Milan: 1960); and Miquel Batllori, *Ramon Llull i el lul·lisme* (Valencia: 1993); Mark D. Johnston, "The Reception of the Lullian Art," *Sixteenth Century Journal* 12 (1981): 31–48; Paola Zambelli, "Il 'De auditu kabbalistico' e la tradizione lulliana nel Rinascimento," *Atti dell'Accademia Toscana di Scienze e Lettere "La Colombaria"* 30 (Florence: 1965): 115–247; all remain useful introductions to sixteenth-century Lullism.

5   Michela Pereira, "Le opere mediche di Lullo in rapporto con la sua filosofia naturale e con la medicina del XIII secolo," *EL* 23 (1979): 5–35.

6   Major studies of Lefèvre include: Charles-Henri Graf, *Essai sur la vie et les écrits de Jacques Lefèvre d'Étaples* (1872; repr. Geneva: 1970); Augustin Renaudet, *Préréforme et*

to purging philosophy of Scholastic corruptions through new commented editions of the Aristotelian oeuvre.[7] The reestablishment and reappreciation of the rational method advocated by the Philosopher were necessary to understanding the material world apprehended by the senses and imagination. However, in order to understand the spiritual world that involved God, Lefèvre concluded that it was necessary to achieve another kind of knowledge beyond the purely rational, namely the intellectual knowledge that best enabled approaching God. This ultimately led him to combine philosophy with religious piety, and so his interest came to focus on thinkers that supported this goal, such as Pseudo-Dionysius, Nicholas of Cusa, and Ramon Llull, all favored with the publication of a good number of their works.[8] Lefèvre's encounter with Lullian thought occurred during a trip to southern France, where a friend provided him a manuscript copy of Llull's *Libre de contemplació* (1271–1273); its reading provoked a profound religious experience, to the point that he wished to abandon worldly life and devote himself to an eremetical existence, seeking God in solitude.[9] Following this experience, Lefèvre undertook an intense Lullian editorial enterprise, which earned him a reputation as the restorer of Lullian studies in France.[10] This achievement involved a group of collaborators who felt no less admiration for Blessed Ramon: Josse Clichtove (1472–1543), Beatus Rhenanus (1485–1547), Charles de Bovelles (Noyon, 1479–1567), and the printer Josse Bade (1462–1532).[11] The support of this group for the restoration of

     Humanisme à Paris pendant les premières guerres d'Italie (1494–1517), 2nd ed. (Paris: 1953); Guy Bedouelle, *Lefèvre d'Étaples et l'Intelligence des Ecritures* (Geneva: 1976); Cesare Vasoli, "Jacques Lefèvre d'Étaples e le origini del 'Fabrismo,'" *Rinascimento* 2 (1959): 221–254; *Jacques Lefèvre d'Étaples (1450?–1536): actes du colloque d'Étaples les 7 et 8 novembre 1992*, (ed.) Jean-François Pernot (Paris: 1995).

7   Carreras i Artau, *Historia de la filosofía*, 2:201–204; David A. Lines, "Lefèvre and French Aristotelianism on the Eve of the Sixteenth Century," in *Der Aristotelismus in der Frühen Neuzeit-Kontinuität oder Wiederaneignung?* (Wiesbaden: 2007), 273–289; Eugene F. Rice, "Humanist Aristotelianism in France: Jacques Lefèvre d'Étaples and his circle," in *Humanism in France at the end of the Middle Ages and in the Early Renaissance*, (ed.) A.H.T. Levi (New York: 1970), 132–149.

8   Eugene F. Rice, *The Prefatory Epistles of Jacques Lefèvre d'Étaples and Related Texts* (New York: 1972). For the works of Pseudo-Dionysius, see 60–71, 350–353; for Nicholas of Cusa, 342–348; and for Ramon Llull, 75–78, 140–145, 373–378.

9   Lefèvre, ep. 45 (to Gabriel, París, 1505), (ed.) Rice, *Prefatory Epistles*, 141.

10   Philip Edgcumbe Hughes, *Lefévre: Pioneer of Ecclesiastical Renewal in France* (Grand Rapids: 1984), 11–15, and 45–52; Jocelyn N. Hillgarth, *Ramon Lull and Lullism in Fourteenth-Century France* (Oxford: 1971), 283–289.

11   On the reception of Lullism in Paris, see: Carreras i Artau, *Historia de la filosofía*, 2:201–216; Hillgarth, *Ramon Lull and Lullism in Fourteenth-Century France*, 281–288; and Armand Llinarès, "Le lullisme de Lefèvre d'Étaples et des ses amis humanistes," in *L'humanisme française au début de la Renaissance* (Paris: 1973), 127–135. For Bade as a publisher of Lullian works and his followers see Philippe Renouard, *Imprimeurs et libraires Parisiens*

a primitive Christianity awakened interest in the figure of Llull as one who exemplified mysticism, the eremetic life, and the apostolic endeavors of preaching and conversion. Lefèvre joins all of these interests in a didactic program intended to achieve reforms in education at Paris and even in the standards of moral behavior for monastic life.[12] Lefèvre believed that the monastic life sketched in Llull's works required a simpler and more direct approach to God, that is, a way or method that would open the possibility for the soul to contemplate God.[13] Fifteenth-century Lullism typically sought to offer a practical and simple version of the Lullian Art, that would be comprehensible to everyone, unlike the abstruse Scholastic speculations of the universities. The instrument that Lefèvre employed for diffusion of these ideas was the printed book, which allowed more rapid circulation of ideas to a wider audience, both geographically and socially.

In 1499 Lefèvre brought forth at Paris, from the press of Guy Marchant, his first collection of Llull's works: *Hic conteninentur libri Raemundi pii eremitae. Primo de laudibus beatissime virginis marie. Secundo Libellus de natali pueri parvuli. Tertio Clericus Raemundi. Quarto Phantasticus Raemundi.*[14] These works deal with the project of a spiritual crusade, founding schools of Oriental languages, the elimination of Averroism, and finally promoting the cult of the Immaculate Conception.[15] Around 1505 Lefèvre edited a second collection of Latin versions of Llull's *Libre de contemplació* and *Libre d'amic e d'amat* (1283).[16] In his introduction, he announces his desire to send copies to distant countries, revealing thus his evangelizing intentions as a mystical ideal within the

---

    du XVIe siècle (Paris: 1969), 2:220–224, 356–357 and 3:44–48; Elies Rogent and Estanislau Durán, *Bibliografía de les Impressions Lul.lianes* (Barcelona: 1927), 43, 49, 56–59, 63–64, 67–68; Carreras i Artau, *Historia de la filosofía*, 2:205–206.

12   Eugene F. Rice, "Jacques Lefèvre d'Étaples and the medieval Christian mystics," in *Florilegium Historiale: Essays presented to Wallace K. Ferguson*, (eds.) J.G. Rowe and W.H. Stockdale (Toronto: 1971), 89–124; Mazour-Matusevich, *Le siècle d'or de la mystique française*, 361–410.

13   Lefèvre, ep. 22 and prolog to the reader from *Hic conteninentur libri Raemundi pii eremitae. Primo de laudibus beatissime virginis marie. Secundo Libellus de natali pueri parvuli. Tertio Clericus Raemundi. Quarto Phantasticus Raemundi* (Paris: 1499), (ed.) Rice, *Prefatory Epistles*, 76–77.

14   On these editions, see Rogent and Durán, *Bibliografía*, 20–23.

15   Peter Walter, "Jacobus Faber Stapulensis als Editor des Raimundus Lullus dargestellt am Beispiel des *Liber natalis pueri parvuli Christi Jesu*," in *Aristotelica et Lulliana*, (eds.) Fernando Domínguez Reboiras et al. (Steenbrugge: 1995), 545–559.

16   *Primum volumen contemplationum Remundi duos libros continens Libellus Blaquerne de amico et amato* (Paris: 1505); Rogent and Durán, *Bibliografía*, 32–33.

secular world, grounded in the figure and personality of Blessed Ramon.[17] Finally, in 1516, Lefèvre publishes together, from the Parisian press of Josse Bade, the *Proverbia Raemundi* and *Philosophia amoris*,[18] dedicating them to Alfonso of Aragon, archbishop of Zaragoza and Valencia; this, his third edition of Lullian works, confirms the favor that Llull's thought enjoyed at the University of Paris.[19] Lefèvre also reiterates the piety found in the works of "that holy hermit," as well as their utility in spiritual matters, and how "despite his sermons written in a plain style, he led a simple life, rejecting the world and professing love for Christ."[20] In the prologue to the last of these editions, he indicates that the doctors and masters of the Sorbonne admire the teaching of Blessed Ramon, which some consider divinely inspired, emphasizing its enormous popularity and academic recognition, taught not just at the University of Paris, but also at those of Rome, Venice, Germany, and Spain.[21] This same interest in Llull led Lefèvre to direct his attention to the thought of Nicholas of Cusa, thanks to the latter's obvious Lullian affiliation. In 1507 Lefèvre journeyed to Rome in search of the Cardinal's manuscripts. In 1510, with the assistance of several contemporary humanists, such as Beatus Rhenanus and the Christian cabbalist Johannes Reuchlin (1455–1522), he began preparing the edition of Cusanus's works that finally appeared at Paris in 1514, as three volumes from the press of Josse Bade.[22] This edition included the French humanist's own theological and philosophical reflections in his commentaries, whether as an introduction or as an afterword to the works of Cusanus.[23]

---

17   Lefèvre, ep. 45 (to Gabriel, París, 1505), (ed.) Rice, *Prefatory Epistles*, 141–143.
18   Rogent and Durán, *Bibliografía*, 59–60. For the involvement of Bade regarding his Lullian editorial politics under the frame of Christian humanism, see Louise Katz, "Les presses badiennes au service des détracteurs d'Érasme et de Jacques Lefèvre d'Étaples: un revirement idéologique?" in *Passeurs de textes: Imprimeurs et libraires à l'âge de l'humanisme*, (eds.) Christine Bénévent et al. (Paris: 2012), 43–56.
19   Lefèvre, ep. 118 (to Alfonso of Aragon, París, 1516), (ed.) Rice, *Prefatory Epistles*, 373–378. See Ricardo García Villoslada, *La universidad de París durante los estudios de Francisco de Vitoria O. P.* (Rome: 1938), 386–390, 413, 429.
20   Lefèvre, ep. 118, (ed.) Rice, *Prefatory Epistles*, 376: "Neque deterrat legentem sancti eremitae sermonis simplicitas quem viventem vita simplex, vilis habitus, et neglectus mundus Christo faciebant carissimum."
21   Ibid., 374–375.
22   *Nicolai Cusae cardinalis opera*, (ed.) Lefèvre d'Étaples (Paris: 1514); Lefèvre, ep. 109 (to Denis Briçonnet, París, 1514), (ed.) Rice, *Prefatory Epistles*, 342–348.
23   On Lefèvre as editor of Cusanus, see Reinhold Weier, *Das Thema vom verborgenen Gott von Nikolaus von Kues zu Martin Luther* (Münster: 1967), 35–43.

11.3   Lullian Influence on Lefèvre

Modern scholars agree that the impact of Lullian doctrines on Lefèvre was pri-marily in the area of mysticism, the soul's contemplation of God. We know that Lefèvre expounded logical techniques for Llull's Great Art in his courses at the College of Cardinal Lemoine and that, like Cusanus,[24] he taught Lullian dialectic as the only method that surpasses reason, because it can acquire knowledge through "conjectures" (*coniecturae*) which thus allow an approach to the divine essence.[25] Lefèvre structures the method employed for achiev-ing this objective in three modes of theological practice: the third and lowest he terms the imaginative way, which corresponds to attempting to know God through the images of things; the second, middle way, is known as the rational, and studies God through logic; the first and highest is the so-called intellectual way, in which the soul attains contemplative knowledge through the coinci-dence of opposites (in divine rapture).[26] The third is found below us, the sec-ond within us, and the first above us. This methodology fuses mainly doctrines from Llull, Cusanus, and Pseudo-Dionysius. On the one hand, Lefèvre adopts Cusanus's theory, derived chiefly from the combinatory exercise of triangles in Llull's Figure T, with its triads such as Agreement, Contrariety, and Difference or Beginning, Middle, and End.[27] This leads the French humanist to postulate the coincidence of opposites, proposed by Cusanus, as the path to experience of God.[28] On the other hand, Cusanus's three realms of human knowledge – the superior world of the intellect (where opposites coincide), the middle world of reason (where knowledge derives from Pseudo-Dionysian negative theology), and the inferior world of sensation (perception with the corporeal senses) – appear visually in the paradigmatic Figure P (Figure 11.1)[29] and projected as well upon the macrocosmic level in the Figure U of the universe (Figure 11.2).[30]

---

24   For his interest in Cusanus, see Maurice de Gandillac, "Lefèvre d'Étaples et Charles de Bouelles, lecteurs de Nicolas de Cues," in *Colloque International de Tours (XIVe stage): L'Humanisme français au début de la Renaissance* (Paris: 1973), 155–171.

25   Carreras i Artau, *Historia de la filosofía*, 2:203; for an in-depth study regarding coniecturae, see Inigo Bocken, *L'art de la collection: Introduction historico-éthique à l'herméneutique conjecturale de Nicolas de Cues* (Paris and Louvain: 2007).

26   Lefèvre, ep. 74, (ed.) Rice, *Prefatory Epistles*, 224, does nonetheless join the imagination to reason (*ratio*) and intellect (*intellectus*); see his preface to Richard of St. Victor, *De super-divina trinitate* (Paris: 1510).

27   On Lull and Cusanus, see Eusebio Colomer, *Ramon Llull y Nicolás de Cusa* (Madrid: 1961).

28   Stephan Meier-Oeser, *Die Präsenz des Vergessenen: Zur Rezeption der Philosophie des Nico-laus Cusanus vom 15. bis zum 18. Jahrhundert* (Münster: 1989), 36–42.

29   Nicholas of Cusa, *De coniecturis*, lib. 1 (Paris: 1514), fol. 46v.

30   Cusa, *De coniecturis*, fol. 49v.

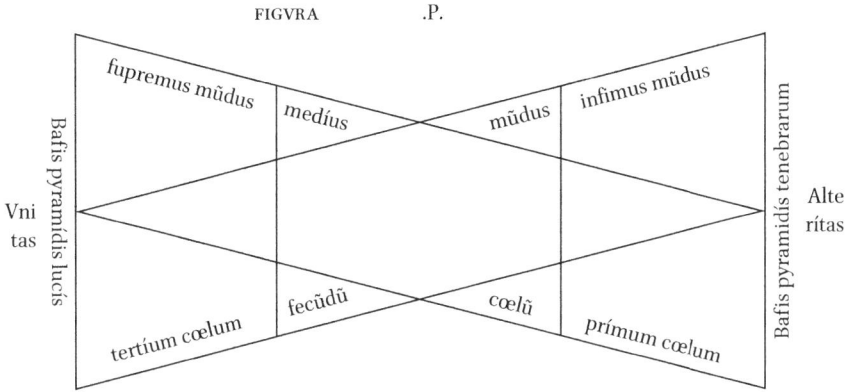

FIGURE 11.1   Cusanus's Paradigmatic Figure, from his *De coniecturis*, in *Nicolai Cusae cardinalis opera*, (ed.) Jacques Lefèvre d'Etaples (Paris: 1514), fol. 46v.

Here the influence of Pseudo-Dionysius is also evident in the structure of the nine hierarchies that organize the celestial universe. One should note that Lefèvre links the mode of knowledge through imagination with Cusanus's realm of sensation, because the imaginative faculty, within the psycho-physiological schemes of the early 16th century, was an internal sense that maintained direct contact with the external senses, and so with the material world, thanks to the information that it received from them.[31] It was thus considered somewhat "impure," unlike reason. Elsewhere, Lefèvre compares the pious mystical behavior of Llull that attracted his attention with Cusanus's figure of the "idiot" (*idiota*),[32] associated in this era with the humble knowledge of the author of the *Contemplationes Idiotae*,[33] who experiences rapture into the heavens

31   As proposed, for example, in the encyclopedia of Gregor Reisch, *Margarita Philosophica* (Freiburg: 1503). The status of the imagination was rather unstable, considered generally below reason until its reappraisal in the 16th century, when the ennoblement of the arts raised it to more elevated status; see *Phantasia-Imaginatio: v Colloquio Internazionale*, (eds.) Marta Fattori and Massimo Bianchi (Rome: 1988). Regarding Llull, see Amador Vega, *Die Sinnlichkeit des Geistigen, die Geistigkeit des Sinnlichen und die metaphorische Sprachverwendung bei Ramon Llull* (Freiburg: 1992).

32   Richard J. Oosterhoff, "Idiotae, Mathematics, and Artisans: The Untutored Mind and the Discovery of Nature in the Fabrist Circle," *Intellectual History Review* 24 (2014): 301–319; and Inigo Bocken, "Visions of Reform. Lay Piety as a Form of Thinking in Nicholas of Cusa," in *Reassessing Reform: An Historical Investigation into Church Renewal*, (eds.) Christopher Bellito and David Zacharias Flanagrin (Washington, D.C.: 2012), 227–231.

33   Lefèvre, prolog to *Contemplationes idiotae* (Paris: 1519). The authorship of this work was unknown until the middle of the 17th century, when Théophile Raynaud attributed it to Raymundus Jordanus, an Augustinian canon and prior of Uzés in 1381.

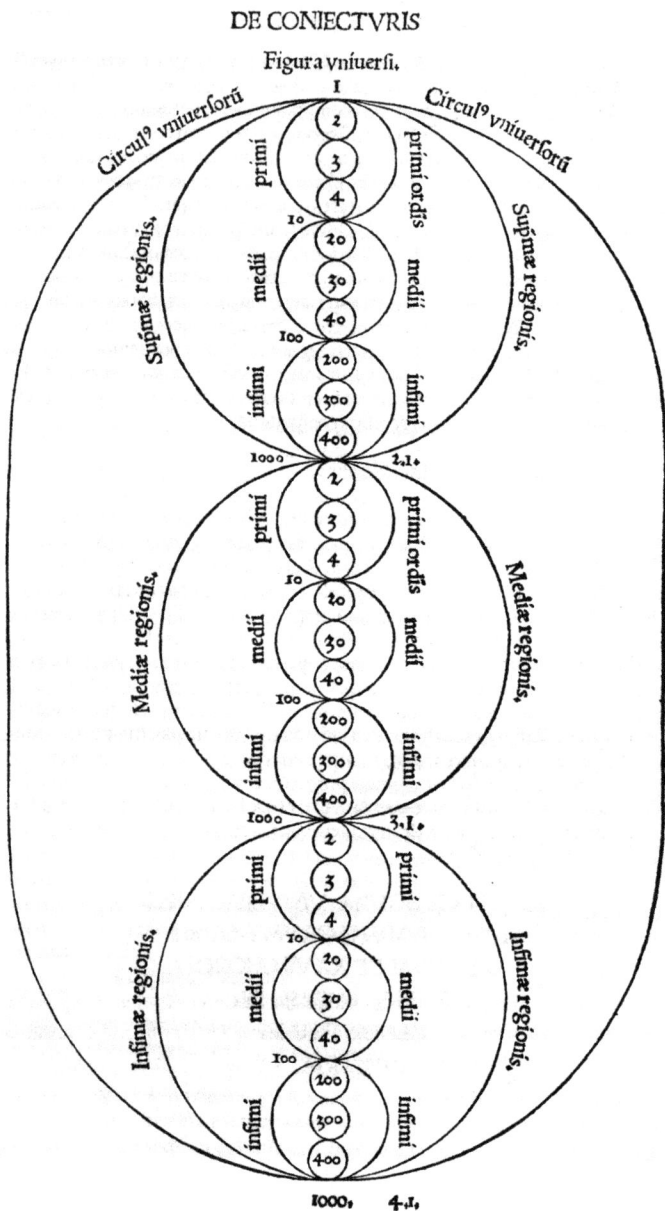

DE CONIECTVRIS

Figura vniuersi.

Híc fupre=
mus / com=
preffus cír=
culus : om=
níno rotũ=
dus intellí=
gídebet.qđ
nõ permifit
fierí: ípref=
foriæ char=
tę anguftía

FIGURE 11.2   Cusanus's Figure U, from his *De coniecturis*, in *Nicolai Cusae cardinalis opera*,
(ed.) Jacques Lefèvre d'Etaples (Paris: 1514), fol. 49v.

through sincere meditation.[34] For Lefèvre, the idiot is therefore identical with the wise Christian of humble style, pure and sincere, who achieves divine illumination through penance and perfection.[35] Lefèvre was successful in promoting Lullism at the editorial level by disseminating Llull's eremitic ideal of contemplation, to the degree that through his editions the acceptance of these ideals became a characteristic phenomenon of contemplative life in this era.[36] However, he did not produce any work of his own that truly incorporated the Lullian Art, which he desired to promote into a more developed and concrete methodological plan. Still, his effort would bear fruit in his disciples and associates, as we will see below.

11.4   Charles de Bovelles and His Relations with the Iberian Lullist Circle

In 1503 and 1509, Charles de Bovelles[37] traveled to Spain and Italy, where he became much more familiar with the Lullian Art thanks to friendships made with some of the most important figures of the era. Bovelles enjoyed the hospitality of Juan de Vera, archbishop of León, and in Toledo of the archbishop and cardinal Francisco Jiménez de Cisneros. Thanks to the Spanish primate he made friends with Lullist academics at the University of Alcalá,[38] among them Nicholas de Pax, for whom Bovelles would become an authority on the theological doctrines of Blessed Ramon. The mystical fervor and messianic expectations that interested him during much of his life,[39] and which he inherited in

---

34 Ep. 22 (prologue to the reader from *Hic conteninentur libri Raemundi pii eremitae*), (ed.) Rice, *Prefatory Epistles*, 77; similarly ep. 188 (to Alfonso of Aragon, París, 1516), (ed.) Rice, *Prefatory Epistles*, 375. Bedouell, *Lefèvre d'Étaples*, 76, discusses the appreciation and importance of Cusanus's "idiot" as emphasized by Lefèvre.

35 Ep. 126 (prolog to *Contemplationes idiotae*), (ed.) Rice, *Prefatory Epistles*, 412.

36 Carreras i Artau, *Historia de la filosofía*, 2:205.

37 On Bovelles's life, see: Karl Hermann Brause, *Die Geschichtsphilosophie des Carolus Bovillus* (Leipzig: 1916); Joseph M. Victor, *Charles de Bovelles (1479–1553: An Intellectual Biography* (Geneva: 1978); and Centre d'études supérieures de la Renaissance de l'Université de Tours, *Charles de Bovelles et son cinquième centenaire (1479–1979): Actes du Colloque International tenu a Noyon, les 14-15-16 septembre 1979* (Paris: 1982). In general: Carreras i Artau, *Historia de la filosofía*, 2:26, 159, 197, 206–209, 243, 252–253, 256, 262, 291, and 357; and Hillgarth, *Ramon Lull and Lullism,* 285–288.

38 Michela Pereira, "Bernardo Lavinheta e la diffusione del Lullismo a Parigi nei primi anni del '500," *Interpres: Rivista di Studi Quattrocenteschi* 5 (1984): 248–250; Bataillon, *Erasmo y España*, 64–65.

39 Curt J. Wittlin, "Charles de Bovelles davant dos models de vida santa i solitària: Nicolau de Flüe (1503) i Ramon Llull (1511)," in *Homenatge a Miquel Batllori,* (ed.) Guillem Alexandre Amengual i Bunyola (Barcelona: 2003), 61–76.

part from the mystical tendencies of his teacher Lefèvre, made him see in Cisneros's apologetic plans and proposals for a Spanish crusade the surest path to the universal spread of Christianity.[40] The cardinal's triumph at Oran, so important after the reconquest of Granada in 1492, seemed to Bovelles the opportunity to initiate a spiritual renewal in which the Cardinal "would fulfill the will of God on earth," making way, using a Vergilian *topos* interpreted to signify Christian reform, for a "new race sent from high heaven in order to establish peace and harmony throughout the world, under one faith and under one universal prince."[41]

Within this context, Bovelles was the first to edit a biography of Ramon Llull, under the title *Epistola in vitam Raymundi Lulli*,which appeared in one volume along with his *Commentarius in primordiale evangelium divi Ioannis*, published at Paris by Josse Bade in 1511.[42] The letter is addressed to a friend, Raymond Boucher, at whose request Bovelles prepared the biography. Bovelles admits that he heard this life of the Blessed one called Ramon Llull, a Spanish-born hermit, "told by a Spanish friend" (*a quodam Hispano amico recenseri audieram*) and so he is composing it from memory and offers it to Boucher in order to increase his piety and devotion.[43] Indeed, this is a version that differs from Llull's *Vita* of 1311: it incorporates legends such as the one about a woman with breast cancer whom Llull loved[44] and another about the pyramid of light that descended after his supposed martyrdom.[45] Bovelles's version does not hide its apologetic purpose and his preferences for embellishing and enhancing the image of Llull as divinely illuminated and a martyr. On the other hand, although the French humanist made use of an oral source, in confecting the catalog of Llull's works that traditionally accompanied his *Vita*,[46] we can see that these are almost the same as those mentioned in the text of 1311. Bovelles omits works such as *Ars generalis ultima, alius Liber intellectus, Liber proverbiorum, Ars medicinae, Liber*

---

40 Bovelles to Cardinal Cisneros, 20 March 1509, from *Philosophicae epistulae*, in *Que hoc volumine continentur: Liber de intellectu. Liber de sensibus. Liber de generatione. Libellus de nihilo. Ars oppositorum. Liber de sapiente. Liber de duodecim numeris. Philosophicae epistulae. Liber de perfectis numeris. Libellus de mathematicis rosis. Liber de mathematicis corporibus. Libellus de mathematicis supplementis* (Paris: 1510), fol. 166v.

41 Bovelles to Cardinal Cisneros, 20 of March, 1509, from *Philosophicae epistulae* in *Que hoc volumine*, f. 167r.: "Iam nova progenies: celo mittatur ab alto. Pax sit et in toto surgat concordia mundo. Una fides, unus iam regnet in omnia princeps."

42 Rogent and Durán, *Bibliografía*, 43–44; for the reprinting of 1514, see Rogent and Durán, *Bibliografía*, 49–50. Modern edition by Joseph M. Victor, "Charles de Bovelles and Nicholas de Pax: Two Sixteenth-Century Biographies of Ramon Lull," *Traditio* 32 (1976): 322–332.

43 Bovelles, *Epistola in vitam Raymundi Lulli Eremita* (Paris: 1511), fol. 34r.

44 Bovelles, *Epistola*, fol. 34r–v. On the *Vita* of 1311, see the first chapter in this volume.

45 Bovelles, *Epistola*, fol. 40r.

46 Bovelles, *Epistola*, fol. 35v–36r.

de centum signis, Liber de maiori agentia Dei, Liber de articulis divinarum ratio-num, and *Ars electionis.* However, he adds, for example, such titles as *De duratio-ne, Liber Fantastici,* and finally the *Liber Alchimiae,* so that the 124 in the original catalog are reduced to 120.[47]

Bovelles went even further in his admiration for the simple life of Blessed Ramon, achieving the integration, within the exposition of his philosophical and theological system, of vital elements of Lullism in order to develop them, following the path of Cusanus, in a very personal way. Likewise, his interest in the theological and philosophical doctrines of Llull and Llull's followers led him to seek inspiration in works from currents of 15th-century Lullism, such as the *Scientia libri creaturarum naturae et scientia de homine* (1436), better known as the *Theologia naturalis,* of Raymond of Sabunde.[48] Also known under many variations of his surname (Sibiuda, Sabiende, Sabond, Sabonde, Sebon, Se-bonde, or Sebeyde), Sabunde was a master of arts, medicine, and theology, and twice rector (1428 and 1435), at the University of Toulouse.[49] His work eventu-ally drew condemnation in the Index of prohibited books of 1559, on suspicion of heresy.[50] Given the recommendation of his book by Bovelles as "very rich and delicious" (*succulentissimus tamen atque uberrimus est*),[51] a brief analysis is worthwhile, because of its significance for the humanist encyclopedic trends of the 16th century that included Bovelles.

Drawing chiefly on Llull's *Libre de home* (1300), *Liber de ascensu et descen-su intellectus* (1305), and *Liber de articulis fidei* (1296), the *Theologia naturalis* reprises Lullian doctrines of conversion at a methodological level, achieving a radicalization of Lullism in the practical, pedagogical, and missiological sense.[52] On the one hand, this is reflected in the accessible language employed to express Lullian concepts, while setting aside their combinatory apparatus, in

47   Ramón de Alós y de Dou, *Los catálogos lulianos: contribución al estudio de la obra de Ramón Llull* (Barcelona: 1918), 17–19.

48   *Theologia naturalis seu Liber creaturarum* (ed. Joachim Sighart), (ed.) Friedrich Stegmül-ler (1852; repr. Stuttgart:1966), 6–16. See Rossi, *Clavis universalis,* 50–51; José María García Gómez-Heras, "El *Liber creaturarum* de Raimundo Sabunde: Estudio bibliográfico," *Cuad-ernos Salmantinos de Filosofía* 3 (1977): 231–271.

49   José Luis Sánchez Nogales, *Camino del hombre a Dios: La teología natural de Raimundo Sibiuda* (Granada: 1995), 77–141; Batllori, *Ramon Llull i el lul·lisme,* 368–371.

50   Mario Scaduto, "Laínez e l'Indice del 1559: Lullo, Sabunde, Savonarola, Erasmo," *Archivum Historicum Societatis Iesu* 24 (1955): 3–32; Lorenzo Riber, "Erasmo en el 'Indice Paulino' con Lulio, Sabunde y Savonarola," *Boletín de la Real Academia Española* (1958): 249–263.

51   Letter to Nicolas de Sainctz (1508) in *Philosophicae epistulae* in *Que hoc volumine,* fol. 54v; and further references in Letter to Jean Cocon (1508), in *Philosophicae epistulae* in *Que hoc volumine,* fol. 53v–54r.

52   *Theologia naturalis,* (ed.) Stegmüller, 35; Jaume de Puig i Oliver, *La filosofia de Ramon Sibiuda* (Barcelona: 1997), 68; Carreras i Artau, *Historia de la filosofía,* 2:101–175.

an attempt to be a unified universal science; on the other hand, in the special attention paid to the religious anthropology of the relationship between humans and God,[53] set in the natural world that bears the functions of representing God and of revealing Christ to fallen humanity.[54] Creation should therefore be understood as the diffusion of divine *dignitates* (comparable to Lullian activity *ad extra*), which thus reveal God's being and trinitarian structure (Lullian activity *ad intra*); creatures are legible as letters from the alphabet of this knowledge, since they "were written by the finger of God" (*digito Dei scripta*) and possess "science and diverse meanings and amazing ideas" (*scientiam et diversas significationes et sententias mirabiles*).[55] Since humans recapitulate the natural world in its various levels—being, living, sensation, and understanding (*esse, vivere, sentire et intelligere*)—along with the addition of free will,[56] only they can restore it to its Creator, through the quest for self-knowledge, which is also knowledge of nature. Thus the latter shows humankind its position in the universe and brings it to understand and remember its reason for being and its purpose: loving its Creator. Bovelles was especially attracted to the ideas of the human being as a recapitulation of the natural world and of acquiring knowledge through the ascent and descent of the Lullian scale of being,[57] so much that in his later work the *scala creaturarum* become a constant element, represented visually in diagrams (Figures 11.3 and 11.4).

These geometric diagrams, derived from long medieval tradition and recycled among humanists for their pedagogical value,[58] are used by Bovelles to articulate a scientific explanation of the cosmos while also establishing the basis for a geometrical-mathematical interpretation of divine creative activity.[59] In this way they become the operative ground where Bovelles develops his

---

53   Alexander Fidora, "La relación entre teología y antropología filosófica en el *Liber creaturarum* de Ramón Sibiuda," *Revista Española de Filosofía Medieval* 8 (2001): 177–185.

54   Puig, *La filosofía*, 270.

55   Sabunde, *Theologia Naturalis*, Prol., (ed.) Stegmüller, 35–36.

56   Sabunde, *Theologia Naturalis*, Pars 1, Tit. 3, (ed.) Stegmüller, 8–9.

57   Sabunde, *Theologia Naturalis*, Prol., intr. Stegmüller, 50–52.

58   See G. Kouskoff, "Tradition et nouveauté dans l'enseignement mathématique de Charles de Bovelles," in *Charles de Bovelles et son cinquième centenaire*, 199–210; Jean-Claude Margolin, "L'enseignement des mathématiques en France (1540–70): Charles de Bovelles, Fine, Peletier, Ramus," in *French Renaissance Studies 1540–70: Humanism and the Encyclopaedia*, (ed.) P. Sharratt (Edinburgh: 1976), 109–155. On diagrams as spiritual-pedagogical tools, see, among others, Christel Meier, "Malerei des Unsichtbaren: Über den Zusammenhang von Erkenntnistheorie und Bildstruktur im Mittelalter," in *Text und Bild, Bild und Text: DFG Symposion 1988*, (ed.) W. Harms (Stuttgart: 1990), 35–65.

59   Anne-Hélène Klinger-Dollé, *Le De sensu de Charles de Bovelles (1511): conception philosophique des sens et figuration de la pensée* (Geneva: 2016), 261–326; and "Making Figures: A Way Of Philosophizing in the De Sapiente," *Intellectual History Review* 21 (2011): 317–339.

N·

Diuus Di=
onyſius.

❡Aſſertiua theologia/a perfectis pergit ad impfecta:a ſublimioribus & potioribus/ ad in=
feriora& potiora deſcedit.Ea naq; iprimis deo aſcribit:que ſuapte natura(vt ait Dionyſi9)
honeſtiora ſunt/ſuaq; natura altius ex humo attollut.Deide ex villioribus etiā materie par
tibus: haud icogruas illi ſimilitudines effingit.Materia quippe & ſi prope nichil ſit/nō en=
tiuicina & entiū extremū/ac minimū:tamen(vt ſactus ille ait)ipſa a ſumo hono nacta ſub=

Diui dio=
nyſij ver=
ba.

ſtātiā:p oēs ſui partes atq; diſtinctiones/intellectualis decoris/quaſdā pre ſe fert imagines
per quas ad ſpiritales/diuinas/primitiuaſq; formas poſſumus aſcendere. Et nō modo aſſer=
tiua theologia a deo/per cūcta media/ad materiāvſq; & entiū extremū deuoluit deſceditq:
ſed& i nichilū vſq; ptraſit.ipſiuſq; nichili nome/deo interdū aſcribit:veraciter pdicās/ac in
myſterio pronūciās nichil eſſe deū:que qd ſit finire eſt ipoſſibile/cuiuſue ratio & cōceptio
nulla eſt.

❡Negatiua theologia/aſſertiue contranititur:a nichilo p materiā cunctaq;   6
media in deum ſcandens.

❡Aſſertiue theologie finis/e toti9negatiue initiū. Ad quod eniſlla extreme deuoluit:ab hoc
iſta eleuari incipit/quoad claudat inferatq; deū.Vtriuſq; theologie eadeſut extrema/ me=
dia eadē.Vnica eſt ambarū linea:qua ſibiiuice/a deo in nichilū aut a nichilo in deū cōtrani
tutur.Quicquid eni eſta deo/vſq; ad materiē:ens eſt & eſſetie particeps. Materia vero vlti
mū eſt entiū:ob nimiā a deo diſtantiā(velut iā ſeneſcēte ſubſtātia)adū nō ens & incōpleta
ſubſtātia & ens ſolū i potētia. Nichil vero ſubeſt materiei:vt quod neq; adu/neq; potētia ſit
ens.Vniuerſorū autē recta lineā/& eorū que ſubſiſtūt ſubſtātiale ordinē:ſeptenis entib9clau
dim9 finimuſq;: deo/angelo/hoie/ aialib9/plātis/mineralib9/& materia/ ſub q̄ nichil, Aut

eni vi cognitionis predita ſūt oia: aut vi
uūt/aut ſūt Porro oculata &cognoſcētia
ſūt quattuor:de9/angel9/hō/aial. Viuūt
autē plāte/mineralia deniq; ſubſiſtūt. Et
hec vltima ſūt:pfecta &ſtatai actu entia.
Nā mixta ipfecta & elemēta:ſub minera=
lib9 clauduñ.vtpote q̄ pfectiorentiū ſūt
ſeminaria:ſuapte natura icōſtātia citeq;
tranſmutationis. Materia vero neq; eſt/
neq; non eſt:ſed potētia quidem eſt/ actu
vero non eſt.

❡Oīa q̄ de deo/ aſſertiua theolo=
gia ſtatuit negatia reſoluit ac tollit
❡Aſſertiua theologia/eūq; cūctisiperitat
quiue oia cōdidit : iprimis deū appellat
theiotē oiaq; vidētē.deide angelū/ ſiue
intellectū.hic oim rationē & cauſa dein
ſeſū multa peragratē. Hinc appellat oim
vitā:poſtea vt vniuerſorū ſubſtātia cōce=
lebrat.Poſtremo vt potētiā/ priuationem
initiū & ichoationē oim eloquif. ſiue vt
oim ſubſidētiā/veraq; baſimintelligit: fere
tem/fulcientē/continentē/ geſtātēq; i ſe=
ſe vniuerſa.Deniq3& nichili nomen/ illi
quoq3 indit acapplicat:nō ens interdum

Deus eſt q̄
eſt :ideſt q̄
vere& ſim=
pliciter eſt.
Diuus dio=
nyſius.

appellās nichilq3 eē dices eū/q p excellē
te eſſētiā/ſe eſſe qui eſt(apparēs in rubo)pfeſſus eſt. Cōtra vero theologia negatiua erigēs
ſeſe i altū:quicqd/affirmatiua poſuit/ac deo itulit/ſapiēter aufert.dices illū iprimis nichil nō
eſſe/nō rerū potētiā:nō ſubſtātiā/ac ſtatū:nō vitā/ neq3 ſenſū/ neq3 rationē/neq3 itellectum
nec deniq3 deū.Diuine ſiquidē poſitiones(vt diu9Dionyſius cēſet)a ſumo & primo nicho=
ant.Ablationes vero diuine ab imis & extremis. Cū eni ingt:ponim9 eū qui ſupra oēm po
ſitionē eſt:ei9 rei ſignificātē affirmationē ponere oportet/ q̄ ſibi ppiquior ſit. Cū vero id tol
lim9 qd oi ablationi eminet:ab his q̄ magis ab eo diſtāt oportet auferre. An vero(ait) de9

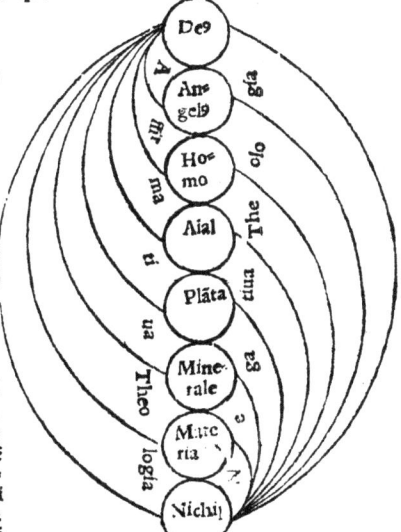

FIGURE 11.3   A typical *scala creaturarum* from the *Libellus de nihilo* of Charles de Bovelles,
in *Que hoc volumine continentur* (Paris: 1510), fol. 74v.

own theory of knowledge, in order to practice the "science of man" (*scientia de
homine*)[60] that we will briefly outline below.

60   Jordi Gayá Estelrich, "Réminiscenses lulliennes dans l'anthropologie de Bovelles," in Centre d'études supérieures de la Renaissance de l'Université de Tours, *Charles de Bovelles*

L.

Generatio creationis implet vacuũ: copulatꝗ lũũ fine creationis initio. 7
Nam creatio/duntaxat ſimplicia & ſeparata conſtituit rerum extrema : abſolutũ inquã
actum angelũ & potentiã abſolutã materiẽ: que ſũt ens maximũ & ens minimũ. Inter hec
antem: latu interhyat chaos/ acuũ & inane: ſenſibilium omniũ actuũ & ſubſtantiarum ca
pax. Hanc igitur nature abyſſum ac imenſum hyans profundum: generatio inchoans ab
imo & materia tanꝗ ab actuũ ſuppoſitione & hypoſtaſi ꝗunctis ſenſibilibus actibus im-

Quidcha-
os creatio-
nis.

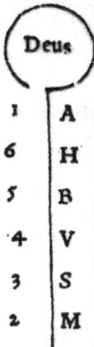

plere ſatagit. aſcendens a materia ad angelici vſꝗ actus viciniam: cui ſupremũ & nobiliſſi
mum ſenſibilium actũ(id eſt rationalē animã)coniungit facitꝗ vicinũ. Eſt enim angelicus
actus et eius creationis initiũ. Humanus vero actus/ generationis finis: coniunctus & atti-
guus creationis initio. Et hec eſt cauſa/ vt liber dē intellectu predocuit)cur cum homo ſit
ſuprema & vltima creatura: proximũ tamen primevis & omniũ antiquiſſimis angelis/ ob-
tineat locum: paulominus ilis/ factus inferior. Sit enim vniuerſorũ linea a m.quã partior
in quinꝗ partes equales punctis h b v s. Sit autē a/ angelus/ m materia/ s ſubſiſtentia/ v vi

Deus

1   A
6   H
5   B
·4   V
3   S
2   M

uentia b bruta animantia/ h homo. Vniuerſa linea a m: haud tota ſimul ſed diuiduẽ orta
eſt manauitꝗ a deo. Primũ ſiquidē ſupremũꝗ eius punctũ a: primitus & ante omnia a deo
proceſſit. Deinde punctũ m/ totius eiuſdē linee finis: ſecundo loco a deo pependit. Ft hec
ſunt vniuerſorũ extrema: que ſummum imũꝗ locum in vniuerſorũ ordine obtinuere: & ꝗ
quanꝗ diſtantiſſima ac diſſimillima ſint(Nam hec abſoluta potētia: ille vero ſimplex & ab-
ſolutiſſimus actus)ſunt tamen ante omnia creata. Productis igitur ſimplicibus c im extremis a & m: medium interhyabat chaos ac vacuũ totius linee medie m a: per quã aliquo pa
cto ipſa extrema copulantur. Hoc autẽ vacuũ: productis deiceps mediis creaturis/ s v b h/
eſt adimpletũ perfectuſꝗ eſt a deo vniuerſorũ ordo. Hic enim ſenis clauditur entibus: An-
gelo materia/ ſubſiſtentibus/ viuentibus animalibus & hominibus: qui merito angelis ꝓxi
mi vicinitꝗ euaſerunt. Deſcendit enim deus imprimis ab a in m: qui demũ reciproca latio-
ne/ ab m in h ſiue in ipſius a vicinia: conſcendiſſe declaratur. progreſſusitaꝗ eſt deus in pri
cipio/ vt in creatione extremorum: a perfectis ad imperfecta. In fine vero & productione

Duplex cre
ationis or-
do.

mediorũ materialiſue actuũ: ab imperfectis proceſſit ad perfecta. In extremis inſuper ꝑ-
creandis: aliquo pacto velitatim & velut per ſaltum & vacuum proceſſiſſe reperitur. In pla
tione autē mediorum actuũ: per plenũ & continuum progreſſus deprehenditur. Sunt eni
(vt diximus)rerum extrema: angelicus actus & potentia materiei/ que & diſtantiſſima ſũt
et primo creata. Media vero quibus vacua eorum impletur intercapedo/ ſunt quattuor cre
aturarum genera: ſubſiſtentium viuentium ſenſibilium & rationalium.

Analogia creationis vniuerſorum ad protentionē linee recte. Cap. III.

Niuerſorum a deo productio/ eo modo facta & abſoluta eſt 1
quo et recta linea ſolet a nobis/ geometrico modo potendi.
Oſtendit palam hec propō: ꝗ ſint mathematice diſcipline/ ad capeſcen-
da intelligendaꝗ diuina exigende. Nam qui rite cognouerit: quo pacto recta a nobis linea/ mathematico more deſcribi protendiꝗ ſolet: no-
ſcet & illico/ quo pacto a deo pependerit manaritꝗ vniuerſorum linea:
in ꝗua ſingula naturali ſue dignitatis & perfectionis ordine diſponun-

Deus
Angelus
Homo
Bruta
Viuentia
Subſiſten-
tia
Materia

tur. Angelus inquam in ſummo: materia in imo. Poſt quam angelum verſus pergendo/
ſubſiſtentia. Deinde viuentia: hinc ſenſibilia: poſtremã homo. Hic enim creationis ꝗdē
ordine ab angelo/ ſextus & vltimus numeratur. dignitate autē/ preſtantia & loco: ab eodē
ſecud⁹ ē. Solet aũt geometrico de more: recta linea/ a nobis deſcribi hoc pacto. Circini pe
dē alterũ imprimis figimus in plano aliquo immobili: quo prim⁹ protendiꝗ linee/ deſi-
gnatur punctus. Et hec ſit angelorum creatio. Reliquus deinde pes a nobis eidem plano
imprimitur: quo future totius linee finis ac meta notatur. Hec autem eſt materie creatio
deinde formatis quidem per ſe duobus totius linee extremis : admouenda eſt ambobus
ipſius circini pedib⁹/ lignea aliqua aut erea regula: cuius directioni innitens pes circini ſe-
cundus: moueatur ac reciprocetur ad primum. ſuoꝗ tractu expetitam rectam lineam. in
plano conficiat: impleatꝗ ſpacium/ quo prius exiſtēte vacuo: ambo puncta ab inuicē diſclu
ſa ſeparataꝗ manebant. Hoc ſenſibili ſigno/ hac lucidiſſima analogia: deprehendes quo-
nãmodo ſunt rerum extrema/ prius a deo facta. Primum prius Secundum poſterius. Dei
de media ab eodem/ contrario extremorũ ordine producta: aſcendente ab ſecũdo extre-

FIGURE 11.4   In the left margin: a typical *scala creaturarum* from the *Liber de generatione* of
Charles de Bovelles, in *Que hoc volumine continentur* (Paris: 1510), fol. 98v.

11.5   Lullian Epistemology and Cosmology in the Theory of Knowledge
         of Bovelles

Bovelles develops the ideal of human wisdom based on the Lullian anthropology
expressed best in the *Libre de home* of Blessed Ramon. However, where for
Llull human perfection only becomes complete through Christology, Bovelles
expounds a more philosophical conception of human perfection, as properly human, and crystalized in the figure of the wise man.[61] He delineates this
thesis in the *Liber de Sapiente* and the *Liber de intellectu*, where he defines a
theory of knowledge developed from elements of the Lullian Art.[62] For example, Bovelles asks how a human being attains divine knowledge. Here he forges
his specular theory of knowledge by employing the metaphor of the mirror
and the light, following closely the arguments found in Llull's *Libre de ànima
racional* and *Libre dels àngels*,[63] which offer a comparative study of human
and angelic intellection. For Bovelles there are two kinds of mirrors.[64] One is
transparent and does not change the luminous rays or represented objects,
and corresponds to angelic understanding. The other is not transparent, but
instead receives images, actively reproduces them, and is specific to human
understanding; its opacity comes from the materiality reflected from the created universe. An engraving illustrates all this at the beginning of the *Liber
de intellectu*.[65] Still, we should remember that a human being, as a reflection
of nature, therefore reflects the different levels in the scale of being where
humans occupy the highest level: a human recapitulates all the levels and is
responsible for developing and leading them to achieve their goal, which is
their Creator. The contemplation of nature thus becomes a path to attaining
knowledge of the divine, since to read the book of creatures is to read the book
of the universe; recall here the influence of the "natural theology" inspired by
Llull's *Libre de meravelles* (1288–1289) or Sabunde's *Theologia naturalis*.[66] Nature contains all the creatures – from the levels of *esse, vivere, sentire* to that of

61   Ernst Cassirer, *Individuum und Kosmos in der Philosophie der Renaissance* (Leipzig and
        Berlin: 1927); Emmanuel Faye, *Philosophie et perfection de l'homme: de la Renaissance à
        Descartes* (Paris: 1998), 33.
62   Gayà Estelrich, "Réminiscences Iuliennes"; Cesare Vasoli, *Immagini umanistiche* (Naples:
        1983), 251–272.
63   Bovelles, *Liber de intellectu*, in *Que hoc volumine*, cap. 2, prop. 2, fol. 4v; compare Llull,
        Libre dels àngels 4.3.1, ORL 21:360. On Cusanus and this topic, see Cesare Catà, "Viewed
        through the Looking-Glass: Human Nature as a Mystical Mirror in Charles de Bovelles'
        Conception of Sapientia," *Intellectual History Review* 21 (2011): 297–306.
64   Bovelles, *Liber de intellectu*, in *Que hoc volumine*, cap. 2, prop. 2, fol. 2v.
65   *Liber de intellectu*, in *Que hoc volumine*, f. 2v.
66   Letter to Jean Cocon (1508), in *Commentarius*, fol. 54r.

intelligere, which correspond respectively to stones, plants, animals, and humans – available to observation and thus lead the human intellect to ascend toward God.[67] Because human beings can rise so high, they become wiser in so far as they understand themselves, attaining thus knowledge of the universe: "only the wise becomes human" (*solus sapiens sit veraciter homo*).[68] In this way one glimpses the possibility of a renewal and rebirth destined to achieve the regeneration of human nature, and an unshakeable faith in the power of the individual who makes use of the Lullian Art to attain this objective.

To understand further the cognitive processes described by Bovelles, one must remember that his concept of "wisdom" results from the joint operation of three faculties of the soul: intellect, memory, and contemplation. For Bovelles, the initial intellective act arises from the apprehension of the intellective species; then, in a second act, these species are deposited into memory, which serves as a receptacle that retains them for presentation subsequently to the speculative and contemplative intellect.[69] In this passage, Bovelles reprises in his epistemology the importance of the Lullian imagination as a mediator between the material and spiritual worlds when processing the data of experience; only through the imagination is it possible to advance to the superior forms of intellectual knowledge.[70] For Bovelles, imagination makes a constant effort to visualize abstract concepts as images. The final act of contemplation proceeds from the memory and the intellect, since it occurs when the intellect considers the species preserved in memory. This cognitive model obviously relies on a triadic relationship, in which the intellect and memory function as opposite extremes, but join together in contemplation, which serves as a third, mediating element. Bovelles develops this scheme very fully in his *In artem oppositorum introductio*, published at Paris by Wolfgang Hopyl in 1501. In his letter of dedication for this work, Lefèvre emphasizes the importance of human understanding in relation to the divine based on the opposition between reason (as multiplicity) and intellect (as unity), but which are inconceivable except as united in a bond of agreement, an idea developed by

---

67   *Liber de sensibus*, in *Que hoc volumine*, fols. 53r–54r.

68   *Liber de sapiente*, in *Que hoc volumine*, fol. 122 v. On this subject see also Tamara Albertini, "Der Mensch als *metamorphische* Weltmitte: Reflexionen zu einer Denkfigur der Renaissance (Bovelles, Ficino, Pico)," in *Sapientiam amemus: Humanismus und Aristotelismus in der Renaissance: Festschrift für Eckhard Keßler zum 60. Geburstag*, (eds.) Paul Richard Blum and Charles Lohr (Munich: 1999), 89–108; Jean-Claude Margolin, "Reflections on the Nature of the *Homo sapiens* and On the Ideal of Wisdom According to Charles de Bovelles," *Intellectual History Review* 21 (2011): 281–295.

69   Bovelles, *Liber de intellectu*, cap. 7, prop. 7, in *Que hoc volumine*, fols. 10v–11r.

70   Vega, *Die Sinnlichkeit des Geistigen*, 99–106.

Nicholas of Cusa from the Lullian Art.[71] In other words, the structural bases of the human cognitive process function as an *ars* that puts in operation opposing extremes such as beginning (intellect) and end (memory), joined and reconciled through a middle (contemplation); this triadic scheme reproduces the forces of opposition and reconciliation in one of the segments from the second Lullian Figure T. It extends as well to all knowledge, since any science or discipline (including theology) operates according to the same internal mechanism of the Lullian principles of beginning, middle, and end, which are applicable to all learning. These trinitarian structures permeate not only the interior of the individual (as microcosmos) but the entire created universe as well (as macrocosmos), postulating unity within the diversity of every triadic relationship. Bovelles structures his *Commentarius* in thirty segments, alluding to the age of Christ or to multiplication of the number ten (symbolizing human nature) by three (the Trinity). The first verses of the Gospel of John recapitulate the mystery of the Trinity, the Incarnation, and the Logos, which is the full revelation of the divine and which reflects the relationship between the Father and the Son as well as the inner nature of God.[72] This reflection implies affirmation of the convertibility among the divine qualities (the Lullian Dignities, different yet equivalent among each other) and their presence in Creation as a reflection of the Trinity.[73] In his *Commentarius in primordiale*, which mentions Llull frequently, Bovelles defines the intra-trinitarian relationships according to the Lullian correlatives: the Father is unity, beginning, and intellect; the Son is equality, middle, memory, and the knowable; the Holy Spirit is connection, end, will, and love.[74] By means of the these analogically transposed triads and by elevating the intellect through them (*asurrectio*), one comprehends the universe and divine mysteries.[75] This *asurrectio* (in its mystical connotation) is one of the key concepts for Bovelles in a theory of knowledge that implies the Lullian ascent and descent of the mind.[76] It is a mental operation based on mathematical relationships visualized through a triangular geometric scheme applied to

---

71   Lefèvre, ep. 29 (to Leonardo Pomar, París, 1501), in Rice, *Prefatory Epistles*, 94–96.

72   Marie-Madeleine de La Garanderie, "Aspectes de l'exégèse de Charles de Bovelles," in *Acta conventus Neo-latini Torontonensis, Proceedings of the Seventh International Congress of Neo-Latin Studies, Toronto, 8 August to 13 August 1988* (Binghamton, New York: 1991), 281–292; Jean-Claude Margolin, "Bovelles et son commentaire de l'évangile johannique," in *Histoire de l'exégèse au XVIe siècle: Actes du Colloque international tenu à Genève en 1976*, (eds.) Olivier Fatio et Pierre Fraenkel (Geneva: 1978), 229–255.

73   Bovelles, *Commentarius*, cap. 1, fol. 8r–v.

74   Ibid., fol. 6v.

75   Ibid., fol. 7v, fol. 9v.

76   Letter to Guillaume Budé (8 March 1511), in Bovelles, *Commentarius*, fol. 48r.

homogeneous realities. The human love of God is a movement from inferior to superior, that is, an ascending motion. Its horizontal axis defines knowledge by analogy (logic, the physical realm, the earth) or what becomes human knowledge of the world, while the vertical axis defines knowledge of the unattainable, the unknown, that is the relationship between humans and God, an upward ascent mediated by angels.[77] The mathematical models that he develops, based on Llull's geometric theology,[78] produce visual demonstrations of both trinitarian theological activity *ad intra* and trinitarian activity projected *ad extra* in Creation.[79] These diagrams are also graphic and schematic means for leading the human soul, in the discourse of the intellect as it reads them, toward contemplation of God. Every geometric form in the work of Bovelles thus expresses a moral, philosophical, and theological truth for epistemological purposes.

11.6   Bernard de Lavinheta and His Lullian Publishing Activity

Bernard de Lavinheta (d. 1523?)[80] was a member of the Franciscan house of Saint Bonaventure in Lyon.[81] After earning the degree of doctor in theology, he taught Lullian doctrine at the universities of Paris and Salamanca.[82] Lefèvre refers to him with singular respect and admiration in his edition of the *Proverbia Raimundi* and *Philosophia amoris* of 1516. From this reference we know that Lavinheta's teaching activity was highly regarded, just as was the doctrine contained in his writings, with the result that these were carefully "kept in the library of that distinguished house of learning, the Sorbonne, most noble in all the world and the home of so many renowned theologians."[83] Lavinheta

---

77   Ibid., fol. 48v–50v.

78   Robert D.F. Pring-Mill, *El Microcosmos Lul.lià* (Oxford: 1962), 59–70 and 87–96.

79   Jean-Claude Margolin, "La function de Modèle dans la pensée créatrice de Bovelles," in *Le modèle à la Renaissance*, (eds.) J. Lafond, C. Balauoine, and P. Laurens (Paris: 1986), 51–75.

80   On his life, see: Bernard Lavinheta, *Explanatio compendiosaque applicatio artis Raymundi Lulli*, (ed.) E.W. Platzeck (1523; Hildesheim: 1977), 1–33; Wolfgang Panzer, *Annales typographici ab artis inventae origine ad annum 1530*, 11 vols. (Nuremberg: 1793–1803), 6:376; *Doctor Illuminatus: A Ramon Llull Reader*, (ed.) Anthony Bonner (Princeton: 1993), 65; Lucas Wadding, *Scriptores Ordinis minorum: quibus accessit syllabus illorum, qui ex eodem Ordine pro fide Christi fortiter ocubuerunt* (Rome: 1650), 56; Rénaudet, *Préreforme et humanisme*, 671–672; and Hillgarth, *Ramon Lull and Lullism*, 288–294, 303–305, and 318–319.

81   Joseph M. Victor, "The Revival of Lullism at Paris, 1499–1516," *Renaissance Quarterly* 28 (1975): 508–509, and Michela Pereira, "Bernardo Lavinheta e la diffusione del Lullismo," 247.

82   Carreras i Artau, *Historia de la filosofía*, 2: 209–210; Victor, "Revival of Lullism," 532–533; Llinarès, "Le lullisme de Lefèvre d'Étaples et des ses amis humanistes," 131–134.

83   Lefèvre, letter to Alfonso of Aragon (1516), in *Proverbia Raemundi. Philosophia amoris* (Paris: 1516), in Rice, *Prefatory Epistles*, 374: "praesertim illa insignis domus Sorbonicae,

was the author, according to his testimony in another of his works, of treatises such as the *De incarnatione Verbi* (Colonia: 1516)[84] and a lost *De conceptione Beatae Virginis Mariae*,[85] the latter with evident echoes of Lullian concepts. He later showed interest in the encyclopedic-scientific aspects of Llull's Art, reasserting their value, which had not received particular attention in the editorial endeavors of Lefèvre.[86] Lavinheta was apparently involved in the edition of the *Arbor scientiae* published at Paris by Josse Bade in 1515; the style of its engravings is very similarly to that of his *Explanatio*.[87] This interest became obvious in the publishing activities to which he contributed: this included not only texts by Llull, such as the *Ars brevis* (Lyon: 1514) and the *Metaphysica nova et compendiosa* (Paris: 1516), but also pseudo-Lullian writings and works by other Lullists, such as a single volume combining the *Dialectica seu logica brevis et nova, Tractatus de conversione subjecti et praedicati per medium,* and the *De venatione medii inter subiectum et praedicatum* (Paris: 1516).[88] He also contributed to publication of the *Janua artis Raymundi Lulli* of Pere Deguí (Cologne: 1516),[89] Llull's *Liber lamentationis philosophiae o duodecim principia philosophiae* (Paris: 1516) and *Ars generalis ultima* (Lyon: 1517) with his own annotations.[90] He inspired his students to produce the pseudo-Lullian *In Rhetoricam Isagoge* (Paris: 1516).[91] Finally, the incorporation of Lullian encyclopedism within his theories of knowledge bore fruit in in his *Explanatio compendiosaque applicatio artis Raymundi Lulli* (Lyon: 1523), which transforms the tenets of Llull's Art into universal principles applicable to all disciplines and fields of learning, and so capable of unifying all knowledge.[92]

---

quae nobilissimum est in toto terrarium orbe tam nominatissiorum theologorum quam publicorum theologicorum certaminum domicilum."

84   Lavinheta, *Explanatio*, pars 2, lib. 2, fol. 26v; Carreras i Artau, *Historia de la filosofía*, 2:210.

85   Lavinheta, *Explanatio*, pars 3, lib. 6, fol. 71r; Carreras i Artau, *Historia de la filosofía*, 2:210.

86   See Pereira, "Bernardo Lavinheta e la diffusione del Lullismo," 242–265; "Le opere mediche di Lullo," 31–33; and "L'uso del 'Panepistemon' del Poliziano nella 'Isagoge in rhetoricam' pseudolulliana," *Physis: Rivista Internazionale di Storia della Scienza* 16 (1974): 231–233. See also: Rossi, *Clavis universalis*, 74–78; and Carreras i Artau, *Historia de la filosofía*, 2:210–214.

87   Rogent and Durán, *Bibliografía*, 53–54.

88   Rogent and Durán, *Bibliografía*, 50, 57 and 58; and for subsequent editions, 63–64.

89   Rogent and Durán, *Bibliografía*, 58–59; Carreras i Artau, *Historia de la filosofía*, 2:72–73.

90   Rogent and Durán, *Bibliografía*, 58–59, 56–57, and 61–62.

91   Rogent and Durán, *Bibliografía*, 56; Carreras i Artau, *Historia de la filosofía*, 2:214–215; published later by Lazarus Zetzner, with an alchemical and cabbalistic corpus, in *Raymundi Lullii Opera* (1598; repr. 1617 and 1651).

92   Rogent and Durán, *Bibliografía*, 71. See Cesare Vasoli, "Gli scritti logici di Lefèvre d'Étaples e della sua scuola," in *La dialettica e la retorica dell'Umanesimo: "Invenzione" e "Metodo" nella cultura del XV e XVI secolo* (Milan: 1968), 213; and Rossi, *Clavis universalis*, 74–78.

11.7   The *Explanatio Compendiosaque Applicatio Artis Raymundi Lulli*

The *Explanatio* became, for its era, the expression of the new didactic and
epistemological paths typically pursued by every *ars* in the 16th century. These
proposed overall the idea of a necessary connection between logical processes
and their figurative expression, both displayed through images, preferably geometric.[93] This was linked to the arts of memory that reached one their culminating points of development within the space provided by engraving in
the fifteenth and sixteenth centuries.[94] Beginning with the Parisian school of
Lefèvre, and especially in Bovelles, we see Aristotelian logic mixed with a Pla-
tonizing symbolic approach, reflected in imagery, above all in geometrical imagery that offers philosophical and theological concepts in sensory form to the
eyes. These charts and diagrammatic trees seek to contain and classify in their
structures the encyclopedia of knowledge based on logical principles from
Llull's Art, linked in turn to a system of *imagines* and *loci* from the classical *ars
memoriae*. Lavinheta thus mentions that he taught "the art of memory of the
Lullian Art at Toulouse" (*Tholose quaedam iuristam hanc artem*).[95]

When introducing Llull's Great Art for his *Explanatio*, Lavinheta proposes
the Lullian Art as an encyclopedic method,[96] because for him there should exist
a general art containing all the common, basic, and necessary principles from
which the principles of all other fields of knowledge can be proven and studied.[97] He introduces practice of the First Figure – of the one and triune God
(Figure 11.5)[98]—by explaining how one applies in it the ascent and descent
of the intellect, all the while emphasizing Neoplatonic theories of emanation
neatly interwoven with concepts from Aristotelian metaphysics and physics.[99]

His treatment of the levels of being brings into play Llull's Second Figure
T, which Lavinheta uses as an opportunity to develop the Scotist doctrine of
formal distinctions in a string of these.[100] The Third Figure summarizes the
process of creation explained through Llull's theory of correlatives, constituting in this way a treatise on natural philosophy that expounds the scale of being.[101] The *Regulae* and *Quaestiones* of Llull's Art are condensed into one long

---

93   Vasoli, *La dialettica*, 199.
94   Fernando Rodríguez de la Flor, *Emblemas: lecturas de la imagen simbólica* (Madrid: 1995).
95   Lavinheta, *Explanatio*, "De memoria artificiali," pars 3, lib. 9, fol. 256v.
96   Lavinheta, *Explanatio*, pars 1, lib. 2, fols. 19v–22r.
97   Lavinheta, *Explanatio*, pars 1, lib. 2, fol. 21r.
98   Lavinheta, *Explanatio*, pars 2, lib. 2, fols. 22v–26r.
99   Lavinheta, *Explanatio*, pars 2, lib. 2, fol. 26r–v.
100   Lavinheta, *Explanatio*, pars 3, lib. 2, fosl. 27v–30v.
101   Lavinheta, *Explanatio*, pars 3, lib. 2, fols. 31r–44r.

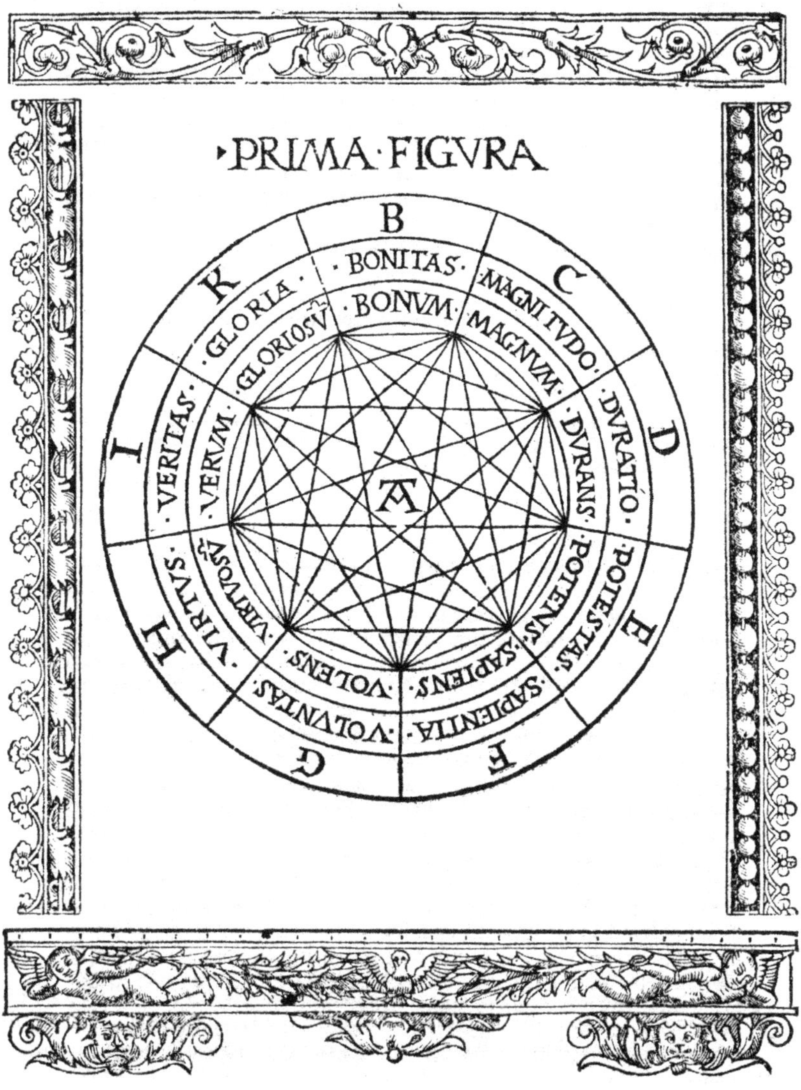

FIGURE 11.5   Lavinheta's Figure A, from his *Explanatio* (Lyon: 1523), pars 1, lib.2, fol. 22v.

section,[102] followed by his Fourth Figure and General Table (*Tabula Generalis*), which prompts questions, such as the necessity of Incarnation, that serve as examples for use in preaching.[103] The work's epilog explains the purpose and

---

102   Lavinheta, *Explanatio*, pars 3, lib. 3, fol. 44v–54v.
103   Lavinheta, *Explanatio*, pars 3, lib. 3, fol. 59v–68r.

function of this encyclopedia and advises that the best *ars memoriae* is one based on logic or that facilitates retaining ideas, like the Lullian Art.[104] Lavinheta also reveals the Christo-centric objectives of his encyclopedia through a beautiful engraving of a tree,[105] as well as the apologetic nature of the treatise, which proposes defending the faith to unbelievers and their conversion by application of its *ars* and necessary reasons,[106] with the requisite visualizations of encyclopedic trees (Figure 11.6).

Lavinehta proposes directing encyclopedic knowledge, along with his mnemonic system, toward the conversion of Saracens and unbelievers to Catholicism,[107] because "this Art of the Illuminated Doctor Ramon Llull is most useful for defending the faith and acting against unbelievers."[108] Lavinheta thus reaffirms the value of the Lullian Art as a method of disputation (with respect to its logical functions) and as rational demonstration for religious purposes within the tradition of apologetics.

11.8   Cardinal Cisneros as a Patron of Lullism and His Collaborators

The Iberian Lullism consolidated in the work of Pere Deguí (1435–1500),[109] with protections and privileges provided by Isabel and Ferdinand,[110] found

---

104   Lavinheta, *Explanatio*, pars 3, lib. 9, fol. 255r–256r.
105   Lavinheta, *Explanatio*, pars 3, lib. 9, fol. 257v–262v.
106   Lavinheta, *Explanatio*, pars 3, lib. 3, fol. 262v.
107   Lavinheta, *Explanatio*, pars 3, lib. 9, fol. 261v.
108   Lavinheta, *Explanatio*, pars 3, lib. 9, f. 263r: "cum hac arte illuminati doctoris magistris Raymundi: quae supra omnes alios modos utilissima est: maxime ad defendendum fidem nostram: agendumque contra infideles."
109   On Deguí and his influence, see Chapter 15 in this volume; Carreras i Artau, *Historia de la filosofía*, 2:65–67, 69, 72–76, 77–79; Norbert Angermann, Robert Auty, Robert-Henri Bautier et al., (ed.) *Lexikon des Mittelalters*, 10 vols. (Stuttgart: 1980–1999), 3:431; Lorenzo Pérez Martínez, "El maestro Pedro Deguí y el lulismo mallorquín de fines de siglo XV," *EL* 4 (1960): 10; Rafael Ramis Barceló, "En torno al escoto-lulismo de Pere Deguí," *Medievalia* 16 (2013): 235–264; Hillgarth, "An unpublished Lullian sermon by Pere Deguí," 561–569; J. Anselm M. Albareda, "Lul·lisme a Montserrat al segle XVè: l'ermità Bernat Boil," *EL* 9 (1965): 13–21; and Maria Barceló i Crespí and Ricard Urgell Hernández, "La Universitat de Mallorca: origen i evolució fins al segle XVIII," in *Les universitats de la Corona d'Aragó*, (eds.) Joan J. Busqueta and Juan Pemán (Barcelona: 2002), 15, 160–161, and 170–171; Marta Romano, "Aspetti del lullismo spagnolo: Pere Deguí," *Estudios de Latín Medieval Hispánico. Actas del V Congreso Internacional de Latín Medieval Hispánico (Barcelona, 7-10 de septiembre de 2009)*, (eds.) José Martínez Gázquez, Óscar de la Cruz Palma and Cándida Ferrero Hernández (Florence: 2011), 275–280. For the works of Deguí see Rogent and Durán, *Bibliografía*, 58, 6–9, 11–14, 20, and 23–27.
110   José María Pou y Martí, "Sobre la doctrina y culto del beato Raimundo Lulio," *Archivo Ibeoramericano* 41 (1921): 13.

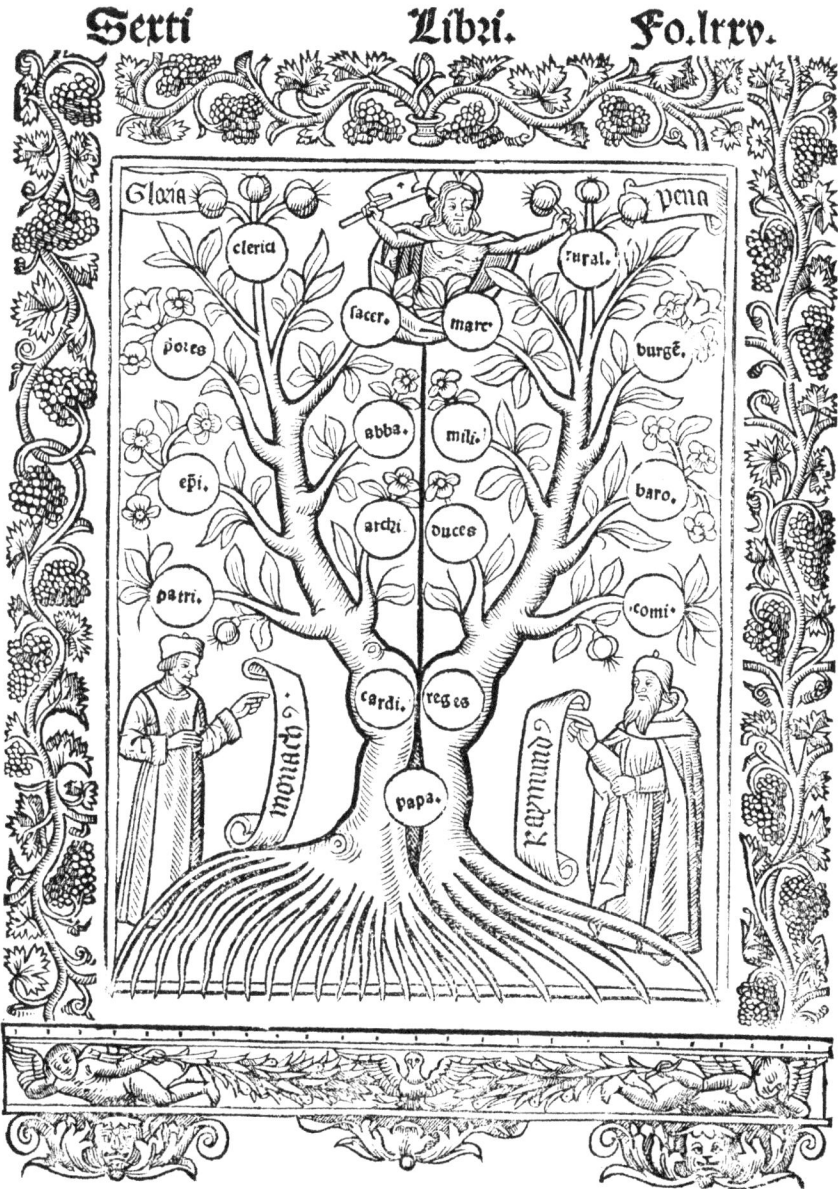

FIGURE 11.6 Lavinheta's Arboreal Figure, from his *Explanatio* (Lyon: 1523), pars 2, lib.6, fol. 75r.

their continuation in Cardinal Francisco Jiménez de Cisneros, Archbishop of Toledo.[111] Observant Franciscans, predominantly Castilian, were also the heirs

---

111   Joseph Pérez, (ed.), *La hora de Cisneros* (Madrid: 1995); José García Oro, *El cardenal Cisneros*, 2 vols. (Madrid: 1992).

and the proponents of a spiritual ideology infused with features nourished by Lullian philosophical and theological doctrines.[112] For this reason, the Spanish primate appears to us in history not only as a spiritual reformer and organizer of the Spanish observant movement,[113] but also as an admirer of the life and work of Blessed Ramon. Cisneros gathered various thinkers and editors and charged them with putting into practice his reformist plans, among which Lullian thought enjoyed ample favor. The foundation of the University of Alcalá in 1508 represented one of the most important fulfillments of those plans, since it served as a university center for cultivating various spiritual trends, including Lullism. Gonzalo Gil, a disciple of Charles de Bovelles from Burgos, was named a professor of moral theology, and the famed theologian Nicholas de Pax was summoned to occupy a chair in Lullian philosophy and theology.[114] The Lullian sympathies of Cisneros are also obvious from an important document that relates how the cardinal enjoyed reading Lullist works when resident in his palace; in addition, during his travels, he took pleasure in hearing Lullian philosophy and theology explained to him, at his request, by Nicholas de Pax himself.[115]

Meanwhile, the Spanish primate maintained contact, as noted above, with the circle of Jacques Lefèvre d'Étaples, whose editions he praised to Bovelles.[116] Cisneros also strengthened Lullism in Castile and reinforced it in Valencia through Jaume Janer and the Lullist chair at the city's *studium generale*, where various important figures gathered, such as the Genovese merchant Bartolomeo Fallamonica Gentile, a promoter and patron of Lullism, the Tarragonese priest Joan Bonllabi and the humanist Alonso de Proaza, who in turn maintained correspondence with Lullists from Barcelona and Majorca: Joan Baró, Gregori Genovart, Jaume Oleza and again Nicholas de Pax.[117] To Cisneros we owe as well the preparation, probably done largely by Pax, of a catalogue of the cardinal's Lullian works, the *Index librorum illuminati doctoris Raymundi Lulli qui sunt apud Reverendissimum dominum meum hispaniae Cardinalem, anno domini 1515 mense junii.*[118] Cisneros's rich collection contained 74 volumes

---

112   Carreras i Artau, *Historia de la filosofía*, 2:251; Andrés, *Historia*, 280.

113   Quintín Aldea, Tomás Marín, et al., (ed.) *Diccionario de Historia Eclesiástica de España*, 5 vols. (Madrid: 1972–1987), 2:957–959; José Fernández Meseguer, "La bula *Ite vos* (29 de mayo de 1517) y la reforma cisneriana," *Archivo Ibeoramericano* 17 (1958): 257–381.

114   Andrés, *Historia*, 291; Erika Rummel, *Jiménez de Cisneros: On the Threshold of Spain's Golden Age* (Tempe: 1999).

115   Nicholas de Pax, *Vita divi Raimundi Lullii* (Alcalà de Henares: 1519), (ed.) Victor, "Charles de Bovelles and Nicholas de Pax: Two Sixteenth-Century Biographies of Ramon Lull," 338.

116   Letter to Charles de Bovelles, *Philosophicae epistulae*, in *Que hoc volumine*, fol. 167r.

117   Carreras i Artau, *Historia de la filosofía*, 2:254.

118   De Alós, *Catálogos lulianos*, 55–67. The catalog appears in *Ars inventiva veritatis, seu ars intellectiva veri quae est instrumentum intellectivae potentiae. Tabula generalis. Lectura*

comprising some 280 Lullian texts, and its importance consists not only in its considerable size, but also in the fact that its inventory was the first Lullian catalogue published in Spain, thanks to his secretary Alonso de Proaza.[119] In short, Cisneros was for the Iberian Peninsula what Lefèvre was for France in regard to Lullism: he was dedicated not only to the wide dissemination of Lullian texts through printing and through the collaborators that he assembled for that end, "because I truly have great esteem for all his works, for their learning and value," but also because he managed to support, nourish, and enrich spiritual reform with these works because "you must believe that in so far as I can, I intend to promote them, and work for their publication and reading in all the [schools]."[120]

11.9   Alonso de Proaza

Alonso de Proaza (ca. 1445–1519), poet and rhetorician, collaborated actively in the edition of the Lullian works that appeared under the direction of Cardinal Cisneros, whom he served as secretary during the last years of his life.[121] From 1506 to a 1515 he sent to press a total of four volumes, containing nine of Llull's original writings, along with others that he translated into Catalan, and various Lullist texts. In 1506 he brought forth at Valencia, from the press of Lleonart Hutz, with funding provided by Bartolomeo Fallamonica Gentile, the *Liber artis metaphysicalis* of Jaume Janer.[122] The latter was a discipline of Pere Deguí and taught Lullism in Valencia thanks to a royal privilege granted by Ferdinand of Aragon, which appears printed in this work.[123] It also includes a brief text entitled *Officium gloriosisimi et beatissimi martyris magistri Raymundi Lullii*, which declares that Llull's martyrdom by stoning in Tunis should

---

super artem inventivam et tabulam generalem. Index librorum Raymundi Lullii, (ed.) Alonso de Proaza (Valencia: 1515), fols. 220v–222v.

119   De Alós, *Catálogos lulianos*, 19.

120   Cisneros, Alcalá de Henares, 8 October 1513, *Testimonia*, in MOG 1:21: "quia in veritate teneo magnam affectionem erga omnia sua Opera, quia sunt magnae doctrinae et utilitatis: citaque credatis, quod in omnibus, quibus potero, illa favore prosequar, et laborabo, ut publicentur et legantur per omnia [studia]." Cf. the Spanish version in Jaime Costurer, *Disertaciones históricas del Beato Raymundo Lullio Doctor Iluminado y Mártir con un apéndiz de su vida* (Mallorca: 1700), 364–365.

121   Carreras i Artau, *Historia de la filosofía*, 2:254–257; D.W. McPheeters, *El humanista español Alonso de Proaza* (Valencia: 1961), 152–168.

122   Rogent and Durán, *Bibliografía*, 34–36; Batllori, *Ramon Llull i el lul.lisme*, 301–303.

123   Jaume Janer, *Liber artis metaphysicalis* (Valencia: 1506), fol. 268r–v.

be sufficient to ensure his canonization.[124] Proaza defends Llull's style and his terminology for the Lullian correlatives as neologisms necessary and required to express new ideas.[125] He also composed for this edition a poem in Latin, *Carmen endecasyllabum in laudem Artis Raymundi Lulli*; it describes how Llull flies, inspired by divine fire, to the second heaven, where he forges a bronze mirror created through a Great Art and that makes visible the secrets of nature.[126] That is, Blessed Ramon receives divine illumination from the Creator in order to design a Great Art that, like a mirror, reflects all Creation and its creatures. Subsequently, in 1510, and again with funding from Bartolomeo Fallamonica Gentile, Proaza published at the Valencian press of Joan Joffre these works by Llull: *Liber qui est disputatio Raymundi christiani et Homerii sarraceni, Liber de demonstratione per equiparantiam, Disputatio quinque hominum sapientum, Liber de accidente et substantia.*[127] Proaza included a *Sententia definitiva in favorem lullianae doctrinae* against the attacks of the Dominicans who had reemerged prominently in the early 16th century with new editions of the anti-Lullist writings of Nicholas Eymerich.[128] From his *Sententia* and the texts that he published, which can be classified as practical guides to missionizing, we perceive in Proaza's endeavors not simply a defense of Lullian thought, but also of its dissemination for evangelizing and apologetic purposes, following thus the objectives of the program for converting unbelievers to Christianity that Cisneros had promoted. The edition features one engraving that depicts Llull, jailed at Bougie, disputing with unbelievers.[129]

By 1512 Proaza prepared and published, in a single volume from the Valencian press of Jordi Costilla, Llull's *Logica nova, Liber correlativorum innatorum,* and *Liber de ascensu et descensu intellectus.*[130] The introductory letter of this volume is addressed to another famous Lullist editor from the school of Alcalá de Henares, Joan Bonllabi, who, sometime after 1521, brought forth a beautiful edition of Llull's *Blaquerna* in the vernacular.[131] In his letter, Proaza defends Lullian logic, explaining how it allows the reader to comprehend the Creator

---

124   Janer, *Liber artis*, fol. 281v.
125   Janer, *Liber artis*, sig. giiii2r. For other testimonies of Proaza's defense of Llull's doctrine, see *Testimonia*, in MOG 1:1–2.
126   Janer, *Liber artis*, fol. 281r–v.
127   Rogent and Durán, *Bibliografía*, 40–42.
128   Cfr. Carreras i Artau, *Historia de la filosofía*, 2:280–281.
129   *Disputatio*, fol. 1r.
130   Rogent and Durán, *Bibliografía*, 46–48.
131   Rogent and Durán, *Bibliografía*, 68–71; Jordi Pardo Pastor, "El cercle lul·lià de València: Alonso de Proaza i Joan Bonllavi," *Zeitschrift für Katalanistik* 14 (2001): 33–45; Rosalía Guilleumas, "La biblioteca de Joan Bonllavi: Membre de l'escola lul.lista de València al segle XVI," *Revista valenciana de filología* 4 (1954): 23–73.

and His creatures, causes and effects, and things and their likenesses. It also calls upon "all those who wish to adopt the teaching of Ramon to read, interpret, and disseminate his works" and urges those who "profess to expound his teaching not to be afraid and flee to avoid conflicts."[132] The volume features two engravings: one, at the beginning of the *Logica nova*, depicts a tree of nature and logic.[133] Another, which introduces the *Liber de ascensu et descensu*, depicts the scale of being, beginning with stones and reaching to the realm of divine wisdom. Llull raises in his hands the two final levels of the intellect's ascent, with its respective terms summarized in a spinning wheel: *ens, actus, passio, actio, natura, substantia, accidens, simplex, compositum, individuum, species, genus; sensibile, imaginabile, dubitabile, credibile, intelligibile.*[134]

In 1515 Proaza edited his last Lullian work, published in Valencia by the press of Diego Gumiel, printed at the expense of Cisneros, and done in collaboration with Nicholas de Pax. The volume consists of the following Latin works by Llull, edited by Proaza: *Ars inventiva veritatis, seu ars intellectiva veri quae est instrumentum intellectivae potentiae, Tabula generalis*, and *Lectura super artem inventivam et tabulam generalem.*[135] It includes a poem about Llull, written by Nicholas de Pax in forty-five hexameters and pentameters, and dedicated to Cardinal Cisneros: *Divi Raymundi Lulli Doctoris illuminati ad Reverendissimum patrem dominum D. Franciscum Ximenez Cardinalem Hispaniarum Carmen.*[136] Following this is a long letter from Proaza to the Spanish primate, *Epistola ad reverendissimum Franciscum Ximenez*, in which Proaza recounts how Jesus Christ, upon recognizing human limitations in acquiring universal wisdom, inspired Llull to devise a general method for attaining this knowledge and to expound it through principles and rules.[137] Similarly, the works contained in the volume serve as a universal cure for "our wounds of ignorance" (*ignorantiae nostrae vulnera*) which is deemed necessary "for discovering all truths" (*ad omnes veritates inveniendas*).[138] Immediately after this comes a first engraving, depicting Mount Randa.[139] A second shows Llull martyred by stoning at the

---

132 *Joanni Bonlabii epistola*, in Ramon Llull, *Logica nova*, (ed.) Alonso de Proaza (Valencia: 1512), fol. 62r: "...totus ad Raymundum vertaris, ipsique suos dumtaxat libellos, legendo, interpretando et bono publico assidue comunicando opem feras. Ceteros uate que in eum se perfitentur expositores cum non sint, valere finas et tanquam simple procul aufugias."

133 *Logica nova*, (ed.) Proaza, fol. 2v.

134 *Liber de ascensu et descensu*, (ed.) Proaza, fol. 1r.

135 Rogent and Durán, *Bibliografia*, 51–53.

136 *Ars inventiva veritatis*, (ed.) Proaza, fol. 1v.

137 *Ars inventiva veritatis*, (ed.) Proaza, fol. 2r.

138 Ibid., fol. 2r.

139 Ibid., fol. 2v.

hands of Saracens in Bougie, with a chart in its lower portion that shows the Dignities, Relative Principles, Rules, and General Questions of the Lullian Art; from Llull's mouth issues a banner with the inscription "Only the Christian religion is a true Art" (*sola christianorum religio sit vera ars*).[140] At the end of the volume appears the already mentioned *Index librorum Raymundi Lullii* of Cisneros, about which Proaza states that the listed works were seen by him or cited by Llull, but that "nonetheless many seem to have been lost due to human negligence" (*quos adhuc iniuria hominum efficit ut delitescant*).[141] Next comes the decree by king Ferdinand of Aragon in favor of Llull's teachings, which contains a letter by Alfonso of Aragon from 1499.[142] Finally, notice exists of an early 17th-century manuscript, held in the library of the University of Alcalá but now lost, ascribed to Proaza and entitled *Arte de Raimundo Lulio*, but it is unclear whether this was a vernacular version of a known work or an original treatise.[143]

Proaza's engagement with Lullian writings is reflected in a remarkable editorial activity, that strengthened, on the one hand, boundaries between Lullian editors within the Iberian peninsula. On the other, it not only defended Lullian terminology and literary style, but broadened basic Lullian concepts and their operation in many aspects of human life: how to attain knowledge of God's manifestation by contemplating and understanding nature, how to argue from necessary reasons, and finally how to put all this into practice within a missionary program promoted by the Cardinal Jiménez de Cisneros at the beginning of the 16th century.

11.10   Nicholas de Pax

Lastly, the Majorcan Nicholas de Pax,[144] who was a student of the Lullist Joan Cabaspre (1455–1529) and of Gregorio Genovard, enjoyed the protection and support of Cardinal Cisneros.[145] On Majorca, Pax copied in his own hand old

---

140   Ibid., fol. 100v.
141   Ibid., fol. 220v.
142   Ibid., fols. 223r–226r.
143   Carreras i Artau, *Historia de la filosofía*, 2:255.
144   Carreras i Artau, *Historia de la filosofía*, 2:207–209, 252–254, 261, 267; Joan Avinyó, *Historia del lulisme* (Barcelona: 1925), 370–374; Joaquín María Bover de Roselló, *Biblioteca de escritores Baleares*, 2 vols. (Palma de Majorca: 1868), 2:76–80, and 590; Gonzalo Díaz Díaz, *Hombres y documentos de la filosofía española*, vol. 6 (Madrid: 1998), 295–296; and Pereira, "Bernardo Lavinheta e la diffusione del Lullismo," 249, 259.
145   Nicholas de Pax, *Vita divi Raymundi*, (ed.) Victor, 333 and 338.

Lullian manuscripts,[146] then later pursued the teaching of Lullism in the class-rooms of the University of Alcalá,[147] and maintained ties with the French cir-cle of Lefèvre thanks to Charles de Bovelles. The correspondence exchanged by Bovelles and Pax confirm's Bovelles's stay in the Iberian Peninsula, as well as the esteem that the French Lullists enjoyed, at this time, as authorities on Lullism.[148] A letter from 1514 reveals the desire of Pax to have Bovelles respond to him regarding nine philosophical and theological questions, and with it he sends to Bovelles a Lullian manuscript containing the *Disputatio super aliqui-bus quaestionibus Sententiarum Petri Lombardi*, expressing the fervent desire that Bovelles, as one most competent for this task, might edit it. Among other things, the Majorcan mentions that he has read eagerly Bovelles's biography of Llull, which apparently inspired him to prepare a second printed edition of the biography.[149]

In 1518 Pax sent to the Alcalá printer Arnao Guillén de Brocar an introduc-tory study of the Lullian tree of knowledge, under the title *Dyalecticae introduc-tiones illuminati doctoris et martyris Raymundi Lulli*,[150] which probably reflects in part his teachings at Alcalá.[151] In 1519 the presses of the same printer bring forth the *Vita divi Raymundi Lulli, doctoris illuminati et martyris*.[152] At the end of this work appear an epitaph for the tomb of Cisneros and an epigram on the fu-neral of king Ferdinand of Aragon, both composed by Pax. This second printed version of Llull's life shows how Pax sought to prove the orthodoxy of the Illu-minated Doctor, thanks to which the biography becomes an apologetic speech that skillfully cites authorities who support Lullian doctrine in order to give it more force, credibility, and corroboration of its Christian truth for ecclesiasti-cal officials. Similarly, for the same purpose, he presents both ecclesiastical and

---

146   Jesús García Pastor, Jocelyn N. Hillgarth, and Lorenzo Pérez Martínez, *Manuscritos lulia-nos de la Biblioteca Pública de Palma* (Barcelona: 1965), 21–23, 59, and 82–83; Jocelyn N. Hillgarth, *Readers and Books in Majorca, 1229–1550*, 2 vols. (Paris: 1991), 1:212, 227, 228, 230; vol. 2, docs. 557, 568.

147   Bover de Roselló, *Biblioteca*, 2:76; Carreras i Artau, *Historia de la filosofía*, 2:280, 584.

148   Caroli Bovilli Samarobrini Responsiones ad novem quesita Nicolai Paxii Maioricensis seu Balearici in arte lullistarum peritissimi (Paris: 1521/1522); Rogent and Durán, *Bibliografia*, 67–68.

149   *Responsiones*, fol. 2 r.

150   Rogent and Durán, *Bibliografia*, 64–65; Carreras i Artau, *Historia de la filosofía*, 2:254. Some authorities have attributed this work, also known as the *Logica parva*, to Llull him-self: Angel d'Ors, "Raimundo Lulio, Nicolás de Paz y la *Logica parva*," *Documenti e Studi sulla tradizione filosofica medievale* 7 (1996): 115–130.

151   Carreras i Artau, *Historia de la filosofía*, 2:254.

152   Rogent and Durán, *Bibliografia*, 66–67; Carreras i Artau, *Historia de la filosofía*, 2:253, 261, 357.

royal decrees, and offers a parade of prominent Lullist proponents and experts from various eras: Nicholas of Cusa, Pere Deguí, Pico della Mirandola, Lefèvre d'Étaples and Charles de Bovelles.[153]

Among the other Lullist endeavors that occupied Pax were a Castilian translation of Llull's *Desconhort* under the title *Desconsuelo muy piadoso del illuminado Doctor Raimundo Lullio mallorquin, autor del Arte general*, although this did not see publication until 1540, at Palma.[154] A similar labor was a Latin translation of Llull's *Félix* as *Liber de mirabilibus orbis* and his manuscript papers include notice of a *Commentaria super artem divi Raymundi Lulli*,[155] consisting of commentaries and expositions given to his students while teaching at Alcalá. In addition, he left various witnesses that testify to his poetic activity regarding the figure of Llull.[156]

Pax's activities translating Lullian works, as well as his teaching career at Alcalá de Henares with the support of Cardinal Cisneros, contributed to a greater extent to catching the attention not only of religious congregations outside the monastic life, but also of scholarly and secular milieus. Moreover, as a defender of Llull, he attempted to resolve the debate concerning the orthodoxy of Llull's doctrine by quoting respectable authorities in his biography of Llull. At the same time, his close relations with Charles de Bovelles reinforced the dialectical exchange of Lullian exegesis and understanding among French and Iberian humanists who worked together on establishing a renewal of spiritual life, which enhanced philosophy and religion in a more secular and practical way.

11.11   Conclusion

The beginning of the 16th century becomes a remarkable era for the history of Lullian thought. The success of the promotion of his doctrine, supported by the defense of Catholicism, and missionary aims of the Spanish Crown and the Church under the guidance of Cardinal Jiménez de Cisneros, can also be

---

153   *Vita divi Raymundi*, 337–338.

154   Rogent and Durán, *Bibliografía*, 78–79; Carreras i Artau, *Historia de la filosofía*, 2:253, 267.

155   Carreras i Artau, *Historia de la filosofía*, 2:253–254; Bover de Rosselló, *Biblioteca*, 2:78; Avinyó, *Historia del lulisme*, 371.

156   Avinyó, *Historia del lulisme*, 373, notes the several Latin poems by Pax included in the re-edition of his *Vita divi Raymundi Lulli, doctoris illuminati et martirys* published in 1708 by the Jesuit Joan Solerius; Bover de Rosselló, *Biblioteca*, 2:590 (appendix to item 896), includes yet another of these.

attributed to the following factors: the faster dissemination of Lullian doctrine by means of printed media (books and engravings) and the efforts for explaining Lullian concepts and making them more feasible for a wider public (through the practice of pedagogical skills and establishment of schools). Finally, but not least, the humanist network that involved the interests of French and Iberian scholarship lead to a fruitful dialogue, advancing and developing Llull's thought in a more differentiated and thus pluralistic way. This last feature showed the adaptability and flexibility of a Lullian system that would serve as a point of departure for missionary initiatives in the territories of the New World.

Works Cited

Primary Works

Bonllabi, Joan, *Joanni Bonlabii epistola*, in Ramon Llull, *Logica nova*, (ed.) Alonso de Proaza (Valencia: 1512), fol. 62r.

Bovelles, Charles de, *In artem oppositorum introductio* (Paris: 1501).

Bovelles, Charles de, *Commentarius in primordiale evangelium divi Ioannis* (Paris: 1511).

Bovelles, Charles de, *Epistola in vitam Raymundi Lulli Eremita* (Paris: 1511).

Bovelles, Charles de, *Que hoc volumine continentur: Liber de intellectu. Liber de sensibus. Liber de generatione. Libellus de nihilo. Ars oppositorum. Liber de sapiente. Liber de duodecim numeris. Philosophicae epistulae. Liber de perfectis numeris. Libellus de mathematicis rosis. Liber de mathematicis corporibus. Libellus de mathematicis supplementis* (Paris: 1510).

Bovelles, Charles de, *Caroli Bovilli Samarobrini Responsiones ad novem quesita Nicolai Paxii Maioricensis seu Balearici in arte lullistarum peritissimi* (Paris: 1521/1522).

Costurer, Jaime, *Disertaciones históricas del Beato Raymundo Lullio Doctor Iluminado y Mártir con un apéndiz de su vida* (Mallorca: 1700).

Deguí, Pere, *Janua artis Raymundi Lulli* (Cologne: 1516).

Janer, Jaume, *Liber artis metaphysicalis* (Valencia: 1506).

Jourdain, Raymond, *Contemplationes idiotae*, (ed.) Jacques Lefèvre d'Étaples (Paris: 1519).

Lavinheta, Bernard de, *De incarnatione Verbi* (Cologne: 1516).

Lavinheta, Bernard de, *Explanatio compendiosaque applicatio artis Raymundi Lulli*, (ed.) E.-W. Platzeck (1523; repr. Hildesheim: 1977).

Nicholas of Cusa, *Nicolai Cusae cardinalis opera*, (ed.) Jacques Lefèvre d'Étaples (Paris: 1514).

Nicholas of Cusa, *De coniecturis* (Paris: 1514).

Panzer, Wolfgang, *Annales typographici ab artis inventae origine ad annum 1530*, 11 vols. (Nuremberg: 1793–1803).

Pax, Nicholas de, Desconsuelo muy piadoso del illuminado Doctor Raimundo Lullio mallorquin, autor del Arte general (Palma: 1540).

Pax, Nicholas de, *Dyalecticae introductiones illuminati doctoris et martyris Raymundi Lulli* (Alcalá de Henares: 1518).

Pax, Nicholas de, *Vita divi Raymundi Lulli, doctoris illuminati et martyris* (Alcalá de Henares: 1519); (ed.) Joseph M. Victor, "Charles de Bovelles and Nicholas de Pax: Two Sixteenth-Century Biographies of Ramon Lull," *Traditio* 32 (1976): 332–345.

Pseudo-Lullian, *In Rhetoricam Isagoge* (Paris: 1515).

Pseudo-Lullian, *In Rhetoricam Isagoge*, in *Raymundi Lulli Opera*, (ed.) Lazarus Zetzner (1598; reprints 1617 and 1651).

Reisch, Gregor, *Margarita Philosophica* (Freiburg: 1503).

Richard of St. Victor, *De superdivina trinitate*, (ed.) Jacques Lefèvre d'Étaples (Paris: 1510).

Raymond of Sabunde, *Theologia naturalis seu Liber creaturarum* (ed. Joachim Sighart), (ed.) Friedrich Stegmüller (1852; repr. Stuttgart: 1966).

Primary Works: Llull

Arbor scientiae (Lyon: 1515).

Ars brevis (Lyon: 1514).

Ars generalis ultima (Lyon: 1517).

Ars inventiva veritatis, seu ars intellectiva veri quae est instrumentum intellectivae potentiae. Tabula generalis. Lectura super artem inventivam et tabulam generalem. Index librorum Raymundi Lullii, (ed.) Alonso de Proaza (Valencia: 1515).

Blanquerna qui tracta de sinch estaments de persones: de Matrimoni, de Religio, de prelatura, de apostolica senyoria ... y del estat de vida hermitana contemplativa debax los quals tots son contenguts (Valencia: 1521).

Dialectica seu logica nova Venerabilis Eremitae Raemmundi Lulli diligenter reposita: restitutis quae nuper fuerant sublata. Et additis Tractatu de inventione medii. Item Tractatu de conversione subjecti et praedicati per medium (Paris: 1516).

Doctor Illuminatus: A Ramon Llull Reader, (ed.) Anthony Bonner (Princeton: 1993).

Doctrina Pueril, (ed.) Joan Santanach i Suñol, NEORL 7.

Hic conteninentur libri Raemundi pii eremitae. Primo de laudibus beatissime virginis marie. Secundo Libellus de natali pueri parvuli. Tertio Clericus Raemundi. Quarto Phantasticus Raemundi, (ed.) Jacques Lefèvre d'Étaples (Paris: 1499).

Liber de anima rationali. Vita divi Raymundi Lulli, doctoris illuminati et martyris (Alcalá: 1519).

Liber de ascensu et descensu intellectus, (ed.) Alonso de Proaza (Valencia: 1512).

Liber de articulis fidei, (ed.) Pere Posa (Barcelona: 1504) and MOG 4:505–530.

Liber lamentationis philosophiae o duodecim principia philosophiae (París: 1516).

Liber qui est disputatio Raymundi christiani et Homerii sarraceni. Liber de demonstra-
   tione per equiparantiam, Disputatio quinque hominum sapientum. Liber de accidente
   et substantia, (ed.) Alonso de Proaza (Valencia: 1510).

Libre d'amic e d'amat, (ed.) Salvador Galmés, Els Nostres Clàssics 14 (Barcelona: 1927),
   19–105.

Libre de ànima racional, (ed.) Miquel Tous Gayà, ORL 21:161–304.

Libre de contemplació en Déu, (eds.) M. Obrador, M. Ferrà, A. Alcover and S. Galmés,
   ORL 2–8.

Libre de home, (ed.) Miquel Tous Gayà, ORL 21:1–159.

Libre de meravelles, (ed.) Miquel Batllori, *OE* 1:319–509.

Libre dels àngels, (ed.) Miquel Tous Gayà, ORL 21:305–375.

Logica nova. Liber correlativorum innatorum. Liber de ascensu et descensu intellectus,
   (ed.) Alonso de Proaza (Valencia: 1512).

Primum volumen contemplationum Remundi duos libros continens Libellus Blaquerne de
   amico et amato, (ed.) Jacques Lefèvre d'Étaples (Paris: 1505).

Proverbia Raemundi & Philosophia amoris, (ed.) Jacques Lefèvre d'Étaples (Paris: 1516).

Secondary Works

Anselm, J. M. Albareda, "Lul·lisme a Montserrat al segle XVè: l'ermità Bernat Boil," *EL*
   9 (1965): 5–21.

Albertini, Tamara, "Der Mensch als *metamorphische* Weltmitte: Reflexionen zu einer Denkfigur der Renaissance (Bovelles, Ficino, Pico)," in *Sapientiam amemus:*
   Humanismus und Aristotelismus in der Renaissance: Festschrift für Eckhard Keßler
   zum 60. Geburstag, (eds.) Paul Richard Blum and Charles Lohr (Munich: 1999),
   89–108.

Aldea, Quintín, Tomás Marín, et al., (eds.), *Diccionario de Historia Eclesiástica de Es-*
   paña, 5 vols. (Madrid: 1972–1987).

Alós y de Dou, Ramon de, *Los catálogos lulianos: contribución al estudio de la obra de*
   Ramón Llull (Barcelona: 1918).

Andrés, Melquíades, *Historia de la mística de la Edad de Oro en España y América*
   (Madrid: 1994).

Angermann, Norbert, Robert Auty, Robert-Henri Bautier, et al., (eds.) *Lexikon des Mit-*
   telalters, 10 vols. (Stuttgart: 1980–1999).

Avinyó, Joan, *Història del lulisme* (Barcelona: 1925).

Barceló i Crespi, Maria and Ricard Urgell Hernández, "La Universitat de Mallorca: origen i evolució fins al segle XVIII," in *Les universitats de la Corona d'Aragó*, (eds.) Joan
   J. Busqueta and Juan Pemán (Barcelona: 2002), 157–192.

Bataillon, Marcel, *Erasmo y España: Estudios sobre la historia espiritual del siglo XVI*,
   trans. Antonio Alatorre, 2nd ed. (Mexico: 1966).

Batllori, Miquel, *Ramon Llull i el lul·lisme* (Valencia: 1993).

Bedouelle, Guy, *Lefèvre d'Étaples et l'Intelligence des Écritures* (Geneva: 1976).

Bocken, Inigo, *L'art de la collection: Introduction historico-éthique à l'herméneutique conjecturale de Nicolas de Cues* (Paris and Louvain: 2007).

Bocken, Inigo, "Visions of Reform: Lay Piety as a Form of Thinking in Nicholas of Cusa," in *Reassessing Reform: An Historical Investigation into Church Renewal,* (eds.) Christopher Bellitto and David Zacharias Flanagrin (Washington, D.C.: 2012), 214–231.

Bover de Roselló, Joaquín María, *Biblioteca de escritores Baleares,* 2 vols. (Palma: 1868).

Brause, Karl Hermann, *Die Geschichtsphilosophie des Carolus Bovillus* (Leipzig: 1916).

Carreras i Artau, Joaquín and Tomás Carreras i Artau, *Historia de la filosofía española,* 2 vols. (Madrid: 1939–1943).

Cassirer, Ernst, *Individuum und Kosmos in der Philosophie der Renaissance* (Leipzig and Berlin: 1927).

Catà, Cesare, "Viewed through the Looking-Glass: Human Nature as a Mystical Mirror in Charles de Bovelles' Conception of Sapientia," *Intellectual History Review* 21 (2011): 297–306.

Centre d'études supérieures de la Renaissance de l'Université de Tours, "No author" *Charles de Bovelles et son cinquième centenaire (1479–1979): Actes du Colloque International tenu a Noyon, les 14-15-16 septembre 1979* (Paris: 1982).

Colomer, Eusebio, *Ramon Llull y Nicolás de Cusa* (Madrid: 1961).

Díaz, Gonzalo Díaz, *Hombres y documentos de la filosofía española,* vol. 6 (Madrid: 1998).

D'Ors, Ángel, "Raimundo Lulio, Nicolás de Paz y la *Logica parva,*" *Documenti e Studi sulla tradizione filosofica medievale* 7 (1996): 115–130.

Fattori, Marta and Massimo Bianchi, (eds.), *Phantasia-Imaginatio: V Colloquio Internazionale* (Rome: 1988).

Faye, Emmanuel, *Philosophie et perfection de l'homme: de la Renaissance à Descartes* (Paris: 1998).

Meseguer, José Fernández, "La bula *Ite vos* (29 de mayo de 1517) y la reforma cisneriana," *Archivo Ibeoramericano* 17 (1958): 257–381.

Fidora, Alexander, "La relación entre teología y antropología filosófica en el *Liber creaturarum* de Ramón Sibiuda," *Revista Española de Filosofía Medieval* 8 (2001): 177–185.

Gandillac, Maurice de, "Lefèvre d'Étaples et Charles de Bouelles, lecteurs de Nicolas de Cues," in *Colloque International de Tours (XIVe stage): L'Humanisme français au début de la Renaissance* (Paris: 1973), 155–171.

García Gómez-Heras, José María, "El *Liber creaturarum* de Raimundo Sabunde: Estudio bibliográfico," *Cuadernos Salmantinos de Filosofía* 3 (1977): 231–271.

García Oro, José, *El cardenal Cisneros,* 2 vols. (Madrid: 1992).

García Pastor, Jesús, Jocelyn N. Hillgarth, and Lorenzo Pérez Martínez, *Manuscritos lulianos de la Biblioteca Pública de Palma* (Barcelona: 1965).

García Villoslada, Ricardo, *La universidad de París durante los estudios de Francisco de Vitoria O. P.* (Roma: 1938).

Gayà Estelrich, Jordi, "Réminiscenses luliennes dans l'anthropologie de Bovelles," in Centre d'études supérieures de la Renaissance de l'Université de Tours, *Charles de Bovelles et son cinquième centenaire (1479–1979): Actes du Colloque International tenu a Noyon, les 14-15-16 septembre 1979* (Paris: 1982), 143–156.

Graf, Charles-Henri, *Essai sur la vie et les écrits de Jacques Lefèvre d'Étaples* (1872; repr. Geneva: 1970).

Guilleumas, Rosalía, "La biblioteca de Joan Bonllavi: Membre de l'escola lul.lista de València al segle XVI," *Revista valenciana de filología* 4 (1954): 23–73.

Hillgarth, Jocelyn N., *Ramon Lull and Lullism in Fourteenth-Century France* (Oxford: 1971).

Hillgarth, Jocelyn N., "An unpublished Lullian sermon by Pere Deguí," in *Aristotelica et Lulliana*, (eds.) Fernando Domínguez Reboiras et al. (Steenbrugge: 1995), 561–569.

Hillgarth, Jocelyn N., *Readers and Books in Majorca, 1229–1550*, 2 vols. (Paris: 1991).

Hughes, Philip Edgcumbe, *Lefévre: Pioneer of Ecclesiastical Renewal in France* (Grand Rapids: 1984).

Johnston, Mark D., "The Reception of the Lullian Art," *Sixteenth Century Journal* 12 (1981): 31–48.

Katz, Louise, "Les presses badiennes au service des détracteurs d'Érasme et de Jacques Lefèvre d'Étaples: un revirement idéologique?" in *Passeurs de textes: Imprimeurs et libraires à l'âge de l'humanisme*, (eds.) Christine Bénévent et al. (Paris: 2012), 43–56.

Klinger-Dollé, Anne-Hélène, *Le De sensu de Charles de Bovelles (1511): conception philosophique des sens et figuration de la pensée* (Geneva: 2016).

Klinger-Dollé, Anne-Hélène, "Making Figures: A Way Of Philosophizing in the *De Sapiente*," *Intellectual History Review* 21 (2011): 317–339.

Kouskoff, G., "Tradition et nouveauté dans l'enseignement mathématique de Charles de Bovelles," in *Charles de Bovelles et son cinquième centenaire (1479–1979): Actes du Colloque International tenu a Noyon, les 14-15-16 septembre 1979* (Paris: 1982), 199–210.

La Garanderie, Marie-Madeleine de, "Aspectes de l'exégèse de Charles de Bovelles," in *Acta conventus Neo-latini Torontonensis, Proceedings of the Seventh International Congress of Neo-Latin Studies, Toronto, 8 August to 13 August 1988* (Binghamton, New York: 1991), 281–292.

Lines, David A., "Lefèvre and French Aristotelianism on the Eve of the Sixteenth Century," in *Der Aristotelismus in der Frühen Neuzeit-Kontinuität oder Wiederaneignung?* (Wiesbaden: 2007), 273–289.

Llinarès, Armand, "Le lullisme de Lefèvre d'Étaples et des ses amis humanistes," in *L'Humanisme française au début de la Renaissance* (Paris: 1973), 127–135.

Margolin, Jean-Claude, "Bovelles et son commentaire de l'évangile johannique," in *Histoire de l'exégèse au XVIe siècle: Actes du Colloque international tenu à Genève en 1976*, (eds.) Olivier Fatio and Pierre Fraenkel (Geneva: 1978), 229–255.

Margolin, Jean-Claude, "L'enseignement des mathématiques en France (1540–70): Charles de Bovelles, Fine, Peletier, Ramus," in *French Renaissance Studies 1540–70: Humanism and the Enyclopaedia*, (ed.) P. Sharratt (Edinburgh: 1976), 109–155.

Margolin, Jean-Claude, "La function de Modèle dans la pensée créatrice de Bovelles," in *Le modèle à la Renaissance*, (eds.) J. Lafond, C. Balauoine, and P. Laurens (Paris: 1986), 51–75.

Margolin, Jean-Claude, "Reflections on the Nature of the *Homo sapiens* and on the Ideal of Wisdom According to Charles de Bovelles," *Intellectual History Review* 21 (2011): 281–295.

Mazour-Matusevich, Yelena, *Le siècle d'or de la mystique française: un autre regard: étude de la littérature spirituelle de Jean Gerson (1363–1429) à Jacques Lefèvre d'Étaples (1450?–1537)* (Milan: 2004).

Meier, Christel, "Malerei des Unsichtbaren: Über den Zusammenhang von Erkenntnistheorie und Bildstruktur im Mittelalter," in *Text und Bild, Bild und Text: DFG Symposion 1988*, (ed.) W. Harms (Stuttgart: 1990), 35–65.

Meier-Oeser, Stephan, *Die Präsenz des Vergessenen: Zur Rezeption der Philosophie des Nicolaus Cusanus vom 15. bis zum 18. Jahrnundert* (Münster: 1989).

Nogales, José Luis Sánchez, *Camino del hombre a Dios: La teología natural de Raimundo Sibiuda* (Granada: 1995).

Oosterhoff, Richard J., "Idiotae, Mathematics, and Artisans: The Untutored Mind and the Discovery of Nature in the Fabrist Circle," *Intellectual History Review* 24 (2014): 301–319.

Pardo Pastor, Jordi, "El cercle lul·lià de València: Alonso de Proaza i Joan Bonllavi," *Zeitschrift für Katalanistik* 14 (2001): 33–45.

Pereira, Michela, "Bernardo Lavinheta e la diffusione del Lullismo a Parigi nei primi anni del '500," *Interpres: Rivista di Studi Quattrocenteschi* 5 (1984): 242–265.

Pereira, Michela, "Le opere mediche di Lullo in rapporto con la sua filosofia naturale e con la medicina del XIII secolo," *EL* 23 (1979): 5–35.

Pereira, Michela, "L'uso del 'Panepistemon' del Poliziano nella 'Isagoge in rhetoricam' pseudolulliana," *Physis: Rivista Internazionale di Storia della Scienza* 16 (1974): 223–233.

Pérez, Joseph, (ed.), *La hora de Cisneros* (Madrid: 1995).

Pérez, Lorenzo, "El maestro Pedro Daguí y el lulismo mallorquín de fines de siglo XV," *EL* 4 (1960): 1–16.

Pernot, Jean-François (ed.), *Jacques Lefèvre d'Etaples (1450?–1536): actes du colloque d'Etaples les 7 et 8 novembre 1992* (Paris: 1995).

Pou y Martí, José María, "Sobre la doctrina y culto del beato Raimundo Lulio," *Archivo Iberoamericano* 41 (1921): 5–23.

Pring-Mill, Robert D.F., *El Microcosmos Lul.lià* (Oxford: 1962).

Puig i Oliver, Jaume de, *La filosofia de Ramon Sibiuda* (Barcelona: 1997).

Ramis Barceló, Rafael, "En torno al escoto-lulismo de Pere Daguí," *Medievalia* 16 (2013): 235–264.

Renaudet, Augustin, *Préréforme et Humanisme à Paris pendant les premières guerres d'Italie (1494–1517)*, 2nd ed. (Paris: 1953).

Renouard, Philippe, *Imprimeurs et libraires Parisiens du XVIe siècle* (Paris: 1969).

Riber, Lorenzo, "Erasmo en el 'Indice Paulino' con Lulio, Sabunde y Savonarola," *Boletín de la Real Academia Española* 38 (1958): 249–264.

Rice, Eugene F., "Humanist Aristotelianism in France: Jacques Lefèvre d'Étaples and his circle," in *Humanism in France at the end of the Middle Ages and in the Early Renaissance*, (ed.) A.H.T. Levi (New York: 1970), 132–149.

Rice, Eugene F., "Jacques Lefèvre d'Étaples and the Medieval Christian Mystics," in *Florilegium Historiale: Essays presented to Wallace K. Ferguson*, (eds.) J.G. Rowe and W.H. Stockdale (Toronto: 1971), 89–124.

Rice, Eugene F., *The Prefatory Epistles of Jacques Lefèvre d'Étaples and Related Texts* (New York: 1972).

Rodríguez de la Flor, Fernando, *Emblemas: lecturas de la imagen simbólica* (Madrid: 1995).

Rogent, Elies and Estanislau Durán, *Bibliografia de les Impressions Lul.lianes* (Barcelona: 1927).

Romano, Marta, "Aspetti del lullismo spagnolo: Pere Daguí," *Estudios de Latín Medieval Hispánico: Actas del V Congreso Internacional de Latín Medieval Hispánico (Barcelona, 7-10 de septiembre de 2009)*, (eds.) José Martínez Gázquez, Óscar de la Cruz Palma and Cándida Ferrero Hernández (Florence: 2011), 275–280.

Rossi, Paolo, *Clavis universalis: Arti della memoria e logica combinatoria da Lullo a Leibniz* (Milan: 1960).

Rummel, Erika, *Jiménez de Cisneros: On the Threshold of Spain's Golden Age* (Tempe: 1999).

Scaduto, Mario, "Laínez e l'Indice del 1559: Lullo, Sabunde, Savonarola, Erasmo," *Archivum Historicum Societatis Iesu* 24 (1955): 3–32.

Vasoli, Cesare, *Civitas mundi: Studi sulla cultura del cinquecento* (Rome: 1996).

Vasoli, Cesare, "Jacques Lefèvre d'Étaples e le origini del 'Fabrismo,'" *Rinascimento* 2 (1959): 221–254.

Vasoli, Cesare, *Immagini umanistiche* (Naples: 1983).

Vasoli, Cesare, *L' enciclopedismo del Seicento* (Naples: 1978).

Vasoli, Cesare, *La dialettica e la retorica dell'Umanesimo: "Invenzione" e "Metodo" nella cultura del XV e XVI secolo* (Milan: 1968).

Vega, Amador, *Die Sinnlichkeit des Geistigen, die Geistigkeit des Sinnlichen und die metaphorische Sprachverwendung bei Ramon Llull* (Freiburg: 1992).

Victor, Joseph M., "Charles de Bovelles and Nicholas de Pax: Two Sixteenth-Century Biographies of Ramon Lull," *Traditio* 32 (1976): 332–345.

Victor, Joseph M., "The Revival of Lullism at Paris, 1499–1516," *Renaissance Quarterly* 28 (1975): 504–534.

Victor, Joseph M., *Charles de Bovelles (1479–1553): An Intellectual Biography* (Geneva: 1978).

Walter, Peter, "Jacobus Faber Stapulensis als Editor des Raimundus Lullus dargestellt am Beispiel des *Liber natalis pueri parvuli Christi Jesu*," in *Aristotelica et Lulliana*, (eds.) Fernando Domínguez Reboiras et al. (Steenbrugge: 1995), 545–559.

Weier, Reinhold, *Das Thema vom verborgenen Gott von Nikolaus von Kues zu Martin Luther* (Münster: 1967).

Wittlin, Curt J., "Charles de Bovelles davant dos models de vida santa i solitària: Nicolau de Flüe (1503) i Ramon Llull (1511)," in *Homenatge a Miquel Batllori*, (ed.) Guillem Alexandre Amengual i Bunyola (Barcelona: 2003), 61–76.

Zambelli, Paola, "Il 'De auditu kabbalistico' e la tradizione lulliana nel Rinascimento," *Atti dell'Accademia Toscana di Scienze e Lettere "La Colombaria"* 30 (1965): 115–247.

CHAPTER 12

Academic Lullism from the Fourteenth to the Eighteenth Century

Rafael Ramis Barceló

12.1 Introduction

Developing a brief history of the teaching of Lullism from the 14th to the 18th century involves, first, establishing its scope of study and, second, proposing a scheme that helps to define best the relationship between Lullism and its teaching. I do not enter into the life of Llull here, in which one can trace, among others, two permanent obsessions: on the one hand, making his books "multiply" lavishly throughout the world; on the other, founding "schools" to teach his Art. Llull was the first author who proposed to inundate every place he knew with his manuscripts, in order to make his works imperishable. At the same time, he demanded that all interpretations of his works come only from those who had a full command of his Art.

Llull was not a cleric, but rather a secular man of the courtly world. He compensated for his lack of university customs and methods through a plethora of views that were not confined to the University. He spread his own work among the diverse levels of society, and above all, made his Art a dialectical weapon for the conversion of the infidels. Llull's contacts with the University were relevant, but not permanent or exclusive. If the Majorcan thinker befriended some of the teachers in Paris and Montpellier, it was not so much for the interest in the knowledge they could provide him as for the facilities they could offer him in order to expose his thought. Llull thought that if he was capable of convincing the teachers of his era of the goodness of his Art, his work would be accepted and disseminated. The result of teaching Lullism, thus, was not only a chapter in history, but also a consequence completely beloved by the Illuminated Doctor, who wished to spread his work.

12.2 Methodology and Schematic Process

The concept of the University, at the end of the Middle Ages and into the modern era, was very flexible. The teaching of many public and private schools had a quasi-university quality, which, in the case of Lullism, was to be studied

© KONINKLIJKE BRILL NV, LEIDEN, 2019 | DOI:10.1163/9789004379671_013

simultaneously in public, private, and convent schools, as well as in universities and para-universities. The underlying reason that Lullism did not form part of Scholastic doctrines from the beginning was due to the fact that his teachings took time to officially become a valid part of university or school curricula. It is worth mentioning that Lullism is a doctrine that was not transmitted in schools, but rather it was frequently dispersed privately and simultaneously in different places with diverse orientations. It is not my intent here to outline a genealogy of the history of the transmission of Lullism in Europe, but rather to draw a cartography of the main centers of academic Lullism in order to underscore its institutional structure, its commonalities, and its differences.

Given the advances in the historiography of the University, it is not possible to follow the great 20th-century historians of Lullism (Avinyó, Carreras i Artau, Batllori) with generic schemes that refer to the Lullian *cátedras* (professorships or chairs) in various universities. With the tools now available, we can identify and provide a more adequate account of each teacher's positions, within the history of university institutions. We must insist that in the history of Lullism, despite the huge advances in the last years, the field continues to expand and that what is proposed here should continue to be revised, refined, and amended in the future.

In a previous work I have covered the diffusion of Lullism in Hispanic universities.[1] To specify the terrain of each educational institution connected to

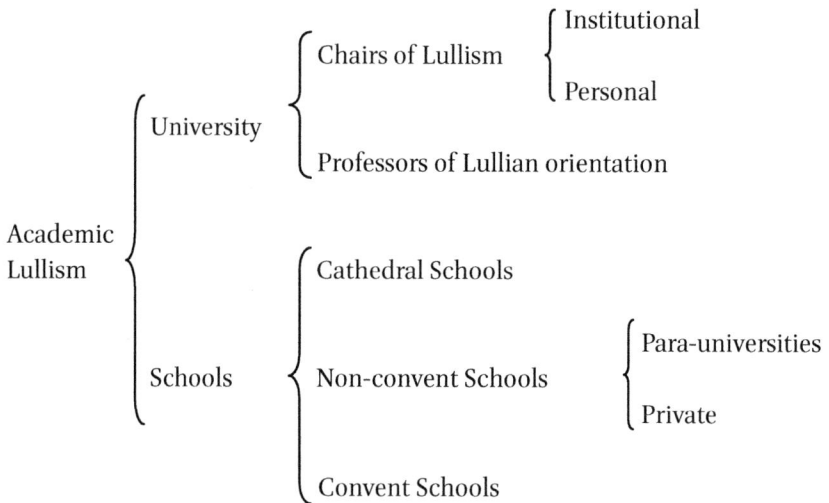

---

1   Rafael Ramis Barceló, "Un esbozo cartográfico del lulismo universitario y escolar en los Reinos Hispánicos," *Cuadernos del Instituto Antonio de Nebrija* 15 (2012): 61–103, for further information on teaching Lullism in the Hispanic Kingdoms. To avoid unnecessarily extending subsequent footnotes and quotations, the following pages do not cite archival data or sources.

Lullism, I proposed a schematization, which I reproduce here. It is my contention that the same schema proves useful to study Lullism within the framework of academic institutions in all of Europe.

Within the realm of academic Lullism, there is an important distinction between academic and Scholastic Lullism. There are two types of university Lullism: the first consists of chairs of Lullism and the second of professors with Lullist orientation. The former can be further divided into those of institutional nature (those that established chairs dedicated to Lullism) and those of personal nature (those that installed "ad hoc" chairs in the university to enrich the course of study). Professors with a Lullian orientation were those that explained Lullism from their professorships, even if the end goal was to explain another discipline besides Lullism, such as Philosophy, Mathematics, or Theology.

Regarding Lullism in the schools, one must consider the cathedral, Franciscan convent, and non-convent schools. These are divided into para-universities, which can be compared to a University, even without that designation, or private schools in which Lullism was explained in a particular way. As we will see, these borders are very subtle, and this chapter intends to show these differences and their problems because for the most part, academic Lullism cannot be understood well without including all of these schools. We must also distinguish between the teachers that dedicated themselves exclusively to the explanation of Lullism and those that used Lullism as an important element for the construction of their own systems of thought. In general, in the Iberian Peninsula and, in part, in Italy, with notable exceptions, the first model was followed. In France and in the Holy Roman Empire, teachers generally followed an eclectic model in which Lullism was a relevant part of the curriculum, but not the only one.

12.3   The Birth of Lullism

While Llull publicly expounded his Art in Montpellier and in other places, it was in Paris where he presented his thought with most fervor. In the Sorbonne, he had disciples whose role, especially that of Thomas Le Myésier (d. 1336), was foundational for the preservation of Llull's works and the diffusion of Lullian thought.[2] The Lullian collections at the Sorbonne and the Carthusian house of Vauvert were objects of interest from the 14th century. A large part of them,

---

2 Charles Lohr, "Die Überlieferung der Werke Ramón Llulls," *Freiburger Universitätsblätter* 78 (1982): 14–15.

along with the *Electorium* of Lullian material compiled by Le Myésier, were known during this century in Toulouse, Barcelona, and Valencia.[3]

In parallel fashion, it seems that at the end of Llull's life certain academic activity in Palma facilitated Llull establishing a school there. According to documentation we can say that a Lullian school was present on the margin of the cathedral school run by Bishop Guillem de Vilanova, even though the origins of Lullism in Majorca remain unclear.[4] One hint with regards to this school is the figure of the priest Guillem Mestre, whose profile is becoming clearer. Apparently, a grammar professor at the cathedral school and a transcriber of Lullian manuscripts, he was most likely Llull's disciple and his ideas were arguably in harmony with those of Llull's close friend Bishop Vilanova.[5] We also know that in the 14th century, the Domincans were instrumental in the inquisitorial persecution of Lullism, and only by a stroke of luck, this persecution did not end as intended. This makes us think that Lullism in Majorca in the second half of the 14th century did not have a clear institutional dimension, but a more eremitical one.[6] As we will see, the shadow of the Dominican Inquisitor Nicholas Eymerich (ca. 1316–1399) fell over the entire Crown of Aragon and his influence was long-lasting. However, we cannot deny that Lullism was a common element in the different stratums of the Crown of Aragon and the Crown of Majorca during the 14th century, just as Eymerich recognized.[7] The question of which were the itineraries of 14th-century Lullism remains open.[8]

While the Lullian connections between Valencia and Majorca are more or less well-known, those with Barcelona are less clear. We do not know with certainty if some Majorcan Lullist inspired interest in Barcelona—just as was done in Valencia, according to Perarnau[9]—or if a Lullian nucleus already existed in Barcelona in Llull's life.[10] There were, of course, people who owned Lullian texts in Barcelona during the 14th century, but it is unknown if they were organized through some academic connection.

---

3   Jocelyn N. Hillgarth, *Ramon Llull i el naixement del lul·lisme* (Barcelona: 1998), 363.

4   Ibid., 178; cf. Jocelyn N. Hillgarth, *Readers and Books in Majorca, 1229–1550*, 2 vols. (Paris: 1991), 1:29.

5   Hillgarth, *Ramon Llull i el naixement*, 178.

6   Josep Amengual Batle, *El bisbe ermità de Miramar: Jaume Badia, exponent del lul·lisme mallorquí del segle XIV* (Palma: 2011), 11. Cf. Jocelyn N. Hillgarth, "Some notes on Lullian Hermits in Majorca saec. XIII-XVII," *Studia Monastica* 6 (1964): 299–328.

7   Nicolau Eymeric, *Diàleg contra els lul·listes* (Barcelona: 2002), 28.

8   See Jordi Pardo Pastor, "El lulismo hispánico del trescientos," in *Ramon Llull, caballero de la fe: El arte luliana y su proyección en la Edad Media* (Pamplona: 2001), 111–127.

9   Josep Perarnau i Espelt, "El lul·lisme de Mallorca a Castella a través de València: Edició de l'Art abreujada de confessió," *Arxiu de Textos Catalans Antics* 4 (1985): 61–172.

10   Sebastiá Trias Mercant, *Història del pensament a Mallorca* (Palma: 1985), 68.

Castilian Lullism had one nucleus in Andalusia and another in Castile, but for now whether it settled in other areas is unknown. It appears that the means of transmission was first from the Hieronymites and later from observant Franciscans.[11] New research suggests there is more information about Lullism in Seville and the Old College of San Bartolomé in Salamanca, as well as in other connective centers.

As Perarnau affirms, perhaps the origins of Valencian Lullism began with the figure of Bernat Garí, a priest of the diocese of Majorca, who was considered a disciple of Llull and who later went to Valencia. In this sense, we can argue that a "hidden Lullism" started in Majorca, namely a Lullism that did not have a public presence.[12] The figure of Garí, as well as other anonymous documents, are the first manifestations of Valencian Lullism, which had in itself a certain continuity during its time and influenced Lerida, the only university town in the good graces of the Crown, as well as Cervera and Barcelona. The most attractive figure of Alcoyan Lullism was the hermit Pere Rossell,[13] doctor of Theology, who taught there.[14]

In 1376 Eymerich obtained a papal bull to prohibit the teaching of Llull's Art. This bull had no effect due to the protection of Lullism sanctioned by the

11   Francisco José Díaz Marcilla, "I lullismi: ambiti tematici d'interesse a confronto," in *Ramon Llull und Nikolaus von Kues: Eine Begegnung im Zeichen der Toleranz*, (eds.) E. Bidese et al. (Turnhout: 2005), 227–245, and "El hilo luliano de la madeja cultural castellana medieval: Nuevos aportes al lulismo castellano medieval laico y religioso," in *Knowledge, Contemplation, and Lullism: Contributions to the Lullian Session at the SIEPM Congress – Freising, August 20-25, 2012*, (ed.) José Higuera Rubio, Subsidia Lulliana 5 (Turnhout: 2015), 165–190; and Fernando Domínguez Reboiras, "La recepción del pensamiento luliano en la Península Ibérica hasta el siglo XIX: Un intento de síntesis," *Revista de lenguas y literaturas catalana, gallega y vasca* 15 (2010): 372–375.

12   Pardo Pastor, "El lulismo hispánico," 117, has defended, among other things, the independence of the Lullian school saying that: "the first Lullian school, more mystical than doctrinal, was created in Valencia by the Franciscans and the Joachimite *fraticelli*. Situated in Alcoi, the latter became a school on Lullist doctrine run by *sacerdotes minimi* and formed by merchants and artisans of different guilds" ("la primera escuela luliana, más mística que doctrinal, se crea en Valencia de manos de franciscanos y fraticelos joaquinistas. Fijada en Alcoi, ésta se convirtió en una escuela de doctrina lulista a cargo de *sacerdotes minimi* y formada por mercaderes y artesanos de distintos gremios"). However, the way in which this Levantine Lullism was established and the motives behind this Lullian movement in Valencia are unknown. Hillgarth notes the possibility that Parisian Lullism spread to Valencia, *Ramon Llull i el naixement*, 321–323.

13   Amengual, *El bisbe ermità*, 44, affirms that Rossell could have been Majorcan, along with Bernat Garí, and that he had been exiled due to the harsh persecution of Lullists on the island.

14   Jaume de Puig i Oliver, "El procés dels lul·listes valencians contra Nicolau Eimeric en el marc del Cisma d'Occident," *Boletín de la Sociedad Castellonense de Cultura* 56 (1980): 374–377.

kings of the Crown of Aragon. Berenguer de Fluvià, a Valencian merchant, was granted a privilege in 1369 by Peter III of Aragon to teach Llull's Art.[15] Said privilege allowed him–and those he considered adept—to divulge and expound Lullian philosophy. There is no doubt that Rossell found refuge in this privilege and that his notoriety as an interpreter of Llull was well recognized. Also, the Valencian Francesc de Llúria, who had studied Lullian medicine, added his efforts and formed part of the nucleus of this Levantine school. On September 12, 1392, in Sant Cugat del Vallès, King John I granted him a privilege to establish a Lullist school, which would create more opportunities to teach philosophy, liberal arts, medicine, and surgery, according to the principles of Llull's Art.

On October 10, 1398, King Martin "the Humane" granted to Rossell the hermitage at Miramar, even though it is unknown whether or not he visited regularly. Josep Amengual assumes that this fact reveals Rossell's familiarity with the activities of the Beguines of Majorca, signaling that maybe he was born on the island.[16] When Eymerich intervened and accused Rossell of heresy, he and his group took refuge in Rome. Thanks to the intervention of the courts of Valencia, Eymerich was removed from office and King John renewed Rossell's *licentia docendi*, which was confirmed in 1399 by King Martin.[17] In 1403 Rossell appealed to Cervera to teach Lullian doctrine there, at the request of a small group of teachers in the area; a little later, Rossell was master of Lullian doctrines at Cervera.[18] The King also granted a privilege to Francesc de Pereta to house the Lullian school of Barcelona, where the priest Thomas Eiximeno began to teach.[19]

Lullism also reached the University of Lerida, through Valencian students and Franciscan friars, which suggests a connection to Rossell.[20] The most renowned figure of this Lullism in Lerida was the Valencian Antoni Riera.[21] Eymerich initiated Inquisitorial prosecution of Riera, as a representative of the Valencian heterodoxy, but Riera resisted, and with the support of the other university teachers and of the Valencian courts, launched a counter-claim

---

15   Jaume de Puig i Oliver, "Documents inèdits referents a Eimeric i al lul·lisme," *Arxiu de Textos Catalans Antics* 2 (1983): 324–339.

16   Amengual, *El bisbe ermità*, 44–45.

17   Pardo Pastor, "El lulismo hispánico del trescientos," 118.

18   Jaume de Puig i Oliver, "El 'Dialogus contra lullistas' de Nicolau Eimeric, O.P. Edició i estudi," *Arxiu de Textos Catalans Antics* 19 (2000): 25–26.

19   Pardo Pastor, "El lulismo hispánico," 126.

20   Pedro Sanahuja, "La enseñanza de la teología en Lérida: Cátedras regentadas por maestros franciscanos (siglos XIV-XV)," *Archivo Ibero-Americano* 38 (1935): 429–430. The study of Lullism at Lérida in the first decades of the fourteenth century is unexplored territory that should be studied as another component of Franciscanism in this era.

21   Puig i Oliver, "El procés dels lul·listes," 427–429.

against the inquisitor. Eymerich had to release his claims and maintain silence until his death in 1399. Thanks precisely to Eymerich, we know that the rector of Madrona gave lessons on Lullism in Valencia until 1390,[22] which suggests that the Lullism of the time was more prevalent than it appears.

In tandem with these conflicts, at the end of the century, Jean Gerson (1363–1429), rector at the University of Paris, prohibited the reading of Llull's Art in the School of Theology. This prohibition reveals that Llull was an important author, and even if his works were not publicly taught, he was well-read and commented on by Parisian teachers and by their disciples. The university transmission of Llull's texts in Paris was essential for the establishment of the diverse Lullism of the 15th and 16th centuries.

12.4   The Onset of the Renaissance

In the 15th century, various nuclei of Lullism in universities and schools were established in Europe: one in the most western part of the Holy Roman Empire; another in Paris, where despite Gerson's condemnations between 1402 and 1426, the teachers of the Sorbonne studied Llull with much interest. There were other nuclei in Italy and more in the Hispanic kingdoms, including Portugal, where there were Lullian works in the Cistercian abbey at Alcobaça and in the regular canons' house of Santa Cruz in Coimbra.[23] The most renowned Lullian teacher from the first third of the 15th century was Raymond of Sabunde (ca. 1385–1436), professor and rector at the University of Toulouse, who can be considered a professor of Lullian orientation. In his work there are traces of Parisian Lullism and his influence was well-known in the centuries that followed.

The most eclectic Lullist from Central Europe was Emmerich van den Velde (1395–1460), who studied arts and theology at Paris and Cologne. It is possible that he was familiar with Llull's works in Paris. He was a professor in the Universities of Cologne and Louvain and the students directly and indirectly associated with him include a large number of Lullists from the period.[24] Despite being

---

22 Joaquín and Tomás Carreras i Artau, *Historia de la filosofía española: Filosofía cristiana de los siglos XIII al XV*, 2 vols. (Madrid: 1939–1943), 2:18.

23 José María da Cruz Pontes, "Raimundo Lulo e o lulismo medieval português," *Biblos* 62 (1986): 51–76, considers these the basis for the teaching and transmission of Lullian thought in Portugal.

24 Ruedi Imbach, "Theologia Raymundi Lulli memoriter epylogata," *EL* 23 (1979): 185–193. It seems that Lullism in Lovaina also spread since it was taught not only in the University, but also in the monastery of Bethlehem to clerics such as Jean Cornelissen, author of *Omne scibile pauperis*, a lost commentary in verse about the *Arbor Scientiae*.

formally an Albertist, his presence was undoubtedly vital later to awareness of Llull in Cologne, among authors such as Andreas Canter, an arts professor in the University. However, Emmerich's most important student was Nicholas of Cusa (1401–1464), who taught Lullism, but did not widely promote it.[25] Nicholas of Cusa had a relationship with three of the Lullian centers of his time: the Italian, primarily centered in Padua, and the aforementioned centers in Cologne and Paris. It cannot be said that Emmerich taught Lullism to Nicholas, but rather that they mutually enriched each other through comparisons of sources.[26] Both formed the bases for Lullian studies in Central Europe, which had direct connections with the Italian and Parisian, and more indirectly, with the Catalonian-Aragonese centers. Llull's work must have been studied in other zones of the Holy Roman Empire, even though no specific teaching of his texts is known.[27]

Not very far from Cologne, a curious author, Johannes Trithemius (1462–1516), dedicated himself to Lullism, and was in correspondence with his teacher, Libanius Gallus, who at the same time seemed to have been influenced by a "wise Majorcan" named Pelagius. It is unknown which type of hermetic-Lullian teachings Trithemius taught[28] to attract the interest and the visits of Cornelius Agrippa (1486–1535) or Charles of Bovelles (ca. 1465-ca. 1566). These two scholars took full advantage to spread Lullism, as did Paracelsus (ca. 1493–1541), yet another author influenced by Trithemius. Agrippa learned of Lullism in Bologna with Andreas Canter,[29] who was later a disciple of Trithemius, and finally became entrenched in the Parisian Lullian circle. His teaching at universities in Dole, but above all in the public and private lessons he gave at Turin and other cities of the Holy Roman Empire,[30] served to diffuse his Lullian ideas, mixed with many others. Agrippa was principally a theorist and a reformer of Llull's Art, and had much influence on later generations.[31]

---

25   Eusebi Colomer i Pous, *De la Edad Media al Renacimiento: Ramon Llull, Nicolás de Cusa, Juan Pico della Mirandola* (Barcelona: 1975), 78–118; and Marta M.M. Romano, "Quale incontro tra Cusano e Lullo? Elementi per un paradigma di Lullismo," in *Niccolò Cusano, l'uomo, i libri, l'opera: Atti del LII Convegno storico internazionale, Todi, 11-14 ottobre 2015* (Spoleto: 2016), 125–148.

26   Eusebi Colomer i Pous, "Nicolau de Cusa i el lul·lisme europeu quatrecentista," *Randa* 27 (1990): 71–84.

27   Johannes Stöhr, "Stephan Bodeker, O. Praem, Bischof von Brandenburg und Raimundus Lullus," *EL* 4 (1960): 199–202.

28   Noel L. Brann, *Trithemius and Magical Theology: A Chapter in the Controversy over Occult Studies in Early Modern Europe* (Albany: 1999), 170.

29   Franz Josef Worstbrock (ed.), *Die deutsche Literatur des Mittelalters: Deutscher Humanismus 1480–1520*, Verfasserlexikon, 1 (Berlin: 2008), 25 and 360.

30   Marc Van der Poel, *Cornelius Agrippa, The Humanist Theologian and His Declamations* (Leiden: 1997), 25.

31   Paolo Rossi, *Clavis universalis: Arti mnemoniche e logica combinatoria da Lullo a Leibniz* (Milan and Naples: 1960), 42–45.

The circle at Cologne was intimately linked to the Parisian, headed by Jacques Lefèvre d'Étaples (ca. 1455–1536), an eclectic Lullist heavily influenced by Nicholas of Cusa, and the most important figure for the diffusion of Lullism in Paris.[32] He taught in the College of Cardinal Lemoine at the Sorbonne. Without a doubt, the figure of Lefèvre was essential in the formation of a Lullian group in Paris, along with disciples such as Charles Bovelles[33] (the most relevant of them), Josse van Clichtowe, and Beatus Rhenanus, who spread an eclectic Lullism in Alsace, his birthplace, and whose writings illustrate best the spread of Lullism from contact between the Parisian and German circles.[34] Thanks to the labors of Lefèvre d'Étaples as a professor and editor, Llull was a very well-known author in Central Europe. Nonetheless, his teaching and editorial labors involved not only Llull, but also Aristotelian humanism and the *devotio moderna*. He maintained contact with Pico della Mirandola and Marsilio Ficino, whom he made participants in his Lullian interests.

The Franciscan Bernard de Lavinheta (d. ca. 1530), who taught courses at the Sorbonne, constituted the peak of Parisian Lullism.[35] It seems that his position was private in nature and facilitated through Lefèvre d'Étaples, since the University of Paris had great flexibility and allowed for multiple approaches. Lavinheta was a professor of Lullism, but he did not want to use Lullism to construct his own eclectic system (like Emmerich van den Velde and partly like Sabunde). Rather, he wanted to present Lullism in a clear, academic exposition. Lavinheta was well versed and was very knowledgeable in Scotism and Lullism, especially the Schools of Barcelona and Pere Daguí, and in Paris he came into contact with Lefèvre d'Étaples' spiritual Lullism. His teaching and works constitute the most perfectly finished exposition of the Renaissance Lullism that recovers its medieval heritage, and it serves as a point of departure for later encyclopedism. His objective was to show how Llull, through his Art, had created the foundation for a general science by demonstrating the primordial principles of all knowledge structures. Lavinheta was, in essence, a master of Lullism, who dedicated his whole life to the study and the explanation of Llull's ideas.

One can say that Lavinheta, through his intellectual journey, connected the main Lullian centers of his time in Salamanca, Toulouse, Lyon, Paris, and

---

32   See the preceding chapter in this volume for detailed analysis of the development of Lullism in Paris and the work of Lefèvre d'Étaples and his circle.

33   Joseph M. Victor, *Charles de Bovelles, 1479–1553: An Intellectual Biography* (Paris: 1978), 12–15.

34   Armand Llinarès, "Le lullisme de Lèfevre d'Etaples et ses amis humanistes," *Colloque International de Tours (XIV stage)* (Paris: 1973), 127–136.

35   Michela Pereira, "Bernardo Lavinheta e la diffusione del Lullismo a Parigi nei primi anni del '500," *Interpres: Rivista di Studi Quattrocenteschi* 5 (1984): 242–265.

Cologne. Without a doubt, during this century, the intellectual relationships between Castille, Aragon, and the French Midi were frequent. Salamanca, thanks to its university tradition, was a Castilian city that Lullism permeated most intensively. Xirau, among others, indicates that "until the 16th century a chair of Lullism existed at the University of Salamanca,"[36] but this has not been confirmed. The abundance of Lullian manuscripts in the University of Salamanca and various references to Llull are evidence that there was much interest at the university in Llull's works. Nonetheless, at this time, I do not know of any data that can corroborate the existence of a specific Lullist chair. Perarnau has demonstrated the connecting threads between Valencian Lullism—stemming from Majorca—and Salamanca.[37] The textual transmission from Valencia to Salamanca may have had some humanistic bases, but the persistence of Lullism in Salamanca, beyond the fashions of reform and counter-reform, was primarily due to a scholarly Franciscan interest.[38]

The most famous Lullian school of the century was that of Barcelona, in which all of the aforementioned lines of thought converged, namely those of Valencia and Castile. According to Madurell, this was due to a certain Pedro de Mena (or Pedro de Nieva) who apparently taught Llull's Art in the Lullian School of Barcelona.[39] Among the teachers of this school are Tomàs Eximeno (the Jiménez Tomás previously mentioned), Pere Martí, Antoni Sedacer, Joan Bulons, Bernat Frigola, Joan Llobet, Joan Ros, Gabriel Desclapés, Joan Baró, Fra Jaume Costa, Joan Comte, and Bartomeu Far. The priest Antoni Sedacer secured economic and institutional stability for the school,[40] and other teachers, such as his nephew Joan Bulons,[41] expanded the school's curriculum. Some

---

36   Ramón Xirau, *Introducción a la historia de la filosofía* (México: 2009), 181, n. 73: "hasta el siglo XVI existió en la Universidad de Salamanca una *Cátedra Raimundo Lulio.*"

37   Perarnau i Espelt, "El lul·lisme de Mallorca a Castella," 89–92.

38   Josep Perarnau i Espelt, "La traducció castellana medieval del 'Llibre de Meravelles' de Ramon Llull," *Arxiu de Textos Catalans Antics* 4 (1985): 16–17.

39   José María Madurell Marimón, "La Escuela de Ramón Llull de Barcelona; sus alumnos, lectores y protectores," *EL* 6 (1962): 199–200. Mark D. Johnston, "Sacrum Studium: The Lullist School of Fifteenth-Century Barcelona," *Homenaje a Alberto Porqueras Mayo* (Kassel:1989), 385–400, describes some of the general characteristics of this school. Regarding the intellectual environment and some programs of study, see Josep Hernando i Delgado, "Escoles i programes acadèmics a la Barcelona del segle XV: L'escola de mestre Ramon Llull i l'ensenyament de disciplines gramaticals i d'arts," *Acta historica et archaeologica mediaevalia* 20–21 (1999–2000): 633–662.

40   José María Madurell Marimón, "Antonio Sedacer, profesor de la escuela luliana de Barcelona," *Analecta Sacra Tarraconensia* 17 (1947): 1–66; and Josep Perarnau i Espelt, "Sobre mestre Antonio Sedacer i l'ambient de l'Escola Lul·liana de Barcelona," *Estudios Históricos y Documentos de los Archivos Protocolarios* 7 (1979): 132–153.

41   Sebastià Trias Mercant, *Diccionari d'Escriptors lul·listes* (Palma: 2009), 89.

students at the school, such as Bernat Frígola,[42] the Valencian Franciscan Fra Joan Ros,[43] and Joan Llobet became teachers there, and the latter settled in Majorca. Similar to these students, many teachers were authorized by the Aragonese Crown to expound Lullian doctrine wherever they lived: Alfonso v "the Magnanimous" gave the Carmelite Landolfo of Columbia a license to teach Lullism on May 17, 1446.

The Italian diffusion of Lullism from the School of Barcelona has some well-developed components. Ros and Bulons went to the Italian Peninsula and taught Llull's doctrines in Bologna, Venice, and Padua.[44] In Padua Lullism received official protection from Bishop Fantino Dandolo, who had already influenced Nicholas of Cusa. It seems that Bulons gave some private lessons about the Art of Llull in Fantino Dandolo's home. Lullism continued in Padua[45] during the successive decades, not through his Art, but rather through cabbalistic interpretation at the hands of Pietro Mainardi, a professor of surgery.[46] According to Batllori,[47] Giovanni Barone (Joan Baró) returned from the School of Barcelona to his birthplace in Sicily, where he took on as his disciple Mariano Accardi, who edited various works of Llull in Venice. There is much more to be investigated about Sicilian Renaissance Lullism, along with Venetian Lullism. Isolated facts, as well the quantity of Lullian works printed there, are evidence of an important Lullian nucleus connected with Central Europe and, above all, with the School at Barcelona.

The Lullian School at Barcelona endured until the 16th century and its last traces can be seen in the heart of the faculty of the University of Barcelona.[48] The prestige of this Lullian school was equivalent to the school of the city and some teachers taught in both. The most noteworthy aspect of this Lullian school was its capacity to produce private teachers with the ability to read the

---

42   Madurell Marimón, "La Escuela de Ramón Llull," 195–197.

43   Hillgarth, *Readers and Books*, 206–207 and 214–215.

44   Marta M.M. Romano (ed.), *Il Lullismo in Italia: itinerario storico-critico* (Palermo: 2015) and "Il primo lullismo in Italia: tradizione manoscritta e contesto della Lectura di Joan Bolons," *SL* 47 (2007): 71–115; Francesco Fioretino, "Il lullismo in Veneto: Glosse alla *Lectura* di Bolons sullo sfondo del cenacolo quattrocentesco di Fantino Dandolo," in *Il Lullismo in Italia: itinerario storico-critico*, (ed.) Marta M.M. Romano (Palermo: 2015), 239–255.

45   On the contrasts between Lullism in northern and southern Italy, see Francesco Santi, "Episodis de lul·lisme genovés a les acaballes del segle XIV: la confluencia amb l'ockhamisme," *Randa* 27 (1990): 57–69.

46   Paola Zambelli, *L'apprendista stregone: astrologia, cabala e arte lulliana in Pico della Mirandola e seguaci* (Venice: 1995), 55–172.

47   For Italian Lullism in general, see Miquel Batllori, "El lul·lisme a Itàlia: un esbós de síntesi," in *Ramon Llull i el Lul·lisme*, Obra completa 2 (Valencia: 1993), 221–335.

48   Antonio Fernández Luzón, *La Universidad de Barcelona en el siglo XVI* (Barcelona: 2005), 47.

Art. Teachers and students came from all parts of the Aragonese Crown, as well as from Italy. Many philosophers, theologians, and lawyers from Catalonia, Valencia, and, above all, Majorca, educated in Italian universities, served also as a bridge to Italian Humanism.

Two members of the Barcelona School settled on Mount Randa in Majorca: Joan Llobet and Gabriel Desclapés. Their notable teaching efforts did not last long, but they succeeded in making Randa an important place for Lullian teaching. After Llobet's death in 1460, a Valencian named Mario de Passa arrived at Randa, attracted by Lullism.[49] He must have had a good relationship with the Court since he was given a hermitage close to the mountain to reinstate the Lullian school at Randa. In 1477 Beatriz de Pinós donated her goods to the Kingdom of Majorca to finance Lullian teaching at Randa. She wanted to revive the Lullian plan of educating thirteen students in the Art so they could go forth and preach, especially to the infidels. Funding was supposed to last for three years with full support assured. Unfortunately for Lullism, her donation was revoked by her daughter, in a lawsuit that lasted almost 100 years.

Above all, the most important Lullian figure of this century was the Catalan priest Pere Daguí (1435–1500), apparently self-educated in Llull's Art, and who taught in Barcelona at a different place than the Lullian school there.[50] He moved to Majorca because another Catalan woman, Agnès de Quint, established in 1481 a notarial agreement for endowing a Lullian institution to expound the Art.[51] This school was supposed to support two young clerics for two years and to teach Llull's works to them. The courses, moreover, had to be public and free.[52]

In 1483 King Ferdinand II "the Catholic" of Aragon granted a privilege to found a *Studium Generale* in Majorca with the same prerogatives as the University of Lerida. While its ultimate intention is clear, the Lullian nature of the university was never specified, neither in the petitions of local officials nor in the privilege's successive confirmations. At the beginning, the monarch counted on two Lullian professorships (endowed by Quint and Pinós) to be the center of the new University.[53] Legal and ideological problems ensued, preventing the effective function of the endowed chairs. On the one hand, the

49   Hillgarth, *Readers and Books*, 213–215.
50   Rafael Ramis Barceló, "En torno al escoto-lulismo de Pere Daguí," *Medievalia* 16 (2013): 235–264. For more details of Daguí's career, see Chapters 12 and 14 in this volume.
51   María Barceló Crespí, "Agnès de Pacs i l'entorn humanista," *Memòries de l'Acadèmia d'Estudis Genealògics, Heràldics i Històrics* 10 (2000): 34–40.
52   Álvaro Santamaría, *La promoción universitaria en Mallorca* (Palma: 1983), 49.
53   Jaime Lladó Ferragut, *Historia del Estudio General Luliano y de la Real Universidad Literaria de Mallorca* (Palma: 1973).

revocation of Pinós' donation prevented the creation of one chair, and on the other Master Daguí was accused of heterodoxy by the Dominican Guillem Caselles, two years after the profitable initiation of instruction.[54] This was the official beginning of a long and tortuous confrontation between the Lullists and the Dominicans in Majorca. Daguí had to defend himself against the Inquisitor of Aragon and had to defend the orthodoxy of his works in Rome. King Ferdinand intervened in his favor and the Holy See proclaimed the orthodoxy of Daguí's writings. The Catalan teacher took advantage of this to exert his magisterium in the itinerant court of the Catholic monarchs, spreading Lullism to the places they visited.[55] In particular, he heavily influenced Cardinal Cisneros, who henceforth was a devotee of Llull.

Meanwhile, Bartomeu Caldentey, a former student of Daguí in Barcelona, established a school of Lullism in Palma. Around 1485, Caldentey, accompanied by a series of disciples, went to Miramar and in 1492, obtained the rights to the hermitage there from King Ferdinand. At the same time, local officials demanded that Daguí return or name a substitute. After Daguí's death, around 1500, the patrons of the foundation, perhaps pressured to close the conflict between the Lullian schools, apparently chose Caldentey as his successor in the Lullian chair.[56]

Daguí was the most important Lullist of the century. At court he influenced the monarchs' and Cisneros' favor toward Lullism; he established the intellectual bases of the Lullian *Studium generale* in Majorca; and his disciples spread Lullism in Valencia and in Montserrat. Valencian Lullism began to flourish again in the first decade of the 16th century. Meanwhile, in Monserrat, Bernat Boïl (ca. 1440-ca. 1507) was a central figure in the last third of the 15th century,[57] even though he was more of a Lullist master at Montserrat than a Lullian professor. One of Daguí's principle disciples was the Cistercian Jaume Gener, who in 1500 obtained a privilege from King Ferdinand II to found a school of Lullism at Valencia. In the city of Turia he had three important disciples: the Italian Bartolomeo Gentile (1450–1500), Joan Bonllavi, and Alfonso de Proaza (ca. 1445–1519), who made Lullian studies flourish in Valencia during the first two decades of the 16th century. Gener's works had great influence on the

54   Lorenzo Pérez Martínez, "El maestro Daguí y el lulismo mallorquín de fines del siglo xv," *EL* 4 (1960): 291.

55   Santamaría, *La promoción*, 96–116.

56   Rafael Ramis Barceló, "Sobre la denominación histórica de la Universidad de Mallorca: cuestiones institucionales e ideológicas en torno al lulismo," *Cuadernos del Instituto Antonio de Nebrija de Estudios sobre la Universidad* 13 (2010): 242–245.

57   Anselmo Maria Albareda, "Lul·lisme a Montserrat al segle XVè: L'ermità Bernat de Boil," *EL* 9 (1965): 5–21. See also the chapter on Boïl by Dagenais in this volume.

Barcelona school, to the extent that, during the 16th century, Lullism at that institution was heavily influenced by Daguí's ideas.[58]

Although much has been written about the chair of Lullism at the University of Valencia,[59] archival investigations into the history of the institution seem to show that in the 16th century there was no such chair, but rather Lullist teachers who taught in its school. It cannot be affirmed either that such a school (unlike Barcelona) had a para-university nature. Instead, it seems that the Lullian school at Valencia was a Lullian humanistic circle under Gener's direction. Proaza was a humanist and a publicist, as well as a great friend of Cardinal Cisneros, and put the Valencian Lullian nucleus in contact with the incipient University of Alcalá. His disciple Joan Bonllavi benefited from this connection with Alcalá, and apparently was also a disciple of the Lullian professors in the *Studium Generale* of Majorca.[60] At the same time, at the end of his life, Bonllavi was a professor of Lullism in the Lullian school at Barcelona, and thus Daguí's Lullism re-entered, albeit indirectly, into the Barcelona institution.[61]

Ultimately, the Valencian Lullism initiated by the Catalan Cistercian was long-lived in various Lullian centers (Barcelona, Alcalá, and Majorca), as well as in Italy. This was due in part to the Italian Bartolomeo Gentile,[62] who had studied in Barcelona with the Valencian Lullists, returned to his birthplace in Genoa, and provided a poetic image of Llull.[63] Still, the most mature fruit of Valencian Lullism was Gener's *Ars metaphysicalis*, jointly edited by his disciples Gentile and Proaza, in which he gathered and perfected Daguí's Scoto-Lullian concepts. The syntheses of Daguí, Lavinheta, and Gener were the most elaborate expositions of Lullism in the transition to modernity.[64] They were the basis both of Scoto-Lullism and the encyclopedism of later generations.

---

58   Carreras i Artau, *Historia de la filosofía española*, 2:251–256, provides a general overview, and continues to be essential, even though it assumes the existence of Lullian *cátedras* that archival records do not support. See Chapter 11 of this volume for detailed analysis of Proaza and his circle.

59   Echoing a long-rooted tradition, Jordi Pardo Pastor, "El cercle lul·lià de València: Alonso de Proaza i Joan Bonllavi," *Zeitschrift für Katalanistik* 14 (2001): 38, n. 37, mentions that Gabriel Bellviure founded a "chair" (*cátedra*) of Lullian philosophy at Valencia.

60   Albert Soler, "Joan Bonllavi, lul·lista i editor eximi," *Estudis de Llengua i Literatura Catalanes: Miscel·lània Germà Colón*, vol. 4 (Barcelona: 1995), 131–132; and Pardo Pastor, "El cercle lul·lià de València," 40–42.

61   Madurell Marimón, "La Escuela de Ramón Llull," 208–209.

62   Marta M.M. Romano, "I Canti di Bartolomeo Gentile Fallamonica (1450–1510/20): Poesia, scienza e studio di Lullo," *PAN: Studi del Dipartimento di Civiltà Euro-Mediterranee e di Studi Classici, Cristiani, Bizantini, Medievali, Umanistici* 24 (2008): 273–299.

63   Bartolomeo Gentile Fallamonica, *Canti*, (ed.) Giuseppe Gazzino (Genoa: 1877).

64   Pereira, "Bernardo Lavinheta," 252–259; and Rafael Ramis Barceló, "La filosofía luliana en la universidad durante los siglos XV y XVI," *Anuario filosófico* 49 (2016): 177–196.

Teachers in the Lullian *Studium Generale* at Palma, during the first third of the 16th century, included Joan Cabaspre, Gregori Genovard, and Nicholas de Pax, heirs of Daguí's ideas, and also connected to the Valencian school and to Cisneros. It was precisely Cisneros who called Nicholas de Pax personally to teach Lullism in Alcalá. It seems Pax did not hold an official and permanent chair of Lullism like the one at the Lullian *Studium generale,* but an individual position, designed to enrich the landscape of university opinions and to spread Lullism within the institution.[65] The University of Alcalá quickly acquired great prestige and served as a trampoline for the spread of Lullism in the Castilian Court, whose penetration Pere Daguí had already begun. Pax was well connected to the Parisian Lullists. For example, Bovelles greatly influenced him and, it seems, the influence was reciprocal when Bovelles visited Alcalá.[66] The connection of the Lullian *Studium generale* with the University of Alcalá was not only linked to Pax, but also in 1565 to the Majorcan professor Francesc Riera, who was invited to Alcalá to give a course on Lullism.[67] In Alcalá, Pedro de Orduña, with his colleague and friend Gil López de Béjar, formed a Lullian nucleus, which eventually disappeared.[68]

Lullism enjoyed the privilege of great protection during the reign of Philip II, a devoted follower of Llull and sponsor of an academy of mathematics, founded by Juan de Herrera. In this para-university institution, logical-mathematic Lullism formed a large part of the plan of study. Herrera tried to infuse Lullism of a mathematic nature into the university. The Lullian texts for this academy were written by Pedro de Guevara and emphasized the *Ars brevis.* At the same time, Lullism was also a polemical current. In 1505, the College of Saint Mary of Jesus in Seville prohibited the teaching of nominalism and Lullism in its statutes, due to Rodrigo of Santaella's unfavorable views of both Lullism and nominalism.[69] A little later, the first rector of the College, the canon Martín Navarro, apparently eliminated these strong interdictions, although whether Lullism spread at Seville in the following century remains unknown.

---

65   Trias Mercant, *Història del pensament,* 140–143. On Pax, see also Chapter 12 in this volume.

66   Joseph M. Victor, "Charles de Bovelles and Nicholas de Pax: Two Sixteenth-Century Biographies of Ramon Llull," *Traditio* 22 (1976): 313–345.

67   Virgilio Pinto Crespo, "La censura inquisitorial, inquietud e incertidumbre: el caso de Ramon Llull (1559–1610)," *Miscelánea de la Universidad Autónoma de Madrid* (Cantoblanco: 1982), 304.

68   José García Oro, *El Cardenal Cisneros: Vida y empresas,* vol. 2 (Madrid: 1993), 490. See also Marcel Bataillon, *Erasmo y España* (Mexico: 1966), 54–55, n. 12 and 172, n. 24.

69   Vicente Beltrán de Heredia, "La teología en nuestras universidades del Siglo de Oro," in *Miscelanea Beltrán de Heredia,* vol. 4 (Salamanca: 1973), 447–448. Beltrán de Heredia accurately notes that Santaella was critical of these currents and could not separate them, which aptly corroborates that the majority of Hispanic Lullism was essentially of Scotist orientation.

The Lullism of Salamanca and of the school of Barcelona came together with the help of Joan-Lluís Vileta (d. 1583),[70] professor for life at the University of Barcelona since 1559 and regent of the Lullian school in the same city. Before him, Joan Bonllavi from the Lullian school of Valencia taught logic at the *Studium generale* of Barcelona, as well as Lullism at the Lullian School until his death in 1526. Vileta was not a professor of Lullism, but rather a professor of theology, from an essentially Aristolelian perspective, who also taught Lullism.[71] None of Vileta's disciples, except Dimas de Miguel, continued teaching the Lullism of their master at the University of Barcelona due, among other factors, to Tridentine reforms. In 1604, the secretary of the pope and the Congregation of the Inquisition wrote to the Bishop of Barcelona, proclaiming "that it was prohibited to read and dispute Llull's doctrine and that the doctors of the *Studium generale* be notified."[72] This end result indicates a long decline of Lullism at the end of the 16th century, which brought with it the extinction of the Barcelona Lullian school, along with Lullism at the university in the city.

The Spanish Inquisition, along with the Roman Inquisition, became belligerent toward Lullism at the end of the 16th century and at the beginning of the 17th. In 1610, Pedro Fernández de Cea, attorney of the Tribunal of the Inquisition in Zaragoza, requested that the reading of Llull's Art be prohibited in the University of Zaragoza.[73] The professor in question was the Carmelite Agustín Núñez Delgadillo, a professor of Scholastic theology who continued the logico-mathematical Castilian Lullism of Pax and Herrera.[74] During these years,

---

70   José María Madurell Marimón, "Luis Juan Vileta," *Analecta Sacra Tarraconensia* 37 (1964): 19–76; Rafael Ramis Barceló, "Aristotelismo, lulismo y ramismo en Barcelona durante el siglo XVI: Joan-Lluís Vileta y sus discípulos," *Cauriensia* 10 (2015): 385–407.

71   The diverse Artistotelianisms to which Charles B. Schmitt alludes, *Aristotle and the Renaissance* (Cambridge, Mass.: 1983), can also be found in the scholarly re-elaboration and convergence of Llull and Aristotle, with very different approaches.

72   Fernández Luzón, *La Universidad de Barcelona*, 232: "que no se permitiera leer y disputar acerca de la doctrina de Llull y que se notificara el decreto a los doctores del Estudio General."

73   Rafael Ramis Barceló, "El proceso de la Inquisición contra la lectura del Arte de Ramon Llull en la Universidad de Zaragoza (1610)," *Hispania Sacra* 66, extra 1 (2014): 131–160; and Rafael Ramis Barceló and Pedro Ramis Serra, "'Comentaria in Artem magnam et paruam' de Agustín Núñez Delgadillo: un curso luliano manuscrito del siglo XVII," *Cuadernos salmantinos de filosofía* 43 (2016): 33–54.

74   Gonzalo Díaz Díaz, *Hombres y documentos*, 7 vols. (Madrid: 1980–2003), 5:841–843, indicates that there were also Lullian chairs in the Univerisities of Córdoba, Granada, Valencia and Alcalá. Concerning Nuñez Delgadillo's professorship in Valencia, see, for example, Ramón Menéndez Pidal, *Historia de España* (Madrid: 1935), 456; no extant data confirm this assertion.

Aragonese members of the Spanish College in Bologna instructed the Celestine Placido Perilli on Llull's works.[75] Perilli had problems with the Inquisition: he was accused of having books by prohibited authors such as Llull.[76] Thanks to a letter that Perilli sent to officials in Majorca, it is known that Lullism in the University of Bologna had become a problematic doctrine and booksellers did not want to sell books on the subject. In the Spanish College of Bologna, no one knew anything of Llull, except Antonio Lorenzo de Quintaniella, who showed him some Lullian books in the college library, and Doctor Jerónimo Arbizu, originally from Daroca, who taught him Lullian doctrine.

The difficulties of Giordano Bruno (1548–1600) with the Inquisition famously led to his death, burnt at the stake. Bruno was an eclectic Lullist, heavily influenced by reading Nicholas of Cusa. He taught his own doctrines, soaked in Lullism, in different Universities. Unlike Lavinheta or Daguí, he was not a professor of Lullism, but rather a teacher who used Llull for constructing his own thought. Despite his problems with Calvinism and with Protestantism, it was mostly in Lutheran Universities (Marburg, Wittenberg, the Academia Julia at Helmstedt) where Bruno spread Lullism, both in his classes and in his writings.[77] Bruno's Lullism, due to its peculiarities, comprised different facets: Llull's Art, logic, medicine, and metaphysics.[78] His teaching at different European academic centers undoubtedly fostered interest in Llull's work in France and the Holy Roman Empire. He also left traces in Oxford and in other parts of England where Lullism spread as a doctrine of Hermeticism and Alchemy.[79] Bruno is the author most often included in an anthology of Lullian texts, edited by Strasbourg publisher Lazarus Zetzner (1551–1616) and frequently republished, which became the main instrument for spreading Lullian and pseudo-Lullian thought in the 17th century.[80] Bruno's work—along with that of Cornelius Agrippa and the school of Lefèvre d'Étaples–thus contributed to the cultivation of Lullian thought in Central Europe by authors such as Giulio Pace, a jurist and philosopher que taught law in various universities (Geneva,

75   Lorenzo Pérez Martínez, "Lulismo e inquisición a principios del siglo XVII," in *Perfiles jurídicos de la Inquisición española*, (ed.) J.A. Escudero (Madrid: 1989), 738–739.

76   Antonio Mercanti, *Il sommario del proceso di Giordano Bruno* (Vatican City: 1961), 106; Rafael Ramis Barceló, "El proceso inquisitorial a Dom. Placido Perilli: contexto y nuevos documentos," *Revista de la Inquisición* 20 (2016): 63–88.

77   Ingrid D. Rowland, *Giordano Bruno: Philosopher/Heretic* (Chicago: 2009), 100–121.

78   Rossi, *Clavis Universalis*, 109–123.

79   Frances A. Yates, *Giordano Bruno and the Hermetic Tradition* (London: 1964); Michela Pereira, *The Alchemical Corpus Attributed to Raymond Lull* (London: 1989).

80   Anthony Bonner, "El lul·lisme alquímic i cabalístic i les edicions de Llàtzer Zetzner," *Randa* 27 (1990): 99–111.

Heidelberg, Montpellier, Nimes), even though his interest in Lullism, it seems, was not the objective of his teaching.[81]

Among the teachers that taught an eclectic pseudo-Lullism were Paracelsus, who taught at the University of Basel, and Cornelius Agrippa. From the end of the 16th century forward, Paracelsus' works and the editions of Zetzner fostered the production of manuals and commentaries on pseudo-Lullian alchemical and medical works, which were the subjects of academic debates. I have not been able to document any professor that held a chair of Lullism on medical, magical and hermetic subjects, although there were professors who used pseudo-Llull in their lectures. That said, commentaries and references to the alchemist Llull spread widely from the 16th to the 18th centuries.

In particular, it is important to note that during the 16th and 17th centuries, at universities in the center of Europe, there was a battle among different methods that sought a universal scope. Specifically, there was a confrontation among the Aristotelian, Lullist, and Ramist methods. While most professors aligned more with Peter Ramus and Philip Melanchthon's Aristotelian-Ramist vision, Llull was popular for his complexity. With the exception of Agrippa and Bruno, there were few Central European teachers that adopted Lullism as a point of departure for the construction of their own thought. Central European Lullism remained marginalized, a para-university, rather than a university, doctrine.[82]

12.5   Encyclopedism and the Enlightenment

The brothers Carreras i Artau argued that Hispanic Lullism in the 17th century contracted into the Majorcan chairs and the Franciscan Order.[83] This

---

81   Rafael Ramis Barceló, "Giulio Pace (1550–1635): humanismo jurídico, ramismo y lulismo," in *Historia y Derecho: Estudios dedicados al profesor Santos Coronas* (Oviedo: 2014), 1325–36.

82   Grazia Tonelli Olivieri, "Ideale lulliano e dialettica ramista: le 'Dialecticae Institutiones' del 1543," *Annali della Scuola Superiore di Pisa* 32 (1992): 885–929; Anthony Bonner, "El arte luliana como método, del Renacimiento a Leibniz," *Constantes y fragmentos del pensamiento luliano: Actas del simposio sobre Ramon Llull en Trujillo, 17-20 septiembre 1994,* (eds.) Fernando Domínguez and J. de Salas, (Tübingen: 1996), 161–172; Anita Traninger, "The Secret of Success: Ramism and Lullism as Contending Methods," in *Ramus, Pedagogy and the Liberal Arts: Ramism in Britain and the Wider World,* (ed.) S.J. Reid and E.A. Wilson (Aldershot: 2011), 113–131; Rafael Ramis Barceló, "Nuevas perspectivas para la historia del lulismo: referencias lulianas desconocidas en textos impresos del siglo XVI," *Antonianum* 90 (2015): 583–606.

83   Carreras i Artau, *Historia de la filosofía española*, 2:271.

century in fact saw the creation of Lullian chairs in the *Studium generale* of Majorca and the establishment of a Lullian education for students on the island. The *Studium generale* was able to obtain royal and pontifical privileges that gave it the authority to grant all degrees and it began to function as a University from 1692.[84] Its chairs formally taught Lullian philosophy and theology.[85] They promoted the fact that the Majorcan students could have a complete Lullian formation, which had started in grammar schools (Palma, Randa, Monti-Sion) and continued as the core of the university. They developed a broad plan of study that replaced the traditional logic, ethics and metaphysics of Aristotle with others that cultivated the texts of Llull. At the same time, theology was to be studied systematically. Thus, beginning in the 17th century, a Lullian scholasticism appeared on Majorca,[86] ready for academic study.

The Pontifical College of La Sapiencia on Majorca was the nucleus where the most prominent Majorcan Lullists were educated. Founded by the canon Bartomeu Llull (1565–1634) in 1633, it was conceived for training priests and for the diffusion of Lullian doctrines.[87] In 1567, a will had provided for creation of a chair of Lullian philosophy, supported by the guild of Saint Peter and Saint Bernard. This chair led an apparently erratic existence due to the lack of prepared teachers and students, but I do see, since the establishment of the College of La Sapiencia, a continuity in the Lullist schools and the training of many generations of Lullists. The *Studium generale*, once converted into a University, enjoyed protection of its secular and regular clergy. Its faculty included not only secular and Franciscan clergy, who had always favored Lullism, but also Mercedarians, Augustinians, Carmelites, Cistercians, and Minims. Only the Dominicans displayed criticism, which became stronger until it reached its height in the 18th century.

At the beginning of the 17th century, the Franciscans accepted a doctrinal openness that included study of the texts of Duns Scotus and Ramon Llull; they also sought Llull's canonization at Rome (the *Causa Pia Lulliana*), which allowed for fluid contact between Rome and Majorca. In fact, an edict inaugurating a chair of Lullism exists in the Franciscan Convent in Palma from 1600. The evolution of the convent chair has not been studied to date, but it coincides

---

84   Lladó Ferragut, *Historia del Estudio General Luliano*, 61.
85   Rafael Ramis Barceló, "Las cátedras lulianas de la Universidad de Mallorca (1692–1830)," *Bolletí de la Societat Arqueològica Lul·liana* 70 (2014): 185–205; and Albert Cassanyes Roig and Rafael Ramis Barceló, "Los grados en teología luliana en la Universidad de Mallorca (1692–1824)," *Bolletí de la Societat Arqueològica Lul·liana* 71 (2015): 93–127.
86   Sebastián Trias Mercant, *Filosofía y Sociedad: Una ecología del neolulismo* (Palma: 1973).
87   Rafael Ramis Barceló, "El Pontificio Colegio de la Sapiencia de Mallorca durante el siglo XVII: constituciones y colegiales," *Historia de la educación* 33 (2014): 167–192.

with the time period of the greatest splendor of Majorcan Franciscan Lullism. Within this context arose contact (the fruit of Daguí's ideas) between Majorcan Lullism, European Lullism, and the resurgence of Scotism. This effort included the works of Pere Fullana, who taught Lullism and left mystical commentaries, but above all the works of Francesc Marçal (1591–1688), a professor at Araceli in Rome and in the Convent of San Francisco on Majorca,[88] as well as an apologist and procurator of the *Causa Pia Lulliana*. His work displays an approach, stemming from Llull, to the modern logic proposed by Juan Caramuel and to the philosophical and theological positions of Scotus. Marçal's work as a teacher and a procurator was continued by Josep Hernández, an expert Lullist and Scotist.

Franciscan Lullism was a common current in the 17th century in the Hispanic kingdoms, France, and the Italian Peninsula. Together with Scotist Lullism, and more protection for teachers, there also existed tendencies that focused on the Art as an instrument of knowledge (or art of memory) and others of encyclopedic nature. Among those who studied the Art as an instrument were: the Franciscans Basile de Poligny (d. 1645), who focused on the Art as metaphysics, and Hugues Carbonel, who pursued a rhetorical-utilitarian vision in his *Artis Lullianae seu Memoriae artificialis secretum explicitum* of 1620; and the Carmelite Léon de Saint Jean (1600–1671), who promoted encyclopedism. No record remains of their Lullian teaching. The most representative encyclopedist was Yves of Paris (1588–1678), even though it is not known for a fact that he practiced Lullian teaching. Without a doubt, Yves of Paris greatly influenced later Lullists through his didactic elaboration of the Art,[89] in a moment when Lullism was well-known in France, as Descartes and Gassendi, among others, testify.

By contrast, the efforts in teaching of Italian Franciscans are well known. The Capuchin monk Vittorio da Palermo (d. 1635) was a reader in Philosophy and Theology at the University of Palermo, offering a late Lullian synthesis.[90] He apparently first made contact with Lullism in Valencia. Also worthy of mention is the Capuchin monk Ruffini of Nonsberg (1672–1749), reader in Theology, who learned about Llull indirectly and attempted to write a synthesis of Sabunde's theology with Scholastic Theology.[91] Last, and perhaps more important, I must

---

88   Sebastián Trias Mercant, "El lulismo barroco y fray Francisco Marçal," *Cuadernos Salmantinos de Filosofía* 16 (1989): 107–125.

89   Cesare Vasoli, "El 'Digestum sapientiae' di Yves di Parigi," *Revista di filosofia neo-scolastica* 70 (1978): 245–265.

90   Marta M.M. Romano, "Vittorio da Palermo commentatore di Lullo: un *link* tra Sicilia e Catalogna (con note sul fondo lulliano della Biblioteca Centrale della Regione Siciliana)," *Il mediterraneo del '300: Raimondo Lullo e Federico III d'Aragona, re di Sicilia, Omaggio a Fernando Domínguez Reboiras*, (eds.) Alessandro Musco and Marta M.M. Romano, Subsidia Lulliana 3 (Turnhout: 2008), 467–484.

91   Jaume de Puig i Oliver, "Un lul·lista sibiudià modern: Juvenal Ruffini de Nonsberg (Juvenalis Ananiensis)," *Arxiu de Textos Catalans Antics* 12 (1993): 394–405.

mention Luigi Sabatini, who taught Metaphysics at the University of Bologna. These three authors can be considered "of Lullian orientation": they tried to integrate Llull's doctrines into the framework of encyclopedic rationalism in their works.

Lullian encyclopedism spread very little in Spain and the influence on universities was very limited. One stand-out is the aforementioned Agustín Núñez Delgadillo (1570–1631), who published a defense of Llull's Art in Alcalá. In Aragon, a certain interest in Llull is documented among the nucleus of authors familiar with his work, such as Pedro Sánchez de Lizárazu, who traveled to Italy and returned to Spain, writing and spreading an eclectic Lullism. Also noteworthy is Francisco José de Artiga (1650–1711), professor of Mathematics at the University of Huesca, who was significantly interested in Llull's rhetoric and combinatory art. Artiga served as a bridge between declining Renaissance Humanism and the Enlightenment.

Parallel to the Franciscan line was the interest in Llull among Scholastic philosophers and theologians, evident in numerous Lullian references from their commentaries on Peter Lombard and Saint Thomas in the 17th century. Specifically, through the references of Francisco Suárez and Gabriel Vázquez to Llull's works, Jesuits knew of the Illuminated Doctor and took a very critical stance toward him.[92] Among the Jesuits, there were true specialists on Llull, such as Sebastián Izquierdo (1601–1681), who taught at Alcalá and Madrid, and Athanasius Kircher (1602–1680), who taught in Rome. Izquierdo and Kircher disassociated Llull from Scholasticism, integrated him into the encyclopedism of their time, and influenced other erudite Jesuits such as Gaspar Knittel (1644–1702) and Gaspar Schott (1608–1666).[93] At the same time, their Lullian affinity allowed them to open pathways in mathematics and logic, which resulted in numerous writings with great influence on European authors.

Other authors of philosophy and theological scholasticism, especially the Carmelites and Minims in France and the Benedictines in Spain, made frequent reference to Lullian thought in the 17th and 18th centuries. They integrated these references into scholastic manuals that still have not been deeply studied. Among the French Minims were Jean Lalemandet (1595–1647),

---

92   Aloisius Madre, *Die theologische Polemik gegen Raimundus Lullus: eine Untersuchung zu den Elenchi auctorum de Raimundo male sentientium* (Münster: 1973), 86–146; Rafael Ramis Barceló, "La presencia de Ramon Llull en la filosofía escolástica del siglo XVII," *Argumenta Philosophica* 2 (2016): 51–68.

93   Kircher's Lullism seems posterior to his teaching in the Roman College (1633–1646). See Paula Findlen, *Athanasius Kircher: The Last Man Who Knew Everything* (London: 2004), 11. All of Kircher's thought can be understood as a revision of Lullism, although without direct application to teaching, opting instead for indirect discussion of the development of mathematics, linguistics, and the experimental sciences.

Emmanuel Maignan (1601–1676), and Pierre de Rians (1672–1750), the author of an introduction to Llull's Art. Among these authors, we nonetheless find no evidence of teaching with a Lullian orientation.

However, while Lullism was waning in Southern Europe, due to frequent problems with the Inquisition, it was alive and healthy in Central Europe, mostly among the Lutherans and Calvinists. Lullism was introduced by Johann Heinrich Alsted (1588–1638) in the Hohe Schule Herborn, a para-university institution in which he was first a student and later a professor of philosophy and theology. The Hohe Schule Herborn was one of the most important Calvinist academic institutions that promoted an ambitious program of theological humanism.[94]

Alsted conceived of an encyclopedism that integrated Aristotle, Ramus, and Llull, among other authors.[95] His intellectual eclecticism had enormous repercussions on rationalism in Central Europe and his influence lasted until the 18th century. Alsted combined his teaching duties with his editorial labors. In collaboration with the editor Lazarus Zetzner, he re-edited Lavinheta and published some unedited works by Giordano Bruno.[96] His efforts to publicize Llull were the reason that the hermetic-Lullian syntheses were known throughout Central Europe and in Transylvania, where he was a professor at the University of Weissenburg. Alsted's most important disciples were J.A. Comenius (1592–1670) and Johann Heinrich Bisterfeld (1605–1655), who was also a professor at Weissenburg. While it cannot be said that Comenius became a professor in centers of university or para-university rank, Lullian influence is undeniable in his pedagogical ideas, above all in his *Didactica magna, Schola pansophica*, and *Unum necessarium*.[97] Bisterfeld had a decisive influence on Leibniz's Lullism, above all during the years in which Leibniz was in Mainz.[98]

This interest in Llull crystalized in the last great Lullian school in the Holy Roman Empire, established at Mainz by the Catholic priest Ivo Salzinger

---

94   See Gerhard Menk, *Die Hohe Schule Herborn in ihrer Frühzeit (1584–1660)* (Wiesbaden: 1981), 274–281.

95   Aloisius Madre, "Raimundus Lullus und Johann Heinrich Alsted," *EL* 4 (1960): 167–178.

96   Howard Hotson, *Johann Heinrich Alsted 1588–1638: Between Renaissance, Reformation and Universal Reform* (Oxford: 2000), treats the complex relationship between Alsted, Lullism, and millenarianism.

97   Comenius and Kircher were, indirectly, the inspirations of Slavic Lullism, whose most important authors were K. Kuhlmann, A.N. Bialobodsky, and his student, A. Dennisov. It seems that Slavic Lullism did not have a teaching focus. See Eugeniusz Gorski, "Apuntes sobre el conocimiento de Ramon Llull en Polonia," *SL* 31 (1991): 41–52 and Vsevolod Bagno, "El lulismo ruso como fenómeno de cultura," *SL* 33 (1993): 33–44.

98   Leroy E. Loemker, "Leibniz and the Herborn Encyclopedists," *Journal of the History of Ideas* 22 (1961): 323.

(1669–1728). Before establishing the school, he had lived in in Düsseldorf, as a chaplain to the court elector Johann Wilhelm, whom he convinced to promote and finance an edition of Llull's works. Salzinger was capable of taking rationalist ideas and opening himself up to new science, without renouncing alchemical Lullism. Trias Mercant describes him as "a perfect illuminated man, since he knows the classical, Semitic, and modern languages, while also mastering theology, philosophy, physics, and mathematics."[99] The principle objective of this school was the study of Lullism, and as a first step, they needed to publish the complete works of Llull. Salzinger managed to publish three volumes, but the project remained incomplete. Due to various circumstances, his disciples were not able to finish his undertaking. Salzinger's private teaching assumed that his students already had a solid philosophical and theological formation. To expand and specify his Lullian explanation, Salzinger discussed with his students some mystical readings, including authors such as Eckhart, Nicholas of Cusa, Albert the Great, Dietrich von Freiberg, Saint Teresa, and Johannes Tauler. He also expounded Lullian themes and taught Llull's Art as universal science, integrating it within the framework of Enlightenment ideas.[100]

Salzinger built his project in close connection with the teachers at the Lullian University, who tacitly recognized that his private lessons were at the para-university rank. The Lullian University named Salzinger a *Doctor honoris causa* in 1726 and around that time there came to study with him eight advanced students from the Majorcan university, who lived at the school with seven other German students. Among the Majorcan students were Antonio R. Pasqual (1708–1791), a Cistercian; the Fornés brothers, observant Franciscans; Bartomeu Rubí (1705–1774), also an observant; and Andreu Oliver, physician. Some of them studied with Salzinger during the last years of his life. Others did not know him personally, but did learn from his students Johann-Melchior Kurhummel, and Franz-Philipp Wolff,[101] who continued editing Llull's works. When the students returned to Majorca, all of them, in their time, became professors in their specialty at the Lullian University. Their work represented an opening of Lullism to the Enlightenment bubbling in Europe, by comparing Llull's thought to other authors. Even though Lullian logic prevailed at the Majorcan university, many schools of thought (Scotist, Thomist, Suarist) were allowed, making it easy to introduce new ideas from European authors. The Lullian University, despite its scholastic orientation, was reading Descartes, Gassendi, Hobbes, Locke, or Newton during the 18th century, even though

---

99   Trias Mercant, *Diccionari*, 389: "era un perfecto ilustrado, pues conocía las lenguas clásicas, semíticas y modernas, amén de dominar la teología, la filosofía, la física y la matemática."

100   Trias Mercant, *Diccionari*, 171.

101   Adam Gottron, *L'edició maguntina de Ramon Llull* (Barcelona: 1915).

these authors conflicted with the university's different schools of thought, especially the Suarist and the Lullist.[102]

The university environment at the Lullian University of Majorca was marked by the problem of the reception of modern philosophical doctrines, such as the struggle between philosophy and theology within the overall realm of knowledge. In the Lullian university doctrine, theology and philosophy formed part of the same structure of thought. In the works of Pasqual, Rubí, and the Fornés brothers, there was an eagerness to harmonize Lullism with thought and modern science. It was, according to Trias Mercant, a "Neolullism" that integrated Lullism into the issues of the era.[103] The other professors not educated at Mainz did not consider this opening to be a good one, and even less so the idea of alchemical Lullism. Majorcan Lullism was characterized by its similarity to Scotus and by its negation of alchemical works. The Mainz students, influenced by Salzinger, defended a "European integration" of Majorcan Lullism that demanded the acceptance of a universal science that "integrated" the empirical sciences. Consequently, those who studied with Salzinger accepted alchemy as a part of Lullian doctrine, whereas other Majorcan teachers were vehemently opposed to it. Lullian medicine as universal knowledge was defended by Andreu Oliver, a professor in the School of Medicine.

Lullism would probably have been reduced to teaching in the schools of Majorca and Mainz (and, of course, in some Franciscan convents) if two great Lullian polemical movements had not emerged in the 18th century: one in the Germanic region, which encompassed the zone that had historically been most receptive to Lullism (Mainz, Cologne, Bamberg, Frankfurt), and another in Spain and Portugal.

The Germanic polemic began in the middle of the century with the plan to publish some of the anti-Lullian works written by the Benedictine Andreas Gordon (1712–1751) and the Jesuit Michael Froehling in Mainz.[104] The dispute involved Johann Köchling from the Mainz circle, chaplain to the Court Elector. In 1742 an anonymous *Dialogus maguntinus* appeared from Miquel Fornés, a professor at the Lullian University who participated actively in the Lullian polemics at Mainz. At the same time, Sebastian Krenzer, a Jesuit, abandoned his order–which, in the German territories, unlike Majorca, did not support Llull's doctrines—and wrote a theological treatise refuting the theses of the

102   Sebastián Trías Mercant, "Las tesis filosóficas de la Universidad Luliana," *EL* 8 (1964): 191–214.

103   Trias Mercant, *Diccionari*, 16 and 432–433.

104   Anton P. Brück, "L'Institut lulliste de Mayence," *Studia Monographica et Recensiones* 14 (1955): 14–20.

anti-Lullists. The polemic ultimately involved Franz Philipp Wolff, another member of the Mainz school, who refuted the previous writings through a defense of Lullism as an improvement on traditional scholasticism.[105] Following the same line as Wolff, Honorius Cordier, a Franciscan from Cologne and reader in philosophy, also wrote that he was in contact with Pasqual to perfect his interpretation of Llull's works. In the end, Krenzer's work was banned. The Lullian debate contributed to Llull's vindication in the schools at a moment when the German Enlightenment was advancing toward criticism and to overcoming the rationalism of Leibniz and Wolff.

A similar debate took place in Spain, where the work of Francisco José de Artiga curiously led the way to a revival of hermetic Lullism. To stop it, the renowned Benedictine scholar Benito J. Feijóo (1676–1764), a professor at Oviedo, printed a piece openly attacking Lullism in 1742.[106] Feijóo spoke out against a theme he only tangentially knew, and his complete rejection of Lullism lacked even minimal documentation.[107] His attacks unleashed a wave of writings and responses that revived the debate about Lullism among professors and scholars in Spain and Portugal. The Lullist professors and all of the Franciscan Order spoke out against Feijóo. Antonio R. Pasqual was his main critic and wrote many works denying all of his ideas. The polemic between the two came to such extremes that it involved a large part of the Spanish intellectuals of the time. The Capuchin Luis de Flandes was a central figure in the polemic against Feijóo. He was a reader in Theology at Valencia and wrote numerous Lullian treatises. Thanks to his Lullian ardor, he convinced the General of the Capuchins to authorize the teaching of Lullism and to establish a chair of Lullism in the Capuchin convent at Palma. This was another "convent school" on Lullism, whose first professor was Fray Bernardino of Majorca.[108] The chair was solemnly inaugurated in April of 1758 and its existence is documented until the end of the century. At the same time, the Capuchin interest in Llull can be traced through the 17th century in convents at Valencia and Barcelona.

During the same period, Pere Vaquer, an observant Franciscan and professor of Scotist theology at the Lullian University, defended Scotist and Lullist conclusions. Bartomeu Fornés (b. 1691), a doctor at the University of Salamanca, was evidently named professor of Hebrew and reader in theology

105   Gottron, *L'edició maguntina*, 98.
106   Benito J. Feijóo, "Sobre el arte de Raimundo Lulio," *Cartas eruditas* 22 (Madrid: 1742).
107   García M. Colombàs, "Feijóo y el lulismo," *EL* 7 (1963): 113–130.
108   Andreu de Palma, "Els fra-menors caputxins i el Beat Ramon Lull," *Estudis Franciscans* 47 (1935): 8–9.

at the University.[109] There he established a parallel Lullian nucleus[110] and in the city of Tormes he published in 1742 a Castilian translation of Llull's *Doctrina Pueril*, along with an apologetic exposition of the *Ars Magna*. Meanwhile, especially during the mid-18th century, there was a proliferation of scholastic and scientific writing that defended Llull.[111] Some wished to remove Llull and Lullism from the schools, while others wanted to use them to develop an authentic and renewed encyclopedia of knowledge.

According to Feijóo, Lullism was a doctrine already surpassed by modern science, while for Pasqual, it represented a suitable base to achieve enlightened knowledge. Manuel do Cenáculo (1724–1814) became involved in the polemic, and for him, Lullism was a framework for organizing the philosophical and scientific thought of the time.[112] Cenáculo, a Franciscan Tertiary, later promoted to bishop, was one of the most educated men in Portugal. An implacable critic of Scholasticism, he was a defender of public instruction and study of the sciences and humanist disciplines, as well as a supporter of the mathematical sciences, logic, and empirical realism. Cenáculo's reformist ideals had a Lullian base, but never came to fruition. During the Napoleonic invasion, Cenáculo was condemned and imprisoned. He represented the decline of Portuguese Lullism, an important component of Peninsular Lullism that had remained since the end of the Middle Ages.

The end of Lullism in Spain was brought on by King Charles III (1716–1788), a proponent of Thomism and royalism, and not a fan of extravagances. The king's anti-Jesuit views, and those of his ministers, implemented vigorously after his ascension to the throne in 1759, caused the Lullian University to lose some of its most distinguished professors with the expulsion of the Jesuits from Spain in 1767. In Majorca, there began an anti-Lullian, anti-Jesuit initiative that ended with elimination of the "Lullian" denomination of the University.[113] Bishop Juan Díaz de la Guerra dismissed Lullian devotion, delivering a hard blow to university Lullism. Professors Pasqual and Bartomeu Fornés,

---

109   Trias Mercant, *Diccionari*, 171–172.

110   Joan Santanach, "La Magúncia de Salzinger i altres records lul·lians de fra Bartomeu Forners," *SL* 47 (2007): 151.

111   Miguel Ángel Álvarez Soaje, "Antonio y Anselmo Arias Teixeiro: Dos lulistas gallegos en el siglo de la Ilustración," Ph.D. Dissertation, University of Santiago de Compostela, 2012.

112   Francisco da Gama Caeiro, *Frei Manuel do Cenáculo: Aspectos da sua actuação filosófica* (Lisbon: 1959).

113   Rafael Ramis Barceló, "En torno a la supresión del connotativo 'luliana' de la denominación histórica de la Universidad de Mallorca," *Memòries de la Reial Academia mallorquina d'Estudis Genealògics, Heràldics i Històrics* 21 (2011): 103–119; Francisco José García Pérez and Rafael Ramis Barceló, "Un conflicto universitario y los orígenes de la represión antiluliana del obispo Juan Díaz de la Guerra en el seminario de Mallorca," *Studia Historica: Historia Moderna* 37 (2015): 323–350.

already elderly men, reacted against the attack with apologetic works that vindicated Lullism as a form of universal knowledge. Without the Jesuits and with frequent attacks from the Dominicans, Lullism had nothing more than a feeble university life in its future. Study of the works of the Illuminated Doctor would not be the basis for the reformation of knowledge, but rather a simple philosophical-theological culture for certain sectors of the clergy.

Among some professors of Lullism at the end of the eighteenth and beginning of the 19th century we can detect a certain turn toward eclectic positions. Their Lullism already formed part of the historical baggage that served to confront other social and cultural questions of the time. They were specialists in the material, but there was no communion or identification with Llull's ideas, as there had been with Marçal, Fornés, and Pasqual. The Literary University of Majorca was closed in 1830 and converted into a Conciliar Seminary. Llull's ideas remained in the diocesan seminary and in the Colegio de la Sapiencia, where they survived somewhat longer.[114]

12.6   Conclusions

The study of university and school Lullism complements the history of the transmission of texts and ideas. It offers a more institutional idea of Lullism, based on circles of teachers and disciples, which helps to formulate an idea about the presence of and changes in Lullism in European institutions of education. Since it has not been a well-studied topic until now, there are certain terminological and conceptual confusions (such as the definition of "chairs" and "schools"), rooted in historiography, that I have tried to correct at the beginning of this chapter.

We can now clarify these concepts and also draw some general conclusions about the academic configurations of European Lullism. We can confirm that, in the centers where Lullist authors were already well-known (Paris, the eastern Holy Roman Empire, Northern Italy, Rome, Majorca, Valencia, Barcelona, Salamanca) there were more or less permanent educational establishments. If until now the ideological transmission based on textual transmission has not been studied in great detail, investigation of the academic centers and their institutional nature helps to understand the "intellectual traditions" of each school and city. In the grand scheme, European Lullism in the universities and schools can be divided geographically into two main threads: the northern, which encompassed France, the Holy Roman Empire, and Northern Italy; and the southern, which consisted of the Hispanic kingdoms, Rome, and Southern Italy.

---

114   Ramis Barceló, "Sobre la denominación," 257–259.

Southern Lullism had three main axes with continuous intellectual interactions: Paris, Venice-Padua, and the eastern Holy Roman Empire. It was distinguished by its eclectic and disconnected nature. The presence of Lullism in the schools and the universities was linked with other philosophical and scientific movements (Aristotelianism, Nominalism, Hermeticism) in which the figure of Llull was used in some way during intellectual debates. The Lullian collections at Paris (including Vauvert) and at the cities of Northern Italy guaranteed direct and continuous access to textual resources. In this eclectic landscape, the figures of Ramon Sibiuda, Emmerich van den Velde, Nicholas of Cusa, Jacques Lefèvre d'Étaples, Charles Bovelles or Johnn Heinrich Alsted stand out. The most stable Lullian schools were Herborn (eclectic) and Mainz (specifically Lullian, even though open to other disciplines and currents). With the exception of the Salzinger school, which was almost only one person, there were no institutionalized Lullist schools in the north of Europe. Rather, there were teachers who read and transmitted Llull within other systems of thought.

Southern Lullism also had important axes in Majorca, Valencia, and Barcelona, which extended in nearby regions to Alcoy, Huesca, and Zaragoza; westward to Alcalá, Salamanca and Portugal; and eastward to Rome and Southern Italy, principally Sicily. This Lullism was intimately connected with Scotism and its institutional presence was much more stable. The universities, the para-universities, and the Franciscan convents were a framework within which Lullism could advance. The Lullists of the Crown of Aragon prior to Daguí, which included nearly all the teachers from the School of Barcelona, Valencia, and the *Studium generale* of Majorca, supported an interpretation of Llull that was very close to Scotism. The sounds of harmony between Aristotelianism and Lullism were growing fainter at the end of the 16th century. However, the Scotist-Lullist readings maintained strength in the heart of the Franciscan family, which then expanded to the convents of the Italian and Iberian peninsulas.

At the end of the 16th and 17th centuries, there was a multiplication of writings about Llull in four directions: scholastic, encyclopedic, medical-alchemic, and the study of his Art. While the first is a resource for information about the nature of Lullism in schools and universities, the others only provide a glimpse of Llull in manuals and treatises written for students and "initiates."

In the end, during the 18th century, academic Lullism was confined to the Lullian University in Majorca, (the only one that had specific chairs of Lullism), to the Franciscan Order (which had created convent chairs), and to the school of Mainz, along with other isolated scholastic teachings, which indicated an interest in Lullism among educated ecclesiastical circles of Jesuits, Benedictines, and Minims.

Salzinger wanted to read Llull from the context of the Enlightenment, which gave rise to an enlightened, eclectic, and alchemical Lullism that was different from the Scoto-Lullist principles of the Fransciscans and the Lullian University. In the eastern Holy Roman Empire and in the Hispanic kingdoms, the last pro- and anti-Lullian debates occurred, while at the same time scholarly Lullist historiography began. During the 19th century Lullism became a cultural substratum to be studied historically. At that time, it ceased to be a live doctrine and came to be recognized as an important, long-standing current of European thought.

This chapter has only begun to synthesize some ideas, to propose an institutional perspective on the history of Lullism and to show many areas that need further attention. The current vigor of university research on Lullism and the pace of publication surrounding the topic indicates that this chapter should be revised very soon. Lullism clearly remains a viable and necessary subject of academic study.

Works Cited

Primary Works
Eymeric, Nicolau, *Diàleg contra els lul·listes* (Barcelona: 2002).

Feijóo, Benito J., "Sobre el arte de Raimundo Lulio," *Cartas eruditas* 22 (Madrid: 1742).

Gentile Fallamonica, Bartolomeo, *Canti,* (ed.) Giuseppe Gazzino (Genoa: 1877).

Secondary Works
Albareda, Anselmo Maria, "Lul·lisme a Montserrat al segle XVè: L'ermità Bernat de Boil," *EL* 9 (1965): 5–21.

Álvarez Soaje, Miguel Ángel, "Antonio y Anselmo Arias Teixeiro: Dos lulistas gallegos en el siglo de la Ilustración," Ph.D. Dissertation, University of Santiago de Compostela, 2012.

Amengual Batle, Josep, *El bisbe ermità de Miramar: Jaume Badia, exponent del lul·lisme mallorquí del segle XIV* (Palma: 2011).

Bagno, Vsevolod, "El lulismo ruso como fenómeno de cultura," *SL* 33 (1993): 33–44.

Barceló Crespí, María, "Agnès de Pacs i l'entorn humanista," *Memòries de l'Acadèmia d'Estudis Genealògics, Heràldics i Històrics* 10 (2000): 21–47.

Bataillon, Marcel, *Erasmo y España* (Mexico: 1966).

Batllori, Miquel, "El lul·lisme a Itàlia: un esbós de síntesi," in *Ramon Llull i el Lul·lisme*, Obra completa 2 (Valencia: 1993), 221–335.

Beltrán de Heredia, Vicente, "La teología en nuestras universidades del Siglo de Oro," in *Miscelanea Beltrán de Heredia*, vol. 4 (Salamanca: 1973), 439–466.

Bonner, Anthony, "El arte luliana como método, del Renacimiento a Leibniz," *Constantes y fragmentos del pensamiento luliano: Actas del simposio sobre Ramon Llull en Trujillo, 17-20 septiembre 1994*, (eds.) Fernando Domínguez and J. de Salas, (Tübingen: 1996), 161–172.

Bonner, Anthony, "El lul·lisme alquímic i cabalístic i les edicions de Llàtzer Zetzner," *Randa* 27 (1990): 99–111.

Brann, Noel L., *Trithemius and Magical Theology: A Chapter in the Controversy over Occult Studies in Early Modern Europe* (Albany: 1999).

Brück, Anton P., "L'Institut lulliste de Mayence," *Studia Monographica et Recensiones* 14 (1955): 1–32.

Carreras i Artau, Joaquín and Tomás, *Historia de la filosofía española: Filosofía cristiana de los siglos XIII al XV*, 2 vols. (Madrid: 1939–1943).

Cassanyes Roig, Albert and Rafael Ramis Barceló, "Los grados en teología luliana en la Universidad de Mallorca (1692–1824)," *Bolletí de la Societat Arqueològica Lul·liana* 71 (2015): 93–127.

Colombàs, García M., "Feijóo y el lulismo," *EL* 7 (1963): 113–130.

Colomer i Pous, Eusebi, *De la Edad Media al Renacimiento: Ramon Llull, Nicolás de Cusa, Juan Pico della Mirandola* (Barcelona: 1975).

Colomer i Pous, Eusebi, "Nicolau de Cusa i el lul·lisme europeu quatrecentista," *Randa* 27 (1990): 71–84.

Cruz Pontes, José María da, "Raimundo Lulo e o lulismo medieval portugués," *Biblos* 62 (1986): 51–76.

Díaz Díaz, Gonzalo, *Hombres y documentos*, 7 vols. (Madrid: 1980–2003).

Díaz Marcilla, Francisco José, "I lullismi: ambiti tematici d'interesse a confronto," in *Ramon Llull und Nikolaus von Kues: Eine Begegnung im Zeichen der Toleranz*, (eds.) E. Bidese et al. (Turnhout: 2005), 227–245.

Díaz Marcilla, Francisco José, "El hilo luliano de la madeja cultural castellana medieval: Nuevos aportes al lulismo castellano medieval laico y religioso," in *Knowledge, Contemplation, and Lullism. Contributions to the Lullian Session at the SIEPM Congress – Freising, August 20-25, 2012*, (ed.) José Higuera Rubio, Subsidia Lulliana 5 (Turnhout: 2015), 165–190.

Domínguez Reboiras, Fernando, "La recepción del pensamiento luliano en la Península Ibérica hasta el siglo XIX: Un intento de síntesis," *Revista de lenguas y literaturas catalana, gallega y vasca* 15 (2010): 361–385.

Fernández Luzón, Antonio, *La Universidad de Barcelona en el siglo XVI* (Barcelona: 2005).

Findlen, Paula, *Athanasius Kircher: The Last Man Who Knew Everything* (London: 2004).

Fioretino, Francesco, "Il lullismo in Veneto: Glosse alla *Lectura* di Bolons sullo sfondo del cenacolo quattrocentesco di Fantino Dandolo," in *Il Lullismo in Italia: itinerario storico-critico*, (ed.) Marta M.M. Romano (Palermo: 2015), 239–255.

Gama Caeiro, Francisco da, *Frei Manuel do Cenáculo: Aspectos da sua actuação filosófica* (Lisbon: 1959).

García Oro, José, *El Cardenal Cisneros: Vida y empresas*, 2 vols. (Madrid: 1993).

García Pérez, Francisco José and Rafael Ramis Barceló, "Un conflicto universitario y los orígenes de la represión antiluliana del obispo Juan Díaz de la Guerra en el seminario de Mallorca," *Studia Historica: Historia Moderna* 37 (2015): 323–350.

Gorski, Eugeniusz, "Apuntes sobre el conocimiento de Ramon Llull en Polonia," *SL* 31 (1991): 41–52.

Gottron, Adam, *L'edició maguntina de Ramon Llull* (Barcelona: 1915).

Hernando i Delgado, Josep, "Escoles i programes acadèmics a la Barcelona del segle XV: L'escola de mestre Ramon Llull i l'ensenyament de disciplines gramaticals i d'arts," *Acta historica et archaeologica mediaevalia* 20–21 (1999–2000): 633–662.

Hillgarth, Jocelyn N., *Ramon Llull i el naixement del lul·lisme* (Barcelona: 1998).

Hillgarth, Jocelyn N., *Readers and Books in Majorca, 1229–1550,* 2 vols. (Paris: 1991).

Hillgarth, Jocelyn N., "Some notes on Lullian Hermits in Majorca saec. XIII-XVII," *Studia Monastica* 6 (1964): 299–328.

Hotson, Howard, *Johann Heinrich Alsted 1588–1638: Between Renaissance, Reformation and Universal Reform* (Oxford: 2000).

Imbach, Ruedi, "Theologia Raymundi Lulli memoriter epylogata," *EL* 23 (1979): 185–193.

Johnston, Mark D., "Sacrum Studium: The Lullist School of Fifteenth-Century Barcelona," in *Homenaje a Alberto Porqueras Mayo* (Kassel: 1989), 385–400.

Lladó Ferragut, Jaime, *Historia del Estudio General Luliano y de la Real Universidad Literaria de Mallorca* (Palma: 1973).

Llinarès, Armand, "Le lullisme de Lèfevre d'Etaples et ses amis humanistes," in *Colloque International de Tours (XIV stage)* (Paris: 1973), 127–136.

Loemker, Leroy E., "Leibniz and the Herborn Encyclopedists," *Journal of the History of Ideas* 22 (1961): 323–338.

Lohr, Charles, "Die Überlieferung der Werke Ramón Llulls," *Freiburger Universitätsblätter* 78 (1982): 13–28.

Madre, Aloisius, "Raimundus Lullus und Johann Heinrich Alsted," *EL* 4 (1960): 167–178.

Madre, Aloisius, *Die theologische Polemik gegen Raimundus Lullus: eine Untersuchung zu den Elenchi auctorum de Raimundo male sentientium* (Münster: 1973).

Madurell Marimón, José María, "Antonio Sedacer, profesor de la escuela luliana de Barcelona," *Analecta Sacra Tarraconensia* 17 (1947): 1–66.

Madurell Marimón, José María, "La Escuela de Ramón Llull de Barcelona; sus alumnos, lectores y protectores," *EL* 6 (1962): 187–209.

Madurell Marimón, José María, "Luis Juan Vileta," *Analecta Sacra Tarraconensia* 37 (1964): 19–76.

Menéndez Pidal, Ramón, *Historia de España* (Madrid: 1935).

Menk, Gerhard, *Die Hohe Schule Herborn in ihrer Frühzeit (1584–1660)* (Wiesbaden: 1981).

Mercanti, Antonio, *Il sommario del proceso di Giordano Bruno* (Vatican City: 1961).

Palma, Andreu de, "Els fra-menors caputxins i el Beat Ramon Lull," *Estudis Franciscans* 47 (1935): 5–24.

Pardo Pastor, Jordi, "El cercle lul·lià de València: Alonso de Proaza i Joan Bonllavi," *Zeitschrift für Katalanistik* 14 (2001): 33–45.

Pardo Pastor, Jordi, "El lulismo hispánico del trescientos," in *Ramon Llull, caballero de la fe: El arte luliana y su proyección en la Edad Media* (Pamplona: 2001), 111–127.

Pereira, Michela, *The Alchemical Corpus Attributed to Raymond Lull* (London: 1989).

Pereira, Michela, "Bernardo Lavinheta e la diffusione del Lullismo a Parigi nei primi anni del '500," *Interpres: Rivista di Studi Quattrocenteschi* 5 (1984): 242–265.

Perarnau i Espelt, Josep, "El lul·lisme de Mallorca a Castella a través de València: Edició de l'Art abreujada de confessió,'" *Arxiu de Textos Catalans Antics* 4 (1985a): 61–172.

Perarnau i Espelt, Josep, "Sobre mestre Antonio Sedacer i l'ambient de l'Escola Lul·liana de Barcelona," *Estudios Históricos y Documentos de los Archivos Protocolarios* 7 (1979): 132–153.

Perarnau i Espelt, Josep, "La traducció castellana medieval del 'Llibre de Meravelles' de Ramon Llull," *Arxiu de Textos Catalans Antics* 4 (1985b): 7–60.

Pérez Martínez, Lorenzo, "El maestro Daguí y el lulismo mallorquín de fines del siglo XV," *EL* 4 (1960): 291–306.

Pérez Martínez, Lorenzo, "Lulismo e inquisición a principios del siglo XVII," in *Perfiles jurídicos de la Inquisición española*, (ed.) J.A. Escudero (Madrid: 1989), 727–752.

Pinto Crespo, Virgilio, "La censura inquisitorial, inquietud e incertidumbre: el caso de Ramon Llull (1559–1610)," in *Miscelánea de la Universidad Autónoma de Madrid* (Cantoblanco: 1982), 293–314.

Puig i Oliver, Jaume de, "El 'Dialogus contra lullistas' de Nicolau Eimeric, O.P. Edició i estudi," *ATCA* 19 (2000): 7–296.

Puig i Oliver, Jaume de, "Documents inèdits referents a Eimeric i al lul·lisme," *Arxiu de Textos Catalans Antics* 2 (1983): 369–381.

Puig i Oliver, Jaume de, "Un lul·lista sibiudià modern: Juvenal Ruffini de Nonsberg (Juvenalis Ananiensis)," *Arxiu de Textos Catalans Antics* 12 (1993): 394–405.

Puig i Oliver, Jaume de, "El procés dels lul·listes valencians contra Nicolau Eimeric en el marc del Cisma d'Occident," *Boletín de la Sociedad Castellonense de Cultura* 56 (1980): 297–388.

Ramis Barceló, Rafael, "Aristotelismo, lulismo y ramismo en Barcelona durante el siglo XVI: Joan-Lluís Vileta y sus discípulos," *Cauriensia* 10 (2015): 385–407.

Ramis Barceló, Rafael, "Las cátedras lulianas de la Universidad de Mallorca (1692–1830)," *Bolletí de la Societat Arqueològica Lul·liana* 70 (2014): 185–205.

Ramis Barceló, Rafael, "En torno a la supresión del connotativo 'luliana' de la denominación histórica de la Universidad de Mallorca," *Memòries de la Reial Academia mallorquina d'Estudis Genealògics, Heràldics i Històrics* 21 (2011): 103–119.

Ramis Barceló, Rafael, "En torno al escoto-lulismo de Pere Daguí," *Medievalia* 16 (2013): 235–264.

Ramis Barceló, Rafael, "Un esbozo cartográfico del lulismo universitario y escolar en los Reinos Hispánicos," *Cuadernos del Instituto Antonio de Nebrija* 15 (2012): 61–103.

Ramis Barceló, Rafael, "La filosofía luliana en la universidad durante los siglos XV y XVI," *Anuario filosófico* 49 (2016a): 177–196.

Ramis Barceló, Rafael, "Giulio Pace (1550–1635): humanismo jurídico, ramismo y lulismo," in *Historia y Derecho: Estudios dedicados al profesor Santos Coronas* (Oviedo: 2014a), 1325–56.

Ramis Barceló, Rafael, "Nuevas perspectivas para la historia del lulismo: referencias lulianas desconocidas en textos impresos del siglo XVI," *Antonianum* 90 (2015): 583–606.

Ramis Barceló, Rafael, "El Pontificio Colegio de la Sapiencia de Mallorca durante el siglo XVII: constituciones y colegiales," *Historia de la educación* 33 (2014b): 167–192.

Ramis Barceló, Rafael, "La presencia de Ramon Llull en la filosofía escolástica del siglo XVII," *Argumenta Philosophica* 2 (2016b): 51–68.

Ramis Barceló, Rafael, "El proceso de la Inquisición contra la lectura del Arte de Ramon Llull en la Universidad de Zaragoza (1610)," *Hispania Sacra* 66, extra 1 (2014c): 131–160.

Ramis Barceló, Rafael, "El proceso inquisitorial a Dom. Placido Perilli: contexto y nuevos documentos," *Revista de la Inquisición* 20 (2016c): 63–88.

Ramis Barceló, Rafael, "Sobre la denominación histórica de la Universidad de Mallorca: cuestiones institucionales e ideológicas en torno al lulismo," *Cuadernos del Instituto Antonio de Nebrija de Estudios sobre la Universidad* 13 (2010): 237–263.

Ramis Barceló, Rafael and Pedro Ramis Serra, "'Comentaria in Artem magnam et paruam' de Agustín Núñez Delgadillo: un curso luliano manuscrito del siglo XVII," *Cuadernos salmantinos de filosofía* 43 (2016): 33–54.

Romano, Marta M.M., "I Canti di Bartolomeo Gentile Fallamonica (1450–1510/20): Poesia, scienza e studio di Lullo," *PAN: Studi del Dipartimento di Civiltà Euro-Mediterranee e di Studi Classici, Cristiani, Bizantini, Medievali, Umanistici* 24 (2008): 273–299.

Romano, Marta M.M., "Il primo lullismo in Italia: tradizione manoscritta e contesto della Lectura di Joan Bolons," *SL* 47 (2007): 71–115.

Romano, Marta M.M., "Quale incontro tra Cusano e Lullo? Elementi per un paradigma di Lullismo," *Niccolò Cusano, l'uomo, i libri, l'opera: Atti del LII Convegno storico internazionale, Todi, 11-14 ottobre 2015* (Spoleto: 2016), 125–148.

Romano, Marta M.M., "Vittorio da Palermo commentatore di Lullo: un *link* tra Sicilia e Catalogna (con note sul fondo lulliano della Biblioteca Centrale della Regione Siciliana)," in *Il mediterraneo del '300: Raimondo Lullo e Federico III d'Aragona, re di Sicilia, Omaggio a Fernando Domínguez Reboiras*, (eds.) Alessandro Musco and Marta M.M. Romano, Subsidia Lulliana 3 (Turnhout: 2008), 467–484.

Romano, Marta M.M. (ed.), *Il Lullismo in Italia: itinerario storico-critico* (Palermo: 2015).

Rossi, Paolo, *Clavis universalis: Arti mnemoniche e logica combinatoria da Lullo a Leibniz* (Milan and Naples: 1960).

Rowland, Ingrid D., *Giordano Bruno: Philosopher/Heretic* (Chicago: 2009).

Sanahuja, Pedro, "La enseñanza de la teología en Lérida: *Cátedras* regentadas por maestros franciscanos (siglos XIV-XV)," *Archivo Ibero-Americano* 38 (1935): 418–448.

Santamaría, Ángel, *La promoción universitaria en Mallorca* (Palma: 1983).

Santanach, Joan, "La Magúncia de Salzinger i altres records lul·lians de fra Bartomeu Forners," *SL* 47 (2007): 141–174.

Santi, Francesco, "Episodis de lul·lisme genovés a les acaballes del segle XIV: la confluencia amb l'ockhamisme," *Randa* 27 (1990): 57–69.

Schmitt, Charles B., *Aristotle and the Renaissance* (Cambridge, Mass.: 1983).

Soler, Albert, "Joan Bonllavi, lul·lista i editor eximi," in *Estudis de Llengua i Literatura Catalanes: Miscel·lània Germà Colón*, vol. 4 (Barcelona: 1995), 125–150.

Stöhr, Johannes, "Stephan Bodeker, O. Praem, Bischof von Brandenburg und Raimundus Lullus," *EL* 4 (1960): 191–201.

Tonelli Olivieri, Grazia, "Ideale lulliano e dialettica ramista: le 'Dialecticae Institutiones' del 1543," *Annali della Scuola Superiore di Pisa* 32 (1992): 885–929.

Traninger, Anita, "The Secret of Success: Ramism and Lullism as Contending Methods," in *Ramus, Pedagogy and the Liberal Arts: Ramism in Britain and the Wider World*, (eds.) S.J. Reid and E.A. Wilson (Aldershot: 2011), 113–131.

Trias Mercant, Sebastià, *Diccionari d'Escriptors lul·listes* (Palma: 2009).

Trias Mercant, Sebastià, *Filosofía y Sociedad: Una ecología del neolulismo* (Palma: 1973).

Trias Mercant, Sebastià, *Història del pensament a Mallorca* (Palma: 1985).

Trias Mercant, Sebastià, "El lulismo barroco y fray Francisco Marçal," *Cuadernos Salmantinos de Filosofía* 16 (1989): 107–125.

Trias Mercant, Sebastià, "Las tesis filosóficas de la Universidad Luliana," *EL* 8 (1964): 191–214.

Van der Poel, Marc, *Cornelius Agrippa, The Humanist Theologian and His Declamations* (Leiden: 1997).

Vasoli, Cesare, "El 'Digestum sapientiae' di Yves di Parigi," *Revista di filosofia neo-scolastica* 70 (1978): 245–265.

Victor, Joseph M., *Charles de Bovelles, 1479–1553: An Intellectual Biography* (Paris: 1978).

Victor, Joseph M., "Charles de Bovelles and Nicholas de Pax: Two Sixteenth-Century Biographies of Ramon Llull," *Traditio* 22 (1976): 313–345.

Worstbrock, Franz Josef (ed.), *Die deutsche Literatur des Mittelalters: Deutscher Humanismus 1480–1520*, Verfasserlexikon 1 (Berlin: 2008).

Xirau, Ramón, *Introducción a la historia de la filosofía* (México: 2009).

Yates, Frances A., *Giordano Bruno and the Hermetic Tradition* (London: 1964).

Zambelli, Paola, *L'apprendista stregone: astrologia, cabala e arte lulliana in Pico della Mirandola e seguaci* (Venice: 1995).

CHAPTER 13

Llull in Seventeenth-Century England

Roberta Albrecht

13.1   Introduction

The influence of Ramon Llull (1232–1316?) upon seventeenth-century English culture can be traced in four separate but related areas: linguistics, science, music, and Reformed millenarianism. Llull's thought was refitted to suit the age, and the common denominator was a quest for harmony. Linguists sought to invent an artificial universal language which would be free from the ambiguities inherent in natural languages and which could be more easily and quickly learned than Latin. The new science demanded that all natural phenomena be catalogued in encyclopedic form, categorized, and, by the inductive process, attached to some recognizable and intelligible unified principle. Music, which already had harmony, needed to be made easier to master. Reformed millenarians sought to resolve the dissonance between Christians and Jews, a necessary prerequisite to the Apocalypse. Theorists in all disciplines employed Lullian constructs to define harmony. Seventeenth-century poets and writers of prose reflect this concern in poems, sermons, devotions, and essays.

All these endeavors were dependent upon an art of memory. Almost without exception, these thinkers employed Llull's mnemotechnics. English linguists and philosophers—Francis Bacon, John Wilkins, William Petty, Samuel Hartlieb, George Dalgarno, Cave Beck, and Robert Boyle—joined others on the Continent—René Descartes, Theodore Haak, Jan Amos Comenius, Sebastian Izauierdo, Jean d'Aubry, Johann Heinrich Alsted, and Gottfried Wilhelm Leibniz—in an effort to develop an *ars memoria* compatible with the new science and with new developments in logic and rhetoric. Alsted's *Clavis artis lullianae* (1609) and *Panacea philosophica seu ... de armonia philosophiae aristotelicae lullianae et rameae* (1610) are evidence that early in the century Lullian mnemotechnics remained influential in spite of the pseudo-Lullian charlatanry that sometimes, like a lamprey, attached itself to it.

Those who demand neatness and order—those who insist upon an orderly progression of ideas from beginning to middle to end—should try to avoid the 17th century, which is an era marked (or marred) by contrary forces moving in different directions simultaneously. Paolo Rossi's assessment is apt: "[A]round 1600 the English intellectual was more than half medieval and around 1660

© KONINKLIJKE BRILL NV, LEIDEN, 2019 | DOI:10.1163/9789004379671_014

he was more than half modern."[1] Many seventeenth-century intellectuals, men like Robert Fludd (1574–1637) and Athanasius Kircher (1601–1680), insisted that medieval magic remain central to any system of thought. Paracelsus, to whom "Lullian medical theories were known,"[2] developed from these some intriguing concepts of how natural phenomena corresponded with divine principles. Sometimes, in fact, Paracelsus's work was confused with Llull's.[3] Paracelsus's theory of *tria prima*, for example, attributed to sulfur, salt, and mercury a triadic spiritual analogue, echoing what Anthony Bonner calls "the ternary phase" of Llull's Art that was so popular during the Renaissance.[4] Possibly Paracelsus's *tria prima* derived from Llull's *Arbor scientiae*, which examines the triangle, a symbol of divine unity, as a shape "nearer to the soul of man and to God the Trinity" than other shapes.[5] Other intellectuals resisted this fascination with outmoded superstition, urging a program that deciphered and rearranged natural phenomena in more logical (in the sense of early modern logic) and scientific ways. Blaise Pascal (1623–1662), in true Lullian fashion, insisted that seemingly chaotic phenomena could be "sorted out, analyzed, [and] related to each other." For this purpose, he devised a triangular array of binomial coefficients—not unlike Llull's concept of triangle—organizing all information in his treatise, *Traité du triangle arithmétique* (1653). Hence, Pascal joined others—Copernicus, Kepler, and Galileo—who, like Llull before them, sought to bring "order out of chaos."[6] Magic and early modern science coexisted throughout the era, even as late as 1687, when Caspar Knittel published his exposition of the rules of the *combinatoria* (a dissertation on magic), the same year that Isaac Newton published his *Principia*. This coincidence demonstrates the intellectual schizophrenia of the age. Llull (or pseudo-Llull) sits squarely in the middle of both camps.

How the spiritual logic and *ars combinatoria* of Ramon Llull became such a compelling influence throughout this period, at least in England, is an intriguing question. Johann Heinrich Alsted (1588–1638) complained about "the

---

1   Paolo Rossi, *Francis Bacon: From Magic to Science*, trans. Sacha Rabinovitch (Chicago: 1968), x.

2   Frances Yates, "The Art of Ramon Lull: An Approach to it through Lull's Theory of the Elements," *Journal of the Warburg and Courtauld Institutes* 17 (1954): 166. For examples of Paracelsian thought in Donne, see Roberta Albrecht, *The Virgin Mary as Alchemical and Lullian Reference in Donne* (Selinsgrove, Pennsylvania.: 2005), Ch. 4.

3   *Lists of Manuscripts Formerly Owned by Dr. John Dee: With Preface and Identifications*, (ed.) M.R. James (Oxford: 1921), 17. A manuscript catalogued as one by "Ramundi Lullii" is corrected as follows: "Non est Ramundi Lullii, sed collectanea diversa ex Paracelso."

4   Bonner, *AL* 19. For discussion of Paracelsus's medical theories, see Albrecht, *The Virgin Mary*, 96–97.

5   Frances Yates, *The Art of Memory* (Chicago: 1966), 183.

6   Manuel Duran, "Ramon Llull: An Introduction," *Catalan Review* 4 (1990): 12.

lack of vigour amongst German Lullists,"[7] evidence that German linguists, cosmographers, and logicians were atypical. In England, for example, Francis Bacon (1561–1626) seems to have appropriated certain features of Llull's spiritual logic for his new scientific method. Although Bacon derided pseudo-Lullist charlatanry, he nevertheless devised a system of scientific investigation that, Bonner observes, was "not without points of similarity to Llull's system"[8] in that it incorporated, for example, the Lullian triadic categories of beginning/middle/end, doubt/affirmation/negation, and superiority/equality/inferiority, which triads convey the idea that unity and diversity can be duly reconciled in harmony. The upshot is that both camps—those who insisted that memory serve magic and those who insisted that memory serve the new logic and the new science—proved by their work that the Lullist tradition of memory-aids, whatever form it assumed, was very much alive.

The emphasis here is placed on those intellectual reforms which developed Llull's thought in new and interesting ways. Readers interested in the phenomenon of pseudo-Lullism in the 17th century should consult the studies by Pereira and Linden.[9] One example of Llull's popularity among those many English enamored of alchemy is George Ripley's *The Compound of Alchemy* (1591). The Sloan collection, Linden observes, "includes at least eight manuscripts of the *Compound*, all of which are complete or nearly so and date from the 16th and 17th centuries."[10] Llull, he points out, was "Ripley's most frequently cited source."[11] Benjamin Farrington affirms this view, citing the first English translation of Henry Cornelius Agrippa of Nettesheim's *Three Books of Occult Philosophy* (1651) as evidence of "the hold magic still had on an educated public on the eve of the foundation of the Royal Society."[12]

This study concerns the various universal language schemes initiated by Bacon and later linguists, particularly those associated with the Royal Society. How these language projects developed in early modern culture is illustrated by English poets, beginning with Donne and ending with Dryden. As preface to the intellectual history and the poetry, a survey of seventeenth-century libraries

---

7   Paolo Rossi, *Logic and the Art of Memory: The Quest for a Universal Language*, trans. Stephen Clucas (New York: 2006), 131.

8   Bonner, *SW* 1:87.

9   Michela Pereira, *The Alchemical Corpus Attributed to Raymond Lull* (London: 1989); Stanton J. Linden, "Expounding George Ripley: A Huntington Alchemical Manuscript," *Huntington Library Quarterly* 61 (2000): 411–28, and "The Ripley Scrolls and *The Compound of Alchemy*," in *Emblems and Alchemy*, (eds.) Alison Adams and Stanton J. Linden (Sherborne, Dorset: 1998), 73–94.

10   Linden, "Expounding George Ripley," 413.

11   George Ripley, *George Ripley's Compound of Alchymy (1591)*, (ed.) Stanton J. Linden (Brookfield, Vermont: 2001), 109, n. 13.

12   Benjamin Farrington, *The Philosophy of Francis Bacon* (Chicago: 1966), 53.

explains how Llull's thought, and particularly his idea of the nine Dignities of God and principles relating to this schema, was disseminated.[13]

The famous library of Dr. John Dee (1527–1608) illustrates the importance of Llull in England. In addition to two copies of *Duodecim Principia Philosophiae* (dating from 1412 and 1417), he owned nineteen authorial works and numerous others attributed to Llull. The authorial works included: *Opera* (1421), *Arbor scientiae* (1415), *Ars brevis* (1424), *Ars demonstrativa* (undated), *Ars inventiva* (1408), *Ars magna* (1418), *Compendium artis demonstrativae* (undated), *Codicillus* (1403), *De regionibus sanitatis et infirmitatis* (1421), *Dialectica* (1411 and 1416), *In rhetoricen isagoge* (1414), *Janua artis Lulli* (1410 and 1423), *Liber principiorum medicinae* (1421), *Liber proverbiorum* (1409), *Mercuriorum liber* (1406), *Metaphysica nova* (1413), *Practica compendiosa artis* (1422), and *Testamentum* (1402).[14] This list indicates a wide range of subjects, all of which continued to compel the interest of seventeenth-century thinkers in England. In addition to Llull's own works and works attributed to him, Dee owned manuscripts and books by his imitators and disciples, including Giulio Camillo (ca. 1480–1544) and Agrippa von Nettesheim (1486–1535).[15] Anthony Bonner notes that Agrippa's commentary on Llull's *Ars brevis* "was printed fifteen or sixteen times between 1531 and 1651."[16] This is one way that ideas of such Lullists as Agrippa came to be appropriated by poets such as Henry Vaughan (1621–1695).[17]

When Dee died, Sir Symonds D'Ewes acquired many priceless manuscripts and books from his library. As part of an exchange, many of these were appropriated by Sir Robert Cotton (1586–1631), who added them to his own impressive collection. Eventually Cotton's library seems to have served as a sort of national library, in the sense that he freely loaned books and manuscripts to scholars and friends, among whom were Inigo Jones (designer of sets for Ben Jonson's masques), John Bond (the Somerset classical scholar), and Robert Fludd. Jonson, a near neighbour of Cotton's in Westminster, is noted in 1621 as having had "Aelfric's *Saxon Grammar* and the *Vita Henrici quinta per Titum*

---

13   Anthony Bonner, *AL* 126, cautions against confusing the terms "dignities" and "principles." "The word 'dignities,'" he says, at least in the ternary phase of Llull's thought, is "reserved for these principles when referred solely to the first subject, that of God." However, Renaissance thinkers, in post-Lullian fashion, may not have respected this distinction.

14   *John Dee's Library Catalogue*, (eds.) Julian Roberts and Andrew G. Watson (London: 1990), 220.

15   *The Private Diary of Dr. John Dee, and the Catalogue of his Library of Manuscripts, from the Original Manuscripts in the Ashmolean Museum at Oxford, and Trinity College Library, Cambridge*, (ed.) James Orchard Halliwell (London: 1842), Index I, n.p.

16   Bonner, *AL* 11.

17   Jonathan Nauman, "Herbert the Hermetist: Vaughan's Reading of *The Temple*," *George Herbert Journal* 17 (1993): 32.

Livium and a great boundell of Originall things of Hen. 5 unbound." Cotton even "lent books to Sir Walter Raleigh during his captivity in the Tower."[18] "Few," Kevin Sharpe observes, "were denied a visit to the books at Cotton's house."[19] These facts begin to indicate the range of Cotton's collection and the kinds of persons who took advantage of it. Since he corresponded with linguists working on the "new theory" of "the Adamic vernacular,"[20] it is not unreasonable to conclude that his library also contained works pertaining to it.

Cotton's library was destroyed by fire in 1731, one hundred years after his death. Some of what remained was in the hands of descendants of people who had borrowed books and manuscripts from Cotton but never returned them. Even were this not the case, tracking down the fate of Lullian texts in Cotton's library (or in the libraries of any other) is an extremely difficult task, especially where manuscripts (which were sometimes taken apart and then sewn back together according to subject or size) are concerned. Cotton himself was not averse to excising pages from various authors writing on the same subject and compiling them into a single work. This seems not to have been an unusual practice during a time when catalogues were designed to classify works in broad subject areas such as astronomy, music, mathematics, cosmography, dialectics, rhetoric, grammar, etc. Since Lullism was associated with all of these, works by Llull—his antecedents and his disciples—would have been nestled among these. Sometimes, however, works by Llull (and his antecedents and disciples) were catalogued in private libraries.

William Crashaw, father of the poet, owned the *Theologia naturalis* of the famous Lullist, Raymond of Sabunde (fl. 1432–1436).[21] Sabunde reinvented Llull's ladder image, from the *Liber de ascensu et descensu intellectus*, as the Great Chain of Being, an image that, like Llull's ladder, referenced the various levels of creation. This schema came to England via John Florio's translation of Montaigne's translation of Sabunde. Hence, E.M.W. Tillyard observes, Sabunde's Great Chain of Being (and Llull's ladder) became "the common property" of every Englishman.[22] Crashaw's large library had been set up near the Inner and Middle Temples in London, where he sometimes preached. After his death (in 1625 or 1626), the bulk of his collection was given to St. John's

---

18   Francis Wormald and C.E. Wright, *The English Library before 1700* (London: 1958), 203.

19   Kevin Sharpe, *Sir Robert Cotton, 1586–1631: History and Politics in Early Modern England* (New York: 1979), 74.

20   David Katz, *Philo-Semitism and the Readmission of the Jews to England, 1603–1655* (Oxford: 1982), 56.

21   P.J. Wallis, "The Library of William Crashawe," *Transactions of the Cambridge Bibliographical Society* 8 (1963): 226.

22   E.M.W. Tillyard, *The Elizabethan World Picture* (London: 1943), 27.

College, Cambridge. Included were two hundred manuscripts, now the core of that library's collection of medieval manuscripts.

Another example of Llull in private libraries is that of John Donne (1572–1631). Although Donne does not cite Llull directly, he cites his disciples—Agrippa, Raymond of Sabunde, Pico della Mirandola (1463–1494), and Johann Reuchlin (1455–1522). Moreover, Donne had first-hand knowledge of Llull's spiritual logic. Among his collection is Llull's *Duodecim Principia Philosophiae* (1516), bearing his signature and motto on the title page, and pencil markings in the margins.[23] Augmenting these private libraries were the commentaries of Johannes Paepp (1617 and 1619), one of which surveys *Ars memoriae*, a work by Lambert Schenkel, which, Paolo Rossi says, the young Descartes "knew well."[24] Finally, Llull's ideas were developed to fit the age as various logicians, linguists, and cosmographers collaborated, hammering out ways to resolve religious strife and social upheaval, and, at the same time, support the new science and the new philosophy.

Descartes openly admitted his debt to Llull, saying his system "was present in his mind when he conceived his new method of constituting a universal science."[25] Walter Ong adds that Bacon and Descartes inherited rather than invented their methodologies and ironically used them like bombardiers dropping explosives on vast "ammunition dumps, stocked by whole centuries of scholasticism."[26] Paepp himself was familiar with the Lullist tradition and with works by contemporary Lullists such as Alsted, whom Ong describes as one who had assimilated the doctrines of "Aristotle, Ramus, and Raymond Lully" in that he defined logic as "the art of knowing" and teaching as "the instrument of knowing."[27] Finally, Llull's pansophism and cosmography came to England in the form of a visitor.

In 1641–42 the Lullist, Jan Amos Comenius (1592–1670), visited England, where he exchanged ideas with linguists interested in developing a new universal language, a language that everyone, whatever his or her linguistic background, could read. One problem to be resolved was the question of images or characters. In less than a year, because of the Civil War, Comenius returned to the Continent, but not before giving to Samuel Hartlieb and John Wilkins his

---

23   Geoffrey Keynes, *A Bibliography of Dr. John Donne: Dean of Saint Paul's*, 4th ed. (Oxford: 1973), 271.

24   Rossi, *Logic and the Art of Memory*, 92. Bonner, *AL* xiii, notes that Descartes was also familiar with the pseudo-Lullian *In rhetoricam isagoge*, published at Paris in 1515.

25   Yates, "The Art of Ramon Lull,"166.

26   Walter Ong, S.J., *Ramus, Method and the Decay of Dialogue: From the Art of Discourse to the Art of Reason* (Cambridge, Mass.: 1983), 230.

27   Ibid., 160.

Via Lucis, a pansophical work (at this point in manuscript form) containing a program for the improvement of religion, society, and the arts and sciences. Wilkins's *Mercury* (1641), the first English textbook on cryptography, is evidence that Comenius had left behind more than a manuscript.

The debate over what kind of characters should be used continued both in England and abroad. Bacon urged the "use of hieroglyphics ... being held in veneration, especially among that most ancient nation, the Egyptians."[28] The purpose of this new universal language he declared to be "an antidote against the curse of Babel, the confusion of tongues."[29] He also warned against "rhetorical ornamentation," saying it hindered communication, "insisting that '*things* are better than words, as real understanding is beyond *elegancy of speech*.'"[30]

John Wilkins (1614–1672) agreed, thinking that the universal language should be reduced to the simplest ideas and things, sacrificing imagination. All that was vague, inaccurate, or ambiguous should be eliminated. His purpose, as stated in his dedicatory epistle to *An Essay Towards a Real Character, and a Philosophical Language* (1668), was to relieve mankind from "the Curse of the Confusion [suffered at Babel], with all the unhappy consequences of it." In order to accomplish this feat, he determined to reduce all things and notions to figures and tables, which "would prove the shortest and plainest way for the attainment of real Knowledge, that hath been yet offered to the World"[31] (see Figure 13.1).

Wilkins's agenda, however, differed from that of the earlier Bacon and Descartes in that he saw the purpose of the new universal language to be the encouragement of commerce. George Dalgarno (1626–1687) disagreed with Wilkins in that he wanted the universal characters to indicate abstract concepts or spiritual things, such as "wretchedness," "adoration," "praying," or "miracle."[32] Henry More (1614–87), who "deeply felt the spiritual threat of the widening gulf between traditional religion and the 'new philosophy,' i.e., science, and especially the new cosmology," joined Robert Boyle (1627–1691), offering "an alternative to the Bacon-Descartes line by elaborating a system

---

28   Francis Bacon, "The Advancement of Learning," in *The Physical and Metaphysical Works of Lord Bacon: Including his Dignity and Advancement of Learning, in Nine Books, and his Novum Organum*, (ed.) Joseph Devey and trans. William Wood (London: 1853), 216.

29   Ibid., 217.

30   Rossi, *Logic and the Art of Memory*, 167, quoting Bacon.

31   John Wilkins, *An Essay Towards a Real Character, and a Philosophical Language: A facsimile of the London edition* (London: 1968), sine pag.

32   Rossi, *Logic and the Art of Memory*, 166.

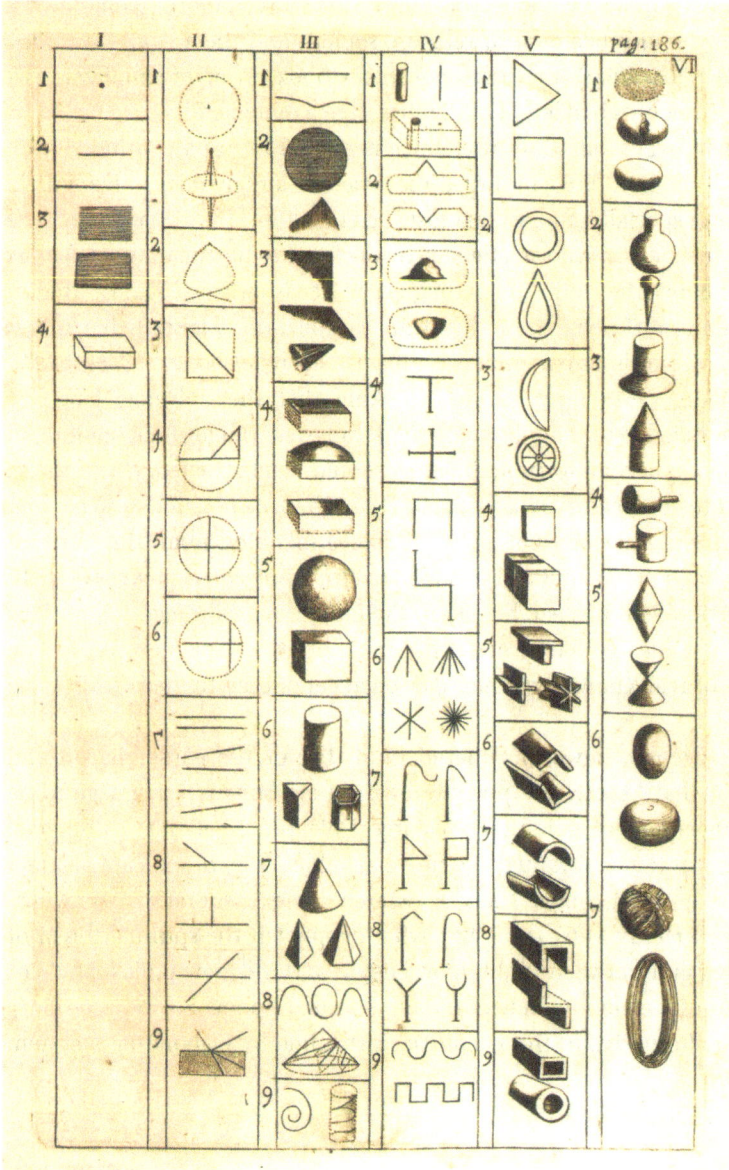

FIGURE 13.1   Shapes from John Wilkins's "Of Space" in *An Essay Towards a Real Character, and a Philosophical Language* (London: 1668), p. 186.

based on a more unified outlook."[33] Actually, Descartes, who was familiar with Agrippa's commentaries on Llull and had read Comenius's *Pansophiae Prodromus* (1639), agreed with Llull and Comenius "that there is a profound unity concealed beneath the apparent multiplicity of the sciences, a law of connection, a common logic which unites them."[34]

William Bedell (1571–1642), an English Comenian, emulated Wilkins in that he too devised an artificial language, which he called *Wit-Spell.* This language, Norman Vance explains, resembled "Raymond Lull's systematizing of all knowledge in terms of a universal symbolized set of divine attributes or perfections."[35] Like Dalgarno and More, Bedell meant his *Wit-Spell* to surmount language barriers in order to promote religious unity. His work was complete and the plates engraved when the 1641 Rebellion broke out. "In the ensuing confusion," Vance explains, "it seems that the manuscript fell into the hands of Franciscan friars who suspected heresy in a scheme to reverse the confusion of Babel and tore it up. The plates were used by tinkers to mend kettles."[36] The irony is that it was Franciscans who first disseminated Llull's art throughout the Western world.

Robert Boyle proposed that the "translinguistic character of mathematical symbols" be used to devise an artificial language "composed of real characters."[37] In this he emulated Llull's own preference for abstract (as opposed to corporeal) images. John Beale (c. 1608–1683), another member of the Royal Society, recommended "'mnemonical characters' … because of their ability to introduce order into all the possible combinations of letters, syllables and words."[38] Leibniz believed "that ideas are analysable, and … can be represented symbolically," adding that "figures of circles, squares and triangles, arranged in various ways, could be used to represent concepts and fundamental notions."[39] Eventually, he devised a language using the methods of algebra or symbolic logic.

These are but a few examples of how English linguists thought and what they hoped to accomplish, inspired by Llull's example. On the Continent, Comenius, Alsted, and Knorr von Rosenroth pursued similar projects.[40] Comenius's ideas about *ars memorativa*, Rossi notes, "had become closely associated

---

33   R.J. Zwi Werblowsky, "Milton and the Conjectura Cabbalistica," *Journal of the Warburg and Courtauld Institutes* 18 (1955): 93.

34   Rossi, *Logic and the Art of Memory*, 114.

35   Norman Vance, *Irish Literature: A Social History: Tradition, Identity and Difference* (Oxford: 1990), 29.

36   Ibid., 30.

37   Rossi, *Logic and the Art of Memory*, 152.

38   Ibid., 169.

39   Ibid., 177.

40   See Chapter 12 in this volume for a review of the work of Contintental Lullists.

with the revival of Lullism."[41] This revival took various shapes, including implementation of Llull's volvelle (discussed below), the millenarianism of Johann Heinrich Alsted (Comenius's teacher), and various concomitant attempts—to reconcile Christians with Jews, Catholics with Protestants, and Lutherans with Calvinists.

Because German and English linguists were in close contact during this period, it is impossible to ignore entirely contributions from Germans such as Adam Bruxius, whose mnemotechnical work, *Simonides redivivus sive ars memoriae et oblivionis* (Leipzig, 1610), Rossi observes, "was widely read in the 17th century."[42] Another German contribution to Lullian thought was Alsted's *Thesaurus chronologiae* (1624), which Howard Hotson describes as "one of his most popular works, not least in England and New England, where it remained a standard component of learned libraries into the 18th century."[43] The *Thesaurus*, Hotson says, is Alsted's version of "the *ars magna* of the medieval philosopher and mystic, Ramon Lull, and the bewilderingly complex mnemonic arts of the heretical ex-Dominican friar, Giordano Bruno."[44] Lord Herbert of Cherbury, brother of the poet, owned a copy.[45]

Most certainly, Joseph Mede (1586–1638), a fellow at Christ's College Cambridge and joint founder with Alsted of the Reformed millenarian tradition, transmitted Alsted's ideas to his students, among whom were John Milton and Henry More. Having designed a peculiar brand of millenarianism that emerged from his study of Llull's theories, Alsted's *Thesaurus chronologiae* was an attempt "to reduce the whole of history to circular [or cyclical] form"—similar to Llull's revolving devices meant to combine related concepts. Hotson explains how Alsted's system of thought resembles a kind of universal combinatorial machine: "The basic idea was simple [as simple as Llull's]: if all of knowledge could be reduced to a finite cycle of intellectual disciplines, if each of these disciplines could be reduced to a finite number of fundamental terms, and if these terms could be inscribed on a system of concentric circles, then the rotation of these circles would combine these fundamental terms with one another in all possible ways and thus yield knowledge of the whole of reality."[46] Alsted, Hotson says, employed this "historical wheel ... at least five times" in his

---

41   Rossi, *Logic and the Art of Memory*, 134.
42   Ibid., 189.
43   Howard Hotson, *Paradise Postponed: Johann Heinrich and the Birth of Calvinist Millenarianism* (Boston: 2000), 29.
44   Ibid., 76.
45   Ibid., 29, n. 90.
46   Ibid., 76.

writings.[47] Obviously he believed that men should learn to read the world (and its fluctuating circumstances) alongside the true Church (and its constancy). This way of understanding, he argued, would restore the world to health.

13.2   Seventeenth-Century Poetry and Prose

To what extent did such millenarian ideas influence early modern English culture? One way to answer this question is to study examples of seventeenth-century poetry and prose. Here are discovered some of the same Lullian themes—Babel, the problem of fragmentation, the importance of remembering names, the dignities of God, health, etc.

John Milton (1608–1674) ranks among Llull's antagonists. He once remarked disparagingly: "I am of those who believe it will be a harder alchemy than Lullius ever knew to sublimate any good use out of such an invention."[48] This barb, however, shows Milton's antipathy towards pseudo-Lullist charlatanry. Sometimes, like Bacon, Milton appropriates Lullian constructs of thought. In his treatise, "The Reason of Church Government," Milton argues that "all earthly things which have the name of good," represent "that knowledge that rests in the contemplation of natural causes and dimensions, which must needs be a lower wisdom," a wisdom that leads us "to know anything distinctly of God."[49] Merritt Hughes thinks Milton is alluding to Bacon's *Advancement*, "which distinguishes the knowledge of divine things from the knowledge that comes after 'the contemplation of God's creatures and works.'"[50] Indeed, this may be, but the way Milton frames his thought is very like Llull's. Mark D. Johnston has described Llull's predication and corresponding propositions as an analogical method whereby he could "express the basic role of identity and difference."[51] Such logical constructs lead to congruence with the divine principle, what Llull called *Sapientia*, one of nine dignities attributed to God. This kind of logical

---

47   Ibid., 77.

48   John Milton, *Areopagitica*, in *Complete Poems and Major Prose*, (*ed.*) Merritt Y. Hughes (Indianapolis: 1976), 725. Ben Jonson's *The Alchemist* (1610) also pokes fun at pseudo-Lullist charlatans: "What is that? A Lullianist? a Ripley? *Filius artis*? Can you sublime and dulcify? Calcine?" (2.5, ll. 7–10).

49   Milton, "Church Government," in *Complete Poems and Major Prose*, 665.

50   Hughes, *Complete Poems and Major Prose*, 665, n. 147, suggests that, like Bacon, Milton also is distinguishing the knowledge of divine things from the knowledge that comes after "the contemplation of God's creatures and works."

51   Johnston, *SL* 74.

construct seems to lurk behind Milton's distinction between "lower wisdom," which is "imperfect," and the higher wisdom "of God."

The sources for Llull's names of his divine dignities cannot be exactly determined. Among them are "John Scotus Erigena, Algazel, the Jewish *sephiroth*, and Islamic *hadras* (Divine Attributes)."[52] Johnston cautions that Llull may not have followed any particular model, but Moshe Idel, as Frances Yates before him, thinks that "Lull was [probably] influenced by Christian Neo-Platonic sources such as Pseudo-Dionysius."[53] Bonner observes that the divine names of the sixth-century Pseudo-Dionysius the Areopagite could join Islamic *hadras* and the Jewish *sephiroth* as "something that would set up resonances with the three religions": Christianity, Judaism, and Islam.[54] Certainly Llull was in a position to appropriate from these (and others) his own theory of names that correspond to the attributes of God. Among John Dee's manuscripts was *Maximi Monachi* by Pseudo-Dionysius.[55] Certain seventeenth-century texts, both poetry and prose, indicate continuing interest in Pseudo-Dionysius's system of divine names.

Richard Crashaw (ca. 1613–1649) cites (or otherwise seems to allude to) Pseudo-Dionysius in his poems. Crashaw entered Pembroke Hall at Cambridge on 6 July, 1631, but he did not formally matriculate until 1632. He received his B.A. in 1634 and became a fellow at Peterhouse in 1635. In fact, it may be argued that the organizing principle of his poem "In The Glorious Epiphanie of our Lord" is the restorative power of "The right-ey'd Areopagite" (l. 192). And "Hymn in the Assumption" expresses the Pseudo-Dionysian and Lullian doctrines that names are invested with Power: "never let goe/ Thy gracious name" (l. 39).

The earlier Donne also celebrates the importance of God's name in the *Devotions*, using the Lullian concept of *contrarietas* in order to conclude that "These [plaguey] spots are but the letters, in which thou hast written thine owne Name, and conveyed thy selfe to mee."[56] In the *Sermons* he cites Pseudo-Dionysius on the subject of names, declaring "His Knowledge, his Wisdome, his Power, his Mercy, his Justice, all his Attributes are alwayes manifested in all his works."[57] Since Donne owned a copy of *Duodecim Principia Philosophiae*,

---

52   Ibid., 19. See Chapters 4 and 5 in this volume for detailed analysis of this question.

53   Moshe Idel, "Ramon Lull and Ecstatic Kabbalah: A Preliminary Observation," *Journal of the Warburg and Courtauld Institutes* 51 (1988): 170.

54   Bonner, *AL* 284.

55   *Lists of Manuscripts Formerly Owned by Dr. John Dee*, 17.

56   John Donne, *Devotions Upon Emergent Occasions*, (ed.) Anthony Raspa (Montreal: 1975), 70.

57   *The Sermons of John Donne*, (eds.) George R. Potter and Evelyn M. Simpson, 10 vols. (Berkeley: 1953–1962), 3: 212.

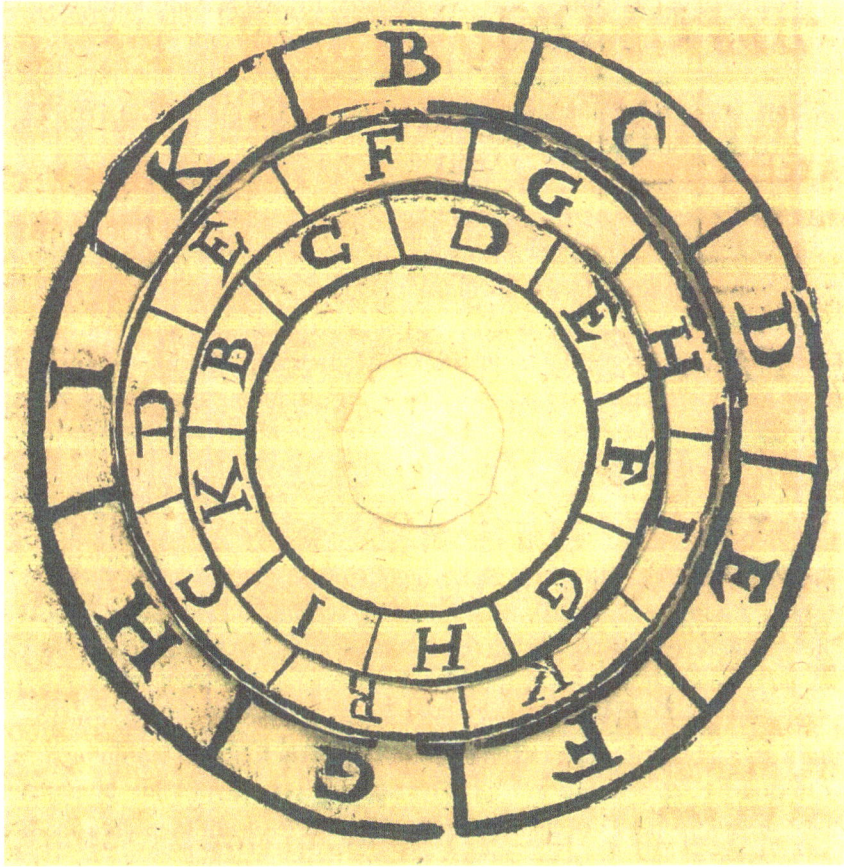

FIGURE 13.2   Figure Four (with moveable inner circles) from Ramon Llull, *Opera omnia*
(Strasburg: 1609), s. p.

it is not unreasonable to understand this list of divine attributes as references
to Llull's Dignities and to infer that Donne's visual imagination included Llull's
volvelle device (see Figure 13.2).

Donne's *Essays* refer to the power invested in names that are meant "to
instruct us, and express natures and essences. This *Adam* was able to do."[58]
He seems to have had in mind some version of Llull's system of names when
he distinguishes the same name for God among "the *Turk* almost as Misti-
cally as the Hebrew, in *Abgd*, almost ineffably."[59] Donne thus embraces Llull's
original agenda, an agenda that dovetails with seventeenth-century Reformed

---

58   *Essays in Divinity*, (ed.) Evelyn M. Simpson (Oxford: 1952), 23.
59   Ibid., 24.

millenarianism, that three religions—Christianity, Islam, and Judaism—join as one true church, a church founded on the same Name.

George Herbert (1593–1633) also develops this theme, using Llull's nine *Dignities* as an organizing principle in his famous poem, "The Pulley." The wit of Herbert's poem resides in "Rest," which is eternal rest or Llull's *Aeternitas*. Herbert distinguishes, even emphasizes, Llull's dignities when he lists seven of them-- "rest" (l. 10), "goodnesse" (l. 19), "strength" (l. 6), "beautie," "wisdom," "honour," "pleasure" (l. 7)--the last of which may be interpreted in the Freudian sense as the pleasure of exercising one's will. That Herbert slyly omits "the rest," which is the other two--truth (or *Veritas*) and greatness (or *Magnitudo*)--is witty. Herbert expects his savvy readers to supply these missing two. He also expects them to understand the coessential relationship among the nine *Dignities*. Rest can only be had, he argues, when man remembers its coessential others: *Bonitas, Magnitudo, Potestas, Sapientia, Voluntas, Virtus, Veritas,* and *Gloria*.[60] "The Pulley" is Herbert's most overt celebration of Llull's spiritual logic.

A more subtle exercise by Herbert are "Easter-wings I" and "Easter-wings II." The first concerns Llull's universal principle of the "Lord, who createst man in wealth and store" (l. 1). Written into that "wealth and store" are all of the coessential attributes, an apt survey of who God is. The second poem is personal (as opposed to universal) in that it articulates the speaker's relation to that divine principle. Without God, the speaker admits, he is "Most thin" (l. 5). But if he is able to "imp my wing on thine" (l. 9), then he will "combine" (l. 7) with God--and, by implication, all of his attributes--in perfect harmony. Since these are companion poems, Herbert seems to have meant them as a version of Llull's corresponding propositions, identity and difference. Herbert's "combine" expresses congruence with God in the same way that Milton's distinction between imperfect and higher wisdom does.

As mentioned above, Raymond of Sabunde was among Llull's later disciples, and seventeenth-century writers sometimes cite him. Donne, for example, says of Sabunde's *Theologia naturalis* that "*Sebund*, when he had digested this book into a written book, durst pronounce, that it was an Art, which teaches al things, presupposes no other, is soon learned, cannot be forgotten, requires no books, needs no witnesses, and in this, is safer then the Bible it self, that it cannot be falsified by Hereticks."[61] Sir Thomas Browne (1605–1682) pulls on the same thread when he praises Sabunde's work of "natural theologie, demonstrating therein the Attributes of God, and attempting the like in most points

---

60   Roberta Albrecht, "'The Pulley': Rundles, Ropes and Ladders in John Wilkins, Ramon Lull, and George Herbert," *The George Herbert Journal* 30 (2006–07):14.

61   Donne, *Essays*, 7.

of Religion."[62] Such comments as these illustrate how Llull's spiritual logic and divine attributes continued to grip the seventeenth-century imagination.

Further evidence of Llull's influence during the period can be found in the work of Thomas Traherne (ca. 1636–1674). He does not name Llull as his model, but *Centuries of Meditations* proves that Llull's volvelle device, or something very like it, remained a memory aid, even late in the period:

> For as there is an immovable Space wherin all finit Spaces are enclosed, and all Motions carried on, and performed: so is there an Immovable Duration, that contains and measures all moving Durations. Without which first the last could not be ... All Ages being but successions correspondent to those Parts of the Eternitie wherin they abide ... the infinit immovable Duration is Eternitie, the Place and Duration of all Things ... the Cause and End.[63]

The "immovable ... eternity" is the outer stationary ring of Llull's volvelle. For Traherne it represents God, the final cause, from which we reason backwards, which is the essence of Llull's spiritual logic. The other moving rings in Llull's volvelle are also here in the *Centuries*: "all finite spaces," "all motions," and "all moving durations." In order to understand natural things that are found in perpetual motion, Traherne says, we must look to an "immovable" God. As Donne and Herbert before him, Traherne celebrates the Lullian art as a way to get back to God.

Finally, late in the period, John Dryden (1631–1700) expresses a similar view in *Religio Laici: Or A Layman's Faith* (1682), where he argues that the most enlightened men "have been led/ From cause to cause, to nature's secret head" (ll. 12–13). This reference to Deism resembles Llull's vision in that both build upon the assumption that any non-Christian can attain salvation by means of his or her own conscience and reason. Edward Herbert, the first English deist, had adopted the same stance, claiming that no one religion can assume authority over others. Dryden's argument in *Religio Laici*, even his defense of Christianity, concedes the deist view that no religion can make sole claim to divine inspiration and authenticity. In this sense his thought concurs with Llull's idea of the Church universal, saying "that one first principle must be" (l. 14) to acknowledge "that UNIVERSAL HE" (l. 15).

---

62   Frank Livingstone Huntley, *Sir Thomas Browne: A Biographical and Critical Study* (Ann Arbor: 1968), 21.

63   Thomas Traherne, "The Fifth Centurie," in *Poems, Centuries and Three Thanksgivings*, (ed.) Anne Ridler (London:1966), 370.

Altogether, these voices argue for Llull's active and pervasive influence during the early modern period in England. Such texts as these show how wide-ranging was Llull's influence not only upon the new logic and the new science but also upon such disparate fields as theology, philology, poetry, and music. Although music may seem a strange field for Llull to land in, neither Jan Amos Comenius nor Johann Heinrich Alsted thought so.

13.3   Music and Llull

Anthony Bonner notes that "the *only* common medieval subject on which Llull wrote almost nothing was music."[64] One notable exception was Llull's definition of music in *Ars brevis*: "Music is the art devised to arrange many voices so that they be concordant in a single song."[65] It is perhaps significant that two early modern disciples of Llull—Comenius and Alsted—developed this theme. Comenius defined music as "the profound harmony which binds the universe together," adding that "God ... is the source of all harmony."[66] Perhaps this idea derived from his teacher Alsted's *Elementale Mathematicum: Templum Musicum* (Frankfurt, 1611), republished in translation in England in 1664.

Alsted says that "The first Cause [of music] is GOD the Author of all Symphony."[67] This is a Lullian way of reasoning backwards from the End (or the Final Cause) to the rest. "The second [Cause]," Alsted says, "is partly Nature, the Mother of all Sounds." "The ultimate End," he says, "is GOD that Archetype of Harmony."[68] Alsted's music theory is too long and complicated to review here, but some of his comments come teasingly close to theories expounded by those linguists engaged in the international language project.

Using the Egyptians and Greeks as his models, he proposes that aspiring musicians learn to consider "the seven *Voyces*" as they correspond to "seven *Vowells*," as well as to the "seven Planets."[69] He proceeds to explain what he calls the "Musical Trias," which "arise from three sounds and as many Dyads."[70] Having discussed "Trias," he next discusses what he calls "Compounded Melodie," which he compares to the "four humours," explaining that "Compounded

---

64   Bonner, *SW* 1: 623, n. 46.

65   Ibid., 1:623.

66   Rossi, *Logic and the Art of Memory*, 138.

67   Johann Heinrich Alsted, *Elementale mathematicum: Templum musicum: A facsimile of the Frankfort edition*, trans. John Birchensha (1664; repr. New York: 1967), 9.

68   Ibid., 10.

69   Ibid., 36–37.

70   Ibid., 55.

Melodie" is analogous to "the four Elements, *Earth*, *Water*, *Air*, and *Fire* ... For as a body mixed of four Elements, is a temperament of four humours: So every harmonical *Polyphony* doth arise from four simple *Melodies*."[71] It is significant that the traditional qualities—*caliditas*, *humiditas*, *frigiditas*, and *siccitas*—as suggested here, intermesh with Llull's system of correlatives, as well as with Llull's quaternary phase of thought.[72] Robert Pring-Mill explains how these correlatives function as "qualitative links" in Llull's web of *contrarietas* and *concordantia*.[73] In fact, Pring-Mill observes, Llull's "entire world-picture ... interlocks with ... the quaternity of the 4 elements."[74] Alsted employs this same construct of correlatives as a way to define harmony. He reserves discussion of his favorite musical instrument for last, declaring that "[T]he Lute is the chiefest of all Instruments of Musick."[75]

What is perhaps most intriguing about Alsted's music theory is the fact that he declares it to be a kind of memory-aid. Whereas the usual methods of musical training require "many Observations which burthen the Memory," he has changed what was heretofore "concealed and mysterious" into something "fully discovered." The usual methods are many and obscure, but he has made them "few and plain." A final note on this Lullian journey into music theory is Alsted's declaration that what has heretofore required "many years," may now, by this method, "be performed without any difficulty in a few Weeks, or Months at the farthest."[76]

Lord Herbert of Cherbury (1583–1648), a famous lutenist, was the brother of the poet (who also played the lute). Lord Herbert owned Alsted's *Thesaurus* (1628), so perhaps he also knew about Alsted's developing music theory. Francis Bacon sometimes visited the Herberts' Chelsea home, where he heard the brothers play their lutes and sing their songs.[77] The rest is surmise, except that Herbert's "Denial" depicts the soul as an instrument "Untun'd, unstrung" and is designed so that the rhyme is frustrated—until the end. The poem ends with a prayer that God "tune my heartless breast" so that "my mind may chime."

---

71   Ibid., 64.

72   For discussion of the techniques of Llull's quaternary phase, see Bonner *AL*, Chap. 2, and Chapter 4 in this volume.

73   Robert D.F. Pring-Mill, "The Role of Numbers in the Structure of the *Arbor scientiae*," in *Arbor scientiae der Baum des Wissens von Ramon Lull*, (eds.) Fernando Domínguez Reboiras, Pere Villalba Varneda, and Peter Walter (Turnhout: 2002), 60.

74   Ibid., 57.

75   Alsted, *Elementale mathematicum: Templum musicum*, 90–91.

76   Birchensha on Alsted, "To the Reader," *Elementale mathematicum: Templum musicum*, 10.

77   Cristina Malcolmson, "George Herbert and Coterie Verse," in *George Herbert in the Nineties: Reflections and Reassessments*, (eds.) Jonathan F.S. Post and Sidney Gottlieb (Fairfield, Connecticut: 1995), 163.

This prayer is answered when the divine principle becomes congruent with the human instrument, restoring harmony so that the "mind may chime" and "mend my rhyme."

13.4   The Jews in England

Gregory Stone observes that Llull's thinking was "marked by its celebration of diversity and its liberal tolerance."[78] One great obstacle to harmonizing the three religions, Llull realized, was the doctrine of the Trinity. Associated with this was another doctrine central to Christianity, the Incarnation. Neither were acceptable to Muslims and Jews. "Tactically," Anthony Bonner observes, "Llull knew full well that, along with the Incarnation, [the Trinity] was for Muslims and Jews the most controversial aspect of Christianity, and ... if he were incapable of proving it, his entire project would be destined for the scrap-heap."[79] Consequently, Llull devised a system of spiritual logic so abstract that anyone of any faith could accept all Christian doctrines, eventually.

Llull's *Liber predicationis contra Judeos*, for example, argued, by analogy, that the Christian God is also the God of the Jewish *sephiroth*. The Trinity, he said, encompasses all: "God, by understanding himself, conceives himself good, great, eternal, powerful, wise, willing, virtuous, true, and glorious."[80] The Incarnation, he said, is a manifestation of these same attributes distributed throughout Creation, and memory will sustain them: "In truth he has a Trinity such as memory, intellect, and will, and he also has unity, because all three are one God."[81] This theory, according to Pring-Mill, evolved (from a regrouping of four initial members) as Llull's "Trinitarian hylomorphic doctrine."[82]

By the time Llull's wheels rolled into the 17th century, his plan for the conversion of the Jews seems to have taken on other aspects. David Katz's study of philo-semitism during the period focuses on how Llull's art was embedded in the philosophical language systems being developed by such men as Descartes, Wilkins, and Comenius. Citing Yates and Rossi, Katz says that the efforts

---

78   Gregory B. Stone, "Ramon Llull vs. Petrus Alfonsi: Postmodern Liberalism and the Six Liberal Arts," *Medieval Encounters: Jewish, Christian and Muslim Culture* 3 (1997): 76.

79   Bonner, *AL* 286.

80   Llull, *El "Liber predicationis contra Judeos" de Ramón Lull*, (ed.) José M. Millás Vallicrosa (Madrid and Barcelona: 1957), 101: "Deus intelligendo seipsum concipit seipsum bonum, magnum, eternum, potentem, sapientem, volentem, virtuosum, verum atque gloriosum."

81   Ibid., 92: "Trinitatem vero habet sicut memoriam, intellectum et voluntatem, et unitatem etiam habet, quia omnes tres sunt unus Deus."

82   Pring-Mill, "The Role of Numbers," 59.

of such linguists as these "came straight out of the memory tradition with its search for signs and symbols to use as memory images." The "real characters" that they were developing, he observes, "originated with the magic images of occult tradition and in the art of Ramon Lull."[83] This marriage between philo-semitism and language is illustrated by the literature of the period. The position of Jews in England during the 17th century must be reviewed in order that the literature be understood.

James I was tolerant towards Jews, but Wilfred Prest records a notable exception. In 1621, Sir Henry Finch, the king's sergeant-at-law and a radical Calvinist millenarian, published a treatise, *The Calling of the Jewes*. This tract prophesied that one day England's king would be required to bow before a governor elected by the Jews.[84] James's response was swift and decisive: Finch was arrested. Evidently, toleration can be carried too far. Nevertheless, Joseph Mede, a popular teacher at Cambridge, was so impressed with Finch's book that, six years later, he published his famous *Clavis Apocalyptica*.[85]

Puritan leader Oliver Cromwell was also a realist. Consequent to the appointment of Abraham Wheelocke (1593–1653) as professor of Arabic and reader in Anglo-Saxon at Cambridge (a Puritan stronghold since the Hampton Court Conference of 1604), interest in the people of the Old Testament had burgeoned. In 1629 Wheelocke was appointed librarian of St. John's College, and in this capacity he supervised the addition of new materials, such as orientalia and works on the Apocalypse, among which were manuscripts and books formerly belonging to William Crashaw, whose library included such prophetic works as "Bede on the Apocalypse from Ramsey Abbey with outline drawings."[86] This renewed interest in Hebrew studies, Cromwell knew, demanded a tolerant stance towards Jews in England. In addition, Cecil Roth suggests, Cromwell's philo-semitism may have been somewhat tainted by his desire for "the protection and encouragement of English commerce."[87]

After the Restoration, Charles II demonstrated "good-natured indifference [towards] the Anglo-Jewish community."[88] When James II came to the throne, he "followed his brother's example, issuing an Order in Council" that allowed Jews to "enjoy the free exercise of their Religion, whilst they behave themselves

83   Katz, *Philo-Semitism*, 78.
84   Wilfred R. Prest, "The Art of Law and the Law of God: Sir Henry Finch (1558–1625)," in *Puritans and Revolutionaries: Essays in Seventeenth-Century History*, (eds.) Donald Pennington and Keith Thomas (Oxford: 1978), 108.
85   Katz, *Philo-Semitism*, 95.
86   Wallis, "The Library of William Crashawe," 226.
87   Cecil Roth, *A History of the Jews in England*, 2nd ed. (Oxford: 1949), 157.
88   Ibid., 182.

dutifully and obediently to his [Majesty's] Government."[89] This brief history indicates that, with few exceptions, Jews in England enjoyed a degree of freedom and general acceptance rare in the 17th century.

On the Continent, where (except for Holland) Jews were generally repressed, another haven was the intellectual center established at Sulzbach in 1666 by Pfalzgraf Christian August von Sulzbach (1622–1708). The "Sulzbach Simultaneum" granted equal rights to Protestants, Catholics, and Jews. In 1668 Christian Knorr von Rosenroth came to Sulzbach in order to study the Kabbalah, wherein (like Llull) he found proofs for the doctrine of the Trinity. Hence, Rosenroth joined other Lullists and Christian kabbalists—such as Pico and Reuchlin—who adduced "proof from kabbalistic texts for the Trinity and other Christological dogmas."[90] Of course, when Christian August von Sulzbach invited Jews to join the Sulzbach community, he anticipated their eventual conversion to Christianity.

13.5   The Jews as Subject of Literature in Seventeenth-Century England

How this Lullist agenda played out in England is illustrated in poetry and prose. Andrew Marvell's "To his Coy Mistress" argues that the speaker's lady should not demure until the "conversion of the Jews," for that (the implication is) will never happen. Other literature, however—Donne's *Essays* and the poetry of Herbert, Vaughan, and Dryden—shows a different stance. In fact, all four seem to agree that someday Jews will join Christians, worshipping the same God.

In the *Essays* Donne describes the Anglican Church as a church disunited from the Jews. Originally, he says, "[W]hen the Gentiles were assum'd into the Church, they entred into the same fundamentall faith and religion with the Jews ... One fold and one shepherd."[91] Now, he says, "though we branch out *East* and *West*, that Church concurs with us in the root, and sucks her vegetation from one and the same ground."[92] So, he continues, "Synagogue and Church is the same thing ... journying to one *Hierusalem*, and directed by one guide, Christ Jesus." This is Donne's way of expressing tolerance towards Jews, even as he anticipates reunion: "Even to such an Unity, I do zealously wish."[93]

---

89   Ibid., 183.
90   Werblowsky, "Milton and the Conjectura Cabbalistica," 92.
91   Donne, *Essays*, 49.
92   Ibid., 50.
93   Ibid., 51.

George Herbert, who resided at Cambridge during Wheelocke's tenure, continues this theme. Moreover, his poem, "The Jews," employs some overt Lullian principles, constructing an argument by means of Llull's modes of proposition—affirmation and negation, antecedence and consequence, and possibility and impossibility—that someday the Jewish and Christian faiths will merge. The problem, as Herbert explains it, is that Christians have stolen the essence of God from the Jews, leaving them poor: "Poor nation, whose sweet sap, and juice/ Our scions have purloin'd, and left you dry" (ll. 1–2). Hope, nevertheless, is written into these lines, mainly because "dry" is not "dead." Still, because the Apostles use these same stolen fluids, even "in baptism," the Jews are left in a condition so dire that they "pine and die." Discovering the cause of this problem will be a way of finding the solution.

Herbert offers the solution of Llull's "pattern of the Trinity," a pattern, Pring-Mill observes, that is "imprinted on Llull's universe in terms of the 'correlative' unfolding of the divine attributes."[94] The key to escape, Herbert's poem argues, is to remember "the letter" (l. 6), that divine dignity which will reconnect the Jews with God. The "letter" alludes to the "jot" and the "tittle" of Hebrew texts, not one of which, according to Jewish theology, can be eliminated from the law. Like Henry More after him and John Reuchlin before, Herbert argues that the Jews cannot afford to forget Christ, the fulfillment of the law. As More put it, "Christ is nothing but Moses unveiled."[95] As Reuchlin put it, "the penta-grammaton IHSUH fulfils and completes that which was only partially revealed in the kabbalistic letter-mysticism of the tri- and tetra-grammaton."[96] Herbert's "the letter" is a witty way of naming Christ the fulfillment of Jewish law and his way of completing Llull's Trinitarian universe. Forgetting that "jot" renders the Jew forever "a debter." The problem, "not keeping once" (l. 5), implies the solution.

The second stanza shows Herbert, like Donne, anticipating the reunion of Christians and Jews in one church. Whether Herbert had read Alsted's *Clavis artis lullianae* (1609) or his *Panacea philosophica seu*, etc. (1610) is unknown, but that he anticipates some apocalyptic event is indicated by the Angel's call: "Oh that some Angel might a trumpet sound; / At which the Church falling upon her face / Should cry so loud, until the trump were drown'd, / And by that cry of her dear Lord obtain, / That your sweet sap might come again!" (ll. 7–12). Although this last stanza is a prayer, Herbert intends that his prayer

---

94   Pring-Mill, "The Role of Numbers," 56.

95   More, quoted by Werblowsky, "Milton and the Conjectura Cabbalistica," 92–93.

96   Ibid., 93.

will be answered, that the Jews will yet possess the Trinity, will yet have their "sweet sap ... again!" (l. 12) Herbert was at Cambridge with both Bacon and Mede. This poem illustrates how some of their linguistic and millenarian programs crop up in his poems.

Henry Vaughan, who was among Herbert's imitators, writes in the same vein. By Vaughan's time, the end of the 17th century, the metaphysical style was being replaced by burgeoning Neoclassicism. So Vaughan represents a final flowering of his mentor. Like Herbert, Vaughan anticipated the conversion of the Jews: "When the fair year / Of your deliverer comes, / And that long frost which now benumbs / Your hearts shall thaw" ("The Jews," ll. 1–4), anticipates this prerequisite to the Apocalypse.

As might be expected, Vaughan emulates Herbert by referring to the same problem, that is, the need to convert "dry dust, and dead trees" (l. 13) to "living waters" (l. 12). And, like Herbert, Vaughan anticipates that time when he will "see the olive bear / Her proper branches! which now lie / Scattered each where, / And without root and sap decay" (ll. 14–17). The key to restoration is memory: "for old love / From your dark hearts this veil remove" (ll. 36–37). The veil to be removed is the veil that was rent when Christ died at Golgotha, but "From your dark hearts" alludes to failed memory. Hence Vaughan's prayer is that Jews, "the dear and chosen stock" (l. 39), will remember in order to be saved.

An interesting twist in this conciliatory speech is Vaughan's depiction of Christians as spiteful younger siblings, enjoying the defeat of their Jewish brothers and sisters on account of their "stony hearts" (l. 43): "ev'n the Gentiles then / Were cheered, your jealousy to move" (ll. 43–45). The poem ends with another prayer request: "Thus, righteous Father! ... thy gifts go round / By turns, and timely, and so heal / The lost son by the newly found" (ll. 46–49).

Donne's "The Canonization" imagines poets as architects who "build in sonnets pretty roomes." This metaphor is an apt vehicle by which to understand the presence of Lullism in early modern literature, whether it come in the form of the essay, devotion, poem, or sermon. Alsted, Bacon, Bedell, Comenius, Dalgarno, Dee, Descartes, Donne, Fludd, Herbert, Kircher, Leibniz, Mede, Paracelsus, Pascal, Vaughan, and Traherne—all are "roomes" where ideas related to Llull's system of spiritual philosophy are refashioned to suit the early modern agenda. As chambers and halls, these various literatures cry out for order, demanding that a huge assembly of facts—indeed all phenomena—be organized so they be understood as "UNITY and ... DIVERSITY ... reconciled in HARMONY."[97] As long as the literature of this era remains, so will Llull.

---

97   Pring-Mill, "The Role of Numbers," 38.

Works Cited

Primary Works

Alsted, Johann Heinrich, *Elementale mathematicum: Templum musicum: A facsimile of the Frankfort edition*, trans. John Birchensha (1664; repr. New York: 1967).

Bacon, Francis, "The Advancement of Learning," in *The Physical and Metaphysical Works of Lord Bacon: Including his Dignity and Advancement of Learning, in Nine Books, and his Novum Organum*, (ed.) Joseph Devey and trans. William Wood (London: 1853), 27–379.

Crashaw, Richard, *The Poems English, Latin and Greek of Richard Crashaw*, (ed.) L.C. Martin (Oxford: 1927).

Dee, John, *John Dee's Library Catalogue*, (eds.) Julian Roberts and Andrew G. Watson (London: 1990).

Dee, John, *Lists of Manuscripts Formerly Owned by Dr. John Dee: With Preface and Identifications*, (ed.) M.R. James (London: 1921).

Dee, John, *The Private Diary of Dr. John Dee, and the Catalogue of his Library of Manuscripts, from the Original Manuscripts in the Ashmolean Museum at Oxford, and Trinity College Library, Cambridge*, (ed.) James Orchard Halliwell (Oxford: 1842).

Donne, John, *Devotions Upon Emergent Occasions*, (ed.) Anthony Raspa (Montreal: 1975).

Donne, John, *Essays in Divinity*, (ed.) Evelyn M. Simpson (Oxford: 1952).

Donne, John, *The Sermons of John Donne*, (eds.) George R. Potter and Evelyn M. Simpson, 10 vols. (Berkeley: 1953–1962).

Dryden, John, *Selected Works*, (ed.) William Frost, 2nd. ed. (New York: 1971).

Herbert, George, *The Complete English Works*, (ed.) Ann Pasternak Slater (1908; rprt. New York: 1995).

Milton, John, *Complete Poems and Major Prose*, (ed.) Merritt Y. Hughes (Indianapolis: 1976).

Ripley, George, *George Ripley's Compound of Alchymy (1591)*, (ed.) Stanton J. Linden (Brookfield, Vermont: 2001).

Traherne, Thomas, "The Fifth Centurie," in *Poems, Centuries and Three Thanksgivings*, (ed.) Anne Ridler (London: 1966), 367–372.

Vaughan, Henry, *Henry Vaughan: A Selection of his Finest Poems*, (ed.) Louis L. Martz (New York: 1995).

Wilkins, John, *An Essay Towards a Real Character, and a Philosophical Language: A facsimile of the London edition* (London: 1968).

Primary Works: Llull

Ars Brevis, in Bonner, *SW* 1: 615–625.

El "Liber predicationis contra Judeos" de Ramón Lull, (ed.) José M. Millás Vallicrosa (Madrid and Barcelona: 1957).

Secondary Works

Albrecht, Roberta, "'The Pulley': Rundles, Ropes and Ladders in John Wilkins, Ramon Lull, and George Herbert," *The George Herbert Journal* 30 (2006–07): 1–18.

Albrecht, Roberta, *The Virgin Mary as Alchemical and Lullian Reference in Donne* (Selinsgrove, Pennsylvania.: 2005).

Duran, Manuel, "Ramon Llull: An Introduction," *Catalan Review* 4 (1990): 11–29.

Farrington, Benjamin, *The Philosophy of Francis Bacon* (Chicago: 1966).

Fletcher, Harris, *Milton's Semitic Studies* (Chicago: 1926).

Hotson, Howard, *Paradise Postponed: Johann Heinrich and the Birth of Calvinist Millenarianism* (Boston: 2000).

Huntley, Frank Livingstone, *Sir Thomas Browne: A Biographical and Critical Study* (Ann Arbor: 1968).

Idel, Moshe, "Ramon Lull and Ecstatic Kabbalah: A Preliminary Observation," *Journal of the Warburg and Courtauld Institutes* 51 (1988): 170–174.

Katz, David, *Philo-Semitism and the Readmission of the Jews to England, 1603–1655* (Oxford: 1982).

Keynes, Geoffrey, *A Bibliography of Dr. John Donne: Dean of Saint Paul's*, 4th ed. (Oxford: 1973).

Linden, Stanton J., "Expounding George Ripley: A Huntington Alchemical Manuscript," *Huntington Library Quarterly* 61 (2000): 11–28.

Linden, Stanton J., "The Ripley Scrolls and *The Compound of Alchemy*," in *Emblems and Alchemy*, (eds.) Alison Adams and Stanton J. Linden (Sherborne, Dorset: 1998), 73–94.

Malcolmson, Cristina, "George Herbert and Coterie Verse," in *George Herbert in the Nineties: Reflections and Reassessments*, (eds.) Jonathan F.S. Post and Sidney Gottlieb (Fairfield, Connecticut: 1995), 159–184.

Nauman, Jonathan, "Herbert the Hermetist: Vaughan's Reading of *The Temple*," *George Herbert Journal* 17 (1993): 25–40.

Ong, S.J., Walter, *Ramus, Method and the Decay of Dialogue: From the Art of Discourse to the Art of Reason* (Cambridge, Mass.: 1983).

Pereira, Michela, *The Alchemical Corpus Attributed to Raymond Lull* (London: 1989).

Prest, Wilfred R., "The Art of Law and the Law of God: Sir Henry Finch (1558–1625)," in *Puritans and Revolutionaries: Essays in Seventeenth-Century History*, (eds.) Donald Pennington and Keith Thomas (Oxford: 1978), 94–117.

Pring-Mill, Robert D.F., "The Role of Numbers in the Structure of the *Arbor scientiae*," in *Arbor scientiae der Baum des Wissens von Ramon Lull*, (eds.) Fernando Domínguez Reboiras, Pere Villalba Varneda, and Peter Walter (Turnhout: 2002), 35–78.

Rossi, Paolo, *Francis Bacon: From Magic to Science*, trans. Sacha Rabinovitch (Chicago: 1968).

Rossi, Paolo, *Logic and the Art of Memory: The Quest for a Universal Language*, trans. Stephen Clucas (New York: 2006).

Roth, Cecil, *A History of the Jews in England,* 2nd ed. (Oxford: 1949).

Sharpe, Kevin, *Sir Robert Cotton, 1586–1631: History and Politics in Early Modern England* (New York: 1979).

Stone, Gregory B., "Ramon Llull vs. Petrus Alfonsi: Postmodern Liberalism and the Six Liberal Arts," *Medieval Encounters: Jewish, Christian and Muslim Culture* 3 (1997): 70–93.

Tillyard, E.M.W., *The Elizabethan World Picture* (London: 1943).

Vance, Norman, *Irish Literature: A Social History: Tradition, Identity and Difference* (Oxford: 1990).

Wallis, P.J., "The Library of William Crashawe," *Transactions of the Cambridge Bibliographical Society* 8 (1963): 245–262.

Werblowsky, R.J. Zwi, "Milton and the Conjectura Cabbalistica," *Journal of the Warburg and Courtauld Institutes* 18 (1955): 90–102.

Wormald, Francis and C.E. Wright, *The English Library before 1700* (London: 1958).

Yates, Frances, *The Art of Memory* (Chicago: 1966).

Yates, Frances, "The Art of Ramon Lull: An Approach to it through Lull's Theory of the Elements," *Journal of the Warburg and Courtauld Institutes* 17 (1954): 115–173.

PART 5

Lullist Missions to the New World

∵

CHAPTER 14

A Lullist in the New World: Bernat Boïl

John Dagenais

14.1   Introduction

The missionary impulse is the very first that Llull feels at the moment of his conversion: "it seemed to him that no one could offer a better or greater service to Christ than to give up his life and soul for the sake of His love and honor, and to accomplish this by carrying out the task of converting to His worship and service the Saracens who in such numbers surrounded the Christians on all sides."[1] It is from this recognition that the three great resolutions that will drive the rest of Llull's life and ceaseless activity derive: the determination to accept martyrdom in the act of converting unbelievers, the resolve to write "the best book in the world" against the errors of the unbelievers, and the recognition of the need to gain the support of secular and religious authorities in the foundation of monasteries where future missionaries would be taught the languages of the peoples they would later be sent to convert.[2]

It should be remembered, too, that Llull's illumination on Mount Randa is not about the Art. The Art is merely the tool that was given Llull there for carrying out his missionary work: "the Lord suddenly illuminated his mind, giving him the form and method for writing the aforementioned book against the errors of the unbelievers."[3] At the heart of the Art of Finding Truth is the art of conversion.

Llull himself never lost sight of this fact. Still in 1311–1312, at the Council of Vienne, he was pursuing his goals, with some success, to have missionaries learn the languages of the "unbelievers." And our last documentary evidence for Llull's life is from Tunis in December 1315, where he had gone, at age 83, perhaps because of certain teasers, sent out by the usurper sultan Abu Yahya

---

1   *Vita coaetanea* 1.5, ROL 8:274: "Et uisum est, quod melius siue maius seruitium Christo facere nemo posset, quam pro amore et honore suo uitam et animam suam dare"; trans. Anthony Bonner, *Doctor Illuminatus: A Ramon Llull Reader* (Princeton: 1993), 12.

2   *Vita coaetanea* 1.6, ROL 8:275: "unum librum, meliorem de mundo."

3   *Vita coaetanea* 3.14, ROL 8:280: "quod subito Dominus illustrauit mentem suam, dans eidem formam et modum faciendi librum, de quo supra dicitur, contra errores infidelium;" tr. Bonner, *Doctor Illuminatus,* 18.

Ibn al-Lihyani, suggesting an interest in converting to Christianity.[4] Llull died, whether in Tunis, in Majorca, or between the two, some time in the next three or four months. His own "dream of conversion" was never fulfilled exactly as he had dreamed it.[5] Over the next two to three centuries the attitude of Christians toward their Jewish and Muslim neighbors would harden, not soften (as we like to imagine Llull would have wished), with increasing pogroms, forced conversions, a new Inquisition and expulsions. The time for the Art as a tool of conversion was largely finished. The Art as theology or philosophy or contemplative tool or alchemy became the focus of Llull's many, many followers over later centuries.

But new missionizing possibilities had begun to open up already in Llull's lifetime: the Genoese sailor Lancelotto Malocello may have landed in the Canary Islands as early as 1312. Llull was in Genoa briefly in late 1290 or early 1291 when the Vivaldi brothers were preparing to set out on their apparently ill-fated voyage *per mare Oceanum ad partes Indiae*.[6] Llull returned for a longer stay in Genoa in 1293 (when he underwent a great spiritual crisis) so he may have known of the Vivaldi's efforts. The 1339 map by Angelino Dulcert, produced in Palma de Majorca, is the first modern map to depict accurately some of the Canary Islands. In 1346, the Majorcan seaman Jaume Ferrer set off south along the west coast of Africa, perhaps beyond Cape Bojador, in search of the "River of Gold." Llompart Moragues identifies Ferrer as a second-generation immigrant to Majorca from Genoa, which would do much to explain his

---

4 Bonner, *Doctor Illuminatus*, 42–43.

5 Robert Ignatius Burns, "Christian-Islamic Confrontation in the West: The Thirteenth-Century Dream of Conversion," *American Historical Review* 76 (1971): 1386–434; Ramon Sugranyes de Franch, "Ramon Llull, docteur des missions," *Studia monographica et recensiones* 5 (1951): 3–44. See also Mark D. Johnston, "Ramon Llull and the Compulsory Evangelization of Jews and Muslims," in *Iberia and the Mediterranean World of the Middle Ages: Studies in Honor of Robert I. Burns*, (ed.) Larry J. Simon, 2 vols. (Leiden:1995): 1:3–37 and Pamela Drost Beattie, "'Pro Exaltatione Sanctae Fidei Catholicae': Mission and Crusade in the Writings of Ramon Llull," in *Iberia and the Mediterranean World of the Middle Ages: Studies in Honor of Robert I. Burns*," (ed.) Larry J. Simon, 2 vols. (Leiden:1995): 1:113–129.

6 1312 is the conventional date, but Malocello's voyage may have been later. Pierre Chaunu, *L'expansion européene du XIIIᵉ au XVᵉ siècle* (Paris: 1969), 94, puts it in "le premier tiers du XIVe." See also Bailey W. Diffie and George D. Winnius, *Foundations of the Portuguese Empire, 1415–1580* (Minneapolis: 1977), 24–34. On the Vivaldi voyage, see Chaunu, *L'expansion européene*, 93–95, and Florentino Pérez Embid, *Los descubrimientos en el Atlántico y la rivalidad castellano-portuguesa hasta el tratado de Tordesillas* (Seville: 1948), 51–58. On early explorations of the Canary Islands, see also Josep Amengual i Batle, "L'herència lul·liana i la missió mallorquina a Canàries: la missió sense espasa," *Randa* 61 (2008): 73–91; Buenaventura Bonnet Reverón, "Las expediciones a las Canarias en el siglo XIV," *Revista de Indias* 5 (1944): 577–610 and 6 (1945): 7–31, 189–220, 389–418.

interest in following the paths of Malocello and other early Genoese explorers of the West African coast.[7] So far as we know, Ferrer and his crew were not heard from again, but the epoch of African exploration and exploitation had begun. Already the Canary Islands had come back into the European world and into the sights of popes and kings. In 1344, the Avignonese Pope Clement VI had named the nobleman Luis de España "Prince of the Fortunate Isles." The newly encountered people of the Canary Islands are neither Jews nor Muslims, nor do they seem to possess the sophistication of Llull's wise gentile in his *Libre del gentil e dels tres savis* [Book of the Gentile and the Three Wise Men].[8] This introduces a whole new missionizing game, laid out by Clement VI in the course of a sermon presented on the occasion of Luis's coronation. In this new game "it is one thing to kill for worldly reasons, another to kill for Christ" (*unum est occidi pro mundo, aliud est occidi pro Christo*).[9] Clement's art of conversion is what he calls "coercion through circumstances (*coactio conditionata*) in which people are forced to convert, not at swordpoint, but rather through the taking of their lands, their enslavement or the "subtraction" (*substractio*) of their material goods.[10] These are ideas that will inform much of the European conquest and conversion of the world over the next four centuries.

That is not to say that the hard line was the only line. There seem to have been, at the very least, good intentions of the Lullian sort toward the conversion of the inhabitants of the Canary Islands. Recent modern scholarship, beginning with Vincke,[11] has suggested a positive view of the missionizing activity of the Majorcans and its relation to Llull's thought. Hillgarth also supports the idea that the conversion of the Canarians was undertaken "along what seem to be Lullian lines," without, unfortunately, specifying what those lines might have been.[12] Amengual provides a thorough and balanced study of these questions; among his most interesting points is the observation that in large part the Majorcan impulse for the evangelization of the Canary Islanders

---

7   Gabriel Llompart Moragues "La identitat de Jaume Ferrer el navegant (1346)," *Memòries de la Reial Acadèmia Mallorquina d'Estudis Genealògics, Heràldics i Històrics* 10 (2000): 7–14.

8   *Libre del gentil e dels tres savis*, NEORL 2.

9   Clement VI, "Sermón de Clemente VI Papa acerca de la otorgación del Reino de Canarias a Luis de España, 1344," (ed.) Marcos G. Martínez, *Revista de Historia Canaria* 29 (1963–1964): 90. I have modified the transcription slightly for readability. On Clement's efforts, see John Dagenais, "The Postcolonial Laura," *Modern Language Quarterly* 65 (2004): 383–388, and references cited there.

10   Clement VI, "Sermón," 103.

11   Johannes Vincke, "Comienzos de las misiones cristianas en las Islas Canarias," *Hispania Sacra* 12 (1959): 193–207; "Die Evangelisation der Kanarischen Inseln im 14. Jahrhundert im Geiste Raimund Lulls," *EL* 4 (1960): 307–316.

12   Jocelyn N. Hillgarth, *Readers and Books in Majorca, 1229–1550*, 2 vols. (Paris: 1991), 1:237.

came from merchants and other lay people, which might reflect the influence
of a popular Lullism, very different from what Amengual's identifies as the
"eccelesiocentric" missionary plans of the popes.[13] Several efforts, originat-
ing in Majorca, to send friars to preach to the Canarians in a peaceable way,
are recorded, although it is not clear how many of these planned expeditions
took place.[14] One of these was to have involved freed Canarian slaves from
Majorca (enslavement of Canarians preceded these missionizing initiatives)
who would instruct the friars in the language of the natives as an aid to their
conversion or serve as interpreters. It is understandable that some have seen
in this an echo of Llull's missionizing spirit, for after all, learning the language
of potential converts was essential to his ideas, and certainly Majorcan friars
would have heard of Llull and his ideas. Some may even have known him personally. But is an effort to learn the language of those one hopes to convert a
peculiarly Lullian idea, or is it simply one of the logical moves that any missionary who wishes to convert by words rather than the sword would hit upon?
Whatever the influence of Llull's ideas may have been, we have come a very
long way from the open-ended dialogue of Llull's *Libre del gentil e dels tres savis*, even while acknowledging that Llull himself, of course, was in favor of military crusades under certain conditions, and not just at the end of his career.[15]

In this and a subsequent chapter I look at two missionaries to the New World
from two distinct periods who had documented connections to Lullist thought:
the 15th-century Bernat Boïl, "First Apostle to the Indies," who accompanied
Columbus on his second voyage (1493–1496), and the 18th-century Junípero
Serra, now St. Junípero, a missionary in both what is now Mexico and what is
now California. Both are fascinating figures in their own right and their very
different interests in and approaches to Lullian ideas make them key figures to
examine as we seek to understand the continuing impact of Llull's thought on
later generations. Boïl and Serra are not the only New World figures for whom
Lullian connections or inspiration have been suggested. Most prominent is
Bartolomé de las Casas, defender of the native inhabitants.[16] In each case, the
connection to Llull is there, but the ways in which this connection may have
informed their missionizing efforts are difficult to establish.

---

13   Amengual i Batle, "L'herència lul·liana," 86–87.
14   Amengaul i Batle, "L'herència lul·liana," with ample recent bibliography in his notes; Bon-
       net Reverón, "Las expediciones a las Canarias," *Revista de Indias* 6 (1945): 194–214; and
       Diffie and Winnius, *Foundations of the Portuguese Empire*, 31–32.
15   Sugranyes de Franch, "Docteur des missions," 36–44.
16   Ramón Sugranyes de Franch, "Bartolomé de Las Casas: ¿Discípulo de Raimundo Lulio?"
       Etudes de lettres 2 (1986): 3–17 and *Ramon Llull a les Amèriques: Bartolomé de las Casas
       deixeble del doctor mallorquí?* (Palma: 1996).

14.2   Bernat Boïl

Bernat Boïl is an extraordinarily complex figure and, despite the extensive paper trail he left behind through his worldly activities, much about him, including his place of birth, remains unclear.[17] A document recently discovered in the Arxiu de la Corona d'Aragó by Jaume Riera and cited by Josep M. Prunés states that Boïl was from Zaidin, a town located in the Catalan-speaking "fringe" (*franja*) of eastern Aragon, not far from Lleida.[18] He lived from 1440–1450 to 1505–1507.[19] Vilallonga provides a succinct list of his many and varied activities: he was "secretary for the Archpriest of Zaragoza, Pere Zapata, as well as of King Ferdinand II "the Catholic" of Aragon, chief administrator of galleys for Admiral Bernat de Vilamarí, royal ambassador to the French court to negotiate the return of the counties of the Roussillon and Cerdanya, a priest, a hermit at Montserrat and superior of the hermits there, Vicar General of the Order of Minims, companion to Christopher Columbus on his second voyage to the Indies, first Apostolic Vicar of the West Indies named by Pope Alexander VI, and commendatory abbot of the Monastery of Sant Miquel de Cuixà [in Roussillon; at the instances of Ferdinand II], where he died."[20] This was a man who lived at the extremes of worldly engagement and solitary contemplation, one who was entrusted with important worldly embassies by kings

---

17   I wish to thank Daniel K. Gullo of the Hill Museum and Microfilm Library for his generous assistance as I was completing the final proofs of this article. Any inaccuracies that remain in my appreciation of Boïl are mine.

18   Josep M. Prunés, "Nuevos datos y observaciones para la biografía de Fray Bernardo Boyl," *Bollettino ufficiale dell'Ordine dei Minimi* 49.4 (2004): 558. This document would seem to put to rest the many other theories, ranging as far afield as Valencia, that had attempted to fix Boïl's birthplace. Mariàngela Vilallonga, *La literatura llatina a Catalunya al segle XV* (Barcelona: 1993), 38–43, together with some details provided by Prunés, is the basis for the following biography. See also Anselm J. Albareda, "Lul·lisme a Montserrat al segle XVᵉ: L'ermità Bernat Boïl," *EL* 9 (1965): 10, who calls Boïl a "polymorphous, interesting, and disconcerting personage" (*personatge polimorf, interessant i desconcertant*). Boïl's name appears in sources as Buïl, Boyl, and Buyl. I use the modern Catalan form. There is now an important doctoral thesis on Boïl by Daniel K. Gullo: "Eremitic Reform at Fifteenth-Century Montserrat, 1472–1497," Dissertation, University of Chicago, 2009.

19   Prunés, "Nuevos datos," 559, favors the earliest date.

20   Vilallonga, *La literatura llatina a Catalunya*, 38–39: "secretari de l'arxiprest de Saragossa, Pere Zapata [but see Prunés, "Nuevos datos," 560–561], i del rei Ferran II de Catalunya, comissari general de les galeres de l'almirall Bernat de Vilamarí, ambaixador reial a la cort de França per gestionar-hi la devolució dels comtats del Rosselló i la Cerdanya, sacerdot, ermità de Montserrat i superior dels ermitans, vicari general de l'orde dels mínims, company de Cristòfor Colom en el seu segon viatge a les índies, primer vicari apostòlic de les índies Occidentals nomenat pel papa Alexandre VI, i abat comendatari del monestir de Sant Miquel de Cuixà, on morí ja al començament del segle XVI."

and spiritual ones by pontiffs and abbots. His life took him from the courts of France, Rome and Aragon to the solitary heights of Montserrat to the wilds of the West Indies when they were scarcely known by Europeans. My own sense is that, however much Boïl may have protested the calls to worldly duties as interruptions to his desired contemplative life, he was a man who needed, perhaps enjoyed, both. In this he was a man not unlike Ramon Llull.

Boïl interests us here primarily because, from one of his would-be contemplative phases, before he set out for the New World, we have several letters that he exchanged with Arnau Descós, an ardent Majorcan Lullist, expressing an interest in learning the Lullian Art. Lullism flourished in Majorca in the latter half of the 15th century.[21] Descós and, in particular, Pere Deguí, author of the widely influential *Ianua artis excellentissimi magistri Raimundi Lull*,[22] were leaders in this movement, which was a source of significant controversy in Llull's native island.[23] It seems that Boïl's first expression of interest in Llull was in correspondence sent to Deguí,[24] not to Descós, from Montserrat, where he dwelt in the Hermitage of the Holy Trinity on the mountain's top, a strenuous walk from the monastery below. Deguí was perhaps in Rome at the time, defending the orthodoxy of Llull's works, and of his own. In any case, he may have passed Boïl's initial inquiry, now lost, on to Descós.[25] Descós writes to Boïl in citing the latter's expression to Deguí: "of your desire for the study of our divine Ramon, to which you would eagerly dedicate yourself, as you say, if you

21 Albareda, "Lul·lisme a Montserrat;" Mark D. Johnston, "The Reception of the Lullian *Art, 1450–1530*," *The Sixteenth Century Journal* 12 (1981): 31–48.

22 Pere Deguí, *Ianua artis excellentissimi magistri Raimundi Lull* (Barcelona, 1482).

23 Miguel Ferrer Flórez, "Controversias y luchas entre lulistas y antilulistas en el siglo XVIII," *Memòries de la Real Acadèmia Mallorquina d'Estudis Genealògics, Heràldics i Històrics* 16 (2006): 157–166. On Deguí, see also Villalonga, *La literatura llatina a Catalunya*, 89–92; Hillgarth, *Readers and Books*, 1:219–220; and Rafael Ramis Barceló, "En torno al escoto-lulismo de Pere Deguí," *Medievalia* 16 (2013): 235–264. On Descós, see Hillgarth, *Readers and Books*, 1:221–228. For the intellectual atmosphere among Lullists in the 15th century, see Hillgarth, *Readers and Books*, 1:204–228 and Johnston, "The Reception of the Lullian *Art*." The name Deguí also appears as Daguí, De Gui, etc. Hillgarth, *Readers and Books*, 1:221, n. 207, suggests that "Dezcors" is perhaps a more correct form for Descós.

24 Fidel Fita, "Fray Bernal Boyl y Cristóbal Colón: Nueva colección de cartas reales," *Boletín de la Real Academia de la Historia* 19 (1891): 173–237; "Escritos de fray Bernal Boyl, ermitaño de Monserrate: Correspondencia latina con don Arnaldo Descós," *Boletín de la Real Academia de la Historia* 19 (1891): 267–348. Hillgarth, *Readers and Books*, 1:221–228, cites portions of Descós's correspondence from a manuscript not seen by Fita: Archivo de la Catedral de Majorca, Ms. 15530.

25 Albareda, "Lul·lisme a Montserrat," 13 and n. 29, dates Boïl's letter to Deguí as prior to October 1483; he places Deguí in Rome in late 1483 and early 1484.

had the possibility of a teacher."[26] Descós seems to have understood right away that the hermit from Montserrat would be most interested in the contemplative Llull; the study of Llull brings,

> not only the knowledge of many things, but also reveals some comprehensiveness of religion and morals. This, this, I say, is what removes all his followers, as I have observed, from all vices, and, clinging so closely to God that they despise wealth, rank and the other deadly pleasures of this world with steadfast hearts, they are brought to the contemplation of the Creator and all his works, forgetful of fleeting things. What, indeed, is sweeter than to understand God? What more delightful than the contemplation of lofty matters? What, finally, is more beneficial than knowing the "dignities" of God through assiduous meditation, grasping them with the mind and all one's strength?[27]

It seems likely that Boïl was aware of the tradition of Lullian hermits of Majorca and that this may have played a role in his interest in Llull.[28] Further evidence of Boïl's interest in the contemplative life is his translation of Isaac of Nineveh's *De religione* into Aragonese dialect "or, if you prefer, Castilian" ("o si mas querres, Castellano"), he says.[29] Descós offers his own home as a place for Boïl to come and study the Lullian Art.[30] In a letter now lost, Boïl apparently

---

26   Fita, "Escritos," 292: "de tua ipsa voluntate erga doctrinam nostri Divi Raimundi, cui libenter, ut ais, operam dedisses, si opportunitatem praeceptoris habuisses." I suppress italics used by Fita to indicate what he considered quotations or paraphrases by Boïl or Descós of each other in their correspondence.

27   Fita, "Escritos," 293: "non solum cognitionem tantarum rerum importat, verum etiam prae se fert nescio quam religionis morumque integritatem. Haec est, haec, inquam, est, quae omnes ejus sequaces, ut compertum habeo, a cunctis detrahit vitiis; et Deo conjunctissime adhaerendo, divitias honores et reliquas hujus saeculi laethiferas delectationes constanti animo contemnunt; et ad contemplationem Creatoris et omnium suorum operum, obliti rerum fragilium, ducuntur. Quid igitur dulcius quam Deum intelligere? Quid jucundius quam res altas contemplari? Quid denique salutarius, quam cognoscendo dignitates Dei adsidua cogitatione, eas mente ac totis viribus complecti?"

28   Hillgarth, *Readers and Books*, 1:207–210.

29   Madrid, Biblioteca Nacional, Inc. 502; BETA [*Bibliografía Española de Textos Antiguos*] manid 2334, Web: http://vm136.lib.berkeley.edu/BANC/philobiblon/beta_en.html. Consulted: October 12, 2014. See Fita, "Escritos," 267; and Sebastià Janeras, "Presència d'Isaac de Nínive a Catalunya," *Revista Internacional d'Humanitats* 18 (2010): 44. In the only surviving manuscript of this translation, made for the monks of Montserrat, the work is attributed to Boïl: *Libro Del Reverendo frai buil De Vita CONtemplatiua*, Madrid, Real Biblioteca II/795, BETA manid 3650.

30   Fita, "Escritos," 293.

begs off, saying something has come up. It seems that the king himself has called on Boïl's services.[31] Once again, we have only Descós's paraphrase of Boïl's letter: "[you said that] you wished for the Art of the Divine Ramon with fervent heart, that you wanted to come to us in order to learn it, if it were not that certain affairs impeded you."[32]

This back and forth goes on for another five years. At one point Descós sends a friar to tutor Boïl since the latter cannot come to Majorca.[33] Descós tells Boïl that with a little application, a gifted man like Boïl could become another Deguí.[34] Descós also sends him jugs of Majorcan olives and capers and twelve cheeses, since Boïl is leading the *vita apostolica*.[35] It is difficult to judge Boïl's actual zeal for learning the Lullian Art, though at one time he says he will use his influence with King Ferdinand II to get him to intervene with the Pope on behalf of Deguí, whose Lulian works are on trial as heretical in Rome.[36] Boïl appears rather circumspect and all he says in this correspondence is that the letters "would already have been sent were it not" for Holy Week.[37] What is certain is that Deguí was subsequently cleared of charges of heresy in Rome and was able to reprint the *Ianua* at Rome itself in 1485, and with papal approval.[38] He tells Descós in a letter of 26 June 1488 that he has finally been able to attend two of Deguí's lectures on the Lullian Art in Zaragoza.[39] In the brief and spotty correspondence that has survived, one gets the sense that Descós was more eager to have a man of Boïl's distinction and connections as a Lullist than Boïl was to become one. Boïl sums up the state of his own Lullism in a letter dated from the Hermitage of the Holy Trinity in February 1484. Although yet another royal command has caused him to put off an announced trip to Majorca, his thirst for learning has not died "but it lurks inside until the fount appears by which it will be revived."[40] For his part, Descós emerges as a rather self-conscious Humanist, larding his own letters with citations from Classical authors and praising Boïl for his eloquence.[41] At one point, in a letter of 10 March 1488, he also feels obliged to apologize for the roughness of Llull's language: "although the reading itself of Ramon does not afford as much delight as do

---

31   Fita, "Escritos," 294–296.
32   Fita, "Escritos," 294: "te flagranti animo peroptare artem divi Raimundi, ob quam addiscendam ad nos commigrare volebas, nisi quaedam negotia essent tibi impedimento."
33   Letter of February 1484; Fita, "Escritos," 296–297.
34   Letter of mid 1488; Fita, "Escritos," 323–324.
35   Letter of late 1489; Fita, "Escritos," 307–309.
36   Letter of 23 February 1484; Fita, "Escritos," 297–298.
37   Letter of 20 April 1484; Fita, "Escritos," 299–302.
38   Hillgarth, *Readers and Books*, 1:219.
39   Fita, "Escritos," 321–322.
40   Fita, "Escritos," 296: "sed latet intrinsecus quousque fons appareat quo reficiatur."
41   Johnston, "Reception of the Lullian *Art*," 38–39.

Cicero, Quintilian or Virgil, we contemplate and examine its majesty and subtlety of ideas rather than only the eloquence of its words."[42]

Columbus sets off on his second voyage in late September of 1493. Already
on 29 May of that year the Catholic Monarchs had told Columbus that he
would be taking Boïl with him. In their letter they outline the missionary work
they expect Boïl and the religious who accompany him to undertake,

> and to help [with the conversion of the natives], their Highnesses send
> there the devout Father Brother Boïl, together with other religious, whom
> the aforementioned Admiral shall take with him, who, with the help
> and effort of the Indians who came here, make sure that they are well
> informed in the matters of our Holy Faith, for they will know and under-
> stand by now a great deal of our language, and try to instruct them in it
> as best they can."[43]

The plan, then, is to use the natives who have returned with Columbus as as-
sistants in this cause because they will already know a good deal of Castilian,
and could, presumably, once they were themselves sufficiently instructed in
matters of the faith, serve as interpreters for the missionaries. On 7 June 1493,
the Monarchs write to the Pope asking him to give Boïl permission and authority for these tasks,

> so that he may go to some islands of the infidels in order that being there,
> with divine aid, he can convert them to faith in Christ. May it please our
> most holy lord pope to give him license and authority so that in each city,
> fort, town, lands and place in the aforementioned islands, personally or
> through persons deputized by him, he can, as long as he shall live, preach
> the word of God to the people and build and construct and have built and
> constructed some churches, chapels and holy places.[44]

---

42 Fita, "Escritos," 319: "si tantum oblectationis ipsa Raymundi lectio non affert quantum illa
    Ciceronis, Quintiliani vel Maronis, intueamur atque perscrutemur ipsam majestatem ac
    sublimitatem sententiarum potius quam solam verborum elegantiam."

43 Fita, "Colón," 184–185: "para ayuda á ello [the conversión of the natives], sus Altezas envi-
    an allá al devoto P. Fr. Buil juntamente con otros Religiosos, quel dicho Almirante consigo
    ha de llevar, los cuales, por mano é industria de los indios que acá vinieron, procure que
    sean bien informados de las cosas de nuestra Santa Fe, pues ellos sabrán é entenderán ya
    mucho de nuestra lengua, é procurando de los instruir en ella lo mejor que se pueda." The
    text seems a bit rough to me and my translation offers an interpretation of what I under-
    stand to be its sense.

44 Fita, "Colón," 186: "ad nonnullas insulas infidelium, ut eos, auxilio divino sibi assistente,
    ad fidem christi convertat. Placeat Sanctissimo domino nostro pape dare sibi licenciam et
    potestatem ut in singulis Civitatibus, castris, villis, terris et locis dictarum Insularum, per

These were to be the lofty goals of the Monarchs' mission to the natives. This was to be Boïl's life "as long as he shall live."

On 25 June 1493, the papal bull *Piis fidelium* is issued, granting Boïl "apostolic authority" (*auctoritas apostolica*) in the New World.[45] It appears that Boïl undertakes his royal and papal commission as Apostle to the Indies without informing his Majorcan correspondent Descós. But Descós hears second-hand and writes a letter to Boïl in September of 1493, a few weeks before Columbus's second expedition sets sail from Cadiz. It is highly significant that Descós himself makes no reference to Llull's missionizing zeal in his farewell to his friend. Appropriately enough, he cites Ovid, *Tristia* 3.5–10, on exile in strange lands, and compares Boïl to Saint Bartholomew, who went to preach in the Indies. His specific advice on techniques of conversion is to use a loud voice, as Christ used to wake Lazarus from the dead:

> Cry, you preachers of truth and raise your voices so that "in all the lands are heard the sound" [Ps. 18:5] of your correction, your rebuke, your love, and your holiness. And so, for converting those peoples not only words are needed, or prayer, or weeping and wailing, but a great voice. For your Master, wishing to resuscitate a man dead for four days "cried in a loud voice" [JOHN 11:43].[46]

Descós closes by citing Psalm 66:8: "And the ends of the earth shall fear him" (*Et metuent* [sic] *eum omnes fines terrae*). This sounds rather ominous in light of subsequent events in the history of European colonization.

The expedition arrives in the New World on 4 November 1493. We can perhaps glimpse the hand of Boïl in the fact that Columbus names one of the first islands he encounters on this voyage "Montserrate."[47] Columbus founds a new

---

se vel personam ab eo deputandam possit, quoad vixerit, verbum dei populo predicare, ac quecumque, ecclesias, capellas el [sic] loca pia erigere, construere, ac erigi et construi facere."

45   Fita, "Colón," 187–190. István Szászdi León-Borja, "Después de la *Inter Caetera*, ruptura y cambio en la política indiana de Alejandro VI," in *Memoria del X Congreso del Instituto Internacional de Historia del Derecho Indiano*, 2 vols. (Mexico City: 1995), 1577–1630, studies in detail this bull and other matters regarding Boïl's appointment as Apostolic Vicar.

46   Fita, "Escritos," 346–347: "Clamate, vos, praedicatores veritatis, et exaltate vocero vestram ut in omnem terrana audiatur sonus vestrae correctionis, increpationis, charitatis et sanctitatis vestrae. Ad has itaque convertendas gentes non opus est solummodo verbis, orationibus, planctu ac fleta, sed voce magna. Nam magister vester, quatriduanum mortuum volens resuscitare, voce magna clamavit."

47   Samuel Eliot Morison, *The European Discovery of America: The Southern Voyages A.D. 1492–1616* (New York: 1974), 108.

colony, the town of Isabela, on the island of Hispaniola at the beginning of
the next year. Antonio de Torres returns to Spain on 2 February 1494, bearing a
letter from Boïl, who apparently expresses frustration at the difficulties in communication with the native population. The Monarchs respond, on 16 August
1494, to a Boïl who seems rather unenthusiastic about this mission and who
wants to come home:

> And as for what you wrote that you thought that your presence there
> does not offer as much benefit as you thought because of the lack of an
> interpreter (for there is no way to make interpreters out of the Indians)
> and that for this reason you want to come home in our service: this is not
> necessary, for now, in any way. We firmly believe that, since the time that
> you wrote us, there will have been some sort of translator so that your
> presence there can begin to bear fruit.[48]

Boïl's attitude toward missionizing seems, if anything, to be anti-Lullian: the
lack of an interpreter (and the difficulty of training the Indians to be interpreters) is a reason to abandon missionizing, not a challenge to be overcome
in service of God and an obvious sign that he and others need to learn these
langauges. The Catholic Monarchs order Boïl to stay in the New World in no
uncertain terms, despite these issues, and refer to the "many things" that he
does for them there: "we know that your presence there is very necessary and
beneficial for now and for many things."[49] They also give him an out, however –
his health:

> And so we command you and require you, if your health should permit it,
> that for our service you stay with it until we write to you, and if your con-
> dition will not permit it and you should be obliged to come back, leave

---

48   Fita, "Colón," 196–197: "Y quanto á lo que nos escrivistes que pensais que vuestra estada
     allá no aprovecha tanto como pensábades por falta de la lengua, que no ay para facer
     yntépretes con los yndios, y que por esto vos querríades venir por servicio nuestro: que
     esto no se falta por agora en manera alguna. Bien creemos que después que nos escrivistes
     avrá avido alguna forma de lengua para que comience á dar fruto vuestra estada allá." It
     is not clear to me whether in complaining of the "falta de la lengua" Boïl is referring to
     the lack of an interpreter or to his own lack of knowledge of the indigenous languages
     in this passage. I have translated it with the first of these possible readings. León-Borja,
     "Despúes" 1616, n. 67, offers a slightly different version of this text that unfortunately does
     not clarify this particular question.

49   Fita, "Colón," 197: "sabemos que vuestra estada allá es muy necesaria y provechosa por
     agora y para muchas cosas."

there a reverend fit to fulfill your responsibilities, so that he can provide for all spiritual matters there.[50]

They mention the utility of his presence there for them: "you will do us great service in writing to us frequently all that you have found out there and will come to know."[51] But by the date of this letter Boïl may already have decided to return.

Boïl's credentials as a Lullist are difficult to establish, reduced, perhaps, to good intentions and attendance at two lectures by Deguí. Albareda argues that the large number of works by and on Llull held at the Monastery of Montserrat at that moment would have provided ample training for Boïl in Llull's ideas. However, Albareda concludes: "We don't know concretely what progress the aspiring disciple [Boïl], always in search of a teacher, achieved in the study of the Lullian Art. Nor do we know the concrete features of that Lullism and the degree of its penetration into the cultured environment of Montserrat."[52]

Boïl's credentials as a missionary are equally problematic. He did not last long on his mission to the New World. The reasons for his return to Spain after less than a year as Vicar Apostolic are far from clear; Poole estimates that Boïl left Isabela in the second half of September 1494.[53] It seems, however, that there had been dissension and perhaps the monarchs deemed it better in the end for Boïl and other parties to the dispute to remain in Spain, rather than return to the New World. Oviedo's version describes a series of standoffs between Boïl and Columbus;[54] Poole has argued that the Columbus in question

---

50   Fita, "Colón," 197: "Por ende nos vos mandamos é encargamos, si vuestra salud da logar á ello, que por servicio nuestro en todo esto sobreseays en ello, fasta que nos vos escrivamos; é si vuestra dispusición no diere lugar á ello é oviéredes de venir, dexad allá el R.° qual convenga con vuestro poder, para que en todo lo espiritual de allá pueda proveer." In a letter of 16 February 1495 to their ambassador in Rome, the Monarchs acknowledge that Boïl is too sick to return to New World; Fita, "Colón," 199.

51   Fita, "Colón," 197: "nos fays mucho servicio en que de contino nos escrivays todo lo que de allá más aveys sabido y supierdes."

52   Albareda, "Lul·lisme a Montserrat," 21: "No sabem en concret quins foren els progressos aconseguits en l'estudi de l'Art lul.lià per l'aspirant deixeble, sempre a la recerca d'un mestre. Ignorem també la concretització d'aquest lul.lisme i el grau de la seva penetració en l'ambient culte de Montserrat."

53   T.F. Poole, "Case Reopened: An Enquiry into the 'Defection' of Fray Bernal Boyl and Mosen Pedro Margarit," *Journal of Latin American Studies* 6 (1974): 199. See also Prunés, "Nuevos datos," 567–568 and 572–573, regarding Boïl's activities during the second voyage, and Josep M. Prunés, "Bernard Boil: Primo delegato apostolico nel nuovo mondo (datos, interrogantes y documentos olvidados)," *Bollettino Ufficiale dell'Ordine dei Minimi*, 47.1 (2001): 116–121.

54   Cited in Poole, "Case Reopened," 204–205.

was Bartolomé, not Christopher.[55] The accumulated evidence suggests that Boïl may have been sent to the New World by the monarchs more as a person of trust, an observer, perhaps, than as a missionary to the natives. Albardaner has put it more bluntly: Boïl was sent by the Catholic Monarchs to spy on Columbus.[56]

There is no surviving evidence that Boïl engaged in missionary activities in the New World and therefore no evidence of any impact of Llull on this aspect of Boïl's life: Stevens-Arroyo dates the first actual baptism of natives in the New World to 21 September 1496, though he notes that rudimentary conversions, involving simple catechistic repetitions, occurred before that.[57] Boïl seems to have been at best a reluctant missionary. It may be that in the final years of his life at the Pyrenean monastery of Sant Miquel de Cuixà he was able to pursue the contemplative life he had sought. But whether Llull was a part of his contemplative program, we do not know. As all who study Boïl agree, he was a fascinating and complex figure, one whose role in so many of the key events of late 15th-century Europe is yet to be appreciated in full. For our purposes, Boïl serves best, not as an example of "Lullism" in the New World or of missionizing in the Lullian spirit, but as a reminder that for every Lullist disciple, such as Le Myésier or Deguí or Salzinger, there were no doubt many individuals of equal or greater gifts who were drawn to the figure of Llull from a variety of avenues. It is those many ways into Llull that have caused interest in him to endure so long and to take so many forms. The story of Boïl's brush with Lullism serves to remind us of the impact of Llull's ideas far beyond a relatively small set of canonical "Lullists." Llull's apppeal was deep, but it was also broad.

Works Cited

Primary Works

Boïl, Bernat, in (ed.) Fidel Fita, "Fray Bernal Boyl y Cristóbal Colón: Nueva colección de cartas reales," *Boletín de la Real Academia de la Historia* 19 (1891): 173–237.

---

55   Ibid., 205–206.

56   Francesc Albardaner i Llorens, "John Cabot and Christopher Columbus Revisited," *The Northern Mariner/Le Marin du nord* 10 (2000): 97; Morison, *European Discovery*, 137, the great admirer of Columbus, does not like Boïl and refers to his "calumnies" to the Monarchs against Columbus.

57   Anthony M. Stevens-Arroyo, "Juan Mateo Guaticabanú, September 21, 1496: Evangelization and Martyrdom in the Time of Columbus," *The Catholic Historical Review* 82 (1996): 614; "The Inter-Atlantic Paradigm: The Failure of Spanish Medieval Colonization of the Canary and Caribbean Islands," *Comparative Studies in Society and History* 35 (1993): 535.

Boïl, Bernat, in (ed.) Fidel Fita, "Escritos de fray Bernal Boyl, ermitaño de Monserrate: Correspondencia latina con don Arnaldo Descós," *Boletín de la Real Academia de la Historia* 19 (1891): 267–348.

Clement VI, Pope, "Sermón de Clemente VI Papa acerca de la otorgación del Reino de Canarias a Luis de España, 1344," (ed.) Marcos G. Martínez, *Revista de Historia Canaria* 29 (1963–1964): 88–107.

Deguí, Pere, *Ianua artis excellentissimi magistri Raimundi Lull* (Barcelona: 1482).

Isaac of Nineveh, *Ysaac de religione*; Madrid, Biblioteca Nacional, Inc/502; BETA [*Bibliografía Española de Textos Antiguos*], manid 2335, Web: http://vm136.lib.berkeley.edu/BANC/philobiblon/beta_en.html. Consulted: October 12, 2014.

Isaac of Nineveh, *De religione*, trans. Bernat Boïl (San Cugat del Vallès: 1484): *Libro Del Reverendo frai buil De Vita CONtemplatiua*. Madrid, Biblioteca Real [Palacio], II 795; BETA [*Bibliografía Española de Textos Antiguos*], manid 3650, Web: http://vm136.lib.berkeley.edu/BANC/philobiblon/beta_en.html.

Primary Works: Llull

Doctor Illuminatus: A Ramon Llull Reader, (ed.) and trans. Anthony Bonner (Princeton: 1993).

Libre del gentil e dels tres savis, (ed.) Anthony Bonner, 3rd. ed., NEORL 2.

Vita coaetanea, (ed.) Hermogenes Harada, ROL 8:271–309.

Vita coaetanea, trans. Anthony Bonner, in *Doctor Illuminatus: A Ramon Llull Reader* (Princeton: 1993), 10–40.

Secondary Works

Albardaner i Llorens, Francesc, "John Cabot and Christopher Columbus Revisited." *The Northern Mariner/Le Marin du nord* 10 (2000): 91–102.

Albareda, Anselm J., "Lul·lisme a Montserrat al segle XVè: L'ermità Bernat Boïl," *EL* 9 (1965): 5–21.

Amengual i Batle, Josep, "L'herència lul·liana i la missió mallorquina a Canàries: la missió sense espasa," *Randa* 61 (2008): 73–91.

Beattie, Pamela Drost, "'Pro Exaltatione Sanctae Fidei Catholicae': Mission and Crusade in the Writings of Ramon Llull," in *Iberia and the Mediterranean World of the Middle Ages: Studies in Honor of Robert I. Burns*," (ed.) Larry J. Simon, 2 vols. (Leiden: 1995): 1:113–129.

BETA [*Bibliografía Española de Textos Antiguos*], dir. Faulhaber, Charles B., Ángel Gómez Moreno, and Óscar Perea Rodríguez (Berkeley: 1997-). Web: http://vm136.lib.berkeley.edu/BANC/philobiblon/beta_en.html. Consulted: October 12, 2014.

Bonnet Reverón, Buenaventura, "Las expediciones a las Canarias en el siglo XIV," *Revista de Indias* 5 (1944): 577–610 and 6 (1945): 7–31, 189–220, 389–418.

Burns, Robert Ignatius, "Christian-Islamic Confrontation in the West: The Thirteenth-Century Dream of Conversion," *American Historical Review* 76 (1971): 1386–434.

Chaunu, Pierre, *L'expansion européene du XIIIe au XVe siècle* (Paris: 1969).

Dagenais, John, "The Postcolonial Laura," *Modern Language Quarterly* 65 (2004): 365–389.

Diffie, Bailey W. and George D. Winnius, *Foundations of the Portuguese Empire, 1415–1580* (Minneapolis: 1977).

Ferrer Flórez, Miguel, "Controversias y luchas entre lulistas y antilulistas en el siglo XVIII," *Memòries de la Real Acadèmia Mallorquina d'Estudis Genealògics, Heràldics i Històrics* 16 (2006): 157–166.

Fita, Fidel (ed.), "Fray Bernal Boyl y Cristóbal Colón: Nueva colección de cartas reales," *Boletín de la Real Academia de la Historia* 19 (1891): 173–237.

Fita, Fidel (ed.), "Escritos de fray Bernal Boyl, ermitaño de Monserrate: Correspondencia latina con don Arnaldo Descós," *Boletín de la Real Academia de la Historia* 19 (1891): 267–348.

Gullo, Daniel K.: "Eremitic Reform at Fifteenth-Century Montserrat, 1472–1497," Dissertation, University of Chicago, 2009.

Hillgarth, J.N., *Readers and Books in Majorca, 1229–1550*, 2 vols. (Paris: 1991).

Janeras, Sebastià, "Presència d'Isaac de Nínive a Catalunya," *Revista Internacional d'Humanitats* 18 (2010): 41–47.

Johnston, Mark D., "Ramon Llull and the Compulsory Evangelization of Jews and Muslims," in *Iberia and the Mediterranean World of the Middle Ages: Studies in Honor of Robert I. Burns*," (ed.) Larry J. Simon, 2 vols. (Leiden: 1995): 1:3–37.

Johnston, Mark D., "The Reception of the Lullian *Art*, 1450–1530," *The Sixteenth Century Journal* 12 (1981): 31–48.

León-Borja, István Szászdi, "Después de la *Inter Caetera*, ruptura y cambio en la política indiana de Alejandro VI," in *Memoria del X Congreso del Instituto Internacional de Historia del Derecho Indiano*, 2 vols. (Mexico City: 1995), 1577–1630.

Llompart Moragues, Gabriel, "La identitat de Jaume Ferrer el navegant (1346)," *Memòries de la Reial Acadèmia Mallorquina d'Estudis Genealògics, Heràldics i Històrics* 10 (2000): 7–14.

Morison, Samuel Eliot, *The European Discovery of America: The Southern Voyages A.D. 1492–1616* (New York: 1974).

Pérez Embid, Florentino, *Los descubrimientos en el Atlántico y la rivalidad castellano-portuguesa hasta el tratado de Tordesillas* (Seville: 1948).

Poole, T.F., "Case Reopened: An Enquiry into the 'Defection' of Fray Bernal Boyl and Mosen Pedro Margarit," *Journal of Latin American Studies* 6 (1974): 193–210.

Prunés, Josep M., "Bernard Boil: Primo delegato apostolico nel nuovo mondo (datos, interrogantes y documentos olvidados)," *Bollettino Ufficiale dell'Ordine dei Minimi,* 47.1 (2001): 116–121.

Prunés, Josep M., "Nuevos datos y observaciones para la biografía de Fray Bernardo Boyl," *Bollettino ufficiale dell'Ordine dei Minimi* 49.4 (2004): 558.

Ramis Barceló, Rafael, "En torno al escoto-lulismo de Pere Daguí," *Medievalia* 16 (2013): 235–264.

Stevens-Arroyo, Anthony M., "The Inter-Atlantic Paradigm: The Failure of Spanish Medieval Colonization of the Canary and Caribbean Islands," *Comparative Studies in Society and History* 35 (1993): 515–543.

Stevens-Arroyo, Anthony M., "Juan Mateo Guaticabanú, September 21, 1496: Evangelization and Martyrdom in the Time of Columbus," *The Catholic Historical Review* 82 (1996): 614–636.

Sugranyes de Franch, Ramón, "Bartolomé de Las Casas: ¿Discípulo de Raimundo Lulio?," *Etudes de lettres* 2 (1986): 3–17.

Sugranyes de Franch, Ramón, *Ramon Llull a les Amèriques: Bartolomé de las Casas deixeble del doctor mallorquí?* (Palma: 1996).

Sugranyes de Franch, Ramón, "Ramon Llull, docteur des missions," *Studia monographica et recensiones* 5 (1951): 3–44.

Vilallonga, Mariàngela, *La literatura llatina a Catalunya al segle XV* (Barcelona: 1993).

Vincke, Johannes, "Comienzos de las misiones cristianas en las Islas Canarias," *Hispania Sacra* 12 (1959): 193–207.

Vincke, Johannes, "Die Evangelisation der Kanarischen Inseln im 14. Jahrhundert im Geiste Raimund Lulls," *EL* 4 (1960): 307–316.

CHAPTER 15

Lullism in New Spain

Linda Báez Rubí

15.1 Introduction

The European discovery of the Americas in 1492 offered for the Lullian Art new prospects for applying and implementing its features within the realms of education and pedagogical practice that humanist theories had opened. The first cleric familiar with Lullism to set foot on American soil was Friar Bernat Boïl (1445–1506),[1] whose interests John Dagenais describes in the preceding chapter of this volume.

15.2 Missions to the Caribbean Islands

The second instance of Lullist presence in the New World pertains to a group of Franciscan missionaries sent by Cardinal Francisco Jiménez de Cisneros on Columbus's second expedition to the Americas. Among them is recorded a Friar Juan de Robles, OFM, who owned a manuscript that contained works by Llull.[2] We know little or nothing about the evangelizing efforts of Robles on the islands or how his reading in Lullian texts might have influenced his activity. We can only surmise the provenance of his Lullian manuscript: an environment imbued with eschatological and apocalyptic dreams, suffused with Lullian hopes for universal Christianity and a tone of millenarianist prophecy.[3] Manuscripts of Llull's writings, together with two Marian works attributed to him, as well as other texts promoting the cult of the Immaculate Conception,

---

1 Odette d'Allerit, "Ramon Llull y la tradición del eremitismo apostólico," *EL* 6 (1962): 105–115; J. Anselm M. Albareda, "Lul.lisme a Montserrat al segle XVè: l'ermità Bernat Boïl," *EL* 9 (1965): 5–21; Quintín Aldea, Tomás Marín, et al. (eds.), *Diccionario de Historia Eclesiástica de España*, 5 vols. (Madrid: 1972–1987), 1:282.

2 Isaac Vázquez Janeiro, "¿Un lector de Raimundo Lulio y de Arnaldo de Vilanova entre los evangelizadores de la América Colombina?," *Humanismo, Reforma y Teología* 4 (1979): 1–36.

3 Josep Perarnau, "Los manuscritos lulianos en las bibliotecas Casanatense y Angélica," *Anthologica Annua* 21 (1974): 190–200, especially 192–193 (on Ramon Llull, *Liber de ente reali et rationis* and *Liber de notitia dei*) and 198–200 (on Arnold of Vilanova, *De elemosina et sacrificio* and *Dyalogus de elementis catholicae fidei*).

were copied and composed by the circle of Iberian beguines of the fourteenth and fifteenth centuries.[4] Robles unfortunately left to history no record of the methods of conversion that he directed toward the indigenous peoples of the islands, but simply insists on the need for protecting the Indians from destruction by the explorers, and for "some clergy to come here because the land is vast and the people so numerous that they are very necessary" for carrying out the labor of conversion.[5]

We thus find, only a decade after the discovery of the Americas, the first missionary projects and their clergy linked in one way or another with the Lullism promoted in beguine circles, but these faded in the face of conditions on the islands that impeded realization of a systematic evangelizing operation. This could only be achieved on the mainland, where it was possible to find a more stable social structure, with a political and religious system whose vestiges after the conquest allowed their restructuring—even though imposed—under the banner of the humanist utopianism that spread its ideals of universal harmony and concord to the American territories.

15.3   From Spain to the Viceroyalty of New Spain: Missionaries in the Context of the Lullian Art

The spirituality that arose on the mainland of New Spain was highly influenced by the Observant movements of Spain that culminated not only in the mysticism of the Golden Age, but also nourished the environment of spiritual renewal and reform encouraged by Cardinal Cisneros at the beginning of the 16th century. It is worth emphasizing that one of the chief literary sources of this spirituality in the peninsula was the *Theologia naturalis* of Raymond of

---

4   E.g. Ramon Astruc de Cortielles, *Disputacio secularis et jacobite*, (ed.) Pedro de Alva y Astorga, in *Monumenta antiqua seraphica pro Immaculata Conceptione Virginis Mariae* (Louvain: 1665), 441–463. Cf. Isaac Vázquez Janeiro, "'Disputatio saecularis et iacobiate,' actores y autor de un tratado inmaculista pseudoluliano del siglo XV," *Salmanticensis* 44 (1997): 25–87; Isaac Vázquez Janeiro, (ed.), *Tratados castellanos sobre la predestinación y sobre la Trinidad y la Encarnación, del maestro Fray Diego de Valencia OFM (siglo XV)* (Madrid: 1984), 103–157 and 161–173. On these doctrinal interests of the era, see Jaume de Puig i Oliver, "Nicolau Eimeric i Ramon Astruc de Cortielles: Novedades a propòsit de la controvèrsia mariana entorn de 1395," *Annals de l'Institut d'Estudis Gironins* 25 (1979–80): 304–311.

5   Robles, letter to Cisneros (Santo Domingo, 12 October 1500), in Ángel Ortega, *La Rábida: Historia documental crítica*, 4 vols. (Seville: 1925), 2:30: "vengan aqui algunos religiosos porque la tierra es tan grande e tanta la gente que son muy necesarios."

Sabunde,[6] from which it took, as a guiding principle, the duty of humankind to acknowledge the "blessings" (*beneficia*) offered in created nature. This "way of the blessings" found literary expression in various mystical and devotional works circulating at the time, such as the *Viola Animae* of Petrus Dorlandus (Toledo: 1500; Castilian version, Valladolid: 1549), written under the patronage of Cardinal Cisneros.[7] The *Viola* in turn was recast in the work *Lumbre del alma* (Valladolid: 1528 and Seville: 1542) by the *alumbrado* Juan de Cazalla, head chaplain of Cardinal Cisneros, collaborator in his religious reforms, partici-pant in the campaign at Oran, and familiar with the work of Jacques Lefèvre d'Étaples.[8] Cazalla's work contributed much to developing the practice of the "way of divine blessings," especially those provided through creation and God's love. For Cazalla, revelation was clearly available both from the Book of Nature and from Holy Scripture: "thanks to God's love for humankind, creatures join with God and attain the purpose of their creation, humans on their own and creatures through humankind."[9] Another interesting reworking of the *Viola* appeared in the anonymous *Despertador del alma adormida* (Seville: 1544 and Zaragoza: 1552),[10] which expounds, in a chart with painted figures, the secrets distilled in four colloquies, by concluding that "all [the figures] together make a book and each one of them is a chapter ... and if created beings are well studied and understood, they bring us to knowledge of ourselves and of the perfections that are in God."[11]

Within the framework of this environment of optimism, idealism, and utopianism among groups connected with Lullism, some recent scholarship has drawn attention to the possible Lullian affiliations of three missionaries sent to the Americas in the early 16th century: Friar Bartolomé de las Casas

6   Melquíades Andrés, *La teología española en el siglo XVI*, 2 vols. (Madrid: 1976), 2:259–270; Israël Salvator Révah, *Une source de spiritualité péninsulaire au XVI siècle: "La theologie naturelle" de Raimond Sebond* (Lisbon: 1953); cf. Jaume de Puig i Oliver, *La filosofia de Ramon Sibiuda* (Barcelona: 1997), 45.

7   Juan de Cazalla, *Lumbre del alma*, (ed.) Jesús Martínez de Bujanda (Madrid: 1974), 24–25.

8   Cf. Marcel Bataillon, *Erasmo y España: Estudios sobre la historia espiritual del siglo XVI*, trans. Antonio Alatorre, 2nd ed. (Mexico: 1966), 65–71.

9   Cazalla, *Lumbre*, cap. 16, part 1, (ed.) Martínez de Bujanda, 110: "por el amor que Dios tiene al hombre, las criaturas se juntan a Dios y alcanzan el fin de su creación; el hombre por sí mismo y las criaturas por medio del hombre."

10   Martínez de Bujanda, introduction to *Lumbre del alma*, 26–30; Melquíades Andrés, *Histo-ria de la mística de la Edad de Oro en España y América* (Madrid: 1994), 160.

11   Cited by Martínez de Bujanda, introduction to *Lumbre del alma*, 27–30: " todas [las figu-ras] juntas hacen un libro y cada una de ellas es un capítulo [...] y si las cosas criadas son bien miradas y bien entendidas, nos traen en conocimiento de nosotros mesmos y de las perfecciones que hay en Dios."

(ca. 1484–1566), Friar Alonso de Molina (1513–1580), and Toribio de Benavente Motolinía (1482–1568). Regarding Bartolomé de las Casas, his missionological treatise *De unico vocationis modo omnium gentium ad veram religionem* (1536–1537)[12] eschews Scholastic argumentation and proposes instead that, for people to accept the truths of the Christian faith, one must offer to their intellect reasons capable of persuading them.[13] Sugranyes de Franch has noted as Lullian elements in such arguments the use of necessary reasons, evangelization achieved only with spiritual weapons, and the peace necessary for the temporal and spiritual welfare of the indigenous peoples.[14] In the case of Molina, it was believed for some time that his *Doctrina cristiana breve* (Mexico: 1546) borrowed its structure from Llull's *Doctrina pueril.*[15] However, a more recent analysis has denied this relationship, associating Molina's structure with traditions of Christian instruction rather than with Lullian influences.[16] Finally, with Benavente Motolinía, it is possible to find traces, however vague, of the Lullism typical of the 16th-century Castilian Observants who enjoyed the patronage of the Counts of Benavente.[17]

More compelling evidence is available regarding Friar Juan de Zumárraga and Friar Diego de Valadés, who are therefore the principal subjects of this chapter. The proximity of these authors to the constellation of Lullist influences varies, thanks to certain differences regarding the use of sources or their interpretation. Nonetheless, both clearly manifest a common denominator that includes Lullian concepts of mission and conversion based on the use of rhetoric.

---

12   Bartolomé de las Casas, *De unico vocationis modo omnium gentium ad veram religionem,* (ed.) and trans. Antonio Millares Castro and Lewis Hanke (Mexico: 1942).

13   Ramón Sugranyes de Franch, "¿Bartolomé de las Casas, discípulo de Raimundo Lulio?," in *De Raimundo Lulio al Vaticano II* (Lausanne: 1991), 107–121; Las Casas, *De unico vocationis modo,* 5.1–4, cited in Sugranyes de Franch, "¿Bartolomé de las Casas?," 110.

14   Sugranyes, "¿Bartolomé de las Casas?," 111–112.

15   Robert Ricard, *La conquista espiritual de México,* trans. Ángel María Garibay (México: 1947), 215–216; León Lopetegui and Félix Zubillaga, *Historia de la Iglesia en la América Española,* 2 vols. (Madrid: 1965), 1:402.

16   Josep Maria Riera i Sans, "La actividad pastoral de fr. Alonso de Molina (1546–1565): una aproximación a las fuentes teológicas," *Excerpta e dissertationibus in Sacra Theologia* 19 (1991): 475–499.

17   Linda Báez Rubí, "La jerarquía imperial: imagen del deseo y de la crítica en el franciscanismo novohispano de evangelización," *Convenit Selecta* 4 (2000): 19–38. Regarding the twelve works of Llull in the library of the Counts of Benavente, see "Inventari de la biblioteca d'Alonso de Pimentel, tercer comte de Benavente (entre 1440 i 1461)," Archivo Histórico Nacional, Osuna (Spain), leg. 4210, núm. 2; cf. Isabel Beceiro Pita, "Los libros que pertenecieron a los Condes de Benavente, entre 1434 y 1530," *Hispania* 43 (1983): 237–280.

15.4 Friar Juan de Zumárraga, OFM (1468–1548)

Friar Juan de Zumárraga OFM, the first bishop and archbishop of Mexico, came to New Spain in 1527 to undertake one of the great defining endeavors of the colonial era in the 16th century: the evangelization of its native population and the organization of the missionary orders, along with their work amidst the recently demolished indigenous society.[18] Zumárraga was familiar with Llull's written oeuvre: he possessed the first printed biography of Blessed Ramon, by Charles de Bovelles, and in addition we know that he owned a copy of Llull's *Liber del amic et amat*, which unfortunately seems to have disappeared.[19] Several important characteristics link Zumárraga to Llull.

First are the three key points at the center of his catechetic doctrine: reason, faith, and devotion. By means of "reasons or credible ideas" (*razones o motivos de credibilidad*), which echo Llull's *rationes necessariae*, the Franciscan prelate attempts to lay a foundation for the origin of the revealed Word, since "understanding gives faith to faith" (*entender da fe a la fe*).[20] He explains, in addition, that this instruction is directed to everyone without distinction, as long as it makes clear the errors of the ancient philosophers and the unbelievers, and instills a noble and exalted knowledge of God and humankind.

Second, the theme of the "debt of love" (*debitum amoris*), linked to the "way of blessings" popularized by Raymond of Sabunde, appears in various parts of the work of Zumárraga, as for example when he invites "prayer, meditation, and contemplation" (*orar meditar y contemplar*) in order "to recall the blessings of God in order to give thanks for these and one's sins in order to repent of them."[21] Insistence on this theme is also evident in his *Regla cristiana breve*, which offers "instruction on how a Christian should give thanks to God," explaining thus a way or method of thanking God for the blessings that He has granted.[22] Zumárraga presents the path of deeply knowing and understanding these received blessings as an experience of love: "one should love God with all one's strength," because "He has given to humankind a power called

---

18   Joaquín García Icazbalceta, *Don Fray Juan de Zumárraga, primer obispo y arzobispo de México* (México: 1947).

19   Ildefonso Adeva Martín and Carmen José Alejos Grau, "Fuentes de inspiración de la *Regla Cristiana Breve* de Fray Juan de Zumárraga," *Archivum Franciscanum Historicum* 85 (1992): 96; Bataillon, *Erasmo y España*, 55, n. 12.

20   Juan de Zumárraga, *Regla cristiana breve*, doc. 5, (ed.) José Almoina (Mexico: 1951), 217.

21   Juan de Zumárraga, *Doctrina cristiana* (México: 1546), Suplemento, fol. n/3r: "traer a la memoria los beneficios de Dios para le dar gracias y sus pecados para arrepentirse de ellos."

22   Zumárraga, *Regla*, doc. 1, (ed.) Almoina, 23–25: "instrucción de cómo el christiano ha de dar gracias a Dios luego en la mañana."

the 'irascible' with which one organizes the memory for loving God."[23] In this way one comprehends and recalls the blessings given by God, and understands as well the Creator's plan for devoting all of one's interior faculties (memory, intellect, will) and exterior powers (the senses, body, and life) to service of the Lord.[24] Thus, the act of thanks should be one more fruit of the experience that arises from loving knowledge, something that encompasses the entire person.[25] For this reason, among the blessings from the creation, preservation, and recreation of life, the most important is the gift of the image and likeness of God.[26] Here we glimpse the tradition of Lullian and Sabundian anthropology, in which a human being, composed of a body and a soul, is capable of rising, through its faculties (memory, intellect, and will) above its natural condition and toward God.[27]

We could conclude that Zumárraga employs a Lullism without figures but guided by them. For example, by means of exercising Llull's Figure S, humans are capable of rising above their natural condition and toward the state in which, by participating in the image and likeness of God, they attain contemplation of the divine. For Zumárraga, humans, unlike other creatures, are the only beings that can rise up to God through their rational souls: "The second power of the soul is called understanding or reason, through which we are similar to the angels and different from beasts. And with this power we should recognize God, Lord and Creator of all creation, who is innately all-powerful, just, and good."[28] Zumárraga reprises this doctrine thus:

---

23   Juan de Zumárraga, *Doctrina breve* (México: 1543), fol. c 1r: "el hombre debe amar a Dios también con todas las fuerzas" ... "le ha dado al hombre una fuerza virtual llamada irascible con la cual ordena su memoria al amor de Dios."

24   Zumárraga, *Doctrina breve*, fol. c1r-v: "aviendo memoria de los infinitos bienes que nos ha hecho y haze de continuo ... avemos de amarle con la memoria como dicho es; y con el entendimiento pensando y entendiendo con nuestra inteligencia con la virtud y fuerza de la racional que nos enseña a alzar el entendimiento a las cosas del cielo ... le devemos de amar con la voluntad la qual avemos de regir y governar ... en manera que nuestra voluntad toda sea puesta en el amor de Dios ... Avemos assi mismo de amar a Dios con todas las fuerzas del cuerpo: como son los cinco sentidos ... mas que los ordenemos al servicio y amor de Dios, y que con todos los otros miembros y partes de nuestro cuerpo, como es la cabeça, el cuerpo, brazos, piernas y todos los miembros, en manera que todo quanto es en nos de dentro y de fuera se ocupe en alabanzas y servicio de Dios."

25   Fernando Gil, *Primeras doctrinas del Nuevo Mundo* (Buenos Aires: 1993), 540.

26   Zumárraga, *Doctrina cristiana*, Suplemento, fol. l/7r.

27   Linda Báez Rubí, "La herencia del *ars lulliana* contemplativa en el orbe cultural de la evangelización franciscana: fray Juan de Zumárraga y la vía de los beneficios en la Nueva España," *Antonianum* 80 (2005): 533–562.

28   Zumárraga, *Doctrina breve*, fol. k/2r: "La segunda potencia del ánima se llama entendimiento o razón, por la qual somos semejantes a los ángeles y desemejantes a las bestias.

... and above all by giving to God the first things that are most essential in your soul—intellect, will, and memory—since He declared these to be so, asking to be loved with all your heart and all your soul and all your strength. That is to say, that we contemplate His greatnesses in our prayer. Let our will pay the price, loving Him for them, since love is always repaid with love. Finally, let our memory not forget to thank our generous Lord, who never ceases to give such great gifts.[29]

Thus we see that he recommends organizing in prayer the three powers of the rational soul, which are most essential to it, namely intellect, will, and memory. The correct order to which he refers consists in each power fulfilling the functions that correspond to it: in intellect to understanding and contemplating the greatnesses of God, in will to making payment (that is, to rewarding love), and in memory to recalling the thanks due to God for the gifts received in nature, since God puts in action His properties (*dignitates*) in order give such great gifts (like that of creation) to humankind.[30] The argument of Zumárraga, seen according to the mechanism of the Lullian Figure S, would be:

Figure S: Species E

Individual components:	Acts:	Divine Dignities (from Figure A):
B – Intellect	E – contemplates	greatnesses
C – Will	E – makes payment by loving Him	for them
D – Memory	E – remembers to give thanks to	our generous Lord

Y que conozcamos con esta potencia al criador, Dios y Señor nuestro y de todas las criaturas, que es todopoderoso, justo y bueno escencialmente."

29 Zumárraga, *Regla*, doc. 1, (ed.) Almoina, 34: "y aun dando a Dios las primicias que es lo más primo de vuestra alma, entendimiento, voluntad y memoria. Pues El, estas primicias declaró assí, pidiendo ser amado de todo coraçón y de toda nuestra ánima y con todas nuestras fuerças. Esto es decir, que en la oración nuestro entendimiento contemple sus grandezas. Nuestra voluntad haga la paga, amándole por ellas, pues amor no se paga sino con amor. Finalmente nuestra memoria se acuerde de dar gracias a tan liberal Señor que jamás cansa de hazer tan largas mercedes."

30 Zumárraga, *Doctrina breve*, fol. k/2r, mentions the dignities "all-powerful," "just," and "good."

This is what Zumárraga terms "loving with all your heart and all your soul and all your strength," that is, the acts of the individual components (BCD) of the first species E are guided in an orderly manner in the Figure S of the rational soul. In this way, we can say that Zumárraga was surely influenced by the Lullism disseminated in his era and that he made use of certain Lullian elements, interweaving them into his doctrines and methodology for conversion.

15.5   Friar Diego de Valadés (1533–ca. 1583)

Born probably at Tlaxcala,[31] Friar Diego de Valadés entered the convent of Saint Francis at Mexico in 1545, where he learned Otomí, Nahuatl and Tarasco in order to convert indigenous peoples to Christianity using their own languages.[32] He also studied painting, philosophy, and theology in the Franciscan college at Santiago de Tlatelolco,[33] designed for the Christian education of the natives.[34] He was warden of the convent at Tlaxcala,[35] served as secretary to Friar Pedro de Gante, and was a missionary to regions in the north of Mexico until 1571, when he traveled to Europe to meet with Franciscan

---

31   Luke Wadding, *Annales Minorum*, 32 vols. (Lyon: 1625–54), 21:19; Agustín de Vetancourt, *Menologio Franciscano* (1698; repr. México: 1971), 142, and *Crónica de la Provincia del Santo Evangelio de México*, (1697–1698; repr. México: 1971), 47 and 109; Francisco de la Maza, "Fray Diego Valadés, escritor y grabador franciscano del siglo XVI," *Anales del Instituto de Investigaciones Estéticas* 13 (1945): 16; Esteban J. Palomera Quiroz, *Fray Diego de Valadés, O.F.M. evangelizador humanista de la Nueva España: Su obra* (Mexico: 1962) and *Fray Diego de Valadés, Evangelizador humanista de la Nueva España: El hombre y su época* (Mexico: 1963); Isaac Vázquez Janeiro, "Fray Diego Valadés: Nueva aproximación a su biografía," in *Actas del II Congreso Internacional sobre los franciscanos en el Nuevo Mundo, La Rábida, 21–26 de septiembre de 1987* (Madrid: 1988), 843–873.

32   Fray Diego de Valadés, *Rhetorica Christiana ad concionandi, et orandi usum accommodata, utriusque facultatis exemplis suo loco insertis, qua quidem, ex Indorum maxime deprompta sunt historiis unde praeter doctrinam, summa quoque delectatio comparabitur*, pars 4, cap. 11, (eds.) Esteban J. Palomera, Alfonso Castro Pallares, and Tarcisio Herrera Zapién (Mexico: 1989), 184.

33   José María Kobayashi, *La educación como conquista (empresa franciscana en México)* (México: 1985), 271; Pauline Moffitt Watts, "Hieroglyphs of conversion: Alien Discourses in Diego Valadés's *Rhetorica Christiana*," *Memorie Domenicane* 22 (1991), 409.

34   Fernando Ocaranza, *El Imperial Colegio de Santa Cruz de Santiago de Tlatelolco* (México: 1934); Francisco Borgia Steck, *El primer Colegio de América: Santa Cruz de Tlatelolco*, (México: 1944); Ricard, *La conquista espiritual de México*, 333–342; cf. Georges Baudot, *Utopía e historia en México: Los primeros cronistas de la civilización mexicana (1520–1569)* (Madrid: 1983).

35   George Kubler, *Mexican Architecture of the Sixteenth Century*, 2 vols. (New Haven: 1948), 2:375.

Minister General Christopher de Chaffontaines at the order's Chapter General in Paris, and continued on to Spain, charged with presenting to Juan de Ovando, president of the Council of the Indies, the work of the Franciscan missions in New Spain.[36] Valadés was named Procurator General of the Order in 1575, but deposed from this office in 1577 due to King Philip's policy against the excessive power that the Franciscans had accumulated in the Indies.[37] Valadés ended up taking refuge at San Pietro in Montorio, where he produced a manuscript entitled *Catholicae assertiones contra praecipuos aliquot hereticorum errores*.[38]

During his stay in Europe Valadés published the *Itinerarium Catholicum* (Seville: 1574) of Juan Focher, which treats catechizing and the organization of the missions in America.[39] Thus far, the *Rhetorica Christiana* is the only known original writing that Valadés managed to publish, and with some difficulty, since dismissal from his position in Rome interrupted its printing, and it finally appeared at Perugia in 1579.[40] The work is dedicated to Pope Gregory XIII, and its purpose is to serve as a manual for missionaries, seeking to endow them with a range of knowledge comparable to a "summa of summas of all learning" (*summam summarum scientiarum omnium*),[41] transmission of which would best be achieved through rhetoric and the arts of memory. In the *Rhetorica* one can detect the kind of Lullism cultivated by those disciples in the circle of Lavinheta that promoted transmission of the Lullian encyclopedic ideal through a peculiar work, long attributed to Llull, the *In Rhetoricam Isagoge* (París: 1515).[42] It combines elements derived from the Pythagorean, magical, cabbalistic, and mystical traditions,[43] presented through an effective method of transmission that would be ideal for the task of converting indigenous

---

36   Joaquín García Icazbalceta, *Nueva Colección de Documentos para la Historia de México*, 5 vols. (Mexico: 1886–92), 1:140.

37   Carmen José Alejos Grau, *Diego Valadés, Educador de la Nueva España* (Pamplona: 1994), 80.

38   *Catholicae assertiones contra praecipuos aliquot hereticorum errores*, (eds.) Bent Löfstedt and Scott Talkovic (Lund: 1998).

39   Juan Focher, *Itinerarium catholicum proficiscentium ad infideles convertendos*, (ed.) Antonio Eguiluz, 2 vols. (Madrid: 1960).

40   Valadés, *Rhetorica*, pars 4, cap. 11, (eds.) Palomera et al., 184.

41   Valadés, *Rhetorica*, praefatio ad lectorem, (eds.) Palomera et al., sig. b 2v.

42   Cf. Michela Pereira, "L'uso del Panepistemon del Poliziano nella *Isagoge in Rhetoricam* pseudo Lulliana," *Revista Internazionale di Storia della Scienza* 16 (1974): 223–233; 214–226; Elies Rogent and Estanislau Durán, *Bibliografia de les Impressions Lul.lianes* (Barcelona: 1927), 56; Joaquín Carreras i Artau and Tomás Carreras i Artau, *Historia de la filosofía española*, 2 vols. (Madrid: 1939–1943), 2:214–215.

43   Paola Zambelli, "Il *De audito kabbalistico* e la tradizione lulliana nel Rinascimento," *Atti dell'Accademia toscana di scienze e lettere La Colombaria* 30 (1965): 115–246; Rita

inhabitants of the Americas: rhetoric. The great popularity of the printings by Josse Bade and of Lefèvre d'Étaples's circle in the lands of New Spain is evident today in the legacies of convent libraries,[44] and was very likely due to the strong bonds between Cardinal Cisneros and the French Lullists.

In Valadés's rhetorical encyclopedia, the reality of the Americas supports a model of description and representation through rhetorical criteria drawn from the classical tradition, including the arts of memory.[45] The universe created by God reflects His order, His measure, and His essence. The background for this is woven from the vision of a Christian Neoplatonism necessary for reaffirming the divine harmony born of the order that sustains it. Consequently, the American worldview at first appears necessarily enclosed within the orderly Humanist vision of the encyclopedia,[46] then later fueling and expanding the categories of scientific knowledge.[47]

The specifically Lullian elements that appear in the work of Valadés are the nine Dignities, called instruments of God or predicates, since things are predicated from them and they are the beginning, middle, and end of everything.[48] Likewise, Valadés names the nine Lullian Subjects from the scale of being, about which one accomplishes refutations or confirmations.[49] This scale allows the preacher to ascend and descend through levels of causation, from the very highest to the very lowest and from the very lowest to the very highest (Figure 15.1).[50]

Valadés eschews using Llull's geometric figures to represent the functioning of the Lullian Principles and their interaction, attempting instead a figurative visualization of the nine Subjects, as done previously by the humanists associated with Lefèvre d'Étaples, specifically in the geometric diagrams of

---

Sturlese, "Lazar Zetzner, 'Bibliopola Argentinensis:' Alchimie und Lullismus in Strassburg an den Anfängen der Moderne," *Sudhoffs Archiv* 75 (1991): 142–162.

44   Eduardo Báez Macías, Jorge Guerra, and Judith Puente León, *Libros y grabados en el Fondo de Origen de la Biblioteca Nacional*, 2 vols. (Mexico: 1988–89).

45   Watts, "Hieroglyphs of conversion;" and René Taylor, "El arte de la memoria en el Nuevo Mundo," in *Iconología y sociedad, arte colonial hipanoamericano: XLIV Congreso Internacional de Americanistas* (Mexico: 1982), 43–76.

46   Wolfgang Neuber, *Fremde Welt im europäischen Horizont. Zur Topik der deutschen Amerika-Reiseberichte der Frühen Neuzeit* (Berlin: 1991).

47   Bernardino de Sahagún, *Florentine Codex: General History of the Things of New Spain*, book 1, Prologue, (eds.) Charles E. Dibble and Arthur Anderson, (Salt Lake City: 1982), 46, and book 11, "To the reader," 88. Cf. the outstanding effort for the classification of plants by Francisco Hernández, *De materia medica Novae Hispaniae libri quatuor*, (eds.) Raquel Álvarez Peláez and Florentino Fernández González (Aranjuez and Valladolid: 1998).

48   First noticed by Mauricio Beuchot, "Retórica y lulismo en Diego de Valadés," *EL* 32 (1992): 153–161; cf. Valadés, *Rhetorica*, pars 2, cap. 7, (eds.) Palomera et al., 57.

49   Ibid., pars 2, cap. 6, (eds.) Palomera et al., 56.

50   Ibid., pars 2, cap. 17, (eds.) Palomera et al., 72.

FIGURE 15.1   Diego de Valadés, The Levels of Creation, from his *Rhetorica christiana*
(Perugia: 1579), between 220–221.

Bovelles and in the engravings from the *Explanatio* of Bernardo de Lavinheta
regarding encyclopedic trees.[51] The peculiarity of Valadés consists in his attempt to clothe the Lullian Subjects with American fashions. That is, he tries

---

51   As described above in the chapter "Lullism Among French and Spanish Humanists of the
Sixteenth Century."

to adapt them to the reality of the flora and fauna of the region, combined with the classificatory tradition of classical rhetoric and Lullist encyclopedic models, in which the art of memory was a key factor not only for organizing knowledge, but also for facilitating its study.[52] The result is a curious mix of European and American cultures in which the visual evidence of engraving expresses that situation, while the solutions employed by Valadés for depicting the Lullian Subjects reveal for us the processes of acculturation in the lands of New Spain, where the rich body of images drawn from the early 16th-century editions of Charles de Bovelles and Bernardo de Lavinheta was enormously influential.[53]

With regard to the latter, it is possible to consider his *Explanatio* as a source for the interesting testimony to Lullist influence apparent in the motif of arboreal hierarchies, first found in the mural paintings of New Spain when Motolinía describes their use in celebrating festivities at Tlaxcala in 1539.[54] Since Valadés was warden of the Franciscan convent at Tlaxcala, it is very likely that the engravings published in his *Rhetorica* were based on images sketched on the walls of the chapel open to natives at the convent. Valadés offers two engravings, of the temporal and ecclesiastical hierarchies (Figures 15.2 and 15.3).[55]

While this is a common theme in the medieval era, based on the model of the hierarchical ordering of the created universe from Pseudo-Dionysius,[56] Valadés clearly combines it with representation of the Lullian "Apostolic Tree" and "Imperial Tree" found in editions of Lavinheta's *Explanatio*, since it visualizes the organization of society and functions of its members (from the Pope, cardinals, archbishops and so forth to the emperor, kings, dukes, and others), all directed toward maintaining the order, concord, peace, and conditions essential for loving God.[57] Valadés puts Lullist concepts to work in images and visualization, because their function corresponds exactly to one of Llull's original goals: conversion and evangelization. But he applies it on another continent, among the natives of New Spain, where the transmission of knowledge

52   Valadés, *Rhetorica*, praefatio ad lectorem, (eds.) Palomera et al., sig. b 2v.
53   Linda Báez Rubí, *Die Rezeption der Lehre des Ramon Llull in der* Rhetorica Christiana *des Franziskaners Fray Diego de Valadés* (*Perugia, 1579*) (Frankfurt: 2004).
54   Toribio Benavente Motolinía, *Historia de los indios de la Nueva España*, trat. 1, cap. 15, (ed.) Edmundo O'Gorman (Mexico: 1990), 149, 164–165; George Kubler, *Mexican Architecture*, 2:174–177.
55   Valadés, *Rhetorica*, pars 4, cap. 10, (eds.) Palomera et al., 180–181.
56   Valadés, *Rhetorica*, pars 4, cap. 9, ed Palomera et al., 177.
57   Báez Rubí, *Die Rezeption*, 181–213.

FIGURE 15.2   Diego de Valadés, The Temporal Hierarchy, from his *Rhetorica christiana*
(Perugia: 1579), between 180–181.

through images was deeply rooted in the humanist pedagogical culture that
sought to sow spiritual renewal in the conquered territories. Its successes and
failures relate for us the complex processes of acculturation that wove the history of these missions in the Americas.

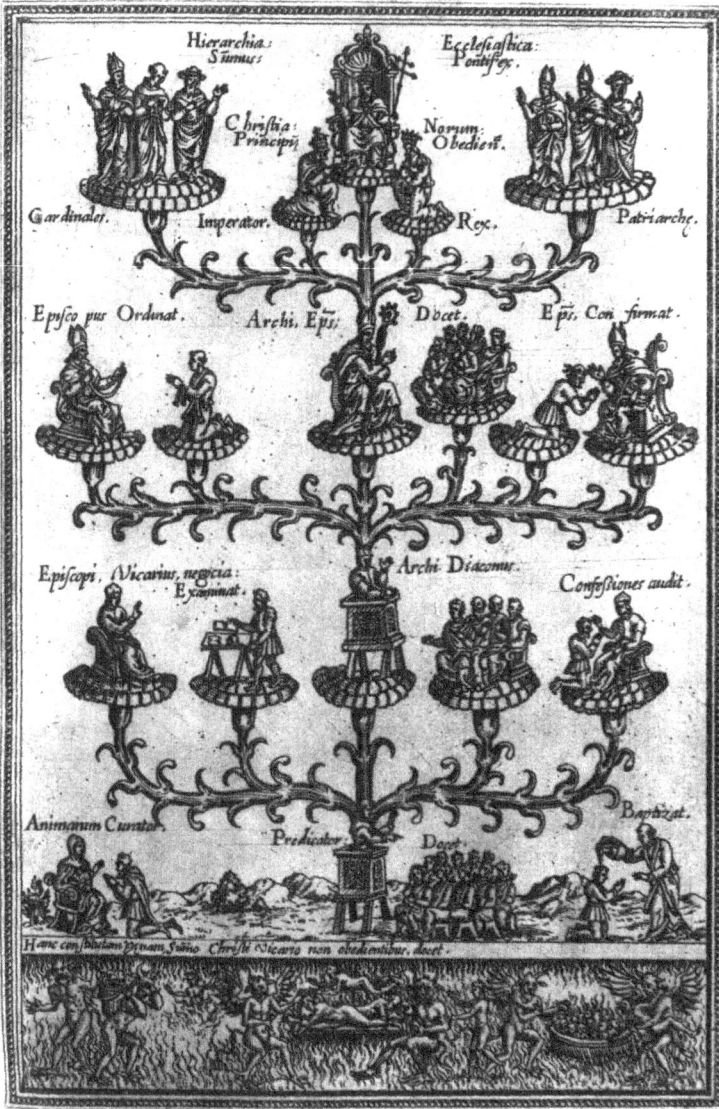

FIGURE 15.3   Diego de Valadés, The Ecclesiastical Hierarchy, from his *Rhetorica christiana*
(Perugia: 1579), between 180–181.

15.6   Conclusion

The movement of spiritual renewal, undertaken originally by Franciscan
Observants in the Iberian peninsula, gave rise to the dissemination of Lullist
doctrines that constituted a model to follow, both in contemplation and in
evangelizing aims, among the first missionaries who were sent on behalf of

the Spanish Crown to the New World. In this era, the first generations of friars, products of this religious reformation and charged with organizing the spiritual life of the conquered indigenous peoples, favored adaptations of the Lullian Art, reformulating it within the humanist legacy forged by the French and Iberian scholars encouraged by Cardinal Cisneros. Exemplary works by Zumárraga, Bartolomé de las Casas, Alonso de Molina, Toribio de Benavente, and Diego de Valadés illustrate broadly the different strains of Lullian influence, reception, and reformulation in their endeavors. Especially noteworthy are the visualizations of Lullian concepts and their operation in pictorial figurations, such as the engravings published by Valadés in his *Rhetorica*. They show us how inventively and flexibly the friars reflected on the Lullist heritage when converting the indigenous population to Christianity, despite cultural differences. The enterprise of religious organization undertaken by these missionaries undoubtedly shaped indigenous Christian spirituality, laying the foundation of successful spiritual life in the viceroyalty of New Spain for centuries to come.

Works Cited

Primary Works

Anonymous, *Despertador del alma adormida* (Seville: 1544 and Zaragoza: 1552).

Astruc de Cortielles, Ramon, *Disputacio secularis et jacobite*, (ed.) Pedro de Alva y Astorga, in *Monumenta antiqua seraphica pro Immaculata Conceptione Virginis Mariae* (Louvain, 1665).

Benavente Motolinía, Fray Toribio, *Historia de los indios de la Nueva España*, (ed.) Edmundo O'Gorman (Mexico: 1990).

Bartolomé de las Casas, *De unico vocationis modo omnium gentium ad veram religionem*, (ed.) and trans. Antonio Millares Castro and Lewis Hanke (Mexico: 1942).

Cazalla, Juan de, *Lumbre del alma*, (ed.) Jesús Martínez de Bujanda (Madrid: 1974).

Dorlandus, Petrus, *Viola animae* (Toledo: 1500; Castilian version of Valladolid: 1549).

Focher, Juan, *Itinerarium catholicum proficiscentium ad infideles convertendos*, (ed.) Antonio Eguiluz, 2 vols. (Madrid: 1960).

Hernández, Francisco, *De materia medica Novae Hispaniae libri quatuor*, (eds.) Raquel Álvarez Peláez and Florentino Fernández González (Aranjuez and Valladolid: 1998).

Molina, Alonso de, *Doctrina cristiana breve* (Mexico: 1546).

Pseudo-Lullian, *In Rhetoricam Isagoge* (Paris: 1515).

Pseudo-Lullian, *In Rhetoricam Isagoge*, in *Raymundi Lulli Opera*, (ed.) Lazarus Zetzner (Strasbourg: 1598; repr. 1617 and 1651).

Sahagún, Bernardino de, *Florentine Codex: General History of the Things of New Spain*, (eds.) Charles E. Dibble and Arthur Anderson, 12 vols. in 13 books (Salt Lake City: 1950–1982).

Valadés, Diego de, *Catholicae assertiones contra praecipuos aliquot hereticorum errores*, (eds.) Bent Löfstedt and Scott Talkovic (Lund: 1998).

Valadés, Diego de, *Rhetorica christiana ad concionandi, et orandi usum accommodata, utriusque facultatis exemplis suo loco insertis, qua quidem, ex Indorum maxime deprompta sunt historiis unde praeter doctrinam, summa quoque delectatio comparabitur*, (eds.) Esteban J. Palomera, Alfonso Castro Pallares, and Tarcisio Herrera Zapién (1579; repr. Mexico: 1989).

Valencia, Diego de, *Tratados castellanos sobre la predestinación y sobre la Trinidad y la Encarnación, del maestro Fray Diego de Valencia OFM (siglo XV)*, (ed.) Isaac Vázquez Janeiro (Madrid: 1984), 161–173.

Vetancourt, Agustín de, *Crónica de la Provincia del Santo Evangelio de México*, (1697–98; repr. Mexico: 1971).

Vetancourt, Agustín de, *Doctrina cristiana* (Mexico: 1546).

Vetancourt, Agustín de, *Menologio Franciscano* (1697–98; repr. Mexico: 1971).

Vetancourt, Agustín de, *Regla cristiana breve*, (ed.) José Almoina (Mexico: 1951).

Wadding, Luke, *Annales Minorum*, 32 vols. (Lyon: 1625–54).

Zumárraga, Juan de, *Doctrina breve* (Mexico: 1543).

Secondary Works

Adeva Martín, Ildefonso and Carmen José Alejos Grau, "Fuentes de inspiración de la *Regla Cristiana Breve* de Fray Juan de Zumárraga," *Archivum Historicum Franciscanum* 85 (1992): 77–98.

Albareda, Anselm Maria, "Lul.lisme a Montserrat al segle XVè: l'ermità Bernat Boïl," *EL* 9 (1965): 5–21.

Aldea, Quintín, Tomás Marín, et al., (eds.), *Diccionario de Historia Eclesiástica de España*, 5 vols. (Madrid: 1972–1987).

Alejos Grau, Carmen José, *Diego Valadés, Educador de la Nueva España* (Pamplona: 1994).

Andrés, Melquíades, *Historia de la mística de la Edad de Oro en España y América* (Madrid: 1994).

Andrés, Melquíades, *La teología española en el siglo XVI*, 2 vols. (Madrid: 1976).

Báez Macías, Eduardo, Jorge Guerra, and Judith Puente León, *Libros y grabados en el Fondo de Origen de la Biblioteca Nacional*, 2 vols. (Mexico: 1988–1989).

Báez Rubí, Linda, "La herencia del *ars lulliana* contemplativa en el orbe cultural de la evangelización franciscana: fray Juan de Zumárraga y la vía de los beneficios en la Nueva España," *Antonianum* 80 (2005): 533–562.

Báez Rubí, Linda, "La jerarquía imperial: imagen del deseo y de la crítica en el franciscanismo novohispano de evangelización," *Convenit Selecta* 4 (2000): 19–38.

Báez Rubí, Linda, *Die Rezeption der Lehre des Ramon Llull in der Rhetorica Christiana des Franziskaners Fray Diego de Valadés (Perugia, 1579)* (Frankfurt: 2004).

Bataillon, Marcel, *Erasmo y España: Estudios sobre la historia espiritual del siglo XVI*, trans. Antonio Alatorre, 2nd ed. (Mexico: 1966).

Baudot, Georges, *Utopía e historia en México: Los primeros cronistas de la civilización mexicana (1520–1569)* (Madrid: 1983).

Beceiro Pita, Isabel, "Los libros que pertenecieron a los Condes de Benavente, entre 1434 y 1530," *Hispania* 43 (1983): 237–280.

Beuchot, Mauricio, "Retórica y lulismo en Diego de Valadés," *Estudios Lulianos* 32 (1992): 153–161.

Carreras y Artau, Joaquín and Tomás Carreras y Artau, *Historia de la filosofía española*, 2 vols. (Madrid: 1939–1943).

D'Allerit, Odette, "Ramon Llull y la tradición del eremitismo apostólico," *EL* 6 (1962): 105–115.

García Icazbalceta, Joaquín, *Don Fray Juan de Zumárraga, primer obispo y arzobispo de México* (Mexico: 1947).

García Icazbalceta, Joaquín, *Nueva Colección de Documentos para la Historia de México*, 5 vols. (Mexico: 1886–92).

Gil, Fernando, *Primeras doctrinas del Nuevo Mundo* (Buenos Aires: 1993).

"Inventari de la biblioteca d'Alonso de Pimentel, tercer comte de Benavente (entre 1440 i 1461)," Archivo Histórico Nacional, Osuna (Spain), leg. 4210, núm. 2.

Kobayashi, José María, *La educación como conquista (empresa franciscana en México)* (Mexico: 1985).

Kubler, George, *Mexican Architecture of the Sixteenth Century*, 2 vols. (New Haven: 1948).

Lopetegui, León and Félix Zubillaga, *Historia de la Iglesia en la América Española* (Madrid: 1965).

Maza, Francisco de la, "Fray Diego Valadés, escritor y grabador franciscano del siglo XVI," *Anales del Instituto de Investigaciones Estéticas* 13 (1945): 15–44.

Neuber, Wolfgang, *Fremde Welt im europäischen Horizont: Zur Topik der deutschen Amerika-Reiseberichte der Frühen Neuzeit* (Berlin: 1991).

Ocaranza, Fernando, *El Imperial Colegio de Santa Cruz de Santiago de Tlatelolco* (Mexico: 1934).

Ortega, Ángel, *La Rábida: Historia documental crítica*, 4 vols. (Sevilla: 1925).

Palomera Quiroz, Esteban J., *Fray Diego de Valadés, evangelizador humanista de la Nueva España: El hombre y su época* (Mexico: 1963).

Palomera Quiroz, Esteban J., *Fray Diego de Valadés, O.F.M. evangelizador humanista de la Nueva España: Su obra* (Mexico: 1962).

Perarnau, Josep, "Los manuscritos lulianos en las bibliotecas Casanatense y Angélica," *Anthologica Annua* 21 (1974): 190–200.

Pereira, Michela, "L'uso del Panepistemon del Poliziano nella *Isagoge in Rhetoricam* pseudo Lulliana," *Revista Internazionale di Storia della Scienza* 16 (1974): 223–233.

Puig i Oliver, Jaume de, *La filosofia de Ramon Sibiuda* (Barcelona: 1997).

Puig i Oliver, Jaume de, "Nicolau Eimeric i Ramon Astruc de Cortielles: Novedades a propòsit de la controvèrsia mariana entorn de 1395," *Annals de l'Institut d'Estudis Gironins* 25 (1979–80): 304–311.

Révah, Israël Salvator, *Une source de la spiritualité péninsulaire au XVI siècle: "La theologie naturelle" de Raimond Sebond* (Lisbon: 1953).

Ricard, Robert, *La conquista espiritual de México*, trans. Ángel María Garibay (Mexico: 1986).

Riera i Sans, Josep Maria, "La actividad pastoral de Fr. Alonso de Molina (1546–1565): una aproximación a sus fuentes teológicas," *Excerpta e dissertationibus in Sacra Theologia* 19 (1991): 473–532.

Rogent, Elies and Estanislau Durán, *Bibliografia de les Impressions Lul.lianes* (Barcelona: 1927).

Steck, Francisco Borgia, El primer colegio de América: Santa Cruz de Tlatelolco (Mexico: 1944).

Sturlese, Rita, "Lazar Zetzner, 'Bibliopola Argentinensis:' Alchimie und Lullismus in Strassburg an den Anfängen der Moderne," *Sudhoffs Archiv* 75 (1991): 142–162.

Sugranyes de Franch, Ramón, "¿Bartolomé de las Casas, discípulo de Raimundo Lulio?," in *De Raimundo Lulio al Vaticano II* (Lausanne: 1991), 107–121.

Taylor, René, "El arte de la memoria en el Nuevo Mundo," in *Iconología y sociedad, arte colonial hipanoamericano: XLIV Congreso Internacional de Americanistas* (Mexico: 1982), 43–76.

Vázquez Janeiro, Isaac, "'Disputatio saecularis et iacobiate,' actores y autor de un tratado inmaculista pseudoluliano del siglo XV," *Salmanticensis* 44 (1997): 25–87.

Vázquez Janeiro, Isaac, "Fray Diego Valadés. Nueva aproximación a su biografía," in *Actas del II Congreso Internacional sobre los franciscanos en el Nuevo Mundo, La Rábida, 21–26 de septiembre de 1987* (Madrid: 1988), 843–873.

Vázquez Janeiro, Isaac, *Tratados castellanos sobre la predestinación y sobre la Trinidad y la Encarnación, del maestro Fray Diego de Valencia OFM (siglo XV)* (Madrid: 1984).

Vázquez Janeiro, Isaac, "¿Un lector de Raimundo Lulio y de Arnaldo de Vilanova entre los evangelizadores de la América Colombina?," *Humanismo, Reforma y Teología* 4 (1979): 1–36.

Watts, Pauline Moffitt, "Hieroglyphs of conversion: Alien Discourses in Diego Valadés's *Rhetorica Christiana*," *Memorie Domenicane* 22 (1991): 405–433.

Zambelli, Paola, "Il *De audito kabbalistico* e la tradizione lulliana nel Rinascimento," *Atti dell'Accademia Toscana di Scienze e Lettere La Colombaria* 30 (1965): 115–246.

CHAPTER 16

A Lullist in the New World: Junípero Serra

John Dagenais

The Lullian and the missionary vocations of Friar Junípero Serra (1713–1784) are far easier to establish than those of Bernat Boïl, though these two aspects of Serra's calling do not necessarily overlap. Like Llull, Serra was a Majorcan. He was born in the town of Petra and christened Miquel Joseph Serra. Unlike Llull, whose "conversion" and rededication to the Christian faith came when he was well into adult life, Serra was immediately drawn to the religious life and professed his calling at the earliest possible opportunity, remaining in the Franciscan order until his death. He is most remembered today as the founder of nine missions in Alta California, many of which survive, though in much modified form. Like Llull, he worked not only at direct evangelization – in his case, of the native populations of New Spain – but understood that an infrastructure, both material and political, was necessary to support the work of conversion.

His professional career can be divided into two parts: his years as Franciscan novice, then student and professor in the Convent of Saint Francis in Palma (1730–1749); and his radically different life in New Spain following his missionary calling (1749–1784). It is during the first period that we find the first documented evidence of Serra's life-long devotion to Llull. Serra made his profession in the Franciscan order in 1731, taking on the name of Saint Francis's beloved companion Junípero: it seems that Serra took this name in its Castilian form, rather than in his native Catalan of Majorca; I have not encountered any documents, including his letters in Catalan, in which he uses possible Catalan forms. Each day during his time of residence in the convent of Saint Francis, Serra must have walked past the magnificent Gothic tomb of Ramon Llull which has occupied a space behind the main altar since the mid 15th century.[1]

Serra had a distinguished career as a preacher and professor in his native Majorca, a part of his life little understood and little studied, and always in the shadow of his reputation as "the founder of the California missions." In fact, he did not travel to the Americas until he was 36 years old, spending almost half of his life, then, in his native Majorca. The life of Serra is most intimately told

---

[1] Miguel Ferrer Flórez, "Culte a Ramon Llull: Discòrdies i controvèrsies," *SL* 41 (2001): 66, n. 4, notes that there were, in fact, three chapels dedicated to Llull in the Convent of Saint Francis.

Ⓒ KONINKLIJKE BRILL NV, LEIDEN, 2019 | DOI:10.1163/9789004379671_017

by his companion and former student Francesc Palou.[2] Palou was a student in a class taught by Serra, a class for which we are fortunate to have three years of lecture notes written by another student in the class, Francesc Noguera.[3]

The question of a possible relation, an intellectual affiliation, between the 13th century Majorcan missionary-philosopher Ramon Llull and the eighteenth century Majorcan founder of the California missions Junípero Serra is an intriguing one. Both Majorcans, separated in time by more than four centuries, dedicated the bulk of their efforts to missionary work, Llull's work being largely, but by no means exclusively, theoretical (his Art) and strategic (his petitioning of Christian rulers to support missions), Serra's being largely practical, tactical, on the ground. Llull inhabited the Mediterranean world and was primarily interested in the conversion of Muslims and Jews. Serra's missionary work was among the native inhabitants of Mexico's Sierra Gorda and the Californias. Did Junípero Serra know about Ramon Llull and about his ideas on missions? Was Serra's missionary work in California in any way informed by the ideas of Ramon Llull? Did the arcana of Llull's Art or the practical example of Llull's life serve in any way in the evangelization of New Spain?[4] These questions can be answered, to some extent, by materials found in the archives of the Santa Barbara (Calif.) Mission Archive and Library, especially the Serra collection held there, and in the libraries of Palma de Majorca, especially that of

---

2   Francesc Palou, *Relación Histórica de la Vida y Apostólicas Tareas del Venerable Padre Fray Junípero Serra...* (1787; repr. New York: 1966); Francesc Palou, *Palóu's Life of Fray Junípero Serra*, trans. Maynard J. Geiger (Washington, D.C.: 1955). Geiger has also written his own account of Serra's life and its context: *The Life and Times of Fray Junípero Serra, O.F.M. or The Man Who Never Turned Back (1713–1784)*, 2 vols. (Washington, D.C.: 1959). James A. Sandos, "Junípero Serra's Canonization and the Historical Record," *The American Historical Review* 93 (1988): 1253–1269, and Steven W. Hackel, "The Competing Legacies of Junípero Serra," *Common-Place: The Interactive Journal of Early American Life* 5.2 (2005) [Web: http://www .common-place.org/vol-05/no-02/hackel/index.shtml], seek to provide balanced summaries of Serra's life, the attendant controversies regarding his conduct as missionary, and his legacy. See also now James A. Sandos, *Converting California; Indians and Franciscans in the Missions* (New Haven and London: 2004) and Steven W. Hackel, *Junípero Serra: California's Founding Father* (New York: 2013). Daniel Fogel, *Junípero Serra, the Vatican, and Enslavement Theology* (San Francisco, Calif.: 1988), gives an anti-Serra viewpoint.

3   Francesc Noguera, *Compendium Scoticum elaboratum tamquam ab auctore Patre Fratre Iunipero Serra, et tamquam ab scriptore Francisco Noguera studente in conventu Seraphici Patris Nostri sancti Francisci ab Assissio. Fuit inceptus luce nona mensis Septembris anno a Nativitate Domini nostri 1740*, Palma de Majorca, Biblioteca de Sant Felip Neri, item 68900.

4   I wish to express here my gratitude to Lynn Bremer, formerly of the Santa Barbara Mission Archive and Library, for her help with this project and to the late Marc Vallori, C.O., of Sant Felip Neri, for his kindness and generosity in allowing me to view the Noguera manuscript held there.

Sant Felip Neri and the Biblioteca Pública. But before taking a look at Serra's documented contacts with Lullism and Lullian thought, it is worthwhile to understand the general Lullian atmosphere in Majorca in Serra's early years.

According to the brothers Carreras i Artau, by the 18th century, the main European centers of interest in Ramon Llull had been reduced to Majorca and to Germany, where Ivo Salzinger was preparing his great edition of Llull's Latin works, *Raymundi Lulli Opera omnia*.[5] In Majorca, Enlightenment values gave rise, on the one hand, to what Carreras i Artau called "critical and learned Lullism" (*el lulismo crítico y erudito*) – works of edition, biography, and bibliography, inspired in part by Salzinger's editorial activities in Mainz. Numerous studies and editions of Lull's works were published in Majorca during the 18th century, beginning with Custurer's *Disertaciones históricas del culto inmemorial del B. Raymundo Lullio* in 1700.[6] Llull's *Liber proverbiorum* was published at Majorca in 1735 and his *Doctrina pueril* the following year.[7] Perhaps most important were the series of Llull's Latin and Catalan works published as *Opuscula* and *Opera parva*,[8] inspired by Salzinger's collection and initiated in 1744, and thus during Serra's time in Majorca.

On the other hand, Carreras i Artau note, there was a polemical form of Lullism, a reaction, in part, to the perennial anti-Lullism of the Dominicans. Planas describes how throughout the 18th century "a flood of hymns, pamphlets, edicts and printed papers of all kinds circulated throughout Majorca, both for and against [Llull], claiming sainthood for Llull or besmirching his name and dragging it down to the crudest level of histrionic debate."[9] As Planas remarks, this conflict took place at the "street level." The parties even had their own nicknames. Llull's supporters (chiefly the Franciscans) were known

---

5 Joaquín Carreras i Artau and Tomás Carreras i Artau, *Historia de la filosofía española: Filosofía cristiana de los siglos XIII al XV*, 2 vols. (Madrid: 1939–1943), 2:354–386. See also Ferrer, "Controversias" and "Culte;" and Rosa Planas Ferrer, "La projecció de Llull," in Fundació "La Caixa," *Ramon Llull: Història, Pensament i Llegenda* (Palma: 2008), 97–106, 201–208 (English text) for the various controversies centered on Llull in this century. *Raymundi Lulli Opera omnia*, (ed.) Ivo Salzinger, 8 vols. (Mainz: 1721–42).

6 Jaime Custurer, *Disertaciones históricas del culto inmemorial del B. Raymundo Lullio Dr. Iluminado y Mártir, y de la inmunidad de censuras, que goza su Dotrina; con un Apendiz de su Vida* (Majorca: 1700).

7 *Liber proverbiorum: in tres partes divisus ... in proverbia de Deo & de naturalibus & de moralibus* (Majorca: 1735–38); *Llibre de Doctrina Pueril compost en llengua llamosina per lo Illuminat Doctor y Martyr invictissim de Christo el B. Ramon Llull mallorqui, Traduit a llengua usual mallorquina per un devot Dexeble seu à utilidat de los miñons de Mallorca* (Majorca: 1736).

8 Elies Rogent and Estanislau Duran, *Bibliografia de les impressions lul·lianes* (Barcelona: 1927), 301–355 provide detailed data about each volume from these series.

9 Planas, "Projecció," 206–207, cites several fascinating cases of pro- and anti-Llull activities, though some of these take place after Serra's departure.

as "swallows" (*gorrions*) and the detractors (chiefly the Dominicans) as *marrells*. Planas translates *marrells* as "black and white ducks," a meaning I have not been able to verify independently, but perhaps relating to the black habits of the Dominicans, as *gorrions* seems to relate to the color of the Franciscan habit. The name *marrells* may also have derived from the surname of the great 14th-century persecutor of Lullism, Nicholas Eymerich y Marrell.[10] At a more intellectual level, during Serra's last years in Majorca, fierce opposition arose to the harsh critiques of Llull by the Galician Benedictine friar Benito Jerónimo Feijóo, a figure generally associated with the Enlightenment in Spanish intellectual history. His critiques were first published in 1742, while Serra was working as professor, and Lullists were quick to respond. Llull's major defender in Majorca was Antonio Raymundo Pasqual, who was born in Andratx just a few years before Serra, in 1708. He had published works on Llull as early as 1740 and his *Examen de la crisis del padre don Benito Gerónimo Feijoo* appeared in April of 1749,[11] as Serra was preparing secretly to leave Majorca behind forever. In 1743, Pasqual preached a sermon on the feast of Llull's conversion on January 25: "The miraculous wisdom of the Blessed Illuminated Doctor Ramon Llull, Martyr, and Patron of the Lullian University of Majorca" (*El milagro de la sabiduria del B. Raymundo Lulio Doctor Illuminado, y Martyr, y Patron de la Luliana Universidad de Majorca*) a sermon that Serra likely heard. (Serra himself would preach a sermon on this date in 1749). Pasqual's four-volume magnum opus *Vindiciae Lullianae* appeared at Avignon in 1778.[12] Carreras i Artau see him as a figure who unites both the learned and the polemical strains of 18th-century Majorcan Lullism, but attribute a sort of "Lullomania" to him when, in his *Descubrimiento de la aguja nautica*, he claims for Llull the discovery of the magnetic compass and of other navigational mysteries, together with the "discovery" by "philosophical observation" (*observación filosófica*) alone that there was land on the other side of the Atlantic, a discovery thence known and acted upon by Columbus.[13] Interestingly, Pasqual devotes the final 25 pages of his treatise to Bernat Boïl.

Ferrer posits 1748, the year before Serra's departure, as the moment when the debates between Lullists and anti-Lullists began to heat up.[14] So, I believe

---

10   Ferrer, "Culte," 69, n. 8.

11   Antonio Raymundo Pasqual, *Examen de la crisis de el R.^mo Padre maestro don Benito Geronimo Feijoo monge benedictino sobre el arte luliana; en el qual se manifiesta la santidad y culto del iluminado doctor y martyr el B. Raymundo Lulio, la pureza de su doctrina, y la utilidad de su arte y ciencia general* (Madrid: 1749–50).

12   Antonio Raymundo Pasqual, *Vindiciae Lullianae: sive demonstratio critica immunitatis doctrinae illuminati Doctoris B. Raymundi Lulli*, 4 vols. (Avignon: 1778).

13   Antonio Raymundo Pasqual, *Descubrimiento de la aguja nautica* (Madrid: 1789).

14   Ferrer, "Controversias," 160.

it is safe to say that Serra was likely well aware of the most controversial issues concerning Llull's legacy in the island of his birth and that Serra was himself a "swallow" (*gorrió*). But perhaps no other issue related to Llull touched Serra more deeply and enduringly throughout his life than the conflicts concerning the doctrine of the Immaculate Conception. This doctrine, too, was a matter of great controversy on the island in the 18th century, a controversy that, once again, pitted Franciscans against Dominicans. It was during Serra's earliest years in Palma that a celebration took place in 1732 of the recent victory in Oran, as well as the doctrine of the Immaculate Conception, that included Lullists, Franciscans and Jesuits.[15]

Our first hints of the nature of the connection between Serra and Llull come from Serra's own study notes, made while he was still a student.[16] In one of his courses, Serra studied Llull's *Liber de angelis* (1276–1283?), as well as a second book on "the speech of angels" from 1312, *Liber de locutione angelorum*.[17] In the exordium to the notes taken by Serra for this class, taught by Joan Pol, we find the following description: "expounding on the theological treatise *De angelis* following the firm path of the Unconquered Martyr of Christ, the Archangelic and Marian Doctor, the Blessed Ramon Llull."[18] So we know that Serra studied at least one aspect of Llull's works in some depth, though in this class scholastic methodology seems to have taken precedence over the actual text by Llull. In his colophon to these course notes, dated 22 June 1737, Serra recognizes Llull

15   *Epílogo breve de los piadosos desvelos con que las tres escuelas del iluminado dotor y mártir el beato Raymundo Lullio, del sutil Escoto y eximio Suárez rindieron las gracias al Dios de las vitorias por la que consiguieron contra Orán las armas católicas de nuestro magnánimo monarca don Felipe quinto, que Dios guarde. Sale a luz consagrándole los alumnos marianos a la puríssima concepción de María santíssima* (Barcelona: 1732).

16   I have used the photocopies of the collected signature pages in "Class Notes in Theology by Serra, 1735–1737," Santa Barbara Mission Archive and Library, Serra Collection 10, Provenance Uncertain, Latin, Phg. 4 Pp., Palma, 06/22/1737, and the full texts of these notes in Palma de Majorca, Biblioteca Pública, MS 76, fols. 153–191 and MS 882. The latter contains notes by Serra from a course on Aristotle taught by Bernardino Castayó, a course very similar in content to one that Serra would eventually teach. See Jesús García Pastor and María Marsá, *Inventario de Manuscritos de la Biblioteca Pública del Estado en Mallorca* (Madrid: 1989); Maynard J. Geiger, *Junipero Serra Collection: Calendar of Documents in the Santa Bárbara Mission-Archive Junípero Serra Collection* (Santa Barbara, Calif.: 2009).

17   *Libre dels àngels*, ed Salvador Galmès, ORL 21:305–375; *Liber de locutione angelorum*, (eds.) Antoni Oliver, Michel Sennellart, and Fernando Domínguez Reboiras, ROL 16:207–236.

18   Palma de Majorca, Biblioteca Pública, MS 76, fol. 153r: "in exponendo tract. Theol. de Angelis inconcussum Xpi Mart. Invictissimi D.ˢ Archangelici et Mariani B. Raymundi tramitem insequendo." See García and Marsá, *Inventario*; J.N. Hillgarth and Lorenzo Pérez Martínez, *Manuscritos lulianos de la Biblioteca Pública de Palma* (Barcelona and Palma: 1965), 88. I am presently preparing an edition and study of this text.

as a defender of the doctrine of the Immaculate Conception of Mary. He refers to "the Blessed Ramon Llull, fierce defender of the pure origin of Mary."[19]

Another connection that should be noted is that in 1749, before traveling to the New World, Serra was elected by his peers to deliver the sermon on the feast day of Ramon Llull on January 25th, a very prestigious honor. The date is doubly important for our purposes because it was in the fall of the previous year that renewed efforts to move the canonization of Llull forward were undertaken in Majorca, hence the annual January 25 sermon may have had additional significance that year.[20] As the story goes, Serra's sermon so impressed one of the religious in attendance, who was not at all a friend of Serra's, that he declared nevertheless that it should be written "in letters of gold" (*con letras de oro*).[21] It seems that letters of gold are not the most enduring ink and unfortunately the sermon has not survived, although evidence exists that money was allocated to print it.

But by far the most substantive connection I have so far found occurs when Serra becomes a professor at the convent of Saint Francis in Palma, where he lectured on the philosophy of Duns Scotus as part of the curriculum of the Lullian University from 1740 to 1749. There were four chairs: the Lullistic, the Suaristic, the Thomistic and the Scotistic. Since 1692 the teaching of the philosophy of Duns Scotus (1266–1308) had fallen to the Franciscans. Duns Scotus was considered a difficult thinker, even in his own day.[22] He was a younger contemporary of Llull. Like Llull and Serra, he was a Franciscan, although in Llull's case we can only speak of what seems to have been a clear attraction to the order, since it remains uncertain whether he was a professed member of the Third Order of Saint Francis. Like Llull and Serra, Scotus was a firm supporter of the doctrine of the Immaculate Conception. Serra held the Scotian chair of Prima, that is, he taught the morning class while someone else taught the Vespertine, or evening course.[23] In the course of those lectures Serra had occasion to refer to the philosophy of Ramon Llull, and, in particular, to the thriving

---

19   Serra, "Class Notes," 10; Palma de Majorca, Biblioteca Pública, MS 76, fol. 191r.: "B. Raymundi Lulli Mariani originei candoris propugnatoris acerrimi."
20   Ferrer, "Culte," 71.
21   Palou, *Relación*, 5; Maynard J. Geiger, "The Scholastic Career and Preaching Apostolate of Fray Junípero Serra, O.F.M., S.T.D. (1730–1749)," *The Americas* 4 (1947): 76–78. See also the important study by Albert Cassanyes-Roig and Rafael Ramis-Barceló, "Fray Junípero Serra y la Universidad Luliana y literaria de Mallorca," *Archivum Franciscanum Historicum* 107 (2014): 427–455.
22   Valentí Serra de Manresa, "El pensament escotista a Catalunya," *Acta historica et archaeologica mediaevalia* 29 (2008): 607–627, on Scotism in Catalonia. I thank Fra Valentí for his kindness and generosity during my visit with him in summer 2012.
23   Geiger, "Scholastic Career," 71–74.

school of Lullism in the Majorca of his day. We know this because one of his students, Francesc Noguera, took detailed and copious notes during his study with Serra. These notes were apparently corrected, or even authored, at least in part, by Serra himself. It is of no little interest that among the other students in class with Noguera were, as we have noted, Francesc Palou, future companion and biographer of Serra, as well as Joan Crespí, who would also follow Serra to the New World. Serra is not the only Majorcan missionary of the 18th century who was familiar with Llull. He is merely the most prominent.

The full title of Noguera's work is *Compendium Scoticum elaboratum tamquam ab auctore Patre Fratre Iunipero Serra, et tamquam ab scriptore Francisco Noguera studente in conventu Seraphici Patris Nostri sancti Francisci ab Assissio. Fuit inceptus luce nona mensis Septembris anno a Nativitate Domini nostri 1740.*[24] The *Compendium* itself seems to be anything *but* a compendium. It is over 800 pages of scholastic Latin prose. There are at least two places in the *Compendium* that refer to Llull or Lullism directly. These take place during the winter term of Serra's first year of teaching, as a part of his course titled *Brevis in Logicam Aristotelis*. In the first reference to Llull, Serra seeks to distinguish Scotus's ideas on *distinctio* from those of the Thomists, the Lullists, and the "neutrals" (that is, the Jesuits).[25] In a second discussion he critiques, gently, the ideas of the "modern Lullists."[26] But there is nothing in this discussion, so far as I can see, that would demonstrate any particular intellectual kinship, positive or negative, between Serra and Ramon Llull. The contents of Serra's course, perhaps not surprisingly, reflect rather closely the course of study Serra himself had followed with Bernardino Castayó from 1731–1733, as we learn from MS 882 in the Biblioteca Pública of Palma de Majorca, which constitutes Serra's own textbook for the class. Thus Serra's comments recorded in Noguera's *Compendium* may reflect a standard curriculum more than a personal perspective on these issues by Serra. Amore refers to a second manuscript that may contain notes from this class.[27] A full comparison of the two (or three) texts should help to resolve this question.

---

24   Palma de Majorca, Biblioteca de Sant Felip Neri, item 68900; Santa Barbara Mission Archive and Library, Junípero Serra Collection 34, is a typed transcript of a portion of this manuscript. See Agostino Amore, Catholic Diocese of Monterey-Fresno (Calif.), and Congregatio pro Causis Sanctorum, *Officium Historicum. Beatificationis et Canonizationis Servi Dei Iuniperi Serra, Sacerdotis Professi O.F.M. (1784): Positio Super Vita et Virtutibus ex Officio Concinnata* (Vatican City: 1981), 12, and n. 36. I am presently preparing a study and edition of the portions of the Noguera manuscript in which Serra refers to Llull.

25   Noguera, *Compendium*, fols. 58v-68r. Two of the passages in which Serra refers to Lullists are discussed by Cassanyes and Ramis, "Fray Junípero Serra," 441–443.

26   Ibid., fols. 76v–79v.

27   Amore, *Officium Historicum,* 16, n. 55.

Where we see the nature of Serra's relation to Llull most clearly is in the small dedications recorded in the Noguera manuscript, with which Serra ends each term. Serra often pauses to mention Llull together with other individuals whose names also have a special resonance in the context of California: Saint Anthony of Padua, Saint Francis of Assisi, Saint Clare of Assisi, Saint Bonaventure. Serra generally refers to Llull as the "Illuminated Doctor" and "Blessed." He mentions those circumstances of Llull's life that allow Serra and his students to identify most closely with him: that he was, as Serra believed, a member of the Third Order of Saint Francis, that he was a Majorcan, that he was from the city of Palma. In the Noguera manuscript we begin to see the nature of Serra's relationship to Llull: it was not as the philosopher or theologian (though Llull's belief in the Immaculate Conception was extremely important for Serra), but as a Majorcan, and a Franciscan tertiary. For example, in the final remarks for his first term as a teacher (16 December 1740), Serra mentions the Virgin, with special reference to the purity of her conception, Saint Francis, his blessed companion Junipero, Saint Bonaventure, Saint Anthony of Padua, John Duns Scotus, and "the illuminated Doctor Blessed Ramon Llull."[28] Noguera repeats the dedication on the following page. He includes a similar list in honor of Saint John's Day (23 June 1742) and refers to "the Illuminated Doctor Blessed Ramon Llull, of our Third Order and illustrious son of the fatherland" (presumably Majorca).[29] Llull is mentioned again, in his usual position following Duns Scotus, at the close of Serra's lectures on Aristotle's *De anima* from 30 April 1743.[30] On Saint John's Day of 1743, at the close of the course, Llull is mentioned as "of this gilded [city of] Palma."[31] A role model, in short, and it seems to me that this role *must* have involved for Serra a recognition of Llull as promoter of missions, as a missionary himself, and, as Serra no doubt believed, also as a martyr to his faith in the course of his missions.

Serra's missionary calling appears less personally traumatic and his work as a missionary far more practical than Llull's. Llull's trips among the Muslims of Cyprus and North Africa were often fraught with emotional conflict, at least as they are portrayed in the *Vita coaetanea*.[32] He seems to have been a person for whom the theory was easier than the practice. Serra got down to the business of missionizing, as we know, and the proof of that is in the series of missions he founded and maintained.

---

28   Noguera, *Compendium*, fol. 48r: "Illuminati D[octoris] Beati Raymondi Lullii."
29   Ibid., fol. 294v: "Illum[inati] D[octoris] Beati Raymundi Lulli nostri 3^i [=tertii] ordinis et patriae preclarisimi filii."
30   Ibid., fol. 400v.
31   Ibid., fol. 401r: "huius deaurate Palme."
32   *Vita coaetanea* 4.20–7.30, (ed.) Harada, 284–293; trans. Bonner, 24–31.

Serra's career in New Spain after his early years in Majorca can be divided into several periods: his journey from Majorca to Mexico City where he arrived on 1 January 1750, his early missions in the Sierra Gorda after only a few months at the Colegio de San Fernando in Mexico City (1750–1758), his return to San Fernando in Mexico City in 1758, and his life as a preacher sent throughout New Spain to deliver sermons *entre fieles*, that is, in missions aimed at the reform of those who were already Christians, a period that lasted until 1767. In this time he also served the Inquisition in investigating several cases of witchcraft and, at his home college, was Master of Novices. What many consider to have been the most important part of his life and certainly the most well-known, his missions to the non-Christian native inhabitants of Baja and Alta California, did not begin until 1767, when Serra was in his mid-50s. The mission venture in Baja California was brief, lasting only until 1769. In that year, he set out overland to found his first Alta California mission: San Diego. He would go on to found nine missions in Alta California, dying at his second mission, and his headquarters, San Carlos Boromeo, in 1784.[33]

It is perhaps one clue to a connection between Llull and Serra that one of Serra's first acts as a missionary in the Sierra Gorda among the indigenous Pame was to take on a native Pame to be his personal language teacher (*maestro*), though Serra seems to have been a much more docile student than Llull, whose Arabic slave language teacher attempted to murder him.[34] Having learned Pame, Serra began to translate Christian catechistic texts into the language of the population he wished to convert, delivering lectures on Christian doctrine in the indigenous language and Castilian on alternating days.[35]

We cannot know, however, whether the ever-practical Serra thought of Llull and Miramar when he began his missionary career among the Pame. In all, Serra seems to have been, at least in the New World, a person chiefly motivated by practical solutions to present needs. He was not the first Franciscan, or even the first Majorcan, to understand the importance of learning the languages of the native inhabitants of the New World in order to facilitate their conversion. Friar Antonio Llinàs i Massanet (1635–1693), from Artà, founded the first missionary Colegio De Propaganda Fidei in Querétaro in 1683.[36] One of the

---

33 Maynard J. Geiger, "Junípero Serra, O.F.M, in the Light of Chronology and Geography (1713–1784)," *The Americas* 6 (1950): 290–333, is the basis of this account.

34 *Vita coaetanea*, 2.11–13, (ed.) Harada, 278–280; trans. Bonner, *Doctor Illuminatus*, 14–17.

35 Palou, *Relación*, 28–29 (errata 342).

36 Maynard J. Geiger, "The Mallorcan Contribution to Franciscan California," *The Americas* 4 (1947): 141–150; Kieran McCarty, "Apostolic Colleges of the Propagation of the Faith – Old and New World Background," *The Americas* 19 (1962): 50–58; Johannes Meier, "The Franciscans in the New World: Their Contribution to the Evangelization of North, Central,

explicit goals of these colleges, as Llinàs had outlined in a proposal of 1681, was to study the languages of potential converts: "the Mexican, Tarasca, Otomí and many other [languages]" (*[las lenguas] mexicana, tarasca, otomí y muchas otras*).[37] After his death a very short-lived missionary college was founded at the Colegio de San Bernardino in Petra on Majorca and it is not impossible that Serra was aware of that former college located in the convent where he had studied as a boy and of its methods.[38]

Serra headquartered at Jalpan in the Sierra Gorda, but oversaw missionaries at the four other missions. He seems to have been involved directly in the construction of the mission church at Jalpan, dedicated to Saint James. Gustin argues that the statue of Saint James on the façade of the Jalpan church used the iconography of "Saint James the Moorslayer" (*Santiago Matamoros*), a violent representation of the saint on horseback with sword in hand trampling over the severed body parts of the Moorish enemies of the Catholic faith.[39] This imagery was adapted in the New World to a form that became known as "Santiago the Indian-slayer" (*Santiago Mataindios*) when new "enemies" of the faith were encountered there. In a final sort of poetic justice, some of the native inhabitants of New Spain adapted the iconography to their own use, creating a figure that has come to be known as "Santiago the Spaniard-slayer" (*Santiago Mataespañoles*). The statue on the façade in Jalpan was destroyed in 1868 so that it could be replaced with a clock! Since we do not know for certain that it was this warlike Saint James that Serra chose to grace the façade of his church, in lieu of more benign representations of Saint James as pilgrim or Saint James enthroned, we can reserve judgment on his choice here. But the figure of *Santiago Matamoros* would, again, seem rather contrary to what we understand of Llull's views of how one converts the non-believers. Gustin makes the additional point, however, that it was probably the figure of Saint James the Apostle that dominated Serra's understanding of the Saint's

---

and South America," in *From La Florida to La California: The Genesis and Realization of Franciscan Evangelization in the Spanish Borderlands*, (eds.) Timothy J. Johnson and Gert Melville (Berkeley: 2013), 71–82; and David Rex Galindo, "Conferences on Theology and Indian Languages: A Program to Train Missionaries in New Spain," in *From La Florida to La California: The Genesis and Realization of Franciscan Evangelization in the Spanish Borderlands*, (eds.) Timothy J. Johnson and Gert Melville (Berkeley: 2013), 251–270. Llinàs's name appears also as "Linaz."

37   Lino Gómez Canedo, *Evangelización y Conquista: Experiencia Franciscana en Hispanoamérica* (Mexico: 1977), 54.

38   Geiger, "Mallorcan," 143.

39   Monique Gustin, *El barroco en la Sierra Gorda: Misiones franciscanas en el Estado de Querétaro, Siglo XVIII* (Mexico: 1969), 142–144.

life: James was the first apostle and first martyr to the new Christian faith.[40] He was, thus, "the model missionary." The presence of a statue of Our Lady of the Pillar, who, according to legend, appeared to James during his evangelizing mission to Iberia, reinforces this more benign interpretation of James's presence on the façade. It is worthwhile to recall that one of Llull's first acts after he received his missionary calling was to make a pilgrimage to Santiago de Compostela, where Saint James's remains were believed to lie. The church standing in Jalpan was already dedicated to Saint James when Serra arrived, but it is interesting to consider this possible connection with Llull as Serra began his first true missions among the native inhabitants of New Spain.

The church also has statues dedicated to Our Lady of the Pillar and to the Virgin of Guadalupe on opposite sides of the façade. We cannot know how directly Serra was involved in creating the facades of the remaining churches, the last of which, in Landa, was probably finished in 1768, well after Serra's return to Mexico City and, indeed, at the beginning of his missions to the Californias. It is clear that Serra and his fellow missionaries did not abandon fully the concerns expressed in the class notes taken by Noguera, most notably, the admiration for Duns Scotus and the promotion of the doctrine of the Immaculate Conception. Tilaco, a church dedicated to Saint Francis himself, also bears an image of the Virgin as a young child, a common representation of the Immaculate Conception. The construction of the mission church at Tilaco was overseen between 1752 and 1767 by Joan Crespí, a fellow student, as we have seen, in Serra's courses in Palma, together with Noguera.[41] The mission of La Purísima Concepción de Landa in the Sierra Gorda, perhaps as an aspect of its dedication to the Immaculate Conception, has a statue of Duns Scotus on its façade, the same Scotus that had occupied Serra and his students in Palma over the course of three years. In her discussion of Landa, Gustin observes that Scotus and Llull were often represented together defending the Immaculate Virgin in engravings produced in Serra's century by the Majorcan printer Guasp.[42] Llull appears together with Scotus as promoter of the doctrine of the Immaculate Conception in the tympanum of the Col·legi de la Sapiència in Palma in a sculpture dated c. 1770.[43] So far as I have been able to determine, Serra never commissioned any statues or other artwork with Llull as their subject, but there is a record of at least one statue of Llull being sent to the

40 Gustin, *El barroco en la Sierra Gorda*, 144.
41 Ibid., 105.
42 Ibid., 195.
43 Catalina Cantarellas Camps, "Sobre la iconografia de Ramon Llull," in Fundació "La Caixa," *Ramon Llull: Història, Pensament i Llegenda* (Palma: 2008), 110 (image), 114, 211; Gustin, *El barroco en la Sierra Gorda*, 194–195, for Scotus in 17th and 18th-century Mexico.

cathedral of Monterrey (Mexico) in the late 18th century.[44] The Llull statue was apparently ordered by the Majorcan Andrés Feliu i Togores, who was overseeing the remodeling of the Monterrey cathedral. I have not so far been able to determine the fate of this statue, but, clearly, like Serra, this Majorcan religious carried a personal and local devotion to Llull with him to the New World.

It gives a sense of the focus of the devotion of Serra, his former students, and the Franciscan missionaries in general, that the same figures who appear on the facades of the churches in the Sierra Gorda – Saint Francis, Saint Anthony of Padua, the Virgin of the Immaculate Conception, Saint Ferdinand, Saint John of Capistrano – will later appear in the names of the missions in Alta California, and that most of these same figures were already mentioned in the prayers Serra offered as he completed each of his courses in Majorca. Nor should we forget that the convent church of Saint Bernardino in Petra, Majorca, where Serra had studied as a boy, had chapels dedicated to several of the same saints: Saint Clare of Assisi, Saint Anthony of Padua, Our Lady Queen of the Angels, Saint Bonaventure, Saint Francis, Saint James, Saint Rose of Viterbo, with an image of Saint Michael above. Vicedo has explored the possibility that Serra was inspired in his naming of the missions of California by these chapels in the little convent church from his boyhood in Petra, but Vicedo's conclusions are negative with respect to this narrow question.[45] I have not been able to determine precisely when the chapel at Petra, formerly dedicated to "The Good Shepherd," was rededicated to Llull, but this was certainly before the dedication of its altarpiece in 1744, five years before Serra set sail for the New World.[46] The presence of such chapels in Serra's native Petra at the very least reminds us of continuities in a life otherwise characterized by deep ruptures.

This brings us to our final, and perhaps deepest, insight into the nature of Serra's connection to Llull: the reliquary crucifix that was buried with Serra at the Carmel mission following his death on 28 August 1784. This crucifix was exhumed, along with Serra's remains, in a highly secret procedure carried out as part of the canonization inquiry for Serra. The crucifix, in the form of the double cross-piece cross of Caravaca, is 4.75 inches by 2.25 inches and rotates "scissorwise" to open, allowing for access to nine small reliquary chambers, which are otherwise viewable through tiny pieces of glass in the back of the crucifix. When the crucifix was opened, pieces of paper (or cloth) with writing

---

44   Anonymous, "Un nuevo documento inédito sobre la extensión del culto al Beat Ramon en América: siglo XVIII," *Studia Monographica et Recensiones* 5 (1951): 59.

45   Salustiano Vicedo, *Convento de San Bernardino de Sena: La escuela del Beato Junípero Serra* (Petra: 1991), 203–215.

46   Ibid., 175.

were found in them, including two pieces bearing the inscription "B. Raydi M.," which Morgado interprets as signifying "of the Blessed Ramon of Majorca."[47]

Morgado affirms that these are "third class relics," writings probably touched to the tomb of Llull in Majorca, so regarding them he suggests only that "at some point they were brought to California and eventually placed in the crucifix buried with Serra." I think it is highly likely, nevertheless, that Serra himself created these third class relics by touching them to the tomb of Ramon Llull before his departure for the New World and placed them in his crucifix, which he carried with him from that point forward. This crucifix, two of whose nine relics seem to belong to Ramon Llull, appears at several *crucial* junctures in Serra's life, as told by him and others.

Serra's former student and lifelong friend Francesc Palou describes the importance of this crucifix in his account of Serra's death:

> He always slept with a crucifix upon his breast, in the embrace of his hands. It was about a foot in length. He had carried it with him from the time he was in the novitiate at the college, nor did he ever fail to have it with him. On all his journeys he carried it with him, together with the blanket and pillow. At his mission and whenever he stopped, as soon as he got up from bed he placed the crucifix upon the pillow. Thus he had it on this occasion when he did not wish to go to bed during the entire night or next morning, on the day when he was to deliver his soul to his Creator.[48]

At least two "chain of evidence" problems occur in the account of Serra and his crucifix that I offer here. First, Palou states that the crucifix was "una tercia de largo." This would make it around 11 inches in length. The actual object is 4.75 inches high, according to Morgado, but the vagueness of both memory and measures and the fact that it seems logical that the crucifix Serra wore when he died was the one he was buried and later exhumed with seems to remove most obstacles to the affirmation that the crucifix Palou describes here is the one later found in Serra's grave.

---

47   Martin Morgado, "Non Recedet Memoria Ejus: The Story of Blessed Junipero Serra's Mission Carmel Grave," *California History* 67 (1988): 156–160, 163 (images).

48   Palou, *Palóu's Life*, trans. Geiger, 246; Palou, *Relación*, 273: "durmiendo siempre con una Cruz en el pecho, abrazado con ella, del tamaño de una tercia de largo, que cargaba desde que estuvo en el Noviciado del Colegio, y jamas la dexó, sino que en todos los viages la cargó, y recogia con la fresada, y almohada, y en su Mision, y en las paradas, en quanto se levantaba de la cama ponia la Cruz sobre la almohada: asi la tenia en esta occasion que no quiso hacer cama, ni en toda la noche, ni por la mañana del dia que habia de entregar su alma al Criador."

More difficult is the significant ambiguity concerning the point in his life at which Serra acquired this crucifix. Does Palou refer to Serra's time as a novice in Majorca (which was not precisely in a "college") or to the place, the house of novices at the Colegio de San Fernando in Mexico City, where Serra was Master of Novices? Palou says "from the time he was in the novitiate at the college." It seems that Palou, if anyone, should know, and Amore asserts that Serra had carried the crucifix with him since 1750, that is, the year he first entered the Colegio de San Fernando.[49] This date, too, could be interpreted differently: Serra was only in San Fernando for a few months in 1750 and did not return there until 1758. However, it seems strange, though not impossible, that Serra, who had so many opportunities to acquire relics of Llull in Palma, would acquire a crucifix with ready-made relics of Ramon Llull in Mexico rather than in Majorca. And Palou's earlier observation concerning the voyage from Cadiz to Puerto Rico – "During the entire voyage, he never laid aside the crucifix which he wore on his breast, even when he slept"[50] – strongly suggests to me that Serra actually had this crucifix since Majorca. Whatever might have been the date of its acquisition, placing this crucifix on his breast seems to have been Serra's last action in this life: "He walked to his little room where he had his bed. He took off only his mantle and lay down over the boards covered with a blanket, with the holy crucifix mentioned above, in order to rest."[51] Serra dies, then, in his sleep, with the crucifix containing the relics of Ramon Llull on his breast.

And so, although in all the writings we have from Serra after his departure from Majorca we have little or no evidence that Serra thought about Llull the philosopher or even Llull the missionary at any point, he must, in fact, have thought about him every day, or at least kept him close to his heart.[52] We see the importance of this crucifix for Serra already in the mention of his voyage from Cadiz to Puerto Rico: "During the entire voyage, he never laid aside the crucifix which he wore on his breast, even when he slept." Of course, if Serra did not acquire the crucifix containing relics of Llull until 1750 or after, the crucifix referred to here is a different one. Serra himself seems to refer to this crucifix in his account of the deadly attack by the native inhabitants against

---

49   Amore, *Officium Historicum*, 319.

50   Palou, *Palóu's Life*, trans. Geiger, 15; Palou, *Relación*, 14: "En todo el tiempo de la navegacion jamas se quitó el Santo Christo del pecho, ni aun para dormir."

51   Palou, *Palóu's Life*, trans. Geiger, 248; Palou, *Relación*, 275: "fué por su pie al Quartito en donde tenia su cama ó tarima, y quitandose solo el manto, se recostó sobre las tablas cubiertas con la fresada con su santa Cruz arriba dicha, para descansar."

52   Neither Palou's *Relación* nor *The Writings of Junípero Serra*, (ed.) Antonine Tibesar, 4 vols. (Washington: 1955–66), which includes Serra's own journal of his trip from Loreto to San Diego, mention Llull.

the recently founded San Diego mission on the Feast of the Assumption, 15 August 1769: "I held [Holy Mary's] picture in one hand, and her Divine Crucified Son in the other when arrows were raining everywhere; and my thoughts were, that with such defense either I would not have to die, or that I would die well, great sinner that I am."[53] Whether Serra thought of the martyrdom of Llull at the precise moment when "arrows were raining everywhere" is unknowable, of course. But it seems quite likely that Serra thought of martyrdom nearly every day during his missionary activities in the Californias and that the relics of Llull in the crucifix he wore signified his deep spiritual and even physical connection to Llull and to what he believed had been Llull's martyrdom in service of the faith. This was a connection between the two Majorcans far more intimate than any intellectual affinity or sedulous imitation of Llull's missionary theories as Serra carried out his own pressing duties as missionary.[54]

As with Boïl, Serra's relationship with Ramon Llull frustrates most of our attempts to characterize him as a Lullist of the erudite variety. It also largely frustrates our attempts to find the intellectual missionizing ideas of Llull directly played out in his missionizing activities. Serra's "life and times" remind us that, over the centuries, there has been a different type of Lullism, a type we often neglect in scholarly studies of the great Majorcan polymath and his difficult Art: Llull has been an object of the most intimate devotion for many individuals over the centuries, from the small towns of Majorca to the wilds of the New World.[55]

---

53   Junípero Serra, Letter to Juan Andrés, 10 February 1770, (ed.) Tibesar, *Writings*, 1:154–155: "Yo la [la Divina Puríssima perlada] tenía en la una mano, y en la otra a su Divino Hijo Crucificado, cuando llovían flechas, y pensé para mí, que con tales defensas, o no havía de morir, o havía de morir bien ahunque tan grande pecador." Tibesar translates the Spanish text as "picture" of Mary, but Serra simply says that he held "her;" Geiger, *Life and Times*, 1:234–235, refers to it as a "statue," but it might also have been a medallion or badge.

54   Cassanyes and Ramis, "Fray Junípero Serra," 453–454, offer measured conclusions, worth citing here, regarding Serra's intellectual debts to Llull: "Mucho se ha especulado sobre el lulismo de Fr. Junípero y si fue la huella luliana la que le impulsó a la misión. Pese a que compartimos el enfoque, en este trabajo aportamos datos que nos permiten corroborar sólidamente que fue un hombre bien formado, con voz propia y opinión precisa, en el marco de la Universidad de su momento. Fue seguidor de Escoto y de Llull, como lo fueron muchos de sus hermanos, pero lo hizo con su propio criterio, algo que muestra la autonomía intelectual de Fr. Junípero."

55   This study has benefitted greatly from conversations and correspondence with my colleague Steven W. Hackel of the University of California at Riverside. I am also grateful for the assistance of Rebecca Dufendach and support from the Center for Medieval and Renaissance Studies at the University of California, Los Angeles.

Works Cited

Primary Works

Custurer, Jaime, *Disertaciones históricas del culto inmemorial del B. Raymundo Lullio Dr. Iluminado y Mártir, y de la inmunidad de censuras, que goza su Dotrina; con un Apendiz de su Vida* (Majorca: 1700).

Epílogo breve de los piadosos desvelos con que las tres escuelas del iluminado dotor y mártir el beato Raymundo Lullio, del sutil Escoto y eximio Suárez rindieron las gracias al Dios de las vitorias por la que consiguieron contra Orán las armas católicas de nuestro magnánimo monarca don Felipe quinto, que Dios guarde. Sale a luz consagrándole los alumnos marianos a la puríssima concepción de María santíssima (Barcelona: 1732).

Noguera, Francesc, *Compendium Scoticum elaboratum tamquam ab auctore Patre Fratre Iunipero Serra, et tamquam ab scriptore Francisco Noguera studente in conventu Seraphici Patris Nostri sancti Francisci ab Assissio. Fuit inceptus luce nona mensis Septembris anno a Nativitate Domini nostri 1740*, Palma de Majorca, Biblioteca de Sant Felip Neri, item 68900.

Noguera, Francesc, *Compendium ...*, Santa Barbara Mission Archive and Library, Junípero Serra Collection 34 (a typed transcript of a portion of Palma de Majorca, Biblioteca de Sant Felip Neri, item 68900).

Palou, Francesc, *Palóu's Life of Fray Junípero Serra*, trans. Maynard J. Geiger (Washington, D.C.: 1955).

Palou, Francesc, *Relación Histórica de La Vida y Apostólicas Tareas del Venerable Padre Fray Junípero Serra...* (1787; repr. New York: 1966).

Pasqual, Antonio Raymundo, *Descubrimiento de la aguja nautica, de la situacion de la America, del arte de navegar, y de un nuevo método para el adelantamiento en las artes y ciencias: disertacion en que se manifiesta que el primer autor de todo lo expuesto es el Beato Raymundo Lulio, martir y doctor, iluminado, con un apendice de la enseñanza publica, de los progresos de la literatura y otros puntos históricos pertenecientes á Mallorca* (Madrid: 1789).

Pasqual, Antonio Raymundo, *Examen de la crisis de el R. ^{mo} Padre maestro don Benito Geronimo Feijoo monge benedictino sobre el arte luliana; en el qual se manifiesta la santidad y culto del iluminado doctor y martyr el B. Raymundo Lulio, la pureza de su doctrina, y la utilidad de su arte y ciencia general* (Madrid: 1749–50).

Pasqual, Antonio Raymundo, *Vindiciae Lullianae: sive demonstratio critica immunitatis doctrinae illuminati Doctoris B. Raymundi Lulli martyris, ab erroribus eidem à Nicolao Eymerico impactis, á censuris ab Albitio Cardinali relatis; reliquisque aliorum lituris. Fundata in collatione textuum Lulli, ex quá proprius ostenditur catholicus sensus, & in consensu doctrinae, imò & modi loquendi ejusdem cum patribus, & doctoribus sacris: cui subnectitur explicatio aliorum quorumdam textuum, quibus aliqui fortè possent offendi. In quatuor tomos divisae, praemittitur vita ejusdem B. Raymundi Lulli, ex ipsius operibus potissimè deprompta*, 4 vols. (Avignon: 1778).

Serra, Junípero, "Class Notes in Theology by Serra, 1735–1737," Santa Barbara Mission
    Archive and Library, Serra Collection 10, Provenance Uncertain, Latin, Phg. 4 Pp.,
    Palma, 06/22/1737.
Serra, Junípero, ["Summaries on Aristotle"], Palma de Majorca, Biblioteca Pública, MS
    882.
Serra, Junípero, ["Treatises on Various Topics"], Palma de Majorca, Biblioteca Pública,
    MS 76.
Serra, Junípero, *The Writings of Junípero Serra*, (ed.) Antonine Tibesar, 4 vols. (Wash-
    ington: 1955–66).

Primary Works: Llull

Doctor Illuminatus: A Ramon Llull Reader, (ed.) and trans. Anthony Bonner (Princeton:
    1993).
Liber de locutione angelorum, (eds.) Antoni Oliver, Michel Sennellart, and Fernando
    Domínguez Reboiras, ROL 16:207–236.
*Liber proverbiorum: in tres partes divisus ... in proverbia de Deo & de naturalibus & de
    moralibus* (Majorca: 1735–38).
Libre dels àngels, ed Salvador Galmès, ORL 21:305–375.
*Llibre de Doctrina Pueril compost en llengua llamosina per lo Illuminat Doctor y Martyr
    invictissim de Christo el B. Ramon Llull mallorqui, Traduit a llengua usual mallorqui-
    na per un devot Dexeble seu à utilidat de los miñons de Mallorca* (Majorca: 1736).
Raymundi Lulli Opera omnia, (ed.) Ivo Salzinger, 8 vols. (Mainz: 1721–42).
Vita coaetanea, (ed.) Hermogenes Harada, in ROL 8:271–309.
Vita coaetanea, trans. Anthony Bonner, in *Doctor Illuminatus: A Ramon Llull Reader*
    (Princeton: 1993), 10–40.

Secondary Works

Amore, Agostino, Catholic Diocese of Monterey-Fresno (Calif.), and Congregatio pro
    Causis Sanctorum, *Officium Historicum. Beatificationis et Canonizationis Servi Dei
    Iuniperi Serra, Sacerdotis Professi O.F.M. (1784): Positio Super Vita et Virtutibus ex
    Officio Concinnata* (Vatican City: 1981).
Anonymous, "Un nuevo documento inédito sobre la extensión del culto al Beat Ramon
    en América; siglo XVIII," *Studia Monographica et Recensiones* 5 (1951): 59.
BETA [*Bibliografía Española de Textos Antiguos*], dir. Faulhaber, Charles B., Ángel Gó-
    mez Moreno, and Óscar Perea Rodríguez (Berkeley: 1997-). Web: http://vm136.lib
    .berkeley.edu/BANC/philobiblon/beta_en.html. Consulted: October 12, 2014.
Camps, Catalina Cantarellas, "Sobre la iconografia de Ramon Llull," in Fundació "La
    Caixa," *Ramon Llull: Història, Pensament i Llegenda* (Palma: 2008), 109–116; 208–212
    (English text).
Carreras i Artau, Joaquín and Tomás Carreras i Artau, *Historia de la filosofía española:
    Filosofía cristiana de los siglos XIII al XV*, 2 vols. (Madrid: 1939–1943).

Cassanyes-Roig, Albert and Rafael Ramis-Barceló, "Fray Junípero Serra y la Universidad Luliana y literaria de Mallorca," *Archivum Franciscanum Historicum* 107 (2014): 427–455.

Ferrer Flórez, Miguel, "Controversias y luchas entre lulistas y antilulistas en el siglo XVIII," *Memòries de la Real Acadèmia Mallorquina d'Estudis Genealògics, Heràldics i Històrics* 16 (2006): 157–166.

Ferrer Flórez, Miguel, "Culte a Ramon Llull: Discòrdies i controvèrsies," *SL* 41 (2001): 65–89.

Fogel, Daniel, *Junípero Serra, the Vatican, and Enslavement Theology* (San Francisco, Calif.: 1988).

Fundació "La Caixa," *Ramon Llull: Història, Pensament i Llegenda* (Palma: 2008).

García Pastor, Jesús, and María Marsá, *Inventario de Manuscritos de la Biblioteca Pública del Estado en Mallorca* (Madrid: 1989).

Geiger, Maynard J., *Junípero Serra Collection: Calendar of Documents in the Santa Bárbara Mission-Archive Junípero Serra Collection* (Santa Barbara, Calif.: 2009). Web: http://sbmal.org/docs/catalog/SBMAL-Serra_Collection.pdf

Geiger, Maynard J., "Junípero Serra, O.F.M, in the Light of Chronology and Geography (1713–1784)," *The Americas* 6 (1950): 290–333.

Geiger, Maynard J., *The Life and Times of Fray Junípero Serra, O.F.M. or The Man Who Never Turned Back (1713–1784)*, 2 vols. (Washington, D.C.: 1959).

Geiger, Maynard J., "The Mallorcan Contribution to Franciscan California," *The Americas* 4 (1947a): 141–150.

Geiger, Maynard J., "The Scholastic Career and Preaching Apostolate of Fray Junípero Serra, O.F.M., S.T.D. (1730–1749)," *The Americas* 4 (1947b): 65–82.

Gómez Canedo, Lino, *Evangelización y Conquista: Experiencia Franciscana en Hispanoamérica* (Mexico: 1977).

Gustin, Monique, *El barroco en la Sierra Gorda: Misiones franciscanas en el Estado de Querétaro, Siglo XVIII* (Mexico: 1969).

Hackel, Steven W., "The Competing Legacies of Junípero Serra," *Common-Place: The Interactive Journal of Early American Life* 5.2 (2005). Web: http://www.common-place.org/vol-05/no-02/hackel/index.shtml.

Hackel, Steven W., *Junípero Serra: California's Founding Father* (New York: 2013).

Hillgarth, J.N. and Lorenzo Pérez Martínez, *Manuscritos lulianos de la Biblioteca Pública de Palma* (Barcelona and Palma: 1965).

Johnson, Timothy J. and Gert Melville, (eds.), *From La Florida to La California: The Genesis and Realization of Franciscan Evangelization in the Spanish Borderlands* (Berkeley: 2013).

McCarty, Kieran, "Apostolic Colleges of the Propagation of the Faith – Old and New World Background," *The Americas* 19 (1962): 50–58.

Meier, Johannes, "The Franciscans in the New World: Their Contribution to the Evangelization of North, Central, and South America," in *From La Florida to La California: The Genesis and Realization of Franciscan Evangelization in the Spanish Borderlands*, (eds.) Timothy J. Johnson and Gert Melville (Berkeley: 2013), 71–82.

Morgado, Martin, "Non Recedet Memoria Ejus: The Story of Blessed Junipero Serra's Mission Carmel Grave," *California History* 67 (1988): 150–167, 205–210.

Planas Ferrer, Rosa, "La projecció de Llull," in Fundació "La Caixa," *Ramon Llull: Història, Pensament i Llegenda* (Palma: 2008), 97–106; 201–208 (English text).

Rex Galindo, David, "Conferences on Theology and Indian Languages: A Program to Train Missionaries in New Spain," in *From La Florida to La California: The Genesis and Realization of Franciscan Evangelization in the Spanish Borderlands*, (eds.) Timothy J. Johnson and Gert Melville (Berkeley: 2013), 251–270.

Rogent, Elies and Estanislau Duran, *Bibliografia de les impressions lul·lianes* (Barcelona: 1927).

Sandos, James A., *Converting California: Indians and Franciscans in the Missions* (New Haven and London: 2004).

Sandos, James A., "Junípero Serra's Canonization and the Historical Record," *The American Historical Review* 93 (1988): 1253–1269.

Serra de Manresa, Valentí, "El pensament escotista a Catalunya," *Acta historica et archaeologica mediaevalia* 29 (2008): 607–627.

Vicedo, Salustiano, *Convento de San Bernardino de Sena: La escuela del Beato Junípero Serra* (Petra: 1991).

Index